Andrew Hooper of McMinn County and Bradley County, Tennessee

Compiled by Harold Reno, Richard Hooper and Barry Hooper

DEDICATION
This book is dedicated to all the Hooper and related families who have helped create the
United States and given us the chance for freedom.

ACKNOWLEDGMENTS

We wish to thank the following for their help in researching the Andrew Hooper family. Barry Hooper and Richard Hooper were very important in locating descendants of Andrew Hooper. Because of Barry's Pedigree Chart, more than 900 family relationships were explained. Also, Richard Hooper translated the *Kinsey Hooper Civil War Diary*, so that other readers could understand what a soldier faced. In addition, Richard explained how the 8th Tennessee Union Infantry Regiment was important to the Hooper family. Richard also contacted the descendants of the Hooper family who moved to the Western part of the United States. Martha Hooper Reno proofread the book and helped correct many errors.

Since the mystery of the father and mother of Sarah Hooper Shelton, Andrew Hooper and Absolom Hooper prevented a complete understanding, we are thankful to those whose research helped us understand the importance of the three children and their families: on the Internet at *Rootsweb* was *The Families of James Shelton of McMinn County, Tennessee* by Arthur Paul Shelton; the interview with Gertrude Hooper Brewer and Albert Hooper in 1975; Clay Hooper at the Internet website, *HooperConnections.com*; William Hayden Hooper's book *Hooper Genealogy and Autobiography of Wm. Hayden Hooper*; and the E. G. Fisher Public Library in Athens, Tennessee. A special thanks to Anne Goodwin who created the Internet website *hoopercompass.com* where she posted Hooper research and allowed her email information to be used.

Mount Ebal research involved the following: Ronald A. Lee at the Tennessee State Library and Archives; Barbara Fagan and Elsie Oneal at the Cleveland Bradley County Public Library, History Branch; Barbara Mathe', Mary DeJong and Ingrid Lennon-Pressey at the American Museum of Natural History Library in New York City; Roy G. Lillard at Cleveland State Community College; George E. Phebus at the Smithsonian Institution, National Museum of Natural History; A. S. Spofford who was Librarian of Congress; Newspapers at the Library of Congress in the section *Chronicling America* and *The Cleveland Weekly Herald, The Cleveland Herald* and *Cleveland Banner* in Cleveland, Tennessee and the *Chattanooga Times* in Chattanooga, Tennessee; Dr. Albert Leighton Rawson who visited Mount Ebal and wrote about it; Harvard University Library of the Museum of Comparative Zoology which included a compilation entitled *TRANSACTIONS OF THE NEW YORK ACADEMY OF SCIENCES LATE LYCEUM OF NATURAL HISTORY VOLUME XI October, 1891, to June, 1892*; and the *American Antiquarian and Oriental Journal* January – November 1892 in Vol. 14.

Finally, this compilation acknowledges all those related families whose histories intertwined with the Andrew Hooper family and helped us understand the total story: the Internet was very important, especially *Ancestry.com* and the many people who published their information; also the Internet information from the King Family Bible and *King with Allied Families* by Joyce Disharoon and the Internet information from the *Salbach - Saulpaw 1700 – 1993* book published by Karl Saulpaw, Jr. I wish to thank Norma Hodgson who loaned a copy of the book *Jay and Lou Graham Family* by Juanita Graham Hinkle and Gertha Hooper Hill.

I have wondered where the birthdate for Andrew Hooper originated, and I think the mystery was solved. The importance of knowing an exact date and the source of that date could help solve many mysteries. On Friday September 7, 2018, Barry Hooper, one of the authors of this compilation on Andrew Hooper, told me that he first heard the date of September 23, 1805 for Andrew's birthdate from Kenneth Cress, a Hooper descendant. Kenneth's mother, Thelma Eloise Tillery Cress, was a great grand daughter of Jahew Hooper, and Kenneth said he got the birthdate from her, but he does not know how she knew. So, one mystery is solved, but the bigger mystery still remains: where did the birthdate originate? Is there a written record of the date?

Written by Harold Reno.

Introduction to Andrew Hooper

After Martha Hooper and I married in 1965, I was fascinated with her family history. I discussed the family with her parents, Earl and Billie Hooper, and listened as they mentioned family members. Earl's brother, John Luther Hooper, Jr., and I would sit and talk about the Hooper Mill and who worked there. Harrison Hooper, Earl's oldest brother, would talk about William Hooper who signed the Declaration of Independence, and he was so proud that a Hooper was one of the signers (William's family has been well documented and no relationship to Andrew Hooper of McMinn County and Bradley County, Tennessee has been established). Sarah Ellen Hooper McDowell, known as Aunt Biddy, (Earl, J. L. and Harrison's sister) would sit and answer questions about the Hooper family. As I listened, I took notes and began to look up information beginning in the 1970s.

One of the best sources for information turned out to be the Gertrude Hooper Brewer, Albert Hooper, Willie Tennessee (Bilie) Hooper and Earl Hooper's visit with Martha and Harold Reno in 1975. Gertrude and Billie Hooper brought family pictures, and Gertrude brought her DAR information. After lunch, Gertrude, Albert, Billie, Earl, Martha and Harold sat and talked. Harold turned on a cassette tape recorder and recorded the conversations. Some of Gertrude's information later was questioned by Harold as more discoveries were made. By using the Internet and the *Ancestry.com* website which contained thousands of records, Harold was able to recheck some of her information and to realize that her enthusiasm might have resulted in a wrong fact or two. Albert remembered some of the old Vernon information that was checked and used to track some descendants of John Vernon in Alabama, but many questions still remain.

Hooper Mill on Candy's/Candies Creek was one of my first main points of interest with Mount Ebal coming later. I did not realize that the Hooper family had run the Mill from about 1862 to 1919. One item that was not discussed for several years was Mount Ebal. It was about the 1980s that J. L.and Earl Hooper and I were riding in a truck Bradley County, Tennessee (about where Lower River Road and Eureka Road join), and J. L. mentioned that they ought to take me to see Mount Ebal. I asked some questions, but Mount Ebal was just a story about their father, John Luther Hooper, and his desire to develop the area and about a Flying Jenny that John Luther brought to a picnic at the site. Several years later Rick Hooper asked me if I had heard of Mount Ebal, and I replied that I had. Rick then found the location of Mount Ebal and visited the site. As I researched the story, I discovered that many errors had creeped into the story.

A phone call in the 1980s from Rick and Pat Hooper to Martha and Harold Reno added to the excitement of discovery. Rick had found the Hooper Box in an old barn and inside the box were some of the old records used in this book. The records included the Kinsey Hooper Civil War Diary, the A Way Bill to the Missouri, Hooper Mill records and the first Andrew Hooper deed in Bradley County, Tennessee.

In the 1990s and later, I found more exciting information about the Ancestors. Barry Hooper designed a large Family Tree chart and had it printed in 1994, and it identified more than 900 members of the Andrew Hooper family and showed how they were related. That information was used in this book in the chapter about Hooper Family Outline of Descendants, but instead of the Family Tree, a number was assigned to each person to show her or his ancestors. Everyone starts with the unknown ancestor listed as the number 1; then Sarah Hooper Shelton became number 2 because she was oldest; after that Andrew Hooper, her brother born about 1805, became number 3; and Absolom who was younger became number 4. So all descendants who begin with 1-2 are the Sarah Shelton family; all with numbers 1-3 are Andrew Hooper descendants; and all that begin 1-4 are Absolom Hooper's relatives. The total number of descendants listed is more than 2021 because some of the obituaries listed grandchildren or great grandchildren and did not designate who the parents were, but the information was included as a unit without giving a separate number to each. Several descendants discovered later were given a number plus a letter to designate each.

Finally, the book is complete after working on it for so many years. Hopefully the information compilation is accurate enough and will benefit anyone who is researching the family.

Harold Reno
September 19, 2018

Table of Contents

Early Hooper History and Andrew Hooper Grants

Hooper, Geren, Hankins, Skagg, Wilhoit, Vernon, Shelton and the other families included in this book opened the Colonial frontier and fought Great Britain in the Revolutionary War.

Nothing has been found that has proven the parentage of Andrew Hooper, Absolom Hooper and Sarah Hooper Shelton who lived in Bradley, Polk and McMinn Counties of Tennessee. From the family names and DNA, a type of ancestry could be gleaned, but records which might prove the connections were lacking. Some believe Andrew was born in Davidson County or Jefferson County or Greene County, Tennessee. Others believe that since Absolom and Andrew were names associated with Hoopers in Georgia, South Carolina, North Carolina and Tennessee, these names might indicate possible family relationships. Perhaps, their sister's name, Sarah, (who married James Shelton), could also indicate a family relationship.

The Hooper name has been in England definitely since William the Conqueror in 1066. *The Norman People* (found at *Internet Archive Bookreader* and digitized by *Google* from the library at Oxford University by *tpb*) published in 1874 by Henry S. King & Company, London on p. 289 stated that most likely the Hooper name originally was a Norman French term *hopere* which meant cloth merchant, but since the cooper (cooperage) made the barrels, then the hoops may have been made by the hooper hence the family name, Hooper. The Internet site, *surnamedb.com/Surname/Hoopper*, stated that the first recorded Hooper record was Adam le Hoper(e), which was dated 1228, in the "*Close Rolls of Wiltshire*", and Ralph le Hopere in *Fines Roll 57* during the reign of King Henry III . C. W. Bardsley in *Dictionary of English and Welsh Surnames* listed some of the other early Hoopers as Alexander le Hopere in Devon in 1273; Andrew le Hopere in 1315; and John le Hopere court summons during the reign of King Edward III.

Another early record in England listed in Fox's *Book of Martyrs* and in other records was that of Bishop John Hooper who was born about 1495 and died February 8, 1555. John was convinced that the Catholic Church needed reforming, but Queen Mary believed the Church should follow the dictates of Rome. John was one of the early Protestants who gave his life rather than recant. In front of thousands of people, he was tied to a stake and placed on top of wood to be burned. The wood was slow to burn and had to be relit several times. John Hooper quietly prayed, "O Jesus, Son of David, have mercy on me, and receive my soul." Once when the fire went out, he exclaimed, "For God's love, good people, let me have more fire!" Whether Bishop John was related to the Hoopers who came to America has not been proven.

Perhaps the first New World Hooper moved to Reading, Massachusetts Bay Company according to *Genealogy.com, Home, User Trees, Douglas-G-Yager* and other researchers; he was William Hooper, "aged 18 years," who came in the ship *James* from London, sailing July 13, 1635. He resided at Reading in 1644, as town records show, but may have been there before that. He was admitted a freeman of the colony May 10, 1648, which implied that he had previously joined the **Congregationalist** church with his wife Elizabeth. William was born about 1617 in Suffolk, England and died Dec. 5, 1678 in Reading, Mass. He may have married Elizabeth Woodruff Marshall born April 13, 1621 in Reading Mass. and christened in 1635 at Reading, Mass. According to *Douglas-G-Yager* at *Genealogy.com*, the children of William and Elizabeth were Mary Hooper born Nov. 24, 1647 in Reading, Mass., died Nov. 17, 1697 in Reading, and she married Thomas Taylor. Other children were James Hooper, born 1649 in Reading, Middlesex, Massachusetts and died 1649 in Reading; Sarah Hooper, born December 7, 1650 in Reading and died in Andover, Massachusetts; Ruth Hooper, born April 15, 1652 in Reading and died January 12, 1714/15 who married Abraham Walcott Sept. 1682 in Reading. Rebecca Hooper was born October 26, 1656 in Reading and died July 12, 1715 in Andover, Essex, Massachusetts. William Hooper, Jr, born November 3, 1658 in Reading and died August 8, 1692 in North Reading; Hannah Hooper, born March 31, 1662 in Reading; Elizabeth Hooper, born August 20, 1665 in Reading and died January 3, 1698/99; Thomas Hooper, Sr, born April 2, 1668 in Reading; John Hooper, Sr, born July 5, 1670 in Reading and died January 9, 1707/08 in Bridgewater, Massachusetts.

Other early Hoopers who arrived in America included John Hooper who along with William Cason received a land grant for 240 acres in 1675 in South Carolina (*Colonial Entry Book Vol. XXIII* pp. 1-5 found on the Internet). Joseph Hooper received a warrant for 50 acres (Internet) when he arrived July 10, 1695 in South Carolina according to A. S. Salley's *Warrants for Land, South Carolina 1692-1711*. The Thomas King Memorial (roadside marker) in South Carolina was for 160 acres on Broad River in Craven County, and it summarized a chain of title to a grant to Thomas Hooper of September 20, 1766.

On the Internet at *Google Books* a book titled *Side-lights on Maryland History: With Sketches of Early Maryland, Volume 2,* Published 1913 by Hester Dorsey Richardson p. 143 told about one of the early settlers in Maryland who was a surgeon, Dr. Henry Hooper, and he died in 1649. At the Internet website *Rootsweb.Ancestry.com* a later Henry Hooper (*Henry Hooper I* by Mrs. Brice Regina Phillips, Shirley Elizabeth Flowers) arrived in the province of Maryland on July 15, 1651, with his wife Sarah Rycroft Hooper and children Elizabeth, Richard, Robert and Henry. Henry Hooper was granted the Lower Cliffs, and this vast tract of land called "Hooper's Neck" remained in the Hooper family until parcels of it were sold by Henry Hooper, 3rd before 1750. On the Internet a *Wickipedia* article told about Hooper Islands grant which included three islands where Henry settled in 1669: Upper Hooper, Middle Hooper and Lower Hooper islands. The islands were surrounded by Chesapeake Bay on one side and the Honga River on the other. Other early Hoopers were John Hooper, James Hooper, Joseph Hooper, and Edward Hooper.

In Virginia, Deanna Baumgardner (her email address *deannabaumgardner@mac.com*) researched the early Hoopers in that state. Her list included William Hooper 1635 to Charles City, Virginia; Richard Hooper 1643 to the Isle of Wight, Virginia. In *Virginia's Colonial Soldiers* compiled by Lloyd DeWitt Bockstruck published in 1988 by Genealogical Publishing Co., Inc. Baltimore, Maryland, several Hoopers were mentioned. In the French and Indian War 1754-1763 chapter, the records were taken from the papers of George Washington. On page 53 "Return of the Second Company of Rangers Commanded by Capt. John Ashby," October 21, 1755, a James Hooper was listed for September 1 and described as five feet 9 inches, fair complexion, 29 years old and a Virginia farmer. In the same chapter on page 59 listed on the Muster Roll of Capt. David Bell's Company at Maidstone which was dated May 12, 1756 were John Hooper dated February 18, 1756, 35 years old, 5 feet four and a half inches tall, a weaver with brown hair from England and a James Hooper dated January 27, 1756, 25 years old, five feet four inches, a weaver with brown hair from England. John was listed in Capt. Christopher Gist's Company for May and June 1756. James was still listed in the Capt. David Bell's Company for April, May 31, and June 1756. On July 13, 1756 the Roll of Capt. David Bell's Company listed James Hooper who enlisted January 1756 at Fairfax, Virginia, 37 years old, five feet 6 inches tall, a weaver from England with fair skin and light hair. Also in Capt. David Bell's Company was a John Hooper who enlisted in February 1756 at Yorktown, Virginia, 26 years old, five feet four inches, a shoemaker from Ireland with swarthy skin and dark hair. On page 311 a Warrant for 50 acres was issued to William Swords, assignee of John Hooper (assigned by John Hooper to William), a soldier under Col. George Washington and a noncommissioned officer in said Regiment, dated April 4, 1780, Frederick County, Virginia. On page 152 William Hooper was listed in Capt. John Murray's Company of Volunteers September 10, 1774 from Botetourt County, Virginia who participated in Dunsmore's War. (As you can see, James and John were favorite Hooper names.)

The *U. S. Revolutionary War Rolls* at *Ancestry.com* listed many Hoopers who participated. The Virginia list included Ames (Amos?) Hooper, James Hooper, John Hooper, Mansfield Hooper and William Hooper. In North Carolina, Anthony Hooper, a private, enlisted as well as William Hooper, Ennis Hooper, James Hooper, Absolam Hooper and Abraham Hooper.

William Hooper from North Carolina signed the Declaration of Independence. In *Historical Sketches of North Carolina* by Col. John H. Wheeler published by Frederick H. Hitchcock, New York reprinted in 1925, on pages 282-288 a biographical sketch gave a history of his life. William was born June 17, 1742 in Boston, Massachusetts to the Rev. William Hooper who was pastor of Trinity Church. By 1767, William Hooper, the signer, had moved to North Carolina to practice law. He married Ann Clark, and their children were William born about 1768 and died July 15, 1804; Elizabeth 1770-1840 who married Col. Henry Watters; and Thomas Hogg Hooper born about 1772 and died after 1795 (Internet, A. C. Goodwin at *homepages. rootsweb.com* posted December 2, 1998). According to Col. John Wheeler as well as A. C. Goodwin in the *Hooper Compass Vol. 2*, William Hooper and his family had to flee their homes several times because of British attempts to capture the Signers of the Declaration of Independence. William

Hooper died October 14, 1790 at Hillsborough, North Carolina. This Hooper family has been well documented, and if the Andrew line of Tennessee were related, it would not be a close kinship.

Two other Revolutionary War Hoopers were Ennis Hooper and Absolom Hooper. According to Zella Armstrong in *The History of Hamilton County and Chattanooga, Tennessee, Volume* 1 Copyright 1931 by The Lookout Publishing Company and reprinted 1993 by The Overmountain Press in the United States of America on page 277, Ennis Hooper was born about 1750 and enlisted in Guilford County, North Carolina in 1777 serving under Captain William Armstrong. He was in the battles of Guilford Court House, Brier Creek, Stone River, General Gates' defeat and Eutaw Springs. He was given a land warrant by North Carolina and before 1830 moved to Marion County, Tennessee where he received a pension. This Ennis has not been connected to the other Hooper families, but may be related to Nashville, TN Hoopers. Absolom Hooper from Georgia, South Carolina and North Carolina named one of his children Enos which may indicate that Ennis of 1750 was related, but name association can be tricky because several other Hooper families used Ennis which in Ireland means island. Absolom Hooper, 1757-1845 (tombstone East LaPorte Cemetery in Jackson County, North Carolina) served in South Carolina, North Carolina and Georgia in the Revolution. He married Sarah Salers/Silars 1762-1856 (East LaPorte Cemetery). According to the Hooper DNA Project Results (p. 267), Absolom (1757) and his family were related to Andrew Hooper (Bradley County, TN), born about 1805 and Andrew's brother, Absolom (Polk County, TN), born about 1810.

There was information on the Internet at *Ancestry.com* in *Roster of South Carolina Patriots in the American Revolution* which listed Absolom's death as December 9, 1845. The record stated that Absolom was living on the Broad River at the mouth of the Green River when he enlisted in 1776 in the Sixth Regiment under Captains Richard Doggett, Jesse Baker and Colonel Henderson. He fought at Sullivan's Island, Stono, Savannah (wounded in the arm), and Charleston (wounded in the thigh). He was taken prisoner but escaped and fled to Georgia where he was captured by Tories. He later joined a Georgia unit.

Other Absolom references included one found on page 1195 of the *History of Tennessee* published in 1887 by Goodspeed Publishing Company of Nashville, Tennessee. Dr. L. W. Hooper (son of John and Margaret Ledbetter Hooper) of Cocke County, Tennessee said that his grandfather Absalom Hooper was a black-smith who was admired by the Cherokee, had lived with the tribe, and they gave him a nickname "steke santone" which meant Little Keg because of his short stature. There was another Absolam Hooper listed on the Internet who served in the American Revolution; he was listed on the Internet in *The Davidson County Cemetery Survey Project*, and he was born about 1740 and died 1813 in Davidson County, Tennessee. Other Hoopers listed who served in South Carolina were Church Hooper, Enock Hooper, James Hooper (may have been more than one?), Thomas Hooper and William Hooper. Hoopers who served in Georgia included Richard Hooper, James Hooper, and Matthew Hooper.

Much of the information in this chapter was based on the areas of Tennessee, South Carolina, Georgia, North Carolina and Virginia. Many of the families searching for land moved among these states as new areas opened. Men who fought in the American Revolution received land through warrants that gave them the right to land in the frontiers which were being settled.

Several Hooper researchers have speculated that a Thomas Hooper was the father of Absolom Hooper. This Thomas might have been a Tory (supported England), and Absolom left his home to serve in the Revolutionary War on the side of the American Colonies who had rebelled. A rebuttal argument by Anne Goodwin to this idea that Thomas was the father can be found in *Newsarch.Rootsweb Hooper L Archives* dated July 20, 2004. Thomas was another case of unproven information which was used as facts.

According to the tradition of naming children, one of the earliest sons was sometimes named for the paternal grandfather and one was named for the maternal grandfather. If this were true, then the first son of Andrew and Martha Hooper, John, might be named for Andrew's father. For that reason, John has been one of the searched and researched names for Andrew's father. Indeed a John Hooper was in McMinn County, Tennessee at the same time as Andrew Hooper, and, possibly, this same John sold land in Monroe County to Andrew, but no proof can be found to support a relationship between John and Andrew. For many years excitement grew when records were found that showed that Elizabeth Presley of Polk County,

Tennessee had sued her husband (who had abandoned her), and she listed the land that her father John Hooper had given her. She was supported by next friend Andrew J. Hooper in the lawsuit. But again this theory fizzled. Most likely, this Elizabeth Hooper Presley was the daughter of John and Margaret Bell Hooper. This Margaret Bell Hooper continued to live in Polk County, Tennessee until after 1880 (Internet, *Ancestry.com, Polk County 1880 Census* p. 26), and Andrew's mother died about 1840 (see pages 19 - 20).

Another search was related to Buncombe County, North Carolina where James Shelton lived before moving to Greene County, Tennessee; later, he married Sarah Hooper. In *A History of Buncombe County North Carolina* by Dr. F. A. Sondley, Volume II published by The Advocate Printing Company of Asheville, North Carolina on page 494 was a record of Hooper's Creek in Buncombe County being mentioned in 1792. Another record on page 457 dated April 16, 1792 was related to Thomas Hooper being summoned to court. In October 1793 on pages 472-473, Thomas Hopper certified that his right ear was bitten off by Philip Williams in a fight. Also on page 840, Thomas Hopper was included in a list of lands which were entered within the bounds of the annexed plat by permission of John Gray Blount for 100 acres on June 20, 1796. Perhaps the Hannah Hooper in the *1810 Census for Buncombe County* on page 293 with 6-1-1 males and 2-0-1 females was the wife of the Thomas Hopper/Hooper mentioned above, but there was no proof of that ancestry. Also, Hannah lived after the 1840 death date for Andrew's mother (page 20).

Some names that might be of interest to the ancestry of Andrew Hooper were James Hooper, Sr. in Blount County, Tennessee (his son James, Jr. probably moved to Rhea County, Tennessee) and another James, son of Hiram and Dorcas Hooper of Monroe County, Tennessee who lived beside James Shelton in McMinn County, Tennessee (p. 297), and a Thomas Hooper was briefly mentioned in a store record in McMinn County before 1840 (see page 9). Could this be the Thomas Hopper/Hooper in Jefferson County, Tennessee who may be a Hooper or a Hopper and had moved to McMinn County, or was this the Thomas listed with Edward Hooper in *Bradley County 1840 Census* (compiled by Sheridan Randolph) on page 49?

Because of the Seaborn/Seabourn connection to Greene and Jefferson Counties in Tennessee, there has been research related to the Hooper/Hopper name in those counties. A Thomas Hopper (not spelled Hooper) did live in Jefferson County in the late 1700s. In the Jefferson County, *Tennessee Court Minutes for 1792-1795*, a John Moulder surrendered the body of Thomas Hopper in discharge of himself as security in open court during the May Session of 1797. On September 27, 1798, a Charles Hopper bought 125 acres on the waters of Tuckahoe Creek from James White for $100.00. (Joseph Seaborn, father of the McMinn and Bradley County Seaborns, signed as a witness to another deed in 1804 for other lands on the same creek, and Edward Seaborn, possibly Joseph's father or grandfather, had a home on the creek.) In the *Jefferson County Tax Records* for District 1 in 1820, a Thomas Hooper owned 105 acres valued at $700.00 and paid a tax of $2.45. According to Hopper family research, Thomas was a Hopper and not Hooper.

Another possibility for a family relationship related to the Hoopers who were in Cocke County, Tennessee was in the *1830 Federal Census* on page 245. Andy Hooper had a male 10-15, another 15-20, two 20-30 and himself 60-70. Females were 5-10, 10-15 and a wife 50-60. On page 246 of the *1830 Cocke County Census* were Clemman Hooper, Sr. and Jr. Most likely this early Andrew was a brother to Clemman, Sr. and also to Absolom Hooper of Haywood County, North Carolina. In the *1800 Federal Census for Greenville, South Carolina*, Absolom Hooper was in house 1612 and Andrew Hooper was in house 1613. Both had been born in the 1760s. Another reference that places them in Greenville, S. C. was the *Kesterson Kollections Newsletter Vol. # 8* which listed an association with William Chesterson (Kesterson) who lived in house 1610 in the 1800 Census. According to the newsletter, Absolam Hooper, Andrew Hooper and William Casterson/Kesterson received a 500 acre grant December 3, 1798, *Book 44* page 364 in the Washington District, Greenville, South Carolina (Grant information came from Internet, *LDS Film #0022531*). (Credit for the Hooper information was given to Anne Goodwin, a Hooper researcher and Editor of the *Hooper Compass*. Emails from Anne Goodwin make up Appendix G in this book.)

Some of the information up until this point was based on conjecture, but Harold Reno believed the Andrew Hooper who married Martha Seabourn was listed in the *McMinn County 1830 Census*, and Kinsey C. Hooper listed his birth place as McMinn County on his Civil War Discharge. Harold Reno found an old microfilm at the E. G. Fisher Public Library in Athens, Tennessee; it listed Andrew Hooper in 1826 with Hiwassee District Grant 618:

Andrew Hooper this day enters as general enterer [not living on the land] 40 acres square in the Southwest corner of the Northwest quarter of Sec. 34 of Tract Township 4 Range 3 West of the Meridian in the county of McMinn, Tennessee Dist. beginning on the Southwest corner of said quarter Dec. 14, 1826 40 acres A. Hooper. I do certify the above to be a true copy of the records of my office Dec. 14, 1826 Nat Smith Ent. Taker. [If this were 40 acres square as stated it would be 1600 acres, so it is most likely just 40 acres.]

Andrew began selling land to his brothers-in-law and others in 1827. Under Grant Number 369, "For a valuable consideration I do assign to James Seabourn all the right that I have to the within names [*sic*] quarter Section of land November 3, 1827. Andrew (his x mark) Hooper." (A quarter section would be 160 acres, a half mile by a half mile.) "Grant No. 3637?? For value received, I do assign my right title interest claim of the within certificate to John Seaborn, his heirs and assigns forever, this the 7th day of August 1832. TEST: Joseph Seaborn." This piece of land was assigned by John Seaborn to William McDowell (his brother-in-law); then, it was reassigned from William to Singleton McKeel whose wife Patsy testified in the Andrew Hooper Court Case in 1855 (pages 20 – 21 in this book). The following was posted on the Internet at *Rootsweb Archives 1998* by R. Clayton Hooper (*claydoh@earthlink*.net): Reba Boyer in 1980 published the *Chancery Court Records of McMinn County, Tennessee*, and one of the records involved Isaac Smart, Exec. of Thomas Smart v. (versus) Widow and heirs, filed Mar. 2, 1867. This file also contains the original grant from James K. Polk, Gov. of Tenn. to Thomas Smart, Nov. 30, 1839, for land entered Dec. 14, 1828 by Andrew Hooper and assigned to Smart.

From other old microfilm tax records found at E. G. Fisher Public Library in Athens, TN, early McMinn County taxes were collected by the use of Captains: in Captain Watkins Company for 1829 Andrew Hooper paid taxes on 120 acres, 1 white poll, .76; John Seabourn 200 acres, 1 white poll 1.06 ¼ ; James Seabourn 200 acres, 1 white poll, 1.06 ¼ ; McKinsey [*sic*] Seaborn no land, 1 white poll, .3 ¼ ; Joseph Seabourn 40 acres, no white poll, .15; James Shelton 366 acres, 1 white poll, 1.69; Edward Sharp (later neighbor of Andrew Hooper in Bradley County whose death was possibly mentioned on pp. 16 and 18) no land, 1 white poll, .3 ¼; Joseph Teague no land, 1 white poll .3 ¼ . The tax list for 1830 in Captain Watkins Company included Andrew Hooper 120 acres (no white poll?), .45; James Seaborn 200 acres, 1 white poll, 1.06; McKinsey [*sic*] Seaborn no acres, 1 white poll, .31 ¼ ; Edward Sharp no land, 1 white poll, .31; James Shelton 368 acres, 1 white poll, 1.68; Joseph Teague no land, 1 white poll, .31 ¼. The Tennessee, McMinn County 1831Tax List was basically unreadable except for Andrew Hooper 120 acres, 1 white poll. In Captain Jamison's Company for 1832, taxes were listed for John Seabourn 360 acres, 1 white poll, 2.11 ¼ ; Kinsy Seabourn no land, 1 white poll, .43; James Seabourn 240 acres, 1 white poll, 1.82; Singleton McKeel no land, 1 white poll, .43; James Shelton 359 acres, 1 white poll, 2.60; Thomas Smart 160 acres, 1 white poll, 1.57. Andrew Hooper in 1836 paid taxes in District 9, McMinn County on 120 acres valued at $200.00 for .30.0. (See page 10 for *Ansearchin* early Bradley County Tax Records.)

Andrew Hooper moved into Bradley County, Tennessee when the land became available for settlement after the Ocoee Purchase. (See Appendix A on pp. 263 – 266 for Ocoee Land information.) The following was a deed made in 1837 and found by Richard (Rick) Hooper in a box of Hooper records:

The State of TenNessee bradley county Now [Know] all men by these present an be that I Lewisay Melton a widow of James Melton deceist [deceased] do bargnan [bargain] sell unto Andrew Hooper the said quarter of land that I am now in possession of at this time this 14 day of December in the six section the Southwest quarter of said section that I am now in possession of an has resiv [received] valu for it from said Andrew Hooper this 14 day of december 1837 for valu resiev [received] of Andrew Hooper I say Reseiv valu for it.

her

Lewisey x Melton

mark

Attest: Rhey Lawson
Attest: A. B. Hooper [Absolom abbreviated AB?]
Attest: Valentine Lawson
Archelaus Melton

Sewed to this deed was another very important document that the family kept (see p. 265 for 2 witnesses):

State of Tennessee   This day came before me Joseph Seabourn and acting Justice of the Peace
Bradley County   of said County John Webb and Benjamin Chester both respectable
sitisans [*sic*] of said County and after being duly sworn deposes and says
that thay are well acquainted with Lewisey Melton and the South East Quarter of Section Six
Township First Range the First west of the Basis Line in the Ocoe [*sic*] district and the said
Lewisey Melton was in possession of and residing upon said quarter section of land at and before
the pasing [*sic*] of the act of the legislature of Tennessee past on the 29th of November 1837
sworn to and subscribed this 3th day of August 1839.

his

John X Webb (Seal)

mark

Joseph Seaburn   his

Justice of the Peace   Benjamin X Chester (Seal)

 BC [Bradley County]   mark

[A Louisa Melton 30-40 lived in Anderson County, TN in 1840 with several young children.]

Notice that Joseph Seabourn was an "acting Justice of the Peace" for Bradley County in 1836, 1837 and1839. In 1836, Samuel Walker applied for a Revolutionary War Pension, and he was living in Bradley County, TN. In 1837, Joseph Laine also applied for a Revolutionary War Pension in Bradley County. Will Graves transcribed the record found on the Internet in *Southern Campaign American Revolution Pensions Statements and Rosters.* Joseph Seaburn was one of the names listed as J. P. (Justice of the Peace) in the records on Dec. 5, 1836 and Sept. 23, 1837. Since the Melton deed was made in 1837, it was important for Andrew to have legal proof for his claim, and Joseph Seaburn signed as the JP confirming the Lewisey Melton deed August 3, 1839. So James and Lewisey Melton must have been very early settlers.

Because of the early date of this land purchase in 1837, Andrew had to be aware of the Cherokee Removal which included nine detachments that left Charleston, Tennessee between August and October 1838 and which took the northern land route to Oklahoma. An Internet record of the "National Register of Historic Places Registration Form" on page 6 which was published Oct. 1990 by the United States Department of the Interior National Park Service, stated that almost 10,000 Cherokee left Charleston, Tennessee and traveled through the Rocky River Crossing and Roadbed to Blythe's Ferry at the confluence of the Hiwassee and Tennessee Rivers to Dayton, Tennessee and up Route 60 to McMinnville. Andrew Hooper's land was close to the Hiwassee River and a few miles from Charleston during the time of the removal.

Tennessee passed a law that allowed two more years for land to be entered and surveyed. Andrew Hooper was occupying the Lewisey Melton 160 acres that he entered August 5, 1839 Certificate Numbered 657 for grant numbered 679 (See grant next page.). The Hooper receipt for the purchase price is below: "Entry Takers Office, Cleveland Aug. 5, 1839, Received of Andrew Hooper in three hundred dollars and twenty dollars in Tenn. money being for Entry No. 679. Luke Lea, Entry Taker of the Ocoee District."

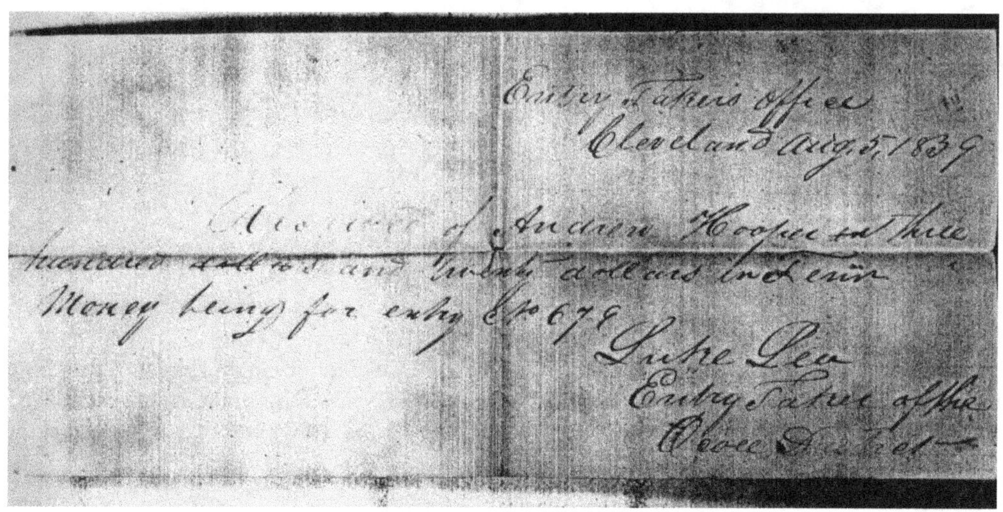

Below is a copy of this Grant (No. 679 written) payment which listed Andrew Hooper as the Occupant Enterer in Range 1 West Section 7 (see pp. 264 – 265). Also included in the Ocoee Grant were Newton Cannon who was the Governor of Tennessee and P. J. R. Edwards who was Register of the Ocoee District.:

THE STATE OF TENNESSEE.

No. 679

TO ALL TO WHOM THESE PRESENTS SHALL COME, GREETING:

KNOW YE, That in consideration of *an Entry made in the Entry Taker's Office of the Ocoee District, of No. 679 dated the 5th day of August 1839, by Andrew Hooper, as Occupant enterer,*

there is granted by the said State of Tennessee, to the said *Andrew Hooper* and *his* heirs, a CERTAIN TRACT OR PARCEL OF LAND, CONTAINING *One hundred and sixty* acres, lying in the County of *Bradley* in said District, situate in the *First* RANGE *West* of the basis line *First* TOWNSHIP, *and the Seventh Section, being the North East quarter of said Section,*

Beginning at the *North East* corner of said first mentioned quarter, with its appurtenances, To HAVE and to HOLD the said TRACT or PARCEL of LAND, with its APPURTENANCES, to the said *Andrew Hooper* and *his* heirs FOREVER.

IN WITNESS WHEREOF, *Newton Cannon,* GOVERNOR of the State of Tennessee, hath hereunto set his hand and caused the GREAT SEAL of the State to be affixed at NASHVILLE, on the *Seventh* day of *September* in the year of our Lord, one thousand eight hundred and thirty-*nine* and of American Independence, the sixty *fourth.*

BY THE GOVERNOR.

Wm. B. Young
SECRETARY.

Andrew Hooper

Hath title to the above described LAND.

P. J. R. Edwards
Register of the Ocoee District.

Next page, a General Enterer grant numbered 753 at top and numbered 790 in entry record for 160 acres in the Ocoee District was entered by Andrew Hooper September 14, 1839 for a grant dated August 7, 1839. This deed was found at *Ancestry.com*. See pp. 264 - 265 for pictures showing Range 1 West in Section 6.

The State of Tennessee,

No. *753*

TO ALL TO WHOM THESE PRESENTS SHALL COME, GREETING:

KNOW YE, That in consideration of an entry made in the Entry Taker's Office of the Ocoee District, of No. *790* dated the *7th* day of *August* 1839 by *Andrew Hooper, as general enterer,*

there is granted by the said State of Tennessee, to the said *Andrew Hooper* and *his* heirs a certain tract or parcel of land, containing *One hundred & sixty* acres, lying in the county of *Bradley* in the said District, situate in the *first* range *West* of the basis line *first* township *Sixth* section, being the *South East* quarter of said section: beginning at the *North East* corner of said quarter; with its appurtenances, to have and to hold the said tract or parcel of land, with its appurtenances, to the said *Andrew Hooper* and *his* heirs forever.

IN WITNESS WHEREOF, *Newton Cannon* Governor of the State of Tennessee, hath hereunto set his hand and caused the Great Seal of the State to be affixed at Nashville, on the *14th* day of *September* in the year of our Lord one thousand eight hundred and *Thirty nine* and of American Independence the sixty *fourth.*

James K. Polk

BY THE GOVERNOR,

John S. Young

SECRETARY.

Andrew Hooper

Hath title to the above described land.

Recorded 25th of January 1840

J. R. Edwards
Register of the Ocoee District

On January 25, 1840, Andrew entered Certificate No. 1587 as Occupant Enterer 80 acres for Grant No. 1711 in the Ocoee District. (See the following copy.) See p. 264 for picture of Range 1 West Section 7.

On the Internet, *Ancestry.com* has a copy of Grant 4377 in Bradley County, Ocoee District where Andrew Hooper was an assignee of the Occupant Enterer for 40 acres in First Range West of the Basis Line in First Township of the Seventh Section of the Northwest Corner dated March 2, 1842. (See pp. 264 – 265 for maps. See p. 10 and p. 288 for 160 acres dated 1848 found by Anne Goodwin of *Hooper Compass.*)

Found in the Hooper Box on a small piece of paper with no date: "40 acres in Section 5 T 1 R1 on the west corner of N W V, 120 a (acres?) in Setion [sic] 32 of T 1 Range 1 South E V". (This could possibly account for some more of the land in McMinn County or Bradley County. This was also listed on p. 186.)

Evidently, Andrew continued to trade across the Hiwassee River in McMinn County because he was listed in the *William Cowen Store Book Vol. 1*. The store record was hand copied by Agnes Maddux in 1965 from the original which was kept by Mrs. Dorothy Roberts of Big Spring, Tennessee. This record was found in the Chattanooga-Hamilton County Bicentennial Library: Andrew Hooper and A. Hooper were listed on page 82 in 1839. Page 25 listed a Thomas Hooper in 1839, and Kinsey C. Seaborn was listed on page 82 in 1839. (This Thomas probably was the Thomas in the *1840 Bradley County Census* (*1840 Census* compiled by Sheridan Randolph. Also, see pp. 289, 290, 291 and 292 for Thomas Hooper.)

In *Ansearchin* on the Internet for 1986 in Vol. 33, No. 1, pp. 9 - 14 early tax records of Bradley County, Tennessee, Andrew Hooper was listed in 1837 in District 1 on page 36, and in 1838 Andrew Hoopper and Absalam Hoopper were listed in District 1 on page 301.   James and Kinsey Seabourn were listed in District 1 in 1838; Kinsey Clabourn and James Claborn in 1837. In 1839, they were listed in Bradley County Taxes as James and Kinsey C. Seabern.   Andrew was also listed in the 1839 tax list with one poll. Mahan/Malin Gilbreath was also listed in 1837 in District 1 on page 36 and in 1839 for District 1 on page 312. (He was the father of Thomas H. Gilbreath who married Andrew and Martha's daughter Dialtha.)

The following record was related to Andrew Hooper of Bradley County. In the *Monroe County Deed Book M* pages 154-155, on April 6, 1839 a deed was made for 285 acres in Monroe County from John Hooper to Andrew Hooper of Bradley County for $1000.00. Nothing has been found to explain what happened to the land. Or, could the 285 acres have been in Bradley County and John Hooper lived in Monroe County?

Email from Anne Goodwin of the *Hooper Compass* March 15, 2016 to Harold Reno (see pp. 288 – 291) :
 There is ALSO a connection between Thomas Hooper and Andrew Hooper:
 Deed, Bradley Co., TN 21 Nov 1845, attachment to the suit of William Brimmer against the estate of
 Thomas Hooper. Mentions that there is no personal property to be found in the county, but there is a
 tract of land:
 NE 1/4 section 12, Twp (unreadable), range two west... 160 acres [another 160 acres of the 900
 acres that Andrew Hooper owned?]
 Case concerns debt to A. P. Brimmer of $8.19 1/4 cents interest, and also $1.35 judgement. Jan. term
 1846 land order sold to satisfy debt and sale held 10 March 1846 by order of circuit court of Bradley,
 and also to pay sum of $4.45... land "struck off to William Brimmer" for $25.63. Afterwards, to wit
 on this 18 day of February 1848, Andrew Hooper (apparently also creditor of Thomas Hooper) land
 from the said William Brimmer at the price of $27.09 and raised the bid to $10.55, the whole sum
 $37.53 ... thus sheriff sells lands of Thomas Hooper to Andrew Hooper 3 May 1848.

 Thus, the deed suggest a strong chance that Thomas Hooper and Andrew Hooper of Bradley County
 were either brothers or else first cousins, with brother being the more likely relationship to explain
 the debt actions.
 That means Elizabeth (Brimmer) Hooper may have been the widowed sister-in-law of Andrew
 Hooper. So, in 1850, she may have been living on the land, formerly that of her husband, which
 Andrew Hooper had bought in 1848.

Was Hiram Hooper related to Andrew Hooper? James, the son of Dorcas and Hiram Hooper, lived for a while in McMinn County next door to James Shelton (p. 297). James Hooper's mother, Dorcas, was mentioned in *Monroe County Deed Book O* numbered 222A. Also, a William Burris who performed the marriage ceremony for an Andrew Hooper to Anna Stephens on April 22, 1840 in Monroe County witnessed deed 222A which also mentioned an Andrew Hooper. This deed in *Deed Book O* involved Ennis C. Hooper and B.B. Babington and was made April 4, 1849 and recorded September 17, 1850 in Monroe County, Tennessee. It was related to 970 acres at Jonathan Smalling's corner with Zachariah Roberts' line, to Isaac Stephens's line, to Jesse Rhea line, to Richard Presley corner. Exempted out of the 970 acres were those owned by Dorcas Hooper of 160 acres; it exempted also 40 acres entered by Joseph Smith, as well as 18 acres entered by an Andrew Hooper, and 30 acres called the Milltract. This was located in District 16, SEC 20, SE corner. The witnesses were William Burris and John Stratton. These records must list a different Andrew? Perhaps this Andrew was the brother of Elizabeth Hooper Presley on pp. 3 and 4?

(Other information about Andrew Hooper can be found in the following chapters: "Andrew Hooper Court Cases" on pp. 11 - 22 for the 1850s; Hooper Descendants on pp. 34 - 131; "The Diary of Kinsey C. Hooper & the 8th Tennessee Volunteer Infantry, Co. A and the Andrew Hooper Estate" on pp. 132 - 161. Also, Appendix G p. 286 – 305 has information related to Andrew and the Hooper family.)

Andrew Hooper Court Cases

The Andrew Hooper court cases were found mostly on microfilm at the History Branch of the Bradley Cleveland Public Library in Cleveland, TN. Harold Reno transcribed the more than 30 pages of Circuit Court records which related to Andrew Hooper becoming a defendant in 1850 when Thomas Caldwell sued him in the Circuit Court of Bradley County, Tennessee.

Small undated record (hard to read):
>(Back of record) Thomas Caldwell Account
>(Front of record) Andrew Hooper to Thomas
>Caldwell July 1849 To one horse beast $20.00
>Cr. by 132 lbs. of bacon at 8 cts per   10.56
>pound Remainder due after credit   9.44

(This small record seemed to indicate that Andrew Hooper had bought a horse for $20.00 and received credit for bacon worth $10.56 leaving a balance of $9.44 to be paid to Thomas Caldwell.)

State of Tennessee To any lawful officer of said county to execute said summons I command
Bradley County   you to summon Andrew Hooper to appear before said Justice of the Peace
for said county to answer the complaint of Thomas Caldwell in a plea of debt due by account under a warrant here-in fail not given under my hand and seal this the 17 day of April 1850.   (Signature Unreadable)
>(seal) JPBC [Justice of the Peace Bradley County]

Thomas Caldwell vs. Andrew Hooper this 10 day of May 1850 J. B. Carter, Constab.

Subpoena Thomas Caldwell vs. Andrew Hooper Issued 25th of May 1850. Came to hand issued executed by Summoning William Caldwell to appear according to this subpoena & return June 1st 1850 to R. M. Swan, Esq. J. B. Carter, Constb.

State of Tennessee To any lawful officer of said county to execute and return, --You are hereby
Bradley County   commanded to summon William Caldwell to appear at the office of R. M.
Swan in the town of Cleveland on Saturday the first day of June next by 2 o'clock in the afternoon, then and there to give evidence in a suit pending in which Thomas Caldwell is plaintiff and Andrew Hooper is defendant on behalf of the plaintiff and this you will not omit under the lawful penalty in such case made and provided and make here return of this writ. Given under my hand and seal May 25th 1850. R. M. Swan JP (seal)

(Another subpoena was issued the same date as above for John Carmichael and Anderson Caldwell, D. D. Lewis, const. [constable?]. A subpoena was issued June 1, 1850 for James Carter to appear on June 22, 1850 by one o'clock in the afternoon.)

Thomas Caldwell In this cause the defendant Andrew Hooper makes oath that Simion Graves
vs.   is a material witness for him in the trial of this cause and that he cannot
Andrew Hooper   safely go to trial without the testimony of the said Simion Graves affiant
further states and makes oath that he believes that he can have the said Simeon Graves on Saturday the 22nd day of June 1850 before Robert M. Swan an acting Justice of the Peace in his office in the town of Cleveland Bradley County. Affiant therefore prays for a continuance of this cause until the said 22nd day of June 1850, not for delay but for the attainment of justice.

Andrew (X) Hooper
mark

Sworn to & subscribed before
me this the 1st day of June 1850
R. M. Swan JPBC

(On the backside of the affidavit of A. Hooper for a continuance are J. Carter 1 day and W. Caldwell 2 day.

Another subpoena was issued for James Carter to appear June 19th 1850 J. B. Carter, const.)
(Many names unreadable) William Eades, summon J. B. Carter, Const. [Constable]?).

Thomas Caldwell	June 22nd 1850 This cause was taken up, the parties being present, the
vs.	Testimony being taken the parties agreed that the Justice shall have
Andrew Hooper	untill [*sic*] Saturday the 29th instant before issuing judgment. Saturday 29th
	June 1850 judgment is given by me against the plaintiff for the cost of this

suit amounting to Six dollars & fifty cents.

Expenses:		2.00
		1.00
		.50
		.50
Houston Gilbreath		.50
	Mulky	75
	Carter	.25
	Carmichael	.25
	Colwell	.50
Judgment:		.25
		$6.50

The plaintiff prays to appeal from said judgment to the Circuit Court of Bradley County which appeal is granted this July 1850 R. M. Swan, JP fee for appeal bond .50 (first decision appealed?):

State of Tennessee Bradley County   We, Thomas Colwell and William Colwell and S. B. Carter bind ourselves to Andrew Hooper in the sum of Fifteen dollars to pay amount Thereof well and timely to be made to the same A. Hooper or his heirs & assigns of their own Thomas Caldwell who has this day appealed to the next term of the Circuit Court for Bradley County the ? to be held at the court house in the town of Cleveland on the first Monday of Sept. for 1850 from a judgment of R. M. Swan a justice of the peace for Bradley County and state aforesaid in favor of Andrew Hooper against the said Thomas Caldwell for six dollars and fifty cents cost rendered the 29th day of June 1850. Shall prosecute said appeal successfully or in case of failure shall comply with and perform the judgment of said court. Given under our hands and seals this 2nd day of July 1850.

Thomas (his X mark) Colwell

Test R. M. Swan   William Caldwell (seal)

Thomas Caldwell	I Thomas Caldwell do solemnly swear that owing to my poverty I am not
vs.	able to bear the expenses of the law suit, which I am to commence and that
Andrew Hooper	I am justly nonbilled to a recovery from the defendant to the best of my
	knowledge and belief an amount within the jurisdiction of the court in
	which I have commenced my suit.

Sworn to & subscribed   Thos. (X) Caldwell
before me this 7th day   mark
of January 1851
John H. Payne clk.

Thomas Caldwell	In this cause the Defendant makes oath that he cannot safely go to trial for
vs.	want of the testimony whose testimony he deems material Simeon Graves
Andrew Hooper	who has been regularly summoned as a witness but does not attend his
	absence is without the consent of procurement of affiant. He believes he can

have said witness at the term. He therefore prays a continuance of the cause not for delay but justice. Sworn in open court Jan. 8th 1851.
John H. Payne clk.   his
                                                         A. (X) Hooper
                                                            mark

STATE OF TENNESSEE TO THE SHERIFF OF Bradley COUNTY, Greeting: We command you to summon Sylvanus Dobbs & John Webb & Jno. T. Carmichael instantly to be and appear before the Judge of our Circuit Court, at a Court now sitting for the county of Bradley at the Court-house in the town of Cleveland to testify, and the truth to depose, in a cause depending in said court, wherein Thos. Caldwell is plaintiff, and Andrew Hooper is defendant, on behalf of the plaintiff and this they shall not omit under the lawful penalty. WITNESS, John H. Payne clerk of our said court, at Office in Cleveland the 1st Monday of May 1851, and of American Independence the 75. John H. Payne, Clerk (Issued May 5, 1851 and executed May 6, 1851 on J. T. Carmichael by T. L. Batey.)

(The dates in the preceding court case were very confusing and hard to understand. The compiler, Harold Reno, placed the Subpoenas in 1850 or 1851 contingent upon whether R. M. Swan, J. P. issued them or whether John H. Payne, Clerk issued them.)

(Another subpoena for the same date was issued for William Edds [Eads?], T. H. Gilbreath and William McPherson to appear on behalf of the Defendant. Issued by John H. Payne, Clerk. The copy was very dark and hard to read but it seemed to have been issued Aug. 1851 for Sept. 1851 Court date. The summons seemed to have been delivered by William Edes [Eads?].)

(The Plaintiff, Thomas Caldwell, also had Subpoenas delivered to Starling Shelton, John Webb, John T. Carmichael, William Caldwell, James Carter and Anderson Caldwell for them to appear the 1st Monday of May 1851 and of American Independence 76 by John H. Payne, Clerk.)

(A subpoena was issued May 8th 1851 and delivered by S. L. Harris ? Sheriff?.)

(On July 17th 1851 a subpoena was issued for John Webb, Starling Shelton, and Wm Coldwell to appear Aug. 27, 1851 and delivered by S. L. Harris Dept. Sheriff with a note that J. T. Carmichael and Andrew Caldwell, [and] James Carter not found.)

A long expense list was also found but not dated:

Andrew Hooper	State Tax	2.50
Thomas Caldwell	filing papers	.75
	documenting cause	.20
	of=taking and filing affidavit	.06¼
	1 order	.25
	1 continuance	.37 ½
	10 subpoenas	1.25
	1 probate	.06 ¼
	materials 25 copies of each	
	25 bill of suit	
	25 recording cause	1.62 ½
		5.07

Plaintiff Judgment 75 cts – 2 orders 50 1 cont	.37 ½
taking and filing of 2 aff. 12 ½ 1 aff.	.06 ¼
3 spons. (subpoenas?) 37 ½	2.43 ¾
T. S. Batey 6 spus. (subpoenas?) executed	1.50
S. L. Harris 4 “ “ 2 not found	1.25
J. B. Carter court [unreadable]	
McPherson & Edds 2 days each [unreadable]	
Gilbreath & Caldwell	1.00
David Mulkey	.75
J. B. Carter	.25
J. T. Carmichael	.25
Justice Swan	.75
Witness: William Caldwell 3 days & 26 miles	3.21
“ Starling Shelton 9 “ “ 24 “	7.71

"	Wm. P. Edds	16 "	" 96 "	15.84
"	Wm. McPherson	17 "	" 96 "	<u>16.59</u>

(total unreadable)

Thomas Coldwell	Circuit Court Sept. term 1851 In this cause before (unreadable)
vs.	makes oath that he is informed the security guarantee by the plaintiff in his
Andrew Hooper	appeal bond is [unreadable] and wholly insufficient to secure the costs

which may be recovered against him in this court wherefore he prays a rule
in plaintiff to satisfy his court security & to subscribe in open court this second day of Sept. 1851.

Andrew (X) Hooper
mark

John H. Payne, clerk

Thomas Caldwell	This day came into open court A. A. Clingan and C. J. Price ? and
vs.	made oath that they are acquainted with the parties in the above suit and
Andrew Hooper	the security guarantee the plaintiff in his appeal bond in this cause that

they are informed and believe that said security is wholly insufficient to
recover the costs of the suit be as affiant believe having little if any property unable to ascertain
from to and ? in open court this 2nd day of Sept. 1851

A. A. Clingan

John H. Payne, clerk   C. J. Price ?

After the Thomas Caldwell versus Andrew Hooper case ended, several bad things happened to Andrew's family. His second wife died, and another son died (see pages 19 and 20). Andrew brought the next lawsuit against several individuals who were operating a grist mill near the mouth of Candy's Creek at the Hiwassee River. They had bought the Mill built by James Shelton, and it used a dam to block Candy's Creek to store the water necessary to power the mill. Andrew Hooper identified the stagnant mill pond as the cause of several families being sick and several people dying from diseases caused by bad air (stinking air). (The term malaria means "bad air," but the Malaria parasite was not discovered until 1880 and the mosquito that carried the disease was not understood until 1897 – 1898. See the Internet article from *Centers for Disease Control*, "The History of Malaria".)

In August of 1854, K. C. Hooper, acting as agent for Andrew Hooper, appealed to Justice of the Third Judicial District, John C. Gaut, in Hamilton County, Tennessee to indict the mill dam because it was causing sickness. John Gaut agreed with the cause on August 4, 1854:

State of Tennessee.

      To the Sheriff of Bradley County Greeting. Whereas Andrew Hooper did on the 4th day of August 1854, present his bill of complaint to the Honorable John C. Gaut, one of the Judges of the Circuit Courts of Law in the State of Tennessee, against Thomas Townsly, Francis Hayes, Carter T. Hayse, David Harvy, Thomas Swafford, William Humphrey, George Millard, Marion Owens, William Shelton, Nathan Ross, Thomas Ross, Elija Ballenger, Levi Carter, Benjamin Harden, Solomon Harden, Silas Avery, John Webb, John Willson, David Wilson, William Duncan, Andrew Duncan, George Kirby, William T. Eades, John Swafford & John Finly, praying among other things in said Bill of Complaint for an injunction to Issue, Restraining the above named persons and all others from rebuilding or constructing a mill dam near the mouth of Candy's Creek in the place formerly known as Shelton's Mill, and whereas also the said John C. Gaut Judge as aforesaid, was pleased to order that an injunction issue as prayed for in said bill of complaint.

Now these are therefore to command you the said Sheriff, that you make known to the above named defendants and all others that these are hereby enjoined from rebuilding or constructing a mill dam near the mouth of Candy's Creek at the place formerly known as Shelton's Mill, until the final hearing of this cause herein delay not and see that you make due return of this writ in the next of said Chancery Court to be held at the Court House in Cleveland on the 4th Monday of next

1854. Witness James Berry Clerk & Master of said court at office in Cleveland the 4th Monday of
February 1854.   [Signature] James Berry C&M

A few months later in the same year, Danis/Daniel G. Foster, a neighbor who married Rutha Geren (a sister
to K. C. Hooper's wife, Elizabeth) joined the suit with Andrew. Danis (known as D. G. Foster) might, also,
be brother-in-law to Andrew, and entered the lawsuit because his sister may have been Mary Foster Hooper
who was the second wife who died (see pages 20, 21 and 30):

> Know all men by these present that we Andrew Hooper and Danis G. Foster, are jointly and
> severally held and firmly bound unto Thomas Townsley, Francis Hayse, Carter T. Hayse, Robert
> Hayse, David Harvey, Thomas Swafford, William Humphreys, George Millard, Marion Owens,
> William Shelton, Nathan Ross, Thomas Ross, Elija Ballenger, Levi Carter, Benjamin Harden,
> Solomon Harden, Silas Avery, John Webb, John Wilson, David Wilson, William Duncan, Andrew
> Duncan, George Kirby, William T. Eeds, John Swaford, & John Finly, in the Sum of Two
> thousand dollars for the payment of which we bind ourselves our heir executors and administrator
> jointly and severally firmly by these present, sealed with our seals and dated the 4th day of August
> 1854. [John Hooper testified that Mary Foster Hooper died August 1854. See p. 20.]
>
> The condition of the above obligation is such that whereas the said Andrew Hooper has this day
> filed his bill of complaint in the Chancery Court at Cleveland Bradley County Tennessee against
> Thomas Townsley and others as above mentioned wherein it is prayed that an Injunction Issue
> restraining the above persons and all others from rebuilding or constructing a mill dam near the
> mouth of Candy's Creek at the place formerly known as Shelton's Mill, until the further order of
> said Chancery Court.
>
> Now if the said Andrew Hooper shall with effect prosecute his said Bill of Complaint or in cause
> he fail therein will well and truly pay all such damages as may be decreed against him by the
> honorable chancellor for wrongfully suing out said injunction then the above obligation to be void
> otherwise to remain in full force and virtue.

Since the Chancery Court Case hinged on depositions made under oath, James Berry, Clerk of Chancery
Court, filed a form entitled "RULES RELATIVE TO TAKING DEPOSITIONS" with Andrew Hooper and
the people being sued listed. This was dated the 4th Monday of August, 1855 (August 27, 1855). These
depositions covered 123 pages including the Rules and the list of people to be deposed.

(Rick Hooper sent part of this trial to George Francis Hooper in Missouri and asked him to transcribe the
pages. Harold Reno had copies made of 123 microfilm pages and transcribed the information using the
parts done by George Francis Hooper to confirm interpretation.) On November 20, 1855, Dennis D. Taylor
began taking depositions at the home of Andrew Hooper for the Fifth Chancery Division of Tennessee.
The Clerk Master of the Court at Cleveland, Tennessee was James Berry. The witnesses for the
Complainant who were served subpoenas on October 22, 1855 were John T. Carmichael 50 years old; Dr.
Calvin Atchley 36 years old; Christopher Graves 30 years old; Henry Earnest 33 years old; John Wilson 47
years old; William John Lane 62 years old; William Farmer 60 years old; John Hooper 29 years old and
Patrick Graham 50 years old. John Brannum's deposition records covered 30 pages and Dennis Taylor
wrote 93 more pages. Each time a different person took depositions, the records began with page one.

John T. Carmichael was questioned by the Complainant's (Andrew Hooper) Solicitor about the length of
time he lived near Shelton Mill, and he answered for eleven years. He also testified that it was the same
mill for which Jesse Wood and John Newman had received a prior indictment. When asked about the
health of the Hoper [sic] family before Wood and Newman were indicted, the Deponent answered that their
health was very bad since he arrived. He stated that Mr. and Mrs. Hooper and a child had come to see him
when he was sick. He stated that he had gone by the Hoopers and had seen Mr. Hooper and some of his
children chilling. Mr. Carmichael was asked how close he lived to the pond and mill and he answered
about a half mile to the pond and farther to the mill. He also described an offensive smell that came from
the pond. He further stated that he had had intermitting fever and then chills and that out of 16 members of
his family, 15 had been sick (slaves and family members). He stated that the pond extended through land

that Andrew Hooper cultivated. He also mentioned orchards on the Hooper farm. The testimony included information regarding the death of a tenant, Mr. Whaley, who lived on Mr. Hooper's farm about thirty or forty yards from the pond. When asked to name who died while living near the pond during last summer and fall, he said a daughter of Mrs. Hayes died, Samuel McCracking and wife, and Joseph McCracking, Patrick Grayham had a child to die and Miss Young died. They had had intermittent fever and chills. He also stated that Andrew Hooper's mother and wife died before the dam was pulled down the first time. Others, who died before the dam was pulled down, included Mr. Morten, Mr. Branham, Edward Sharp, Rudy Archer and several children. After being asked where the defendants lived in relation to the mill, he stated that John Webb lived something over a mile from the pond, Silas Avery lived four miles away in the settlement, Wm Dunbar lived two miles or further from the mill, did not know how far George Millerd lived and Andrew Duncan lived near William Dunbar.

Cross examination by the Respondents' Solicitor included how far William Shelton, a defendant, lived from the pond, and Carmichael answered that it must be a half mile. He also testified that Thomas Ross lived about a half mile from the pond, and Nathaniel Ross lived about a mile and a half from the pond. Mr. Carmichael was then asked where Andrew Hooper lived eleven years ago when Mr. Carmichael moved to the area, and he stated that Mr. Hooper lived a quarter of a mile from the creek, and Mr. Hooper moved to the house where he now lives about a year ago. According to testimony, a Shelton had sold the mill to Young, and the Solicitor wanted to know if Carmichael and Hooper had discussed buying the land where the mill was located and dividing the land. Carmichael testified that he and Hooper had never had such a discussion. So, the Solicitor asked about a conversation that Carmichael had had with Mr. Eads about buying the land. Carmichael responded that the land he was talking about was land that Hooper already owned and was not the mill quarter. (See close- up Ocoee Map saved by David Johnson showing James Shelton land which is to the left of Andrew Hooper on p. 265 where dam was located on Candy's Creek.)

When asked if the mill was operating when Mr. Hooper entered the land, Carmichael stated that he did not know when Hooper entered the land. The cross examination also questioned whether flooding of the springs was caused by freshet (fresh rain) falling into the creek or by the backwaters of the Hiwassee? He answered that he remembered one time when there was high water with a swift current running down the creek, and the springs were covered that time. Another question related to a conversation with John T. Milliway about Mr. Carmichael threatening to have the dam pulled down by force. Carmichael answered that while he was sick, he said if able he would go to the dam and destroy it. He was then asked if he told Alfred Fitzgerald and Wm Day that the dam was not the cause of the sickness, and he replied that he did not remember that conversation.

The Respondents' Solicitor then inquired about Mr. Carmichael being examined as a witness in the Circuit Court of Bradley County, Tennessee relating to the character of the pond and if he testified to an agreement made between him and Hooper about buying the mill and then selling some of the land to Carmichael. He answered that he was examined in Circuit Court during the September term of 1854, and he remembered a conversation between him and Mr. Hooper about Hooper possibly buying the mill and making gates to let the water run off to alleviate some of the sickness in the area. Mr. Carmichael also said that he told Hooper that his (Mr. Carmichael's) land had already been ditched to drain the water off, and if that didn't help he would bring suit against the dam. When asked if he told Wm Edes (Eads) that Hooper ought to sell land on Carmichael's side of the creek if he (Hooper) bought the mill quarter, Carmichael stated that he did not remember that conversation. He also stated that he thought the mill could grind about ten bushels during the dry season of the year. He said that the mill had two sets of stones and about four feet of water to turn the stones. John T. Carmichael testified for two days at 75 cents a day.

The next person to give a deposition was Dr. Calvin Atchly/Atchley who was called on behalf of the Complainant. He testified that he had been a practicing physician for four years. He described the pond as having a green scum with a very disgraceful odor. When asked what influence the smell would have on neighbors, he said that it would be capable of producing chills, fever and other malarious diseases (they thought Malaria was caused by bad air). The people who were sick had the intermittent chills and fever. He described the deaths of women in the neighborhood as being for female complaint and one of hydroespholates. He further testified that he saw one little girl who had chills, saw Mrs. McCrackin at Grahams when she had chills (he later learned she died); also, he learned that Joseph McCrackin died with a congestive chill (but the doctor never went to see him) and admitted that Joseph McCrackin had come earlier to ask Dr. Atchley to come see his sick daughter, but the doctor never went to see her. He stated that he was asked to see Mr. Whaley when he was sick, but since he had another physician at the time, Dr. Atchley did nothing for him. Later when he was asked to see Mrs. Peoples, he learned that Mr. Whaley was dying. He further described Mr. Whaley's sickness as a Billious Remittent fever, but said it was difficult to diagnose because fever can change from one type to another. He said that Mr. Whaley lived about three or four hundred yards from the pond. When asked if he attended Patrick Graham's family when they were sick, he admitted to doctoring the Graham family, and they had an intermittent disease with one boy suffering from pneumonia. Later he learned that one of the children died after the doctor quit tending to the family. Under cross examination he said the McCrackin family lived on the banks of the Hiwassee River, and one was aged from 45 to 55 and the other from 65 to 75. He also testified that the disease was extensive and as bad in other sections of the county. When asked if he had been attending to the John T. Carmichael family, he stated that he had during last summer and fall, and that Mrs. Carmichael was afflicted with a chronic liver affliction with chills and fever and neuralgia which was of a malarious origin. He stated that a pond on S. C. Woods' farm and a filthy creek that runs through the S. C. Wood and Charles Tillery farms also had people suffering from chills and fever that could cause malaria. When questioned about curing a patient living close to the stagnant water, he said that it was almost impossible to cure someone who lived close to the cause. He also testified that he treated five white members of the John T. Carmichael family and four black members. Dr. Calvin Atchley served as a witness for two days, and traveled from Meigs County, Tennessee for a distance of twelve miles.

Another witness for the Complainant Andrew Hooper was Dr. James M. Campbell who said he had been practicing medicine for 16 years. He said he passed the pond frequently and did not notice a smell. When asked about the types of diseases that were produced when water was in a pond, he said that intermittent chills and fever usually occurred. He was asked if he was practicing before the pond was pulled down and also did he testify in Circuit Court of Bradley County in the case against Wood and Newman? He admitted that he was practicing at that time and that he did testify in Circuit Court. He also stated that before the dam was destroyed, the people suffered intermittent chills and fever, and after the dam was removed, the health improved. The families he attended were Mr. Young, Holt, Hays, Whaley, Graham and Z. Lawson who lived within three quarters of a mile from the pond. He believed that Whaley and Graham lived on Mr. Hooper's land. Under cross examination by the Respondents' Solicitor, Dr. Campbell testified that intermitting fever and chills have extended through the ridges and hills, and that there were no more cases close to the pond than anywhere else. He testified that Mrs. Young probably died from a breast complaint with a very bad cough, and Mr. Whaley died because of a lack of nursing. Under reexamination of the Complainant's Solicitor, the doctor said that disease was more likely where the creek is dammed, or a large drift slowed the flow of the creek. He described another mill pond on the same creek above Shelton's that was pulled down, and the health of the neighbors was much better. Under reexamination by the Respondents' Solicitor, the doctor testified that a large drift above the dam was on Mr. Hooper's land, and it was made of timber. Dr. J. M. Campbell witnessed two days, lived in Meigs County and traveled ten miles.

The next to testify for the Complainant was Christopher Graves. He described a yellowish scum that was on the pond. He knew that Carmichael, his wife and two sons were sick, along with John Hayse, Robert Hayse and Silas Avery who had been chilling. He heard that Jesse M. Woods and children were sick along with Elisha Hayse and several others who looked unhealthy. Christopher stated that he also had bad health with the chills. He also had seen Patrick Graham whose health had been bad, and Patrick said his family had been chilling, and they lost one child. When asked if he was familiar with the sickness in the Complainant's family, he said he had no knowledge of their sickness. Under cross examination by the Respondents' Solicitor, Christopher said that he had been informed that Andrew Hooper was his wife's uncle. (Christopher had married Elizabeth Shelton, a daughter of James Shelton and Sarah Hooper Shelton. Elizabeth died young.) He admitted that he had seen the drifts above and below the mill dam. Under reexamination by the Complainant's Solicitor, he described Rogers Creek on the opposite side of the Hiwassee as nasty looking. Christopher testified three days at 75 cents a day.

Kinsey Seaborn, aged about fifty years old, was also a witness for the Complainant, Andrew Hooper. Kinsey testified that he was acquainted with the creek before the pond was created, and that he had been acquainted with the pond ever since it had been raised in 1835 or 1836. When asked about the health of the neighborhood before the pond, he stated that it was thinly settled, and he was not aware of sickness before that. When asked about Andrew Hooper's first wife's health, he said that it had been good before she took sick. He also said that he had been to the Hooper house about two weeks before Mrs. Hooper died, and she had been chilling. He said he had seen John Hooper's children chilling frequently when he lived on the creek; he also said he knew of Andrew Hooper's mother dying, and he was at Andrew Hooper's when his second wife died. He was asked if he was present when the injunction was served at the dam and how much water was in the pond. He answered that he was present when the injunction was served and the water was about sixteen inches deep. Under cross examination by the Respondents' Solicitor, Kinsey testified that there was not more sickness on Candy's Creek before the dam was built. When asked to name the men who were present at the mill when the injunction was served, he said that S. S. Harris, Thomas H. Gilbreath, K. C. Hooper, John Hooper, Silas Avery, Thomas Ross, Solomon Harden and R. S. Holt were present. When asked if he was related to the Complainant's first wife, he stated that she was his sister and the third wife of Andrew was Kinsey's cousin. (Margaret was a cousin; was she a Beaty or Carson? See pp. 25 and 288 - 291.) K. C. Seaborn testified for 2 days at 75 cents a day, and he traveled 20 miles.

Henry Earnest, about 33 years old, was called to testify on behalf of the Complainant. He stated that he had lived close to the dam for thirteen years. He said that he knew that Mr. Hooper's wife and mother died before the dam was pulled down. He also stated that his sister and mother died; Alan Blair had a child to die; Edward Sharp died; Linsey Edwards had a child to die; Wm Shelton had a child to die, and Rhody Archer died while living near the pond. In fact the general health of the people living around the pond was bad with fever and chills. He described the pond as having a dark green scum and an offensive smell. The smell was worse after they had been grinding all day and the pond water level was low. When asked to name the people who lived on the Complainant's land, Henry replied that Andrew Hooper with two sons and a son-in-law lived there. Also, Washington Whaley and Patrick Graham lived on the farm. All of the families had sickness and some had deaths. He also named other families living close to the pond that had sickness: McCrackings, Simeon Graves, Carmichael, Miss McKeel, Wm Harris, Elisha Hayes, R. S. Holt, James Young, Esquire Davis, Jesse Wood, Dunn; Samuel McCracking and wife died; Joseph McCracking died, and Miss Young and her daughter died.

Henry was then asked to describe Mr. Hooper's land and to describe the mill. He said that some of the bottom land was first rate and other land was not as good. The springs were as good as any in this country. He said he would describe the mill as a tub mill. Under cross examination by the Respondents' Solicitor, he was asked about how bad the sickness was last summer and fall, and he said he thought that there was more sickness than common and compared it to 1838 or 1840 when there was a lot of sickness. He also said that he did not know what Mrs. Hooper died of, but heard that Andrew Hooper's mother died of yellow jaundice. He admitted that he did not know what diseases caused the people to die, and he could not remember the year they died. He was asked the size of the area where the deaths occurred, and he said it was two miles square and thickly settled. Henry was asked if any of the families who were sick lived below the mill pond, and he answered that he lived about three hundred yards from the river, Duncan lived about a quarter of a mile from the river and Dunn lived about a mile from the river. Also Simeon Graves lived about two hundred yards from the river, and McCracking lived on the bank of the river. Mr. Earnest was then asked about a drift in Candy's Creek below the dam, and he replied that a large drift did exist below the mill with the McCracking family living a mile from the drift; Simeon Graves lived some farther; Henry stated he lived three quarters of a mile from the dam; Dunn lived two hundred yards nearer the drift; Miss McKeel lived a half mile away; Wm Hays lived about a quarter of a mile from the dam; Dunn lived about three quarters of a mile, and Carmichael lived about three quarters of a mile from the drift. He said his mother died of a liver complaint, and she was about sixty years old. His sister died of fever. Under reexamination by the Complainant's Solicitor, Mr. Earnest said the mill pond was in the two mile area he had designated earlier where there was much sickness, and he said the mill dam backed the water up two miles in Candy's Creek. Henry Earnest testified three days at 75 cents a day.

The next witness for the Complainant Andrew Hooper was John Lane. He said he was acquainted with the pond and described it as green with a green scum and bad smell. He further testified that the sick families included the Carmichaels, McKeel, Hays, Henry Earnest and Graves. He said the sickness included chills and fever. Under cross examination by the Respondents' Solicitor, he also admitted that there had been a great deal of sickness in the country. He also said the drift below the dam seemed to stop the current of the creek. He said that he had fished where the drift was. He also admitted that the green scum was also on other mill ponds. John Lane testified three days.

Patrick Graham, fifty years old, was a witness for the Complainant. He stated that he had lived on Andrew Hooper's land for three years. He and his sons became sick the first fall with the ague, and this summer and fall all six of his children were sick with five having chills and fever, one with fever and one of his sons died of chills and fever. He said the scum on the pond had different colors and a bad smell. Patrick Graham testified four days. (See page 27 for more information about the Graham/Hooper family.)

John McPherson, aged about fifty seven years, next testified for the Complainant. He stated that the dam was first erected between 1836 and 1839. He said he lived about three miles above the dam. When asked how far the smell of the pond reached, he said about two miles. He also said that there used to be several ponds on the creek, and now that some had been abated the health had improved. He also said that the people who lived above him were healthier than the ones below. Two of the people he visited while they were sick were John Carmichael and Robert Holt. Under cross examination by the Respondents' Solicitor, Mr. McPherson said the first people he knew to live on the mill quarter were James Shelton and Singleton McKeel. When asked if Hooper was the owner of the land at the same time that Shelton filed on the mill quarter, he said he did not know from personal knowledge. He was asked if sickness was worse, and he said that it was worse on the water courses. Mr. McPherson testified that the mills closest to the Shelton Mill were in Cleveland, five miles away, and Castillers' Mill, about six miles away. He also said the Shelton Mill was a tub mill that could grind about eight to twelve bushels of corn in the dry season and grind about fifteen to twenty bushels of wheat. He said they usually only ran one pair of stones at a time. John McPherson testified three days at 75 cents a day.

The Complainant's Solicitor called William Farmer, age about 61, to give a deposition. He said he was acquainted with the mill and had seen the pond with a white color and also a green color. He said that he had smelled the pond from about a mile. He said that the families who lived on Andrew Hooper's land were Whaleys, Grahams, Kinsey Hooper and Daniel Foster's family. He stated he had seen Kinsey Hooper with a fever, Graham's son who was sick and Peoples who lived close to the Whaleys. When asked how long he had known Andrew Hooper, he said several years. Under cross examination by the Respondents' Solicitor, William stated that he lived in the Ridges, and the health was about the same there as on the low lands. He also stated that there were two drifts in the creek on Andrew Hooper's land. He was then asked if there are other mills, other than the one on James Young's farm, and he said that Spivy's Mill was about two and a half miles away, but it was a sorry mill for grinding in the summer. If a person wanted to go to a better mill, it would be five or more miles, and the bridge was not a very good one. Under reexamination by the Complainant's Solicitor, the witness stated that there was another swamp near Kincannon's ferry called the Flag Pond that was said to cause sickness. He said that Spivy's Mill had two ponds, and there was more sickness close to that area also. Mr. Farmer was asked how long the drifts had been there, and he stated several years. He was also asked if Mr. Hooper had enough time to remove the drifts after the dam was pulled down, and he said he didn't suppose there was enough time. Under reexamination by the Respondents' Solicitor, he said that the area was not more thickly settled. He admitted that the sickness was all over the country and not just on the low grounds. He also said that there were two springs on the Hooper farm, and one was flooded by the pond, but the other flooded when it rained heavily. He said one of the springs was small and had been found when the dam was pulled down. William Farmer testified for 4 days at 75 cents a day.

The next witness to give a deposition was John Hooper, age about 29. He stated that he was the son of Andrew Hooper, and his mother died of yellow jaundice (he had heard this from others). He said she died after the first mill pond was abated. He also remembered his grandmother's death and said she died of Ague and fever. He had had three brothers to die, and two of them died of scarlet fever. He was not at home when the third brother died. When asked if his first step-mother (Mary Foster) was sickly for years before her death, he answered that she had the sick head (fell down) and the ague. He said he saw a green scum on the pond and smelled the pond when the water was drawn down. He said that the people who lived on the farm were Whaley and Peoples who lived across the creek; Whaley was sick and died. Patrick Graham, Caleb Dobbs, Kinsey Hooper, T. H. Gilbreath and Daniel Foster lived on Andrew Hooper's farm.

Kinsey had the ague, and father's (Andrew's) wife and two of the children were sick along with two of Dobb's children this past summer and fall. When John was asked about the mill dam after the two injunctions were served, he said the pond has been full to running over since the bill was served. He identified Thomas Ross, Silas Avery, John Barrett, Solomon Hardin and others who had carried dirt to repair the dam. He said that while the pond was lowered after the Circuit Court injunction, they burned the drift and removed a great part of it. He said his father owned 920 acres, and the mill pond extended through two quarters of his father's farm creating pools and ponds of stagnant, stinking water. Under examination by the Respondents' Solicitor, he stated that his grandmother (Hooper) was in her sixtys when she died. He said that his mother died over fifteen years ago (1839), grandmother died about fourteen years ago (1840), his first brother died twelve years ago (1843), another brother died ten years ago (1845) and the other brother died twelve months ago (1854). When he was asked about his first step-mother's death, he said she died August a year ago (August 1854). (That means that Andrew Hooper was married to Martha Seaborn about 1825 in McMinn County, Tennessee; married Mary Foster about 1840 in Tennessee and Margaret [last name unknown but a Seaborn cousin] about 1854. If Margaret was a cousin, could she be a Beaty or Carson [p. 290] related to Polly Wilhite Seaborn whose mother might be Missy Baty/Beaty?)

The case continued on November 23, 1855 with John Brannum/Branham in charge. The depositions totaled 30 pages. The witnesses who were called for the Chancery Court proceeding were George Hotchkisson who was 26; Caleb Dobbs who was 60; Rebecca Whaley who was 26 and Patsy McKeel who was 64 years old. John Brannum began the deposition taking with "being duly sworn on the Holy Evangelist of almighty God deponeth and saith the following."

All of the deponents were called on behalf of the Complainant, Andrew Hooper. Most of the testimonies centered around the dam and the sickness in close proximity. George Hotchkisson was questioned regarding a drift of logs and trash above the dam, people who lived close by, whether the pond smelled and who was ill. He was cross examined by the defendants' (Respondents) Solicitor who questioned George about whose land the drift was on, and he said Andrew Hooper's. He also was asked about the importance of the mill to the people in the community, the distance to another mill and to describe the chills and fever that the people had. He had to admit that some of the people who lived close by were not sick. Families who were mentioned in his testimony included Widow Witt, Simeon Witt, Mr. Calvin, Widow Kirkpatrick, Nathaniel Ross, William Shelton, James Kirkpatrick, John Hooper, Mr. Whaley (Jesse Wood made Mr. Whaley's coffin), Peoples and Graham. George Hotchkisson testified for five days for 75 cents a day.

Caleb Dobbs testified that he had been acquainted with the Shelton Mill since 1841. He also said he saw Andrew Hooper's whole family sick with the Ague and fever. Under cross examination, he testified to the scum above the drift, about a spring close to the creek, and to whether the springs were useless because of the distance from the houses. He said that the Whaley house was close enough to the spring that they may have used it. Also he was questioned about flooding from the Hiwassee River and from heavy rainfall. He was asked if the people would suffer if the mill was not there, and he said they would suffer an inconvenience. Further questioning revealed that the dam was four miles from the Hiwassee River. When he was asked if Mr. Hooper could ditch his fields, so the excess water could be drained off, he answered that ditches could not be dug that deep. He also estimated that the mill could grind approximately 20 bushels a day. Other families that were included in his testimony were John Hooper and Whaley. Caleb Dobbs testified five days and received 75 cents a day.

Rebecca Whaley testified that her husband and his brother had died and talked about the smell of the pond. She said that she had the ague, fever and chills and that her son had also been sick. On cross examination by the Respondents' Solicitor, she admitted that her husband's brother had died on the other side of the river. Rebecca Whaley was in attendance for four days. (Since the other witnesses were paid 75 cents a day, she probably also received that amount.)

Patsy McKeel knew the area before the mill and mill pond were erected. (There was a record made on February 16, 1838 in McMinn County, Tennessee for Singleton McKeel purchasing land from William McDowell.) She testified that Andrew Hooper's first wife was never healthy after they moved too close to the pond. She said Andrew's mother died and two or three Hooper children also died. Patsey knew of Andrew's second wife (Foster) having chills, fever and the shaking ague. She also said she had lived on

James Shelton's land fourteen years across the river (*1830 Census for McMinn County, Tennessee* listed Singleton McKeel next to James Shelton). She had also lived at Mr. Carmichael's three years on this side, then moved to a different location and lived there two years, moved south and lived three years, moved to the state of Illinois for three years, lived at John McPherson's three years, William Shelton's a year and then moved back to Mr. Carmichael's for the last year. She said that Alen Blair had two to die, and Andy Hooper had two to die. She testified that Mr. Hooper's second wife was sickly. Some of the other families she mentioned included another McKeel family, Mr. Sharp, Calvin Sharp, John Robinson, Absolom Hooper, Jo Teague, William Lovel, Ward, Cane, Hardin, Mark and Turner. She received 75 cents for testifying one day. This finished the 30 pages of depositions that John Branham took.

A list of Costs:

Justice D. D. Lay 11 Depositions			$11.00
Witnesses:	John T. Charmichael	2 days	1.50
	Calvin Atchley	2 days	1.50
	James M. Campbell	2 days	1.50
	Henry Earnest	3 days	2.25
	John Lane	3 days	2.25
	John McPherson	3 days	2.25
	Kinsey Seborn	3 days	2.25
	William Farmer	4 days	3.00
	John Hooper	5 days	3.75
	Patrick Graham	4 days	3.00
	Christopher Graves	3 days	2.25
Constable John K. Branum			
service of notices on defts	$1.00		
Summoning the Witnesses	5.25		6.25
			42.50 (Total?)

State of Tennessee
Bradley County
Dennis D. Taylor an acting Justice of the Peace for the county of Bradley aforesaid do hereby certify that the foregoing depositions was reduced to writing by me accept (except) the writing for Calvin Atchley, James Campbell, John McPherson & Christopher Graves who wrote their own Depositions that said depositions was respectfully signed by the deponents in my presents [*sic*] that the counsel for the complainant & defts was present during the examination that   I am not of counsel or attorney or of kin of either of the parties nor interested in said cause. Given under my hand and seal this the 24th day of November 1855.
          D. D. Taylor

The final judgment was issued by G. Nixon Van Dyke Chancellor presiding and holding the Chancery Court at Cleveland, Bradley County, Tennessee on February 26, 1856:

Andrew Hooper vs. Thomas Townsley, Francis Hayes, Carter Hayes, Robert Hayes, David Henry, Thomas Swafford, William Humphreys, George Millard, Marion Owens, William Shelton, Nathaniel Ross, Thomas Ross, Elijah Ballanger [*sic*], Levi Carter, Benjamin Hardin, Solomon Hardon [*sic*], Silas Avery, John Webb, John Wilson, William Duncan, George Kerby, William I. or J. Eads, David Wilson, Andrew Duncan, John Swafford, John Finley and James Young.

Be it remembered this cause came on to be heard before his Honor G. Nixon Van Dyke Chancellor presiding and holding the Chancery Court at Cleveland Bradley County Tennessee, on this 26th day of February 1856 upon Bill answers. Judments proconfessor [Pro Confesso means since the defendants offered no defense, it was taken as a confession of guilt.] regularly taken in said cause and the proof taken in said cause.

And because it appears to the satisfaction of his Honor, the Chancellor, from Bill, answers, judgments proconfessor and proof taken in said cause, the complainant is a resident citizen of Bradley County settled upon valuable lands situated upon both sides of Candy Creek with four wholesome springs situated thereon; that the defendants was at the time of the complainant filing his Bill in this cause rebuilding and erecting a mill dam upon said creek known by the name of Shelton Mill which had been lately abated by an indictment as a public nusance [*sic*] to health and did go on creek and rebuilt said mill dam which [page 2. of Chancellor's Decree] the complainants lands and springs were drowned over flowed, and his land and residence became sickly by reason of said mill dam ponding up the water in said Candy's Creek, and the same being stagnated, poisoned and corrupted and his habitation becoming unhealthy and his springs becoming drowned and the water thence corrupted; and his farming lands became to a considerable extent drowned and rendered useless; and the neighborhood, as well as the residence of the complainant, become sickly in consequence of said mill dam, and pond becoming stagnated, and poisoning the air and atmosphere.

His Honor is therefore pleased to order adjudge and decree that said mill dam and pond was and is a nuisance to the complainant his lands and habitation; and that the complainant is entitled to the relief prayed for in his said Bill. His Honor is further pleased to order adjudge and decree that said mill pond and dam be fully and entirely abated and removed from and out of said creek until said stream of water runs in its natural channels unobstructed as though said dam had never been there; and that said Respondents have until the fifteenth of April next to abate and remove said dam out of said creek so as to let said water run and flow in its natural channel unobstructed as though said dam had not been in said creek, and in default thereof that upon the application of the complainant the Clerk & Master issue a writ of abatement to the Sheriff of Bradley County and that he take so much of the power of the county as may be necessary for that purpose and go and fully and entirely abate said dam according to the directions of the foregoing part of the decree at the costs of the Respondents; and that the complainant here in open court having waived the prosecution of the attachment of this cause. It is further ordered adjudged and decreed by the court that complainant recover of the Respondents all the costs in this cause, as well as the costs of the attachment as the other costs of this suit, for which execution may issue as at law, but, no costs are adjudged against Wm Shelton as to the attachment. The complaint being responsible therefore, it is decreed against him, for which execution may issue.

Sometime after this decree, Andrew Hooper opened Hooper Mill on Candy's Creek. By the time of the *1862 United States Direct Tax Commission* for 9th District Bradley, Andrew Hooper had a mill valued at $600.00.

Seaburn/Seabourne and Wilhite/Wilhoit Families

Two of the earliest families related to Andrew Hooper's descendants were the Seaburn/Seabourne and Wilhite/Wilhoit families from Greene County and Jefferson County, Tennessee. The histories of these families remain incomplete, but perhaps these notes will aid in solving some of the mysteries that exist.

On the Internet at *Google.com*, a Seabourn family name origin was found at *A Dictionary of English Surnames* by Percy Hide Reaney and Richard Middlewood Wilson, Third Edition published in 1991 by Routledge of London, England and New York, United States. On page 2766, Seaborn, Seaborne, Seabourn, Seabourne, Sebbom, Sibborn, Sibbons, Siborne, Sibnrn, and Sayburn variations listed Nel, John Sebern in 1190 as the earliest listing. The name originally was Old English and translated as Sea Warrior from sae (sea) beorn (warrior). Another Internet site, *surnamedb.com*, listed Geoffrey Sebern 1173, Sayer Sabern 1327 and John Sabern 1377 as other early Seabourns.

On the Internet, there were references to Edward Seaborns who lived in England, but no definite connection to the Seaborn family in the United States has been established. Some of the Maryland Seaborne or Seborne records in the United States were summarized on the Internet in the book of *Anne Arundel County Church Records of the 17th and 18th Centuries* by F. Edward Wright published by Westminster, MD Family Line Publications: Anne b. October 22, 1681 and baptized; Thomas Seborne son of Thomas and Anne b. February 16, 1689 and baptized; Edward Seborne son of Thomas and Anne b. July 28, 1693 and baptized (from page 1). Elizabeth Seaborn married William Smith on January 28, 1702 (page 17). Phillip Green and Sarah Seaborn married October 25, 1711 (page 25).

Found on the Internet at *Ancestry.com*, *Abstracts of Land Records*, Anne Arundel County, Maryland, Vol 1 by R. Dodd and P. M. Bausell for 1684 was a deed from Joseph Williams, Anne Arundel County planter, to Thomas Seaborne, planter for 100 acres called Velmead near the bridge over Patuxent River which was part of 400 acres formerly laid out for Jno Deering (See p. 26 of this book for 1636 reference to a Nicholas and a Thomas Seaburne.). This parcel was part of a dividend sold to Benjamin Williams on the north line of Hickory Hills. Witnesses were Nicholas Gassaway and Henry Haslap; Mary Williams released dower (*Abstracts of Land Records, Anne Arundel County, Maryland, Volume I,* by RB Dodd and PM Bausell).

Another record, related to Richard Williams, Sr., showed that Richard witnessed a deed in Anne Arundel County from Thomas Seaborne to Edward Seaborn for land near Hiccory Hills in 1714. In 1740 an Edward Seaborn was a testator for the will of Joseph Williams, Sr. in Maryland. On February 3, 1774 in the *Berkeley County, Virginia Deed Book 2* on page 347, William Chapline of Frederick County, Maryland (the oldest son of Joseph and Ruhamah Chapline and oldest daughter of William Williams deceased) empowered John Smith and Jerome Williams to retain the authority granted in a power of attorney that expired in settling the estate of the said William Williams. The witness to this was Edward Seaborn.

In the *Maryland Probate Records for 1674-1774* (Internet) Edward Seabourn and his wife Mary were executors for Samuel Richards on December 20, 1753. Mary Seabourn was formerly Mary Richards.

Barbara Brinkley on March 3, 2001 posted an Internet message on *Genforum.com* that said she had information from the *South Carolina Journal for 1766* that an Edward Seaborn from Virginia with wife and 1 child under 16 received 200 acres in Berkeley County on December 16, 1766 from the king. This land was between the Broad and Saluda Rivers on Bush River which located the land in Laurens or Newberry County of South Carolina. (It seems possible that this Edward Seaborn might have continued to accumulate land in Georgia and Tennessee.)

Most likely there was more than one Edward Seabourn. In the *Colonial Records of the State of Georgia Volume 12* (Internet) for March 1772 compiled by Allen D. Candler, Edward Seaborn on pages 231-232 presented a petition that stated he had lived in the Province for four years. His petition for one hundred acres in St. George's Parish joining land surveyed for William Downey was granted.

There was also an Internet Revolutionary War record for a Private Edward Seaborn on the *Muster Roll for Washington County, Pennsylvania* in Ensign Benjamin Powell's Company on p. 248. In 1784 the *Pennsylvania Archives* on page 289 listed Captain Edward Seaburn in the Fifth Battalion with 55 men. According to later tax records, this Edward remained in Washington County, Pennsylvania.

Could Edward Seabourn of Greene County and Jefferson County, TN be related to Joseph Seaburn from Hyde County, North Carolina and John Seabourn from Virginia? Joseph Seaburn served in the Revolutionary War and since one of Edward's children was named Joseph, it would seem possible. Joseph received a warrant of 274 acres for serving in the Revolutionary War in North Carolina. Also, John, the older son of Edward in Tennessee, could show a relationship to John Seabourn who also served in the Revolutionary War in Virginia and received a 100 acre warrant. Joseph and John Seaburn received these warrants for land according to *Revolutionary War Bounty Land Grants* on page 470 listed on *Ancestry.com*. A John Seabourn was born in 1740 in Virginia according to the *American Genealogical-Biographical Index Volume 155* on page 220 (Internet, *Ancestry.com*). No records have proven Edward's ancestry.

Also a William Seaborn was listed in 1723 in the Pasquotank, NC list of free men on jury duty (Internet *Google Books*: Pasquotank District p. 63 Freeholder listed in *History of North Carolina: With Maps and Illustrations Volume 2* by Francis Lister Hawks and published in 1858 by E. J. Hale and Son in Fayetteville, NC). A William Seaborn was listed at *Ancestry.com* on *U. S. Revolutionary War Rolls* for September 9, 1778 in the Second Battalion for 1775 – 1783 on page 20 or 29 in Captain John Ingles Company.

All of the preceding records were for reference purposes, but the following records do seem to be related to the ancestry of Joseph Seabourn who moved to McMinn County, Tennessee in the 1820s and to Bradley County in the 1830s with Andrew Hooper. One of the earliest records was related to the *Greene County, Tennessee County Court of Common Pleas 1783-1795* on page 93 where Edward Seeburs makes a mortgage bond to John Hill on July 31, 1788. The *Land Deeds of Jefferson County, Tennessee Volume C* page 49 from the Register of Deeds (September 1792-1797) listed a conveyance from William Hadley to Jesse Kimbrough on Dumplin Creek in June 1793 which mentioned the land to be above Edward Seburn's, and Edward was also listed as a witness.

Edward Seaborne/Seabourne received several land grants from North Carolina in the area that became Greene County, TN. On February 13, 1790 the *North Carolina and Tennessee, Early Land Records, 1753 – 1931* Roll18: Book 7 p. 401(Internet *Ancestry.com*) listed a land sale where Edward Seaburn bought 200 acres on Dumpling Creek in Greene County, TN (became Tennessee in 1796) and paid 50 shillings for every 100 acres. At *Ancestry.com* a land survey for Edward Seaburn for 100 acres was made on March 1, 1790 in Washington County, NC. In the North Carolina *Land Grants Book 73 File 852* (Warrant No. 831), Edward Seaborn on Feb. 13, 1791 received Grant 833 for 200 acres in Greene County (originally entered Oct. 29, 1783 by Samuel Williams). On page 27 of the *Jefferson County, Tennessee Court Minutes 1792-1795* was a deed from Edward Seabourn to John Vanhooser which was proved in court and recorded in 1792. In the North Carolina *Land Grants Book 77 File 1207* (Warrant No. 2890), Edward Seaborn received Grant 1051 on March 1792 (paid 10 pounds British for every 100 acres) and bought 200 acres on the north side of Dumplin Creek in Greene County from the State of North Carolina at Hillsborough (originally entered by James Ivey on Dec. 18, 1789). Edward Seburn conveyed 200 acres land on the north side of Dumplin Creek to John Vanhooser on September 7, 1793 for 100 pounds. On May 8, 1794 Edward Seabourne sold 200 acres for 140 pounds to William Legate where Edward now lives. In the North Carolina *Land Grants Book 78 File 1244* (Warrant No. 2111), Edward paid 50 shillings for 200 acres on Jan. 12, 1793 in Greene County on Dumplin Creek for Grant 1094 from the State of North Carolina at New Bern (originally filed by William Davis on Nov. 8, 1779). In the North Carolina *Land Grants Book 78 File 1245* (Warrant No. 1484), on the same date for Grant 1095, he paid another 50 shillings for 100 acres in Greene County on Dumplin Creek (originally filed by John Wright but assigned from Henry Rowen to Edward Seaburn). (On page 7 of *Land Deeds of Jefferson County, Tennessee 1792*-1814 by Richard Porterfield published by Southern Historical Press, Inc. in Greenville, SC and reprinted in 2001, Charles Hooper bought 125 acres for $100.00 on the waters of Tuckahoe Creek where deeds showed that Edward Seaborn lived.)

Edward and John Seeburn [*sic*] were listed in Jefferson County, TN in 1800. Edward Seabourn served on several juries and was listed in *Jefferson County Court Minutes*. In the April session of 1800 John Seebourn was listed as judge (Justice of the Peace) and used the title of Esquire. Also in the *Jefferson County Tax List, 1800* at *Ancestry.com* Edward Seeburn was taxed for 350 acres no white poll (he was more than 50 years old) and John Seeburn was taxed for 174 acres and 1 white poll in Capt. McSpadden's Company. (If Edward Seabourn were more than 50 years old, he would have been born before 1750 and could be the Edward Seabourn in SC with his wife and son [John] who would have been born before 1766.)

A deed dated April 12, 1804 for 127 ½ acres which sold for $300.00 at the head of the Tuckahoe Creek for land adjoining Edward Seabourn listed Joseph Seaborn (22 years old?) as the Testator. A deed dated October 10, 1805 and finalized January 13, 1806 from Edward Seaborn to Henry Creswell listed another 100 acres sold on Dumplin Creek for $333.00. In the *Jefferson County Deeds* dated January 9, 1806 on page 203, Edward Seaborn sold 88 acres of land to William Eaton for $333.00 on Tuckahoe Creek that was proved in open court and recorded November 29, 1808. On page 204 January 9, 1806 – November 29, 1808 Edward Seaborn sold to William Eaton 50 acres for $133.00 and the land was proved in open court and recorded. Page 216 June 4 – November 23, 1808 Edward Seaborn sold 100 acres for $200.00 to Humphrey Mount, and this was proved and recorded in open court. In 1807 the conditional line of Edward Seaborn and John Seaborn where John Seaborn now lives was established. In 1807 on page 27 a deed from John Seaborn to Humphrey Mount for 382 acres of land was proved in court and recorded. Possibly Edward Seaborn died around 1808. John Seaborne was mentioned again in May 9, 1811 in Jefferson County, Tennessee when he was listed as one of the executors of Robert Gentry's will along with Robert's wife Rachel and Thomas Galbraith. According to *Ancestry.com*, a John Seaborn was listed on the Bledsoe County, Tennessee petitioners list in 1811 and *Ansearchin News* for Winter 1989 p. 150 listed a John Seabourn in1813 and p. 188 as a Commissioner (died 1833 in Marion County – see below).

John Seaborn, possibly the same John who was in Jefferson County, TN, was in the *1830 Marion County, Tennessee Census* p. 51 with 1 male 5-10, 1 male 10-15, 3 males 15-20, one male 50-60 (1770s); 3 females under 5, 1 female 15-20, 3 females 20-30; also, a son, Edward Seaborn with 1 male 0-5, 1 male 15-20, 1 male 20-30; 2 females 0-5 and one 20-30. John Seaburn died before February 13, 1833 in Marion County. John Seabourn had entered more than 1200 acres from 1830 to 1832 (Internet, *Marion County Entry Taker's Book Nov. 1823 – August 1895*). His children sold land at various times; one sale was in *Deed Book C* on pages 315 – 316, and his heirs were Edward, Joseph, John, George, Margaret and Jesse B. Sarell (Sherrell), Polly, Sarah, Anne and Elihu Hatchkess (Hotchkiss) and Elizabeth Seaburn heirs and legatees (heirs also found at Barbara Brinkley at *tngenweb.org* on March 6, 1997).

Since the first record was dated 1788, Edward must have been born before 1767. If John Seaborn born in the 1770s were a child of Edward Seaborn, then the birth date for Edward might be pushed back to the 1750s or earlier (he paid no poll tax in 1800, so he could be older than 50 [see above]). Evidence of name and location which linked Seaborns in Jefferson County, Tennessee indicated that Joseph Seaborn/ Seabourne might also be a son of Edward. Another Jefferson County record also linked the Seabourn and Wilhite name in the same area: Charles McClung of Knox County signed a Deed of Release to Joseph Coppock on April 12, 1808 and proven February 28, 1809 which mentioned 316 acres which was part of 20,000 acres to Stockley Donelson and William Tyrrell on the Forks of the Holston and French Broad Rivers adjoining Joseph Seabourn and (unknown) Wilhite (Adam Wilhite?). (See Appendix B on pp. 267 – 268 for Wilhite/Wilhoit information.)

Joseph Seaborn, listed above as testator in a deed and owning land adjoining land that was sold, was definitely in Jefferson County, Tennessee. He also was listed July 18, 1798 when he married Mary Wilhight (Wilhoit/Wilhite) in Jefferson County, Tennessee with Edward Seabourn as bondsman and John and James Wilhite (brothers of Mary?) as witnesses. Joseph and Mary were born about 1782 as shown in the *1850 Census of Bradley County, TN* at House 1594 (Compiled by Ellen Ann Westerberg Campbell 1973) . There was no definite proof for the parentage of Mary, but several have accepted that she was the daughter of Adam Wilhite/Wilhoit, born about 1760 in Virginia and died December 1815 (see page 267) and his wife Missy Beaty. Joseph Seaburn was listed in the War of 1812 from Jefferson County, Tennessee in Bunch's Mounted Regiment in 1813-14 for the East Tennessee Volunteers with a rank of Private. The war record was found at *Ancestry.com* in Box 185, Roll 602.

Adam Wilhight and his wife, Missy Beaty, lived in Jefferson County close to the Seabourns. Children of Adam and Missy included Avy Anne who married Thomas Cate April 20, 1802; Barbara; James; John; Mary who married Joseph Seabourne July 10, 1798 and Nancy who married William Julian July 20, 1802. In a court case dated September 17, 1813 in the *Jefferson County Court Minutes*, Thomas Cate and wife Avy Cate and daughter Elizabeth Cate provide bond that they will testify for the state against Joseph Seabourne in September, and this was also entered June 15, 1814. On March 15, 1815 Thomas Cate, Jesse Cate and Betsy Wilhoit appeared to testify in court, but Joseph Seabourn did not appear. Adam Wilhoit forfeited a $100.00 bail for Joseph Seabourne's failure to appear for petty larceny (Adam possibly died about this time). Evidently something happened to settle the problem because a Thomas Cate and Joseph Seabourne moved to McMinn County, Tennessee. *BH Hooper* at *Ancestry. com* listed Joseph as a Constable in McMinn County in 1820. Joseph Seabourn served as a juror in December 1823 (*Chancery Court Records* for McMinn County, Tennessee p. 101). In the chapter related to the "Andrew Hooper Court Cases" which took place in the 1850's, Kinsey C. Seaborn testified that his sister (Martha?) was the wife of Andrew Hooper (see pages 17 – 18 in this book).

Further proof that the Joseph Seabourn families were in McMinn County in the 1820s involved another court case. On December 2, 1828 in the *McMinn County Minutes 1819-1831* for McMinn County Court Records, Mary Billingsley took Joseph Seaburn and Griffith Dickason to court, and it was continued on page 422 dated March 5, 1829. (See p. 5 for Hooper and Seabourn in McMinn County, TN.)

The Hooper and Seabourn families continued in McMinn County during part of the 1830s as shown by the Census records and the *Court Record* Book. In the *1830 McMinn County, Tennessee Census* on page 142 were Andrew Hooper with 2 males under 5 and one 20-30 with one female 20-30; p. 141 James Seabourne 2 males under 5, one male 5 – 10, one male 30 – 40, with a female 0 – 5 and one 20 – 30; Kinsey Seabourne one male 20 – 30, three females 0 – 5 and one female 20 – 30; p. 142 John Seborne 3 males under 5, one 15-20, one 20-30 with a female 20-30; and Joseph Sebourne one male 5-10 and one 40-50 (1780s) one female 40-50. Ms. Judy Brown transcribed the McMinn County road orders from the *1831 – 1840 Court Record Book* which were extracted by Joyce G. Reece and found on the Internet. (**P-35**) The Court ordered that Jonathan Hugh be appointed Overseer of the road from Calhoun to Washington (Rhea County?) instead of James Seaborn who resigned from overseeing the road from Rogers Creek to the County line and have the same workers as the former Overseer had for a 2nd Class road. (**P-36**) Monday 5th Decr. 1831 Ordered by the Court that Andrew Hooper be appointed Overseer of the road leading from Sheltons to James Bonners up Rogers Creek in the room of John Seaborn who resigned and have the same workers as the former Overseer had. On **P-70**, James and John Seaborn were mentioned in Road Work. (**P-112**) In 1832, John Seaborn, Esquire was mentioned for road work.

Joseph and Mary Seabourn moved to Bradley County, Tennessee with their sons James and Kinsey before the *1840 Bradley County Census* (see pp. 6 and 10 in this book). In the *1840 Census* (compiled by Sheridan Randolph) on page 34 James Seabourn and his wife Sarah Wright had 1 male 0-5, 2 males 10-15, 1 male 15-20, 1 male 40-50; 3 females 0-5, 1 female 5-10, 1 female 10-15, 1 female 30-40; p. 38 had Kinsey Seabrun with 2 males 0-5, 1 male 30-40; 1 female 0-5, 2 females 5-10, 1 female 30-40; p. 38 Joseph Seabourn 1 male 15-20, 1 male 50-60; 1 female 30-40 and 1 female 50-60. In the *1850 Bradley County Census* at House 1594 Joseph and Mary are 68 years old (Compiled by Ellen Ann Westerberg Campbell 1973). The children of Joseph and Mary also included H. Bradford Seaborn born about 1823 who married Catherine Campbell. John Seaborn, born about 1800, was in Meigs County, Tennessee in 1840 and 1850. He married Hester McDowell and moved from Meigs County, Tennessee to Collin County, Texas before 1860. Kinsey Caswell Seaborn b. about 1805 married Martha Weir or Ware. Martha Seaborn b. about 1808 married Andrew Hooper probably in McMinn County, Tennessee about 1825. (Additional information on the Wilhite and Beaty family can be found in Appendix B on pp. 267 - 268 of this book.)

Found at Internet, *Ancestry.com,* (317) John Yates received 200 acres at Elizabeth City (VA) county for the transportation of 4 persons: Mary Yates, Nicholas Seaburne, Thomas Seaburne and Richard Wright. Granted by West on May 4, 1636. Also, at *Google.com*, the information was from *The Virginia Magazine of History and Biography, Volume 4* p. 430 edited by Philip Alexander Bruce, William Glover Stanard.

Andrew Hooper's Children and Their Families

Because of the work of Richard (Rick) Hooper and Barry Hooper, the names of the four Hooper brothers and sister, Tabitha, who, with their uncle Danis Garett Foster, moved west about 1870 were found. Perhaps, they moved west because Union veterans of the Civil War received special homestead rights in 1870 when an amendment to the 1862 Homestead Act gave them the right to claim 160 acres within railroad grant areas (other homesteaders got only 80). Another amendment in 1872 gave Union veterans the right to deduct the length of their war service from the five-year residency needed to prove a homestead (Internet: *Ancestry.com Wiki* article printed first in"Land Records" by Sandra Hargreaves Luebking, FUGA in *The Source: A Guidebook to American Genealogy*). Or, they moved after Andrew Hooper died.

John Hooper, oldest son of Andrew and Martha Seaborn Hooper, may have married Sarah/Sally Farmer about 1845 in Bradley County, Tennessee (several Internet researchers listed her name as Sally Farmer). They were listed in the *1850 Bradley County Census* in House 1300 (Compiled by Ellen Ann Westerberg Campbell 1973); he was 24 years old with Sarah 24, Elizabeth 5, Andrew 3 and William 1. In the *1860 Bradley County, TN Census*, John and Sallie were 33, Betsey 14, Andrew 12, Wm 10, Dealtha 8 and James 5. In the *1862 United States Direct Tax Commission* for 9th District Bradley County, TN on p. 15 found at *Ancestry.com.*, John Hooper paid \$1.26 on 80 acres valued at \$360.00. Sally possibly was the daughter of James Farmer who lived in Bradley County in 1840. The Farmer families who were in the *1840 Bradley Census* (compiled by Sheridan Randolph) included James on page 35: 1 male 0-5, 1 male 5-10, one male 30-40; 1 female 0-5, 1 female 5-10 and one 20-30 and on p. 54 William Farmer, 40-50, who might be his father or his brother. About 1870 John Hooper moved with his brother James to Arkansas. On pages 16 and 17 in the *1870 Sebastian County Census* in Sulphur Township were John Hooper 43 TN, Sarah 43 TN, Dialtha 19 TN, James 15 TN, Martha 12 TN and Margaret 8 TN.

In November 2010, new information indicated that the Patrick Graham family of Bradley County, Tennessee was more related to the Andrew Hooper family than previously thought. In the *Bradley County 1850 Census* in House 226 (Internet, *Ancestry.com*), Patrick Graham was 31, Ellener 31, Mary 14, Marion 10, Samuel 8, Landon 6, William 4, Jasper 1 and Elbert 16. In the *1860 Bradley County Census* in District 9 p. 167 (Internet, *Ancestry.com*), Patrick was 55, Ellener 55, Elbert 25, Marion 21, Samuel 16, Landon 10, William 8, Newton 6, Jimison 5 and Asa 4. It was mentioned in the 1854 Andrew Hooper Chancery Court case that Patrick Graham, who lived on the Andrew Hooper farm, had six sons and five had been sick and also stated that one died (see p. 19). Marion Graham born about 1838, son of Patrick and Ellener, married John Hooper's daughter Elizabeth on August 31, 1865 in Bradley County, Tennessee. In addition to Elizabeth Hooper who married Marion Graham, John Hooper had daughters named Dialtha and Martha who also possibly married other Patrick Graham sons. According to Tammy Graham at Internet *Genforum.com* on Nov. 11, 2001, Newton Graham married Dialtha Hooper in Sebastian County, Arkansas on August 13, 1870 after the Hoopers and Grahams had moved to Arkansas. Tammy also mentioned that Jamison Graham married Martha Hooper.

In the *Sebastian County 1870 Census* of Big Creek Township on p. 15, Patrick Graham was 55, Ellener 54, William 23, Newton J. 20, Jamison 18 and Asa 16. One intriguing cemetery in Sebastian County, Arkansas was the Lavaca City Cemetery where Marion F. Graham, Elizabeth (Hooper) Graham, W. M. Graham, Landon Graham, and Asa Graham were buried. Marion F. Graham died April 28, 1896, 58 years old (born 1838). Elizabeth (Hooper) Graham was born 1846 and died in 1928. Landon Graham died February 5, 1888, and Asa F. Graham was in the same cemetery 1856 – 1882. W. M. Graham died on Sept. 1, 1897 aged 52 years (William Graham in the Tennessee, *Bradley County 1850 Census* was 4.).

Andrew's second son, Kinsey C. Hooper, was listed in the *1850 Bradley County Census* in House 1313 (Compiled by Ellen Ann Westerberg Campbell 1973), as Kin or Kim 20 years old and Elizabeth 19. In the *1862 United States Direct Tax Commission* for 9th District Bradley County, TN on p. 29 found at *Ancestry.com*, K. C. Hooper paid \$1.68 in taxes on 120 acres valued at \$480.00. He married Elizabeth Geren, daughter of Isaac Geren (b. abt. 1795 d. abt. 1860) and Anna Hankins Geren (b. abt. 1795 and d. abt. 1870). Isaac's father, Hiram Geren, was born about 1758 in North Carolina and died in Knox County, TN. Hyram Geran's estate was settled by Susannah and their son, Joseph, on April 28, 1798 in Knox

County, TN (Internet *Allred Family Organization* Ruth Clift Bowen Document). Hiram married Susannah Alred, daughter of John Alred, in North Carolina. John's father was Solomon Allred (1680 to abt. 1740) who moved from Lancaster, England to Chester County, Pennsylvania before 1726 (Internet Dawnell Griffin and Linda Allred Cooper at *Allred Family Organization*). Hiram and his brother Solomon Geren served in the Revolutionary War. Hiram served under Captain John Hinds and completed a tour in the regiment of horsemen for the years 1780-1789. (Credit for the Revolutionary War information was given to *Roane County, Tennessee Pioneer Families* by Emma Middleton Wells found on the Internet and Alfred C. Ellis at *Genforum.com*. A handwritten copy of Captain Hinds soldiers was found also at the Bicentennial Library in Chattanooga, TN.) Hiram moved to Hawkins County, North Carolina before November 3, 1790 because Hiram Girin was named an Ensign on page 38 of *The Blount Journal 1790-1796*. On June 16th 1792 on page 62 of the same journal in Knox County, Hiram Geron is again named an Ensign. Denise Guerin Rice (Internet credit below) listed Hiram's parents as Joseph Guerin/ Geren who was born in New Jersey and Angelique Barbeau. Joseph Geron applied for and received a patent on 300 acres of land including improvements in Randolph County, North Carolina. Tax records for 1779 showed that he had cleared 21 acres, owned no slaves, had 14 head of cattle, 4 horses and 4 pounds 7 shillings of money. The total value was 694 pounds. On September 12, 1786 he sold 100 acres to Richard Beeson and 200 acres to Simon Gerron. Joseph Geren/ Guerin's parents were probably Thomas Guerin and Jane Whitehead who moved from South Carolina to New Jersey. Thomas Guerin's parents were possibly a Huguenot from France named Thomas Guerin, Sr. and Mary Ford . Thomas, Sr. and Mary had children: Thomas, Jr., Susannah and Joseph. Thomas, Jr. had Moses, Joshua, Levi, Epenetus, Joseph (moved to NC), Nathan, Mehetible, Vincent, Sarah and Jemima. All of Thomas' sons fought in the American Revolutionary War. (This early Guerin/Geren information was found on the Internet at *Denise Guerin Rice Collection*, North Jersey History Center, The Morristown and Morris Township Library in Morristown, NJ).

Isaac Geren's wife, Anna Hankins, also had a very interesting family. Isaac and Anna were married November 18, 1817 in Knox County, TN (Internet). According to Internet information, Anna's parents were Absolom Hankins (born about 1770 and died 1820 in Roane County, Tennessee) and Ruthy Skaggs (born about 1770 died about 1840). Ruthy's father (according to a letter date April 1, 1833 from Absolom Hankins to his mother Ruthy found in the McClung Library at *Ancestry.com*) was James Skaggs from Virginia. The Internet Bullock Pen Church Minutes in Roane County, TN indicated that Ruth Hankins joined the church on November 3, 1820 and left March 1840. Anna Geron joined the same church April 14, 1832 and removed her membership May 11, 1833. In the *1840 Census for Bradley County, Tennessee* (compiled by Sheridan Randolph) on page 40 Isaac Gerrin's household included: 1 male 5-10, 1 male 10-15, 2 males 15-20, 1 male 20-30 and 1 male 40-50; 2 females 0-5, 1 female 5-10, 1 female 10-15, 1 female 20-30 and 1 female 50-60. Could the older female be Ruth Hankins? Absolom Hankins, Sr.'s father was Richard Hankins who was born about 1745 in Virginia and died in Jefferson County, Tennessee in 1800. His wife's first name was Deborah, but her last name is unknown. The children in his will dated October 25, 1800 were Thomas, Edward, Richard, Abram (Abraham), John, Becky (Rebecca), Debe (Deborah) and Absolom. Richard's father was probably Thomas Hankins, born about 1700, from New Jersey who married Mary Clevenger (several sources on Internet).

Isaac Geren died before February 17, 1866 because his heirs sold 160 acres to K. C. Hooper, and the deed stated that Isaac Geran was deceased. The only exception to the land sale was "the land where J. S. Witt's sawmill dam and race that conveys the water to said mill with the right to raise the water that part we do not convey as the same has been conveyed to the said Will by Isaac Gearen in his life time." This was found in *Deed Book C* pages 139-140 in Bradley County, Tennessee. The listed heirs were J. S. and Susan K. Witt, J. G. Geren, S. D. Geren, G. K. Geren, D. G. and Ruthy Foster, James and Eliza Hooper, Martha Ross and the widow Anney Geren. On January 2, 1873 K. C. Hooper made a Quit Claim Deed listed in the *Bradley County Deed Book E* on page 183 to J. K. Geren for the same 160 acres with the same exception listed for the sawmill dam and race owned by J. S. Witt. In the *1880 Census for Bradley County, Tennessee* 9th Civil District, on page 65, Ann Geren, 80 years old, lived with Kinsey and Elizabeth Hooper and was listed as mother-in-law.

Andrew and Martha Hooper's first daughter was named Dialtha, and she was born March 10, 1832 and died Feb.17, 1894. She married Thomas Houston Gilbreath born Nov. 24, 1825 and died Feb. 13, 1894. In the *Bradley County 1850 Census* in House 1310 (Compiled by Ellen Ann Westerberg Campbell 1973),

Houston Gilbreath was 26 and Doutha 19. In the *1862 United States Direct Tax Commission* for 9th District Bradley County, TN on p. 30 found at *Ancestry.com* T. H. Gilbreath owned 40 Acres and a Still. According to *Goodspeed Biographies of Marion* County, Tennessee published by Goodspeed in 1886 and transcribed by Betty McBee on the Internet, one of Thomas and Dialtha's sons, John, became Dr. John Gilbreath and moved to Marion County, Tennessee. Thomas' father was Mahlon/Malen Gilbreath listed as Galbreath in the *1840 Bradley County Census* (compiled by Sheridan Randolph) on page 37: 1 male 10-15 and 1 male 30-40; 1 female 10-15 and 1 female 30-40. Mahlon Gilbreath married Polly Campbell in Jefferson County, Tennessee. According to the research by *Bevtwin* at *Ancestry.com*, Mahlon was the son of Thomas Gilbreath (born about 1751 in Bucks County, Pennsylvania and died February 5, 1829 in Jefferson County, Tennessee) who married Elizabeth Hays on May 30, 1779 in Bedford County, Virginia. Thomas Gilbreath served in the Revolutionary War in the Pennsylvania Continental Line and received a pension April 27, 1820 at age 83 and died February 5, 1829 in Jefferson County, Tennessee (*Ralph-L-Temple User Trees* at *Genealogy.com*). Thomas Gilbreath, born 1751, was the son of Alexander Gilbreath/ Galbraith (born in Scotland about 1720 and died 1792 in Campbell County, Virginia. Alexander married Nancy Agnes Miller about 1747 in Bucks County, Pennsylvania. The Thomas Gilbreath in the *1850 Bradley County Census* [Compiled by Ellen Ann Westerberg Campbell 1973] may have been an uncle.)

Another son of Andrew and Martha was Jahue/Jahew who was married twice. Jahue (November 13, 1833-November 14, 1901) married (1) Mary McPherson (November 11, 1835-April 24, 1894) daughter of William McPherson (September 5, 1804-October 7, 1891) and Elizabeth Ketner (March 17, 1814-December 27, 1899) of Bradley County, Tennessee. William McPherson's parents were Henry and Mary Eaton McPherson of Roane County, Tennessee. Mary's ancestry was proven by the affidavit (Internet, *Rootsweb* Dec. 12, 2007 Eaton) made March 28, 1872 by John and William McPherson in front of J. K. Brown, Justice of the Peace in Bradley County, Tennessee. It involved a lawsuit to prove she was the sister of Daniel Eaton of Grainger County, Tennessee. Henry McPherson and Mary Eaton married January 29, 1799 in Grainger County, Tennessee. Henry McPherson was possibly born about 1770 in Montgomery County, Virginia to Richard and Eleanor Barton McPherson. Henry died about 1816 in Roane County, Tennessee. Elizabeth Ketner McPherson's parents were Henry Ketner and Mary Wilkins. Henry's parents were George Michael Ketner/Kettner born about 1745 in Berks, Pennsylvania and died in 1806, and Catherine who was born in the same state. George Kettner was a soldier in the Pennsylvania Rifle Regiment during the Revolutionary War (*Ancestry.*com) and may be the same person who was Henry's father. Much of the McPherson information was taken from *Rootsweb*'s *World Connect Project: Winch/Proffitt Genealogy Database.* Jahue married (2) Amanda Maxwell from Georgia. Her father was probably Emerson Maxwell from Kentucky who lived in Walker County, Georgia in 1840, 1850 and in Catoosa County, Georgia in 1860, 1870 and 1880. Amanda's nephew Morton Cross lived with Jahue and Amanda in 1900 (see *1900 Bradley County Census*, Ninth Dist. p. 9 A; Morton married Leathey Carlton.)

James Hooper, son of Andrew and Martha Hooper, was born about 1838 and married Liza Geren, daughter of Isaac Geren and Anna Hankins. (Look at Kinsey Hooper listed previously for more Geren information.) James was hung by the Confederate Army during the Civil War but survived (see page 157). James and his family moved to Arkansas about 1870 because they were in the *1870 Census for Sulphur Township, Sebastian County, Arkansas* on page 16: James Hooper 35 TN, Eliza 27 TN, Susan 8 TN, Ruth 6 TN, Mary 3 TN and Danl 1 TN. On the same page was John Hooper, and on the next page was Dannis G. Foster his brother-in-law and possibly uncle. In 1880 James Hooper was still listed in the Sulphur Township for Sebastian County, Arkansas on page 10, but his wife was not listed: James Hooper 42 TN, Eliza 16 daughter TN, Mary 13 TN, Annie 8 Ark. and Tobiathe 6 Ark.

After Martha Seabourn Hooper died about 1839 (this was found in the testimony of John Hooper in his deposition in 1855 on pages 19-20 of this book), Andrew Hooper married Mary Foster about 1840/41 in Tennessee. Mary was possibly the daughter of Jarrett/Jarrott Foster and Dorcas Moseley. Greg Foster has researched Jarrett and Dorcas extensively, and some of the Foster background came from his work on the Internet: *These Are My Fosters.* In the *1840 Bradley County Census* p. 41 (compiled by Sheridan Randolph) Andrew Hooper had 2 males 0 – 5, 1 male 5 – 10, 2 males 10 – 15 and 1 male 30 – 40; females were one 5 – 10 and one 15 – 20. The house next door was Jarrott Foster. Mary Foster was the second wife of Andrew Hooper as proved by William Hooper's Certificate of Death in Hickory County, Missouri (this Certificate was found by Barry Hooper August 21, 1996). The File No. for the certificate was 22525 for William Hooper. This information about Mary Foster being the second wife of Andrew was backed up by John Hooper's deposition on December 4, 1855 in *Bradley County Chancery Court* records on microfilm pages 88-89 (on page 88 he was asked how long since your mother's death and he answered, "I recon something over fifteen years since mother died [1839?]." Then on page 89, John was asked to state, "...the exact time of first step-mother's death & give the ...month and day of the month of the death." John's answer, "She died in the first part of last August over a year ago [August 1854].") (In Kinsey Seaborn's deposition found on microfilm page 47 dated December 4, 1855 he testified, "His [Andrew Hooper] first wife was a sister of mine and this third wife is a cozzin (cousin) to me." Margaret would be the third wife.

(Danis/Daniel Garrett Foster [referred to as D. G. Foster] was born in South Carolina and joined Andrew Hooper in the lawsuit against the grist mill owners whose mill dam pond polluted Andrew's springs and possibly caused the sickness that killed Mary Foster Hooper who might be Garrett's sister. (See page 15 for Danis joining the lawsuit in August 1854 which was the same month as Mary Foster Hooper's death. The 1830 and 1840 census information listed below showed the possibility that Mary and Danis Foster could be children of Jarrett Foster who was listed next to Andrew Hooper in 1840.)

Jarrett/Garrett Foster was born about 1795 in Union County, South Carolina and married Dorcas Moseley. He moved to McMinn County before the *1830 Census* (Internet, *Ancestry.com*) where he was found on page 144 with 0 1 1 0 0 1-- 2 1 0 0 1 (1 male 5 – 10, 1 male 10 -15 1 male 30 – 40 and 2 females 0 – 5, 1 female 5 – 10, and 1 20 –30). Danis Garrett Foster could be the male listed as being 5 – 10 years old and John Foster could be the other brother (the letter "J" looks like a "G" in the old records so Garrett could be Jarrett). Mary Foster, the second wife of Andrew Hooper, could be the daughter listed as 5 – 10 in McMinn County. In the *1840 Census* of Bradley County, Tennessee (compiled by Sheridan Randolph) on page 41, the Jarrett Foster family was listed as 0 0 0 1 1 0 1 – 2 0 2 0 0 1 (1 male 15 – 20, 1 male 20 – 30, and one 40 – 50 and 2 females 0 – 5, 2 females 10 – 15 and one 0 – 40). Andrew Hooper's wife, Mary Foster, in 1840 was listed as 15 – 20 in the family of Andrew Hooper. In the *1850 Census for Jasper County*, MO in District 41 House 245 (Internet, *Ancestry.com*), Jarrett Foster was 55 b. SC, Dorcus 49 SC, Lucinda 22 TN, Sarah 20 TN, Martha E. 14 TN, Elizabeth 10 TN, Andrew J. 8 TN and Francis M. 4 born in Arkansas. John Foster 28 b. SC was in the same county with Jane 20 TN, Zachary 3 MO and Mary 2 MO. Jarrett and his family moved to Marmaton in Bourbon County, MO before 1865 and finally to Montgomery County, Kansas before 1875. Dorcas died after Aug. 8, 1865 according to Dr. Barbara Inman Beall at *Historical Footprints 2010* on the web in an article titled "Who Killed John Bass?" found in "Bundles of Twigs". At *Newspapers.com* Michael Roberts clipped an article from *The Coffeyville Weekly Journal* dated Aug. 12, 1876 on p. 3 that listed Jarrett Foster's death as Aug. 9, 1876; he was 83.   Another possible reason for Andrew and Mary Hooper's son being named Fancis Jarrott Hooper could be that Mary's father was Jarrett Foster. (Confusion about Jarrett and Dorcas Foster has not been solved.)

Jarrett Foster's father was John Foster who was born in the 1740s according to the *1830 Union County, SC Census* on p.177 where he lived next to his son Frederick who later moved through Bradley County, TN and died in Lawrence County, MO on Jan. 17, 1864 (Internet, Foster, Linda Elaine Jones at *fredmott97601* at *Ancestry.com*). Databases listed John Foster's wife as Mary McElfresh (*Grindal Shoals Gazette*). John bought land from Nicholas Jasper on the Pacolet River in Union County. Children in John Foster's will were Frederick, John, Jared/Jarrett, Thomas and a grandson Jeremiah listed as Frederick's son. John left one third to Jared Foster's children (Will proven June 6, 1840 Internet, *Ancestry.com*). Perhaps, John Foster was from Virginia and married to Mary (Mollie) McElfresh (*Grindal Shoals Gazette* the "John Jasper Story" dated July 5, 2011). Perhaps John Foster was the son of John Foster, Sr. from VA.

If Jarrett/Jared Foster was the son of John from Union County, SC, then his wife Dorcas Moseley Foster's ancestry was important. Her father James Moseley was a scout during the Revolutionary War and applied for a pension on Oct. 10, 1832 (the *Southern Campaign American Pension Statements* transcribed by Will Graves and numbered S9421 list his campaigns). Since James Moseley married Nancy Anna Jasper, another Revolutionary War aspect was added. *Stub Entries To Indents, Book X, Part II*, p. 188, by A. S. Salley show that John Jasper, Sr. was reimbursed for corn and a wagon during the Revolutionary War. (*Grindal Shoals Gazette* published a lengthy article about the John Foster and John Jasper families dated July 5, 2011.) James Moseley's will was dated October 4, 1839 in Union County, SC, and he left to Jared

Foster's children one shilling. Why did James Moseley only give one shilling to Jared/Jarrett Foster's children? Perhaps, Jared and Dorcas left the old parents, or, perhaps, Jared and Dorcas never legally married? (Dorcas might have married Benjamin Hodge first and left him according to the *Grindal Shoals Gazette* information.)

Possibly Jarrett Foster fought in the Second Seminole War in Florida in 1836. Information from *Statewide County MO Archives Military Records* on the Internet, listed Some Military Land Grants in Missouri for Soldiers of the Indian Wars Part Two from *Indian USGenWeb Archives* by Linda S. Ayres dated October 21, 2010. Jarrett Foster was granted land while he lived in Jasper County, Missouri for serving in the Regiment: Elliott's Company Tennessee Militia Florida War. He lived in Jasper County, MO from about 1850 to 1865. The *Jasper County, Missouri 1850 Census*, House 245 in Franklin Township (Internet, *Ancestry.com*) listed Jarrett Foster 55 born SC on page 752 in District 41 and on page 753 Dorcas Foster 49 born SC, Lucinda 22 b. TN, Sarah 20 b. TN, Martha E. 14 b. TN, Elizabeth 10, b. TN, Andrew J. 8 b. TN and Francis M. 4 b. Arkansas.   John Foster was also living in Jasper County, MO in House 494 in District 41: he was 28 b. SC, Jane 20 b. TN, Zachary 3 b. MO, Mary 2 b. MO and Martha 2 / 12 b. MO.

George Francis Hooper b. April 22, 1910 - d. May 21, 1997 from Missouri wrote to Richard (Rick) Hooper on August 6, 1991 about the Hoopers from Tennessee who moved to Missouri. Andrew and Mary Hooper's son, William Hooper, born September 5, 1842, was married first to Marilla Jane Wilson from Bradley County, Tennessee on June 13, 1866 (*Ancestry.com*). In the *1860 Bradley County, Tennessee Census* (Internet, *Ancestry.com*) on page 176 in District 9, Marilla J. Wilson was 13 and her father was David (a David Wilson was involved in the Shelton Mill lawsuit) and her mother Margaret. David's father was John W. Wilson who married Elizabeth Campbell July 20, 1820 in Knox County, Tennessee according to Internet *bourlandcivilwar.com*. William Hooper and Marilla had a son named David F. Hooper born 1867. On January 7, 1877 in Sebastian County, Arkansas, William married to Nancy E. Thurston; they moved to Fayette County, Illinois according to the *1880 Census of Fayette County, Illinois* in Bear Grove p. 19. Their children were D. F. Hooper 13, Hattie C. Thurston 7, Charles Hooper 2 and Walter W. Hooper 1/12. Nancy must have been married to a Thurston before, and then she and William had Charles and Walter. William married Mrs. Barbara Bowen on Jan. 3, 1886 in Hickory County, MO (Internet, *Ancestry.com*). In the *1900 Census for Hickory County, Missouri* on page 13 B, were William age 58 born September 1842 in Tennessee, Barbara A. was born July 1855, and they had been married 14 years (Internet *Find A Grave*, tombstone in Antioch Cemetery, Hickory Co., MO listed her dates as July 25, 1855 – Nov. 6, 1915). Children were Bertha R. born February 1890, Eza born August 1892 and a step daughter Jessie Bowen born 1878. According to George Francis Hooper, another wife was Elvira Cooper (could her name be Fansler?). On the Internet at *Fayette County, Illinois Queries* p. 1, Elvira Thompson married three times: (1.) Oscar Smith and had son Isaac; (2.) Frederick Fansler and (3.) William Hooper.)

There seemed to be a gap in years between the births of William and Daniel Hooper. This could be partially explained by the deaths of some of Andrew Hooper's children. In John Hooper's Chancery Court deposition on microfilm page 89 dated December 4, 1855, he was asked about his brothers' deaths: "...12 years since my first brother died, one died about 10 years ago & the other one about 12 months ago." If the ages were figured from the testimony in 1855, the deaths would be 1843, 1845 and 1854. Daniel was born June 30, 1846 and died Aug. 12, 1927 according to the Tombstone at Nemo Bethel Baptist Church Cemetery in Hickory County, MO. He married Isabelle Victoria Snow on Aug. 8, 1877 in Hickory County, MO. In *1870 Census of Bradley County, TN*, she was listed as the daughter of John W. Snow and Nancy (Agee). The certificate of the birth of Ida Alice Hooper on Oct. 16, 1883 in Green County, Missouri listed the mother's name as Isabelle Victoria Snow before she married Daniel G. Hooper. Isabelle's father, John W. Snow, was the son of Thomas (born about 1815) and Elizabeth Snow (born about 1823). John must have died before 1880, because Lorena Snow, listed as Step Daughter, was living with Washington Viles and Nancy Viles in 1880 in Polk County, MO. Thomas Snow's father was John Snow born about 1785 in North Carolina, and his mother was Elizabeth R. Dickens. John Snow died February 2, 1845 and Elizabeth died October 5, 1866 in Meigs County, Tennessee according to Glenn Newburn on *Genealogy.com* entry dated July 5, 2000. Isabelle's mother was Nancy Agee who was born about 1842. Nancy's father was Isaac Agee born March 8, 1802 in Abingdon, Virginia. He married Hannah Bounds who was born about 1805 in Goochland, Virginia. She died March 9, 1864 in Bradley County, Tennessee. Isaac died after the

1870 Census because he was living with the family of John W. Snow in District 6, page 7 in the *1870 Bradley County, Tennessee Census* (Internet, *Ancestry.com*).

Francis Jarrott/Jarrett Hooper was born Oct. 10, 1849 in Bradley County, Tennessee and died Dec. 13, 1897 in Hickory County, MO. He married Sarah Clementine Kirkpatrick (born September 26,1849 and died Nov. 21, 1935 Internet, *Find a Grave, Ancestry.com*). (Possibly, Francis was named for his grandfather, Jarrott Foster who lived in Bradley County, TN in 1840.) Francis J. Hooper became President of the Hickory County, Missouri Court in November 1894. According to a descendent, George Francis Hooper in a letter to Rick Hooper dated August 6, 1991, Francis J. Hooper served on the Hickory County, Missouri County Court from 1894 to his death in December 1897. Sarah was the daughter of James Kirkpatrick (born about 1816 died about 1890) and Elizabeth Witt (born August 1826 died after 1900). Francis and Sarah with James and Elizabeth Kirkpatrick moved to Hickory County, Missouri (*Census 1870* pp. 13 &15 found at Internet, *Ancestry.com*). James' parents were Joel Kirkpatrick (born about 1785 and died after 1840 in Bradley County, Tennessee) and Nancy (born about 1790 and died after 1860). A Joel Kirkpatrick had signed the bond for Isaac Geron and Anna Hankins in 1817 in Knox County, Tennessee.

Francis Jarrett Hooper

Picture found at *Ancestry.com* of Francis Jarrett Hooper October 10, 1849 - December 13, 1897 was kept by David McNabb Hooper son of George Francis Hooper.

The youngest child of Mary Foster and Andrew Hooper who lived to maturity was Tabitha who married Clinton Jack on September 30, 1866 in Bradley County, Tennessee. The marriage information was found at the *Ancestry.com* Message Board for the Jack family by Gail Barham from the Clinton Jack family Bible and in the *Memorial and Biographical History of Dallas County, Texas* published in Chicago by The Lewis Publishing Company in 1892 on page 886. Along with John Hooper, K. C. Hooper, William Hooper, James Hooper and Andrew J. Hooper (John's son), Clinton Jack and his father David served in the Union Army during Civil War (p. 158). David Jack married Mary Jane Hall whose father was John Wesley Hall who pastored Methodist churches, but later joined the Baptist church. David and Mary Jane had Clinton, John, Adaline (married G. M. D. Shelton), Flora (married John E. Shelton brother to G. M. D), Hamilton, Jane, Emily and Florence. Possibly, David's father was John Jack (born about 1788 and died after 1850) and his mother Elizabeth (born about 1784 and died after 1850). They lived in houses numbered 1822 and 1823 in the *1850 Bradley County, Tennessee Census* (Internet, *Ancestry.com*). According to *U. S. and International Marriage Records, 1560-1900*, John Jack married Elizabeth Garrett. (The following is unproven, but it is a possibility.) Jeremiah Jack b. abt. 1750 married Martha Gillespie in Virginia, and they might be the parents of John. In his will (*Genealogy.com* by F. Keenan) dated about 1833, the children listed were John, Elizabeth, Margaret, George, Jane, Jeremiah, Martha, James, Thomas, Robert and Allen.

In the *1870 Bradley County Census* (Internet, *Ancestry.com*) in District 8 on page 18, Clinton Jack was 25, a Farmer born in TN and has Real Estate valued at $2500 with Personal Estate $1150; Tabitha is 19 and born in TN; Charles H. is 1 and Margaret Hooper is 55 born in TN. Margaret is Tabitha's step-mother;

later when Tabitha stated that her father was Henry instead of Andrew, possibly Henry was someone related to her step mother. Tabitha Hooper Jack and John Clinton Jack moved to Lee County, Arkansas before 1880. Clinton Jack 36, Tabitha J. 30, Charles H. 10, Oscar 8, Frank 6, Lillia A. 4/12, Flora Shelton 31 (sister who married John E. Shelton December 13, 1866 son of William C. Shelton and Sarah Rymer), William Shelton 12 (nephew), Dalas H. Shelton 10 (nephew), Ensley Jack 28 (sister), Florina Jack 21 (sister) and John H. Jack 19 (brother) were in the *1880 Lee County, Arkansas Census*, Flint Township on page 27 (Internet, *Ancestry.com*). On pages 885-886 in the *Memorial and Biographical History of Dallas County, Texas* published in 1892 in Chicago by the Lewis Publishing Company (Internet), Clinton Jack was described as being a widely-known and highly respected citizen of Oak Cliff, a suburb of Dallas, Texas. He was an Alderman and engaged in the flour and feed business. He was born in Bradley County, Tennessee on November 6, 1844. The book said that Tabitha was daughter of Henry (Census records show her father was Andrew Hooper) and Mary Hooper. In the 1892 book, nine children were listed: Mary (dead), Charles H., Oscar O., Fred H. (dead), Frank L., Lillie E., Maude T., David A. and one died unnamed. In the *1900 Dallas County, TX*, (Internet, *Ancestry.com* 1900, 1910, 1920, 1930 Censuses) Oak Cliff District on page 32 were Clint Jack 55 TN TN TN, Tabitha 49 TN NC TN, Frank son 26 TN TN TN, John C. son 8 TX TN TN, and John H. Kyle (brother-in-law) 50. In the *1910 Tarrant County Census*, TX, Fort Worth on page 3 were Tabitha Jack 57 widow TN NC TN, and John C. 18 son TX TN TN. The *1920 Census* for Dallas County, TX, Justice Precinct on page 13A were John C. Jack 27 TX TN TN, Carrie S. 27 TX TX TN, Mary J. 8 TX TN TN, John C. Jack father 71 TN TN TN and Tabiatha Jack mother 69 TX NC NC. In the *1930 Census* for Dallas County, Texas on page 35A John C. Jack was 38, Carrie L. wife 39, Mary 17, Helen J. 9, John C. 6 and Tabitha J. 79, mother. Texas *Death Certificate* No. 44477 (*Ancestry.com*) listed her birth as August 22, 1850 and her death as Sept. 9, 1936. Her father was listed as Andy Hooper and mother unknown (this corrected the earlier incorrect father as Henry Hooper).

Research at *Ancestry.com* revealed more information related to Clinton and Tabitha Jack. Mystery surrounded John Clinton Jack's death date. Tabitha applied for a Civil War Pension and listed his death as March 24, 1903. Civil War Records list February 19, 1903 as the date for the Headstones Provided for Deceased Union Civil War Veterans at Oak Cliff Cemetery, Dallas, TX. For some reason, Tabitha and John C. Jack were both listed in the 1920 Census living with their son John C. Jack in Dallas County, TX. Yet, each year in the Dallas, TX City Directories, Tabitha listed herself as Clinton Jack's Widow. Most likely the Census taker misunderstood and listed Clinton as alive. Tabitha Jane Jack has a tombstone Aug. 22, 1850 and Sept. 9, 1936 in the Oak Cliff Cemetery in Dallas, TX. Clinton Jack has a military tombstone in the same cemetery which lists Co. A 8 Tenn. Inf. So, Tabitha in 1910 is a Widow and married in 1920 and Widow in 1930. Probably, there was confusion related to the census taker who took the information.

Hooper Family Outline of Descendants

The following outline was based on Barry H. Hooper's Family Tree revised 7-20-94. More recent Census information has also been added. The outline begins with the unknown ancestor listed as number 1. Sarah, an older sister of Andrew and Absolom Hooper, was given number 2. She married James Shelton and their children received numbers 5 through 13. The children of Andrew Hooper, number 3, were designated by numbers 14 through 22. The children of Absolom Hooper, number 4, were given numbers 23 through 35. The idea was to give each descendant a separate number or series of numbers to indicate which Hooper was their ancestor. The most recent discoveries are in bold but do not have a separate number. There are more than 2020 relatives listed. (Note that person 1-2-11-88 is only listed on p. 37 due to an oversight.)

1 Unknown Hooper ancestor, but DNA (p. 268) showed him to be related to Absolom Hooper from SC, GA and NC and other Hoopers who were in the Revolutionary War. Unknown Hooper's wife died at Andrew's home about 1840 (see pp. 19 and 20). The use of names related to this family, i.e. Absolom and Andrew, also indicated a possible kinship.

1-2 Sarah Hooper b. abt. 1795 married James Shelton born in VA. A Chancery Court case in Bradley County, Tennessee in 1854 included testimony that Sarah was a sister to Andrew Hooper (p. 17). James Shelton b. March 1, 1791 moved to Buncombe County, North Carolina about 1795 and d. Oct. 1879 (Internet, *Ancestry.com, 1880 Mortality Schedule*) in McMinn County, Tennessee. Tombstone has a November death month.

1-3 Andrew Hooper b. abt. 1805 (no proof of exact date) d. 1866 married (1) Martha Seabourn b. abt. 1805 d. abt. 1840; (2) Mary Foster b. abt. 1820 d. abt. 1854 and (3) Margaret (cousin to the Kinsey Seabourn family).

1-4 Absolom Hooper b. abt. 1810 married Elizabeth Rymer and later, Mariah Amanda Williams.

1-2 Children of Sarah Hooper and James Shelton were listed in the *1850 McMinn County, Tennessee Census* page 274 (Internet, *Ancestry.com*). Sarah was born 1795 and died in 1851 from drowning (see p. 268). Also, information was available on *Ancestry.com* that included the James Shelton Will which listed the children, except for Lewis who probably died in Greenwood County, Kansas. In the *1900 McMinn County, Tennessee Census* p. 1 A, 16th District (Internet, *Ancestry.com*), William C. Shelton b. Sept. 1820 and his wife, Dorcas b. Sept. 1850, were living with William's half-brother Samuel Shelton b. Oct. 1854, his wife, Viola, and Samuel's step-mother Catherine b. May 1815.

> 5. William C. Shelton b. Sept. 1820
> 6. Andrew Hooper Shelton b. 1824
> 7. Elicy Shelton b. May 27, 1827
> 8. John E. Shelton b. abt. 1829
> 9. Jane Shelton b. Dec. 25, 1830
> 10. Lewis Shelton b. abt. 1833 possibly died in Greenwood, Kansas unmarried.
> 11. Ursula Shelton b. 1834
> 12. Elizabeth Shelton b. abt. 1836
> 13. Catherine Shelton b. abt. 1842

Internet, *MOMILLER@rootsweb.com*. December 12, 2004, a first wife was Betsy Lawson and other possible children were Naomi, Nancy, Cornelia, and Caroline. (*Ancestry.com, SRM1210*) James married Jane Wood (b. 1834 d. 1858) had three young children named Samuel, Cyrus and Sarah named in his Will dated March 1, 1869. James then married Catherine Bell (1815 – 1900).

1-3 Children of Andrew Hooper and Martha Seaborn:
> 14. John Hooper b. abt. 1827 married Sarah Farmer. (John moved to Sebastian Co., Arkansas before 1870 and died before 1880.)
> 15. Kinsey C. Hooper b. 1829 died June 6, 1904 married Elizabeth Geren b. 1833 and she died Feb. 14, 1903
> 16. Dialtha Hooper b. March 10, 1832 d. Feb. 13, 1894 married Thomas Houston Gilbreath b. Nov. 24, 1825 died Feb. 11, 1894
> 17. Jahew Hooper b. Nov. 13, 1833 died Nov. 14, 1902 married Mary McPherson b. Nov. 11, 1835 died April 24, 1894 married (2) Amanda Maxwell
> 18. James Hooper b. abt. 1838 d. May 13, 1892 married Eliza Geren (moved to Sebastian Co., Arkansas before 1870)

1-3 Barry Hooper found a *Death Certificate* for William Hooper born Sept. 5, 1842 in Bradley County, TN and died July 18, 1914 in Green County, Missouri which listed his mother as Mary Foster and his father as Andrew Hooper. John Hooper, Andrew's son, says his first step-mother died in 1854 (see pp. 19 – 20). There is a marriage record for an Andrew Hooper who married Anna Stephens April 22, 1840 in Monroe County, TN, but a different Andrew Hooper must have married her.

    19.   William Hooper b. Sept. 5, 1842 died July 18, 1914 married (1) Marilla Jane Wilson on June 15, 1866 in Bradley County, TN, (2) Mary Ann Crosby, (3) Nancy Thurston b. abt. 1853 and married Jan. 7, 1877 in Sebastian County, Arkansas, (4) Elvira Fansler married 1882 and (5) Barbara Bowen b. July 1855 married Hickory County, MO Jan. 3, 1886 (Internet, *Ancestry.com*)

    20.   Daniel/Danis Hooper b. June 30, 1846 died August 12, 1927 married Isabelle Snow in Hickory County, MO July 22, 1877 (Moved from Arkansas to Hickory Co., Missouri after 1870. Moved to Mills County, IA before 1920, p.11A, Anderson Township .)

    21.   Francis Jarret/ Jarrot/Garrett Hooper b. October 10, 1849 married Sarah Clementine Kirkpatrick b. abt. 1850 married Nov. 4, 1866 Bradley County, TN (Moved to Hickory Co., Missouri before 1870). Francis died December 13, 1897.

    22.   Tabitha J. Hooper b. Aug. 22, 1850 died Sept. 9, 1936 married Clinton Jack b. Nov. 1844 died about 1898 moved to Lee Co., Arkansas before 1880. Moved to Dallas County, Texas before 1900 (see p. 33), TX Death Certificate No. 44477.

1-3 Andrew married Margaret who Kinsey Seaborn (see pages 17 – 18) testified was a cousin. Anne Goodwin of *Hooper Compass* suggested Margaret Carson. (According to Chancery Court testimony by John Hooper on pages 19 – 20 and 29 in this book, Andrew Hooper had three other sons who died.)

Some of the Absolom Hooper family information was taken from *Hooper Genealogy and Autobiography of Wm. Hayden Hooper1898-1966* which was published at Thomas, Custer County, OK on August 4, 1966. On the Internet, *hooperconnections.com* (Bill Hooper, Clay Hooper and Sharon Hooper) also had data for the Absolom Hooper family.

Absolom Hooper married Elizabeth Rymer of Buncombe County, NC. She was the daughter of William Rymer, and they moved to Greasy Creek in Polk County, TN on the Hiwassee River about four miles above Reliance, TN. Census records also helped to trace the family.

1-4 Absolom Hooper b. abt. 1810 and Elizabeth Rymer Hooper's children:

    23.   Alford Hooper b. abt. 1834
    24.   Nancy Hooper b. February, 4, 1837
    25.   Sarah Hooper b. January 24, 1838
    26.   John Hooper b. September 2, 1840
    27.   Mary Letty Hooper b. Sept. 2, 1840
    28.   William Hooper b. December 10, 1842
    29.   Isaac Hooper b. March 27, 1844
    30.   Dialthea Hooper b. March 3, 1846
    31.   Andrew Hooper b. April 26, 1848
    32.   Elizabeth Hooper b. September 22, 1850
    33.   Absolom Hooper b. February 3, 1853 and d. April 11, 1921 in Custer County, OK
    34.   George Hooper b. April 1, 1855
    35.   Margaret Hooper b. March 4, 1857

1-4   Absolom Hooper married a second time to Mariah Amanda Williams on September 19, 1867 in Bradley County, TN. She was born April 1823 and died May 1909.

1-2-5   William C. Shelton b. Sept. 1820 fought against the Seminoles in Florida when he was 15; fought in the Mexican War from 1836 to 1842 and was a Captain in the Union Army in the Civil War (Internet at *Rootsweb The Families of James Shelton of McMinn County, Tennessee* by Arthur Paul Shelton August 1987 pp. 25 - 26) married 1. Sarah Rymer in Bradley County, TN:

    36.   George Shelton b. 1844
    37.   Catherine Shelton b. 1846
    38.   John Shelton b. 1849
    39.   Tempor Shelton b. 1854

1-2-5   William C. Shelton married a second time to Dorcas Paris b. 1850:

    40.   James Shelton b. abt. 1872

41.	Caldona Shelton b. abt. 1874
42.	Laura Shelton b. abt. 1876
43.	Sarah Shelton b. abt. 1878
44.	Landon Shelton b. Feb. 1880
45.	Elise Shelton b. 1882
46.	Myrtle Shelton b. 1884-July 1994 (died sixteen days short of 100)
47.	Julia Shelton b. 1888 (moved to San Bernardino, CA)
48.	Daisy Shelton b. 1890
49.	Jennie Shelton b. 1894 (moved to San Bernardino, CA)

1-2-6	Andrew Hooper Shelton b. 1824 d. abt. 1863 married Alice Sparks born about 1828 (Internet *Fischer Family Tree at Ancestry.com*). They moved to Washington County, MO before 1850.
50.	Mary Shelton b. 1843
51.	Lewis Shelton b. 1844 TN
52.	James Shelton b. 1847 TN
53.	Elizabeth Shelton b. 1849 TN
54.	Oma Shelton b. 1852 MO
55.	Biger Shelton b. 1854. MO
56.	Eliza Shelton b. 1856 MO
57.	Thomas Shelton b. 1858 MO
58.	Ann Shelton b. 1861 MO
59.	Harvy Shelton b. 1863 MO

1-2-7	Elicy/Eliza/Liza Shelton b. May 27, 1827 d. Dec. 1866 married 1. Edward Sharp:
60.	Napoleon Sharp b. 1844 d. abt. 1864
61.	Edward Sharp, Jr. b. 1846 d. abt. 1864

1-2-7	Elicy/Eliza/Liza Shelton Sharp married 2. Simeon Graves about 1849 in Bradley County, TN:
62.	Nancy Graves b. 1849
63.	Elizabeth Graves b. 1852
64.	Lucinda Graves b. 1854
65.	Lewis Graves b. 1857
66.	Daniel Graves b. 1859
67.	Catherine Graves b. 1861
68.	Vilena Graves b. 1862
69.	Simeon Graves b. 1865

1-2-8	John E. Shelton b. Sept. 4, 1829 married Lucinda Perrin on August 12, 1853 (information for John E. Shelton family found on Internet *willownsm on Ancestry.com.*)
70.	James Shelton b. 1854
71.	Samuel Shelton b. Aug. 23, 1856
72.	William Shelton b. Nov. 21, 1857 d. June 14, 1878
73.	Benjamin Shelton b. Jan. 10, 1860
74.	Felix Shelton b. Mar. 5, 1862 d. April 1, 1896
75.	Sarah Elizabeth Shelton b. Aug. 10, 1864 d. Jan. 4, 1947
76.	Catherine Shelton b. Dec. 20, 1866 d. Aug. 19, 1961
77.	Virginia Shelton b. Aug. 30, 1869 d. Jan. 13, 1900
78.	John Shelton b. July 12, 1872 d. Dec. 28, 1872
79.	Jasper Shelton b. July 2, 1874 d. July 23, 1903

1-2-9	Jane Shelton b. Dec. 25, 1830 married Nathaniel Farmer in Bradley County, TN on March 15, 1846 (some information provided at Internet *willownsrn on Ancestry.com* dated July 13, 2011)
80.	Richard Farmer b. 1846
81.	Henry Farmer b. 1848
82.	Caroline Farmer b. 1850
83.	Simeon Farmer b. 1856
84.	John Louis Farmer b. March 8, 1858
85.	Andrew Jackson Farmer b. 1861
86.	Catherine Farmer b. 1862
87.	Thomas Jefferson Farmer b. 1865

1-2-10	Lewis Shelton b. abt. 1833 (probably died in Greenwood, Kansas)

1-2-11   Ursula Shelton married Henry Jacob Cantrell and lived in Bradley County, TN in 1850, Newton
          County, MO in 1860 and father and children lived in Greenwood County, Kansas in 1870. Some
          list a James Cantrell as the oldest child, but in the 1860 Census Mary is the oldest
          (Internet *Ancestry.com Censuses 1850* [family 1304], *1860* [Shoal Creek, MO p. 45] *and 1870*
          [Greenwood, KS, Fallriver p. 16]).
          88.   Mary Cantrell b. 1851   TN married Benjamin F. Lawson ch. J. H., M. C., and W. O.
          89.   Tennessee Cantrell b. 1854   MO
          90.   William Cantrell b. 1856   MO
          91.   Emily Cantrell b. 1858   MO
          92.   Eliza Cantrell b. 1859   MO
1-2-12   Elizabeth Shelton b. Jan. 20, 1836 married to Christopher Graves Aug. 15, 1853 by William
          Walker, JP in McMinn County, TN. Elizabeth died Jan. 3, 1858. On the Internet at *Rootsweb, The
          Families of James Shelton of McMinn County, Tennessee* by Arthur Paul Shelton, August 1987 p.
          98 listed a James Graves born in 1857 who died young. N. B. and Jane Graves lived with William
          Bracket (spelled as Brackit) at *Ancestry.com, 1860 Census of Bradley County, TN* p. 174.
          93.   Napoleon B. Graves b. 1855 (Internet, *Ancestry.com Bradley County 1870 Census*, p.
                    17)
          94.   Jane Graves b. 1858
1-2-13   Catherine Shelton b. abt. 1842 married R. W. Shipley on Sept. 17, 1857 by James Bonner, JP in
          McMinn County, TN
          95.   James Shipley b. 1859   TN
          96.   Mary Shipley b. 1861   TN
          97.   Ada Shipley b. 1863   TN
1-3-14   John and Sarah Farmer Hooper's children:
          98.   Elizabeth (Betsey) Hooper b. 1846 – d. 1928 (Internet *Find A Grave* Lavaca City,
                    Cemetery) married Marion Graham. (See p. 27 for Graham information.)
          99.   Andrew J. Hooper b. Mar. 26, 1846 married (1) Elizabeth Scroggins and (2) Linda
                    Dawson. He died Sept. 5, 1923 and is buried at Hopewell Cemetery at Dallas Co., MO.
                    His tombstone picture is at *Ancestry.com* and was submitted by *flowermom121.*
          100.   William Hooper b. Feb. 1849 married Martha Consada Cobb
          101.   Deltha Hooper b. abt. 1852 married Jasper Newton Graham on Aug. 13, 1870 in
                    Sebastian County, Arkansas (See p. 27 for Graham family information.)
          102.   James Hooper b. abt. 1855 married Margaret Hill on Oct. 24, 1875 in Sebastian County,
                    Ark.
          103.   Martha Hooper b. abt. 1858 married Jamison Graham? (See p. 27 for Graham family.)
          104.   Margaret Hooper b. 1862 d. 1939 married Richard Filmon Johnson on Oct. 10, 1878)
                    (Internet, *Ancestry.com* by *bw36912* in *Walker Family Tree*).
1-3-15   Kinsey C. and Elizabeth Geren Hooper's children:
          105.   James Hooper b. abt. 1856 married Cynthia Hickman
          106.   Isaac Houston Hooper b. Oct. 11, 1858 d. 1915 married Ellen (Ella) C. Allen on June 8,
                    1877 (Internet, Hooper, *Ancestry.com*, Bradley County, Tennessee Marriages).
          107.   Ethalinda Hooper b. abt. 1861 married Henry Brackett Jan. 2, 1878 in Bradley County,
                    TN (moved to TX) (Internet, Texas, Brackett, *Ancestry.com*).
          108.   Jeanetta Hooper b. abt. 1866 – d. May 17, 1930 in Hamilton County, TN married Samuel
                    Isaac Baker
          109.   Martha Hooper b. 1868 d. 1918 married A. U. Miller Jan. 1885
          110.   Allice Hooper b. abt. 1873 married A. W. Millaway
          111.   Andy Hooper b. Sept. 12, 1875 d. May 29, 1951 married Maggie (Margaret) Marr
                    (number 363)
1-3-16   Dialtha Hooper and Thomas H. Gilbreath's children:
          112.   Mary J. Gilbreath b. Mar. 1850 married James L. Marr
          113.   Martha A. Gilbreath b. May 1852 married Samuel Graham
          114.   Maranda Gilbreath b. Aug. 9, 1854 married Robert W. Williamson
          115.   Andrew Gilbreath b. Feb. 8, 1857 married Margaret Cofer
          116.   Dr. John Gilbreath b. Mar. 1860 married Darthula Jane Andes (See pp. 287 – 288.)
          117.   Margaret Gilbreath b. abt. 1863 married Medlin Dunham (Doctor?) on June 15, 1884 in

Bradley County, TN
118. Tabitha Gilbreath b. abt. 1866
119. Genetta Gilbreath b. Oct. 27, 1868 d. March 10, 1936 married on Oct. 27, 1885 in Bradley County, TN to Dr. Med M. Dunham (same as number 116?)
1-3-17 Jahew Hooper b. Nov. 13, 1833 d. Nov. 14, 1902 married (1) Mary McPherson b. Nov. 11, 1835 d. Apr. 24, 1894 children:
120. Martha Elizabeth Hooper b. July 11, 1856 d. Jan. 25, 1919 married Joshua Carlton Aug. 1880
121. Margaret Ellen Hooper married Joel Teague March 10, 1878 in Bradley County, TN (Internet, *Ancestry.com*).
122. William Howard Hooper b. Aug. 23, 1861 d. Sept. 10, 1931 married Letha Ann Carlton
123. Josephine Hooper b. Nov. 2, 1864 married George W. Eads
124. Andrew Jackson Hooper b. Sept. 23, 1867 d. July 10, 1868
125. Charles Hooper b. Sept. 21, 1869 d. Jan. 9, 1945 married Annie McCamish
126. Kenzie Hooper b. Sept. 15, 1872 d. 1933 married number 315, Rosa Hooper b. Dec. 1883 d. 1966.
127. Addie Hooper b. abt. 1875 married D. Frank Ownby
128. Emma Hooper b. July 14, 1879 d. Oct. 22, 1883
1-3-17 Jahew married (2) Amanda Maxwell about 1894.
1-3-18 James and Eliza Geren Hooper's children:
129. Susan Hooper b. May 1860 married on Aug. 31, 1879 in Sebastian County, Arkansas Alexander C. Boggs b. April 1842 (Internet, *Ancestry.com* also see p. 285).
130. Ruth (Eliza) Hooper b. abt. 1864
131. Mary Hooper b. abt. 1867
132. Daniel Hooper b. abt. 1869
133. Annie Hooper b. abt. 1872
134. Tabitha Hooper b. abt. 1874
1-3-19 William Hooper b. Sept. 5, 1842 d. July 18, 1914 and (1) Marilla Wilson Hooper's child:
135. David Francis Hooper b. 1867 d. 1945 married Nancy Duncan in Goodson, MO on July 27, 1884 and (2) Maude E. Devine on March 6, 1914 at Cowley County, Kansas (Internet *teresahoddy* at *Ancestry.com*)
1-3-19 William Hooper married (2) Nancy Thurston abt. 1878
136. Charles T. Hooper b. abt. 1878 d. abt. 1916? married Myrtle Kirkpatrick in Polk County, MO Jan. 29, 1913 (Internet *Ancestry.com*)
137. Walter W. Hooper b. abt. 1880
(Step-children listed Hattie C. Thurston b. abt. 1873 and Flora Thurston b. abt. 1874)
1-3-19 William Hooper married (3) Mary Ann Cosby
1-3-19 William Hooper married (4) Barbara Bowen
138. Bertha Hooper b. Feb. 1890 married Perry Miller
1-3-19 Willam Hooper married (5) Elvira Thompson Fansler
139. Ezza K. Hooper b. August 1892 married Clyde Gilbert
(Jessie Bowen b. April 1878 step-daughter)
1-3-20 Daniel/Danis Hooper and Isabelle Snow Hooper's children:
140. Kinsey L. Hooper b. July 8, 1871 d. Aug. 16, 1963 married Martha Emmaline Taylor and Frances Eads
141. Dona J. Hooper Feb. 1880 married Walter Dobbs
142. Ida Hooper b. Oct. 1883 married Joseph A. Knight
143. Henry J. Hooper b. July 14, 1886 d. Feb. 7, 1967 married Donna B. Taylor b. April 5, 1885 d. Feb. 28, 1964 Married Sept. 2, 1916 (Internet, *Ancestry.com, Find A Grave*)
144. Cordella Hooper Jan. 1890 married James E. Summers
145. John Andrew Hooper b. Sept. 8, 1897 d. Feb. 21, 1987 married Bertha Frances Crawford
146. Noah E. Hooper b. July 8, 1900 d. Aug. 17, 1967 married Treva M. Nicholson
1-3-21 Francis Jarret Hooper and Sarah Clementine Kirkpatrick Hooper's children:
147. James Andrew Hooper b. Sept. 6, 1867 married Rosa Cooper on Sept. 9, 1894 in Hickory County, MO and Ethel R. Pitts on July 31, 1901 in Hickory County, MO
148. John William Hooper b. Nov. 11, 1869 d. Aug. 27, 1957 married Cordelia Alexander

149.	Charles Clinton Hooper b. Feb. 11, 1872 d. Nov. 26, 1932 married Ina May Alexander
150.	Tobitha Hooper b. abt. 1875 married John Johnson
151.	Margaret Hooper b. Feb. 16, 1877 d. Oct. 29, 1937 married John W. Meadors on Nov. 23, 1895 in Hickory County, Missouri (Internet, *Ancestry.com*).
152.	Henry Jahew Hooper b. Nov. 1879 d. Sept. 16, 1974 married Rachel Lyon Mallonee
153.	Arthur Hooper b. Feb. 26, 1882 d. Jan. 2, 1954 married Jewell Mallonee
154.	Benjamin Harrison Hooper b. Jan. 7, 1885 d. June 1, 1970 married Myrtle Larose
155.	Carrie Harrison Hooper b. Jan. 7, 1885 d. 1970 married Ully Roy
156.	Mary E. Hooper b. April 1889 married Thomas Grisham and Douglas L. Pitts

1-3-22	Tabitha Hooper b. Aug. 1850 d. Sept. 9, 1936 in Dallas County, TX married John Clinton Jack b. Nov. 6, 1844 d. abt. 1900?. Nine children were listed on Internet pages 885-886 in the *Memorial and Biographical History of Dallas County, Texas* published in 1892 in Chicago by the Lewis Publishing Company.
157.	Charles H. Jack b. Feb. 1870 married Effie
158.	Oscar Jack b. April 1872 married Lillie D.
159.	Frank Luther Jack b. Dec. 11, 1873 TN d. March 4, 1959 (Internet, *Texas Death Certificate* for Tarrant County, *Ancestry.com*)
160.	Lillia A. Jack b. 1880
161.	John C. Jack b. Nov. 8, 1891
162.	Mary Jack
163.	Fred H. Jack
164.	Maude T. Jack
165.	David A. Jack

1-4-23	Alford Hooper b. abt. 1834
1-4-24	Nancy Hooper b. February 4, 1837
1-4-25	Sarah Hooper b. Jan. 24, 1838 married Miller Perrin b. Jan. 18, 1843 d. April 21, 1877
166.	John Perrin 1869
167.	William Perrin 1872
168.	Isaac Perrin 1873
169.	Mary Perrin 1875

1-4-26	John Hooper b. Sept. 2, 1840 married Susan Barnet
170.	Absolom Hooper b. abt. 1873
171.	Louisa (Eliza?) Hooper b. abt. 1879
172.	Pollie Hooper b. May 1881
173.	Mary Hooper b. Dec. 1884
174.	Susan (Anna?) Hooper b. Nov. 1887

1-4-27	Mary Letty Hooper b. Sept. 2, 1840 married Lee Hickey;
175.	William Hickey;
176.	Media Hickey

1-4-28	William Hooper b. Dec. 10, 1842 (ambushed and killed with his brother Isaac at the end of the Civil War taking corn to the mill in Polk Co., TN according to William Hayden Hooper in OK, 1966) married Cathern Rumels (Cathern Runnels?)
1-4-29	Isaac Hooper b. March 27, 1844 (ambushed and killed with his brother William at the end of the Civil War taking corn to the mill in Polk Co., TN according to William Hayden Hooper 1966 in OK) married Nancy Kirkland
1-4-30	Dialthea Hooper b. March 3, 1846 married Bill Cardin
177.	John W. Cardin
178.	Maggie Cardin
179.	Sadie or Sarah Cardin

1-4-31	Andrew Hooper b. April 26, 1848 married Mary C. b. abt. 1852
180.	James B. Hooper b. abt. 1876
181.	Sarah M. Hooper b. abt. 1878

1-4-32	Elizabeth Hooper b. Sept. 22, 1850 married Jim Shell
182.	Reece Shell

1-4-33	Absolom Hooper was born in Springtown, Polk County, TN Feb. 3, 1853 but moved to OK where he died April 11, 1921. He married in Custer County, OK Mary C. Smith who lived from Jan. 22,

1857 to April 27, 1945.
183.   Sarah M. Hooper Nov. 13, 1875-April 27, 1945 m. Samuel Edgar Harris, Sr. on Oct. 20, 1901 in Oklahoma Territory. Samuel was born March 4, 1872 and died Nov. 23, 1950.
184.   William H. Hooper July 24, 1877-May 20, 1958 married Lou H. Hamons March 20, 1899 in Springtown, Polk County, TN. She lived from May 18, 1879 to Jan. 9, 1954.
185.   John G. Hooper May 4, 1879-July 7, 1953 married Dorothy Pauline Wieland. She lived from July 13, 1883 to Feb. 9, 1944.
186.   Isaac A. Hooper Jan. 20, 1881-July 20, 1959 married Elsie Ethel Smith on Oct. 9, 1913 in Arapaho, OK. She lived from June 20, 1894 to Jan. 22, 1983.
187.   James Enos Hooper Dec. 29, 1882-Nov. 11, 1948 married Mary Elizabeth Pike on March 8, 1908 in Custer County, OK. She lived from Feb. 18, 1890 to Dec. 30, 1950.
188.   Temperance Hooper born Sept. 2, 1884 and married Alonzo Potter in Custer Co., OK.
189.   Maudie Helen Hooper Nov. Oct. 10, 1886-Jan. 12, 1970 married William Carl Campbell on Dec. 11, 1911 in Custer Co., OK.   He lived from July 10, 1879 to Feb. 22, 1967.
190.   Amanda Hooper b. Sept. 1889 married Lee C. Ryan.
191.   Bertha Hooper Jan. 1893-April 9, 1914
192.   Samuel Arthur Hooper March 9, 1898-July 1984 married Myrtle Frances Faw on Jan. 30, 1920 in Custer County, OK. She lived from April 1902 to Nov. 25, 1980.
193.   Jennings Bryan Hooper Sept. 3, 1900-July 30, 1962 in Colorado. On July 28, 1936 in Pittsburgh, KS, he married Nellie Nerina Ross who was born Dec. 16, 1905.

1-4-34   George Hooper April 1, 1855-1886 married Jane Bates b. abt. 1856
194.   Dallas Monroe Hooper Sept. 18, 1876-March 30, 1940 married Ida Ellen Thompson b. April 23, 1877 daughter of John Burley Thompson and Martha Angaline Childress in Springtown, Polk County, TN. Dallas and Ellen married November 8, 1896.
195.   Henry Hooper b. abt. 1879
196.   Granville Jackson Hooper b. Dec. 25, 1879 d. abt. 1961 Etowah, TN married Elizabeth Armstrong on Dec. 23, 1900 in Polk County, TN.
197.   Mollie Hooper b. Nov. 1885 married Charley Davis on Nov. 4, 1900 in Polk County, TN. He was born April 18, 1877 and died Oct. 10, 1949
198.   Margaret Hooper b. Nov. 1885 married 1. Bert R. Cobb on Sept. 21, 1901 in Polk County, TN. She married a second time to William Casteel.

1-4-35   Margaret Hooper b. abt. 1855 married Oliver Cardin;
199.   Vitta R. Cardin Jan. 1883 Polk County, TN
200.   Ida Cardin Feb. 1885 Polk County, TN
201.   Anna Cardin July 1888 Polk County, TN m. Floyd Martin
202.   Newton Swan Cardin Jan. 1891 Polk County, TN m. Anna b. 1894
203.   Thoms Cardin Oct. 1894
204.   Oliver Cardin Dec. 1897 m. Hazel

1-2-5-36   George Shelton b. 1844
1-2-5-37   Catherine Shelton b. 1846
1-2-5-38   John Shelton b. 1849 married Flora Jack on Dec. 13, 1866 in Bradley County, TN (Internet, *Ancestry.com*).
205.   William Douglas "Wylie" Shelton b. Feb. 26, 1868 – d. July 16, 1938 in Rowlett, TX
206.   Dallas Homer Shelton b. April 26, 1871 – d. Jan. 25, 1889 at Monroe County, Arkansas
1-2-5-39   Temperance Shelton b. 1854
1-2-5-40   James A. Shelton b. Oct. 12, 1871
1-2-5-41   Caldona Shelton b. Feb. 23, 1874
1-2-5-42   Laura Shelton b. Sept. 10, 1875 married Thomas A. Walker on Dec. 16, 1894 in McMinn County, TN (Internet, *Ancestry.com*).
207.   Felix Jack Walker 1895-1993
208.   Nathaniel Walker b. 1898 married Ollie M.   ?
209.   Nellie Walker b. 1899
210.   Thomas A. Walker, Jr. 1902
211.   Shelton Reid Walker July 23, 1905-March 20, 1930
212.   Mary Dorcas Walker b. 1912 married Aubrey Mitchell on Dec. 27, 1928 in McMinn County, TN

1-2-5-43   Sarah Shelton b. Feb. 6, 1878
1-2-5-44   Landon Shelton b. Jan. 24, 1880
1-2-5-45   Elsa Shelton b. April 20, 1882
1-2-5-46   Myrtle Shelton b. Aug. 8, 1884 d. July 23, 1983 in San Diego, CA married Arthur Albert
      McKellop in OK. He was born Sept. 4, 1884 and died April 25, 1982. Arthur's father was
      a tribal leader for the Creek Indians in Oklahoma (Internet *willownsrn* at *Ancestry.com*).
   213.   Alberta Pearl McKellop b. 1912 d. Feb. 14, 2001
1-2-5-47   Julia Shelton b. Jan. 2, 1888 d. June 16, 1990 San Bernardino, CA married James David Baugh
      b. May 26, 1889. They married in McMinn County, TN Dec. 30, 1907 (Internet,
      Ancestry.com). He died July 1, 1959 in Yuba County, CA.
   214.   Auda S. Baugh b. 1909
   215.   Fred W. Baugh b. 1911
   216.   Annie Ruth Baugh b. 1916-d. 1918
   217.   Alma J. Baugh b. 1920
   218.   Edith L. Baugh b. 1922
   219.   James D. Baugh, Jr. b. 1923
1-2-5-48   Daisy Arlene Shelton b. Feb. 22, 1890 d. Sept. 20, 1916 married C. G. Hughes on Feb. 21, 1915
      in McMinn County, TN (Internet, *Ancestry.com*).
1-2-5-49   Jennie Shelton b. March 25, 1894 d. August 9, 1991 San Bernardino, CA married 1. Melvin
      Shea Baugh on Dec. 11, 1910 in McMinn County, TN (Internet, *Ancestry.com*). He was born
      April 1891 and died 1915.
   220.   Julia Lois Baugh b. May 22, 1913
1-2-5-49   Jennie Shelton married 2.William J. Tillotson was born 1873 in NY.
   221.   Mildred Georgiana Tillotson b. March 22, 1918
1-2-6-50   Mary Shelton b. 1843 TN
1-2-6-51   Lewis Shelton b. 1844 TN d. June 9, 1921 in OK. He married Sarah Ann Hodge on March 5,
      1866 in Webster County, MO (Internet, *Ancestry.com*).
1-2-6-52   James Shelton b. 1847 TN
1-2-6-53   Elizabeth Shelton b. 1849 TN married Joseph Stephens Jan. 1, 1888 in Washington
      County, MO (Internet, *Ancestry.com*).
1-2-6-54   Oma Shelton b. 1852 MO
1-2-6-55   Biger Shelton b. 1854 MO
1-2-6-56   Eliza Shelton b. 1856 MO married James L. Reel on Dec. 2, 1874 in Washington County,
      MO (Internet, *Ancestry.com*).
1-2-6-57   Thomas Shelton b. 1858 MO
1-2-6-58   Ann Shelton b. 1861
1-2-6-59   Harvy Shelton b. 1863 MO
1-2-7-60   Napoleon Sharp b. 1844 d. abt. 1864
1-2-7-61   Edward Sharp b. 1846 d. abt. 1864
1-2-7-62   Nancy Graves b. 1849
1-2-7-63   Elizabeth Graves b. 1852
1-2-7-64   Lucinda Graves b. 1854
1-2-7-65   Lewis Graves b. 1857 married Julia A. Maddin b. 1857 married August 29, 1873 in McMinn
      County, TN (Internet, *Ancestry.com*).
   222.   Nap Graves b. 1874
   223.   Catherine Graves b. 1876
   224.   Art Graves b. 1879
1-2-7-66   Daniel Graves b. 1859
1-2-7-67   Catherine Graves b. March 31, 1861 d. Nov. 9, 1942 married Caleb Right (Wright) in Meigs
      County, TN Dec. 17, 1874 (Internet information from *Calvin Dodson, Sr.* at *Ancestry.com*)
   225.   John Wright b. 1878
   226.   Lawrence Wright b. 1881
   227.   Savannah Wright b. 1885
   228.   Ella Wright b. 1887
   229.   Minnie Wright b. 1889
1-2-7-68   Vilena Graves b. 1862

1-2-7-69   Simeon Graves b. 1865
1-2-8-70   James Shelton b. 1854 married 1. Easter Moore
    230.   Jane Shelton b. 1877
1-2-8-70   James married Esther Moore before 1880.
    231.   Leon Shelton
1-2-8-71   Samuel Shelton b. Aug. 23, 1856 died 1856
1-2-8-72   William Shelton b. Nov. 21, 1857 d. June 14, 1878
1-2-8-73   Benjamin Shelton b. Jan. 10, 1860 d. Feb. 11, 1909 married Lena J. Finley b. April 24, 1868
1-2-8-74   Felix Shelton b. March 5, 1862 d. April 1, 1896 (Internet, *Ancestry.com*)
1-2-8-75   Sarah Elizabeth Shelton b. August 10, 1864 d. Jan. 4, 1847 married Henry D. Saulpaw b. Sept. 20, 1850 – Sept. 17, 1933 (adopted Allie Saulpaw), (Internet, *Ancestry.com*)
1-2-8-76   Catherine Shelton b. Sept. 20, 1866 d. Aug. 19, 1961 married James F. Henninger and lived in Rhea County, TN before moving to Statesville in Iredell County, NC (Internet *willownsrn* at *Ancestry.com*).
    232.   Elba Henniger b. 1889
    233.   Sophia Henniger b. 1891
    234.   Alice Elizabeth Henniger b. 1892
    235.   Almeda Henniger b. 1895
    236.   James Shelton Henniger b. 1897
    237.   Ruby Catherine Henniger b. 1900
    238.   Mary Frances Henniger b. 1903
1-2-8-77   Virginia Shelton b. Aug. 30, 1869 d. Jan. 13, 1900
1-2-8-78   John Shelton b. July 12, 1872 d. Dec. 28, 1872
1-2-8-79   Jasper Shelton b. July 2, 1874 d. July 23, 1903
1-2-9-80   Richard Farmer b. 1846
1-2-9-81   Henry Farmer b. 1848
1-2-9-82   Caroline Farmer b. Oct. 1850 married John Baff b. June 1846 in Germany. Married at Laclede County, MO June 15, 1872 moved to Lee County, IO (Internet, *Ancestry.com*).
    239.   Myrtle Baff b. 1880   IO
    240.   Mamie Baff b. 1882   IO
    241.   Edward Baff b. 1886 IO
1-2-9-83   Simeon Farmer b. 1856
1-2-9-84   John Louis Farmer b. March 8, 1858 married Helen Taylor in Laclede County, MO on Nov. 14, 1886. Helen was born August 1858 (Internet, *Ancestry.com*).
    242.   Walter S. Farmer b. August 1887
    243.   Maude H. Farmer b. Oct. 1889
    244.   Raymond J. Farmer b. Nov. 1894
1-2-9-85   Andrew Jackson Farmer b. 1861
1-2-9-86   Catherine Farmer b. 1862
1-2-9-87   Thomas J. Farmer b. May 1866 TN moved to Laclede County, MO before 1870 (Internet, *Ancestry.com*)
1-2-11-89   Tennessee Cantrell b. 1854 MO
1-2-11-90   William Cantrell b. 1856 MO
1-2-11-91   Emily Cantrell b. 1858 MO
1-2-11-92   Eliza Cantrell b. 1859 MO
1-2-12-93   Napoleon (Ponie ?) Graves b. 1855 (Internet information *Ancestry.com* by *keithamcdonald*) On July 4, 1878, he married Nellie Clementson. By 1900 Ellen (Nellie) Graves was married to Henry Bolen and living in the Second District (*Meigs County 1900 Census*, TN p. 3 A.)
    245.   Elbert M. Graves b. April 1879
    246.   Leonard Mercer Graves b. Dec. 8, 1883 d. Nov. 6, 1952 *Death Certificate* for Rhea County, TN.
1-2-12-94   Jane Graves (N. B. and Jane Graves living at William Bracket [Brackit]'s house next door to Christopher Graves in the Internet *Ancestry.com* in Dist. 9 *Bradley County, TN 1860 Census* on p. 174.)
1-2-13-95   James Shipley 1859 in McMinn County, TN
1-2-13-96   Mary V. Shipley b. 1861 in TN married James L. Cantrell in Greenwood County, KA (note

this James Cantrell was listed by some as the son of Henry Jacob and Ursula Cantrell, but he arrived in the Internet, *Ancestry.com, 1870 Census Greenwood, KS, Fallriver* p. 16, but may be a nephew?.)

247. Henry Cantrell b. 1876
248. Catherine Cantrell b. Dec. 1881 MO
249. Richard J. Cantrell b. Nov. 1883 MO
250. James L. Cantrell b. Feb. 1886
251. Clarence O. Cantrell b. Oct. 24, 1888 MO
252. Charles M. Cantrell b. Sept. 1890 Indian Territory
253. Cora J. Cantrell b. Jan. 1894 Indian Territory
254. Martha A. Cantrell b. May 1896 Indian Territory
255. Otto B. Cantrell b. May 1897 Indian Territory
256. Alice Cantrell b. 1901 Indian Territory.

1-2-13-97   Ada Shipley b. Oct. 1863 d. April 3, 1949 in Washburn, MO married Benjamin Shipley
257. Claude W. Shipley 1887
258. Earl Shipley 1893
259. Rachel Shipley 1897

1-3-14-98   Elizabeth Hooper b. abt. 1845 alive after 1920 in Sebastian County, Arkansas m. Marion Graham on August 31, 1865 in Bradley County, TN. (Internet, Marriage, *Ancestry.com*)
260. William Graham b. March 1866 married Martha E. Mullin (Mcie) Sept. 23, 1885 in Sebastian County, Arkansas (Internet *Ancestry.com*). She was b. Nov. 1874 and he married (2) Betty Steward on April 16, 1905. She was born 1887.
261. Landon Graham b. July 1868 married Mary P. Jones b. Oct. 1873
262. Louis Graham b. May 1876 in Arkansas
263. Benjamin Graham b. September 1881 in Arkansas
264. Lizzie E. Graham b. April 1884 in Arkansas
265. Oscar L. Graham b. Nov. 1888 in Arkansas

1-3-14-99   Andrew J. Hooper b. March 22, 1846 married 1. Elizabeth Scroggins on June 27, 1865 in Bradley County, TN (Internet, *Ancestry.com*)
266. Samuel Campbell Hooper b. Nov. 21, 1865 d. Sept. 6, 1948 married Gertrude Dixon on August 5, 1888 in McMinn County, TN (Internet, *Ancestry.com*)

1-3-14-99   Andrew J. Hooper b. March 22, 1846 in Bradley County, TN d. Sept. 5, 1923 in Dallas County, MO. He married 2. Malinda Dawson b. Dec. 24, 1853 at Hickory County, MO and died Dec. 5, 1922 in Dallas County, MO. He married Jan. 28, 1870 in Hickory County, MO (Internet information from *Shari913 at Ancestry.com*).
267. Florence Hooper b. abt. 1873 married Joe Honeyman and Adam McDaniel
268. William Hooper b. Feb. 8, 1874 married Allice Wheeler
269. Sarah Jane Hooper b. abt. 1876 married Tom Honeyman
270. Laura Hooper b. abt. 1878 married William Bonner
271. Zadie B. Hooper b. Jan. 1880 married Albert Catlett
272. Josie Hooper b. Aug. 4, 1882 married 1. Rufus Reynolds and 2. Riley Vanlandingham
273. Della May Hooper b. Oct.4, 1884 d. Oct. 4, 1872   married William Wesley Erven
274. Margaret Pearl Hooper b. April 11, 1886 married Fount Sawyer
275. Carrie B. (Tabitha) Hooper b. Aug. 15, 1889 married Wesley Wheeler
276. Lou Ada Hooper July 16, 1891- Oct. 10, 1957 married Joseph Carlton Nasalroad b. June 20, 1888 d. June 22, 1960. They married Jan. 10, 1905 in Dallas County, MO. Some information from Kenneith Bickmore Nasalroad on Internet at *Genealogy.com*, family information section and *Find A Grave* at *Ancestry.com*.
277. James Hooper b. and d. 1892
278. Rosa P. Hooper b. Dec. 31, 1895 married Tom Van Landingham and Harry Huber

1-3-14-100   William Marion Hooper b. Feb. 2, 1849 d. Jan. 30, 1931 in Bryan Co., OK married Martha Cansada Cobb b. June 6, 1857 in Miss. d. July 17, 1933. William Marion Hooper [son of John Hooper and Sarah Farmer Hooper] moved to Choctaw Nation before 1900 with his family. In Bradley County in 1850 and 1860, John had a son William b. 1849, and John moved to (Internet, *Ancestry.com*) *Sebastian County, Arkansas* before the *1870 Census* (pp. 16 and 17 Sulpher Township). William and his family were in *Reveille, Logan County,*

Arkansas in 1880 Census p. 33 with his sister Margaret Johnson (p. 33), and his Uncle Jasper Newton Graham (p. 21). Martha Cobb and her family were also living in Sebastian County, Arkansas in 1870.   Their children's names would seem to indicate a John Hooper relationship also. Names are listed on Internet at *Genforum.com* by Demetra Haggard.)

279.   John W. Hooper b. Jan. 13, 1874 d. Nov. 30, 1892
280.   Nancy Hooper b. Nov. 11, 1876
281.   Rhoda May Hooper b. July 30, 1878 d. June 14, 1969 married George Edward Hammond Oct. 8, 1894. George was born Nov. 25, 1974 d. Oct. 11, 1946.
282.   Florence E. Hooper b. Dec. 7, 1881 married Ray L. Patillo on Jan. 1, 1905
283.   Andrew Albert Hooper b. Jan. 15, 1883 d. Aug. 14, 1934
284.   Francis Marion Hooper b. Dec. 6, 1885 d. Jan. 19, 1979
285.   William Thomas Hooper b. Feb. 29, 1888 d. April 5, 1980 married Katherine Garner b. July 8, 1898 d. Feb. 16, 1983
286.   Sarah Ethel Hooper b. Jan. 11, 1890
287.   Mary D. (Althea) Hooper b. May 4, 1893 d. Feb. 13, 1984
288.   Horatio Hooper Feb. 3, 1894 d. Jan. 16, 1923
289.   Catherine Leona Hooper b. Oct. 16, 1895 d. Jan. 22, 1963 married Wyatt Wallace Walton on May 3, 1918. He was born Jan. 16, 1895 and d. June 18, 1971.
290.   Viola Hooper b. Sept. 16, 1897
291.   Hattie Savannah Hooper b. March 4, 1902 d. December 31, 1986 married (1) Roy Bates and (2) Thomas Grover Richardson on Sept. 17, 1928 (Internet, *Find A Grave.com*).

1-3-14-101   Dealtha Hooper married Jasper Newton Graham on August 13, 1870 in Sebastian County, Arkansas. He was born March 1845 (Internet *Ancestry.com Sebastian County, Arkansas Census 1900* in Big Creek on p. 3 A).

292.   Samuel Graham b. 1872
293.   Sarah E. Graham b. August 1873
294.   John Graham b. 1874
295.   Lee Graham b. October 1877
296.   James Graham b. 1880
297.   Florence Graham b. December 1883
298.   Martha Graham b. March 1885
299.   Minnie Graham b. December 1886
300.   Myrtle Graham b. May 1891

1-3-14-102   James Hooper married Margaret Hill on Oct. 24, 1875 in Sebastian County, Arkansas.
1-3-14-103   Martha Hooper married Jamison Graham who died 1898 according to Tammy Graham in Internet *Genforum.com* in a message dated November 11, 2001; another record found in *Ancestry.com* listed possible children which also were in the Sebastian County Arkansas 1900 (living with sister Lizzie and her husband William Southard) and 1910 Censuses.

301.   George Graham b. 1877 (Internet *Ancestry.com, Find A Grave* Lavaca City Cemetery: married Mary Elsie Hickman. Son Hugh Graham and his father died from Worldwide Flu Epidemic of 1919. Other possible children Albert Graham 1905 – 1970 and Keller E. Graham b. 1909.)
302.   Elizabeth Graham
303.   Arthur Graham b. 1880
304.   Lulu Graham
305.   Richard Graham
306.   William Tackett Graham b. Jan. 1, 1894

1-3-14-104   Margaret Hooper b. abt. 1862 d. 1939 married Richard Filmon Johnson on Oct. 10, 1878 in Sebastian County, Arkansas according to information at Internet *Ancestry.com*.

307.   Florence Johnson
308.   Mary Elizabeth Johnson 1880-1929
309.   John William Johnson 1883
310.   Della May Johnson 1886-1919
311.   Elsie Jane Johnson 1888-1919
312.   Nancy Johnson 1891
313.   Jasper Franklin Johnson 1896-1967

314.	Charlotte Mayme Johnson 1904-1990
1-3-15-105	James Hooper married Synthia Hickman on Dec. 26, 1876 in Bradley County, TN (Synthia Hickman Hooper married 2. William L. Galloway on Oct. 26, 1884 in Bradley County, TN Internet at *Ancestry.com*)
315.	William Oscar Hooper b. Oct. 7, 1878
316.	Lon Hooper b. Feb. 21, 1882 – d. Feb. 12, 1954
1-3-15-106	Isaac Houston Hooper married Ellen (Ella) C. Allen on June 8, 1877 in Bradley County, TN:
317.	John Luther Hooper b. June 4, 1878 d. Oct. 25, 1953 married Maudie Belle Shiflett April 8, 1900 in Bradley County, TN (Internet, *Ancestry.com*). She was born May 7, 1883 and died April 3, 1931.
318.	Sereptha Hooper b. Dec. 27, 1879 d. Aug. 31, 1892
319.	Lennie (Ethalinda) Hooper b. Sept. 18, 1881 d. Aug. 19, 1944 married Thomas Ledford on Feb. 4, 1898 in Bradley County, TN and George W. Geren on Sept. 2, 1903 in Bradley County, TN (Internet, *1900 Census* 9th Dist., p. 10 A listed Lennie Widow Ancestry.*com*)
320.	Rosa Hooper b. Dec. 1883 d. 1966 married on Oct. 29, 1903 in Bradley County, TN to number 126 Kenzie C. Hooper b. 1872 d. 1933 (Internet, *Ancestry.com*)
321.	Lillie Hooper b. Dec. 9, 1883 d. Jan. 11, 1937 married James Madison Calhoun on Feb. 2, 1908 in Bradley County, TN. He was born June 13, 1876 and died July 4, 1930. She also married William F. Mahoney who lived in Knoxville, TN.(Internet, *Ancestry.com, Tennessee, Deaths and Burials Index*).
322.	James William Hooper b. March 27, 1886 d. Oct. 1972 married June 7, 1908 to Mary Taylor b. Nov. 1885 (Internet, *Ancestry.com*)
323.	Ethel Laura Hooper b. July 1888 married on June 30, 1907 to James Taylor in *Bradley County, TN* (Internet, *Ancestry.com*)
324.	Albert Hooper b. May 3, 1890 d. Jan. 31, 1978 married April 28, 1912 in Bradley County, TN to Pearl Beaty (Internet, *Ancestry.com*)
325.	Gertrude Hooper b. May 15, 1900 d. June 5, 1991 married John Logan Brewer on December 29, 1922 in Bradley County, TN (see page 253).
1-3-15-107	Ethalinda Hooper b. Apr. 16, 1861 d. Jan. 17, 1918 in Texas (Internet, *Find A Grave,* Mills Cemetery, Dallas County, TX) married Henry Brackett Jan. 2, 1878 in Bradley County, TN.
326.	Thomas Walter Brackett b. abt. 1879 married Ruth abt. 1911
327.	Saloma Brackett b. abt. 1882 married 1. John Duncan Garrison and 2. ?	Mealer
328.	Emma Brackett b. abt. 1884 unmarried in 1920
329.	John Fred Brackett b. abt. 1889 married Irene bef. 1910
330.	James A. Brackett b. Mar. 13, 1896 d. Jan. 6, 1910 (Internet, Mills Cemetery, TX)
331.	Dolly/Dollie Brackett b. abt. 1893
332.	Roy Brackett b. abt. 1894 married Bertie bef. 1910

(Henry Brackett married second time on March 15, 1922 in Bradley County, TN to Jessie Pierce b. abt. 1890. Henry had moved back to TN bef. 1920, and they had Mary Elizabeth Brackett b. abt. 1923, Henry H. Brackett b. abt. 1925 and Ann C. Brackett b. abt. 1928.)

1-3-15-108	Jeanetta Hooper b. April 24, 1866 married Samuel Isaac Baker on Dec. 28, 1884 in Bradley County, TN. Isaac was born Feb. 3, 1865 and died April 18, 1944. She died May 17, 1930 in Hamilton County, TN (Internet *Ancestry.com* and *Find A Grave*)
333.	Andy Baker b. June 1887
334.	Effie Eudora Baker b. Jan. 12, 1889 – d. May 15, 1969 (Internet M*arthaD8843* at *Ancestry.com)*
335.	Delia Baker b. Oct. 1894
336.	Isaac Homer Baker b. Feb. 1896
337.	Ethalinda Baker b. June 1899
338.	Martha D. Baker b. abt. 1903
339.	Lucil K. Baker b. abt. 1906
1-3-15-109	Martha Hooper married Alden U. Miller Jan. 18, 1885 in Bradley County, TN
340.	Virgie Miller b. June 1887
341.	Henry Miller b. Nov. 1892
342.	Cash Miller b. April 1894
343.	Gracie Miller b. Jan. 1897

344.   Lawrence Miller b. July 1899

345.   M. Z. Miller b. abt. 1902

346.   Ernest Miller b. abt. 1904

347.   Joseph Luther Miller b. abt. 1908

348.   Rilla Mae Miller b. abt. 1911

(Alden U. Miller married a second time to Carrie Dalton and had Caroline Elizabeth Miller b. abt. 1920 and Willie Cate Miller b. abt. 1922.)

1-3-15-110   Allice Hooper b. March 1873 married Alfred W. (William) Millaway b. Dec. 31, 1867-d. Jan. 17, 1953 in Dallas, TX. They married July 17, 1886 in Bradley County, TN (Internet *Ancestry.com*).

349.   Samuel Isaac Millaway b. July 3, 1889 – Oct. 8, 1950 (Internet *Tennessee Death Index at Ancestry.com*)

350.   Arthur Raymond Millaway b. March 24, 1891 – Aug. 9, 1956 (Internet *Ancestry.com* Texas Death Certificate for Dallas County, Texas)

351.   Jasper Millaway b. Dec. 14, 1896 d. Jan. 12, 1933 in Internet Dallas County, Texas Death Record

352.   Betty Millaway b. July 1899

(Alice died and William Millaway was married to Malinda Johnston on December 24, 1902 in Bradley County, TN (Internet, *Ancestry*.com) and they had Ollie Millaway b. abt. 1904, Horace Millaway b. abt. 1906, Alvie Millaway (dau.) 1910, Cletus Millaway 1912, and A. W. Millaway 1915.)

1-3-15-111   Andrew Jackson Hooper b. September 12, 1875 d. May 29, 1951 married Margaret Marr (number 363) on Nov. 8, 1900 in Bradley County, TN. She was born Dec. 31, 1880 and died Aug. 28, 1941(Internet, *Ancestry.com,* Hooper, Bradley County TN Marriages and *Find A Grave*).

353.   K. C. Hooper b. abt. 1901 m. Ruth Buckner

354.   Arnold Hooper b. abt. 1903 m. Icie Lawson

355.   Annie Hooper b. abt. 1905 m. Ernest Thompson

356.   Lake Hooper b. abt. 1909 m. Dorothy Graham (892)

357.   Aldon Hooper b. abt. 1913 m. Almetta Melton

358.   Forrest Hooper b. abt. 1916 d. 1918

1-3-16-112   Mary J. Gilbreath b. Mar. 1850 m. James Lloyd Marr who was born Aug. 1841 (Internet, *Tennessee, Bradley County 1880* Dist. 9 p. 64 and *1900 Census* Dist. 9 p. 3 B and p. 3 A are reversed for House 47.)

359.   Thomas Houston Marr b. Feb. 1868

360.   Daniel Marr b. Sept. 1871

361.   John Marr b. abt. 1876

362.   Tabitha Marr b. abt. 1879

363.   Maggie (Margaret) Marr b. Dec. 1881

364.   Martha Marr b. Aug. 1883

365.   Andrew L. Marr b. Feb. 1887

366.   Dialtha Marr b. July 1891

1-3-16-113   Martha A. Gilbreath b. May 3, 1852 d. July 31, 1908 married Samuel Graham July 6, 1867. Samuel was born Sept. 29, 1844 and died July 31, 1902. Joyce Disharoon has listed a King Family Bible on Internet *King with Allied Families*, which had information about the Samuel Graham and Martha Gilbreath family. Also *Jay and Lou Graham Family* by Juanita Graham Hinkle and Gertha Hooper Hill published in 2004.

367.   Mary Graham b. Aug. 10, 1868 d. Aug. 22, 1896

368.   William Kins Graham b. Nov. 1, 1870-Feb. 5, 1940

369.   Florence Graham b. Feb. 5, 1873

370.   Thomas H. Graham b. Sept. 27, 1875-April 28, 1950

371.   Jahue H. Graham b. Feb. 20, 1878-April 9, 1951

372.   Andy Graham b. July 15, 1880-July 6, 1900

373.   John R. Graham b. Oct. 10, 1883 d. Nov. 18, 1893

374.   Samuel B. Graham b. July 3, 1886-Nov. 14, 1914

375.   Ader Graham (dau.) b. Jan. 27, 1889 d. July 3, 1918

376.   Mala Graham (son) b. Oct. 9, 1891 d. Aug. 1, 1902

1-3-16-114   Maranda Gilbreath b. Nov. 1854 married Robert W. Williamson on May 21, 1878 in Bradley County, TN. According to *Cheyenne Dunbar* on Internet *Ancestry.com* Maranda died in1896 and Robert died Feb. 12, 1922. Some of the information comes from tracing Essie Elmina Williamson who married Monroe Y. Dicks (Internet, *Ancestry.com)*.

377.   Arthur Williamson b. abt. 1879
378.   Charles Thomas Williamson b. 1881
379.   Margaret Dialtha Williamson b. 1882 – 1949
380.   Mary Elizabeth Williamson b. Oct. 10, 1884 – d. June 11, 1974 in Los Angeles, CA
381.   William Audie Williamson July 1886 – 1945
382.   Arminta Jeannette "Minnie" Williamson Feb. 1889
383.   Lula Williamson June 1890
384.   Essie Elmina Williamson Oct. 1893
385.   Fred Williamson 1896

1-3-16-115   Andrew Gilbreath b. Feb. 1857 married Margaret Cofer b. June 1863

386.   Dolly E. Gilbreath b. Dec. 1886
387.   Walter Gilbreath b. Oct. 1889
388.   Jeanetta Gilbreath b. July 1893
389.   William L. Gilbreath b. Sept 1894
390.   Icie May Gilbreath b. Jan. 1898

1-3-16-116   Dr. John Gilbreath b. Mar. 15, 1860 married Darthula Jane Andes b. May 1866 (pp. 288-289)

391.   William Walter Gilbreath b. Jan. 1888
392.   Elbert Hughston Gilbreath b. June 1891
393.   Bula Gilbreath b. Nov. 1893
394.   Carey Gilbreath b. Dec. 1899
395.   Med Gilbreath b. abt. 1905

1-3-16-117   Margaret Gilbreath b. abt. 1863 married Dr. Medlin Dunham on June 15, 1884 in Bradley County, TN. He was born Feb. 24, 1855 d. June 6, 1915 in Georgetown, TN (Internet, *Ancestry.com, Tennessee, Deaths and Burials Index 1874-1955*).

1-3-16-118   Tabitha Gilbreath b. abt. 1866

1-3-16-119   Genetta Gilbreath b. Oct. 27, 1868 d. March 6, 1936 married Dr. Med M. Dunham on Oct. 26, 1885 in Bradley County, TN. He was born Feb. 1855 (evidently the same person married sisters Internet *Ancestry.com*)

396.   Eva Patilla Dunham b. Aug. 1886 married John Earl Bacon
397.   Fred Dunham b. Aug. 1892
398.   Paul Dunham b. abt. 1902

1-3-17-120   Martha Elizabeth Hooper b. July 11, 1854 d. Jan. 26, 1919 married Joshua Carlton August 1880. Joshua was born Sept. 1848.

399.   Leathey Carlton b. Apr. 1884
400.   Frank Carlton b. May 1886
401.   Pearly Carlton b. Aug. 1888
402.   Joseph Carlton b. Sept. 1890
403.   Kinsie Carlton b. Feb. 1894
404.   Lattie Carlton b. Sept. 1896
405.   Arnold Carlton b. abt. 1904

1-3-17-121   Margaret Ellen Hooper b. April 19, 1859 – d. July 24, 1891 (Internet, *Ancestry.com, Find A Grave*) married Joel Teague March 1878

406.   Martha Ida Teague b. Sept 1880
407.   Mary Teague b. Dec. 20, 1885 – d. Sept. 26, 1901
408.   Lula P. Teague b. Feb. 1889

(Internet, *Ancestry.com, Marion County 1900* Census Dist. 3 p. 6 A indicated Joel Teague married a second time in Marion County, TN to Lawil Deakin (*Ancestry.com & Find A Grave* by *KayT* and they had Corine Teague b. Nov. 1894, Sarah C. Teague b. Apr. 1896 and Bertha J. Teague b. Feb. 1899.)

1-3-17-122   William Howard Hooper b. Aug. 23, 1861 d. Sept. 10, 1931 married Letha Ann Carlton b. June 1865

409.   Icie Hooper Aug. 29, 1889 d. Apr. 28, 1969 married Charles Franklin Tillery

410.   Jahue (Jay) Hooper b. 1892 d. Dec. 2, 1945 married Bernola Liner
411.   Robert Lee Hooper b. Sept. 1893 (WW 1 Veteran) married Emy McClean
412.   Grace M. Hooper b. July 1895 married James E. Plank
413.   William Clinton Hooper b. Aug. 23, 1897 (WW 1 Veteran) married Anne Marie McIntire
414.   Roy K. C. Hooper b. Oct. 21, 1899 d. Oct. 8, 1918
415.   Mary Della Hooper b. April 24, 1902 d. Sept. 15, 1903
416.   Charles Clarence Hooper b. Feb. 27, 1904 d. July 3, 1962 married Ersa Baker b. Aug. 20, 1913
417.   Etta May Hooper b. July 19, 1906 d. Aug. 17, 1906
418.   Pauline Hooper b. March 1, 1911 married James Lee Sullivan

1-3-17-123   Josephine Hooper b. Nov. 2, 1864 married on August 12, 1883 to George W. Eads b. Oct. 14, 1863 (*The Heritage of Bradley County, Tennessee, 1836-1998* submitted by Charles J. Eads, Jr.)

419.   Mattie Eads Oct. 15, 1884 d. March 21, 1918 married on March 13, 1904 to Charlie Shamblin b. Feb. 18, 1879 d. Jan. 30, 1950
420.   Icye May Eads Aug. 14, 1887-May 8, 1888
421.   William Telles Eads Jan. 21, 1890-June 10, 1910
422.   Mary Elmiry Eads Nov. 17, 1894-Sept. 18, 1895
423.   Charles Jahew Eads March 22, 1897-March 30, 1979 married on June 26, 1927 to Mary A. Moore April 1, 1906-Nov. 1, 1993
424.   Bertha Eads Oct. 28, 1901-March 2, 1897 married on June 6, 1920 to N. J. Pardue b. Jan. 9, 1886 and d. April 7, 1975
425.   Gurtha Eads Oct. 28, 1901-March 2, 1995 married on Nov. 1943 to Doyle Martin 1900-1968

1-3-17-124   Andrew Jackson Hooper b. Sept. 23, 1867 d. July 10, 1868
1-3-17-125   Charles F. Hooper b. Sept. 21, 1869 d. Jan. 9, 1945 married Annie McCamish
426.   Lee J. Hooper b. April 1900
427.   James Ernest Hooper b. abt. 1902 married Patricia Estelle Leamon (number 807)
428.   Infant March 27, 1911 – April 3, 1911
1-3-17-126   Kenzie Hooper b. Sept. 15, 1872 d. abt. 1933 married number 320 Rosa Hooper b. Dec. 1883
429.   Bruce Hooper b. abt. 1905 married Mable Morgan
430.   Gladys Hooper b. abt. 1907
431.   Boyd Hooper b. abt. 1912 married Mary Smalling
1-3-17-127   Adelie (Addie) Hooper b. abt. 1875 married Doctor Frank Ownbey on Oct. 15, 1889 in Bradley County, TN (Doctor was his first name and not a title [Internet, *Ancestry.com*].)
432.   Mary Olie Ownbey b. Sept. 1892 (Internet, *Ancestry.com, Bradley County Tennessee 1900 Census*)
433.   Lloyd McKinley Ownbey b. Sept. 2, 1896 – d. June 15, 1957 in Los Angeles, CA
434.   Charles Louis Ownbey b. Oct. 2, 1900 – d. Dec. 23, 1978 in Riverside, CA
1-3-17-128   Emma Hooper b. July 14, 1879 d. Oct. 22, 1883
1-3-18-129   Susan Hooper b. May 1860 TN married Alexander Boggs b. April 1842 in Louisiana (p. 285)
435.   Luther L. Boggs b. April 1881 Indian Territory Choctaw Nation
436.   Mary L. Boggs b. June 1888 Indian Territory
437.   Hattie M. Boggs b. Nov. 1889 Indian Territory
438.   Laura G. Boggs b. July 1891 Indian Territory
439.   Henry A. Boggs b. Aug. 1893 Indian Territory
1-3-18-130   Ruth Eliza Hooper b. abt. 1864
1-3-18-131   Mary Hooper b. abt. 1867
1-3-18-132   Daniel Hooper b. abt. 1870
1-3-18-133   Annie Hooper b. June 4, 1871 – Dec. 25, 1934 married Alonzo (Lon) Ellis b. July 1, 1867 – Jan. 15, 1951 buried in Sallisaw City Cemetery in Sallisaw, Oklahoma married March 16, 1890 in Sebastian County, Arkansas (Internet *radnofdixie, Ancestry.com*)
440.   Edgar Ellis b. Feb. 12, 1889 in Arkansas d. Oct. 20, 1972 in Oklahoma
441.   Allie Ellis b. Aug. 1894 in Indian Territory
442.   Jesse Ellis b. Nov. 1897 in Indian Territory
443.   Jami C. Ellis (dau.) 1906 b. Oklahoma

444.	Cora Ellis b. 1908 in Oklahoma
445.	Mary Ellis b. 1911 in Oklahoma
446.	Flora Ellis b. 1913 in Oklahoma
447.	Billy Ellis b. 1915 in Oklahoma

1-3-18-134 Tabitha/Tobiathe Hooper b. abt. 1874

1-3-19-135 David Francis Hooper b. abt. 1867 in TN died abt. 1945 married Nancy Duncan

448.	Walter Hooper b. 1885 d. 1962 married Epsie Bridges b. 1890 d. 1962
449.	Allice Hooper b. 1887 d. 1976 married Robert Jenkins
450.	Jane Hooper b. 1888 d. 1952 married John Brogdon
451.	Norma Hooper b. 1890 d. 1938 married Charles Logan
452.	Bessie Hooper b. 1892 d. 1966 married Earl Griffin

1-3-19-136 Charles T. Hooper b. 1878 in Arkansas d. 1918 married Myrtle Kirkpatrick (Internet *Ancestry.com*)

| 453. | John William Hooper b. 1914 d. 1917 (Internet *Ancestry.com*) |
| 454. | Charles Ray Hooper b. 1916 d. 1966 married Rosaltha Cowelti b. 1922 |

1-3-19-137 Walter W. Hooper b. May 1880 in Illinois

1-3-19-138 Bertha Hooper b. Feb. 1890 in MO married Perry Miller Aug. 18, 1907 in Hickory County, MO

455.	Allen Miller b. abt. 1910 in MO
456.	Edith Miller b. abt. 1912 in MO
457.	Arline Miller b. abt. 1916 in Montana
458.	Roy Miller b. abt. 1918 in Montana

1-3-19-139 Ezza Ray Hooper b. Aug. 1892 in MO – d. Jan. 1959 in Missoula, Montana married Clyde Gilbert on Dec. 25, 1916 in Park County, Montana (Internet, *Ancestry.com Wayne Shenck*)

1-3-20-140 Kinsey L. Hooper b. July 8, 1878 d. Aug. 16, 1963 married Martha Emmaline Taylor b. Nov. 1880 – d. May 15, 1904 (Internet, *The Index* May 30, 1918 Vol 33 No. 48). The marriage date was March 25, 1900 in Hickory County, MO.

| 459. | Burl/Oral D. Hooper b. abt. 1902 MO |

1-3-20-140 Kinsey L. Hooper married Frances Eads Jan. 5, 1909 in Hickory County, MO

460.	Harley Hooper b. abt. 1914 CA (*Ventura County1930 Census*, Sims Township, p. 9 A)
461.	Evelyn Hooper b. abt. 1917 CA
462.	Leonard Hooper b. 1921 CA d. Washington 1972
463.	Meribe Hooper (dau.) b. abt. 1926 CA

1-3-20-141 Dona J. Hooper b. Jan. 1879 married L. Walter Dobbs

464.	Larman Dobbs b. July 1899
465.	Golda C. Dobbs b. abt. 1901
466.	Bethel B. Dobbs b. abt. 1903
467.	Alta M. Dobbs b. abt. 1906

1-3-20-142 Ida Hooper b. Oct. 1883 married Joseph A. Knight b. Jan. 1871 (Marie A. Knight b. Jan. 1897 step-daughter, and her mother was a Patterson)

468.	Lloyd C. Knight b. abt. 1904
469.	Don W. Knight b. abt. 1906
470.	Herman Knight b. abt. 1911

1-3-20-143 Henry J. Hooper b. July 14, 1886 d. Feb. 7, 1967 married Donna B. Taylor b. April 5, 1885 d. Feb. 28, 1964 Married Sept. 2, 1916 (Internet, *Find a Grave* at *Ancestry.com*)

1-3-20-144 Cordella Hooper b. Jan. 1890 married James E. Summers (Internet *Ancestry.com* Mills County, Iowa)

471.	Hobert Lou Summers b. abt. 1908
472.	Blanche Summers b. abt. 1911
473.	Violet Summers b. abt. 1921
474.	Cecil Summers b. abt. 1925
475.	Lyman Summers b. abt. 1929

1-3-20-145 John Andrew Hooper b. Sept 8, 1897 d. Feb. 21, 1987 married Bertha Frances Crawford

1-3-20-146 Noah E. Hooper b. July 8, 1900 d. August 17, 1967 married Treva M. Nicholson

| 476. | Garland Hooper b. abt. 1927 |
| 477. | Marion Hooper b. May 3, 1928 d. April 13, 1964 married Willa Lee Schnitker b. Oct. 9, |

1930 – d. Jan. 4, 2013 married in 1952 (Internet at *Obitsforlive.com* at Missouri.)
478. Harold Hooper b. March 6, 1930 d. March 16, 1992 married Mary Lou Vittetoe
479. Iona May Hooper married Marvin Edge
480. Robert Hooper b. August 12, 1947 married Glatha Goldston
1-3-21-147   James A. Hooper b. Sept. 1867 married Rosa Cooper in Internet *Ancestry.com* Hickory County, Missouri on Sept. 9, 1894.
481. Argus Hooper July 1897
1-3-21-147   James A. Hooper married 2. Ethel R. Pitts b. 1881 married Aug. 1, 1901 in Hickory County, Missouri (Internet *Ancestry.com*)
482. Willis L. Hooper b. abt. 1905
483. Chester R. Hooper b. abt. 1910
484. James Herbert Hooper b. abt. 1914
1-3-21-148   John William Hooper b. Nov. 11, 1869 d. Aug. 27, 1957 m. Cordelia Alexander
485. Clarcie M. Hooper b. April 29, 1901 d. Aug. 14, 1995 married George K. Dechow
486. George Francis Hooper b. April 22, 1910 d. May 21, 1997 married Mary McNabb
1-3-21-149   Charles Clinton Hooper b. Feb. 11, 1872 d. Nov. 26, 1932 married Ina May Alexander b. Sept. 1878 on Nov. 11, 1895 (Internet *Ancestry.com* Hickory County, MO).
1-3-21-150   Tobitha Hooper b. Oct. 2, 1874 d. Feb. 21, 1902 married John Johnson on Jan. 5, 1893 in Hickory County, MO. He was born March 20, 1869 and died Nov. 13, 1942.
487. Minnie Johnson b. April 1895
488. Charles G. Johnson b. Oct. 1897
1-3-21-151   Margaret Hooper b. Feb. 16, 1877 d. Oct. 29, 1937 married on Nov. 23, 1895 Hickory County, MO to John W. Meadors b. May 6, 1875 d. Jan.11, 1941(Internet, *Ancestry.com*)
489. Charles Thomas Meadors b. April 25, 1899 d. Jan. 4, 1990 married Velma Ida Little
1-3-21-152   Henry Jahew Hooper b. Nov. 1879 d. Sept. 16, 1974 married Rachel Lyon Mallonee
490. Gilbert G. Hooper b. June 28, 1912 married Willie Dee Pitts
1-3-21-153   Arthur Hooper b. March 26, 1882 d. Jan. 2, 1954 married Jewell Mallonee
1-3-21-154   Benjamin Harrison Hooper b. Jan. 7, 1885 d. June 1, 1970 married Myrtle Larose on Sept. 15, 1907 in Hickory County, MO (Internet, *Ancestry.com*)
491. Owen Ray Hooper b. abt. 1913 married Irene ?
492. Edna May Hooper b. abt. 1916 married Everett Fletcher
493. Frances Hooper b. abt. 1918
1-3-21-155   Carrie (Dollie) Harrison Hooper b. Jan. 7, 1885 d. 1970 married Ulman (Ully) Wallace Roy b. March 2, 1883 – d. 1960
494. Helen Roy b. Aug. 11, 1910 m. George Figge
495. Thomas L. Roy b. Sept. 1, 1913 – d. March 18, 2010 (*Springfield News-Leader* at Internet, *Ancestry.com*) m. Edna Greenfield
496. Jack Roy b. April 10, 1916
497. Lynn Roy b. March 1922
1-3-21-156   Mary E. Hooper b. April 1889 married 1st. Thomas Grisham 2nd Douglas L. Pitts
498. Garrett Lee Grisham b. Jan. 30, 1907 d. Mar. 23, 1969 m. Leda Richards
499. Lucy Marie Pitts b. June 11, 1915 m. Ivan Noal Breshears
500. Kenneith N. Pitts b. July 26, 1918 m. Virgia M. Green
501. Bonnie Gean Pitts b. March 5, 1921 m. 1st Albert Degraffenreid, 2nd Fred Hulston, 3rd Merlin Shively (Internet, m. Cedar Co., MO Feb. 24, 1940 *Ancestry.com*)
1-3-22-157   Charles H. Jack b. Feb. 22, 1869 married Effie Blessing (according to Terry Harmon at *Internet Ancestry.com, Find A Grave, and* ljohnston29 *[Baker and Decker Family])*
502. Ruth E. Jack b. abt. 1897
503. Clyde Jack (dau.) b. abt. 1902
504. James B. Jack b. abt. 1904
1-3-22-158   Oscar Jack b. April 1872 married Lillie D.
505. Pearl Jack b. abt. 1896
506. Geneva Jack b. abt. 1905
1-3-22-159   Frank Jack b. Dec. 1873 married Ruth b. abt. 1881
507. Mary A. Jack b. abt. 1905
508. Josephine Jack b. abt. 1907

509.   Francis Jack (dau.) b. abt. 1909
510.   Ora Lou Jack b. abt. 1912
1-3-22-160   Lillia A. Jack b. abt. 1880
1-3-22-161   John C. Jack b. Nov. 8, 1891 married Carrie Lou Bardin b. abt. 1893
511.   Mary J. Jack b. May 21, 1912
512.   Helen J. Jack b. March 9, 1921
513.   John C. Jack b. August 8, 1923
1-3-22-162   Mary Jack
1-3-22-163   Fred H. Jack
1-3-22-164   Maude T. Jack
1-3-22-165   David A. Jack

Some of the following Absolom Hooper information was taken from *Hooper Genealogy and Autobiography of Wm. Hayden Hooper1898-1966* which was published at Thomas, Custer County, OK on August 4, 1966. On the Internet, *hooperconnections.com* (Bill Hooper, Clay Hooper and Sharon Hooper) also had data for the Absolom Hooper family.

1-4-25-166   John Perrin abt. 1869
1-4-25-167   William Perrin abt. 1872 married Flora B. Stephens (Internet, *Ancestry.com, 1910 Census of Polk County, TN* p. 2 B Dist. 6 and *Polk County, TN Census 1920* Dist. 2 p. 2B)
514.   Miller Elisha Peron b. Nov. 23, 1894 d. April 9, 1982 in San Bernardino, CA
515.   Isaac F. Peron b. 1896
516.   Johny Green Peron b. April 15, 1898 d. March 17, 1929
517   Sarah E. Peron b. 1900
518.   Vilila N. Peron b. 1902
519.   Absolam Peron b. 1906
520.   Lillie Peron b. 1907
521.   Lester Peron b. 1909
522.   J. P. Perion b. 1912
523.   Sanford Perion b. 1914
1-4-25-168   Isaac Perrin abt. 1873 married Martha (Internet *Polk County, TN Census 1900* in Dist. 11 p. 9A and *Polk County, TN Census* 1910 Dist. 9 p. 10B)
524.   Lizzie Perring 1891
525.   Donil Perring 1898
526.   Harvey Perrin 1908
1-4-25-169   Mary Perrin abt. 1875
1-4-26-170   Absolom Hooper b. abt. 1873
1-4-26-171   Louisa (Eliza?) Hooper b. abt. 1879
1-4-26-172   Pollie Hooper b. May 1881
1-4-26-173   Mary Hooper b. Dec. 1884
1-4-26-174   Susan (Anna?) Hooper b. Nov. 1887
1-4-27-175   William Hickey
1-4-27-176   Media Hickey
1-4-30-177   John W. Carden born March 13, 1885 (WWI Registration McMinn County, TN) married Cinda Allen on March 1, 1906 (Internet *Ancestry.com* Polk County, TN)
527.   Bertha Carden 1908
528.   Lester Carden 1911
529.   Ethel Carden 1913
530.   Clifford Carden Sept. 23, 1914
531.   Hazel Carden 1917
532.   Amos Carden 1918
533.   Rossie Mae Carden 1922
534.   Ruth Carden 1925
535.   Charles Carden 1928
536.   Ruby Evelyn Carden 1930
1-4-30-178   Maggie Cardin married Robert Davis Pike Aug. 29, 1897 in Polk County, TN (Internet *Ancestry.com*)
537.   Cori M. Pike Aug. 1898

1-4-30-179   Sadie or Sarah Cardin married R. D. Pike on April 29, 1905 in Polk County, TN
     538.   Lela Pike 1907
     539.   Bertha Pike 1909
     540.   Helen Pike   1912
     541.   Jesse Pike   1913
     542.   Charlie Pike 1915
     543.   Dorothy Pike 1918
     544.   Morine Pike 1921
     545.   Ivona Pike 1925
1-4-31-180   James B. Hooper b. abt. 1876
1-4-31-181   Sarah M. Hooper b. abt. 1878
1-4-32-182   Reece Shell
1-4-33-183   Sarah M. Hooper Nov. 13, 1875-April 27, 1945 m. Samuel Edgar Harris, Sr. on Oct. 20, 1901 in Oklahoma Territory. Samuel was born March 4, 1872 and died Nov. 23, 1950.
     546.   William C. Harris b. abt. 1903
     547.   Katie Harris b. abt. 1904
     548.   Victoria Harris b. abt. 1906
     549.   James G. Harris b. abt. 1907
     550.   Samuel E. Harris b. abt. 1910
     551.   George Harris b. abt. 1918
1-4-33-184   William H. Hooper July 24, 1877-May 20, 1958 married Lou H. Hamons March 20, 1899 in Springtown, Polk County, TN. She lived from May 18, 1879 to Jan. 9, 1954.
     552.   Hershel Hooper b. abt. 1900
1-4-33-185   John G. Hooper May 4, 1879-July 7, 1953 married Dorothy Pauline Wieland. She lived from July 13, 1883 to Feb. 9, 1944.
     553.   Sanford G. Hooper b. abt. 1909
     554.   Absolom Hooper b. abt. 1915
     555.   Dorothy Hooper b. abt. 1924
1-4-33-186   Isaac A. Hooper Jan. 20, 1881-July 20, 1959 married Elsie Ethel Smith on Oct. 9, 1913 in Arapaho, OK.. She lived from June 20, 1894 to Jan. 22, 1983.
     556.   Lois Hooper b. abt. 1915
     557.   Wayne Hooper b. abt. 1921
     558.   Russell Hooper b. abt. 1927
1-4-33-187   James Enos Hooper Dec. 29, 1882-Nov. 11, 1948 married Mary Elizabeth Pike on March 8, 1908 in Custer County, OK. She lived from Feb. 18, 1890 to Dec. 30, 1950.
     559.   Frank Hooper b. abt. 1913
     560.   Ethel Hooper b. abt. 1915
     561.   Grace Hooper b. abt. 1919
     562.   James E. Hooper b. abt. 1929
1-4-33-188   Temperance Hooper born Sept. 2, 1884 and married Alonzo Potter in Custer Co., OK.
     563.   Olen N. Potter b. abt. 1905
     564.   Henry J. Potter b. abt. 1909
     565.   Dessie Potter b. abt. 1918
1-4-33-189   Maudie Helen Hooper Nov. 10, 1886-Jan. 12, 1970 married William Carl Campbell on Dec. 11, 1911 in Custer Co., OK. He lived from July 10, 1879 to Feb. 22, 1967.
     566.   Elbert Lee Campbell b. abt. 1913
     567.   Paul Hooper Campbell b. abt. 1914
     568.   Opal Campbell b. abt. 1916
     569.   Katherine Campbell b. abt. 1920
1-4-33-190   Amanda Hooper b. Sept. 1889 married Lee C. Ryan.
     570.   Joseph L. Ryan b. 1930
1-4-33-191   Bertha Hooper Jan. 1893-April 9, 1914
1-4-33-192   Samuel Arthur Hooper March 9, 1898-July 1984 married Myrtle Frances Faw on Jan. 30, 1920 in Custer County, OK. She lived from April 1902 to Nov. 25, 1980.
1-4-33-193   Jennings Bryan Hooper Sept. 3, 1900-July 30, 1962 in Colorado. On July 28, 1936 in Pittsburgh, KS, he married Nellie Nerina Ross who was born Dec. 16, 1905.

571.   Frances Clair Hooper
572.   Samuel Edward Hooper

1-4-34-194   Dallas Monroe Hooper b. Sept. 18, 1876 married 1. Nancy E. Hammons on Jan. 16, 1895 in
Polk County, TN. He married Nov. 5, 1896 in Springtown, Polk County, TN 2. Ida Ellen
Thompson April 23, 1877 and later moved to Custer, OK

573.   William Hayden Hooper born in TN Aug. 4, 1898-Oct. 13, 1975 died Custer County, OK
574.   Nora G. Hooper Sept. 11, 1901 in OK Territory died Jan. 4, 1992 in Osage County, OK
575.   Minnie Ola Hooper born Springtown, Polk County, TN Feb. 2, 1904 died July 3, 1925
        OK
576.   Lola Ruth Hooper June 4, 1908 in Conway, AR died Dec. 1, 1936 Oklahoma City, OK
577.   Charley Hooper born Aug. 14, 1912 Custer County, OK died Sept. 2, 1987 Finney
        County, KS
578.   Pearl Hooper April 16, 1916 Custer County, OK
579.   Nelley Hooper May 10, 1918 Custer County, OK
580.   Reece Hooper Feb. 2, 1921-Oct. 6, 1925

1-4-34-195   Henry Hooper b. abt. 1879 d. abt. 1901 OK Territory

1-4-34-196   Granville (Grant) Jackson Hooper b. Dec. 25, 1881 TN d. Sept. 13, 1961 TN married
Elizabeth Armstrong Dec. 23, 1900 in Polk County, TN

581.   Lillie Hooper b. abt. 1902
582.   Stella Hooper b. abt. 1904
583.   Luther Hooper b. 1907
584.   Lonzo (Lon) Hooper July 15, 1907-July 21, 1985
585.   Amos (Bud) Hooper b. abt. 1912
586.   Lucy Hooper b. abt. 1915
587.   Kenneth B. Hooper Sept. 20, 1919-May 11, 1991

1-4-34-197   Mary L. (Mollie) Hooper b. Nov. 1885 married Charley Davis on Nov. 4, 1900 in Polk
County, TN. He was born April 18, 1877 in TN and died Oct. 10, 1949 in Custer County,
OK. ??

588.   Myrtle Davis 1901
589.   Pearl Davis 1903
590.   Arthur Davis 1909
591.   Clyde Davis 1912
592.   Wayne Davis 1916
593.   Thelma Davis 1918
594.   Inez Davis 1922

1-4-34-198   Margaret Hooper b. Nov. 1884 married 1. Bert R. Cobb on Sept. 21, 1901 in Polk County,
TN. She married a second time to William Casteel.

1-4-35-199   Vitta R. Cardin Jan. 1883 Polk County, TN
1-4-35-200   Ida Cardin Feb. 1885 Polk County, TN
1-4-35-201   Anna Cardin July 1888 Polk County, TN m. Floyd Martin
1-4-35-202   Newton Swan Cardin Jan. 1891 Polk County, TN m. Anna b. 1894
1-4-35-203   Thoms Cardin Oct. 1894
1-4-35-204   Oliver Cardin Dec. 1897 m. Hazel

1-2-5-38-205   William Douglas "Wylie" Shelton b. Feb. 26, 1868 – d. July 16, 1938 in Rowlett, TX
married (1) Elizabeth "Bettie" Pannell in 1887 at Ferris County, TX (Internet,
Ancestry.com, Lisa Lynn Allen/Lisa Todd) and (2) Jennie Wells on Jan. 24, 1909 in Fannin
County, TX (found at Internet *Ancestry.com,* Fannin County, TX Marriages)

595.   John Ray Shelton b. Nov. 6, 1890 – d. May 14, 1966 Garland, TX
596.   Ida Hasseltine Shelton b. Apr. 1892 (May 14, 1894) – d. June 1, 1934 Lancaster, TX
597.   Frances May Shelton b. Oct. 25, 1893 – Jan. 22, 1982 Dallas, TX
598.   Beulah Viola Shelton b. June 13, 1896 – d. Feb. 7, 1999 Garland, TX
599.   Havus L. Shelton b. August 1898
600.   Bonita Shelton b. Oct. 20, 1899
601.   Myrtle Shelton b. 1903
602.   Robert Bonner Shelton b. July 19, 1906 – d. Dec. 30, 1983
603.   Mammie Shelton b. 1906

604.	Maggie Shelton b. 1914
605.	W. D. Shelton, Jr. b. 1918
606.	Janine Shelton b. 1920
607.	Robbie L. Shelton (dau.) 1925

1-2-5-38-206 Dallas Homer Shelton b. April 26, 1871- d. Jan. 25, 1889 at Monroe County, Arkansas

1-2-5-42-207 Felix Jack Walker b. 1895 d. 1993

1-2-5-42-208 Nathaniel Walker m. Ollie M.   ?

608.   Virginia Walker b. 1928

1-2-5-42-209 Nellie Walker b. 1899

1-2-5-42-210 Thomas Walker b. 1902

1-2-5-42-211 Reid Walker b. July 23, 1905 d. March 20, 1930 (Internet *Ancestry.com*)

1-2-5-42-212 Mary Dorcas Walker b. 1912 married Elmer B. Ethridge on Dec. 28, 1928 in McMinn County, TN

609.   Bruce Lamar Ethridge b. April 4, 1936

610.   Marla Shelton Ethridge b. March 11, 1939

1-2-5-46-213 Alberta Pearl McKellop b. 1912 d. Feb. 14, 2001 (information from Internet *millerfam* and Joseph C. Tarvin Research owned by *abhoffman* at *Ancestry.com* and Internet research) Alberta was known by the screen name of Marla Shelton. She married John Wesley Dawn (Jack Dawn), a Hollywood make-up man. Later, she married N. Gayle Gitterman of Warner Brothers Studios.

611.   John Wesley Dawn, Jr. 1938-1990

612.   Marla Jo Dawn 1941-1972

1-2-5-47-214 Auda S. Baugh b. 1909 d. March 7, 2010 married Philip Sterns (Baugh information from Internet *Oonagh* at *Ancestry.com*)

1-2-5-47-215 Fred W. Baugh b. March 7, 1911 d. May 1, 2001 married Marion Drayer (Internet, *Bookemon.com* listed two sons Bruce and Craig Baugh.)

1-2-5-47-216 Annie Ruth Baugh b. 1916 - d. 1918

1-2-5-47-217 Alma J. Baugh b. Aug. 20, 1920 d. March 1, 1976

1-2-5-47-218 Edith L. Baugh b. Aug. 30, 1921 (Internet California Birth Index *Ancestry.com*)

1-2-5-47-219 James D. Baugh, Jr. b. March 14, 1923

1-2-5-49-220 Julia Lois Baugh b. May 22, 1913 (Internet, *Ancestry.com, Fisher Harr Family Tree* by Paul Fisher) Julia wed Charles M. Harr on Nov. 11, 1931 in California.

613.   Patricia Joane Harr b. Aug. 2, 1937

1-2-5-49-221 Mildred Georgiana Tillotson b. March 22, 1918 Mildred married on Feb. 10, 1943 to Edward Arthur Furbush b. July 18, 1912 (Internet *Rootsweb, The Families of James Shelton of McMinn County, Tennessee* by Arthur Paul Shelton p. 69).

614.   Sandra Kay Furbush b. Aug. 7, 1944

615.   Jacqueline Lee Furbush b. March 20, 1946

1-2-7-65-222 Nap Graves b. 1874

1-2-7-65-223 Catherine Graves b. 1876

1-2-7-65-224 Art Graves b. 1879

1-2-7-67-225 John Wright b. 1878

1-2-7-67-226 Lawrence Wright b. 1881

1-2-7-67-227 Savannah Wright b. 1885

1-2-7-67-228 Ella Wright b. 1887

1-2-7-67-229 Minnie Wright b. 1889 d. 1969 married Karl D. Saulpaw on Dec. 4, 1904 McMinn County, TN. Karl was born on April 7, 1883 and died in San Francisco, CA on Dec. 9, 1948. **(Saulpaw information came from *Salbach - Saulpaw 1700 – 1993* published by Karl Saulpaw, Jr., Knoxville, TN, April 1994. It was found on the Internet at *rpevans.org*.)**

616.   George Lewis Saulpaw b. Dec. 23, 1905 – Aug. 12, 1976

617.   Zillah Catherine Saulpaw b. Oct. 7, 1907 – March 1, 1990

618.   Hattie Weston Saulpaw b. Feb. 4, 1910 – Dec. 4, 1983

619.   Pyott Davis Saulpaw b. May 14, 1912 – Aug. 21, 1969

620.   Henry Bernard Saulpaw b. Dec. 3, 1914 – July 14, 1983

621.   Karl Davenport Saulpaw, Jr. b. Nov. 2, 1920 – Aug. 5, 1994

622.   Caleb Jackson Saulpaw b. Jan. 16,1924 – Dec. 16, 1995

623.   Doris Ellen Saulpaw b. 1926
624.   Elizabeth Ann Saulpaw b. 1928
1-2-8-70-230   Jane Shelton b. 1877
1-2-8-70-231   Leon Shelton
1-2-8-76-232   Elba Henniger b. 1889
1-2-8-76-233   Sophia Henniger b. 1891
1-2-8-76-234   Alice Elizabeth Henniger b. 1892
1-2-8-76-235   Almeda Henniger b. 1895
1-2-8-76-236   James Shelton Henniger b. 1897
1-2-8-76-237   Ruby Catherine Henniger b. 1900
1-2-8-76-238   Mary Frances Henniger b. 1903
1-2-9-82-239   Myrtle Baff   b. 1880   IO
1-2-9-82-240   Mamie Baff   b. 1882   IO
1-2-9-82-241   Edward Baff b. 1886   IO
1-2-9-84-242   Walter S. Farmer b. August 1887 married Jessie L. Speer (Internet, *Ancestry.com* , *U. S.,
        Social Security Application and Claims Index*)
625.   Raymond Farmer b. 1915
626.   Stanley Gordon Farmer b. Jan. 25, 1919 – Nov. 13, 2006 (see father information)
627.   Naomi Ruth Farmer b. 1927
1-2-9-84-243   Maude H. Farmer b. Oct. 1889 married Shederic Allen Casey (S. A.) on Sept. 27, 1909
        in Laclede County, Missouri. Dr. Shederic Allen Casey died Sept. 20, 1964
        (Internet, *Ancestry.com*).
1-2-9-84-244   Raymond J. Farmer b. Nov. 1894
1-2-12-93-245   Elbert M. Graves
1-2-12-93-246   Leonard Mercer Graves b. Dec. 8, 1883 d. Nov. 6, 1952 *Death Certificate* for Rhea
        County, TN. He married Elizabeth Leuty (Internet, *Rootsweb, The Families of James
        Shelton of McMinn County, Tennessee* by Arthur Paul Shelton p. 98). *Rhea County,
        TN 1940 Census* Second Civil District p. 5 B listed the following children:
628.   Ellen R. Graves b. 1931 married Thomas Castleberry of Pittsburgh, PA
629.   James L. Graves b. 1934
630.   Henry M. Graves b. 1937
631.   Leutina Graves b. 1939
632.   David Lynn Graves
1-2-13-96-247   Henry Cantrell b. 1876
1-2-13-96-248   Catherine Cantrell b. Dec. 1881 MO
1-2-13-96-249   Richard J. Cantrell b. Nov. 1883 MO
1-2-13-96-250   James L. Cantrell b. Feb. 1886
1-2-13-96-251   Clarence O. Cantrell b. Oct. 24, 1888 MO
1-2-13-96-252   Charles M. Cantrell b. Sept. 1890 Indian Territory
1-2-13-96-253   Cora J. Cantrell b. Jan. 1894 Indian Territory
1-2-13-96-254   Martha A. Cantrell b. May 1896 Indian Territory
1-2-13-96-255   Otto B. Cantrell b. May 1897 Indian Territory
1-2-13-96-256   Alice Cantrell b. 1901 Indian Territory
1-2-13-97-257   Claude W. Shipley 1887
1-2-13-97-258   Earl Shipley 1893
1-2-13-97-259   Rachel Shipley 1897
1-3-14-98-260   William Graham b. Jan. 1866 married (1) Martha Mullin (Mcie) b. Nov. 1874 and (2)
        Betty Steward b. 1887 (Internet *Ancestry.com*)
633.   Marion A. Graham b. Dec. 1886 (Big Creek, *1900 Sebastian County Census* p. 3 A)
634.   Eugene T. Graham b. June 1888
1-3-14-98-260   William Graham b. Jan. 1866 married (2) Betty Steward b. abt. 1887
635.   Parker Graham 1896 (appears in Internet, *Ancestry.com*, Graham, *Sebastian County,
        Arkansas Censuses* 1910 in Big Creek p. 3 A but not in 1900 Big Creek pp. 2 B and 3 A)
636.   Andy Graham b. 1906
637.   Lester Graham b. 1908
638.   Lena Graham b. 1910

639.　　Dessie Graham b. 1913
640.　　Guy W. Graham b. 1917

1-3-14-98-261　Landon Graham b. July 29, 1868 d. December 23, 1950 married (1) Mary Philura Jones b. Oct. 1873. They were married March 2, 1893 in Sebastian County, Arkansas. (Internet, Graham, *lynrise* at *Ancestry.com*), and (2) Mattie Arrington 1928 sons (see p. 131)

641.　　Emma J. Graham b. Oct. 1893
642.　　Newt D. Graham b. April 1896
643.　　Elsie Philura Graham b. Dec. 1899
644.　　Ida Graham b. abt. 1902
645.　　William Graham b. abt. 1908
646.　　Early Graham (son) b. abt. 1910
647.　　Ellen Graham b. abt. 1913

1-3-14-98-262　Louis Graham b. May 29, 1875 in Arkansas d. July 3, 1939. He married Gussie Joiner b. 1882 on Sept. 8, 1902 in Sebastian County, Arkansas. (Internet, *Ancestry.com*, Graham, by *lynrise*)

648.　　Lewis Graham, Jr. b. 1903
649.　　Claud Graham b. 1905
650.　　Doss Graham (dau.) b. 1907

1-3-14-98-263　Benjamin Graham b. Sept. 4, 1881 d. June 12, 1951 in Arkansas married on May 15, 1902 in Sebastian County, Arkansas to Roxie Ana Hickman b. 1884. (Internet *MaryElizabeth at Ancestry.com*)

651.　　Oliver Graham b. 1903
652.　　Ethel Graham b. 1905
653.　　Goldie Graham b. 1914
654.　　Rena Graham b. 1916

1-3-14-98-264　Lizzie E. Graham b. April 1884
1-3-14-98-265　Oscar L. Graham, Sr. b. Nov. 29, 1888 d. Sept. 8, 1950 in Sebastian County, Arkansas married Lillie b. 1904

655.　　Benny Graham b. 1915
656.　　Clydie Graham b. 1918
657.　　Oscar Graham, Jr. b. 1920

1-3-14-99-266　Samuel Campbell Hooper b. 1865 d. 1945 married Gertrude L. Dixon on Aug. 5, 1888 in McMinn County, TN. She was born July 23, 1871 – d. Nov. 22, 1936 (Internet, *Ancestry.com*)

658.　　Nettie L. Hooper b. Sept 1889
659.　　James Scott Hooper b. Sept. 28, 1891 d. Dec. 13, 1890 married Martha Jeanette Gilbreath (number 388) Oct. 10, 1909 in Bradley County, TN (Internet, *Ancestry.com*). Martha was b. July 24, 1892 d. June 12, 1984.
660.　　Ollie Elizabeth Hooper b. Oct. 1894
661.　　Louie Hooper (dau.) b. Oct. 1896
662.　　Sim McKinley Hooper b. July 1898
663.　　Glen Campbell Hooper b. abt. 1912

1-3-14-99-267　Florence Hooper b. June 1873 married Joseph Honeyman b. May 1872 (Missouri, or Arkansas or Texas)
1-3-14-99-268　William Hooper b. Feb. 8, 1874 married Alice E. Wheeler

664.　　Mary Hooper
665.　　Merritt Hooper
666.　　Earl Hooper

1-3-14-99-269　Sarah Jane Hooper b. March 6, 1876 married Tom Honeyman
1-3-14-99-270　Laura Hooper b. April 19, 1878 married William Bonner on March 24, 1894 in Dallas County, MO

667.　　Uva L. Bonner b. 1899
668.　　William P. Bonner b. 1900
669.　　Joseph F. Bonner b. 1903
670.　　John L. Bonner b. 1905
671.　　George Y. Bonner b. 1908

672.   Claude Bonner b. 1910

1-3-14-99-271   Zadie Hooper b. Jan. 11, 1880 married Albert B. Catlett b. 1879

     673.   Albert B. Catlett b. abt. 1905

     674.   Odessis Catlett b. abt. 1907

     675.   Dicie Catlett b. abt. 1908

     676.   Ada Catlett b. abt. 1910

     677.   Delvia Catlett b. abt. 1914

     678.   Bonney Catlett b. abt. 1915

     679.   Gore W. Catlett b. abt. 1917

1-3-14-99-272   Josie Hooper b. Aug. 4, 1882 married 1. Rufus Reynolds on August 17, 1902 in Polk County, MO 2. Riley Vanlandigham

1-3-14-99-273   Della May Hooper b. Oct. 4, 1884 d. Oct. 4, 1972 married Wm. Wesley Erven b. abt. 1875

     680.   Lucy Vona Erven b. March 4, 1903 married Dewey Manes

     681.   William Bonnie Erven b. Aug. 25, 1905

     682.   Lowell W. Erven b. Jan. 25, 1915 married Mildred Irene Gibson

     683.   Roscoe Guy Erven b. Aug. 17, 1923 married Mildred Vearl Jenkins

1-3-14-99-274   Pearl Hooper b. April 11, 1886 married Fount Sawyer b. April 1, 1881 d. Aug. 30, 1864 lived in OK. Pearley Hooper married Fount Sawyer on June 18, 1903 in Polk County, MO.

     684.   Anthony Sawyer b. 1905

     685.   Zella Sawyer b. 1908

     686.   Robert Sawyer b. 1911

1-3-14-99-275   Carrie B. (Tabitha) Hooper b. Aug. 15, 1889 married Wesley Wheeler

1-3-14-99-276   Ada Lou Hooper b. July 16, 1891in Missouri d. Oct. 10, 1957 in Santa Paula, CA married Joseph Nasalroad b. June 20, 1888 d. June 22, 1960. They married Jan. 10, 1905 in Dallas County, MO (Internet, *Ancestry.com, Find A Grave* Memorial# 71685514).

     687.   Lady Nasalroad b. Feb. 25, 1906 in Tunas, MO married Mark Taylor

     688.   Glade Nasalroad b. Feb. 17, 1908 d. 1975

     689.   Andrew Nasalroad b. Aug. 1, 1911 d. Jan. 2, 1989 m. Mary Lee Erven

     690.   Lonnie Nasalroad b. Feb. 21, 1914 in Sperry, OK m. Viola Garner

     691.   Hannah Nasalroad b. Nov. 3, 1917 in Shamrock, OK m. Claude Barham

     692.   Riley Carlton Nasalroad June 27, 1923 d. Jan. 26, 1943 (Marine WW II)

     693.   Fred McKinley Nasalroad b. Oct. 30, 1924 in Bristow, OK married Shirley Herzog

     694.   Betty Jo Nasalroad b. Jan. 1, 1926 m. Jim Lytle

     695.   Jaquolee Nasaroad b. Feb. 11, 1928 in Seminole, OK m. Carl Cook

     696.   Willard Ray Doc Nasalroad b. Sept. 23, 1931 in Polk, OK m. Shirley Eileen O'Neil

1-3-14-99-277   James Hooper b. and d. 1892

1-3-14-99-278   Rosa P. Hooper b. Dec. 31, 1895 married 1. Tom Vanlandingham married 2. Harry Huber

     697.   Dennis Huber b. abt. 1920

     698.   Nina Huber b. abt. 1923 married William Bonner

     699.   Zoe Huber b. abt. 1925 married Edward Drussel

     700.   Donal Huber b. abt. 1928

1-3-14-100-279   John W. Hooper b. Jan. 13, 1874 d. Nov. 30, 1892 Indian Territory, OK

1-3-14-100-280   Nancy Hooper b. Nov. 11, 1876

1-3-14-100-281   Rhoda May Hooper b. July 30, 1878 Sebastian Co., Arkansas d. June 14, 1869, Durant, Bryan Co., OK married George Edward Hammond

     701.   Bertha M. Hammond b. Dec. 1895

     702.   Flora D. Hammond b. Feb. 1900

     703.   James V. Hammond b. abt. 1909

     704.   Lowell Hammond b. abt. 1912

     705.   Lula Hammond b. abt. 1915

     706.   Culie Hammond b. abt. 1919

1-3-14-100-282   Florence E. Hooper b. Dec. 7, 1881 Logan Co., Arkansas married Ray L. Patillo b. abt. 1880. They married Jan. 1, 1905 in Bryan County, OK (Internet *sjames9 at Ancestry.com*).

707.   Earzey Patillo (dau.) b. abt. 1907
708.   Roy W. Patillo b. abt. 1909
709.   Owen Patillo b. abt. 1913
710.   Cleo Patillo b. abt. 1915

1-3-14-100-283 Andrew Albert Hooper b. Jan. 15, 1883 d. Aug. 14, 1934 married Mary Nonnie Edwards ? b. abt. 1898

711.   Troy Hooper b. abt. 1914
712.   Mollie Hooper b. abt. 1916
713.   Albert Hooper b. abt. 1917
714.   J. R. Hooper b. abt. 1921
715.   Mildred Hooper b. abt. 1923
716.   Benidict Hooper b. abt. 1927

1-3-14-100-284 Francis Marion Hooper b. Dec. 6, 1885 d. Jan. 19, 1979 married Mattie B. Parker (Internet, *Ancestry.com, Find A Grave*). WWI Registration in 1918 listed a wife and 4 children in Bryan County, OK. By 1930 the ages of Francis and Mattie were wrong, and the Census listed the children separately with a note to correct it (bottom left corner *Bryan County, Oklahoma 1930 Census* see p. 14 A line 1 and p. 15 B at bottom).

717.   Doyle F. Hooper b. 1911
718.   Elsie Hooper b. 1912
719.   J. T. Hooper b. 1913
720.   Lela B. Hooper b. 1918
721.   Haskel Hooper b. 1920
722.   Lucille Hooper b. 1921

1-3-14-100-285 William Thomas Hooper b. Feb. 29, 1888 d. April 5, 1980 married Katherine Garner b. July 8, 1898 d. Feb. 16, 1983

723.   Carroll Hooper (son) b. abt. 1919
724.   Thurman Hooper b. abt. 1922

1-3-14-100-286 Sarah Ethel Hooper b. Jan. 11, 1890

1-3-14-100-287 Mary D. Hooper b. May 4, 1893 d. Feb. 13, 1984

1-3-14-100-288 Horatio Hooper b. Feb. 3, 1895 d. Jan. 16, 1923 married Lorena or Corina (*Bryan County 1920 Census*, OK.) ?

725.   Truman Hooper b. abt. 1918
726.   Wayne Theron Hooper b. abt. 1920

1-3-14-100-289 Catherine Leona Hooper b. Oct. 16, 1895 d. Jan. 22, 1963 married Wyatt Wallace Walton on May 3, 1918 in Grayson County, TX. He was born Jan. 16, 1894 d. June 18, 1971. Walton family information came from Internet *ancestry.com* from *twalton128*.

727.   Douglas W. Walton 1919
728.   Otice or Otis Walton 1923
729.   Mary J. Walton 1925
730.   Kenneth Walton 1927

1-3-14-100-290 Viola Hooper b. Sept. 16, 1897

1-3-14-100-291 Hattie Savannah Hooper b. March 4, 1902 d. Dec. 31, 1986 married (1) Roy Bates and (2) Thomas Grover Richardson Sept. 17, 1928 (Internet, *Find A Grave.com*). Thomas was born June 5, 1885 in Grayson County, TX and died March 10, 1968 in Bryan County, OK.

731.   Thelma Bates 1924 (granddaughter living with William and Martha Hooper in the *Bryan County, Oklahoma 1930 Census*, Internet, *Ancestry.com*)
732.   Johnny Edward Richardson b. Aug. 5, 1929 – July 22, 2000
733.   Earnest Andrew Richardson b. Dec. 12, 1931 – Dec. 19, 1997
734.   Althea Leona Richardson b. April 19, 1934 – Nov. 4, 2009
735.   Joy Fae Richardson b. June 19, 1938

1-3-14-101-292 Samuel Graham b. Nov. 1871 married Nancy Julia Summers b. Jan. 1872. They lived in Sebastian County, Arkansas

736.   Benjamin Graham b. Aug. 31, 1892-June 1985
737.   Walter H. Graham b. Nov. 1894
738.   Stella M. Graham b. Feb. 1897

739.	Elmer Graham May 1899
740.	Ruby Graham 1902
741.	Arthur Graham 1904
742.	Ocie Graham 1908
743.	Linda L. Graham 1911
1-3-14-101-293	Sarah E. Graham b. August 1873
1-3-14-101-294	John Graham b. 1874
1-3-14-101-295	Lee Graham b. Oct. 11, 1877 m. Bertie
744.	Clarence Graham b. 1900
745.	Lillia Graham b. 1906
746.	Cletis Graham b. 1908 m. Ella May ?
747.	Kermit Graham b. 1911 m. Ellen b. 1913
748.	Thelma Graham b. 1914
749.	Jess Graham b. 1917
750.	Leonard Graham b. 1918
751.	Jeanetta Graham b. 1920
752.	Lorene Graham b. 1922
753.	Alta Graham b. 1923
754.	Alma Graham b. 1923
755.	Ilous Graham b. 1925
1-3-14-101-296	James Graham b. 1880
1-3-14-101-297	Florence Graham b. Dec. 1883
1-3-14-101-298	Martha Graham b. March 1885
1-3-14-101-299	Minnie Graham b. Dec. 1886
1-3-14-101-300	Myrtle Graham b. May 1891
1-3-14-103-301	George Graham b. 1877 married Elsie Hickman Nov. 6, 1904 Sebastian County, Ark (Internet, *Ancestry.com*).
756.	Albert Graham b. 1906
757.	Hugh Graham b. 1907
758.	Keller Graham b. 1910
1-3-14-103-302	Elizabeth Graham April 1875 married William Southard on Nov. 1, 1891 in Sebastian County, Arkansas (Internet, *Ancestry.com*)
759.	Gracie Southard b. 1898
1-3-14-103-303	Arthur Graham b. 1880
1-3-14-103-304	Lulu Graham Jan. 1888
1-3-14-103-305	Richard Graham
1-3-14-103-306	William Tackett Graham b. Jan. 1, 1894 d. Jan. 1978
1-3-14-104-307	Florence Johnson
1-3-14-104-308	Mary Elizabeth Johnson 1880-1929
1-3-14-104-309	John William Johnson 1883
1-3-14-104-310	Della May Johnson 1886-1919
1-3-14-104-311	Elsie Jane Johnson 1888-1919
1-3-14-104-312	Nancy Johnson 1891
1-3-14-104-313	Jasper Franklin Johnson Jan. 18, 1896-June 1967 married 1. Josie b. 1898
760.	Jasper Johnson, Jr. b. 1918
1-3-14-104-313	Jasper Franklin Johnson married 2. Linda
761.	Buna Johnson b. 1923
762.	Grady Johnson b. 1926
763.	Joy Johnson b. 1928
1-3-14-104-314	Charlotte Mayme Johnson 1904-1990
1-3-15-105-315	William Oscar Hooper b. Oct. 7, 1878 married 1. Zealie Geren Aug. 13, 1898 in Bradley County, TN and 2. Minnie Laura Stevenson April 5, 1905
764.	Lynn Hooper b. July 18, 1899 d. Sept. 4, 1916 (murdered) Information found at *familytreemaker.genealogy.com/users/s/m/i/Gregory-Smith-New-Carlisle* on Internet.
765.	Mabel Hooper b. July 9, 1902 d. Oct. 4, 1946 (Information found at preceding reference and *Ancestry.com* on the Internet.

766.   Willie P. Hooper b. 1910

1-3-15-105-316 Isaac Lon Hooper b. Feb. 22, 1882 d. Feb. 12, 1954 married Vinie Davis on May 8, 1902 in Bradley County, TN (Internet, *Ancestry.com*) and Maude E. ?

767.   Cecil Hooper (dau.) b. abt. 1904

768.   Paul Hooper b. abt. 1914

1-3-15-106-317 John Luther Hooper b. June 4, 1878 d. Oct. 25, 1953 married on April 8, 1900 in Bradley County, TN (Internet, *Ancestry.com*, Hooper, Bradley County Marriages 1931) to Maudie Belle Shiflett b. May 7, 1883 d. April 3, 1931.

769.   Infant b. August 22, 1901 – d. September 28, 1901

770.   James Harrison Hooper b. July 29, 1903 d. Dec. 16, 1978 married Jewel Cofer b. Nov. 23, 1907 d. May 13, 1999

771.   Sarah Ellen Hooper b. Dec. 25, 1907 d. Dec. 25, 1992 married on Jan. 20, 1926 in Bradley County, TN to Claude Monroe McDowell b. Feb. 18, 1903 d. Feb. 1972

772.   John Luther Hooper, Jr. b. August 21, 1911 d. Dec. 14, 2002 married Eloise Harris b. Feb. 19, 1919 d. Feb. 15, 1996. Marriage is listed on Johnston Cemetery tombstone, Jan. 10, 1936.

773.   Earl Cook Hooper b. July 21, 1913 d. Nov. 19, 1993 married in Meigs County, TN on Nov. 23, 1932 to Willie Tennessee (Billie) Jenkins b. Oct. 4, 1916 d. March 14, 2002

774.   Lennie Hooper b. & d. April 7, 1915

1-3-15-106-318 Sareptha Hooper b. Dec. 11, 1879 d. Aug. 31, 1892

1-3-15-106-319 Lennie Hooper b. Sept. 1881 married 1. Thomas Ledford on Feb. 4, 1898, and he died (*1900 Census* listed her Widow). Lennie Ledford married 2. George W. Geren on Sept. 2, 1903 in Bradley County, TN (Internet, *Ancestry.com*), and he was born June 1878.

775.   Clara Mae Geren b. Dec. 26, 1904 d. May 1, 1999 married on April 28, 1932 in Bradley County, TN (Internet, *Ancestry.com*) to Roy Glenn Caldwell b. Feb. 21, 1905 d. May 22, 1993

776.   Albert Geren b. Nov. 26, 1906 d. Jan. 1978

777.   J. H. Geren b. April 5, 1909 d. Feb. 9, 2001

778.   Kinze Geren b. abt. 1914

779.   Hazel Geren b. abt. 1916

780.   James R. Geren b. abt. 1924

1-3-15-106-320 Rosa Hooper (twin) b. Dec. 9, 1883 d. 1966 married (number 126) Kenzie Hooper b. Sept. 15, 1872 d. 1933

429.   Bruce Hooper b. April 14, 1905 d. Feb. 1985 married Mable Morgan

430.   Gladys Hooper b. abt. 1907 married Buford W. Goins on March 15, 1925 in Bradley County, in Bradley County, TN

431.   Boyd Hooper b. April 4, 1911 d. Oct. 1983 married Mary Smalling

1-3-15-106-321 Lillie Hooper (twin) b. Dec. 9, 1883 married on Feb. 2, 1908 in Bradley County, TN to 1. James Calhoun b. June 13, 1876 d. July 2, 1930 and after James' death to 2. William F. Mahoney

1-3-15-106-322 James William Hooper b. March 27, 1886 d. Oct. 1972 married Mary E. Taylor b. Nov. 1885

781.   Marvin B. Hooper b. Oct. 22, 1910 d. Jan. 8, 1995

782.   Roy L. Hooper b. abt. 1913

1-3-15-106-323 Ethel Laura Hooper b. July 9, 1888 married James Brooks Taylor on June 29, 1907 (Internet, *Ancestry.com*) *Bradley County, Tennessee Marriages* p. 155. James was born on June 30, 1880 and died April 25, 1931.

783.   Alvin A. Taylor b. March 16, 1908 d. June 21, 1991

784.   Dennis K. Taylor b. abt. 1910

785.   J. B. Taylor b. abt. 1913

786.   Eula Myrtle Taylor (dau.) b. Oct. 13, 1915 d. May 12, 2001

787.   Thomas Hooper Taylor b. May 17, 1918 d. Dec. 18, 1981

1-3-15-106-324 Albert Kinsey Hooper b. May 3, 1890 d. Jan. 1978 married Pearl Beaty b. July 9, 1889 d. May 1, 1964

788.   Jewell Hooper b. abt. 1916

789.   Joseph Brackett Hooper b. April 22, 1920 d. April 5, 1998 married Marie Geren

1-3-15-106-325   Gertrude Louetta Hooper b. May 15, 1900 d. June 5, 1981 married John L. Brewer b.
                 Oct. 16, 1886 d. May 27, 1946. The wedding was Dec. 28, 1922 in Hamilton County,
                 TN (see page 253). An infant was born and died in 1929. Emily Brewer was adopted
                 and buried beside her birth parents.
        790.   John L. Brewer, Jr. b. July 10, 1939 d. July 5, 2002 married Jo Ann Yarnell b. June 11,
                 1938 and d. July 27, 1997 (Internet, *Find A Grave.com*)
1-3-15-107-326   Thomas Walter Brackett b. abt. 1879 d. April 9, 1953 married Viola Ruth Wagoner b.
                 abt. 1892 in Dallas County, TX (Internet, *20346glynnys* and TX Death Records at
                 Ancestry.com)
        791.   Elsie Brackett b. abt. 1911
        792.   Howard Brackett b. abt. 1912
        793.   T. W. Brackett, Jr. b. abt. 1927 d. Nov. 2, 1963
1-3-15-107-327   Salome G. Brackett b. July 14, 1881 d. Feb. 28, 1961 (Internet, *Ancestry.com,
                 jpm36161*) married John D. Garrison b. July 22, 1872 in Arkansas d. Oct. 11, 1911 in
                 Dallas County, TX (Internet, *dbm57 at Ancestry.com*) married second to ? Mealer
                 (Internet, *Ancestry.com, Dallas County, TX 1910 Census* p. 8 A&B Justice Precinct)
        794.   Frank R. Garrison b. abt. 1905
        795.   J. D. Garrison b. abt. 1906
        796.   Cora Wilma Garrison b. Feb. 1, 1907 d. Jan. 19, 1972 (Internet, *Ancestry.com, Texas
                 Death Certificate 02167*)
        797.   Dallas Earcel Garrison (dau.) b. abt. 1909
        798.   Henry Garrison b. abt. 1911
        799.   John Garrison b. abt. 1912
1-3-15-107-328   Emma Brackett b. Nov. 1886
1-3-15-107-329   John Fred Brackett b. June 20, 1888 d. Jan. 16, 1962 married Irene Johnson (Internet,
                 Ancestry.com, jcwiener). Irene was b. Sept. 21, 1891 d. April 22, 1972.
        800.   Ethalinda Brackett b. abt. 1914
1-3-15-107-330   James A. Brackett b. Mar. 13, 1896 d. Jan. 6, 1910 (Internet, Mills Cemetery, TX)
1-3-15-107-331   Dolly/Dollie Brackett b. Aug. 6, 1892 – d. Dec. 5, 1966 married (1) Edwin H. McCallum
                 (Internet, *Ancestry.com*, kmoore254, Dallas *County 1910 Census*, Justice Precinct
                 p. 9 A), and (2) Putham H. Lambert (Internet, Brackett, *Ancestry.com, Dolores Lambert*)
        801.   M. Ruth McCallum b. 1911
        802.   Edwin L. McCallum b. 1914
        803.   Trixie J. Lambert b. 1916
        804.   Jimmie R. Lambert (dau.) b. 1919
        805.   Roy B. Lambert b. 1922
        806.   Bettie Lambert b. 1924
1-3-15-107-332   Roy Stephen Brackett b. May 28, 1894 – Dec. 3, 1918, married Winnie D. b. March 28,
                 1892 – d. Nov. 11, 1918 (Internet, *Ancestry.com, Find A Grave*, Mills Cemetery)
1-3-15-108-333   Andy Baker b. June 1887
1-3-15-108-334   Effie Eudora Baker b. Jan. 12, 1889 – May 16, 1969 married James Joseph Leamon b.
                 Oct. 26, 1882 – d. Sept. 2, 1961 (Internet, Leamon, *MarthaD8843 at Ancestry.com*)
        807.   Patricia Estelle Leamon b. March 30, 1908 – d. Dec. 5, 1990 in Oak Ridge, TN
                 (Internet, *KeithMillsStewart* at *Ancestry.com*) (Married 427 and 875.)
1-3-15-108-335   Delia Baker b. Oct. 1894
1-3-15-108-336   Isaac Homer Baker b. Feb. 10, 1896
1-3-15-108-337   Ethalinda Baker b. June 1899
1-3-15-108-338   Martha D. Baker b. abt. 1903
1-3-15-108-339   Lucil K. Baker b. Aug. 24, 1905 in Hamilton Co., TN d. Jan. 30, 1984 d. in Redding, CA
                 according to Internet, *garystandifer1* at *Ancestry.com*. She married James Quintis
                 Standifer b. May 23, 1906 – d. Dec. 19, 1964.
1-3-15-109-340   Virgie Miller b. June 1887
1-3-15-109-341   Henry Miller b. Nov. 1892 married Sept. 14, 1913 in Bradley County, TN to Mae
                 Messer b. abt. 1898 (See Appendix H p. 306 for additional Descendants.)
        808.   Thelma Miller b. 1914
        809.   Lillard Miller (dau.) b. abt. 1920

810.   Luetta Miller b. abt. 1922
811.   Cecil M. Miller (dau.) b. abt. 1924
812.   Opal P. Miller b. abt. 1926
813.   Essadine D. Miller b. abt. 1928

1-3-15-109-342   Cash Miller b. April 30, 1894 served in WW1 during Oct. 2, 1917 to Jan. 20, 1918. Cash married Annie Haney (Internet, Miller, *mahaffjg* at *Ancestry.com*); he lived in a Home for Disabled American Soldiers in Johnson City, TN from July 9, 1921 to May 3, 1922.

1-3-15-109-343   Gracie Miller b. Jan. 1897

1-3-15-109-344   Lawrence Miller b. July 13,1898 married Cecil Varnell b. abt. 1898 (See Appendix H.

     814.   Rathburn Miller b. March 27, 1920-d. Sept. 1, 1989   for other children.)
     815.   Herman H. Miller b. August 19, 1924-d. July 24, 2006
     816.   Cash Edward (Chub) Miller b. Nov. 26, 1926-d. May 3, 2003

1-3-15-109-345   M. Z. Miller b. March 2, 1902 d. Sept. 28, 1987 married (1) Pearl Lee Melton b. abt. 1905 and (2) Ollie Millaway

     817.   Carolyn Miller married Duncan Gibson
     818.   Betty Sue Miller b. abt. 1929 married (1) Charles Fortney and (2) Bud Bowman
     819.   Martha Celestine Miller married David T. Hooper (number 954)
     820.   Judy Miller married Darrell Hooper (838)
     821.   Doug Miller married Mary Lou Callaway

1-3-15-109-346   Ernest Miller b. abt. 1904 married Florence Haney b. abt. 1905

     822.   Earnestine Miller b. abt. 1926
     823.   Bonnie Joe Miller b. abt. 1928 married Lettie Ashford

1-3-15-109-347   Joseph Luther Miller b. abt. 1908

1-3-15-109-348   Rilla Mae Miller b. abt. 1911

(Alden U. Miller married a second time to Carrie Dalton and had Caroline Elizabeth Miller and Willie Cate Miller.)

1-3-15-110-349   Samuel Isaac Millaway b. July 3,1889 – d. Oct. 8, 1950 married Sallie McDowell Dec. 23, 1911 in Bradley County, TN (Internet, *Ancestry.com, Find A Grave*)

     824.   John W. Millaway b. Sept. 27, 1912 – d. April 16, 1981 (*Find A Grave*)
     825.   Auther Raymond Millaway b. Dec. 4, 1914 – d. Feb. 10, 1996
     826.   Gladys Beattrice Millaway b. Feb. 2, 1919 – Nov. 28, 1980 (*Find A Grave*)
     827.   (S. I., Jr.) Earl Millaway b. July 19, 1922 - d. Feb. 5, 1985 (*Find A Grave*)
     828.   Millard L. Millaway b. April 6, 1926 – Feb. 8, 1994 (*Find A Grave*)
     829.   Ina M. Millaway b. April 28, 1929 - d. Oct. 29, 2008 (*Find A Grave*)
     830.   Edward Keith Millaway b. Feb. 15, 1932 – d. Sept. 7, 2013 (Internet, *Ancestry.com, Tennessee, Meigs County 1940 Census ,*First District p. 11 A and *Find A Grave*)
     831.   James Millaway b. 1936 (Internet, *Ancestry.com* 1940 Census)
     832.   Jessie Millaway b. 1936 (Internet, *Ancestry.com* 1940 Census)

1-3-15-110-350   Arthur Raymond Millaway b. March 24, 1891 d. Aug. 9, 1956 Dallas Co., TX married Vela Fletcher b. abt. 1891 d. April 1, 1931 and Ina Martin b. Jan. 8, 1895 d. Nov. 23, 1969. (Dallas County, TX *Death Certificate* listed Alice Cooper as mother instead of Hooper. Information found at Internet, *Rootsweb, The Dallas Morning News* -August 11, 1956 and submitted by Edward Lynn Williams.)

1-3-15-110-351   Jasper Alexander Millaway b. Dec. 14, 1896 d. Jan. 10, 1933 (Dallas County, TX Death Certificate) married before 1930 to Ina Martin b. Jan. 8, 1895 TX d. Nov. 23, 1969.

1-3-15-110-352   Betty Millaway b. July 21, 1899 d. May 17, 1938 in Dallas County, TX. She married Roy Aubrey Garrison b. Aug. 9, 1897 d. Nov. 14, 1962 in Denton County, TX

     833.   Margaret Irene Garrison b. 1920
     834.   Dorothy Nell Garrison b. 1921
     835.   Roy Garrison, Jr. b. 1926

(Alice died before 1902 because on December 24, 1902 William Millaway married Malinda Johnston and had Ollie, Horace and Olivia Millaway.)

1-3-15-111-353   K. C. Hooper b. July 8, 1901 - d. July 10, 1953 m. Ruth Buckner on April 5, 1924 in Bradley County, TN (Internet, *Ancestry.com*)

     836.   Virginia J. Hooper married Marshall Wallace
     837.   Mary Margaret Hooper married Noah Western

1-3-15-111-354   James Arnold Hooper b. Jan. 24, 1903 – d. Dec. 3, 1974 m. Icie Lawson on June 7, 1924 in Bradley County, TN (Internet, *Ancestry.com*)

838.   Darrell Hooper married June 29, 1951 in Bradley County, TN (Internet, *Ancestry.com*) to Judy Miller (number 820)

1-3-15-111-355   Annie Hooper b. 1905- d. 1976 m. Earnest Waller Thompson b. June 30, 1903 – July 5, 1948 (Internet, *Ancestry.com, HAROLDH38*)

839.   Lottie Lee Thompson b. abt. 1929 married Thomas Eddie Wood
840.   J. E. Thompson b. Oct. 10, 1931 – June 16, 1932
841.   Marie Irene Thompson married Harold Baker
842.   Martha Edwyna Thompson married Ralph L. Pierce
843.   Earnest W. Thompson, Jr. married Mildred Smith

1-3-15-111-356   Lake Hooper b. March 3, 1909-d. April 13, 1940 married Dorothy Graham (number 892) b. March 13, 1913 d. April 29, 1988

844.   Gurtha Dean Hooper married Forrest Hill
845.   Hazel Lou Hooper (some name information from Internet *FamilyTreeGuide.com* for Dorothy Graham family and *Jay and Lou Graham by* Juanita Graham Hinkle and Gertha Hooper Hill)
846.   Martha June Hooper
847.   Bobbye Roberta Hooper

1-3-15-111-357   Aldon Hooper b. April 29, 1912 d. Nov. 15, 2001 m. Almetta Melton

848.   Dewayne Cyrus Hooper b. Jan. 1936

1-3-15-111-358   Forrest Hooper b. abt. 1916 d. 1918

1-3-16-112-359   Thomas Houston Marr b. Feb. 1868 married Mary Frances Moore b. April 1872

849.   James Albert Marr b. March 20, 1896
850.   Florence Marie Marr b. Jan. 17, 1898 (*Delayed Certificate of Birth* Chattanooga, TN on May 19, 1952 found at Internet, *Ancestry.com*)
851.   John Marr April 4, 1900 – d. July 2, 1901 (Internet *1_rcmoore at Ancestry.com*)
852.   Loyd T. Marr b. 1903 married Beulah Defriese?
853.   Owen N. Marr b. July 2, 1904 d. May 1972
854.   Lela B. Marr b. abt. 1907
855.   Effie C. Marr b. abt. 1912
856.   Beulah B. Marr b. abt. 1914
857.   Clifford R. Marr b. Dec. 20, 1914 d. May 1975

1-3-16-112-360   Elie Daniel Marr b. b. Oct. 6, 1871 d. June 7, 1923 married "Mollie" Mary Buckner b. June 18, 1872 d. May 15, 1936 (Internet, *Ancestry.com, Find A Grave*)

858.   William C. Marr b. Dec. 6, 1896 married Blanche b. abt. 1900
859.   Maggie F. Marr b. March 1898
860.   Kenzie Marr b. abt. 1903 (See p. 131 for family information.)
861.   George Marr b. abt. 1905
862.   Ollevia Marr b. May 13, 1909 – d. May 24, 1984 (Internet, *Find A Grave*, Bradley County, TN)
863.   Huston Daniel Marr b. abt. 1914

1-3-16-112-361   John Henry Marr b. Dec. 23, 1874 married Partela West b. June 1876. The Marriage was solemnized May 1, 1894 Monroe County, TN (Internet, *Ancestry.com, casiekay1865*).

864.   Elsie Marr b. Sept. 17,1895
865.   Pearl Marr b. June 1896
866.   Loma Marr b. March 1899 (*Bradley County, TN 1900 Census,* 9th Dist. p. 1B)
867.   Ledford Marr b. abt. 1902
868.   Garland Marr b. abt. 1904

1-3-16-112-362   Tabitha Marr b. abt. 1879

1-3-16-112-363   Margaret (Maggie) Marr married Andrew Jackson Hooper (number 111) b. September 12, 1875 d. May 29, 1951 on Nov. 8, 1900 in Bradley County, TN. She was born Dec. 31, 1880 and died Aug. 28, 1941 (see information for 111 and 112 p. 46).

353.   K. C. Hooper b. abt. 1901 m. Ruth Buckner
354.   Arnold Hooper b. abt. 1903 m. Icie Lawson
355.   Annie Hooper b. abt. 1905 m. Ernest Thompson

356. Lake Hooper b. abt. 1909 m. Dorothy Graham (892)
357. Aldon Hooper b. abt. 1913 m. Almetta Melton
358. Forrest Hooper b. abt. 1916 d. 1918

1-3-16-112-364 Martha Marr b. Aug. 1883
1-3-16-112-365 Andrew Lucas Marr b. Feb. 1887 d. Jan 1869 married Letha Moon on Sept. 30, 1907 in
Bradley County, TN. She was b. Sept. 28, 1891 – d. Aug. 2, 1966 (Internet,
Ancestry.com, midgelemke and Internet, *Find A Grave*).
869. Marie Marr b. abt. 1909
870. Ruby Marr 1912 - 1971
871. Martha Marr b. abt. 1913
1-3-16-112-366 Dialtha Marr b. July 1891
1-3-16-113-367 Mary Graham b. 1869 m. M. Boles
872. J. Boles
1-3-16-113-368 William Kins Graham b. Nov. 1870 married Ella M. King b. abt. 1885
873. Eulah L. Graham b. abt. 1910
874. Partella Graham b. abt. 1912
1-3-16-113-369 Florence Graham b. Feb. 1873 m. W. Hindman
1-3-16-113-370 Thomas H. Graham b. Sept. 1875 married (1) Lissie Wagner b. abt. 1882
875. Burley Graham b. abt. 1901
876. Edith Graham b. abt. 1903
877. Hazel Graham b. abt. 1905
878. Thurman Graham b. abt. 1907
879. Sallie May Graham b. abt. 1909
880. Myrtle Graham b. abt. 1914
1-3-16-113-370 Thomas H. Graham married (2) Emma Geren Lee who had Myrtle Lee b. abt. 1909,
Maynard Lee b. abt. 1911, Wayne Lee b. abt. 1913 and Bertie L. Lee by Lester Lee
(information found at *Find A Grave* for Bertie). Thomas and Emma Graham had:
881. Oma Lee Graham b. abt. 1919
882. Hoyt T. Graham b. abt. 1921
883. Cletus G. Graham b. abt. 1923
884. Mary Lou Graham b. abt. 1926
1-3-16-113-371 Jahue H. Graham b. Feb. 20, 1878 d. April 9, 1951. He married Lula Mae Dalton March
20, 1897 in Bradley County, TN. She was born Nov. 15, 1881 and d. Feb. 13, 1964.
(Some of the information came from *Bradley County Cemeteries and Genealogical
Information* by Jo Bryson Callahan Martin printed 2000 by Jo Bryson Callahan Martin.
Also *Jay and Lou Graham Family* by Juanita Graham Hinkle and Gertha Hooper Hill
published in 2004)
885. Nola Graham b. Jan. 1898-April 21, 1967
886. Jasper O. Graham b. Oct. 14, 1899-Sept. 28, 1983 m. Bertie L. Messer
887. Oscar Graham b. 1902 d. Oct. 25, 1923
888. Zenia D. Graham b. Jan. 9,1905 d. Oct. 3, 1981
889. Willie Graham
890. Paul B. Graham b. Aug. 4, 1908 d. Feb. 25, 1976. He married Clara Grisham on July
27, 1928 in Bradley County, TN. She was born Jan. 28, 1912 and died March 24, 1997
(found on Internet, *Ancestry.com, Find A Grave.com*).
891. Arnold Graham b. Nov. 11, 1910 d. Nov. 5, 1982 married Pauline Thompson on
Nov.11, 1933 in Bradley County, TN
892. Dorothy Graham b. March 13, 1913 d. April 29, 1988 married (1) Lake Hooper
(number 356) and (2) Uel Claude Sandidge
893. Ova Graham b. June 12, 1915 d. March 19, 1984
894. Margaret Marie Graham Aug. 3, 1917 d. Oct. 31, 1918
895. James Graham b. Nov. 15, 1919 d. Nov. 21, 2003
896. Jahue Graham, Jr. b. March 15, 1922 d. June 2, 1989
1-3-16-113-372 Andy Graham b. July 1880
1-3-16-113-373 John R. Graham b. Oct. 10, 1883 d. Nov. 18, 1893
1-3-16-113-374 Samuel Bedford Graham b. July 3, 1886 – d. Nov. 14, 1914 married Minnie Shipley b.

May 9,1893 – d. May 17, 1926. Information came from the Internet at *Ancestry.com* by *HaroldH38;* Tennessee, Birth Records; and *Find A Grave;* the marriage was in Walker County, GA on March 26, 1911.

897. Lloyd Eugene Graham b. Nov. 1, 1912 – d. 1982 Internet, *Ancestry.com, U. S., Social Security Death Index* for Rosebush, Isabella, Michigan

898. James Graham b. 1914

1-3-16-113-375 Ada Graham (dau.) b. Jan 1889 m. Thomas Clemmie King on July 22, 1906 in Bradley County, TN (Internet, Graham, *Ancestry.com* by *fpagones1*).

899. Clay Victor King

900. Earl Walker King

1-3-16-113-376 Mala Graham (son) b. Oct. 1891

1-3-16-114-377 Arthur Williamson b. abt. 1879

1-3-16-114-378 Charles Thomas Williamson b. 1881 in the *1920 Los Angeles, CA Census, Malibu* p. 8A and 8 B was married to Clara Schultz. (Internet, *Jacqueline-L-Brusseau-CO, Genealogy.com: Descendants of Robert Thomas Williamson*)

901. Anna M. Williamson b. 1912 in CA

902. John J. Williamson b. 1915 in TN

903. Dorthy L. Williamson b. 1925 in CA

904. Thomas C. Williamson b. 1928 in CA

1-3-16-114-379 Margaret Dialtha Williamson according to *Cheyenne Dunbar, Ancestry.com* b. Oct. 22, 1882 and died Nov. 7, 1949 in Los Angeles, CA. She married William Albert Bunch.

905. Edna Elizabeth Bunch 1904 – 1972

906. Nanalee "Nancy" Bunch 1907 – 1986

907. Margaret Dialtha Bunch   1910 – 1994 moved to Los Angeles, CA before 1940 (Internet *Ancestry.com,1940 Los Angeles, CA Census* Block Numbers 8 – 9 p. 3)

908. Lorrain Evelyn Bunch 1912 - 1996

909. William Albert Bunch, Jr. 1914 – 1973

910. Joseph R. Bunch 1916 – 1970

911. Charles Bunch 1920 - 1968

912. Carl Eugene Bunch 1922 – 1990

1-3-16-114-380 Mary Elizabeth Williamson b. Oct. 10, 1884 – d. June 11, 1974 in Los Angeles, CA married John Ben Goike in 1905 in Hamilton County, TN (Internet, *Rootsweb, Ancestry.com, Williamson Genealogy*)

913. Lillian Goike married Harry Walcott in CA

1-3-16-114-381 William Audie Williamson July 1886 – July 27, 1945 married Beulah Collins (Internet, *Ancestry.com, Tennessee, Deaths and Burials Index, 1874 – 1955*)

914. Mildred Williamson 1914 (Internet *Hamilton County, TN 1920 Census* p. 2 B Dist. 3 at *Ancestry.com*)

915. Reita Williamson 1916

916. Howard Williamson 1918

917. Grove Williamson 1926 (*Hamilton County, TN 1930 Census* p. 20 B Dist. 3 at Internet *Ancestry.com*)

1-3-16-114-382 Arminta Jeannette "Minnie" Williamson Feb. 1889 died Sept. 18, 1939 in Hamilton County, TN (Internet *Ancestry.com Certificate of Death*) married Roderick Bell

918. Jessie May Bell 1912

919. Myrtle Bell 1914

1-3-16-114-383 Lula Williamson June 1890

1-3-16-114-384 Essie Elmina Williamson Oct. 1, 1893 married Monroe Yongue Dicks June 30, 1914 in Hamilton County, TN (*Ancestry.com, patrickkeeney1*). Essie died Dec. 5, 1994 in Las Vegas, Clark County, Nevada.

920. Sarah J. Dicks

1-3-16-114-385 Fred Williamson

1-3-16-115-386 Dolly E. Gilbreath b. Dec. 1886

1-3-16-115-387 Walter G. Gilbreath b. Oct. 7, 1890 married Mayme M. Beaty b. Aug. 30, 1893 – d. Feb. 6, 1975 (Internet, *Pinellastek* at *Ancestry.com*) b. abt. 1894

921. Maree Gilbreath b. abt. 1913

1-3-16-115-388   Martha Jeanetta Gilbreath b. July 24, 1892 d. June 12, 1984 married James Scott Hooper (number 659) b. Sept. 28, 1891 d. Dec. 13, 1990. She married Scott Hooper Oct. 10, 1909 in Bradley County, TN (Internet, *Ancestry.com*).
    922.   Lynn Andrew Hooper b. Oct. 18, 1910 d. Feb. 21, 1973
    923.   James Hoyt Hooper b. August 14, 1913-d. Aug. 22, 1915
    924.   Edith Gertrude Hooper b. Oct. 30, 1918-d. April 24, 2008
1-3-16-115-389   William Leonard Gilbreath b. Sept 1894
1-3-16-115-390   Icie May Gilbreath b. Jan. 1898
1-3-16-116-391   William Walter Gilbreath b. Jan. 1888
1-3-16-116-392   Elbert Hughston Gilbreath b. June 1891
1-3-16-116-393   Bula Gilbreath b. Nov. 1893
1-3-16-116-394   Carey Gilbreath b. Dec. 1899
1-3-16-116-395   Robert Med Gilbreath b. 1904
1-3-16-117-396   Eva P. Dunham b. Aug. 1886 married John Earl Bacon (Internet, *Ancestry.com*, *Paladin1952* at *Ancestry.com*
    925.   Med D. Bacon b. Jan. 3, 1910
1-3-16-117-397   Fred Dunham b. Aug. 1892 married Peditta M. Schoolfield b. March 1, 1893 (Internet *kbraboy171* at *Ancestry.com*
    926.   Fred Dunham b. abt. 1914
    927.   William R. Dunham b. abt. 1924
1-3-16-117-398   Paul Dunham b. abt. 1902
1-3-17-120-399   Leathey Carlton b. Apr. 1884 married Morton Cross on Sept. 20, 1905 in Bradley County, TN (Morton's aunt Amanda Maxwell married Jahue Hooper.).
    928.   Letha Grace Cross b. Aug. 15, 1915 – d. Oct. 21, 1992 (Internet, *Ancestry.com, Social Security Death Index* at *Ancestry.com*
    929.   Betty Cross b. 1919
1-3-17-120-400   Frank W. Carlton b. May 1886 married Mamie Wrinkle March 17, 1912 in Meigs County, TN. Mamie was born 1890. (*Descendants of Rufus Rinkle/Wrinkle* on Internet *Earthlink.net* by K. Callan & Evelyn Wrinkle Cross published Feb. 2001 and updated April 2001)
    930.   Stacy E. Carlton b. July 19, 1913 d. July 1992
    931.   Milton Carlton b. March 1915 d. June 23, 1987
    932.   Joseph F. Carlton b. April 27, 1918 d. Dec. 19, 1989
    933.   William R. Carlton b. abt. 1924
    934.   Naomi Frances Carlton b. Oct. 4, 1930
1-3-17-120-401   Pearly Carlton b. Aug. 1888
1-3-17-120-402   Joseph Carlton b. Sept. 1890 married Mary b. abt. 1895
    935.   Josephine Carlton b. abt. 1914
    936.   Caldwell Carlton b. abt. 1917
1-3-17-120-403   Kinsie Carlton b. Feb. 1894 married Rubie Geren (*Findagrave*.com} b. abt. 1900
    937.   Leland L. Carlton b. abt. 1920
    938.   Margaret L. Carlton b. abt. 1921
    939.   Gale M. Carlton b. abt. 1923
    940.   Kins C. Carlton, Jr. b. abt. 1926
1-3-17-120-404   Lattie Carlton b. Sept. 1896
1-3-17-120-405   Arnold Carlton b. abt. 1904
1-3-17-121-406   Martha Ida Teague b. March 23, 1879 married Jacob Howell Barker (Internet, Teague, *Ancestry.com,* by *llgivens1* and the Social Security Information): **Children discovered recently were Hugh Barker b. 1906, Homer Barker b. 1908 and Margaret Barker b. 1911.**
1-3-17-121-407   Mary Teague b. Dec. 1886
1-3-17-121-408   Lula P. Teague b. Feb. 17, 1889 d. March 27, 1980 married Walter Leonard Richards b. Nov. 27, 1882 d. March 1, 1969 (according to Internet, *FergyMom* at *Ancestry.Com* and the *1920 Census for Marion County*, TN Dist. 5 p. 7 A)
    941.   Clayton Richards b. 1909
    942.   Paul Richards b. 1911

943.   Clyde Richards b. 1914

944   Hershell Richards b. 1916

945.   Margaret Richards b. 1918

(Joel Teague married a second time in Marion County, TN to Lawil V. Deakin, and children listed p. 47.)

1-3-17-122-409   Icie Hooper Aug. 29, 1889 d. Apr. 28, 1969 married on Sept. 9, 1908 in Bradley County, TN to Charles Franklin Tillery b. July 1, 1885 – d. Sept. 26, 1947 in Hamilton County, TN

946.   Thelma Tillery b. Jan. 27, 1911

947.   Edna Tillery b. Aug. 24, 1913 d. April 8, 2009 m. 1. Joseph McSpadden and 2. Cecil Shirley

1-3-17-122-410   Jay Harrison (Jahue) Hooper b. March 22, 1892 d. Dec. 2, 1945 married Bernola Liner b. March 25, 1893 d. June 1969

948.   William Robert Hooper b. June 8, 1913 d. Dec. 29, 1918

949.   Alvin Arthel (Red) Hooper b. Sept. 16, 1914 married Thelma Miller (808) b. abt. 1915

950.   Ruby Ellen Hooper b. August 14, 1916 married Aldon Wayne Harris b. abt. 1915

951.   Roy Frank Hooper b. Sept. 22, 1918 (WW 1 Veteran) married Lorraine Tinsley

952.   Thomas Calvin Hooper b. April 17, 1920 (WW 1 Veteran) married Lois Lawson

953.   Paul Jahue Hooper b. May 22, 1922 (WW 1 Veteran) married Pauline Umphrey

954.   David Thurman Hooper b. Oct. 11, 1925 married Martha Celestine Miller (819)

955.   Marjorie Dellifene Hooper b. July 25, 1930 married Herman Melton

956.   Carl Ray Hooper b. Jan. 7, 1932 married Betty Sneed

957.   Dorothy Marie Hooper b. Feb. 16, 1934 married Bill Carson

958.   Joseph Clinton Hooper b. March 10, 1937 married Rosa Bell Schroyer

959.   Charles Leonard Hooper b. Dec. 8, 1939 d. Nov. 24, 1940

960.   Wayne Harrison Hooper b. Dec. 31, 1941 married Barbara Carden (number 1057)

1-3-17-122-411   Robert Lee Hooper b. Sept. 1893 d. July 6, 1937 married Emy McClean (Internet *Ancestry.com, Alabama Deaths and Burials Index 1881-1974*)

1-3-17-122-412   Grace M. Hooper b. July 14, 1895 married James E. Plank

961.   Louise Plank b. abt. 1924

1-3-17-122-413   William Clinton Hooper b. Aug. 23, 1897 d. Oct. 3, 1937 married Anne Marie McIntire

962.   Frances Hooper b. abt. 1922 married Quinten Brown

963.   Clinton McIntire Hooper b. March 2, 1931 married Sharon Sipple b. Nov. 13, 1939

1-3-17-122-414   Roy K. C. Hooper b. Oct. 21, 1899 d. Oct. 8, 1918

1-3-17-122-415   Mary Della Hooper b. April 24, 1902 d. Sept. 15, 1903

1-3-17-122-416   Charles Clarence Hooper b. Feb. 27, 1904 d. July 3, 1962 married Ersa Baker b. Aug. 20, 1913

1-3-17-122-417   Etta May Hooper b. July 19, 1906 d. Aug. 17, 1906

1-3-17-122-418   Pauline Hooper b. March 1, 1911 married James Lee Sullivan

964.   James Lee Sullivan, Jr. b. Sept. 26, 1937

965.   Joseph E. Sullivan b. Sept. 24, 1940

966.   Jane Sullivan b. Dec. 1, 1944

1-3-17-123-419   Mattie Eads Oct. 15, 1884 d. March 21, 1918 married on March 13, 1904 in Bradley County, TN to Charlie Shamblin b. Feb. 18, 1879 d. Jan. 30, 1950 moved to Maricopa, Arizona before 1920 where he remarried to Ida M. Totten and had a step-son Richard Totten.

967.   Clara M. Shamblin b. 1909

968.   C. L. Shamblin b. 1911

969.   Telles E. Shamblin b. 1912

1-3-17-123-420   Icye May Eads Aug. 14, 1887-May 8, 1888

1-3-17-123-421   William Telles Eads Jan. 21, 1890-June 10, 1910

1-3-17-123-422   Mary Elmiry Eads Nov. 17, 1894-Sept. 18, 1895

1-3-17-123-423   Charles Jahew Eads b. March 22, 1987 d. March 30, 1979 married on June 26, 1927 in Bradley County, TN to Mary Moore b. April 1, 1906 d. Nov. 1, 1993 (*Heritage of Bradley County, Tennessee 1836-1998* submitted by Charles J. Eads, Jr.)

970.   Charles J. Eads, Jr.

971.   Mildred Josephine Eads
972.   Raymond Moore Eads married July 23, 1966 in Bradley County, TN to Etta Louise
        Pulliam b. July 7, 1938 d. March 18, 2008
973.   John Floyd Eads
974.   Calvin Lloyd Eads
1-3-17-123-424   Bertha Eads Oct. 28, 1901-March 2, 1897 married on June 6, 1920 in Bradley County,
        TN to N. J. Pardue Jan. 9, 1886-April 7, 1975
975.   Martha E. Pardue b. 1922
976.   Beulah Pardue b. 1924
1-3-17-123-425   Gurtha Eads Oct. 28, 1901-March 2, 1995 married on Nov. 1943 to Doyle Martin 1900-
        1968
1-3-17-125-426   Lee J. Hooper b. April 1900
1-3-17-125-427   James Ernest Hooper b. Jan. 24, 1903 d. Dec. 1974 married Patricia Estelle Leamon
        (number 807) b. March 30, 1908 – d. Dec. 5, 1990 in Oak Ridge, TN (*KeithMillsStewart*
        at Internet, *Ancestry.com*)
977.   Earnesteen Hooper b. abt. 1924
978.   Anabell Hooper b. abt. 1927
979.   Bettie J. Hooper b. abt. 1929
1-3-17-125-428   Infant March 27, 1911 – April 3, 1911
1-3-17-126-429   Bruce Hooper b. April 14, 1905 d. Sept. 1971 married Mable Morgan b. Feb. 3, 1912 d.
        Jan.1968
980.   Infant Nov. 28, 1934
981.   Lillian Hooper married William L. Hall
982.   Bruce Hooper b. 1940 d. Oct. 22, 2013 married Jo Ann Hughes
983.   Bernard Hooper b. Oct. 17, 1943 d. Dec. 18, 2007 married 1. ?   2. Jenna Morrison
        Guinn (Internet, *The Chattanoogan.com* December 23, 2015) b. June 4, 1936 d. Oct.
        20, 2012
1-3-17-126-430   Gladys Evelyn Hooper b. Dec. 24, 1906 married Buford William Goins on March 15,
        1925 in Bradley County, TN (*Internet, Ancestry.com*)
1-3-17-126-431   Boyd Hooper b. April 4, 1911 d. Oct. 1983 married on Dec. 11, 1933 in Bradley County,
        TN to Mary Louise Smalling b. Jan. 11, 1917 d. Jan. 1982 (Internet, *Ancestry.com*).
984.   Boyd Milton Hooper married Ruth Lawson
985.   William Kins Hooper married Mabel Jones (Internet, *Ancestry.com, Findagrave.com*
        for Imogene "Jean" Gore 2007)
986.   Midge (Rose Margaret) Hooper married 1.   Jim Cody 2. Zeno Beaty
1-3-17-127-432   Mary Olie Ownby b. Sept. 8, 1890 – Oct. 10, 1970 married John M. Crook in Fulton
        County, GA on June 21, 1904. He died April 4, 1951 (Internet *Find A Grave* at
        Ancestry.com).
987.   John M. Crook, Jr. b. Jan. 22, 1905 – Feb. 15, 1978
1-3-17-127-433   Lloyd McKinley Ownbey b. Sept. 2, 1896 in TN d. June 15, 1957 in Los Angeles, CA.
        He married Irene R. Bailey on Jan. 4, 1919 in Los Angeles, CA (Internet, *Ancestry.com,
        lightkeeperswellness, Tennessee Delayed Birth Records* and *California, Death Index*)
988.   Dorothy A. Ownbey b. 1921
989.   Irene M. Ownbey b. 1923
1-3-17-127-434   Charles Louis Ownbey b. Oct. 2, 1900 – d. Dec. 23, 1978 in Riverside, CA (Internet,
        Ancestry.com, lightkeeperswellness, Tennessee Delayed Birth Records and *California,
        Death Index*) married Liliane R.
990.   Jack F. Ownbey b. 1922
991.   Eloise O. Ownbey b. 1926
992.   Robert C. Ownbey b. 1933
1-3-18-129-435   Luther L. Boggs b. April 1881
1-3-18-129-436   Mary L. Boggs b. June 1888 married Tom Woods b. abt. 1889 Pittsburgh, OK
993.   Tommie Woods b. abt. 1910
994.   Samuel Woods b. abt. 1912
995.   Jay R. Woods b. abt. 1916
1-3-18-129-437   Hattie M. Boggs b. Nov. 1889

1-3-18-129-438   Laura G. Boggs b. July 1891
1-3-18-129-439   Henry A. Boggs b. Aug. 1893 married Grace b. abt. 1895
     996.   Harold Boggs b. abt. 1913 Latimer, OK
1-3-18-133-440   Edgar Ellis b. Feb. 12, 1889 in Arkansas d. Oct. 20, 1972 in Oklahoma
1-3-18-133-441   Allie Ellis b. Aug. 1894 in Indian Territory
1-3-18-133-442   Jesse Ellis b. Nov. 3, 1897 in Indian Territory d. May 30, 1984 in Elkhart, Kansas
        married Ollie Vera Matthews on Feb. 24, 1922 in Sequoyah County, OK (*radnofdixie* at
        Internet, *Ancestry.com*)
     997.   Eula May Ellis 1922-1923
     998.   Sula Fay Ellis 1922-1923
     999.   James Theodore Ellis 1924-2002
    1000.   Clifford Hurley Ellis March 7, 1927-July 21, 1932
    1001.   Fonda Bernice Ellis June 19, 1930-Jan. 27, 2010
    1002.   David Dale Ellis 1934-2002
    1003.   Infant 1943
1-3-18-133-443   Jami C. Ellis (dau.) 1906 b. Oklahoma
1-3-18-133-444   Cora Ellis b. 1908 in Oklahoma
1-3-18-133-445   Mary Ellis b. 1911 in Oklahoma
1-3-18-133-446   Flora Ellis b. 1913 in Oklahoma
1-3-18-133-447   Billy Ellis b. 1915 in Oklahoma
1-3-19-135-448   Walter Hooper b. 1885 d. 1962 married Epsie Bridges b. 1890 d. 1962
    1004.   Arlie Franklin Hooper b. Oct. 27, 1910 (MO) d. Nov. 30, 1990 (Internet *California
    Death Index* at *Ancestry.com*)
    1005.   Harlon J. Hooper b. May 9, 1912 (MO) d. Jan. 22, 1990 (Internet *California Death
    Index* at *Ancestry.com*)
1-3-19-135-449   Barbara Allice Hooper b. 1887 d. 1976 married 1. Robert Jenkins b. abt. 1885 2. John
    Hall b. abt. 1878 (lived at Kansas City, Kansas)
    1006.   Ava Jenkins b. abt. 1907
    1007.   Andy Jenkins b. abt. 1909
    1008.   Alba Jenkins (dau.) b. abt. 1911
    1009.   Owen Jenkins b. abt. 1913
    1010.   Billie Jenkins (son) b. abt. 1918
    1011.   Donald Hall Jenkins b. abt. 1929
1-3-19-135-450   Jane Hooper b. 1888 d. 1952 married John Brogdon b. abt. 1884
    1012.   Henry Brogdon b. abt. 1907
    1013.   Pearl Brogdon b. abt. 1911
1-3-19-135-451   Norma Hooper b. 1890 d. 1938 married Charles Logan
1-3-19-135-452   Bessie Hooper b. 1892 d. 1966 married Earl Griffin b. abt. 1884
    1014.   Walter E. Griffin b. abt. 1913
    1015.   David E. Griffin b. abt. 1915
1-3-19-136-453   John William Hooper b. 1914 d. 1917
1-3-19-136-454   Charles Ray Hooper, Sr. b. 1916 d. 1966 married Rosaltha Cowelti b. Oct. 20, 1922 d.
    Oct. 20, 2010
    1016.   Winnie Yvonne Hooper b. 1945 married R. J. Fulton
    1017.   Charles Ray Hooper, Jr. b. Nov. 12, 1948 in Denver, CO and d. Sept. 6, 2006 in
    Cimarron, NM. He married Shirley Cunico b. 1954 (Internet, *Ancestry.com,
    Findagrave.com*)
1-3-19-138-455   Allen Miller b. abt. 1910
1-3-19-138-456   Edith Miller b. abt. 1912
1-3-19-138-457   Arline Miller b. abt. 1916
1-3-19-138-458   Roy Miller b. abt. 1918
1-3-20-140-459   Burl/Oral D. Hooper b. abt. 1902
1-3-20-140-460   Harley Hooper b. abt. 1914
1-3-20-140-461   Evelyn Hooper b. abt. 1917
1-3-20-140-462   Leonard Hooper b. abt. 1922 m. Hazel Kinnamon (See p. 131 for more information.)
1-3-20-140-463   Meribe Hooper (dau.) b. abt. 1926

1-3-20-141-464   Larman Dobbs b. July 1899
1-3-20-141-465   Golda C. Dobbs b. abt. 1901
1-3-20-141-466   Bethel B. Dobbs b. abt. 1903
1-3-20-141-467   Alta M. Dobbs b. abt. 1906
1-3-20-142-468   Lloyd C. Knight b. abt. 1904
1-3-20-142-469   Don W. Knight b. abt. 1906
1-3-20-142-470   Herman Knight b. abt. 1911
1-3-20-144-471   Hobert Lou Summers b. abt. 1908
1-3-20-144-472   Blanche Summers b. abt. 1911
1-3-20-144-473   Violet Summers b. abt. 1921
1-3-20-144-474   Cecil Summers b. abt. 1925
1-3-20-144-475   Lyman Summers b. abt. 1929
1-3-20-146-476   Garland Hooper b. 1927
1-3-20-146-477   Marion Hooper b. May 3, 1928 d. April 13, 1964 married Willa Lee Schnitker in 1952 (Internet, *Ancestry.com, Findagrave.com* and Speaks Family Legacy Chapels)
1018.   Randall K. Hooper (had MS and died at 30 at Independence, MO)
1019.   Belinda G. Hooper (had cancer and died at 25 at Independence, MO)
1020.   Gary Wayne Hooper
1-3-20-146-478   Harold Hooper b. March 6, 1930 d. March 16, 1992 married Mary Lou Vittetoe
1021.   Daniel Hooper
1022.   Dawn Hooper married Sam Wiggins
1023.   David Hooper
1024.   Garland Hooper
1-3-20-146-479   Iona May Hooper married Marvin Edge
1-3-20-146-480   Robert Hooper b. August 12, 1947 married Glatha Goldston
1025.   Gregory Hooper b. Sept. 13, 1969 married Lynn Hogan
1026.   Jeffrey Hooper
1-3-21-147-481   Argus Reed Hooper July 7, 1897 d. Nov. 1970 married Oma D. b. abt. 1895
1-3-21-147-482   Willis L. Hooper b. abt. 1905 married Edith L. b. abt. 1908
1-3-21-147-483   Chester R. Hooper b. June 13, 1909 d. Feb. 1984 married Aline b. abt. 1911
1-3-21-147-484   James Herbert Hooper b. abt. 1914
1-3-21-148-485   Clarcie M. Hooper b. April 29, 1901 married George K. Dechow b. June 6, 1898 d. Oct. 1974
1027.   George K. Dechow b. Sept. 18, 1944 married Karen Dian Springer
1-3-21-148-486   George Francis Hooper b. April 22, 1910 d. May 21, 1997 married Mary McNabb
1028.   William L. Hooper b. Sept. 16, 1931 married Doris Jean Wallace
1029.   Robert Hooper b. July 11, 1936 married Sylvia Bell
1030.   David McNabb Hooper b. Jan. 19, 1942 married Jane Frances Miller
1-3-21-150-487   Minnie Johnson b. April 1895
1-3-21-150-488   Charles G. Johnson b. Oct. 1897
1-3-21-151-489   Charles Thomas Meadors b. April 25, 1899 d. Jan. 4, 1990 married Velma Ida Little
1031.   Betty Jo Meadors b. Nov. 7, 1936 married Lendsie Gardnerr
1-3-21-152-490   Gilbert G. Hooper b. June 28, 1912 d. Nov. 9, 1994 married Willie Dee Pitts
1032.   Shirley Joan Hooper b. June 28, 1912 married Robert E. Mace
1-3-21-154-491   Owen Ray Hooper b. Sept. 25, 1912 d. Jan. 17, 1979 (Los Angeles) married Irene
1033.   Judy Hooper
1-3-21-154-492   Edna May Hooper b. abt. 1916 married Everett Fletcher
1034.   Kay Fletcher
1-3-17-154-493   Francis Hooper b. abt. 1918
1-3-21-155-494   Helen Roy b. Aug. 11, 1910 m. George Figge
1-3-21-155-495   Thomas L. Roy b. Sept. 1, 1913 – d. March 18, 2010 m. Edna Greenfield
1035.   Donna Roy b. Jan. 28, 1939 d. Oct. 8, 1950
1036.   Bill Roy b. Oct. 3, 1940
1037.   Bob Roy b. Feb. 11, 1945
1038.   Helen Roy b. Sept. 19, 1951
1039.   Shirley Roy b. May 28, 1957

1-3-21-155-496 Jack Roy b. April 10, 1916
1-3-21-155-497 Lynn Roy b. March 1922
1-3-21-156-498 Garrett Lee Grisham b. Jan. 30, 1907 d. Mar. 23 1969 m. Leda Richards
  1040. James Lee Grisham April 7, 1935 married Ramadean Taylor
1-3-21-156-499 Lucy Marie Pitts b. June 11, 1915 m. Ivan Noal Breshears
  1041. Joan Marie Breshears b. June 18, 1941 married Thomas A. Northrip
  1042. Mary Ethel Breshears
  1043. Infant son
  1044. Ivan Noel Breshears b. Nov. 5, 1946 married Mary Beth Mayfield
1-3-21-156-500 Kenneth N. Pitts b. July 26, 1918 married Virgia M. Green
  1045. Willeta Kay Pitts b. Nov. 24, 1944 married Robert J. Blake
  1046. Peggy Ann Pitts b. May 16, 1946 married Noel J. Shull
  1047. Gloria Jean Pitts b. Nov. 16, 1949 married James E. McIntire
  1048. Rebecca Ilene Pitts Oct. 30, 1956 married James Reynolds
1-3-21-156-501 Bonnie Gene Pitts b. March 5, 1921 m. 1st Albert Degraffenreid on Feb. 24, 1940 in Hickory County, MO, and 2nd Fred Hulston, 3rd Merlin Shively
  1049. Carolyn Sue Degraffenreid b. March 15, 1942 d. Dec. 29, 1946
1-3-22-157-502 Ruth E. Jack b. abt. 1897 (TX)
1-3-22-157-503 Clyde Jack (dau.) b. abt. 1902 (TX)
1-3-22-157-504 James B. Jack b. Dec. 6, 1903 d. Dec. 1974 (Tarrant Co., Fort Worth, TX)
1-3-22-158-505 Pearl Jack b. abt. 1896 (TX)
1-3-22-158-506 Geneva Jack b. abt. 1905 (TX)
1-3-22-159-507 Mary A. Jack b. abt. 1905 (TX)
1-3-22-159-508 Josephine Jack b. abt. 1907 (TX)
1-3-22-159-509 Francis Jack (dau.) b. abt. 1909 (TX)
1-3-22-159-510 Ora Lou Jack b. abt. 1912 (TX)
1-3-22-161-511 Mary J. Jack b. abt. 1912 (TX)
1-3-22-161-512 Helen J. Jack b. abt. 1921 (TX)
1-3-22-161-513 John C. Jack, Jr. b. Aug. 8, 1923 married Betty J. Young on Sept. 9, 1983 (Hunt County, TX found at Internet *Ancestry.com*)
1-4-25-167-514 Miller E. Peron b. 1895 b. Nov. 23, 1894 d. April 9, 1982 in San Bernardino, CA married Ana b. 1901 in Oklahoma (*1930 San Bernardino, CA Census*, Cucamonga, p. 16 B found at Internet *Ancestry.com*)
  1050. Lois Perian b. 1921 in Oklahoma
  1051. Louise Perian b. 1923
  1052. Arvil Perian b.1930 in California
1-4-25-167-515 Isaac F. Peron b. 1896
1-4-25-167-516 Johny Green Peron b. April 15, 1898 d. March 17, 1929 married Anna Hamby on Nov. 13, 1918 in Polk County, TN
1-4-25-167-517 Sarah E. Peron b. 1900
1-4-25-167-518 Vilila N. Peron b. 1902
1-4-25-167-519 Absolam Peron b. 1906
1-4-25-167-520 Lillie Peron b. 1907
1-4-25-167-521 Luster Peron b. 1909 married Evelin Withrow April 27, 1936 in Polk County, TN
1-4-25-167-522 J. P. Perion b. Feb. 28, 1911 d. Oct. 2, 1971 married Aug. 27, 1933 to Julia Jenkins in Polk County, TN and were in the *1940 Polk County Census* Second Dist. p. 13 B. She was born Jan. 27, 1913 d. Nov. 13, 2001
  1053. J. P. Perian, Jr. b. 1935
1-4-25-167-523 Sanford Perion b. 1914 married Helen Jenkins on Oct. 1, 1933 in Polk County, TN.
  1054. James Sanford Perian b. 1936
  1055. Donnie Coralee Perian b. 1937
  1056. George Winston Perian b. 1939
1-4-25-168-524 Lizzie Perring 1891
1-4-25-168-525 Donil Perring 1898
1-4-25-168-526 Harvey Perrin b. July 15, 1907 d. June 4, 1983
1-4-30-177-527 Bertha Carden 1908

1-4-30-177-528   Lester Carden 1911
1-4-30-177-529   Ethel Carden 1913
1-4-30-177-530   Clifford Carden Sept. 23, 1914 married Naomi Watson on Dec. 15, 1938 in Bradley
        County, TN (Internet *Ancestry.com*)
    1057.   Barbara Carden m. Wayne Harrison Hooper (number 960)
    1058.   Billy Carden m. Jeannie Russell
    1058A. Judy Evelyn Carden m. James Edwin McCracken
    1058B. Carolyn Carden m. Jack Green
    1059.   Ronnie Carden m. Rosie Juanita Prater on Jan. 28, 1972 in Polk County, TN (Internet,
        Ancestry.com, Polk County, TN)
    1059A. Wanda Carden m. Glenn David McCracken on August 28, 1971 in Bradley County, TN
        (Internet, *Ancestry.com*, Bradley County, TN)
    1059B. Gary Carden m. (1) Mary Lisa Hickman; (2) Letha Rene Rodriguez-Chapman; (3)
        Gayla Higgins
1-4-30-177-531   Hazel Carden 1917
1-4-30-177-532   Amos Carden 1918
1-4-30-177-533   Rossie Mae Carden 1922
1-4-30-177-534   Ruth Carden 1925
1-4-30-177-535   Charles Carden 1928
1-4-30-177-536   Ruby Evelyn Carden 1930
1-4-30-178-537   Cori M. Pike Aug. 1898
1-4-30-179-538   Lela Pike 1907 (OK, *Custer County 1930 Census, Ancestry.com*)
1-4-30-179-539   Bertha Pike 1909 b. OK
1-4-30-179-540   Helen Pike 1912 b. OK
1-4-30-179-541   Jesse Pike 1913 b. OK
1-4-30-179-542   Charlie Pike 1915 b. OK
1-4-30-179-543   Dorothy Pike 1918 b. OK
1-4-30-179-544   Morine Pike 1921 b. OK
1-4-30-179-545   Ivona Pike 1925 b. OK
1-4-33-183-546   William Claude Harris b. Oct. 19, 1902 d. Sept. 1, 1972 married Marcella (information
        from Internet *Ancestry.com in grbsr09 Rymer Family*)
1-4-33-183-547   Catherine Lee (Katie) Harris b. Nov. 1, 1903 d. Sept. 30, 1972 married Frank Brundage
        on May 27, 1932 in Custer County, Oklahoma (Internet *Ancestry.com, grbsr09 Rymer*
        Family)
    1060.   Truman Francis (Frank) Brundage
    1061.   Shirley Jean Brundage
    1062.   Billie Gene Brundage
1-4-33-183-548   Victoria Harris b. April 15, 1905 d. Oct. 14, 1996 married Smith Herring (*grbsr09*
        Rymer Family, Internet *Ancestry.com*)
1-4-33-183-549   James Harris b. Jan. 28, 1907 married Lucille (*grbsr09 Rymer Family*)
1-4-33-183-550   Samuel E. Harris b. 1910 married Thelma Matthews (*grbsr09 Rymer Family*)
    1063.   Loraine Harris
1-4-33-183-551   George Harris b. Feb. 22, 1917 d, March 24, 1990 married Maxine Chittenden
    1064.   Sammie E. Harris
    1065.   Ronnie Harris
    1066.   Vickie Jean Harris
1-4-33-184-552   Hershel V. Hooper b. Dec. 30, 1899 married Ruby Bright
    1067.   Jo Helene Hooper
    1068.   William Bright Hooper
    1069.   Hershel Victor Hooper
1-4-33-185-553   Sanford G. Hooper 1909 m. unknown 1. and 2.
    1070.   Sandra Sue Hooper by the first wife
    1071.   John David Hooper by the second wife
1-4-33-185-554   Absolom Hooper 1915 worked for oil companies in South America and Arabia
1-4-33-185-555   Dorothy Hooper b. 1924 married John Cooke
    1072.   Cindy Cooke

1073.	Candi Cooke
1-4-33-186-556	Lois Hooper b. 1915 Ebert Orr Simpson
1074.	Ethel Mae Simpson
1075.	Maxwell David Simpson
1-4-33-186-557	Robert Wayne Hooper b. 1921 married Marjorie Wilson
1076.	Dianne Hooper
1077.	John Robert Hooper b. 1954
1078.	David Wayne Hooper b. 1961
1-4-33-186-558	Russell A. Hooper b. 1926 married Charlene Parks
1079.	Charsell Hooper
1080.	Kevin Isaac Hooper b. 1956
1081.	Kile Parks Hooper b. 1964
1-4-33-187-559	Frank Hooper b. 1913 married Marvel Ferrel
1082.	Richard Enos Hooper
1083.	Gary Hooper
1084.	Thomas Hooper b. 1948
1085.	Douglas Hooper b. 1953
1-4-33-187-560	Ethel Hooper b. 1915 married Theodore Gripe
1086.	Ronnie Gripe
1-4-33-187-561	Grace Hooper b. 1919 married Monar Dickerson
1087.	Stephen Dickerson
1-4-33-187-562	James E. Hooper b. 1928 married Mary Belle Eyster
1088.	James Warren Hooper b. 1953
1089.	Anthony Kent Hooper b. 1955
1090.	Mary Sue Hooper
1-4-33-188-563	Olen Neal Potter b. 1905 married Jennie Coy
1091.	A. L. Potter
1092.	Robert Olen Potter
1093.	Don Coy Potter
1-4-33-188-564	Henry J. Potter b. 1908 married Bernice Floyd
1094.	Bryan Henry Potter
1-4-33-188-565	Dessie Potter b. 1920 married John Morrison
1095.	Gary Morrison
1096.	Nana Beth Morrison
1-4-33-189-566	Elbert Lee Campbell b. 1913 married Avis Applegate
1097.	Billy Gene Campbell
1-4-33-189-567	Paul Hooper Campbell b. 1914 married Clenavive Mitchell
1098.	Pauline Campbell
1099.	Ann Campbell
1-4-33-189-568	Opal Campbell b. 1916 married Devert Hastey
1100.	Beth Hastey
1-4-33-189-569	Katherine Campbell b. 1920 married Bennet Marcoux
1-4-33-190-570	Joseph L. Ryan married Twila Ballew
1101.	Sammy Joe Ryan
1102.	Donnie Wayne Ryan
1103.	Terry Dean Ryan
1-4-33-193-571	Frances Clair Hooper b. 1939 married Stanley Cotts
1104.	Tracy Lee Cotts
1-4-33-193-572	Samuel Edward Hooper b. 1942 married Kay Beach
1-4-34-194-573	William Hayden Hooper b. Aug. 4, 1898 d. Oct. 1975 (Custer, OK) married 1. Madeline Fern Pollett on Oct. 4, 1919 in Custer County, OK
1105.	Carl Truman Hooper b. June 26, 1920 – d. Dec. 30, 2003 in Boulder, CO. He married (1.) Genevieve Green and (2.) Sylvia Gurney on July 4, 1962
1106.	Anita Vyrle Hooper b. Oct. 4, 1926 married H. L. Christensen, Jr.
1107.	Venita Pearl Hooper b. Oct. 4, 1926 married 1. Keith Christensen and 2. Worth Cornelius

1108.   Ann Marie Hooper b. Feb. 7, 1934 married William Kinslow Harrison
1-4-34-194-574 Nora G. Hooper b. abt.1902 (OK) married Hershel Moore
    1109.   Donald Moore
    1110.   Mary Ellen Moore
    1111.   Wanda Moore
    1112.   Joann Moore
1-4-34-194-575 Minnie Ola Hooper b. abt. 1904 (OK) died July 3, 1925 and married Leslie Moore
    1113.   Leslie Ray Moore b. July 3, 1925 d. May 15, 1992 in Texas
1-4-34-194-576 Lola Ruth Hooper b. abt. 1909 (OK) lived to be 11 years old
1-4-34-194-577 Charley Hooper b. abt. 1913 (OK) married Grace Windsor
    1114.   Gary Hooper b. 1941
    1115.   Larry Hooper b. 1953
1-4-34-194-578 Pearl Hooper b. abt. 1915 (OK) married Glenn Ayling
    1116.   Larry Allen Ayling 1941
1-4-34-194-579 Nelley Hooper b. abt. 1918 (OK)
1-4-34-194-580 Reece Hooper Feb. 2, 1921-Oct. 6, 1925
1-4-34-196-581 Lillian Bell Hooper b. March 18, 1902 in Polk County, TN d. Jan. 19, 1994 in Knox
    County, TN (Internet, *Ancestry.com, Dona Lynn Carr Family Tree*) married Roland
    Payne on May 22, 1921 in Polk County, TN
    1117.   Ralph Payne
    1118.   Billy Payne
    1119.   Donald Payne
1-4-34-196-582 Stella Hooper b. Aug. 29, 1903 in Polk County, TN (*Delayed Birth Certificate on
    Internet Ancestry.com*) married Claude Griffith
    1120.   Wilburn Griffith
    1121.   Bobby Ruth Griffith
1-4-34-196-583 Luther Hooper b. 1907 – Oct. 28, 1954 married Oct. 30, 1929 to Toy Birchfield in
    McMinn County, TN. She was born Feb. 14, 1910 - d. Sept. 14, 2002
    1122.   Jackson Hooper
    1123.   Jerry Hooper
1-4-34-196-584 Alonzo (Lon) Hooper July 15, 1907-July 21, 1985 married on March 30, 1940 in
    McMinn County, TN to Nina Grant b. 1918 - d. Dec. 8, 1999
    1124.   Joe Allen Hooper
1-4-34-196-585 Amos (Bud) Hooper 1912 married Ida Pangle Oct. 5, 1914-Feb. 2, 2001
    1125.   Deborah Hooper
1-4-34-196-586 Lucy Hooper b. 1915 married Joseph Smith
    1126.   Deloris Smith
    1127.   Joyce Smith
    1128.   James Smith
    1129.   Kenneth Smith
1-4-34-196-587 Kenneth B. Hooper Sept. 20, 1919-May 11, 1991 married Imogene Black b. Jan. 2,
    1920 - Feb. 1, 2004
    1130.   Tommy Dan Hooper married Laura Hood on March 16, 1962 in McMinn County, TN
    1131.   Eddie Kenneth Hooper married Glenda Wilson
    1132.   Loretta Gail Hooper married (1) B. W. Cooley on April 22, 1966 in McMinn County,
    TN and (2) Arnold Sledge. (Thanks, Gail, for information about the Kenneth Hooper
    family.)
    1133.   Robert Michael Hooper married Mitzi Crabtree
1-4-34-197-588 Myrtle Davis b. 1901
1-4-34-197-589 Pearl Davis b. 1903
1-4-34-197-590 Arthur Davis b. 1909
1-4-34-197-591 Clyde Davis b. 1912
1-4-34-197-592 Wayne Davis b. 1916
1-4-34-197-593 Thelma Davis b. 1918
1-4-34-197-594 Inez Davis b. 1922
1-2-5-38-206-595 John Ray Shelton b. Nov.6, 1890 – d. May 14, 1966 Garland, TX married Monta

Alexander (Texas *Death Certificate* for Edward M. Shelton Dallas, TX)

1134. Edward Shelton b. Nov. 24, 1913 – d. Nov. 8, 1982
1135. Elmo Shelton b. June 8, 1916 – d. Jan. 25, 2009
1136. Ima Well Shelton b. Sept. 3, 1918 – Nov. 18, 2010
1137. John Shelton, Jr. April 15, 1920 – d. Sept. 6, 1990
1138. Imogene Shelton Feb. 22, 1924 – d. March 9, 2000
1139. Maxine Shelton 1927
1140. Kenneth R. Shelton July 12, 1927 – d. Aug. 11, 2007

1-2-5-38-206-596 Ida Hasseltine Shelton b. Apr. 1892 (May 14, 1894) – d. June 1, 1934 Lancaster, TX
1-2-5-38-206-597 Frances May Shelton b. Oct. 25, 1893 – Jan. 22, 1982 Dallas, TX
1-2-5-38-206-598 Beulah Viola Shelton b. June 13, 1896 – d. Feb. 7, 1999 Garland, TX
1-2-5-38-206-599 Havus L. Shelton b. August 1898
1-2-5-38-206-600 Bonita Shelton b. Oct. 20, 1899
1-2-5-38-206-601 Myrtle Shelton b. 1903
1-2-5-38-206-602 Robert Bonner Shelton b. July 19, 1906 – d. Dec. 30, 1983
1-2-5-38-206-603 Mammie Shelton b. 1906
1-2-5-38-206-604 Maggie Shelton b. 1914
1-2-5-38-206-605 W. D. Shelton, Jr. b. 1918
1-2-5-38-206-606 Janine Shelton b. 1920
1-2-5-38-206-607 Robbie L. Shelton (dau.) 1925
1-2-5-42-208-608 Virginia Walker
1-2-5-42-212-609 Bruce Lamar Ethridge
1-2-5-42-212-610 Marla Shelton Ethridge married Aubrey Mitchell
1-2-5-46-213-611 John Wesley Dawn, Jr. 1938-1990 (Internet, *bookemon,* ch. Erin and Anna Dawn)
1-2-5-46-213-612 Marla Jo Dawn 1941-1972 (Internet, *bookemon*, ch. may be Jamie Peters)
1-2-5-49-220-613 Patricia Joane Harr b. Aug. 2, 1937
1-2-5-49-221-614 Sandra Kay Furbush b. Aug. 7, 1944
1-2-5-49-221-615 Jacqueline Lee Furbush b. March 20, 1946
1-2-7-67-229-616 George Lewis Saulpaw b. Dec. 23, 1905 – Aug. 12, 1976 married Estelle Taylor (Internet, Saulpaw, *rpevans.org* see p. 54 for the documentation for Saulpaw.)
1141. George Lewis Saulpaw, Jr. died 1987 in California
1-2-7-67-229-617 Zillah Saulpaw b. Oct. 7, 1907 – March 1, 1990 married Lee Bryant on Feb. 23, 1927 in Rhea County, TN
1142. Charles L. Bryant b. 1928 married Lucille Kays
1143. Lillah Catherine Bryant b. Feb. 23, 1929-May 18, 1929 (Tennessee, *Death Index Ancestry.com*)
1-2-7-67-229-618 Hattie Weston Saulpaw b. Feb. 4, 1910 – d. Oct. 1983 and married (1) Frank Seaton, (2) Claude Jackson and (3) Mack Knight (Internet *rpevans1.home.comcast.net*).
1144. Virginia Lee Seaton married John Morgan Taylor, 3rd in Claiborne Co., TN May 10, 1954 (Internet *Ancestry.com*)
1-2-7-67-229-619 Pyott Davis Saulpaw b. May 14, 1912, d. August 21,1969 married Frances Little (Internet *rpevans1.home.comcast.net*)
1-2-7-67-229-620 Bernard H. Saulpaw b. Dec. 3, 1914
1-2-7-67-229-621 Karl D. Saulpaw, Jr. b. Nov. 2, 1920-Aug. 5, 1994 (Department of Veteran Affairs Death File at *Ancestry.com*) married Dorothy Spearman b. Feb. 14, 1928-Oct. 21, 2011 (*Knoxville News Sentinel* on Oct. 25, 2011) and (Internet *Ron Evans' Genealogy Page rpevans.org*)
1145. Karl Davenport Saulpaw, 3rd
1146. Glen Wright Saulpaw b. July 31, 1951 – June 22, 1998 married Beverly Rogers Crye
1147. Sarah Ann Werman-Saulpaw b. Oct. 19, 1953 – June 11, 1999
1148. James Richard Saulpaw (Saulpaw information on Internet at *rpevans.org*)
1149. Charles Erich Saulpaw
1-2-7-67-229-622 Jack Saulpaw b. Jan. 16, 1924-Dec. 16, 1995
1-2-7-67-229-623 Doris Saulpaw b. 1926 married James E. Brown (Internet *rpevans.org*)
1150. Kathyrn Brown

1151.	Mitchell R. Brown
1152.	Michael L. Brown
1153.	Teresa Brown
1-2-7-67-229-624	Elizabeth Ann (Betty) Saulpaw b. Jan. 11, 1928-d. Jan. 22, 2011 married (1) Wilson Hutcheson and (2) William Raimonde according to *Calvin Dodson, Sr.* on *Ancestry.com*
1154.	Jane Ellen Hutcheson (Internet *Ron Evans' Genealogy Page rpevans.org*)
1155.	Emma Elizabeth Hutcheson
1-2-9-84-242-625	Raymond Farmer b. 1915 married Beulah
1156.	Raymond Farmer b. 1939
1-2-9-84-242-626	Stanley G. Farmer b. Jan. 25, 1919 d. Nov. 13, 2006 married Helen Marie Lowry b. Aug. 12, 1918 d. July 31, 2003 (Internet *U. S. Veterans Gravesites* at *Ancestry.com*)
1-2-9-84-242-627	Naomi Ruth Farmer b. 1927
1-2-12-93-246-628	Ellen R. Graves b. 1931 married Thomas Castleberry of Pittsburgh, PA
1-2-12-93-246-629	James L. Graves b. 1934
1-2-12-93-246-630	Henry M. Graves b. 1937
1-2-12-93-246-631	Leutina Graves b. 1939
1-2-12-93-246-632	David Lynn Graves
1-3-14-98-260-633	Marion A. Graham b. Dec. 1886
1-3-14-98-260-634	Eugene T. Graham b. June 1888
1-3-14-98-260-635	Parker Graham 1896 (appears in 1910 but not in 1900)
1-3-14-98-260-636	Andy Graham b. 1906
1-3-14-98-260-637	Lester Graham b. 1908 married Dec. 16, 1926 in Sebastian County, Arkansas to Edna Webb
1157.	Betty Graham b. 1928
1158.	Coleen Graham b. 1931
1159.	Sue Graham b. 1932
1160.	Kathleen Graham b. 1936
1161.	Jo Ann Graham b. 1938
1-3-14-98-260-638	Lena Graham b. 1910
1-3-14-98-260-639	Dessie Graham b. 1913
1-3-14-98-260-640	Guy W. Graham b. Sept. 28, 1916 died March 1985
1-3-14-98-261-641	Emma J. Graham b. Oct. 1893
1-3-14-98-261-642	Newt D. Graham b. April 1896
1-3-14-98-261-643	Elsie Philura Graham b. Dec. 1899
1-3-14-98-261-644	Ida Graham b. abt. 1902
1-3-14-98-261-645	William Graham b. abt. 1908
1-3-14-98-261-646	Early Graham (son) b. abt. 1910
1-3-14-98-261-647	Ellen Graham b. abt. 1913
1-3-14-98-262-648	Lewis Graham, Jr. b. 1903
1-3-14-98-262-649	Claud Graham b. 1905
1-3-14-98-262-650	Doss Graham (dau.) b. 1907
1-3-14-98-263-651	Oliver Graham b. 1903
1-3-14-98-263-652	Ethel Graham b. 1905
1-3-14-98-263-653	Goldie Graham b. 1914
1-3-14-98-263-654	Rena Graham b. 1916
1-3-14-98-265-655	Benny Graham b. 1915
1-3-14-98-265-656	Clydie Graham b. 1918
1-3-14-98-265-657	Oscar Graham, Jr. b. 1920
1-3-14-99-266-658	Nettie L. Hooper b. Sept 1889
1-3-14-99-266-659	James Scott Hooper b. Sept. 28, 1891 d. Dec. 13, 1890 married Martha Jeanette Gilbreath (number 388) Oct. 10, 1909(Internet, *Ancestry.com*). Martha was b. July 24, 1892 d. June 12, 1984.
922.	Lynn Andrew Hooper b. Oct. 18, 1910 d. Feb. 21, 1973
923.	James Hoyt Hooper b. August 14, 1913-d. Aug. 22, 1915
924.	Edith Gertrude Hooper b. Oct. 30, 1918-d. April 24, 2008

1-3-14-99-266-660   Ollie Elizabeth Hooper b. Oct. 1894
1-3-14-99-266-661   Louie Hooper (dau.) b. Oct. 1896
1-3-14-99-266-662   Sim McKinley Hooper b. July 1, 1898 d. Oct. 1971 married (1) Ethel A. and (2) May
                                  Bell Pierce on June 21, 1967 in Polk County, TN.
        1162.   Mildred Hooper 1921
1-3-14-99-266-663   Glen Campbell Hooper b. abt. 1912
1-3-14-99-268-664   Mary Hooper
1-3-14-99-268-665   Merritt Hooper
1-3-14-99-268-666   Earl Hooper
1-3-14-99-270-667   Uva L. Bonner b. 1899
1-3-14-99-270-668   William P. Bonner b. 1900
1-3-14-99-270-669   Joseph F. Bonner b. 1903
1-3-14-99-270-670   John L. Bonner b. 1905
1-3-14-99-270-671   George Y. Bonner b. 1908
1-3-14-99-270-672   Claude Bonner b. 1910
1-3-14-99-271-673   Albert B. Catlett b. abt. 1905
1-3-14-99-271-674   Odessis Catlett b. abt. 1907
1-3-14-99-271-675   Dicie Catlett b. abt. 1908
1-3-14-99-271-676   Ada Catlett b. abt. 1910
1-3-14-99-271-677   Delvia Catlett b. abt. 1914
1-3-14-99-271-678   Bonney Catlett b. abt. 1915
1-3-14-99-271-679   Gore W. Catlett b. abt. 1917
1-3-14-99-273-680   Lucy Vona Erven b. March 4, 1903 married Dewey Manes
1-3-14-99-273-681   William Bonnie Erven b. Aug. 25, 1905
1-3-14-99-273-682   Lowell W. Erven b. Jan. 25, 1915 married Mildred Irene Gibson
        1163.   Nadine Erven b. March 27, 1935 married Duane R. Buckholz
1-3-14-99-273-683   Roscoe Guy Erven b. Aug. 17, 1923 married Mildred Vearl Jenkins
        1164.   Ronnie Dean Erven b. May 30, 1946 married Marinell Rayfield
1-3-14-99-274-684   Anthony Sawyer b. 1905
1-3-14-99-274-685   Zella Sawyer b. 1908
1-3-14-99-274-686   Robert Sawyer b. 1911
1-3-14-99-276-687   Lady Nasalroad b. Feb. 25, 1906 in Tunas, MO married Mark Taylor
1-3-14-99-276-688   Glade Nasalroad b. Feb. 17, 1908 d. 1975
1-3-14-99-276-689   Andrew Nasalroad b. Aug. 1, 1911 d. Jan. 2, 1989 m. Mary Lee Erven
1-3-14-99-276-690   Lonnie Nasalroad b. Feb. 21, 1914 in Sperry, OK m. Viola Garner
1-3-14-99-276-691   Hannah Nasalroad b. Nov. 3, 1917 in Shamrock, OK m. Claude Barham
1-3-14-99-276-692   Riley Carlton Nasalroad June 27, 1923 d. Jan. 26, 1943 (Marine WW II)
1-3-14-99-276-693   Fred McKinley Nasalroad b. Oct. 30, 1924 in Bristow, OK married Shirley Herzog
1-3-14-99-276-694   Betty Jo Nasalroad b. Jan. 1, 1926 m. Jim Lytle
1-3-14-99-276-695   Jaquolee Nasalroad b. Feb. 11, 1928 in Seminole, OK m. Carl Cook
1-3-14-99-276-696   Willard Ray Doc Nasalroad b. Sept. 23, 1931 in Polk, OK m. Shirley Eileen O'Neil
1-3-14-99-278-697   Dennis Huber b. abt. 1920
1-3-14-99-278-698   Nina Huber b. abt. 1923 married William Bonner
1-3-14-99-278-699   Zoe Huber b. abt. 1925 married Edward Drussel
1-3-14-99-278-700   Donal Huber b. abt. 1928
1-3-14-100-281-701   Bertha M. Hammond b. Dec. 1895
1-3-14-100-281-702   Flora D. Hammond b. Feb. 1900
1-3-14-100-281-703   James V. Hammond b. abt. 1909
1-3-14-100-281-704   Lowell Hammond b. abt. 1912
1-3-14-100-281-705   Lula Hammond b. abt. 1915
1-3-14-100-281-706   Culie Hammond b. abt. 1919
1-3-14-100-282-707   Earzey Pattillo (dau.) b. abt. 1907
1-3-14-100-282-708   Roy W. Pattillo b. abt. 1909
1-3-14-100-282-709   Owen Pattillo b. abt. 1913
1-3-14-100-282-710   Cleo Pattillo b. abt. 1915
1-3-14-100-283-711   Troy Hooper b. abt. 1914

1-3-14-100-283-712   Mollie Hooper b. abt. 1916
1-3-14-100-283-713   Albert Hooper b. abt. 1917
1-3-14-100-283-714   J. R. Hooper b. abt. 1921
1-3-14-100-283-715   Mildred Hooper b. abt. 1923
1-3-14-100-283-716   Benidict Hooper b. abt. 1927
1-3-14-100-284-717   Doyle F. Hooper b. 1911
1-3-14-100-284-718   Elsie Hooper b. 1912
1-3-14-100-284-719   J. T. Hooper b. 1913
1-3-14-100-284-720   Lela B. Hooper b. 1918
1-3-14-100-284-721   Haskel Hooper b. 1920
1-3-14-100-284-722   Lucille Hooper b. 1921
1-3-14-100-285-723   Carroll Hooper (son) b. abt. 1919
1-3-14-100-285-724   Thurman Hooper b. abt. 1922
1-3-14-100-288-725   Truman Hooper b. abt. 1918
1-3-14-100-288-726   Wayne Theron Hooper b. abt. 1920
1-3-14-100-289-727   Douglas W. Walton 1919
1-3-14-100-289-728   Otice or Otis Walton 1923
1-3-14-100-289-729   Mary J. Walton 1925
1-3-14-100-289-730   Kenneth Walton 1927
1-3-14-100-291-731   Thelma L. Bates 1924 (granddaughter living with William M. and Martha Consada
   Hooper in 1930) married Capt. William R. (Bill) Thompson on June 29, 1944 in
   OK (Internet, *Find A Grave.com*).
 1165. William R. Thompson Jr. and his wife, Linda
 1166. Thomas Thompson and his wife, Lesa
 1167. Ann Thompson married Frank Autrey
 1168. Patty Thompson married Tom Shipley
1-3-14-100-291-732   Johnny Edward Richardson b. Aug. 5, 1929 – July 22, 2000 married Dianna Rosetta
   Fairbanks b. July 27, 1940 – d. July 9, 2001 (Internet, *Find A Grave.com*).
 1169. Mark Earl Richardson b. Dec. 11, 1961 d. Dec. 11, 1977
 1170. Ronny Richardson married Sandra
 1171. Linda Sue Richardson married William Earnhart
1-3-14-100-291-733   Earnest Andrew Richardson b. Dec. 12, 1931 – Dec. 19, 1997 married Cleda Mae
   Rhoades on June 28, 1952 in Calera, OK (Internet, *Ancestry.com* by *stormylynn77*
 1172. Dennis Earl Richardson b. Jan. 10, 1959 – d. Oct. 2, 1993 married Vickie Melton on
  Dec. 6, 1980
 1173. Annette Richardson married a Burden
 1174. Sherry Richardson married a Townsend
 1175 Bonnie Richardson married a Rutherford
1-3-14-100-291-734   Althea Leona Richardson b. April 19, 1934 – Nov. 4, 2009 married James Leroy
   Beauchamp b. Jan 1, 1927 – d. Oct. 15, 1987 (Internet, Beauchamp, *Find A*
   Grave.com).
 1176. James Rhea Beauchamp
 1177. Jay Lee Beauchamp
 1178. Jim Ann Beauchamp married a Hill
1-3-14-100-291-735   Joy Fae Richardson b. June 19, 1938 married Walter R. Rambo on March 11, 1955,
   and divorced Feb. 7, 1995.
1-3-14-101-292-736   Benjamin Harrison Graham b. Aug. 31, 1892-June 1985 married Lena H. Pence on
   Aug. 6, 1916 in Sebastian County, Arkansas
 1179. Garrett Graham b. 1918
 1180. Sada Graham b. 1920
 1181. Rollen Graham b. 1923
 1182. Hallas Graham b. 1925
1-3-14-101-292-737   Walter H. Graham b. Nov. 1894
 1183. Unknown
1-3-14-101-292-738   Stella M. Graham b. Feb. 1897
1-3-14-101-292-739   Elmer Graham May 1899

1-3-14-101-292-740   Ruby Graham 1902
1-3-14-101-292-741   Arthur Graham 1904 married Ruby Irene Jones
      1184.   Roy Graham b. 1926
      1185.   Ralph Graham b. 1928
      1186.   Raymon Graham b. 1929
1-3-14-101-292-742   Ocie Graham 1908
1-3-14-101-292-743   Linda L. Graham 1911
1-3-14-101-295-744   Clarence Graham b. 1900
1-3-14-101-295-745   Lillia Graham b. 1906
1-3-14-101-295-746   Cletis Graham b. 1908 m. Ella May ?
1-3-14-101-295-747   Kermit Graham b. 1911 m. Ellen b. 1913
1-3-14-101-295-748   Thelma Graham b. 1914
1-3-14-101-295-749   Jess Graham b. 1917
1-3-14-101-295-750   Leonard Graham b. 1918
1-3-14-101-295-751   Jeanetta Graham b. 1920
1-3-14-101-295-752   Lorene Graham b. 1922
1-3-14-101-295-753   Alta Graham b. 1923
1-3-14-101-295-754   Alma Graham b. 1923
1-3-14-101-295-755   Ilous Graham b. 1925
1-3-14-103-301-756   Albert Graham b. 1906
1-3-14-103-301-757   Hugh Graham b. 1907
1-3-14-103-301-758   Keller Graham b. 1910
1-3-14-103-302-759   Gracie Southard b. 1898
1-3-14-104-313-760   Jasper Johnson, Jr. b. 1918
1-3-14-104-313-761   Buna Johnson b. 1923
1-3-14-104-313-762   Grady Johnson b. 1926
1-3-14-104-313-763   Joy Johnson b. 1928
1-3-15-105-315-764   Lynn Hooper b. July 18, 1899 d. Sept. 4, 1916 (murdered) Information found at *familytreemaker.genealogy.com/users/s/m/i/Gregory-Smith-New-Carlisle* on Internet.
1-3-15-105-315-765   Mabel Margaret Hooper b. July 9, 1902 d. Oct. 4, 1946 married Charles Edward McAmis (Information found at preceding reference and *Michelle_Rowe_k12* at *Ancestry.com* on the Internet.)
      1187.   Mary E. McAmis b. 1922
      1188.   Charles. E. McAmis b. Sept. 2, 1923 d. Dec. 24, 2005
      1189.   John D. McAmis b. 1928
      1190.   Thomas Oscar McAmis b. Dec. 12, 1932 – Sept. 16, 1951 at Harvey, Illinois
1-3-15-105-315-766   Willie Pat Hooper b. March 10, 1909 d. March 28, 1951 in Davidson County, TN married Laura Brown on Feb. 4, 1927 in Bradley County, TN (Internet, *Ancestry.com*)
1-3-15-105-316-767   Cecil Hooper (dau.) b. abt. 1904 married Charles Thomas Cain on Jan. 22, 1925 in Bradley County, TN(Internet, *Ancestry.com*)
1-3-15-105-316-768   Paul Hooper b. abt. 1914
1-3-15-106-317-769   Infant b. abt. 1901
1-3-15-106-317-770   James Harrison Hooper b. July 29, 1903 d. Dec. 16, 1978 married Jewel Cofer b. Nov. 23, 1907 d. May 13, 1999
      1191.   Bobbie Hooper b. 1932 married Dr. Gordon Lawrence Hixson, Sr. b. 1929
1-3-15-106-317-771   Sarah Ellen (Biddy) Hooper b. Dec. 25, 1907 d. Dec. 25, 1992 married Claud McDowell b. Feb. 18, 1903 d. Feb. 1972
      1192.   Barbara McDowell married John Chalker
1-3-15-106-317-772   John Luther Hooper, Jr. b. August 21, 1911 d. Dec. 14, 2002 married Eloise Harris b. Feb. 19, 1919 d. Feb. 15, 1996
      1193.   Judy Hooper married Doyle Gibson
1-3-15-106-317-773   Earl Cook Hooper b. July 21, 1913 d. Nov. 19, 1993 married Willie Tennessee (Billie) Jenkins on Nov. 23, 1932 in Meigs County, TN. Billie was born Oct. 4, 1916 d. March 14, 2002

1194.   Martha Lyn Hooper b. August 16, 1944 married Floyd Harold Reno on Aug. 27, 1965
in Meigs County, TN. He was born Oct. 30, 1943.

1-3-15-106-317-774   Lennie Hooper d. April 7, 1915 (b. & d. on same day)

1-3-15-106-319-775   Clara Mae Geren b. Dec. 26, 1904 d. May 1, 1999 married Roy Glenn Caldwell on
April 28, 1932 (Internet, *Ancestry.com*) in Bradley County, TN. He was born Feb.
21, 1905 and died May 22, 1993.

1195.   Glenda Caldwell married John Cantrell

1196.   Clarestine Roy Caldwell

1-3-15-106-319-776   Albert Geren b. Nov. 26, 1906 d. Jan. 1978 married Nina Knight (information
from *Appletree.com* on the Internet)

1197.   Albert Vernon Geren

1198.   George Williard Geren

1199.   Joyce Ann Geren

1-3-15-106-319-777   J. H. Geren b. April 5, 1909 d. Feb. 9, 2001

1-3-15-106-319-778   Kinze Geren b. Aug. 23, 1913 d. Sept. 30, 1992 married Mellie Loree Melton on
December 23, 1934 in Bradley County, TN (Internet, *Ancestry.com*)

1200.   Billy Don Geren b. May 23, 1939 – d. Dec. 13, 2012

1201.   Barkley Geren b. Nov. 27, 1944 – d. Feb. 7, 2017 (*Cleveland Daily Banner* Obituary on
February 9, 2017)

1-3-15-106-319-779   Hazel Geren b. abt. 1916

1-3-15-106-319-780   James R. Geren b. abt. 1924 (electrocuted while young)

1-3-15-106-320-429   Bruce William Hooper b. April 14, 1905 d. Feb. 1985 married Mable Morgan on
Jan. 4, 1934 in Bradley County, TN.

980.   Infant Nov. 28, 1934

981.   Lillian Hooper married William L. Hall

982.   Bruce (Sonny) Hooper b. April 30, 1940 d. Oct. 22, 2013 married JoAnn Hughes

983.   Bernard Hooper b. Oct. 17, 1943 d. Dec. 18, 2007 married 1. ?   2. Jenna Morrison
Guinn b. June 4, 1936 d. Oct. 20, 2012

1-3-15-106-320-430   Gladys Hooper b. abt. 1907

1-3-15-106-320-431   Boyd M. Hooper b. April 4, 1911 d. Oct. 1983 married Mary Louise Smalling on
Dec. 11, 1933 in Bradley County, TN (Internet, *Ancestry.com*)

984.   Boyd Milton Hooper married Ruth Lawson

985.   William Kins Hooper married Mabel Jones (*Findagrave.com* for Imogene "Jean" Gore
2007)

986.   Midge (Rose Margaret) Hooper married 1. Jim Cody   2. Zeno Beaty

1-3-15-106-322-781   Marvin B. Hooper b. Oct. 22, 1910 d. Jan. 8, 1995 married Sally Brown

1202.   Carolyn Hooper married Steve Bryant

1-3-15-106-322-782   Roy L. Hooper b. abt. 1913 married Irene Maddux on Dec. 31, 1939 in McMinn
County, TN (Internet, *Ancestry.com*)

1203.   Jimmy Hooper married Sandra Graham (number 1343) June 20, 1969 in Bradley
County, TN (Internet, *Ancestry.com*)

1-3-15-106-323-783   Alvin A. Taylor b. March 16, 1908 d. June 21, 1991 married Adele Petty b. Oct. 3,
1921 and d. March 5, 2014 in Rio Linda, California. She was buried with Alvin at
Hamilton Memorial Gardens at Hixson, TN (Internet *Ancestry.com, Find A Grave).*

1204.   Laura Jane Taylor married Wilson B. Garrett

1-3-15-106-323-784   Dennis K. Taylor b. abt. 1910

1-3-15-106-323-785   J. B. Taylor b. abt. 1913

1-3-15-106-323-786   Eula Myrtle Taylor b. Oct. 13, 1915 d. May 12, 2001 married John Acuff on
Feb. 22, 1941 in Bradley County, TN (Internet, *Ancestry.com*)

1-3-15-106-323-787   Thomas Hooper Taylor b. May 17, 1918 d. Dec. 18, 1981

1-3-15-106-324-788   Jewell Hooper b. 1916 married Paul Deackins (John Beaty Family Tree
auvenshine.com)

1205.   Paul Deackins

1-3-15-106-324-789   Joseph Brackett Hooper b. April 22, 1920 d. April 5, 1998 married Marie Geren on
Aug. 18, 1940 in Bradley County, TN (Internet, *Ancestry.com* and *Fike Funeral
Home Memorial Page* for Marie Hooper)

1206.   Larry Hooper married Sandy Debellis (John Beaty Family Tree *auvenshine.com*)
1207.   Judy Hooper married Bill Chandler
1-3-15-106-325-790   John L. Brewer, Jr. b. July 10, 1939 d. July 5, 2002 married Jo Ann Yarnell b. June
          11, 1938 (Internet, *Ancestry.com*) and d. July 27, 1997 buried at Ooltewah
          Cemetery, TN
1208.   Sandra Brewer married 1. Brett Simpson and 2. Jimmy Caldwell
(The descendants of Ethalinda Hooper and Henry Brackett lived in Dallas County, TX.)
1-3-15-107-326-791   Elsie Brackett b. abt. 1911
1-3-15-107-326-792   Howard Brackett b. Jan. 22, 1912 d. Aug. 11, 1951 married on May 27, 1932 to
          Nellie C. b. Oct. 23, 1913 d. May 21, 2003 (found at *Ancestry.com, Find A Grave*
          by EJ Brown and *1940 Dallas County, TX Census* p. 17B Township G. P. 3.)
1209.   Henry Brackett b. 1934
1210.   Jerry Brackett b. 1937
1-3-15-107-326-793   T. W. Brackett, Jr. b. abt. 1927 d. Nov. 2, 1963
1-3-15-107-327-794   Frank R. Garrison b. June 21, 1904 d. April 16, 1988 married Ellen B. Hayes b. abt.
          1908
1211.   Evelyn Faye Garrison b. Dec. 21, 1928
1212.   Maurine F. Garrison b. 1930 (*Ancestry.com, 1940 Dallas County, Texas Census* p. 3 A)
1213.   Mary Catherine Garrison b. 1932
1214.   Ora Mae Garrison b. 1940
1-3-15-107-327-795   John D. Garrison b. Aug. 26, 1905 d. June 10, 1992 married Ruth Lee Hays b. June
          21, 1910 d. Aug. 8, 1989 (*hentras* at *Ancestry.com*)
1215.   Jackie B. Garrison (son) b. 1929 (Texas, *Dallas County1940 Census* p. 19 A)
1216.   Betty R. Garrison b. 1931
1217.   Carrol L. Garrison b. 1934
1-3-15-107-327-796   Cora Wilma Garrison b. b. Feb. 1, 1907 d. Jan. 19, 1972 (Internet, *Ancestry.com,*
          Texas Death Certificate 02167) married Pinkney W. Fletcher b. May 11, 1904
1218.   Pink W. Fletcher b. 1927 (*1930 Wise County Census, Texas p. 2A Precinct 9*)
1219.   Marita Jean Fletcher b. Aug. 22, 1929 d. Oct. 24, 1998
1-3-15-107-327-797   Dallas (Dolly) Ercel Garrison (dau.) b. abt. 1909 married Nodie Keller Stovall b.
          Feb. 29, 1904 d. Dec. 21, 1951 (*halemary_1 at Ancestry.com*)
1-3-15-107-327-798   Henry Harrison Garrison b. May 10, 1910 d. April 21, 1979 (*Death Certificate in*
          Dallas County, Texas no. 34125 at Ancestry.com)
1-3-15-107-327-799   John Thomas Garrison b. Jan. 15, 1912 married Faye Leach (Internet,
          Ancestry.com, mccallumhw)
1220.   John T. Garrison, Jr.
1221.   Donald Ray Garrison
1-3-15-107-329-800   Ethalinda Brackett b. abt. 1914
1-3-15-107-331-801   M. Ruth McCallum b. 1911
1-3-15-107-331-802   Edwin L. McCallum b. 1914
1-3-15-107-331-803   Trixie J. Lambert b. 1916
1-3-15-107-331-804   Jimmie R. Lambert (dau.) b. 1919
1-3-15-107-331-805   Roy B. Lambert b. 1922
1-3-15-107-331-806   Bettie Lambert b. 1924
1-3-15-108-334-807   Patricia Estelle Leamon b. March 30, 1908 – d. Dec. 5, 1990 in Oak Ridge, TN
          (*KeithMillsStewart at Ancestry.com*) married James Ernest Hooper (number 427)
          b. Jan. 24, 1903 d. Dec. 1974 and (2) Burley Graham b. Aug. 27, 1900 d. Jan. 5,
          1991 (number 875)
977.   Earnesteen Hooper b. Nov. 20, 1923
978.   Anabell Hooper b. abt. 1927
979.   Bettie J. Hooper b. abt. 1929
1-3-15-109-341-808   Thelma Miller b. 1914 married on Sept. 6, 1932 Alvin Arthel (Red) Hooper (number
          949)
1222.   Jay H. Hooper b. June 6, 1934 in Bradley County, TN married Doris Lankford
1223.   William Hooper married Jean
1-3-15-109-341-809   Lillard Miller (dau.) b. abt. 1920

1-3-15-109-341-810   Luetta Miller b. abt. 1922
1-3-15-109-341-811   Cecil M. Miller (dau.) b. abt. 1924
1-3-15-109-341-812   Opal P. Miller b. abt. 1926
1-3-15-109-341-813   Essadine Miller b. abt. 1928 (See Appendix H for more Henry Miller children.)
1-3-15-109-344-814   Rathburn Louis Miller b. March 27, 1920-d. Sept. 1, 1989. Married Opal Kaylor
    March 24, 1940 (See Appendix H for additional Lawrence Miller children.)
1-3-15-109-344-815   Herman Lawrence Miller b. Aug. 19, 1924-d. July 24, 2006. Married Reba
    Hamilton in 1944.
    1224.   Gale Miller
    1225.   Ivo (Monty) Miller
1-3-15-109-344-816   Cash Edward (Chub) Miller b. Nov. 26, 1926-d. May 3, 2003. Married Mary Elrod.
    1226.   Randall Edward Miller
    1227.   Brenda Miller
    1228.   Donna Miller
1-3-15-109-345-817   Carolyn Miller married Duncan Gibson
    1229.   Gwen Gibson
    1230.   Melanie Gibson married Tim
1-3-15-109-345-818   Betty Sue Miller b. abt. 1929 married (1) Charles Fortney and (2) Bud Bowman
    1231.   Robert Fortney
1-3-15-109-345-819   Martha Celestine Miller married David T. Hooper (number 954)
    1232.   Connie L. Hooper married Roy Millaway
    1233.   David Dale Hooper married Sable Couch
    1234.   Alice M. Hooper married Fritz Harris
    1235.   Barry H. Hooper married Cheryl Kendrick
1-3-15-109-345-820   Judy Miller married Darrell Hooper (number 838)
    1236.   James Richard Hooper married Partricia Lambert Prince and Marcia McMurray
    1237.   Mark Douglas Hooper married Kim Shehan
1-3-15-109-345-821   Doug Miller married Mary Lou Callaway on Sept. 2, 1967 in Bradley County, TN
    1238.   Aon Douglas Miller
    1239.   Jessica Lea Miller
1-3-15-109-346-822   Earnestine Miller b. abt. 1926
1-3-15-109-346-823   Bonnie Joe Miller b. abt. 1928 married Lettie Ashford
**(Isaac Millaway moved west to Texas with his father Alfred William Millaway before 1912 and to
Oklahoma about 1919 with Alfred William Millaway and his second wife and family. Isaac returned
to Bradley County, TN before 1930.)**
1-3-15-110-349-824   John W. Millaway b. abt. 1913
1-3-15-110-349-825   Arthur Raymond Millaway b. Dec. 4, 1914 – Feb. 10, 1996 in Chatsworth, GA
    married Helen Ware
1-3-15-110-349-826   Gladys Beattrice Millaway b. Feb. 2, 1919 d. Nov. 22, 1980 m. Hubert Murphy
    (number 1329)
    1240.   Charles Hubert Murphy b. 1943
    1241.   Linda Lou Murphy b. 1946
    1242.   Dewayne Murphy b. 1948
    1243.   Alice Lynn Murphy b. 1954
    1244.   Deborah Joyce Murphy b. 1957
1-3-15-110-349-827   Earl Millaway b. July 19, 1922 d. Feb. 1885 married Gladys Marion b. July 22, 1922
    d. April 1, 2004 (*riccrs at Ancestry.com*). Earl in the *Meigs County 1940 Census* in
    First District was listed as S. I., Jr. (Internet, *Ancestry.com*).
    1245.   John Millaway
    1246.   Donna Millaway
    1247.   Sherry Millaway
    1248.   Michael Frank (Frankie) Millaway
1-3-15-110-349-828   Millard L. Millaway b. 1926 married Helen Cofer b. 1933 died 2016
    1249.   Millard Dale Millaway 1953-d. April 23, 2008
    1250.   Gary Lee Millaway
    1251.   Beverley Millaway married Kenneth Lankford

1252. Darla Millaway married John Roberts

1253. Jimmy Millaway married Lisa

1-3-15-110-349-829 Ina M. Millaway b. abt. 1929 d. Oct. 29, 2008 married William Clifford Black born June 18, 1929 – d. Feb. 21, 2003

1254. Phyllis Black b. Oct. 16, 1952 married (1) ? Parris and (2) Dexter Denny

1255. Clifford Lamar Black b. May 17, 1956 married Kay ?

1-3-15-110-349-830 Edward Keith Millaway b. Feb. 15, 1932 d. Sept. 7, 2013 married (1) Barbara Rose and (2) Nita Burns

1256. Edward Keith Millaway, Jr.

1257. Heath Millaway

1258. Alan Millaway

1259. Patricia Millaway

1-3-15-110-349-831 James Millaway married Alma

1-3-15-110-349-832 Jessie Millaway married Elijah Burdette

1-3-15-110-352-833 Margaret Irene Garrison b. 1920

1-3-15-110-352-834 Dorothy Nell Garrison b. 1921

1-3-15-110-352-835 Roy Garrison, Jr. b. 1926

1-3-15-111-353-836 Virginia J. Hooper b. abt. 1929 married Marshall Wallace

1260. Gary Wallace married Suzanne Newman on August 13, 1988 in Bradley County, TN

1261. Mary Kay Wallace married Melvin Elder on Sept. 9, 1978 in Bradley County, TN

1262. Ila Virginia Wallace married Mike Kirkpatrick

1-3-15-111-353-837 Mary Margaret Hooper married Noah Western

1263. Diana Lynn Western married Mitchell Geren

1264. Michael Len Western married Rita Crye

1-3-15-111-354-838 Darrell Hooper married Judy Miller (number 820)

1236. James Richard Hooper married Patricia Lambert Prince and Marcia McMurray

1237. Mark Douglas Hooper married Kim Shehan

1-3-15-111-355-839 Lottie Lee Thompson b. abt. 1929 married Thomas Eddie Wood

1265. Thomas E. Wood, Jr.

1266. Marianna Wood

1-3-15-111-355-840 J. E. Thompson

1-3-15-111-355-841 Marie Irene Thompson married Harold Baker

1-3-15-111-355-842 Martha Edwyna Thompson married Ralph L. Pierce

1-3-15-111-355-843 Earnest W. Thompson, Jr. married Mildred Smith

1-3-15-111-356-844 Gurtha Dean Hooper b. 1933 married Forrest Hill b. Feb. 22, 1928 – May 13, 2012 (See person 113 and 371 Jahue H. Graham information for Graham family sources.)

1267. Forrest Buchanan (Bucky) Hill, 3rd

1268. Robert Hooper Hill

1-3-15-111-356-845 Hazel Lou Hooper b. Nov. 22, 1935 married James Pell b. Feb. 13, 1934 d. Jan. 18, 1996

1269. Ronnie Lee Pell

1270. Richard Lynn Pell

1271. Regina Louise Pell

1-3-15-111-356-845 Hazel Lou Hooper married (2) Francis Erhart Scherer, 3rd

1272. Francis Erhart Scherer, 4th

1-3-15-111-356-846 Martha June Hooper b. 1938 married Bill Franklin Bacon

1273. Steven Franklin Bacon

1-3-15-111-356-847 Bobbye Roberta Hooper b. 1940 married Dennis Robert Whaley

1274. Dennis Robert Whaley, Jr.

1275. Gregory Alan Whaley

1-3-15-111-356-848 Dewayne Cyrus Hooper b. Jan. 1936 married Judy Clayton on July 16, 1963 in Bradley County, TN

1276. Julia Ann Hooper

1-3-16-112-359-849 James Albert Marr b. March 20, 1896 – March 19, 1957 (*Death Certificate at Ancestry.com*) married Mary Lee Fann (*1940 Census Franklin County, TN* at 11th District p. 6B)

1-3-16-112-359-850   Florence M. Marr b. Jan. 1898
1-3-16-112-359-851   John Marr April 4, 1900 - d. July 2, 1901 (*1_rcmoore at Ancestry.com*)
1-3-16-112-359-852   Loyd T. Marr b. 1903 married Beulah Defriese?
1-3-16-112-359-853   Owen N. Marr b. July 2, 1904 d. May 1972 married Mary K. (*1930 Census
        Hamilton County, TN in 2nd District p. 3B*)
    1277.   Mary O. Marr
1-3-16-112-359-854   Lela B. Marr b. March 23, 1906 (Internet, *Ancestry.com,* Marr, *1_rcmoore*)
        married Blankinship d. Dec. 28, 1927 (Internet, *Ancestry.com, Certificate of Death*
1-3-16-112-359-855   Effie C. Marr b. married James Alfred Leamon b. Nov. 6, 1908 – April 21, 1984
        (*lespriebe at Ancestry.com*) married Feb. 27, 1931
1-3-16-112-359-856   Beulah B. Marr b. abt. 1914
1-3-16-112-359-857   Clifford R. Marr b. Dec. 20, 1914 d. May 1975
1-3-16-112-360-858   William C. Marr b. Dec. 6, 1896 married Blanche Logan b. Oct. 20,1899 d. July 10,
        1959 (Internet, Marr, *brenda marr at Ancestry.com*)
    1278.   Florence Marr b. b. Dec. 10, 1917 – d. Feb. 6, 1931
    1279.   Albert Marr b. abt. 1922
    1280.   Thomas Logan Marr b. 1923 d. 2004 married Arlene Coffey
    1281.   Pauline Marr b. abt. 1927
    1282.   Polly Marr died before 2004? Married a Frazier
    1283.   Virginia L. Marr b. abt. 1929 married a Parton and died before 2004
    1284.   Myrtle Marr b. abt. 1934
    1285.   Arnold Marr b. abt. 1937
1-3-16-112-360-859   Maggie Florence Marr b. March 1898
1-3-16-112-360-860   Kenzie Marr b. May 17, 1902 d. Oct. 24, 1981 married (1) Mary Smith b. Feb. 25,
        1902 d. Feb. 28, 1920 (*HAROLDDH38 at Ancestry.com*) and (2) Beulah L. Smith b.
        March 30, 1908 d. Nov. 27, 1978 married Oct. 23, 1925 in Bradley County, TN
        (Internet, *Ancestry.com*) (More information can be found on p. 131.)
1-3-16-112-360-861   George Marr b. abt. 1905
1-3-16-112-360-862   Ollevia Marr b. May 13, 1909 – d. May 24, 1984 (Internet, *Find A Grave*), married
        Roy Lee Johnson b. August 24,1906 –d. May 21, 1997
    1286.   Mamie Wanda Johnson b. and d. 1942
1-3-16-112-360-863   Houston Marr b. Feb. 8, 1913 – d. Sept. 24, 1991 married 1. Pearl Hughes on April
        15, 1933 and 2. Abbie Morgan on June 18, 1938 in Bradley County, TN
        (*Ancestry.com*)
    1287.   Pauline Marr married Warner Bertel Washburn
    1288.   Calvin "Red, Pop" Marr married Jimmie Ruth Farris (**Children are Danny Marr
        married to Cathy and Daniel Marr married to Brenda; Grandchildren are
        Jonathan Marr married to Brenda; Nathan Marr married to Taylor; Great-
        Grandchildren are Wyatt Marr, Drake Marr and Grace Marr. See p. 102.**)
    1289.   Alvin "Speedy" Marr (twin) married Ruby.
    1290.   Pete Marr
    1291.   Kenneth Marr
    1292.   Mary Ann Marr married a Ledford
1-3-16-112-361-864   Elsie Marr b. Sept. 17, 1896 – Jan. 25, 1963 married Horace Jones (Internet,
        Ancestry.com by *MLEubank* also check p. 131 for two more children)
    1293.   Ruby Lee Jones b. Oct. 27, 1914 – May 29, 1955
1-3-16-112-361-865   Pearl Marr b. June 1896
1-3-16-112-361-866   Loma Marr b. March 1899
1-3-16-112-361-867   Ledford Marr b. June 3, 1900 d. Aug. 1985
1-3-16-112-361-868   Garland L. Marr b. Nov. 1, 1902 d. April 15, 1994 married Azzie L. Foote b. May
        29, 1911 – d. April 10, 1997.
1-3-16-112-363-353   K. C. Hooper b. abt. 1901 m. Ruth Buckner
    836.   Virginia J. Hooper b. abt. 1929 married Marshall Wallace
    837.   Margaret Hooper married Noah Western
1-3-16-112-363-354   Arnold Hooper b. abt. 1903 m. Icie Lawson
    838.   Darrell Hooper married June 29, 1951 in Bradley County, TN to Judy Miller (820)

1-3-16-112-363-355   Annie Hooper b. 1905- d. 1976 m. Earnest Waller Thompson b. 1903 – 1948
    839.   Lottie Lee Thompson b. abt. 1929 married Thomas Eddie Wood
    840.   J. E. Thompson
    841.   Marie Irene Thompson married Harold Baker
    842.   Martha Edwyna Thompson married Ralph L. Pierce
    843.   Earnest W. Thompson, Jr. married Mildred Smith
1-3-16-112-363-356   Lake Hooper b. March 3, 1909-d. April 13, 1940 married Dorothy Graham (number 892) b. March 13, 1913 d. April 29, 1988
    844.   Gurtha Dean Hooper married Forrest Hill
    845.   Hazel Lou Hooper **(some information came from *FamilyTreeGuide.com* for Dorothy Graham family and *Jay and Lou Graham by* Juanita Graham Hinkle and Gertha Hooper Hill)**
    846.   Martha June Hooper
    847.   Bobbye Roberta Hooper
1-3-16-112-363-357   Aldon Hooper b. April 29, 1912 d. Nov. 15, 2001 m. Almetta Melton
    848.   Dewayne Cyrus Hooper b. Jan. 1936
1-3-16-112-363-358   Forrest Hooper b. abt. 1916 d. 1918
1-3-16-112-365-869   Marie Marr b. abt. 1909
1-3-16-112-365-870   Ruby Marr 1912 - 1971 married Carl Taylor Gamble 1909 – 1992
    1294.   Ona Virginia Gamble
1-3-16-112-365-871   Martha Marr b. abt. 1913
1-3-16-113-367-872   J. Boles
1-3-16-113-368-873   Eulah L. Graham b. abt. 1910
1-3-16-113-368-874   Partella Graham b. abt. 1912
1-3-16-113-370-875   Burley Graham b. Aug. 27, 1900 d. Jan. 5, 1991 married (1) Aileen Falls on Nov. 7, 1929 in Meigs County, TN; (2) Abbie Morgan on January 1, 1933 in Bradley County, TN (3) Mary Lou Etter (information from *Ancestry.com* and *The Augusta Chronicle* from March 4, 2015 Obituary for Benice Graham who was Burley's stepson.) (4) Patricia Estelle Leamon Hooper (number 807) married Oct. 16, 1968 in Bradley County, TN.
    1295.   Hazel Dean Graham
    1296.   Willard Louis Graham
    1297.   Tommy Lee Graham
    1298.   Lorene Ann Graham
    1299.   Michael J. Graham
    1300.   Mittie Lou Graham
1-3-16-113-370-876   Edith Graham b. abt. 1903
1-3-16-113-370-877   Hazel Graham b. abt. 1905
1-3-16-113-370-878   Thurman Graham b. abt. 1907
1-3-16-113-370-879   Sallie May Graham b. Nov. 3, 1908 d. Feb. 4, 1982 married J. Leonard Geren on Feb. 9, 1925 in Bradley County, TN
    1301.   Drefus (D. L.) Geren (Internet, *Find A Grave,* and *Ancestry.com*)
    1302.   Eugene T. Geren
    1303.   Dean V. Geren married Louise Birdwell (Internet, *Ancestry.com*)
    1304.   Luther E. Geren
    1305.   Tresley Geren
    1306.   Neva June Geren
    1307.   Julia Ann Geren
1-3-16-113-370-880   Myrtle Graham b. abt. 1914
(Thomas H. Graham married (2) Emma Geren Lee who was the widow of Lester Lee; Emma and Lester's children were Myrtle Lee, Maynard Lee, Wayne Lee and Bertie Lee . See p. 64.)
1-3-16-113-370-881   Oma Lee Graham b. 1919 d. March 19, 2010 married Joe Lyle
    1308.   Willis Lyle
    1309.   Linda Lyle
    1310.   Janice Lyle
    1311.   Eddie Lyle

1-3-16-113-370-882   Hoyt T. Graham b. Jan. 17, 1921 d. Feb. 24, 2007 married Dorothy Harris b. April
                28, 1920 d. April 5, 2000
    1312.   Vernard Hoyt Graham b. Aug. 24, 1948
    1313.   La Vonne Graham b. August 5, 1960
1-3-16-113-370-883   Cletus G. Graham b. March 6, 1923 d. July 8, 1993 married Audrey Collins
    1314.   Wesley G. Graham b. Nov. 16, 1949-d. Nov. 16, 1966
    1315.   Stanley Graham
1-3-16-113-370-884   Mary Louellen Graham b. Aug. 6, 1925 – Dec. 22, 2015 married Roy Lee Moore
                (Obituary Dec. 24, 2015 at Jim Rush Funeral Home in Cleveland, TN)
    1316.   Lisa Renee Moore m. 1.   Rogers and 2. Richard L. Calfee
    1317.   Dana Moore married Dale Elkins
    1318.   Randall Moore married Carolyn
    1319.   Mark Moore married Kim

Mary Lou Graham Moore's grandchildren and great grandchildren in the Obituary were: Brad (Suzanne) Pickens, LeeAnn (Wes) Moore, Emily Rogers, Tara (Mark) Miller, Lara Moore, Marka Moore (Cody Ellis), Ariel Bellamy, Matt (Terri) Dillard, Craig (Sandy) Dillard, and Cliffee (Chrissy) Dillard. Great grandchildren were Bailey Rogers, Madison Ingram, Anna Lee Miller, Shiplee Moore, Emma Kate Ellis and Justin Moore.

1-3-16-113-371-885   Nola Graham b. Jan. 13, 1897 m. Jacob Monroe Neeley Aug. 15, 1915 in Bradley
                County, TN. Jake was born May 17, 1898 and died April 22, 1966.
    1320.   Doyle M. Neeley b. Dec. 13, 1918 – d. Dec. 22, 1990
    1321.   Lou Anna M. Neeley b. May 26, 1922 d. Dec. 29, 2012
    1322.   Nola Imogene Neeley b. March 19, 1924 d. Sept. 14, 1996
    1323.   Thelma Neeley (twin died at birth)
    1324.   Delma Neeley   (twin died at birth)
    1325.   Robert Curtis Neeley b. Sept 7, 1930-d. June 14, 1993 married Agnes M. b. Apr. 2,
                1929
1-3-16-113-371-886   Jasper O. Graham b. Oct. 14, 1899-Sept. 28, 1983 m. Bertie L. Messer b. April 20,
                1903 d. Dec. 25, 1985
    1326.   Francis L. Graham
    1327.   Dela M. Graham
    1328.   Jasper Graham, Jr.
1-3-16-113-371-887   Oscar Graham 1902
1-3-16-113-371-888   Delzenia (Zena) Graham b. Jan. 9, 1905 d. Oct. 3, 1981 married Hugh Murphy b.
                July 4, 1901 d. Feb. 10, 1984
    1329.   Hubert Murphy b. July 16, 1922 d. March 11, 2003
    1330.   Clyde Murphy b. Sept. 11, 1923 d. Sept. 10, 1991
    1331.   Frederick Murphy Aug. 27, 1925 d. March 23, 2003
    1332.   Floyd Murphy b. Nov. 11, 1932
1-3-16-113-371-889.   Willie Graham
1-3-16-113-371-890   Paul B. Graham b. Aug. 4, 1909 d. Feb. 24, 1976 married Clara Grissom b. Jan. 27,
                1912 d. March 24, 1997
    1333.   Juanita Elizabeth Graham
    1334.   Charles Paul Graham
    1335.   Billy Joe Graham
1-3-16-113-371-891   Arnold Graham b. Nov. 30, 1910 d. Nov. 5, 1982 married Pauline Thompson on
                Nov.11, 1933 in Bradley County, TN (Internet, *Ancestry.com*). She was born July
                19, 1914 d. April 15, 1989.
    1336.   Harold A. Graham b. August 22, 1934 d. Feb. 22, 2013
    1337.   Murel Graham
    1338.   Jerry M. Graham
1-3-16-113-371-892   Dorothy M. Graham b. May 13, 1913 d. Sept. 7, 1988 m. 1. Lake Hooper on Sept. 6,
                1930 in Bradley County, TN (Lake is number 356.) and 2. Uel Claude Sandidge b.
                Feb. 1, 1904 d. Feb. 2, 1995 (Internet, *Ancestry.com*)
    1339.   Sterling Sandidge
    1340.   Linda La Faye Sandidge b. June 10, 1950

844.	Gurtha Dean Hooper
845.	Hazel Lou Hooper
846.	Martha June Hooper
847.	Bobbye Roberta Hooper
1-3-16-113-371-893	Ova Graham b. 1915 m. 1. Gearl Rogers on Nov. 25, 1933 in Bradley County, TN and. 2. Walter Puckett
1341.	Gearlee Rogers
1-3-16-113-371-894	Margaret Marie Graham Aug. 3, 1917 d. Oct. 31, 1918
1-3-16-113-371-895	James S. Graham b. Nov. 15, 1919 d. Nov. 21, 2003 m. Lucy B. Wooden b. April 12, 1920 d. Aug. 2, 2008 (Internet, *Ancestry.com*)
1342.	James Sherman Graham
1343.	Sandra Graham (married Jimmy Hooper 1203)
1-3-16-113-371-896	Jahue Graham, Jr. b. 1922 m. Helen Geren
1344.	Lanny C. Graham
1345.	Terry L. Graham
1-3-16-113-374-897	Lloyd Eugene Graham married (1) Mary E. Ross on Nov. 29, 1931 in Bradley County, TN and (2) Jean G. Johnston on Jan. 2, 1951 at Cook County, Illinois (Internet *Ancestry.com* and the *Bradley County 1940 Census,* Cleveland, Ward 2 p. 5 B).
1346.	Jayne Graham
1347.	Tereh (Terel?) Graham (son)
1348.	Joan Graham
1-3-16-113-374-898	James R. Graham
1-3-16-113-375-899	Clay Victor King
1-3-16-113-375-900	Earl Walker King
1-3-16-114-378-901	Anna M. Williamson b. 1912 in CA married Marshall Mosher (Internet , *Jacqueline-L-Brusseau-CO, Genealogy.com: Descendants of Robert Thomas Williamson*)
1349.	John S. Mosher Oct. 20, 1943
1350.	James S. Mosher Dec. 18, 1947
1-3-16-114-378-902	John J. Williamson b. 1915 in TN
1-3-16-114-378-903	Dorthy L. Williamson b. 1925 in CA
1-3-16-114-378-904	Thomas C. Williamson b. 1928 in CA
1-3-16-114-379-905	Edna Elizabeth Bunch 1904 – 1972 married Charles Brown Wood
1351.	Betty Margaret Wood 1932 (Internet, *Genealogy.com, Brusseau* see p. 65)
1-3-16-114-379-906	Nanalee "Nancy" Bunch 1907 – 1986 married W. Jackson Watts (Internet, Bunch, *Genealogy.com*, Br*usseau* see p. 65)
1352.	Mary Heaton Watts married Harry Thomas Wilhoit
1-3-16-114-379-907	Margaret Dialtha Bunch July 8, 1910 – 1994 married Carl William Coleman
1-3-16-114-379-908	Lorrain Evelyn Bunch 1912 – 1996 married James Oswald Gilbreath
1353.	Ted Monroe Gilbreath b. 1936
1354.	James Oswald Gilbreath b. 1944
1-3-16-114-379-909	William Albert Bunch, Jr. 1914 – 1973 married Hazel Nowlin
1355.	Billy Lynn Bunch
1-3-16-114-379-910	Joseph R. Bunch 1916 – 1970 married Mildred Powell
1356.	Grayson Bunch (died as an infant)
1357.	Jeanne Bunch (Internet, *Ancestry.com, Find A Grave*, Created by Glenda Rowland)
1358.	Joseph Robert Bunch, Jr.
1-3-16-114-379-911	Charles Bunch 1920 – 1968
1-3-16-114-379-912	Carl Eugene Bunch 1922 – 1990 married Betty Floyd
1359.	Carl Eugene Bunch, Jr.
1360 .	Mary Elizabeth Bunch
1361.	Paul David Bunch
1362.	Brian Andrew Bunch
1-3-16-114-380-913	Lillian Goike married Harry Walcott in CA
1363.	Ronald Walcott 1935 CA

1-3-16-114-381-914   Mildred Williamson 1914 (*Hamilton County, TN 1920 Census* p. 2 B Dist. 3)
married (1) William L. Galbraith and (2) James Lee Hale (Internet,
Genealogy.com Jacqueline-L-Brusseau-CO)
1364.   Roberta Galbraith 1932 (*1940 Walker County, GA Census* Lisbon p. 13 A)
1365.   Charlotte Galbraith 1933
1366.   Tommy C. Galbraith 1936
1367.   William Lee Galbraith, Jr.
1368.   Howard Sam Hale
1369.   James Wesley Hale
1370.   John Audie Hale
1-3-16-114-381-915   Reita Williamson 1916
1-3-16-114-381-916   Howard Williamson 1918 married Dorothy Worley (Internet, *Genealogy.com,*
Brusseau see p. 65)
1371.   David Earle Williamson
1372.   Howard Donald Williamson
1-3-16-114-381-917   Grove Audie Williamson 1926 (*Hamilton County, TN 1930 Census* p. 20 B, 3rd
Dist.) married Annie Gregory
1373.   Dorothy Marie Williamson
1374.   Edna Anne Williamson
1375.   William Gregory Williamson
1376.   Gail Edith Williamson
1377.   Laura Susan Williamson
1-3-16-114-382-918   Jessie May Bell 1912
1-3-16-114-382-919   Myrtle Bell 1914 married Charles William Hassler in 1932 in Hamilton
County, TN (*Genealogy.com, Brusseau* see p. 65)
1378.   Charles William Hassler, Jr. 1933
1379.   Raymond Lee Hassler 1935
1-3-16-114-384-920   Sarah J. Dicks married Robert Lee Henry in Oct. 14, 1948 in Hamilton County,
TN (*Genealogy.com, Brusseau* see p. 65)
1380.   Janel Diane Henry
1381.   Nancy Louise Henry
1-3-16-115-387-921   Maree Gilbreath b. abt. 1913
1-3-16-115-388-922   Lynn Andrew Hooper b. Oct. 18, 1910 d. Feb. 21, 1973
1-3-16-115-388-923   James Hoyt Hooper b. August 14, 1913-d. Aug. 22, 1915
1-3-16-115-388-924   Edith Gertrude Hooper b. Oct. 30, 1918 d. April 24, 2008 married William F.
"Jack" Barger in 1941 in Dandridge, TN. Edith was the daughter of 659 and 388.
(Information was found in Edith Barger's Obituary in the *Cleveland Daily Banner*
dated April 28, 2008 and found at *Ancestry.com.*)
1382.   Martha Lynn Barger
1383.   Maurine Barger
1-3-16-117-396-925   Med D. Bacon b. Jan. 3, 1910
1-3-16-117-397-926   Fred Dunham b. abt. 1914
1-3-16-117-397-927   William R. Dunham b. abt. 1924
1-3-17-120-399-928   Grace Cross b. 1915
1-3-17-120-399-929   Betty Cross b. 1919
1-3-17-120-400-930   Stacy E. Carlton b. July 19, 1913 d. July 1992 m. Floyd Frances Puett (*Descendants*
of Rufus Rinkle/Wrinkle on Internet Earthlink.net by K. Callan & Evelyn Wrinkle
Cross)
1384.   Stacy E. Carlton Sept. 20, 1936-Nov. 9, 2009
1385.   Barbara Frances Carlton
1386.   William Carlton Feb. 1, 1939-Oct. 30, 1962
1-3-17-120-400-931   Milton Carlton b. March 1915 d. June 23, 1987 married Ruby Murray
1387.   Eugene Carlton
1-3-17-120-400-932   Joseph F. Carlton b. April 27, 1918 d. Dec. 19, 1989
1-3-17-120-400-933   William R. Carlton b. June 1925
1-3-17-120-400-934   Naomi Frances Carlton Oct. 4, 1930

1-3-17-120-402-935   Josephine Carlton b. abt. 1914
1-3-17-120-402-936   Caldwell Carlton b. abt. 1917
1-3-17-120-403-937   Leland L. Carlton b. abt. 1920
1-3-17-120-403-938   Margaret L. Carlton b. abt. 1921
1-3-17-120-403-939   Gale M. Carlton b. abt. 1923
1-3-17-120-403-940   Kins C. Carlton, Jr. b. abt. 1926
1-3-17-121-408-941   Clayton Richards b. 1909
1-3-17-121-408-942   Paul Richards b. 1911 married Nettie
1-3-17-121-408-943   Clyde Richards b. 1914
1-3-17-121-408-944   Hershell Richards b. 1916
1-3-17-121-408-945   Margaret Richards b. 1918
1-3-17-122-409-946   Thelma Eloise Tillery b. Jan. 27, 1911- d. Sept. 13, 1993 (Internet *randywhite611at Ancestry.com*) married (1) James H. Ellis on Feb. 16, 1931 in Bradley County, TN and (2) Deward Cress b. Aug. 22, 1911 – d. Aug. 29, 1999 married Oct. 20, 1945 in Bradley County, TN (Internet *Ancestry.com*)

1388.   Eloise Ellis b. 1932 (*1940 Census of Bradley County, TN p. 4 B in Dist. 4*)
1389.   Nancy Ellis b. 1933
1390.   Ellen Ellis b. 1934
1391.   Kenneth Cress
1392.   Mike Cress b. July 5, 1948 married on Oct. 17, 1970 to Janice Anita Jones b. June 20, 1950 in Bradley County, TN
1393.   Karen Edna Cress b. Sept. 9, 1952 married (1) on Nov. 4, 1970 to James Daniel Ledford b. July 9, 1951 and married (2) on Dec. 22, 1979 to Robert Mitchell Hair b. Aug. 13, 1953 in Bradley County, TN

1-3-17-122-409-947   Edna Tillery b. Aug. 24, 1913 d. April 8, 2009 m. 1. Joseph McSpadden on Oct. 9, 1946 in Bradley County, TN and 2. Cecil Shirley (Internet *kidwelml1 at Ancestry.com*)

1394.   Linda Shirley married Luther King
1-3-17-122-410-948   William Robert Hooper b. June 8, 1913 d. Dec. 29, 1918
1-3-17-122-410-949   Alvin Arthel (Red) Hooper b. Sept. 16, 1914 d. Aug. 6, 1988 and married Thelma Miller b. abt. 1915 (number 808)

1222.   Jayhue H. Hooper b. June 6, 1934 married Doris Lankford
1223.   William Hooper married Jean
1-3-17-122-410-950   Ruby Ellen Hooper b. August 14, 1916 married on Dec. 24, 1937 Aldon Wayne Harris b. abt. 1915 in Bradley County, TN.

1395.   Murel Wayne Harris b. Nov. 7, 1938
1396.   Donald Alden "Don" Harris
1397.   Curtis Harris
1398.   Robert Harris
1-3-17-122-410-951   Roy Frank Hooper b. Sept. 22, 1918 married Lorraine Tinsley

1399.   Bennie Hooper
1400.   Herbert Hooper married Janice
1401.   Carl Hooper
1-3-17-122-410-952   Thomas Calvin Hooper b. April 17, 1920 d. Feb. 11, 1868 married Lois Lawson
1-3-17-122-410-953   Paul Jahue Hooper b. May 22, 1922 married Pauline Umphrey

1402.   Carolyn Hooper
1403.   Larry Hooper
1404.   Danny Hooper
1405.   Brian Hooper
1406.   Kathy Hooper
1-3-17-122-410-954   David Thurman Hooper b. Oct. 11, 1925 married Martha Celestine Miller (number 819)

1232.   Connie L. Hooper married Roy Millaway
1233.   David Dale Hooper married Sable Couch
1234.   Alice M. Hooper married Fritz Harris
1235.   Barry H. Hooper married Cheryl Kendrick

1-3-17-122-410-955   Marjorie Dellifene Hooper b. July 25, 1930 married Herman Melton
    1407.   Linda Melton m. (1) Robert George Schichtel ch. Rob and Barratt Schichtel m. (2) Lee
    1408.   Herman Thomas Melton b. June 28, 1951 married Teresa K. Maples on July 3, 1971 in
        Bradley County, TN. b. Jan. 13, 1951. m. (2) Cathy Coe Melton. Brian was a son.
1-3-17-122-410-956   Carl Ray Hooper b. Jan. 7, 1932 married Betty Sneed
    1409.   Randall Hooper
    1410.   Wesley Hooper
    1411.   Cindy Hooper
    1412.   Christie Hooper
1-3-17-122-410-957   Dorothy Marie Hooper b. Feb. 16, 1934 married Bill Carson
    1413.   William Phillip Carson married Angela Lynne Boring
    1414.   Dr. Jeffery Carson married Dawn Rumba
    1415.   Suzanne Carson married Chris Bynum
1-3-17-122-410-958   Joseph Clinton Hooper b. March 10, 1937 married Rosa Bell Schroyer (Internet,
        Ancestry.com Los Angeles Marriage Index for Sept. 2, 1955
    1416.   Rosalee Lee Hooper married Gary Frost
    1417.   Clint Harrison Hooper married Karen Schmidt
    1418.   Vickie Lynn Hooper married Duane Harris
    1419.   Judy Elaine Hooper
    1420.   Gary Allen Hooper married Sheila Bevins
    1421.   Dennis Raymond Hooper married Amy Aultmann
    1422.   Bernola Mae Hooper married Brent L. Webb
1-3-17-122-410-959   Charles Leonard Hooper b. Dec. 8, 1939 d. Nov. 24, 1940
1-3-17-122-410-960   Wayne Harrison Hooper b. Dec. 31, 1941 married Barbara Carden (number 1057)
    1423.   Timothy Wayne Hooper married Andrea Michele Roark on Jan. 28, 1995 in Bradley
        County, TN
    1424.   Tracy Hooper married Leslie Ratcliff
1-3-17-122-412-961   Louise Plank b. abt. 1924
1-3-17-122-413-962   Frances Hooper b. abt. 1922 married Quinten Brown
    1425.   Samuel Brown
    1426.   Ann Brown
    1427.   Wade Brown
1-3-17-122-413-963   Clinton McIntire Hooper b. March 2, 1931 married Sharon Sipple b. Nov. 13, 1939
1-3-17-122-418-964   James Lee Sullivan, Jr. b. Sept. 26, 1937
1-3-17-122-418-965   Joseph E. Sullivan b. Sept. 24, 1940
1-3-17-122-418-966   Jane Sullivan b. Dec. 1, 1944
1-3-17-123-419-967   Clara M. Shamblin b. 1909
1-3-17-123-419-968   C. L. Shamblin b. 1911
1-3-17-123-419-969   Telles E. Shamblin b. 1912
1-3-17-123-423-970   Charles J. Eads, Jr.
1-3-17-123-423-971   Mildred Josephine Eads
1-3-17-123-423-972   Raymond Moore Eads married in Bradley County, TN on July 23, 1966 to Etta
        Louise Pulliam b. July 7, 1938 d. March 18, 2008
    1428.   Michael Eads
1-3-17-123-423-973   John Floyd Eads
1-3-17-123-423-974   Calvin Lloyd Eads
1-3-17-123-424-975   Martha E. Pardue b. 1922
1-3-17-123-424-976   Beulah Pardue b. 1924
1-3-17-125-427-977   Earnestine Hooper b. abt. 1924 m.   Haiskell? Wender??
1-3-17-125-427-978   Anna Lee Hooper b. abt. 1927 m.   Anderson?
1-3-17-125-427-979   Bettie June Hooper b. abt. 1929 m.   Dickerson?
1-3-17-126-429-980   Infant Nov. 28, 1934
1-3-17-126-429-981   Lillian Hooper married William L. Hall
    1429.   Dr. Keyoda Hall
    1430.   Kimitia Hall
1-3-17-126-429-982   Bruce "Sonny" Hooper b. April 30, 1940 d. Oct. 22, 2013 married JoAnn Hughes

(see p. 98)
1-3-17-126-429-983	Bernard Hooper b. Oct. 17, 1943 d. Dec. 18, 2007 (Internet, *Life Legacy* at Grissom Funeral Home, Cleveland, TN) married 1. ? 2. Jenna Morrison Guinn b. June 4, 1936 d. Oct. 20, 2012 (Internet, *The Chatanoogan.com*, May 12, 2016).

    1431.	Troy Hooper

    1432.	Gwen Hooper

    1433.	Renee Hooper

    (Step-children Tim Guinn and Terry Guinn)

1-3-17-126-431-984	Boyd Milton Hooper married Ruth Lawson

    1434.	Barbra Hooper

1-3-17-126-431-985	William Kins Hooper married Mabel Jones

    1435.	William Kins (Kinny) Hooper

    1436.	Greg Hooper married Connie Linkous

    1437.	Lori Hooper married William Chris Hutchins

1-3-17-126-431-986	Rose Margaret (Midge) Hooper married 1. Jim Cody

    1438.	Tim Cody

1-3-17-126-431-986	Rose Margaret (Midge) Hooper married 2. Zeno Beaty

    1439.	Zeno Beaty

1-3-17-127-432-987	John M. Crook, Jr. b. Jan. 22, 1905 – Feb. 15, 1978

1-3-17-127-433-988	Dorothy A. Ownbey b. 1921

1-3-17-127-433-989	Irene M. Ownbey b. 1923

1-3-17-127-433-990	Jack F. Ownbey b. 1922

1-3-17-127-433-991	Eloise O. Ownbey b. 1926

1-3-17-127-433-992	Robert C. Ownbey b. 1933

1-3-18-129-436-993	Tommie Woods b. abt. 1910

1-3-18-129-436-994	Samuel Woods b. abt. 1912

1-3-18-129-436-995	Jay R. Woods b. abt. 1916

1-3-18-129-439-996	Harold Boggs b. abt. 1913 Latimer, OK

1-3-18-133-442-997	Eula May Ellis 1922-1923

1-3-18-133-442-998	Sula Fay Ellis 1922-1923

1-3-18-133-442-999	James Theodore Ellis 1924-2002

1-3-18-133-442-1000	Clifford Hurley Ellis March 7, 1927-July 21, 1932

1-3-18-133-442-1001	Fonda Bernice Ellis June 19, 1930-Jan. 27, 2010

1-3-18-133-442-1002	David Dale Ellis 1934-2002

1-3-18-133-442-1003	Infant 1943

1-3-19-135-448-1004	Arlie Franklin Hooper b. Oct. 27, 1910 (MO) d. Nov. 30, 1990 (Internet *California Death Index* at *Ancestry.com*)

1-3-19-135-448-1005	Harlon J. Hooper b. May 9, 1912 (MO) d. Jan. 22, 1990 (Internet *California Death Index, Ancestry.com*)

1-3-19-135-449-1006	Ava Jenkins b. abt. 1907

1-3-19-135-449-1007	Andy Jenkins b. abt. 1909

1-3-19-135-449-1008	Alba Jenkins (dau.) b. abt. 1911

1-3-19-135-449-1009	Owen Jenkins b. abt. 1913

1-3-19-135-449-1010	Billie Jenkins (son) b. abt. 1918

1-3-19-135-449-1011	Donald Hall Jenkins b. abt. 1929

1-3-19-135-450-1012	Henry Brogdon b. abt. 1907

1-3-19-135-450-1013	Pearl Brogdon b. abt. 1911

1-3-19-135-452-1014	Walter E. Griffin b. abt. 1913

1-3-19-135-452-1015	David E. Griffin b. abt. 1915

1-3-19-136-454-1016	Winnie Yvonne Hooper b. 1945 married R. J. Fulton

    1440.	Jon Fulton married Kathy

    1441.	Wash Fulton

1-3-19-136-454-1017	Charles Ray Hooper, Jr. b. Nov. 12, 1948 in Denver, CO and d. Sept. 6, 2006 in Cimarron, NM. He married Shirley Cunico b. 1954 (Internet, *Ancestry.com, Findagrave.com*)

1442.   Kaycee Hooper

1443.   Kara Hooper married Kevin Mutz

1-3-20-146-477-1018   Randall K. Hooper b. May 3, 1955 – d. July 1, 1984 buried at Nemo Bethel Baptist Church Cemetery in Hickory County, MO (Internet *Ancestry.com, Find A Grave*)

1-3-20-146-477-1019   Belinda G. Hooper b. Feb. 25, 1961 – d. Sept. 7, 1987 buried at Nemo Bethel Baptist Church Cemetery in Hickory County, MO (Internet, *Ancestry.com, Find A Grave*)

1-3-20-146-477-1020   Gary Wayne Hooper (Internet, listed in Willa Schnitker Hooper Obituary at Speaks Family Legacy Chapels.)

1444.   Brandon Hooper

1445.   Krystal Hooper

1446.   Jeffrey Hooper

1-3-20-146-478-1021   Daniel Hooper

1-3-20-146-478-1022   Dawn Hooper married Sam Wiggins

1-3-20-146-478-1023   David Hooper

1-3-20-146-478-1024   Garland Hooper

1-3-20-146-480-1025   Gregory Hooper b. Sept. 13, 1969 married Lynn Hogan

1447.   Blaise Hooper

1-3-20-146-480-1026   Jeffrey Hooper

1-3-21-148-485-1027   George K. Dechow b. Sept. 18, 1944 married Karen Dian Springer

1-3-21-148-486-1028   William L. Hooper b. Sept. 16, 1931 married Doris Jean Wallace

1448.   William L. Hooper b. August 2, 1956 married Karen Lewis

1449.   Carol Ann Hooper b. Feb. 13, 1958 married Peter Allen Cooper

1-3-21-148-486-1029   Robert Hooper b. July 11, 1936 married Sylvia Bell

1450.   Cheryl Lynn Hooper b. June 4, 1960 married Stephen Cunningham

1451.   Phillip Lyle Hooper b. Feb. 26, 1963 married Joy Clark

1452.   David Alan Hooper b. Nov. 1, 1964 married Yvette Fermin

1-3-21-148-486-1030   David McNabb Hooper b. Jan. 19, 1942 married Jane Frances Miller

1453.   Andrew Cordia Hooper b. Aug. 2, 1978

1454.   Caitlin McNabb Hooper b. Oct. 3, 1981

1-3-21-150-489-1031   Betty Jo Meadors b. Nov. 7, 1936 married Lendsie Gardner

1455.   Recinda Lynn Gardner b. March 31, 1959 married Rick Osburn

1456.   Gregory Joe Gardner b. Feb. 24, 1962 married Angie Beasley

1-3-21-152-490-1032   Shirley Joan Hooper b. June 28, 1912 married Robert E. Mace

1457.   Stephen Eugene Mace b. Nov. 12, 1960 married Lisa Cathrine

1458.   Shari Lynn Mace married Steve Olsen

1459.   Scott Allen Mace

1-3-21-154-491-1033   Judy Hooper

1-3-21-154-492-1034   Kay Fletcher

1-3-21-155-495-1035   Donna Roy b. Jan. 28, 1939 d. Oct. 8, 1950

1-3-21-155-495-1036   Bill Roy b. Oct. 3, 1940

1-3-21-155-495-1037   Bob Roy b. Feb. 11, 1945

1-3-21-155-495-1038   Helen Roy b. Sept. 19, 1951

1-3-21-155-495-1039   Shirley Roy b. May 28, 1957

1-3-21-156-498-1040   James Lee Grisham April 7, 1935 married Ramadean Taylor

1460.   Shirley Ann Grisham b. Oct. 3, 1957 married Melvin Douglas Evans

1461.   James Michael Grisham b. March 4, 1961 married Shawna Redd

1-3-21-156-499-1041   Joan Marie Breshears b. June 18, 1941 married Thomas A. Northrip

1462.   Angelia Marie Breshears b. Nov. 10, 1961 married Rufus Eric Blair

1463.   Tommie Lynn Breshears b. Nov. 6, 1965 married Kenneth Dale Blair

1464.   Sarah Jo Breshears b. Jan. 30, 1970 married Larry Payne

1-3-21-156-499-1042   Mary Ethel Breshears

1-3-21-156-499-1043   Infant son

1-3-21-156-499-1044   Ivan Noel Breshears b. Nov. 5, 1946 married Mary Beth Mayfield

1465.   Andrea Michelle Breshears b. Jan. 1, 1968

1466.   Monica Suzanne Breshears b. Jan. 7, 1970

1-3-21-156-500-1045   Willeta Kay Pitts b. Nov. 24, 1944 married Robert J. Blake
      1467.   Barbara Lynette Blake b. Dec. 18, 1965 married Danny N. Morgans
      1468.   Amy Leann Blake b. March 3, 1967 married Gregory J. Morgans
      1469.   Jaqueline Renee Blake b. Nov. 3, 1972 married Scotty K. Rice
      1470.   Robert Justin Blake b. April 5, 1980
1-3-21-156-500-1046   Peggy Ann Pitts b. May 16, 1946 married Noel J. Shull
      1471.   Anthony Von Shull b. August 2, 1964
      1472.   Charles Douglas Shull b. May 28, 1970
1-3-21-156-500-1047   Gloria Jean Pitts b. Nov. 16, 1949 married James E. McIntire
      1473.   Yvette Lorea McIntire b. Dec. 29, 1972
      1474.   Lance Edwin McIntire b. June 1, 1975
1-3-21-156-500-1048   Rebecca Ilene Pitts Oct. 30, 1956 maried James Reynolds
      1475.   Jamie Ileen Reynolds b. Sept. 15, 1978
      1476.   Jacy Leigh Reynolds b. Oct. 9, 1984
1-3-21-156-501-1049   Carolyn Sue Degraffenreid b. March 15, 1942 d. Dec. 29, 1946
(1-3-22 Tabitha Hooper Jack and Clinton Jack had several children in Tarrant County, Fort Worth, TX, but no descendants were listed in the seventh generation.)

Some of the Absolom Hooper family information was taken from *Hooper Genealogy and Autobiography of Wm. Hayden Hooper1898-1966* which was published at Thomas, Custer County, OK on August 4, 1966. On the Internet, *hooperconnections.com* (Bill Hooper, Clay Hooper and Sharon Hooper) also had data for the Absolom Hooper family.
1-4-25-167-514-1050   Lois Perian b. 1921
1-4-25-167-514-1051   Louise Perian b. 1923
1-4-25-167-514-1052   Arvil Perian b.1930 in California
1-4-25-167-522-1053   J. P. Perian, Jr. b. 1935
1-4-25-167-523-1054   James Sanford Perian b. 1936
1-4-25-167-523-1055   Donnie Coralee Perian b. 1937
1-4-25-167-523-1056   George Winston Perian b. 1939
1-4-30-177-530-1057   Barbara Carden m. Wayne Harrison Hooper (number 960)
      1423.   Timothy Wayne Hooper married Andrea Michele Roark on Jan. 28, 1995 in
                Bradley County, TN (Internet, *Ancestry.com*)
      1424.   Tracy Hooper married Leslie Ratcliff
1-4-30-177-530-1058   Billy Carden m. Deloris Jean Russell
      1477.   Tamara Carden
      1478.   Rodney Carden
      1479.   Tina Carden
1-4-30-177-530-1058A Judy Evelyn Carden m. James Edwin McCracken
      1479A.   Jason McCracken
      1479B.   John C. McCracken married Kristi
      1479C.   Cathy McCracken
1-4-30-177-530-1058B Carolyn Carden m. Jack Green
      1479D. Melanie Green
      1479E.   Kristi Green married Michael Mason on May 28, 1993 in Bradley County, TN
                (Internet, *Ancestry.com*)
1-4-30-177-530-1059   Ronald L. Carden b. Aug. 28, 1951 m. Jan. 28, 1972 Rosie Juanita Prater b. Aug.
                15, 1952 in Polk County, TN (Internet, *Ancestry.com*, Polk County, TN)
      1480.   Laura Carden
1-4-30-177-530-1059A Wanda Carden m. Glenn David McCracken on August 28, 1971 in Bradley
                County, TN (Internet, *Ancestry.com*)
1-4-30-177-530-1059B Gary Carden m. (1) Mary Lisa Hickman; (2) Letha Rene Rodriguez-Chapman;
                (3) Gayla Higgins (Internet, *Ancestry.com*, Bradley County Marriages, TN)
1-4-33-183-547-1060   Truman Francis (Frank) Brundage
1-4-33-183-547-1061   Shirley Jean Brundage
1-4-33-183-547-1062   Billie Gene Brundage
1-4-33-183-550-1063   Loraine Harris

1-4-33-183-551-1064   Sammie E. Harris
1-4-33-183-551-1065   Ronnie Harris
1-4-33-183-551-1066   Vickie Jean Harris
1-4-33-184-552-1067   Jo Helene Hooper married Charles Green
    1481.   Barbara Green
    1482.   Charles Green
    1483.   Stephen Green
    1484.   David Green
    1485.   Grace Ann Green
1-4-33-184-552-1068   William Bright Hooper married Janice Mitchell
    1486.   Angelia Hooper
1-4-33-184-552-1069   Hershel Victor Hooper married Marlene Riley
    1487.   Linda Diane Hooper
    1488.   Michael Hooper
    1489.   Karen Jo Hooper
    1490.   Nicholas Hooper
1-4-33-185-553-1070   Sandra Sue Hooper by the first wife
1-4-33-185-553-1071   John David Hooper by the second wife
1-4-33-185-555-1072   Cindy Cooke
1-4-33-185-555-1073   Candi Cooke
1-4-33-186-556-1074   Ethel Mae Simpson
1-4-33-186-556-1075   Maxwell David Simpson
1-4-33-186-557-1076   Dianne Hooper
1-4-33-186-557-1077   John Robert Hooper b. 1954
1-4-33-186-557-1078   David Wayne Hooper b. 1961
1-4-33-186-558-1079   Charsell Hooper
1-4-33-186-558-1080   Kevin Isaac Hooper b. 1956
1-4-33-186-558-1081   Kile Parks Hooper b. 1964
1-4-33-187-559-1082   Richard Enos Hooper married Beverly Day
    1491.   Richard Clayton Hooper
    1492.   Leslie Denise Hooper
    1493.   Terry Hooper
    1494.   Sydney Allison Hooper
1-4-33-187-559-1083   Gary Hooper married Joyce A. Smith
    1495.   Carla A. Hooper
    1496.   Sue A. Hooper
1-4-33-187-559-1084   Thomas Hooper b. 1948
1-4-33-187-559-1085   Douglas Hooper b. 1953
1-4-33-187-560-1086   Ronnie Gripe
1-4-33-187-561-1087   Stephen Dickerson
1-4-33-187-562-1088   James Warren Hooper b. 1953
1-4-33-187-562-1089   Anthony Kent Hooper b. 1955
1-4-33-187-562-1090   Mary Sue Hooper
1-4-33-188-563-1091   A. L. Potter married Barbara Porter
    1497.   Bobby Potter
    1498.   Bruce Potter
    1499.   Donna Potter
    1500.   Janet Potter
1-4-33-188-563-1092   Robert Olen Potter
1-4-33-188-563-1093   Don Coy Potter
1-4-33-188-564-1094   Bryan Henry Potter married Catherine Cone
    1501.   Janice Potter
1-4-33-188-565-1095   Gary Morrison
1-4-33-188-565-1096   Nana Beth Morrison
1-4-33-189-566-1097   Billy Gene Campbell
1-4-33-189-567-1098   Pauline Campbell

1-4-33-189-567-1099   Ann Campbell
1-4-33-189-568-1100   Beth Hastey
1-4-33-190-570-1101   Sammy Joe Ryan
1-4-33-190-570-1102   Donnie Wayne Ryan
1-4-33-190-570-1103   Terry Dean Ryan
1-4-33-193-571-1104   Tracy Lee Cotts
1-4-34-194-573-1105   Carl Truman Hooper b. June 26, 1920 married 1. Genevieve Green
     1502.   Carla Hooper
     1503.   Trudy Hooper
1-4-34-194-573-1105   Carl Truman Hooper b. June 26, 1920 married 2. Sylvia Gurney on July 4,
     1962
     1504.   Kevin Todd Hooper b. Oct. 22, 1965
1-4-34-194-573-1106   Anita Vyrle Hooper b. Oct. 4, 1926 married H. L. Christensen, Jr.
     1505.   Randal Lee Christensen b. Nov. 12, 1950
     1506.   Ranita June Christensen b. Nov. 17, 1955
1-4-34-194-573-1107   Venita Pearl Hooper b. Oct. 4, 1926 married 1. Keith Christensen
     1507.   Deanna Beth Christensen b. June 13, 1945
     1508.   Kent Duane Christensen Oct. 4, 1948
1-4-34-194-573-1107   Venita Pearl Hooper b. Oct. 4, 1926 married 2. Worth Cornelius
     1509.   Bryan Lane Cornelius Feb. 2- Feb. 4, 1961
1-4-34-194-573-1108   Ann Marie Hooper b. Feb. 7, 1934 married William Kinslow Harrison
1-4-34-194-574-1109   Donald Moore
1-4-34-194-574-1110   Mary Ellen Moore
1-4-34-194-574-1111   Wanda Moore
1-4-34-194-574-1112   Joann Moore
1-4-34-194-575-1113   Leslie Ray Moore b. July 3, 1925
1-4-34-194-577-1114   Gary Hooper b. 1941 married Martha Newby
     1510.   Cheryl Ann Hooper b. Jan. 26, 1966
1-4-34-194-577-1115   Larry Hooper b. 1953
1-4-34-194-578-1116   Larry Allen Ayling 1941
1-4-34-196-581-1117   Ralph Payne
1-4-34-196-581-1118   Billy Payne
1-4-34-196-581-1119   Donald Payne
1-4-34-196-582-1120   Wilburn Griffith
1-4-34-196-582-1121   Bobby Ruth Griffith
1-4-34-196-583-1122   Jackson Hooper
1-4-34-196-583-1123   Jerry Hooper
1-4-34-196-584-1124   Joe Allen Hooper
     1511.   Reed Hooper
     1512.   Bryce Hooper
1-4-34-196-585-1125   Deborah Hooper
1-4-34-196-586-1126   Deloris Smith
1-4-34-196-586-1127   Joyce Smith
1-4-34-196-586-1128   James Smith
1-4-34-196-586-1129   Kenneth Smith
1-4-34-196-587-1130   Tommy Dan Hooper married Laura Hood on March 16, 1962 in McMinn County,
     TN (Internet, *Ancestry.com*)
     1513.   Jeffrey Dan Hooper
     1514.   Tonya Jean Hooper
     1515.   Candance Gail Hooper
1-4-34-196-587-1131   Eddie Kenneth Hooper married Glenda Wilson
     1516.   Brian Kenneth Hooper (deceased)
     1517.   Pamela Hooper
     1518.   Cindy Hooper
1-4-34-196-587-1132   Gail Hooper married (1) B. W. Cooley on April 22, 1966 in McMinn County, TN
     (Internet, *Ancestry.com*) and (2) Arnold Sledge.

1519.   David Cooley
1520.   Shannon Cooley
1521.   Jessica Cooley
1-4-34-196-587-1133   Robert Michael Hooper married Mitzi Crabtree
1-2-5-38-206-595-1134   Edward Shelton b. Nov. 24, 1913 – d. Nov. 8, 1982
1-2-5-38-206-595-1135   Elmo Shelton b. June 8, 1916 – d. Jan. 25, 2009
1-2-5-38-206-595-1136   Ima Well Shelton b. Sept. 3, 1918 – Nov. 18, 2010
1-2-5-38-206-595-1137   John Shelton, Jr. April 15, 1920 – d. Sept. 6, 1990
1-2-5-38-206-595-1138   Imogene Shelton Feb. 22, 1924 – d. March 9, 2000
1-2-5-38-206-595-1139   Maxine Shelton 1927
1-2-5-38-206-595-1140   Kenneth R. Shelton July 12, 1927 – d. Aug. 11, 2007
(See p. 54 for the source of the Saulpaw information.)
1-2-7-67-229-616-1141   George Lewis Saulpaw, Jr. died 1987 in California
1-2-7-67-226-617-1142   Charles L. Bryant b. 1928 married Lucille Kays
1522.   Deborah Bryant
1-2-7-67-226-617-1143   Lillah Catherine Bryant b. Feb. 23, 1929-May 18, 1929 (*Tennessee Death Index*)
1-2-7-67-226-618-1144   Virginia Lee Seaton married married John Morgan Taylor, 3rd in Claiborne Co.,
          TN May 10, 1954 (Internet, *Ancestry.com*).
1523.   Carolyn Taylor
1524.   John Taylor
1525.   James Martin Taylor
1526.   Seaton Taylor
1527.   Mary Elizabeth Taylor
1-2-7-67-226-621-1145   Karl Davenport Saulpaw, 3rd
1-2-7-67-226-621-1146   Glen Wright Saulpaw b. July 31, 1951 – June 22, 1998 married Beverly Rogers
          Crye
1-2-7-67-226-621-1147   Sarah Ann Saulpaw b. Oct. 19, 1953 – June 11, 1999 married Steven B.
          Wermann
1528.   Scott Aaron Wermann
1-2-7-67-226-621-1148   James Richard Saulpaw
1-2-7-67-226-621-1149   Charles Erich Saulpaw
1-2-7-67-226-623-1150   Kathyrn Brown married Lan C. Dingess
1529.   Matthew L. Dingess
1530.   Patrick Dingess
1-2-7-67-226-623-1151   Mitchell R. Brown married Melissa Landre
1531.   Margaret Grace Brown
1-2-7-67-226-623-1152   Michael L. Brown married Susan Larkin
1-2-7-67-226-623-1153   Teresa Brown married Reed Harvey
1532.   Ellen Harvey
1533.   Carol Harvey
1-2-7-67-226-624-1154   Jane Ellen Hutcheson married Donnie Ray Womac
1534.   Lucinda Jane Womac
1535.   Rachel Ann Womac
1-2-7-67-226-624-1155   Emma Elizabeth Hutcheson married Richard Keith Jacob
1536.   Richard Keith Jacob, Jr.
1537.   Christian Darr Jacob
1-2-9-84-242-625-1156   Raymond Farmer b. 1939
1-3-14-98-260-637-1157   Betty Graham b. 1928
1-3-14-98-260-637-1158   Coleen Graham b. 1931
1-3-14-98-260-637-1159   Sue Graham b. 1932
1-3-14-98-260-637-1160   Kathleen Graham b. 1936
1-3-14-98-260-637-1161   Jo Ann Graham b. 1938
1-3-14-99-266-659-922   Lynn Andrew Hooper b. Oct. 18, 1910 d. Feb. 21, 1973 (son of Scott Hooper
          659 and Jeanette Gilbreath Hooper 388)
1-3-14-99-266-659-923   James Hoyt Hooper b. August 14, 1913-d. Aug. 22, 1915 (son of Scott Hooper
          659 and Jeanette Gilbreath Hooper 388)

1-3-14-99-266-659-924   Edith Gertrude Hooper b. Oct. 30, 1918-d. April 24, 2008 (daughter of Scott
                        Hooper 659 and Jeanetta Gilbreath Hooper 388) married William F. "Jack"
                        Barger in 1941 in Dandridge, TN. (Information was found in Edith Barger's
                        Obituary in the *Cleveland Daily Banner* dated April 28, 2008 and found at
                        Ancestry.com.)
        1382.   Martha Lynn Barger
        1383.   Maurine Barger
1-3-14-99-266-662-1162   Mildred Hooper 1921
1-3-14-99-273-682-1163   Nadine Erven b. March 27, 1935 married Duane R. Buckholz
1-3-14-99-273-683-1164   Ronnie Dean Erven b. May 30, 1946 married Marinell Rayfield
1-3-14-100-291-731-1165   William R. Thompson Jr. and his wife, Linda
1-3-14-100-291-731-1166   Thomas Thompson and his wife, Lesa
1-3-14-100-291-731-1167   Ann Thompson married Frank Autrey
1-3-14-100-291-731-1168   Patty Thompson married Tom Shipley
**(Thelma Louise Bates Thompson family information for the children listed above came from her
husband William R. Thompson's information from Internet, *Find A Grave.com* and the Brumley-
Mills Funeral Home of McAlester, OK. This included the Obituary from the *McAlester News Capital*
Feb. 19, 2007. Listed are seven grandchildren, Chris Autrey, Clint Autrey and his wife, Alana,
Stephen Thompson, Lauren Wilson and her husband, Brian, Jon Shipley, Matthew Vaughan and
Chelsie, and Matthew Shipley and his wife, Lindsey; also, it included five great-grandchildren,
Kaitlyn Thompson, Carter Vaughan, Parker Shipley, Brynn Shipley, and Cash Autrey.)**
1-3-14-100-291-732-1169   Mark Earl Richardson b. Dec. 11, 1961 d. Dec. 11, 1977
1-3-14-100-291-732-1170   Ronny Richardson married Sandra
1-3-14-100-291-732-1171   Linda Sue Richardson married William Earnhart
**(The Internet, *Find A Grave.com* website by *MATuley* included the Obituary from the *Herald
Democrat* (TX) p. A-22, July 23, 2000 about Johnny Edward Richardson (number 732 above) and
Dianna Rosetta Fairbanks which included granddaughters and husbands: Stephanie and Steven
Brilliant, Misty Dannelley, Tonja Cagle, Chari Landry, Destiny and Teran Richardson, Lisa Blood
and Tiffany Earnhart and grandsons, Blake Leinneweber, Ryan Earnhart and Cameron Richardson
and three great grandchildren.)**
1-3-14-100-291-733-1172   Dennis Earl Richardson b. Jan. 10, 1959 – d. Oct. 2, 1993 married Vickie
                        Melton on Dec. 6, 1980 (Internet, Richardson, *Find A Grave.com*)
        1538.   Dennis Jake Richardson
1-3-14-100-291-733-1173   Annette Richardson married a Burden
1-3-14-100-291-733-1174   Sherry Richardson married a Townsend
1-3-14-100-291-733-1175   Bonnie Richardson married a Rutherford
1-3-14-100-291-734-1176   James Rhea Beauchamp
1-3-14-100-291-734-1177   Jay Lee Beauchamp
1-3-14-100-291-734-1178   Jim Ann Beauchamp married a Hill
1-3-14-101-292-736-1179   Garrett Graham b. 1918
1-3-14-101-292-736-1180   Sada Graham b. 1920
1-3-14-101-292-736-1181   Rollen Graham b. 1923
1-3-14-101-292-736-1182   Hallas Graham b. 1925
1-3-14-101-292-737-1183   Margie Graham b. 1924
1-3-14-101-292-741-1184   Roy Graham b. 1926
1-3-14-101-292-741-1185   Ralph Graham b. 1928
1-3-14-101-292-741-1186   Raymon Graham b. 1929
1-3-15-105-315-765-1187   Mary E. McAmis b. 1922
1-3-15-105-315-765-1188   Charles. E. McAmis b. Sept. 2, 1923 d. Dec. 24, 2005
1-3-15-105-315-765-1189   John D. McAmis b. 1928
1-3-15-105-315-765-1190   Thomas Oscar McAmis b. Dec. 12, 1932 – Sept. 16, 1951 at Harvey, Illinois
                        married Lula Mae Potts 1931 – 2003
        1539.   Debra McAmis
1-3-15-106-317-770-1191   Bobbie Hooper b. 1932 married Dr. Gordon Lawrence Hixson, Sr. b. 1929
        1540.   Karen Hixson b. 1951 married Steve Phillips b. 1954
        1541.   Dr. Gordon (Gary) Lawrence Hixson II b. 1954 married Sherry McPherson b. 1960

1-3-15-106-317-770-1192   Barbara McDowell married John Chalker and adopted David Chalker.
      1542.   Chris Chalker
      1543.   Mark Chalker
1-3-15-106-317-770-1193   Judith (Judy) Hooper married Doyle Gibson
      1544.   Deborah Darlene Gibson (Sept. 5, 1960 – April 9, 1971 Johnston Cemetery, Bradley County, TN)
      1545.   Kim Gibson
      1546.   Pam Gibson
      1547.   Allen Gibson married Rhonda Knight
1-3-15-106-317-770-1194   Martha Lyn Hooper b. married Floyd Harold Reno on Aug. 27, 1965 in Meigs County, TN.
1-3-15-106-319-775-1195   Glenda Clara Caldwell married John Wilson Cantrell in Bradley County, TN on May 15, 1970 (Internet, *Jim Rush Funeral Home* 2017 listed 3 dead grandchildren of John Wilson Cantrell: David Casswell Cantrell, John Wilson Cantrell and Noah Starr Cantrell)
      1548.   Jonathan Roy Cantrell
      1549.   David Christian Cantrell
1-3-15-106-319-775-1196   Clarestine Roy Caldwell born March 8, 1948 died Nov. 14. 1959
1-3-15-106-319-776-1197   Albert Vernon Geren
1-3-15-106-319-776-1198   George Willard Geren married Sharon Matthews (number 1682) on May 2, 1966 in Bradley County, TN
      1550.   Georgina Gay Geren
      1551.   Emily Geren
1-3-15-106-319-776-1199   Joyce Ann Geren
1-3-15-106-319-778-1200   Billy Don Geren b. May 23, 1939 – d. Dec. 13, 2012 married Peggy Vance (Internet, *Find A Grave, Ancestry.com*)
      1552.   Donna Geren
1-3-15-106-319-778-1201   Barkley Geren b. Nov. 27, 1944 – d. Feb. 7, 2017 married Mable Delay (*Cleveland Daily Banner* Obituary on Feb. 9, 2017).
      1553.   Bryan Geren married Pam
      1554.   Kinny Geren married Cindy Pickins
      1555.   Cheryl Geren
      1556.   Amy Geren married Scott McGowan

Barkley and Mable Geren's grandchildren named in the *Cleveland Daily Banner* Obituary dated February 9, 2017: Walker Geren (Breanna); Bradlee Geren; Bradlee Carter; Baylee Carter; Kellee Geren; Sydni Geren; Barkley "Kley" McGowan; Kinslee McGowan; Kason McGowan; Walker McGowan and Baylor McGowan.

1-3-15-106-320-429-981   Lillian Hooper married William L. Hall
      1429.   Dr. Keyoda Hall
      1430.   Kimitia Hall
1-3-15-106-320-429-982   Bruce Hooper b. April 30, 1940 d. Oct. 22, 2013 (Internet, *The Chattanoogan.com,* May 12, 2016) married JoAnn Hughes (step children Jim Hughes and Debbie Hughes)
1-3-15-106-320-429-983   Morgan Bernard Hooper b. Oct. 17, 1943 d. Dec. 18, 2007 married 1. ?   2. Jenna Morrison Guinn b. June 4, 1936 d. Oct. 20, 2012 (see p. 91)
      1431.   Troy Hooper
      1432.   Gwen Hooper b. May 28, 1964
      1433.   Renee Hooper
      (Step-children Tim Guinn and Terry Guinn)
1-3-15-106-320-431-984   Boyd Milton Hooper married Ruth Lawson
      1434.   Barbra Hooper
1-3-15-106-320-431-985   William Kins Hooper married Mabel Jones
      1435.   William Kins (Kinny) Hooper, Jr.
      1436.   Greg Hooper married Connie Linkous
      1437.   Lori Hooper married William Chris Hutchins
1-3-15-106-320-431-986   Midge Hooper married 1. Jim Cody.

1438.   Tim Cody
1-3-15-106-320-431-986   Midge Hooper married 2. Zeno Beaty.
1439.   Zeno Beaty
1-3-15-106-322-781-1202   Carolyn Hooper married Steve Bryant
1557.   David Bryant
1-3-15-106-322-782-1203   James R. (Jimmy) Hooper married Sandra Graham (number 1343)
1558.   Jonathan David Hooper
1559.   Christopher Nicholas Hooper
1-3-15-106-323-783-1204   Laura Jane Taylor married Wilson B. Garrett
1-3-15-106-324-788-1205   Paul Deackins
1-3-15-106-324-789-1206   Joseph Larry Hooper, Sr. married Sandy Debellis (Internet,
          auvenshine.com/beaty and *Fike Funeral Home Memorial Page*)
1560.   Joseph Larry Hooper, Jr.
1561.   Brian Geren Hooper
1-3-15-106-324-789-1207   Judy Hooper married Bill Chandler
1-3-15-106-325-790-1208   Sandra Brewer married 1. Brett Simpson and 2. Jimmy Caldwell
1562.   Alex Simpson
1563.   Alison Simpson
1-3-15-107-326-792-1209   Henry Brackett b. 1934
1-3-15-107-326-792-1210   Jerry Brackett b. 1937
1-3-15-107-327-794-1211   Evelyn Garrison b. Dec. 21, 1928
1-3-15-107-327-794-1212   Maurine F. Garrison
1-3-15-107-327-794-1213   Mary Catherine Garrison
1-3-15-107-327-794-1214   Ora Mae Garrison
1-3-15-107-327-795-1215   Jackie B. Garrison (son) b. abt. 1929
1-3-15-107-327-795-1216   Carrol L. Garrison
1-3-15-107-327-795-1217   Carrol L. Garrison b. 1934
1-3-15-107-327-796-1218   Pink W. Fletcher b. 1927 (Internet, *Ancestry.com,1930 Wise County, Texas
          Census p. 2A Precinct 9*)
1-3-15-107-327-796-1219   Marita Jean Fletcher b. Aug. 22, 1929 d. Oct. 24, 1998 married Ollie
          Martin (Buster) Brem on July 18, 1950 in Red River County, TX
          (*reneflor at Ancestry.com*)
1564.   Henry L. Brem (Internet, *Ancestry.com, joeowen92*, tombstone picture has children
          listed)
1565.   Sheila A. Brem b. Feb. 12, 1951 – d. Feb. 25, 1951 (*joeowen92 at Ancestry.com*)
1566.   Kathie L. Brem
1567.   Ricky M. Brem
1-3-15-107-327-799-1220   John T. Garrison, Jr.
1-3-15-107-327-799-1221   Donald Ray Garrison
1-3-15-108-334-807-977   Earnesteen Hooper b. Nov. 20, 1923 – Oct. 16, 1996 m. a Wender & Heiskell
1-3-15-108-334-807-978   Anabell Hooper b. abt. 1927
1-3-15-108-334-807-979   Bettie J. Hooper b. abt. 1929
1-3-15-109-341-808-1222   Jay H. Hooper married Doris Lankford (See Appendix H p. 306.)
1568.   Debra L. Hooper
1-3-15-109-341-808-1223   William Hooper married Jean   (See Appendix H p. 306.)
1-3-15-109-344-815-1224   Gale Miller married Bernice Kay Clark on Nov. 26, 1966 in Bradley County,
          TN (Bernice Clark traces her ancestry from Absolom Hooper the
          Revolutionary War hero and his wife Sarah Siler)
1569.   Anthony Miller
1570   Neil Miller
1-3-15-109-344-815-1225   Ivo Monroe (Monty) Miller married Diane Hodnett on June 11, 1968 in
          Bradley County, TN (2) Lori Jordan
1571.   Dr. Ivo Aaron Miller b. April 26, 1971
1572.   Joshua Wade Miller
1573.   Jordan Miller b. 2001
1-3-15-109-344-816-1226   Randall Edward Miller was born May 24, 1953 and died July 20, 2011 (found

on Internet at *Web: Tennessee, Find a Grave Index*. He married 1. Deborah
Jean Barber on Dec. 19, 1972, and 2. Melissa Ann Gentry on May 19, 1979 in
Bradley County, TN. Children listed in *Cleveland Daily Banner* Obituary on
July 23, 2011.

    1574.   Zachary Miller
    1575.   Ashley Miller
    1576.   Mollie Miller

1-3-15-109-344-816-1227   Brenda Miller
1-3-15-109-344-816-1228   Donna Jo Miller married Robert Joe Bacon on July 1, 1985 in Bradley
    County, TN
1-3-15-109-345-817-1229   Gwen Gibson
1-3-15-109-345-817-1230   Melanie Gibson married Tim
1-3-15-109-345-818-1231   Robert Fortney
1-3-15-109-345-819-1232   Connie L. Hooper married Roy Millaway
    1577.   Carrie Lee Millaway
1-3-15-109-345-819-1233   David Dale Hooper married Sable Couch
    1578.   William Keith Hooper
    1579.   Natalie Deann Hooper
1-3-15-109-345-819-1234   Alice M. Hooper married Fritz Harris
    1580.   Joey Heather Harris
    1581.   Jenny Lynn Harris
1-3-15-109-345-819-1235   Barry H. Hooper married Cheryl Kendrick
    1582.   Garrett Harrison Hooper
    1583.   Anna Caroline Hooper
1-3-15-109-345-820-1236   James Richard Hooper married Partricia Prince who had a son named Beau
    who died April 19, 2011 (Internet *The Chattanoogan.com* May 11, 2011)
    1584.   Tyler Hooper b. March 13, 1985
1-3-15-109-345-820-1237   Mark Douglas Hooper married Kim Shehan
1-3-15-109-345-821-1238   Aon Douglas Miller married Amanda A. Johnston
    1585.   Morgan Kathryne Miller
    1586.   Mary Alden Miller
1-3-15-109-345-821-1239   Jessica Leigh Miller married James E. Jollie
1-3-15-110-349-826-1240   Charles Hubert Murphy b. 1943 married Marion Mysinger
    1587.   Lillian Murphy b. 1965
    1588.   Michael Murphy b. 1967
1-3-15-110-349-826-1241   Linda Lou Murphy b. 1946 married Charles Hobert Cook, Jr.
    1589.   Lesa Cook
1-3-15-110-349-826-1242   Dewayne Murphy b. 1948 married (1) Virginia Baker and (2) Anna Lee
    Grissom
1-3-15-110-349-826-1243   Alice Lynn Murphy b. 1954 married Dennis Taylor
    1590.   Jason Taylor
    1591.   Curtis Taylor
1-3-15-110-349-826-1244   Deborah Joyce Murphy b. 1957 m. Junior Scroggins
    1592.   Adam Murphy
1-3-15-110-349-827-1245   John Millaway
1-3-15-110-349-827-1246   Donna Millaway
1-3-15-110-349-827-1247   Sherry Millaway married Steve Harden on Feb. 15, 1985 in Bradley County,
    TN (Internet, *Ancestry.com*)
    1593.   Tracey Harden
    1594.   Valerie Harden
1-3-15-110-349-827-1248   Michael Frank (Frankie) Millaway married 1. Vickie Poole on May 26, 1977
    in Bradley County, TN; 2. Susan Jones on April 3, 1992 in Bradley County,
    TN (Internet, *Ancestry.com*)
    1595.   Joel Millaway
1-3-15-110-349-828-1249   Millard Dale Millaway 1953 – d. April 23, 2008
1-3-15-110-349-828-1250   Gary Lee Millaway b. May 6, 1960

1-3-15-110-349-828-1251   Beverley Millaway married Kenneth Lankford
      1596.   Tyler Lankford
1-3-15-110-349-828-1252   Darla Millaway married John Roberts
      1597.   Jonathan Roberts
      1598.   Rachel Roberts
1-3-15-110-349-828-1253   Jimmy Millaway married Lisa
      1599.   Jimmy Millaway
      1600.   Laura Millaway
1-3-15-110-349-829-1254   Phyllis Elaine Black b. Oct. 16, 1952 married in Bradley County, TN Dexter Denny on June 8, 1974 (*Ancestry.com*). He was born Feb. 13, 1949.
      1601.   Deidre Denny
1-3-15-110-349-829-1255   Lamar Black married Kay ?
1-3-15-110-349-830-1256   Edward Keith Millaway, Jr.
1-3-15-110-349-830-1257   Heath Millaway
1-3-15-110-349-830-1258   Alan Millaway married Rhonda Ball on Feb. 19, 1983 in Bradley County, TN
      1602.   Dustin Millaway
1-3-15-110-349-830-1259   Patricia Millaway
1-3-15-111-353-836-1260   Gary Marshall Wallace married Suzanne Newman Aug. 13, 1988 in Bradley County, TN
      1603.   Karen Wallace
      1604.   Ken Wallace
      1605.   Amanda Wallace
1-3-15-111-353-836-1261   Mary Kay Wallace married Melvin Elder Sept. 9, 1978
      1606.   Adam Elder
      1607.   Laura Elder
1-3-15-111-353-836-1262   Ila Virginia Wallace b. Sept. 16, 1964 married Mike Kirkpatrick
      1608.   Chase Kirkpatrick
      1609.   Olivia Kirkpatrick
1-3-15-111-353-837-1263   Diana Lynn Western married Mitchell Geren
1-3-15-111-353-837-1264   Michael Len Western married Rita Crye
1-3-15-111-354-838-1236   James Richard Hooper married (1) Patricia Lambert Prince, and she already had a son named Beau who died April 19, 2011(Internet *The Chattanoogan.com*) . Rick married (2) Marcia McMurray.
      1584.   Tyler Hooper b. March 13, 1985
1-3-15-111-354-838-1237   Mark Douglas Hooper married Kim Shehan
1-3-15-111-355-839-1265   Thomas E. Wood, Jr.
1-3-15-111-355-839-1266   Marianna Wood
1-3-15-111-356-844-1267   Forrest Buchanan (Bucky) Hill, 3rd
1-3-15-111-356-844-1268   Robert Hooper Hill
1-3-15-111-356-845-1269   Ronnie Lee Pell married Tammy Laverne Walden
1-3-15-111-356-845-1270   Richard Lynn Pell married Mary Ann Goolet
      1610.   James Pell
      1611.   Jennifer Pell
      1612.   Mary Ann Pell
1-3-15-111-356-845-1271   Regina Louise Pell married Tony Pantalucas
      1613.   Anthony Pantalucas
1-3-15-111-356-845-1272   Francis Erhart Scherer, 4th married Lori
      1614.   Desiree Scherer
1-3-15-111-356-846-1273   Steven Franklin Bacon married (1) Regina Daniels, no children, (2) Susan E. Brown (one child), (3) Teresa Walker and (4) Pamela M. Loveday
      1615.   Justin Franklin Bacon
1-3-15-111-356-847-1274   Dennis Robert Whaley, Jr. married Susan Hunsucker
      1616.   Amber Nichole Whaley
      1617.   Dennis Robert Whaley, 3rd
1-3-15-111-356-847-1275   Gregory Alan Whaley married Zandra Orr

1618.	Carmen Alise Whaley
1619.	Alana Bree Whaley
1-3-15-111-356-847-1275	Gregory Alan Whaley married (2) Jessica Helton
1620.	Megan Faye Whaley
1-3-15-111-356-848-1276	Julia Ann Hooper
1-3-16-112-359-853-1277	Mary O. Marr
1-3-16-112-360-858-1278	Florence Marr b. Dec. 10, 1917 – d. Feb. 6, 1931
1-3-16-112-360-858-1279	Albert Daniel Marr, Sr. (b. 1921) married Dorothy Randolph
(Internet, Marr, *The Chattanoogan.com* obit Dec. 24, 2013)
1621.	Debbie Marr
1622.	Danny Marr Jr.
1623.	Bill Marr
1624.	David Marr
1-3-16-112-360-858-1280	Thomas Marr b. Oct. 26, 1923 – May 6, 2004 married Nancy Arlene Coffey
1625.	Sandra Marr
1626.	Pamela Marr
1627.	Thomas Logan Marr, Jr.
1628.	Tammy Marr
1-3-16-112-360-858-1281	Pauline Marr b. abt. 1927
1-3-16-112-360-858-1282	Polly Marr married a Frazier
1-3-16-112-360-858-1283	Virginia L. Marr b. abt. 1929
1-3-16-112-360-858-1284	Myrtle Marr b. abt. 1934
1-3-16-112-360-858-1285	Arnold Marr b. abt. 1937
1-3-16-112-360-862-1286	Mamie Johnson
1-3-16-112-360-863-1287	Pauline Marr married Warner Bertel Washburn
1-3-16-112-360-863-1288	Calvin "Red, Pop" Marr married Jimmie Ruth Farris. **(Internet,
Ancestry.com, Find A Grave listed sons Danny Marr (Cathy) and Daniel Marr (Brenda); grandsons
Jonathan Marr (Jennifer) and Nathan Marr (Taylor); great-grandchildren are Wyatt Marr, Drake
Marr and Grace Marr.)**
1-3-16-112-360-863-1289	Alvin "Speedy" Marr (twin) married Ruby.
1-3-16-112-360-863-1290	Pete Marr
1-3-16-112-360-863-1291	Kenneth Marr
1-3-16-112-360-863-1292	Mary Ann Marr married a Ledford
1-3-16-112-361-864-1293	Ruby Lee Jones b. Oct. 27, 1914 – May 29, 1955
1-3-16-112-363-353-836	Virginia J. Hooper b. 1928 – d. 2017. She married Marshall Wallace.
1260.	Gary Wallace married Suzanne Newman on August 13, 1988 in Bradley County, TN
1261.	Mary Kay Wallace married Melvin Elder on Sept. 9, 1978 in Bradley County, TN
1262.	Ila Virginia Wallace married Mike Kirkpatrick
1-3-16-112-363-353-837	Mary Margaret Hooper married Noah Western
1263.	Diana Lynn Western married Mitchell Geren
1264.	Michael Len Western married Rita Crye
1-3-16-112-363-354-838	Darrell Hooper married June 29, 1951 in Bradley County, TN to Judy Miller
(number 820)
1236.	Richard Hooper
1237.	Mark Hooper
1-3-16-112-363-355-839	Lottie Lee Thompson b. abt. 1929 married Thomas Eddie Wood
1265.	Thomas E. Wood, Jr.
1266.	Marianna Wood
1-3-16-112-363-355-840	J. E. Thompson
1-3-16-112-363-355-841	Marie Irene Thompson married Harold Baker
1-3-16-112-363-355-842	Martha Edwyna Thompson married Ralph L. Pierce
1-3-16-112-363-355-843	Earnest W. Thompson, Jr. married Mildred Smith
1-3-16-112-363-356-844	Gurtha Dean Hooper married Forrest Hill
1267.	Forrest Buchanan (Bucky) Hill, 3rd
1268.	Robert Hooper Hill
1-3-16-112-363-356-845	Hazel Lou Hooper (some name information from *FamilyTreeGuide.com* for

Dorothy Graham family and *Jay and Lou Graham* by Juanita Graham Hinkle and Gertha Hooper Hill)

    1269.   Ronnie Lee Pell
    1270.   Richard Lynn Pell
    1271.   Regina Louise Pell

1-3-16-112-363-356-845   Hazel Lou Hooper married (2) Francis Erhart Scherer, 3rd
    1272.   Francis Erhart Scherer, 4th

1-3-16-112-363-356-846   Martha June Hooper b. 1938 married Bill Franklin Bacon
    1273.   Steven Franklin Bacon

1-3-16-112-363-356-847   Bobbye Roberta Hooper b. 1940 married Dennis Robert Whaley
    1274.   Dennis Robert Whaley, Jr.
    1275.   Gregory Alan Whaley

1-3-16-112-363-357-848   Dewayne Cyrus Hooper b. Jan. 1936 married Judy Clayton on July 16, 1963 in Bradley County, TN
    1276.   Julia Ann Hooper

1-3-16-112-365-870-1294   Ona Virginia Gamble married Wendell McKinley Goodwin in Bradley County, TN 1954.
    1629.   Tim Goodwin
    1630.   Mickey Goodwin

1-3-16-113-370-875-1295   Hazel Dean Graham married Jimmy Dill Shook
    1631.   Cheryl Yvonne Shook

1-3-16-113-370-875-1296   Willard Louis Graham married Wilma Sue Ensley
    1632.   Nancy Louise Graham

1-3-16-113-370-875-1297   Tommy Lee Graham married Roberta Ann Shults
    1633.   Tony Lee Graham
    1634.   Robert Douglas Graham

1-3-16-113-370-875-1298   Lorene Ann Graham married Larry Stewart
    1635.   Tammy Michelle Stewart
    1636.   Charles Douglas Stewart
    1637.   Cherie Renee Stewart

1-3-16-113-370-875-1299   Michael J. Graham married Imogene Smith
    1638.   Michael Franklin Graham
    1639.   Carolyn Faye Graham

1-3-16-113-370-875-1300   Mittie Lou Graham

1-3-16-113-370-879-1301   Drefus Geren (D. L.) married Juanita Blair (maiden name from Dale Geren's marriage to Sherry Osment in 1972 in Bradley County, TN (see p. 116)
    1640.   Jo Geren
    1641.   Wanda Jean Geren
    1642.   Dale Geren

1-3-16-113-370-879-1302   Eugene Thomas Geren married Betty Curtis
    1643.   Thomas Ray Geren
    1644.   Kim Geren
    1645.   Sandi Geren

1-3-16-113-370-879-1303   Dean Van Geren married Louise Birdwell
    1646.   Marcy Waynn Geren
    1647.   Ronnie Geren
    1648.   Terry Geren
    1649.   John Geren
    1650.   Chris Geren
    1651.   Greg Geren
    1652.   Jan Geren

1-3-16-113-370-879-1304   Luther E. Geren married Betty Jean Brand (Internet, Geren, *Heartfelt Connections,* Jim Rush Funeral Home Obituary)
    1653.   Darlene Geren
    1654.   Eddie Geren

1-3-16-113-370-879-1305   Tresley Geren married Wynona

1-3-16-113-370-879-1306   Neva June Geren
1-3-16-113-370-879-1307   Julia Ann Geren married Joe Collins
    1655.   Joe Collins
    1656.   Corey Collins
1-3-16-113-370-881-1308   Willis Lyle married 1. Martha Jane Cartwright Dec. 11, 1959 in Bradley County, TN (Internet, *Ancestry.com*)
    1657.   Mike Lyle
    1658.   Shelley Lyle
1-3-16-113-370-881-1308   Willis married (2) Juanita Gail Withrow August 20, 1969 in Bradley County, TN (Internet, *Ancestry.com*)
    1659.   Doug Lyle
1-3-16-113-370-881-1308   Willis married (3) Sarah Elizabeth Thomas April 2, 1983 in McMinn County, TN (Internet, *Ancestry.com*)
    1660.   Josh Lyle
1-3-16-113-370-881-1309   Linda Lyle married Billy Eugene Whaley Dec. 4, 1965 in Bradley County, TN (Internet, *Ancestry.com*)
    1661.   Lori Whaley
    1662.   Jeff Whaley
1-3-16-113-370-881-1310   Janice Lyle married Dennis Garner (Garner)
1-3-16-113-370-881-1311   Eddie Lyle married Karen Grissom on March 18, 1978 in Bradley County, TN (Internet, *Ancestry.com*)
1-3-16-113-370-882-1312   Vernard Hoyt Graham Aug. 24, 1948 married Willie Carolyn Bunch in Bradley County, TN on Nov. 21, 1969. She was born Nov. 22, 1950 (Internet, *Ancestry.com*).
    1663.   Patty Graham
    1664.   Sandra Graham
    1665.   Kevin Graham
1-3-16-113-370-882-1313   La Vonne Graham married Donald Caldwell Jan. 15, 1980 in Meigs County, TN (Internet, *Ancestry.com*). He was born Sept. 13, 1959.
    1666.   Chris Caldwell
    1667.   Chrystal Caldwell
1-3-16-113-370-883-1314   Wesley G. Graham b. Nov. 16, 1949-d. Nov. 16, 1966
1-3-16-113-370-883-1315   Stanley Dean Graham b. Nov. 7, 1956 married 1. Connie Sue Rayfield June 24, 1977 in Bradley County, TN. She was born June 22, 1961. Stanley married 2. Linda Darlene Redman Oct. 2, 1982 in Bradley County, TN (Internet, *Ancestry.com*).
    1668.   Nathan Graham
    1669.   Timmy Graham
1-3-16-113-370-883-1315   Stanley Graham married 2. Linda Darlene Redman Oct. 2, 1982 in *Bradley* County, TN (Internet, *Ancestry.com*)
    1670.   Christian Graham
    1671.   T. D. Graham
1-3-16-113-370-884-1316   Lisa Renee Moore m. 1.   Rogers and 2. Richard L. Calfee **(See p. 86.)**
1-3-16-113-370-884-1317   Dana Moore married Dale Elkins
1-3-16-113-370-884-1318   Randall Moore married Carolyn
1-3-16-113-370-884-1319   Mark Moore married Kim
1-3-16-113-371-885-1320   Doyle M. Neeley b. Dec. 13, 1918 d. Dec. 12, 1990 m. (1) Pauline Beck; (2) Mildred Parker on July 2, 1965; and (3) Beulah Gelene Burgner March 28, 1980. Each marriage was in Bradley County, TN (Internet, *Ancestry.com*).
    1672.   Wendell Neeley
    1673.   Wayne Neeley
    1674.   Doyline Neeley
1-3-16-113-371-885-1321   Lou Anna M. Neeley b. May 26, 1922 and d. Dec. 29, 2012 married Amos Caldwell on Feb. 10, 1940 in Bradley County, TN. Amos was born Aug. 10, 1913 and died in Oct. 23, 1997 (Internet, *Ancestry.com*).
    1675.   Norma Caldwell

1676.   Patsy Caldwell
1677.   Delbert L. Caldwell
1678.   Sherry Caldwell
1679.   Donna Caldwell

1-3-16-113-371-885-1322   Nola Imogene Neeley b. March 19, 1924-d. Sept. 14, 1996 married Roy
Matthews b. May 7, 1923 and d. Jan. 24, 2008

1680.   Carolyn Matthews
1681.   Bunny (Laverne) Matthews
1682.   Sharon Matthews

1-3-16-113-371-885-1323   Thelma Neeley
1-3-16-113-371-885-1324   Delma Neeley
1-3-16-113-371-885-1325   Robert Curtis Neeley b. Sept. 7, 1930-d. June 14, 1993 m. Agnes Farmer in
1948

1683.   Bobbie Neeley
1684.   Dinah Neeley
1685.   Jackie Neeley

1-3-16-113-371-886-1326   Francis L. Graham married Kenneth Francisco

1686.   Carol Ann Francisco

1-3-16-113-371-886-1327   Dela M. Graham
1-3-16-113-371-886-1328   Jasper Graham, Jr.
1-3-16-113-371-888-1329   Hubert Murphy b. July 16, 1922 d. March 11, 2003 married Gladys
Beatrice Millaway (number 826) b. Feb. 2, 1919 d. 11-22-1980

1240.   Charles Hubert Murphy b. 1943
1241.   Linda Lou Murphy b. 1946
1242.   Dewayne Murphy b. 1948
1243.   Alice Lynn Murphy b. 1954
1244.   Deborah Joyce Murphy b. 1957

1-3-16-113-371-888-1330   Clyde Murphy b. Sept. 11, 1923 d. Sept. 10, 1991 married (1) Virgie Lois
Owenby and (2) Martie Headrick

1687.   Barbara Ann Murphy
1688.   Margaret Rose Murphy
1689.   Richard Lynn Murphy

1-3-16-113-371-888-1331   Frederick Murphy Aug. 27, 1925 d. March 23, 2003 married Mary
Matthews

1690.   Fred Anthony (Ted) Murphy
1691.   Marilyn Gayenell Murphy

1-3-16-113-371-888-1332   Floyd Murphy b. Nov. 11, 1932 married (1) Deloris Baker and (2) Betty Jean
Bunch. Floyd died Sept. 10, 2016. **(In his *Cleveland Daily Banner*
obituary, he listed grandsons Jason Davis and Andy Hardy.)**

1692.   Cynthia Mechell Murphy
1693.   Oglevia Cornelles Murphy

1-3-16-113-371-890-1333   Juanita Elizabeth Graham married Walter Hinkle, Jr. on Jan. 25, 1950 in
Bradley County, TN **(see p. 85 for Graham Sources)**
1-3-16-113-371-890-1334   Charles Paul Graham married (1) Ann Haglar, (2) Shirley Bell and
(3) Judy Beck.

1694.   Michael Graham

1-3-16-113-371-890-1335   Billy Joe Graham married (1) Wanda Hennessee.

1695.   Cathy Graham
1696.   Wyman Graham

1-3-16-113-371-890-1335   Billy Joe Graham married (2) Sheri Cooley.

1697.   Tyler Graham

1-3-16-113-371-891-1336   Harold Arnold Graham b. Aug. 22, 1934 d. Feb. 22, 2013 married Shirley
Drucilla Gibson

1698.   Yolanda Marline Graham

1-3-16-113-371-891-1337   Murel Graham married Mary Louise Paul on August 10, 1963 in Bradley
County, TN.

1699.   Robert F. Graham

1700.   Mary Lajane Graham

1701.   David Murel Graham

1-3-16-113-371-891-1338   Jerry M. Graham married Doris Wilson on Sept. 6, 1962 in Bradley County, TN.

1702.   Karen Eileen Graham

1703.   Rhonda Graham

1704.   Jerry M. Graham, Jr.

1-3-16-113-371-892-1339   Sterling Sandidge b. 1945 married Peggy Geneva Pierce

1-3-16-113-371-892-1340   Linda La Faye Sandidge b. June 10, 1950 married Eddie Joe Wells b. Sept. 22, 1947 in Bradley County, TN on July 29, 1966

1705.   Lisa Renaee Wells

1706.   Mark Alan Wells

1707.   James Edward Wells

1-3-16-113-371-892-844   Gurtha Dean Hooper m. Forrest Buchanan Hill, Jr. b. Feb. 22, 1928 – May 13, 2012

1267.   Forrest Buchanan (Bucky) Hill, 3rd

1268.   Robert Hooper Hill

1-3-16-113-371-892-845   Hazel Lou Hooper b. Nov. 22, 1935 married James Pell b. Feb. 13, 1934 d. Jan. 18, 1996

1269.   Ronnie Lee Pell

1270.   Richard Lynn Pell

1271.   Regina Louise Pell

1-3-16-113-371-892-845   Hazel Lou Hooper married (2) Francis Erhart Scherer, 3rd

1272.   Francis Erhart Scherer, 4th

1-3-16-113-371-892-846   Martha June Hooper b. 1938 married Bill Franklin Bacon

1273.   Steven Franklin Bacon

1-3-16-113-371-892-847   Bobbye Roberta Hooper b. 1940 married Dennis Robert Whaley

1274.   Dennis Robert Whaley, Jr.

1275.   Gregory Alan Whaley

1-3-16-113-371-893-1341   Gearlee Rogers married Nancy Yvonne Galyon

1708.   Dennis Lee Rogers

1709.   Denise Lynne Rogers

1710.   Karen Renee Rogers

1711.   Kevin Randall Rogers

1-3-16-113-371-895-1342   James Sherman Graham married (1) Teresa Lane on June 24, 1966 in Bradley County, TN (Internet, *Ancestry.com*) and (2) Martha

1712.   Susan Graham married Christopher Vernon

1713.   Richard Darrell Graham

1714.   Doug Graham

1715.   Rachel Graham

1-3-16-113-371-895-1343   Sandra K. Graham married James Richard (Jimmy) Hooper (1203) on June 20, 1969 in Bradley County, TN (Internet, *Ancestry.com*)

1558.   Jonathan David Hooper

1559.   Christopher Nicholas Hooper

1-3-16-113-371-895-1344   Lanny C. Graham married Bonita Link

1716.   Stephanie Dawn Graham

1-3-16-113-371-896-1345   Terry L. Graham b. Dec. 2, 1949 married (1) Debra Lee Hooper (1568) b. Jan. 14, 1953 in Wisconsin, married in Bradley County, TN on June 6, 1972 (Internet, *Ancestry.com*), (2) Sandra Kay Pendergrass, (3) Susan Denise Allmon, and (4) Judy Davis.

1717.   Terry Derrick Graham

1718.   Andrew Jeremiah Graham

1-3-16-113-371-897-1346   Jayne Graham

1-3-16-113-371-897-1347   Tereh Graham (son)

1-3-16-113-371-897-1348   Joan Graham

1-3-16-114-378-901-1349 John S. Mosher Oct. 20, 1943 (Internet, *Jacqueline-L-Brusseau-CO, Genealogy.com: Descendants of Robert Thomas Williamson*)
1-3-16-114-378-901-1350 James S. Mosher Dec. 18, 1947 (*Genealogy.com, Brusseau*)
1-3-16-114-379-906-1352 Mary Heaton Watts married Harry Thomas Wilhoit
1-3-16-114-379-908-1353 Ted Monroe Gilbreath b. 1936 married Lamartine Edwards (Br*usseau*)
1-3-16-114-379-908-1354 James Oswald Gilbreath b. 1944
1-3-16-114-379-909-1355 Billy Lynn Bunch married Larry Jenno (*Brusseau*)
1-3-16-114-379-910-1356 Grayson Bunch (died as an infant)
1-3-16-114-379-910-1357 Jeanne Bunch married Bill Trewhitt (Internet, *Find A Grave*, Created by Glenda Rowland at *Ancestry.com*)

1719.   Bill Trewhitt, Jr.
1720.   Elizabeth Trewhitt
1721.   Christopher Trewhitt
1722.   Shannon Trewhitt

1-3-16-114-379-910-1358 Joseph Robert Bunch, Jr. married Debbie Tyni (*Genealogy.com, Brusseau* see p. 65)

1723.   Michelle Bunch married Ryan Nelson
1724.   Alissa Bunch married   ?   Pope
1725.   Christina Bunch

1-3-16-114-379-912-1359 Carl Eugene Bunch, Jr. married Nancy Windom (*Brusseau* see p. 65)
1-3-16-114-379-912-1360 Mary Elizabeth Bunch married Jeff Ganaway (*Brusseau* see p. 65)
1-3-16-114-379-912-1361 Paul David Bunch
1-3-16-114-379-912-1362 Brian Andrew Bunch
1-3-16-114-380-913-1363 Ronald Walcott 1935 CA
1-3-16-114-381-914-1364 Roberta Galbraith 1932 (*1940 Walker County, GA Census* Lisbon p. 13 A) married Rev. Kenneth E. Brown. Roberta died Feb. 15, 2003 found at *Ancestry.com* in *The Social Security Death Index*, and her Obituary was published Sept. 24, 2016 on the Internet at *The Chattanoogan.com*.

1726.   Kenneth E. Brown, Jr.
1727.   Steve R. Brown
1728.   Deborah Ann Brown married an Allgood
1729.   Patricia Kay Brown married a Gentry
1730.   Constance Lynn Brown married a Ruth
1731.   Cynthia Annette Brown married a Woodward

1-3-16-114-381-914-1365 Charlotte Galbraith 1933 married Hobert E. Anderson (*Brusseau* see p. 65)
1-3-16-114-381-914-1366 Tommy C. Galbraith 1936 married Wanda Ashmore (*Brusseau*)
1-3-16-114-381-914-1367 William Lee Galbreath, Jr. married Pamela Hixson (*Brusseau*)
1-3-16-114-381-914-1368 Howard Sam Hale
1-3-16-114-381-914-1369 James Wesley Hale
1-3-16-114-381-914-1370 John Audie Hale
1-3-16-114-381-916-1371 David Earle Williamson married (1) Judith Netherly and (2) Marianne Walden (*Brusseau*)
1-3-16-114-381-916-1372 Howard Donald Williamson
1-3-16-114-381-917-1373 Dorothy Marie Williamson married Lamar Bryson (*Brusseau* see p. 65)
1-3-16-114-381-917-1374 Edna Anne Williamson married Kirby Airhart, 3rd (*Brusseau*)
1-3-16-114-381-917-1375 William Gregory Williamson married Cynthia Kaye Maxi (*Brusseau*)
1-3-16-114-381-917-1376 Gail Edith Williamson married Donnie Melton (*Brusseau*)
1-3-16-114-381-917-1377 Laura Susan Williamson married Wayne Moore (*Brusseau*)
1-3-16-114-382-919-1378 Charles William Hassler, Jr. 1933
1-3-16-114-382-919-1379 Raymond Lee Hassler 1935
1-3-16-114-384-920-1380 Janel Diane Henry
1-3-16-114-384-920-1381 Nancy Louise Henry
1-3-16-115-388-924-1382 Martha Lynn Barger (grand dau. of 659 and 388) married David Vernon Dryden

1732.   Carol Lynn Dryden b. March 30, 1968 (Internet Texas Birth Records at *Ancestry.com*)
1733.   David Scott Dryden b. Feb. 3, 1970 (Texas Birth Records at *Ancestry.com*)

1-3-16-115-388-924-1383   Willa Maurine Barger (grand dau. of 659 and 388) b. May 29, 1948 married
Harry Psemeneki on June 15, 1974 in Anderson County, TN (Internet,
Ancestry.com, Find A Grave by Randy Shepherd) .

1734.   Tiffany Psemeneki
1735.   Stacy Psemeneki

1-3-17-120-400-930-1384   Stacy E. Carlton Sept. 20, 1936-Nov. 9, 2009
1-3-17-120-400-930-1385   Barbara Frances Carlton married (1) Edward Jackson Rogers July
15, 1956 in Cleveland, Bradley County, Tennessee. He was born 1936 in
Bradley County, Tennessee. She married (2) Ray Daniel 1976. He died
June 02, 1978. (Information from *Wrinkle History* on the Internet p. 66.)

1736.   Edward Jackson Rogers, Jr.
1737.   Connie Frances Rogers
1738.   Brad Stewart Rogers
1739.   Stacey Nay Rogers

1-3-17-120-400-930-1386   William Carlton Feb. 1, 1939-Oct. 30, 1962
1-3-17-120-400-931-1387   Eugene Carlton
1-3-17-122-409-946-1388   Eloise Ellis married Frank Melvin Swafford (See p. 131 for her information.).
1-3-17-122-409-946-1389   Nancy Ellis
1-3-17-122-409-946-1390   Ellen Ellis
1-3-17-122-409-946-1391   Kenneth Cress
1-3-17-122-409-946-1392   Mike Cress
1-3-17-122-409-946-1393   Karen Edna Cress
1-3-17-122-409-947-1394   Linda Shirley married Luther King

1740.   Shelley King

1-3-17-122-410-949-1222   Jayhue H. Hooper married Doris Lankford (See Appendix H p. 306.)

1568.   Debra L. Hooper

1-3-17-122-410-949-1223   William Hooper married Jean (See Appendix H p. 306.)
1-3-17-122-410-950-1395   Murel Wayne Harris married Margie Marie Reasonover

1741.   Monte Gale Harris
1742.   Mark Wayne Harris
1743.   Michael Troy Harris

1-3-17-122-410-950-1396   Donald Alden "Don" Harris married Frances Harmon on Oct. 8, 1960 in
Meigs County, TN (Internet, *Ancestry.com*)

1744.   Alden Dewayne "Dee" Harris
1745.   Donna Faye Harris

1-3-17-122-410-950-1397   Curtis Harris married Patsy Collins

1746.   Karen Harris
1747.   Amy Harris
1748.   Kellie Harris

1-3-17-122-410-950-1398   Robert Harris b. Dec. 15, 1950 married (1) Linda Headrick on Feb. 28,
1970. She was born July 18, 1953. He married (2) Phyllis Loraine Hinkle
on July 25, 1994. Both marriages were in Bradley County, TN (Internet,
Ancestry.com).

1-3-17-122-410-951-1399   Bennie Hooper
1-3-17-122-410-951-1400   Herbert Hooper married Janice
1-3-17-122-410-951-1401   Carl Hooper
1-3-17-122-410-953-1402   Carolyn Hooper
1-3-17-122-410-953-1403   Larry Hooper
1-3-17-122-410-953-1404   Danny Hooper
1-3-17-122-410-953-1405   Brian Hooper
1-3-17-122-410-953-1406   Kathy Hooper
1-3-17-122-410-954-1232   Connie L. Hooper married Roy Millaway

1577.   Carrie Lee Millaway

1-3-17-122-410-954-1233   David Dale Hooper married Sable Couch

1578.   William Keith Hooper
1579.   Natalie Deann Hooper

1-3-17-122-410-954-1234   Alice M. Hooper married Fritz Harris
       1580.   Joey Heather Harris
       1581.   Jennie Lynn Harris
1-3-17-122-410-954-1235   Barry H. Hooper married Cheryl Kendrick
       1582.   Garrett Harrison Hooper
       1583.   Anna Caroline Hooper
1-3-17-122-410-955-1407   Linda Melton married (2) Lee Owens.
1-3-17-122-410-955-1408   Thomas Melton married Teresa K. Maples and Cathy Coe ?
1-3-17-122-410-956-1409   Randall Hooper married Betsey Giles on March 7, 1984 in Bradley County,
          TN (Internet, *Ancestry.com*)
       1749.   Brady Hooper
1-3-17-122-410-956-1410   Wesley Hooper
1-3-17-122-410-956-1411   Cindy Hooper married (1) David Ownbey on Nov. 4, 1978 in Bradley County,
          TN; (2) Married Joey Chastain on Sept. 11, 1991 in Bradley County, TN
          (Internet, *Ancestry.com*); and (3) Tom Helton
       1751.   Wesley Lebron Ownbey
       1752.   Torie Chastain
1-3-17-122-410-956-1412   Christie Hooper married Allen Hartley
       1750.   Kelsie Hartley   (One Obituary said Hooper and another listed Hartley.)
       1753.   Taylor Hartley
       1754.   Jacob Hartley
1-3-17-122-410-957-1413   William Phillip Carson married Angela Lynne Boring on August 2, 1986 in
          McMinn County, TN (Internet, *Ancestry.com*)
       1755.   Phillip Carson
       1756.   Landin Carson
       1757.   Mary Claire Carson
1-3-17-122-410-957-1414   Dr. Jeffery Alan Carson married Dawn Marie Rumba on July 22, 1995 in
          Bradley County, TN (Internet, *Ancestry.com*)
       1758.   McKenna Joyce Carson
       1759.   Kellar Bryce Carson
1-3-17-122-410-957-1415   Suzanne Maria Carson married Christopher Lee Bynum on May 24, 1990 in
          Bradley County, TN (Internet, *Ancestry.com*)
       1760.   Chase Bynum
       1761.   Madison Bynum
1-3-17-122-410-958-1416   Rosalee Lee Hooper married Gary Frost
1-3-17-122-410-958-1417   Clint Harrison Hooper married Karen Schmidt
1-3-17-122-410-958-1418   Vickie Lynn Hooper married Duane Harris
1-3-17-122-410-958-1419   Judy Elaine Hooper
1-3-17-122-410-958-1420   Gary Allen Hooper married Sheila Bevins
1-3-17-122-410-958-1421   Dennis Raymond Hooper married Amy Aultmann
1-3-17-122-410-958-1422   Bernola Mae Hooper married Brent L. Webb
1-3-17-122-410-960-1423   Timothy Wayne Hooper married Andrea Michele Roark on Jan. 27, 1995
          in Bradley County, TN (Internet, *Ancestry.com*)
       1762.   Abby Hooper
       1763.   Andrew Hooper
1-3-17-122-410-960-1424   Tracy Hooper married Leslie Ratcliff
       1764.   Kenley Harrison Hooper
       1765.   Kiana Faith Hooper
       1766.   Mattea Danielle Hooper
1-3-17-122-410-962-1425   Samuel Brown
1-3-17-122-410-962-1426   Ann Brown
1-3-17-122-410-962-1427   Wade Brown
1-3-17-123-423-972-1428   Michael Eads
1-3-17-126-429-981-1429   Dr. Keyoda Hall b. April 22, 1957 d. April 8, 1999 married Dr. Mark Bookout
          on Dec.26, 1980 in Bradley County, Tennessee (Internet, *Ancestry.com*)
       1767.   Megan Lynsey Bookout

1-3-17-126-429-981-1430   Kimitia Subrena Hall married Jon Thomas Rymer July 2, 1983 in Bradley
                County, Tennessee (Internet, *Ancestry.com*)
1-3-17-126-429-983-1431   Troy Hooper married Connie Norwood
    1768.   Justin Hooper   (Lillian Hooper Hall's obituary online at *Cleveland Daily Banner*
    1769.   Cody Hooper   Oct. 2, 2018 listed two great grandnephews Asher and Steele Hooper.)
1-3-17-126-429-983-1432   Gwen Hooper married Alton Beavers
    1770.   Kelci Beavers
1-3-17-126-429-983-1433   Renee Hooper married ? Pfleuger
1-3-17-126-429-984-1434   Barbra Hooper
1-3-17-126-429-985-1435   William Kins (Kinny) Hooper, Jr. married 1. Sherry Ann Cate on July 10,
                1985 in Bradley County, TN (Internet, *Ancestry.com*) and 2. Jennifer Walden
    1771.   Sidney Hooper
    1772.   Madison Hooper
    1773.   Kins Hooper
1-3-17-126-429-985-1436   Greg Hooper married Connie Linkous
    1774.   Hays Hooper
    1775.   Alexander Hooper
1-3-17-126-429-985-1437   Lori Jean Hooper married William Chris Hutchins on Oct. 11, 1999 in Bradley
                County, TN (Internet, *Ancestry.com*)
    1776.   Garett Hutchins
1-3-17-126-429-986-1438   Tim Cody
1-3-17-126-419-986-1439   Zeno Beaty
1-3-19-136-454-1016-1440   Jon Fulton married Kathy
1-3-19-136-454-1016-1441   Wash Fulton
1-3-19-136-454-1017-1442   Kaycee Hooper
1-3-19-136-454-1017-1443   Kara Hooper married Kevin Mutz
1-3-20-146-477-1020-1444   Brandon Hooper
1-3-20-146-477-1020-1445   Krystal Hooper
1-3-20-146-477-1020-1446   Jeffrey Hooper
1-3-20-146-480-1025-1447   Blaise Hooper
1-3-21-148-486-1028-1448   William L. Hooper b. August 2, 1956 married Karen Lewis
    1777.   Nathan Andrew Hooper b. Nov, 24, 1982
    1778.   Natalie Claire Hooper b. April 19, 1984
    1779.   Sarah Ann Hooper . Nov. 26, 1985
1-3-21-148-486-1028-1449   Carol Ann Hooper b. Feb. 13, 1958 married Peter Allen Cooper
    1780.   Claire Emily Cooper b. Dec. 15, 1990
    1781.   Kate Elizabeth Cooper b. Dec. 16, 1993
1-3-21-148-486-1029-1450   Cheryl Lynn Hooper b. June 4, 1960 married Stephen Cunningham
    1782.   Billie Jo Summers Cunningham b. March 5, 1997
    1783.   Christopher Ross Cunningham b. Aug. 10, 1981
    1784.   Joshua Stephen Cunningham b. Feb. 4, 1983
1-3-21-148-486-1029-1451   Phillip Lyle Hooper b. Feb. 26, 1963 married Joy Clark
    1785.   Adam Lyle Hooper b. Aug. 16, 1986
    1786   Ashley Joy Hooper b. Nov. 24, 1987
    1787.   Kendra Michelle Hooper b. May 27, 1989
1-3-21-148-486-1029-1452   David Alan Hooper b. Nov. 1, 1964 married Yvette Fermin
    1788.   Levi Lane Hooper b. July 29, 1993
1-3-21-148-486-1030-1453   Andrew Cordia Hooper b. Aug. 2, 1978
1-3-21-148-486-1030-1454   Caitlin McNabb Hooper b. Oct. 3, 1981
1-3-21-150-489-1031-1455   Recinda Lynn Gardner b. March 31, 1959 married Rick Osburn
    1789.   Cassie Nichole McPherson Osburn b. Aug. 16, 1983
1-3-21-150-489-1031-1456   Gregory Joe Gardner b. Feb. 24, 1962 married Angie Beasley
    1790.   Garrett Thomas Gardner b. March 30, 1993
1-3-21-152-490-1032-1457   Stephen Eugene Mace b. Nov. 12, 1960 married Lisa Cathrine
    1791.   Laura Catherine Mace b. Dec. 11, 1987
    1792.   Linda Michele Mace b. March 24, 1990

1-3-21-152-490-1032-1458   Shari Lynn Mace married Steve Olsen
1-3-21-152-490-1032-1459   Scott Allen Mace
1-3-21-156-498-1040-1460   Shirley Ann Grisham b. Oct. 3, 1957 married Melvin Douglas Evans
      1793.   Airanna Lee Evans b. Dec. 23, 1976
      1794.   Billy Joe Evans b. April 6, 1978
      1795.   Patricia Sue Evans b. Jan. 16, 1980
1-3-21-156-498-1040-1461   James Michael Grisham b. March 4, 1961married Shawna Redd
      1796.   Dalton Michael Grisham b. Jan. 22, 1992
1-3-21-156-499-1041-1462   Angelia Marie Breshears b. Nov. 10, 1961 married Rufus Eric Blair
1-3-21-156-499-1041-1463   Tommie Lynn Breshears b. Nov. 6, 1965 married Kenneth Dale Blair
1-3-21-156-499-1041-1464   Sarah Jo Breshears b. Jan. 30, 1970 married Larry Payne
1-3-21-156-499-1044-1465   Andrea Michelle Breshears b. Jan. 1, 1968
1-3-21-156-499-1044-1466   Monica Suzanne Breshears b. Jan. 7, 1970
1-3-21-156-500-1045-1467   Barbara Lynette Blake b. Dec. 18, 1965 married Danny N. Morgans
      1797.   Taylor Lee Morgans b. 1992
1-3-21-156-500-1045-1468   Amy Leann Blake b. March 3, 1967 married Gregory J. Morgans
      1798.   Eric Gregory Morgans b. Jan. 22,1989
1-3-21-156-500-1045-1469   Jaqueline Renee Blake b. Nov. 3, 1972 married Scotty K. Rice
1-3-21-156-500-1045-1470   Robert Justin Blake b. April 5, 1980
1-3-21-156-500-1046-1471   Anthony Von Shull b. August 2, 1964
1-3-21-156-500-1046-1472   Charles Douglas Shull b. May 28, 1970
1-3-21-156-500-1047-1473   Yvette Lorea McIntire b. Dec. 29, 1972
1-3-21-156-500-1047-1474   Lance Edwin McIntire b. June 1, 1975
1-3-21-156-500-1048-1475   Jamie Ileen Reynolds b. Sept. 15, 1978
1-3-21-156-500-1048-1476   Jacy Leigh Reynolds b. Oct. 9, 1984
1-4-30-177-530-1057-1423   Timothy Wayne Hooper married Andrea Roark on Jan. 28, 1995 in Bradley
      County, TN (Internet, *Ancestry.com*)
      1762.   Abby Hooper
      1763.   Andrew Hooper
1-4-30-177-530-1057-1424   Tracy Hooper married Leslie Ratcliff
      1764.   Kenley Harrison Hooper
      1765.   Kiana Faith Hooper
      1766.   Mattea Danielle Hooper
1-4-30-177-530-1058-1477   Tamara Michele Carden married Jeffery Glenn King on June 27, 1987 in
      McMinn County, TN (Internet, *Ancestry.com*)
      1799.   Jared King
1-4-30-177-530-1058-1478   Rodney Carson Carden married Susan Annette Evans on Aug. 25, 1990 in
      Bradley County, TN (Internet, *Ancestry.com*)
      1800.   Emily Carden
      1801.   Sydney Carden
1-4-30-177-530-1058-1479   Tina Renee Carden married Mitchell Todd Shoemaker on Nov. 27, 1994 in
      Bradley County, TN (Internet, *Ancestry.com*)
      1802.   Ashley Shoemaker
      1803.   Clay Shoemaker
1-4-30-177-530-1058A-1479A   Jason McCracken (Internet, *The Chattanoogan.com* Tuesday, May 30,
      2017, Obituary for Judy Evelyn McCracken)
1-4-30-177-530-1058A-1479B   John C. McCracken married Kristi (*The Chattanoogan.com*)
      1803A.   Courtney McCracken married Brandon Dietrich (*The Chattanoogan.com*)
      1803B.   Cody McCracken (*The Chattanoogan.com*)
1-4-30-177-530-1058A-1479C   Cathy McCracken (*The Chattanoogan.com*)
1-4-30-177-530-1058B-1479D   Melanie Green
1-4-30-177-530-1058B-1479E   Kristi Green married Michael Mason on May 28, 1993 in Bradley
      County, TN
      1803C.   Dawson Mason
1-4-30-177-530-1059-1480   Laura Carden married (1)   Jones; and (2) Matthew Wittmaier.
      1804.   Christian Jones

1-4-33-184-552-1067-1481   Barbara Green
1-4-33-184-552-1067-1482   Charles Green
1-4-33-184-552-1067-1483   Stephen Green
1-4-33-184-552-1067-1484   David Green
1-4-33-184-552-1067-1485   Grace Ann Green
1-4-33-184-552-1068-1486   Angelia Hooper
1-4-33-184-552-1069-1487   Linda Diane Hooper
1-4-33-184-552-1069-1488   Michael Hooper
1-4-33-184-552-1069-1489   Karen Jo Hooper
1-4-33-184-552-1069-1490   Nicholas Hooper
1-4-33-187-559-1082-1491   Richard Clayton Hooper
1-4-33-187-559-1082-1492   Leslie Denise Hooper
1-4-33-187-559-1082-1493   Terry Hooper
1-4-33-187-559-1082-1494   Sydney Allison Hooper
1-4-33-187-559-1083-1495   Carla A. Hooper
1-4-33-187-559-1083-1496   Sue A. Hooper
1-4-33-188-563-1091-1497   Bobby Potter
1-4-33-188-563-1091-1498   Bruce Potter
1-4-33-188-563-1091-1499   Donna Potter
1-4-33-188-563-1091-1500   Janet Potter
1-4-33-188-564-1094-1501   Janice Potter married Billy Bob Droke
        1805.   Martin Lynn Droke
1-4-34-194-573-1105-1502   Carla Hooper
1-4-34-194-573-1105-1503   Trudy Hooper
1-4-34-194-573-1105-1504   Kevin Todd Hooper
1-4-34-194-573-1106-1505   Randal Lee Christensen
1-4-34-194-573-1106-1506   Ranita June Christensen
1-4-34-194-573-1107-1507   Deanna Beth Christensen
1-4-34-194-573-1107-1508   Kent Duane Christensen
1-4-34-194-573-1107-1509   Bryan Lane Cornelius
1-4-34-194-577-1114-1510   Cheryl Ann Hooper
1-4-34-196-584-1124-1511   Reed Hooper
1-4-34-196-584-1124-1512   Bryce Hooper
1-4-34-196-587-1130-1513   Jeffrey Dan Hooper
1-4-34-196-587-1130-1514   Tonya Jean Hooper
1-4-34-196-587-1130-1515   Candance Gail Hooper
1-4-34-196-587-1131-1516   Brian Kenneth Hooper (deceased)
1-4-34-196-587-1131-1517   Pamela Hooper
1-4-34-196-587-1131-1518   Cindy Hooper
1-4-34-196-587-1132-1519   David Cooley
1-4-34-196-587-1132-1520   Shannon Cooley
1-4-34-196-587-1132-1521   Jessica Cooley
1-2-7-67-226-618-1142-1522   Deborah Bryant (see p. 54 for Saulpaw information)
1-2-7-67-226-618-1144-1523   Carolyn Taylor
1-2-7-67-226-618-1144-1524   John Taylor
1-2-7-67-226-618-1144-1525   James Martin Taylor
1-2-7-67-226-618-1144-1526   Seaton Taylor
1-2-7-67-226-618-1144-1527   Mary Elizabeth Taylor
1-2-7-67-226-621-1147-1528   Scott Aaron Wermann
1-2-7-67-226-623-1150-1529   Matthew L. Dingess
1-2-7-67-226-623-1150-1530   Patrick Dingess
1-2-7-67-226-623-1151-1531   Margaret Grace Brown
1-2-7-67-226-623-1153-1532   Ellen Harvey
1-2-7-67-226-623-1153-1533   Carol Harvey
1-2-7-67-226-624-1154-1534   Lucinda Jane Womac
1-2-7-67-226-624-1154-1535   Rachel Ann Womac

1-2-7-67-226-624-1155-1536   Richard Keith Jacob, Jr.
1-2-7-67-226-624-1155-1537   Christian Darr Jacob
1-3-14-99-266-659-924-1382   Martha Lynn Barger (grand dau. of 659 and 388) married David V. Dryden
    1732.   Carol Lynn Dryden b. March 30, 1968
    1733.   David Scott Dryden b. Feb. 3, 1970
1-3-14-99-266-659-924-1383   Maurine Barger (grand dau. of 659 and 388) married Harry Psemeneki
    1734.   Tiffany Psemeneki
    1735.   Stacy Psemeneki
1-3-14-100-291-733-1172-1538   Dennis Jake Richardson (Internet, *Find A Grave.com*)
1-3-15-105-315-765-1190-1539   Debra McAmis
1-3-15-106-317-770-1191-1540   Karen Hixson b. 1951 married Steve Phillips b. 1954
    1806.   Eric Steven Phillips b. 1985
    1807.   Emily Blair Phillips b. 1987
1-3-15-106-317-770-1191-1541   Dr. Gordon (Gary) Lawrence Hixson b. 1954 married Sherry McPherson
        b. 1960
    1808.   Gordon (Trey) Lawrence Hixson, 3rd b. 1983
    1809.   John Benjamin Hixson b. 1988
    1810.   Catherine Lane (Laney) Hixson b. 1993
1-3-15-106-317-770-1192-1542   Chris Chalker
1-3-15-106-317-770-1192-1543   Mark Chalker
1-3-15-106-317-770-1193-1544   Deborah Darlene Gibson b. Sept. 5, 1960 – d. April 9, 1971
1-3-15-106-317-770-1193-1545   Kim Gibson married Gary White on June 16, 1990 in Bradley County,
        TN (Internet, *Ancestry.com*)
    1811.   Brently White
    1812.   Riley White
1-3-15-106-317-770-1193-1546   Pam Gibson married Nicholas Burnette on June 17, 1995 in Bradley
        County, TN (Internet, *Ancestry.com*)
    1813.   Nicolas Doylene Burnette
    1814.   Avery Watson Burnette Jan. 28, 2004
    1815.   Noah Burnette
1-3-15-106-317-770-1193-1547   Allen Gibson married Rhonda Knight and Judy
    1816.   Brooklyn Gibson
1-3-15-106-319-775-1195-1548   Jonathan Roy Cantrell married Sarah McGee
    1817.   Caroline Cantrell
    1818.   Caldwell Cantrell
1-3-15-106-319-775-1195-1549   David Christian Cantrell married Jeanine Jamerson of McMinn County,
        TN
    1819.   Christian Cantrell
    1820.   Gabriel Cantrell
1-3-15-106-319-776-1198-1550   Georgina Gay Geren b. Feb. 17, 1972 married Dr. Ivo Aaron Miller
        (1571) on Aug. 7, 1993 in Bradley County, TN (Internet, *Ancestry.com*)
    1821.   Ivo Aaron Miller, Jr.
    1822.   Joshua Wade Miller
    1823.   Jordan Miller
1-3-15-106-319-776-1198-1551   Emily Geren married Justin McCulley on June 4, 2011 (Internet,
        Cleveland Daily Banner, May 20, 2012)
1-3-15-106-319-778-1200-1552   Donna Geren married Jeff Frazier (Internet, *Find A Grave,
        Ancestry.com*)
    1824.   Chandler Vance Frazier
1-3-15-106-319-778-1201-1553   Bryan Geren married Pam (See information below.)
1-3-15-106-319-778-1201-1554   Kinny Geren married Cindy Pickins (See information below.)
1-3-15-106-319-778-1201-1555   Cheryl Geren (See information below.)
1-3-15-106-319-778-1201-1556   Amy Geren married Scott McGowan (See information below.)
Bryan, Kinny, Cheryl and Amy Geren's children were named in the *Cleveland Daily Banner*
Obituary dated February 9, 2017: Walker Geren (Breanna); Bradlee Geren; Bradlee Carter; Baylee

Carter; Kellee Geren; Sydni Geren; Barkley "Kley" McGowan; Kinslee McGowan; Kason McGowan; Walker McGowan and Baylor McGowan.

1-3-15-106-320-429-981-1429   Dr. Keyoda Hall b. April 22, 1957 d. April 8, 1999 married Dr. Mark Bookout on Dec. 6, 1980 in Bradley County, TN (Internet, *Ancestry.com*)

    1767.   Megan Lynsey Bookout

1-3-15-106-320-429-981-1430   Kimitia Hall married Jon Thomas Rymer on July 2, 1983 in Bradley County, TN (Internet, *Ancestry.com*)

1-3-15-106-320-429-981-1431   Troy Hooper married Connie Norwood on July 22, 1988 in Bradley County, TN (Internet, *Ancestry.com*)

    1768.   Justin Hooper   (Lillian Hooper Hall's obituary online at *Cleveland Daily Banner*

    1769.   Cody Hooper   Oct. 2, 2018 listed two great grandnephews Asher and Steele Hooper.)

1-3-15-106-320-429-981-1432   Gwen Hooper married Alton Beavers

    1770.   Kelci Beavers

1-3-15-106-320-429-981-1433   Renee Hooper married   Pfleuger

1-3-15-106-320-431-984-1434   Barbra Hooper

1-3-15-106-320-431-985-1435   William Kins (Kinny) Hooper married (1) Sherry Ann Cate on July 10, 1985 in Bradley County, TN (Internet, *Ancestry.com*) and (2) Jennifer .

    1771.   Sidney Hooper

    1772.   Madison Hooper

    1773.   Kins Hooper

1-3-15-106-320-431-985-1436   Greg Hooper married Connie Linkous

    1774.   Hays Hooper

    1775.   Alexander Hooper

1-3-15-106-320-431-985-1437   Lori Jean Hooper married William Chris Hutchins on Oct. 11, 1999 in Bradley County, TN (Internet, *Ancestry.com*)

    1776.   Garett Hutchins

1-3-15-106-320-431-986-1438   Tim Cody

1-3-15-106-320-431-986-1439   Zeno Beaty

1-3-15-106-322-781-1202-1557   David Bryant married Emily

1-3-15-106-322-782-1203-1558   Jonathan David Hooper married Dedra Diane Thummel on Feb. 11, 1995 in Bradley County, TN (Internet, *Ancestry.com*)

1-3-15-106-322-782-1203-1559   Christopher Nicholas Hooper

1-3-15-106-324-789-1206-1560   Larry Hooper

1-3-15-106-324-789-1206-1561   Brian Hooper

1-3-15-106-325-790-1208-1562   Alex Simpson

1-3-15-106-325-790-1208-1563   Alison Simpson

1-3-15-107-327-796-1219-1564   Henry L. Brem (*Ancestry.com, joeowen92* tombstone picture of Ollie Martin Brem has children listed.)

1-3-15-107-327-796-1219-1565   Sheila A. Brem b. Feb. 12, 1951 – d. Feb. 25, 1951 (*joeowen92* at *Ancestry.com*)

1-3-15-107-327-796-1219-1566   Kathie L. Brem

1-3-15-107-327-796-1219-1567   Ricky M. Brem

1-3-15-109-341-808-1222-1568   Debra L. Hooper married Terry L. Graham (1345)

    1717.   Terry Derrick Graham

    1718.   Andrew Jeremiah Graham

1-3-15-109-344-815-1224-1569   Anthony Clark Miller married Julie Marie Sauder on June 16, 1990 in Bradley County, TN (Internet, *Ancestry.com*)

    1825.   Morgan Nichole Miller

    1826.   Gareth Alan Miller

    1827.   Gwyneth Ann Miller

1-3-15-109-344-815-1224-1570   Neil Darren Miller married Stacey Nichole Hobbs on Nov. 16, 1993 in Bradley County, TN (Internet, *Ancestry.com*)

    1828.   Parker Hobbs Miller

    1829.   Payton Miller

1-3-15-109-344-815-1225-1571   Dr. Ivo Aaron Miller married Georgina Gay Geren (1550) on Aug. 7,

1993 in Bradley County, TN (Internet, *Ancestry.com*)

1821. Ivo Aaron Miller, Jr.
1822. Joshua Wade Miller
1823. Jordan Miller

1-3-15-109-344-815-1225-1572 Joshua Wade Miller
1-3-15-109-344-815-1225-1573 Jordan Miller b. 2001
1-3-15-109-344-816-1226-1574 Zachary Miller married Maranda

1830. Caittie Miller
1831. Toby Miller
1832. Anna Miller

1-3-15-109-344-816-1226-1575 Ashley Miller married Michael Sovastion
1-3-15-109-344-816-1226-1576 Mollie Miller married Matt Childs
1-3-15-109-345-819-1232-1577 Carrie Lee Millaway
1-3-15-109-345-819-1233-1578 William Keith Hooper
1-3-15-109-345-819-1233-1579 Natalie Deann Hooper
1-3-15-109-345-819-1234-1580 Joey Heather Harris
1-3-15-109-345-819-1234-1581 Jenny Lynn Harris
1-3-15-109-345-819-1235-1582 Garrett Harrison Hooper
1-3-15-109-345-819-1235-1583 Anna Caroline Hooper
1-3-15-109-345-820-1236-1584 Tyler Hooper b. March 13, 1985 married Fawn Hall

1833. Ella Grace Hooper

1-3-15-109-345-821-1238-1585 Morgan Kathryne Miller
1-3-15-109-345-821-1238-1586 Mary Alden Miller
1-3-15-110-349-826-1240-1587 Lillian Murphy b. 1965 married William Morfield

1834. Amber L. Morfield

1-3-15-110-349-826-1240-1588 Michael Murphy b. 1967 married June Pettit

1835. Angel Faye Murphy
1836. Aaron Murphy

1-3-15-110-349-826-1241-1589 Lesa Cook married Marvin Freeman

1837. Erick Freeman

1-3-15-110-349-826-1243-1590 Jason Taylor
1-3-15-110-349-826-1243-1591 Curtis Taylor
1-3-15-110-349-826-1244-1592 Adam Murphy
1-3-15-110-349-827-1247-1593 Tracey Harden married Jeremy Noble on July 12, 1991 in Bradley County, TN (Internet, *Ancestry.com*)

1838. Victoria Noble
1839. Christian Noble

1-3-15-110-349-827-1247-1594 Valerie Harden married 1. Matthew Lynn on Nov. 9, 1994 in Bradley County, TN; 2. Howard Callaway on Jan. 27, 1996 in Bradley County, TN (Internet, *Ancestry.com*); 3. Richard Holt

1840. Montgomery Callaway
1841. Richard Holt

1-3-15-110-349-827-1248-1595 Joel Millaway
1-3-15-110-349-828-1251-1596 Tyler Lankford
1-3-15-110-349-828-1252-1597 Jonathan Roberts
1-3-15-110-349-828-1252-1598 Rachel Roberts
1-3-15-110-349-828-1253-1599 Jimmy Millaway
1-3-15-110-349-828-1253-1600 Laura Millaway
1-3-15-110-349-829-1254-1601 Deidre Denny
1-3-15-110-349-830-1258-1602 Dustin Millaway married Megan Jones
1-3-15-111-353-836-1260-1603 Karen Wallace d. Oct. 30, 2014 married Russell Brent Musgrove; they died Oct. 30, 2014 (Karen and Russell died in an auto accident: Internet, *Life Legacy*, Lakeside Funeral Home at Woodstock, GA.)

1842. Russell Brent Musgrove, Jr.
1843. Jake Marshall Musgrove
1844. Emily Suzanne Musgrove

1-3-15-111-353-836-1260-1604   Kenneth Marshall Wallace married Sharon Renae Melton in Meigs
                                 County, TN on July 26, 1991 (Internet, *Ancestry.com*)
        1845.   Garrett Wallace
        1846.   Grayson Wallace
1-3-15-111-353-836-1260-1605   Amanda Wallace married Duane Gilbert on June 16, 2009 in St.
                                 Thomas, Virgin Islands (Internet, *Ancestry.com*, in the *U.S.
                                 Marriages in Newspapers*)
        1847.   Grace Gilbert
        1848.   Alexis Gilbert
        1848A. Jay Gilbert
1-3-15-111-353-836-1261-1606   Adam Elder
        1848B. David Elder
1-3-15-111-353-836-1261-1607   Laura Elder married a Gregory
        1848C. Wyatt Gregory
1-3-15-111-353-836-1262-1608   Chase Kirkpatrick
        1849.   Karma Kirkpatrick
1-3-15-111-353-836-1262-1609   Olivia Kirkpatrick married a Callahan
        1849A. Jackson Callahan
1-3-15-111-354-838-1236-1584   Tyler Hooper b. March 13, 1985 married Fawn Hall
        1833.   Ella Grace Hooper
1-3-15-111-356-845-1270-1610   James Pell married Jennifer Williams
        1850.   Destiny Pell
        1851.   Cameron Pell
        1852.   Kennedy Pell
1-3-15-111-356-845-1270-1611   Jennifer Pell
        1853.   Alexis Pell
1-3-15-111-356-845-1270-1612   Mary Ann Pell
1-3-15-111-356-845-1271-1613   Anthony Pantalucas
1-3-15-111-356-846-1273-1614   Desiree Scherer
1-3-15-111-356-846-1273-1615   Justin Franklin Bacon
1-3-15-111-356-847-1274-1616   Amber Nichole Whaley
1-3-15-111-356-847-1274-1617   Dennis Robert Whaley, 3rd
1-3-15-111-356-847-1275-1618   Carmen Alise Whaley
1-3-15-111-356-847-1275-1619   Alana Bree Whaley
1-3-15-111-356-847-1275-1620   Megan Faye Whaley
1-3-16-112-360-858-1279-1621   Debbie Marr married a   ?   Sullivan (Internet, *Chattanoogan.com*
                                 Feb. 19, 2017 Obituary for Dorothy Randolph Marr
1-3-16-112-360-858-1279-1622   Albert Daniel Marr, Jr. married Pam Moss on June 2, 1975 (Internet
                                 Ancestry.com Bradley County Marriages)
1-3-16-112-360-858-1279-1623   Bill Marr (companion Laura Franklin)
1-3-16-112-360-858-1279-1624   David Lynn Marr married Sharon Annette Odom on June 23, 1989
                                 (Internet *Ancestry.com*, Bradley County Marriages)
1-3-16-112-360-858-1280-1625   Sandra Faye Marr married (1) Gary William Clark on July 2, 1965 in
                                 Bradley County, TN and (2) Tom Rowland.
1-3-16-112-360-858-1280-1626   Pamela Kay Marr married Charles David Johnson July 1, 1968 in
                                 Bradley County, TN (Internet, *Ancestry.com*).
        1854.   Jeff Johnson married Dana
        1855.   Michelle Johnson married   Roberts
        1856.   Jason Johnson married Lindsey
**(Internet, *Life Legacy* at Ralph Buckner Funeral Home: Charles David Johnson died April 11, 2006
and his Obituary listed the grandchildren: Drew, Robbie, Dustin, Jesse, Hailey, Heather and Jailyn)**
1-3-16-112-360-858-1280-1627   Thomas Logan Marr, Jr. married (1) Trudy Gail Coffman on May 28,
                                 1975 in Bradley County, TN (Internet, *Ancestry.com*) (2) Sheila
        1857.   Derrick Marr married Cindy   **(Derrick and Chris' wives from Trudy Marr's**
        1858.   Chris Marr married Meaghan   **Obituary in the *Cleveland Daily Banner* 3-22-18)**
        1859.   Bryan Marr

116

1860.	Tiffany Marr
(From the Internet, Tommy Marr worked for Southern Valley Services in Athens, AL and it listed his children and his grandchildren: Sarah, Brooklyn, Hannah, Josiah, Logan, Claire.)
1-3-16-112-360-858-1280-1628	Tammy Marr married Jeffrey Wayne Bentley
1861.	Caitlin Bentley
1862.	Courtney Bentley
1-3-16-112-363-353-836-1260	Gary Wallace married Suzanne Newman on August 13, 1988 in Bradley County, TN
1603.	Karen Wallace
1604.	Ken Wallace
1605.	Amanda Wallace
1-3-16-112-363-353-836-1261	Mary Kay Wallace married Melvin Elder on Sept. 9, 1978 in Bradley County, TN
1606.	Adam Elder
1607.	Laura Elder
1-3-16-112-363-353-836-1262	Ila Virginia Wallace married Mike Kirkpatrick
1608.	Chase Kirkpatrick
1609.	Olivia Kirkpatrick married a Callahan
1-3-15-112-363-353-837-1263	Diana Lynn Western married Mitchell Geren
1-3-16-112-363-353-836-1264	Michael Len Western married Rita Crye
(Ona Virginia Goodwin died 2016 and the *Cleveland Daily Banner* on Dec. 16, 2016 listed her survivors: sons Tim married to Kim and Mickey married to Aimee and four grandchildren and six great-grandchildren: Nathan and wife, Jamie Goodwin and their children, Taylor, LaShay and Lilly; Tiffany and her husband, Casey and their children, Eli, Landon and Logan; Brogen Goodwin, McKinley Goodwin. See pages 85 and 102 for more information.)
1-3-16-112-365-870-1294-1629	Tim Goodwin married Kim
1-3-16-112-365-870-1294-1630	Mickey Goodwin married Aimee
1-3-16-113-370-875-1295-1631	Cheryl Yvonne Shook
1-3-16-113-370-875-1296-1632	Nancy Louise Graham
1-3-16-113-370-875-1297-1633	Tony Lee Graham
1-3-16-113-370-875-1297-1634	Robert Douglas Graham
1-3-16-113-370-875-1298-1635	Tammy Michelle Stewart
1-3-16-113-370-875-1298-1636	Charles Douglas Stewart
1-3-16-113-370-875-1298-1637	Cherie Renee Stewart
1-3-16-113-370-875-1299-1638	Michael Franklin Graham
1-3-16-113-370-875-1299-1639	Carolyn Faye Graham
1-3-16-113-370-879-1301-1640	Jo Geren married Alan Newberry
1-3-16-113-370-879-1301-1641	Wanda Jean Geren married Don E. Lewis
1-3-16-113-370-879-1301-1642	Dale Geren married Sherry Osment on Oct. 19, 1972 in Bradley County, TN (Internet, *Ancestry.com*, mothers names listed on record)
1-3-16-113-370-879-1302-1643	Thomas Ray Geren
1-3-16-113-370-879-1302-1644	Kim Geren
1-3-16-113-370-879-1302-1645	Sandi Geren
1-3-16-113-370-879-1303-1646	Marcy Waynn Geren married Janice Kay Ratcliffe
1863.	Michelle Geren
1864.	Meleah Geren
1-3-16-113-370-879-1303 -1647	Ronnie Geren married Charlene Blankinship on March 11, 1970 in Bradley County, TN (Internet, *Ancestry.com*)
1-3-16-113-370-879-1303 -1648	Rev. Terry Chandler Geren married Mary Lucille Shoemaker in Bradley County, TN on Dec. 28, 1970 (Internet, *Ancestry.com*)
1865.	Brad Geren
1866.	Nathan Geren
1-3-16-113-370-879-1303-1649	John Geren
1-3-16-113-370-879-1303-1650	Chris Geren married Margaret
1-3-16-113-370-879-1303-1651	Greg Geren
1-3-16-113-370-879-1303-1652	Jan Geren married Tommy Bedingfield

1-3-16-113-370-879-1304-1653   Darlene Geren married Don Akins
    1867.   Julia Akins married Mitchell Humphreys
    1868.   Jenni Akins
    1869.   Emily Akins married Coby Goins
1-3-16-113-370-879-1304-1654   Eddie Geren married Elaine
    1870.   Christie Geren married David Wright
    1871.   Shelley Geren
1-3-16-113-370-879-1307-1655   Joe Collins married Holli Broughton Biggs on May 20, 2000 in
        Bradley County, TN (Internet, *Ancestry.com*)
    1872.   Josie Collins
    1873.   Trent Collins
1-3-16-113-370-879-1307-1656   Corey Collins
    1874.   Sallie Collins
1-3-16-113-370-881-1308-1657   Mike Lyle
1-3-16-113-370-881-1308-1658   Shelley Lyle
1-3-16-113-370-881-1308-1659   Doug Lyle
1-3-16-113-370-881-1308-1660   Josh Lyle
1-3-16-113-370-881-1309-1661   Lori Whaley married Eddie Howard
    1875.   Olivia Howard
1-3-16-113-370-881-1309-1662   Jeff Whaley married Debbie
    1876.   Bryson Whaley
1-3-16-113-370-882-1312-1663   Patty Graham married Brian Swafford
    1877.   Cody Swafford
    1878.   Courtney Swafford
1-3-16-113-370-882-1312-1664   Sandra Graham married Clay Matthews
    1879.   Casey Matthews
    1880.   Brody Matthews
1-3-16-113-370-882-1312-1665   Kevin Graham married Christy
1-3-16-113-370-882-1313-1666   Chris Caldwell married Misty
    1881.   Isaiah Caldwell
    1882.   Malachi Caldwell
    1883.   Nehemiah Caldwell
1-3-16-113-370-882-1313-1667   Chrystal Caldwell
1-3-16-113-370-883-1315-1668   Nathan Daniel Graham
1-3-16-113-370-883-1315-1669   Timmy Graham
1-3-16-113-370-883-1315-1670   Christian Graham
1-3-16-113-370-883-1315-1671   T. D. Graham
1-3-16-113-371-885-1320-1672   Wendell Neeley married Jimmie Gill
    1884.   Wendy Neeley
    1885.   Amy Neeley
    1886.   Cliff Neeley
1-3-16-113-371-885-1320-1673   Wayne Neeley married Nellie Cawood
    1887.   Brian Neeley
    1888.   Ginger Neeley
1-3-16-113-371-885-1320-1674   Ada Doyline Neeley married Donald Park on Nov. 29, 1963 in Bradley
        County, TN (Internet, *Ancestry.com*) (2) Johnny Davis Cheek, (3)
        Samuel Howard Cooper
    1889.   Karen Park
    1890.   Sabrena Park
1-3-16-113-371-885-1321-1675   Norma Caldwell married John Vance Hodgson on Dec. 21, 1960 in
        Bradley County, TN (Internet, *Ancestry.com*)
    1891.   Lamar Hodgson
    1892.   Neil Hodgson
1-3-16-113-371-885-1321-1676   Patsy Caldwell married Claude Robert (Bobby) Neeley May 31, 1966 in
        Bradley County, TN (Internet, *Ancestry.com*)
    1893.   Beth Neeley

1894.   Leah Neeley
1-3-16-113-371-885-1321-1677   Delbert Leon Caldwell married Minnie Quinsetta Grissom Nov. 19,
            1971 in Bradley County, TN (Internet, *Ancestry.com*) (adopted child
            Melinda Caldwell)
1895.   Janet Caldwell
1896.   Jason Caldwell
1-3-16-113-371-885-1321-1678   Sherry Caldwell married Barry Franklin Stephens on Dec. 20, 1977 in
            Bradley County, TN (Internet, *Ancestry.com*)
1897.   Brett Stephens
1898.   Matthew Stephens
1899.   Kristen Stephens
1-3-16-113-371-885-1321-1679   Donna Caldwell married Ron Dunaway
1900.   Tyler Dunaway
1901.   Taylor Dunaway
1-3-16-113-371-885-1322-1680   Carolyn Matthews married Larry Dunn
1-3-16-113-371-885-1322-1681   Laverne (Bunny) Matthews married William L. Farmer (Junior) May 19,
            1961 in Bradley County, TN (Internet, *Ancestry.com*)
1902.   Debbie Farmer
1903.   Darlene Farmer
1-3-16-113-371-885-1322-1682   Sharon Matthews married George Willard Geren (number 1198) on May
            2, 1966 in Bradley County, TN (Internet, *Ancestry.com*)
1550.   Georgina Gay Geren
1551.   Emily Geren
1-3-16-113-371-885-1325-1683   Bobbie Neeley married (1) Pete Grady and (2) Leon Ledford.
1904.   Terrie Lynn Grady
1905.   Mitchell Grady
1906.   Bradley Grady
1-3-16-113-371-885-1325-1684   Dinah Neeley married Steve Ellis
1907.   Angie Ellis
1908.   Karen Ellis
1-3-16-113-371-885-1325-1685   Jackie Neeley married Ricky Carver
1909.   Eric Carver
1910.   Jillian Carver
1-3-16-113-371-886-1326-1686   Carol Ann Francisco married (1) Kenneth Waters and (2) Mike Martin.
1911.   Kendra Lynn Waters
1-3-16-113-371-888-1329-1240   Charles Hubert Murphy b. 1943 married Marion Mysinger
1587.   Lillian Murphy b. 1965
1588.   Michael Murphy b. 1967
1-3-16-113-371-888-1329-1241   Linda Lou Murphy b. 1946 married (1) Bobby Cook and (2) Hubert Ray
            Cook on Dec. 20, 1966 in Bradley County, TN (Internet, *Ancestry.com*).
1589.   Lesa Cook
1-3-16-113-371-888-1329-1242   Dewayne Murphy b. 1948 married (1) Virginia Baker and (2) Anna Lee
            Grissom
1-3-16-113-371-888-1329-1243   Alice Lynn Murphy b. 1954 married Dennis Taylor
1590.   Jason Taylor
1591.   Curtis Taylor
1-3-16-113-371-888-1329-1244   Deborah (Debbie) Joyce Murphy b. 1957
1592.   Adam Murphy
1-3-16-113-371-888-1330-1687   Barbara Ann Murphy married Wayne Lacy, Jr.
1912.   Stephanie Paige Lacy
1913.   Bridgette Renea Lacy
1-3-16-113-371-888-1330-1688   Margaret Rose Murphy
1-3-16-113-371-888-1330-1689   Richard Lynn Murphy
1-3-16-113-371-888-1331-1690   Fred Anthony (Ted) Murphy married Sandra Caywood
1914.   Anthony Matthew (Tony) Murphy
1915.   John David Murphy

1-3-16-113-371-888-1331-1691   Marilyn Gayenell Murphy married Daniel Phelps
     1916.   Tim Phelps
     1917.   Christopher Daniel Phelps
1-3-16-113-371-888-1332-1692   Cynthia Mechell Murphy married Terry Lewis
     1918.   Alisha Lewis
     1919.   Shannon Lewis
1-3-16-113-371-888-1332-1693   Oglevia Cornelles Murphy married Cary Belcher
     1920.   Atchley Murphy
1-3-16-113-371-890-1334-1694   Michael Graham
1-3-16-113-371-890-1335-1695   Cathy Graham married Brian Matthews
     1921.   Erin Matthews
     1922.   Chad Matthews
1-3-16-113-371-890-1335-1696   Wyman Graham married (1) Lisa Dixson;
     1923.   Holli Graham
1-3-16-113-371-890-1335-1696   Wyman Graham married (2) Sharon Trew.
     1924.   Hanna Graham
     1925.   Hayden Graham
1-3-16-113-371-890-1335-1697   Tyler Graham
1-3-16-113-371-891-1336-1698   Yolanda Marline Graham married David Allen on Sept. 12, 1981 in
            Bradley County, TN (Internet, *Ancestry.com*)
     1926.   Jonathan Heath Allen married Jill Myers
     1927.   Jared Houston Allen married Carissa Faith Ellenwood on Oct. 19, 2013 *Cleveland Daily
        Banner*
1-3-16-113-371-891-1337-1699   Robert F. Graham
1-3-16-113-371-891-1337-1700   Mary Lajane Graham married (1) Robert Morrow;
     1928.   Mary Elizabeth Morrow
1-3-16-113-371-891-1337-1700   Mary Lajane Graham married (2) Jean-Francois Riand.
     1929.   Sophie Michelle Riand
1-3-16-113-371-891-1337-1701   David Murel Graham married Crissy
     1930.   Ashland Marie Graham
     1931.   Ava Grace Graham
     1932.   Weston David Graham
1-3-16-113-371-891-1338-1702   Karen Eileen Graham
1-3-16-113-371-891-1338-1703   Rhonda Graham m. (1) Charles Standlee Williams, 3rd on Oct. 7, 1986
            in Bradley County, TN (Internet, *Ancestry.com*) and (2) Michael Torbett
     1933.   Haley Williams
     1934.   Christian Torbett
1-3-16-113-371-891-1338-1704   Jerry M. Graham, Jr. (Jay) married (1) Stephanie Irene Powell May 21,
            1993 in Bradley County, TN (Internet, *Ancestry.com*) and (2) Lisa
            Peacock.
     1935.   Karen Destiny Graham
     1936.   Bailey Andrew Graham
1-3-16-113-371-892-1340-1705   Lisa Renaee Wells married Matthew C. Wiley
     1937.   Leslie Nichole Wiley
1-3-16-113-371-892-1340-1706   Mark Alan Wells married Yvonne Allen
     1938.   Cody Wells
     1939.   Kevin Wells
1-3-16-113-371-892-1340-1707   James Edward Wells married Angie Stokes
1-3-16-113-371-892-844-1267   Forrest (Bucky) Buchanan Hill, 3rd
1-3-16-113-371-892-844-1268   Robert Hooper Hill
1-3-16-113-371-892-845-1269   Ronnie Lee Pell married Tammy Laverne Walden
1-3-16-113-371-892-845-1270   Richard Lynn Pell married Mary Ann Goolet
     1610.   James Pell
     1611.   Jennifer Pell
     1612.   Mary Ann Pell
1-3-16-113-371-892-845-1271   Regina Louise Pell married Tony Pantalucas

1613.   Anthony Pantalucas

1-3-16-113-371-892-845-1272   Francis Erhart Scherer, 4th married Lori

     1614.   Desiree Scherer

1-3-16-113-371-892-846-1273   Steven Franklin Bacon married (1) Regina Daniels, no children, (2) Susan E. Brown (one child), (3) Teresa Walker and (4) Pamela M. Loveday.

     1615.   Justin Franklin Bacon

1-3-16-113-371-892-847-1274   Dennis Robert Whaley, Jr. married (1) Susan Hunsucker and (2) Lori Green.

     1616.   Amber Nichole Whaley

     1617.   Dennis Robert Whaley, 3rd

1-3-16-113-371-892-847-1275   Gregory Alan Whaley married (1) Melanie Pendergrass on Feb. 29, 1984 in Bradley County, TN and (2) Zandra Orr on Jan. 22, 1985 in Bradley County, TN (Internet, *Ancestry.com*)

     1618.   Carmen Alise Whaley

     1619.   Alana Bree Whaley

1-3-16-113-371-892-847-1275   Gregory Alan Whaley married (3) Jessica Helton on Jan. 28, 1999 in Bradley County, TN (Internet, *Ancestry.com*)

     1620.   Megan Faye Whaley

1-3-16-113-371-893-1341-1708   Dennis Lee Rogers

1-3-16-113-371-893-1341-1709   Denise Lynne Rogers married (1) Kenneth Ray Craig;

     1940.   Kenneth Ray Craig, 3rd

1-3-16-113-371-893-1341-1709   Denise Lynne Rogers married (2) Tim Sedam.

     1941.   Adam Brandon Sedam

1-3-16-113-371-893-1341-1710   Karen Renee Rogers

     1942.   Taylor Renee Rogers-Settnek

1-3-16-113-371-893-1341-1711   Kevin Randall Rogers

1-3-16-113-371-895-1342-1712   Susan Graham married Christopher Vernon March 28, 1987 in Bradley County, TN (Internet, *Ancestry.com*)

     1943.   Victoria Ann Vernon

1-3-16-113-371-895-1342-1713   Richard Darrell Graham married Julie Wright

     1944.   Emily Lucinda Graham

1-3-16-113-371-895-1342-1714   Douglas Graham married Heather Strickland

     1945.   Daisy Ann Graham

1-3-16-113-371-895-1342-1715   Rachel Graham

1-3-16-113-371-895-1343-1558   Jonathan David Hooper married Dedra Diane Thummel on Jan. 17, 1995 in Bradley County, TN (Internet, *Ancestry.com*)

1-3-16-113-371-895-1343-1559   Christoper Nicholas Hooper

1-3-16-113-371-895-1344-1716   Stephanie Dawn Graham

1-3-16-113-371-895-1345-1717   Terry Derrick Graham

1-3-16-113-371-895-1345-1718   Andrew Jeremiah Graham

1-3-16-114-379-910-1357-1719   Bill Trewhitt, Jr. (Internet, Trewhitt, *Ancestry.com, created by Glenda Rowland, Find A Grave*)

     1946.   Zachary Trewhitt married to Taylor (Internet *Find A Grave*)

1-3-16-114-379-910-1357-1720   Elizabeth Trewhitt (Internet *Find A Grave*)

1-3-16-114-379-910-1357-1721   Christopher Trewhitt (Internet *Find A Grave*)

1-3-16-114-379-910-1357-1722   Shannon Trewhitt married Michael McAbee (Internet *Find A Grave*)

     1947.   Caden McAbee (Internet *Find A Grave*)

     1948.   Milla McAbee (Internet *Find A Grave*)

1-3-16-114-379-910-1358-1723   Michelle Bunch married Ryan Nelson

1-3-16-114-379-910-1358-1724   Alissa Bunch married   ? Pope

1-3-16-114-379-910-1358-1725   Christina Bunch

1-3-16-114-381-914-1364-1726   Kenneth E. Brown, Jr.

1-3-16-114-381-914-1364-1727   Steve R. Brown

1-3-16-114-381-914-1364-1728   Deborah Ann Brown married an Allgood

1-3-16-114-381-914-1364-1729   Patricia Kay Brown married a Gentry

1-3-16-114-381-914-1364-1730   Constance Lynn Brown married a Ruth
1-3-16-114-381-914-1364-1731   Cynthia Annette Brown married a Woodward
1-3-16-115-388-924-1382-1732   Carol Dryden married Derrel G. Bush on June 22, 1990 in Dallas, TX
                                (Internet, *Texas, Marriage Collection* at A*ncestry.com)*
1-3-16-115-388-924-1382-1733   David S. Dryden married Amy J. Alderman on Oct. 30, 1993 (found in
                                the Internet, *Collin County, Texas Marriage Index at Ancestry.com*)
1-3-16-115-388-924-1382-1734   Tiffany Psemeneki
1-3-16-115-388-924-1382-1735   Stacy Psemeneki
1-3-17-120-400-930-1385-1736   Edward Jackson Rogers, Jr.
1-3-17-120-400-930-1385-1737   Connie Frances Rogers
1-3-17-120-400-930-1385-1738   Brad Stewart Rogers
1-3-17-120-400-930-1385-1739   Stacey Nay Rogers
1-3-17-122-409-947-1394-1740   Shelley King
1-3-17-122-410-949-1222-1568   Debra L. Hooper
1-3-17-122-410-950-1395-1741   Monte Gale Harris b. Aug. 22, 1960 married Tanya Elizabeth Baldree
                                on June 12, 1981 in Bradley County, TN (Internet, *Ancestry.com*). She
                                was born Nov. 22, 1961.

    1949.   Julia Ann Harris
    1950.   Joseph Corey Harris
    1951.   Stephen Daniel Harris
    1952.   Lilly Kathryn Elizabeth Harris
1-3-17-122-410-950-1395-1742   Mark Wayne Harris married Lisa Gaye Young on Sept. 14, 1985
                                in Bradley County, TN (Internet, *Ancestry.com*).
    1953.   David Wayne Harris
    1954.   Rachel Marie Harris
1-3-17-122-410-950-1395-1743   Michael Troy Harris
1-3-17-122-410-950-1396-1744   Alden Dwayne "Dee" Harris married (1) Heather Anne Cruden on Oct.
                                18, 1987 in Bradley County, TN (Internet, *Ancestry.com*). (2) Daphney
    1955.   Alden Craig Harris
    1956.   Hooper Haywood Harris
    1956A.   Neyland Harris (found in Frances Harris Obituary in *Cleveland Daily Banner*)
(*Cleveland Daily Banner* Obituary for Frances Harris named Aubrey Harris as Great Grandchild.)
1-3-17-122-410-950-1396-1745   Donna Faye Harris married David Scott
1-3-17-122-410-950-1397-1746   Karen Harris married (1.) ? Bonner, (2) ? Auday and (3) Thomas Ray
                                Edwards, 3rd
    1957.   Jessica Bonner
1-3-17-122-410-950-1397-1747   Amy Harris married Russ Filyah
    1958.   Amber Filyah
1-3-17-122-410-950-1397-1748   Kellie Harris married Brad Young
    1959.   Corey Young
    1960.   Logan Young
    1961.   Jerrod Young
1-3-17-122-410-954-1232-1577   Carrie Lee Millaway
1-3-17-122-410-954-1233-1578   William Keith Hooper
1-3-17-122-410-954-1233-1579   Natalie Deann Hooper
1-3-17-122-410-954-1234-1580   Joey Heather Harris
1-3-17-122-410-954-1234-1581   Jennie Lynn Harris
1-3-17-122-410-954-1235-1582   Garrett Harrison Hooper
1-3-17-122-410-954-1235-1583   Anna Caroline Hooper
1-3-17-122-410-956-1409-1749   Brady Hooper
1-3-17-122-410-956-1410-1750   Kelsie Hartley
1-3-17-122-410-956-1411-1751   Wesley Lebron Ownbey
1-3-17-122-410-956-1411-1752   Torie Chastain
1-3-17-122-410-956-1412-1753   Taylor Hartley
1-3-17-122-410-956-1412-1754   Jacob Hartley
1-3-17-122-410-957-1413-1755   Phillip Carson

1-3-17-122-410-957-1413-1756   Landin Carson
1-3-17-122-410-957-1413-1757   Mary Claire Carson
1-3-17-122-410-957-1414-1758   McKenna Joyce Carson
1-3-17-122-410-957-1414-1759   Kellar Bryce Carson
1-3-17-122-410-957-1415-1760   Chase Bynum
1-3-17-122-410-957-1415-1761   Madison Bynum
1-3-17-122-410-960-1423-1762   Abby Hooper
1-3-17-122-410-960-1423-1763   Andrew Hooper
1-3-17-122-410-960-1424-1764   Kenley Harrison Hooper
1-3-17-122-410-960-1424-1765   Kiana Faith Hooper
1-3-17-122-410-960-1424-1766   Mattea Danielle Hooper
1-3-17-126-429-981-1429-1767   Megan Lynsey Bookout married Erick Georges Bergmann on Dec. 20, 2008 in Hamilton County, TN (*Times Free Press* March 1, 2009)
1-3-17-126-429-983-1431-1768   Justin Hooper
1-3-17-126-429-983-1431-1769   Cody Hooper
1-3-17-126-429-983-1432-1770   Kelci Beavers
1-3-17-126-429-985-1435-1771   Sidney Hooper
1-3-17-126-429-985-1435-1772   Madison Hooper
1-3-17-126-429-985-1435-1773   Kins Hooper
1-3-17-126-429-985-1436-1774   Hays Hooper
1-3-17-126-429-985-1436-1775   Alexander Hooper
1-3-17-126-429-985-1437-1776   Garett Hutchins
1-3-21-148-486-1028-1448-1777   Nathan Andrew Hooper b. Nov, 24, 1982
1-3-21-148-486-1028-1448-1778   Natalie Claire Hooper b. April 19, 1984
1-3-21-148-486-1028-1448-1779   Sarah Ann Hooper. Nov. 26, 1985
1-3-21-148-486-1028-1449-1780   Claire Emily Cooper b. Dec. 15, 1990
1-3-21-148-486-1028-1449-1781   Kate Elizabeth Cooper b. Dec. 16, 1993
1-3-21-148-486-1029-1450-1782   Billie Jo Summers Cunningham b. March 5, 1997
1-3-21-148-486-1029-1450-1783   Christopher Ross Cunningham b. Aug. 10, 1981
1-3-21-148-486-1029-1450-1784   Joshua Stephen Cunningham b. Feb. 4, 1983
1-3-21-148-486-1029-1451-1785   Adam Lyle Hooper b. Aug. 16, 1986
1-3-21-148-486-1029-1451-1786   Ashley Joy Hooper b. Nov. 24, 1987
1-3-21-148-486-1029-1451-1787   Kendra Michelle Hooper b. May 27, 1989
1-3-21-148-486-1029-1452-1788   Levi Lane Hooper b. July 29, 1993
1-3-21-150-489-1031-1455-1789   Cassie Nichole McPherson Osburn b. Aug. 16, 1983
1-3-21-150-489-1031-1456-1790   Garrett Thomas Gardner b. March 30, 1993
1-3-21-152-490-1032-1457-1791   Laura Catherine Mace b. Dec. 11, 1987
1-3-21-152-490-1032-1457-1792   Linda Michele Mace b. March 24, 1990
1-3-21-156-498-1040-1460-1793   Airanna Lee Evans b. Dec. 23, 1976
1-3-21-156-498-1040-1460-1794   Billy Joe Evans b. April 6, 1978
1-3-21-156-498-1040-1460-1795   Patricia Sue Evans b. Jan. 16, 1980
1-3-21-156-498-1040-1461-1796   Dalton Michael Grisham b. Jan. 22, 1992
1-3-21-156-500-1045-1467-1797   Taylor Lee Morgans b. 1992
1-3-21-156-500-1045-1468-1798   Eric Gregory Morgans b. Jan. 22,1989
1-4-30-177-530-1057-1423-1762   Abby Hooper
1-4-30-177-530-1057-1423-1763   Andrew Hooper
1-4-30-177-530-1057-1424-1764   Kenley Harrison Hooper
1-4-30-177-530-1057-1424-1765   Kiana Faith Hooper
1-4-30-177-530-1057-1424-1766   Mattea Danielle Hooper
1-4-30-177-530-1058-1477-1799   Jared King
1-4-30-177-530-1058-1478-1800   Emily Carden married Blake Justice
1-4-30-177-530-1058-1478-1801   Sydney Carden
1-4-30-177-530-1058-1479-1802   Ashley Shoemaker
1-4-30-177-530-1058-1479-1803   Clay Shoemaker
1-4-30-177-530-1058A-1479B-1803A   Courtney McCracken married Brandon Dietrich (*The Chattanoogan.com* Tuesday May 30, 2017 Obituary)

1-4-30-177-530-1058A-1479B-1803B   Cody McCracken (*The Chattanoogan.com*)
1-4-30-177-530-1058B-1479E-1803C   Dawson Mason
1-4-30-177-530-1059-1480-1804   Christian Jones
1-4-33-188-564-1094-1501-1805   Martin Lynn Droke
1-3-14-99-266-659-924-1382-1732   Carol Lynn Dryden
1-3-14-99-266-659-924-1382-1733   David Scott Dryden
1-3-14-99-266-659-924-1383-1734   Tiffany Psemeneki
1-3-14-99-266-659-924-1383-1735   Stacy Psemeneki
1-3-15-106-317-770-1191-1540-1806   Eric Steven Phillips b. 1985
1-3-15-106-317-770-1191-1540-1807   Emily Blair Phillips b. 1987 and Josh Key
  1962.   Madelyn Key
1-3-15-106-317-770-1191-1541-1808   Gordon (Trey) Lawrence Hixson, 3rd b. 1983
1-3-15-106-317-770-1191-1541-1809   John Benjamin Hixson b. 1988
1-3-15-106-317-770-1191-1541-1810   Catherine Lane (Laney) Hixson b. 1993
1-3-15-106-317-770-1193-1545-1811   Brently White
1-3-15-106-317-770-1193-1545-1812   Riley White
1-3-15-106-317-770-1193-1546-1813   Nicolas Doylene Burnette
1-3-15-106-317-770-1193-1546-1814   Avery Watson Burnette
1-3-15-106-317-770-1193-1546-1815   Noah Burnette
1-3-15-106-317-770-1193-1547-1816   Brooklyn Gibson
  1963.   Allie Grace Gibson
1-3-15-106-319-775-1195-1548-1817   Caroline Cantrell
1-3-15-106-319-775-1195-1548-1818   Caldwell Cantrell
1-3-15-106-319-775-1195-1549-1819   Christian Cantrell
1-3-15-106-319-775-1195-1549-1820   Gabriel Cantrell
1-3-15-106-319-776-1198-1550-1821   Ivo Aaron Miller, Jr.
1-3-15-106-319-776-1198-1550-1822   Joshua Wade Miller
1-3-15-106-319-776-1198-1550-1823   Jordan Miller
1-3-15-106-319-778-1200-1552-1824   Chandler Vance Frazier
1-3-15-106-320-429-981-1429-1767   Megan Lynsey Bookout married Erick Georges Bergmann on Dec. 20, 2008 in Hamilton County, TN (*Times Free Press* March 1, 2009)
1-3-15-106-320-429-981-1431-1768   Justin Hooper
1-3-15-106-320-429-981-1431-1769   Cody Hooper
1-3-15-106-320-429-981-1432-1770   Kelci Beavers
1-3-15-106-320-429-981-1435-1771   Sidney Hooper
1-3-15-106-320-429-981-1435-1772   Madison Hooper
1-3-15-106-320-429-981-1435-1773   Kins Hooper
1-3-15-106-320-429-981-1436-1774   Hays Hooper
1-3-15-106-320-429-981-1436-1775   Alexander Hooper
1-3-15-106-320-429-981-1437-1776   Garett Hutchins
1-3-15-109-341-808-1222-1568-1717   Terry Derrick Graham
1-3-15-109-341-808-1222-1568-1718   Andrew Jeremiah Graham
1-3-15-109-344-815-1224-1569-1825   Morgan Nichole Miller
1-3-15-109-344-815-1224-1569-1826   Gareth Alan Miller
1-3-15-109-344-815-1224-1569-1827   Gwyneth Ann Miller
1-3-15-109-344-815-1224-1570-1828   Parker Hobbs Miller
1-3-15-109-344-815-1224-1570-1829   Payton Miller
1-3-15-109-344-815-1225-1571-1821   Ivo Aaron Miller, Jr.
1-3-15-109-344-815-1225-1571-1822   Joshua Wade Miller
1-3-15-109-344-815-1225-1571-1823   Jordan Miller
1-3-15-109-344-816-1226-1574-1830   Caittie Miller
1-3-15-109-344-816-1226-1574-1831   Toby Miller
1-3-15-109-344-816-1226-1574-1832   Anna Miller
1-3-15-109-345-820-1236-1584-1833   Ella Grace Hooper
1-3-15-110-349-826-1240-1587-1834   Amber L. Morfield

1-3-15-110-349-826-1240-1588-1835   Angel Faye Murphy
1-3-15-110-349-826-1240-1588-1836   Aaron Murphy
1-3-15-110-349-826-1240-1589-1837   Erick Freeman
1-3-15-110-349-827-1247-1593-1838   Victoria Noble married Jared Tilley
1-3-15-110-349-827-1247-1593-1839   Christian Noble
1-3-15-110-349-827-1247-1594-1840   Montgomery Callaway
1-3-15-110-349-827-1247-1594-1841   Richard Holt
1-3-15-111-353-836-1260-1603-1842   Brent Musgrove
1-3-15-111-353-836-1260-1603-1843   Jake Musgrove
1-3-15-111-353-836-1260-1603-1844   Emily Musgrove
1-3-15-111-353-836-1260-1604-1845   Garrett Wallace
1-3-15-111-353-836-1260-1604-1846   Grayson Wallace
1-3-15-111-353-836-1260-1605-1847   Grace Gilbert
1-3-15-111-353-836-1260-1605-1848   Alexis Gilbert
1-3-15-111-353-836-1260-1605-1848A   Jay Gilbert
1-3-15-111-353-836-1260-1606-1848B   David Elder
1-3-15-111-353-836-1260-1607-1848C   Wyatt Gregory
1-3-15-111-353-836-1262-1608-1849   Karma Kirkpatrick
1-3-15-111-353-836-1262-1609-1849A   Jackson Callahan
1-3-15-111-354-838-1236-1584-1833   Ella Grace Hooper
1-3-15-111-356-845-1270-1610-1850   Destiny Pell
1-3-15-111-356-845-1270-1610-1851   Cameron Pell
1-3-15-111-356-845-1270-1610-1852   Kennedy Pell
1-3-15-111-356-845-1270-1611-1853   Alexis Pell
1-3-16-112-360-858-1280-1626-1854   Jeff Johnson married Dana
1-3-16-112-360-858-1280-1626-1855   Michelle Johnson married   Roberts
1-3-16-112-360-858-1280-1626-1856   Jason Johnson   married   Lindsey
1-3-16-112-360-858-1280-1627-1857   Derrick Marr
1-3-16-112-360-858-1280-1627-1858   Chris Marr
1-3-16-112-360-858-1280-1627-1859   Bryan Marr
1-3-16-112-360-858-1280-1627-1860   Tiffany Marr
1-3-16-112-360-858-1280-1628-1861   Caitlin Bentley
1-3-16-112-360-858-1280-1628-1862   Courtney Bentley

(Tammy Marr Bentley and Jeff Bentley's son-in-law is Adrian Rymer and their grandson is Nathaniel Rymer.)

1-3-16-112-363-353-836-1260-1603   Karen Wallace d. Oct. 30, 2014 married Russell Brent Musgrove; they died Oct. 30, 2014 (Karen and Russell died in an auto accident: Internet, *Life Legacy*, Lakeside Funeral Home at Woodstock, GA.)

 1842. Russell Brent Musgrove, Jr.
 1843. Jake Marshall Musgrove
 1844. Emily Suzanne Musgrove

1-3-16-112-363-353-836-1260-1604   Kenneth Marshall Wallace married Sharon Renae Melton in Meigs County, TN on July 26, 1991 (Internet, *Ancestry.com*)

 1845. Garrett Wallace
 1846. Grayson Wallace

1-3-16-112-363-353-836-1260-1605   Amanda Wallace married Duane Gilbert on June 16, 2009 in St. Thomas, Virgin Islands (Internet, *Ancestry.com*, in the *U.S. Marriages in Newspapers*)

 1847. Grace Gilbert
 1848. Alexis Gilbert
 1848A. Jay Gilbert

1-3-16-112-363-353-836-1261-1606   Adam Elder

 1848B. David Elder

1-3-16-112-363-353-836-1261-1607   Laura Elder married a Gregory

 1848C. Wyatt Gregory

1-3-16-112-363-353-836-1262-1608   Chase Kirkpatrick
       1849.   Karma Kirkpatrick
1-3-16-112-363-353-836-1262-1609   Olivia Kirkpatrick married a Callahan
       1849A.   Jackson Callahan
1-3-16-113-370-879-1303-1646-1863   Michelle Geren married Ramsey? and Robert Steven
                                Anderson
       1964.   Matthew Ramsey
       1965.   Trevor Ramsey
       1966.   Colton Ramsey
       1967.   Olivia Anderson
       1968.   Phallyn Anderson
1-3-16-113-370-879-1303-1646-1864   Meleah Geren
       1969.   Dakota Geren
1-3-16-113-370-879-1303-1648-1865   Brad Geren married Andrea
       1970.   Cole Geren
       1971.   Callie Geren
1-3-16-113-370-879-1303-1648-1866   Nathan Geren married Leslie
       1972.   Savanna Geren
       1973.   Chase Geren
1-3-16-113-370-879-1304-1653-1867   Julia Akins married Mitchell Humphreys
1-3-16-113-370-879-1304-1653-1868   Jenni Akins
1-3-16-113-370-879-1304-1653-1869   Emily Akins married Coby Goins
1-3-16-113-370-879-1304-1654-1870   Christie Geren married David Wright
1-3-16-113-370-879-1304-1654-1871   Shelley Geren
1-3-16-113-370-879-1304   Luther Edward Geren's **grandchildren: Taylor Brooks, Mack Suits, Chelsey Humphreys, Carlie Ann Wright and Luke Goins: great-grandchild: Micah Brooks (Information from the *Heartfelt Connections*, Obituary at Jim Rush Funeral Home Nov. 21, 2013)**
1-3-16-113-370-879-1307-1655-1872   Josie Collins
1-3-16-113-370-879-1307-1655-1873   Trent Collins
1-3-16-113-370-879-1307-1656-1874   Sallie Collins
1-3-16-113-370-881-1309-1661-1875   Olivia Howard
1-3-16-113-370-881-1309-1662-1876   Bryson Whaley
1-3-16-113-370-882-1312-1663-1877   Cody Swafford
1-3-16-113-370-882-1312-1663-1878   Courtney Swafford
1-3-16-113-370-882-1312-1664-1879   Casey Matthews
1-3-16-113-370-882-1312-1664-1880   Brody Matthews
1-3-16-113-370-882-1313-1666-1881   Isaiah Caldwell
1-3-16-113-370-882-1313-1666-1882   Malachi Caldwell
1-3-16-113-370-882-1313-1666-1883   Nehemiah Caldwell
1-3-16-113-371-885-1320-1672-1884   Wendy Neeley married Brad Benton on June 3, 1995 in Bradley
                               County, TN (Internet, *Ancestry.com*).
       1974.   Neeley Benton
       1975.   Luke Benton
       1976.   Parker Benton
1-3-16-113-371-885-1320-1672-1885   Amy Neeley married John Owenby on March 25, 2000 in Bradley
                               County, TN (Internet, *Ancestry.com*).
       1977.   Anna Grace Owenby
       1978.   Abbie Bess Owenby
1-3-16-113-371-885-1320-1672-1886   Cliff Neeley married Kristine Lang on July 21, 2007 in Nashville,
                               TN (Internet, Belmont University Sept. 6, 2007).
       1979.   Virginia May Neeley
       1980.   Emmett Reinier Neeley
       1981.   Hayden Michael Neeley
1-3-16-113-371-885-1320-1673-1887   Brian Monroe Neeley married Tonya Lynn Lewallen on March 4,
                               2000 in Bradley County, TN (Internet, *Ancestry.com*).
       1982.   Jacob Monroe Neeley

1983.	Amanda Neeley

1-3-16-113-371-885-1320-1673-1888	Ginger Neeley married Don Summers

1984.	Chelsie Summers

1-3-16-113-371-885-1320-1674-1889	Karen Park

1985.	Michaela Park

1-3-16-113-371-885-1320-1674-1890	Sabrena Park

1-3-16-113-371-885-1321-1675-1891	Lamar Hodgson married Lisa Marie Dalton on Dec. 18, 1987 in Bradley County, TN (Internet, *Ancestry.com*).

1986.	Dalton Hodgson

1-3-16-113-371-885-1321-1675-1892	Neil Hodgson married Pam Samples

1987.	Haley Hodgson

1-3-16-113-371-8851321-1676-1893	Beth Neeley married Thomas Michael Kammer on Aug. 1, 1992 in Bradley County, TN (Internet, *Ancestry.com*).

1-3-16-113-371-885-1321-1676-1894	Leah Neeley married Oliver Perry Hovey, Jr. on April 27, 1997 in Bradley County, TN (Internet, *Ancestry.com*).

1988.	Olivia Hovey
1989.	Zachary Hovey

1-3-16-113-371-885-1321-1677-1895	Janet Caldwell married Steven Howard

1990.	Tanner Caldwell
1991.	Haley Caldwell

1-3-16-113-371-885-1321-1677-1896	Jason Caldwell married Kellie Ots

1992.	Eston Caldwell
1993.	Shelby Caldwell
1994.	Keegan Caldwell

1-3-16-113-371-885-1321-1678-1897	Brett Stephens
1-3-16-113-371-885-1321-1678-1898	Matthew Stephens
1-3-16-113-371-885-1321-1678-1899	Kristen Stephens
1-3-16-113-371-885-1321-1679-1900	Tyler Dunaway
1-3-16-113-371-885-1321-1679-1901	Taylor Dunaway
1-3-16-113-371-885-1322-1681-1902	Debbie Farmer married Bobby Lee Myers, Jr. on Oct. 26, 1991 in Bradley County, TN (Internet, *Ancestry.com*).

1995.	Corey Myers
1996.	A. J. Myers
1997.	Ethan Myers

1-3-16-113-371-885-1322-1681-1903	Darlene Farmer married Ivan Richard Murray, Jr. on Feb. 6, 1979 in Bradley County, TN (Internet, *Ancestry.com*).

1998.	Adam Murray
1999.	Dusty Murray

1-3-16-113-371-885-1322-1682-1550	Georgina Gay Geren married Dr. Ivo Aaron Miller (number 1381 on Aug. 7, 1993 in Bradley County, TN (Internet, *Ancestry.com*).

1821.	Ivo Aaron Miller, Jr.
1822.	Joshua Wade Miller
1823.	Jordan Miller

1-3-16-113-371-885-1322-1682-1551	Emily Geren married Justin McCulley on June 4, 2011 (*Cleveland Daily Banner* May 20, 2012)

1-3-16-113-371-885-1325-1683-1904	Terrie Lynn Grady married Kenny Bryant

2000.	Taylor Bryant
2001.	Ashlynne Bryant

1-3-16-113-371-885-1325-1683-1905	Mitchell Grady married Dana Jones

2002.	Dylan Grady

1-3-16-113-371-885-1325-1683-1906	Bradley Grady
1-3-16-113-371-885-1325-1684-1907	Angie Ellis married Dustin Hicks
1-3-16-113-371-885-1325-1684-1908	Karen Ellis married Heith Lamon

2003.	Caleb Lamon
2004.	Nathaniel Lamon

1-3-16-113-371-885-1325-1685-1909	Eric Carver

1-3-16-113-371-885-1325-1685-1910   Jillian Carver
1-3-16-113-371-886-1326-1686-1911   Kendra Lynn Waters married Gary Owens
    2005.   Gary L. Owens, Jr.
    2006.   Brittany Leann Owens
    2007.   Valerie Michelle Owens
    2008.   Melanie Renaee Owens
1-3-16-113-371-888-1329-1240-1587   Lillian Murphy b. 1965 married William Morfield
    1834.   Amber L. Morfield
1-3-16-113-371-888-1329-1240-1588   Michael Murphy b. 1967 married June Pettit
    1835.   Angel Faye Murphy
    1836.   Aaron Murphy
1-3-16-113-371-888-1329-1241-1589   Lesa Cook married Marvin Freeman
    1837.   Erick Freeman
1-3-16-113-371-888-1329-1243-1590   Jason Taylor
1-3-16-113-371-888-1329-1243-1591   Curtis Taylor
1-3-16-113-371-888-1329-1244-1592   Adam Murphy
1-3-16-113-371-888-1330-1687-1912   Stephanie Paige Lacy
1-3-16-113-371-888-1330-1687-1913   Bridgette Renea Lacy married Billy Joe Byers
    2009.   Brayden Joe Byers
1-3-16-113-371-888-1331-1690-1914   Anthony Matthew (Tony) Murphy married Leanna Moore
    2010.   Hannah Elizabeth Murphy
    2011.   Elliott Murphy
    2012.   Hudson Murphy
1-3-16-113-371-888-1331-1690-1915   John David Murphy married (1) Kristie Woody and (2) Gina
    2013.   Jordan Dakota Murphy   (Step-Daughter: Maria)
1-3-16-113-371-888-1331-1691-1916   Tim Phelps married Leslie Wagner
    2014.   Kathleen (Katie) Elizabeth Phelps
1-3-16-113-371-888-1331-1691-1917   Christopher Daniel Phelps married Michelle Champagne
1-3-16-113-371-888-1332-1692-1918   Alisha Lewis
1-3-16-113-371-888-1332-1692-1919   Shannon Lewis
1-3-16-113-371-888-1332-1693-1920   Atchley Murphy
1-3-16-113-371-890-1335-1695-1921   Erin Matthews
1-3-16-113-371-890-1335-1695-1922   Chad Matthews
1-3-16-113-371-890-1335-1696-1923   Holli Graham
1-3-16-113-371-890-1335-1696-1924   Hanna Graham
1-3-16-113-371-890-1335-1696-1925   Hayden Graham
1-3-16-113-371-891-1336-1698-1926   Jonathan Heath Allen married Jill Myers
    2015.   Kendall Reese Allen
    2016.   Kipton Heath Allen
1-3-16-113-371-891-1336-1698-1927   Jared Houston Allen married Carissa Faith Ellenwood on Oct. 19,
                    2013 according to the *Cleveland Daily Banner*
    2017.   Addyson Grace Allen
1-3-16-113-371-891-1337-1700-1928   Mary Elizabeth Morrow
1-3-16-113-371-891-1337-1700-1929   Sophie Michelle Riand
1-3-16-113-371-891-1337-1701-1930   Ashland Marie Graham
1-3-16-113-371-891-1337-1701-1931   Ava Grace Graham
1-3-16-113-371-891-1337-1701-1932   Weston David Graham
1-3-16-113-371-891-1338-1703-1933   Haley Williams married Durelle Wood
1-3-16-113-371-891-1338-1703-1934   Christian Torbett
1-3-16-113-371-891-1338-1704-1935   Karen Destiny Graham
1-3-16-113-371-891-1338-1704-1936   Bailey Andrew Graham
1-3-16-113-371-892-1340-1705-1937   Leslie Nichole Wiley
1-3-16-113-371-892-1340-1706-1938   Cody Wells
1-3-16-113-371-892-1340-1706-1939   Kevin Wells
1-3-16-113-371-892-845-1270-1610   James Pell married Jennifer Williams
    1850.   Destiny Pell

1851.	Cameron Pell
1852.	Kennedy Pell
1-3-16-113-371-892-845-1270-1611	Jennifer Pell
1853.	Alexis Pell
1-3-16-113-371-892-845-1270-1612	Mary Ann Pell
1-3-16-113-371-892-845-1271-1613	Anthony Pantalucas
1-3-16-113-371-892-845-1271-1614	Desiree Scherer
1-3-16-113-371-892-845-1272-1615	Justin Franklin Bacon
1-3-16-113-371-892-847-1274-1616	Amber Nichole Whaley
1-3-16-113-371-892-847-1274-1617	Dennis Robert Whaley, 3rd
1-3-16-113-371-892-847-1275-1618	Carmen Alise Whaley
1-3-16-113-371-892-847-1275-1619	Alana Bree Whaley
1-3-16-113-371-892-847-1275-1620	Megan Faye Whaley
1-3-16-113-371-893-1341-1709-1940	Kenneth Ray Craig, 3rd
1-3-16-113-371-893-1341-1709-1941	Adam Brandon Sedam
1-3-16-113-371-893-1341-1710-1942	Taylor Renee Rogers-Settnek
1-3-16-113-371-895-1342-1712-1943	Victoria Ann Vernon
1-3-16-113-371-895-1342-1713-1944	Emily Lucinda Graham
1-3-16-113-371-895-1342-1714-1945	Daisy Ann Graham
1-3-16-114-379-910-1357-1719-1946	Zachary Trewhitt married to Taylor (Internet, *Ancestry.com, Find A Grave created by Glenda Rowland*)
1-3-16-114-379-910-1357-1722-1947	Caden McAbee (*Find A Grave*)
1-3-16-114-379-910-1357-1722-1948	Milla McAbee (*Find A Grave*)
1-3-17-122-410-950-1395-1741-1949	Julia Ann Harris
1-3-17-122-410-950-1395-1741-1950	Joseph Corey Harris
1-3-17-122-410-950-1395-1741-1951	Stephen Daniel Harris
1-3-17-122-410-950-1395-1741-1952	Lilly Kathryn Elizabeth Harris
1-3-17-122-410-950-1395-1742-1953	David Wayne Harris
1-3-17-122-410-950-1395-1742-1954	Rachel Marie Harris
1-3-17-122-410-950-1396-1744-1955	Alden Craig Harris
1-3-17-122-410-950-1396-1744-1956	Hooper Haywood Harris
1-3-17-122-410-950-1396-1744-1956A	Neyland Harris
1-3-17-122-410-950-1397-1746-1957	Jessica Bonner
1-3-17-122-410-950-1397-1747-1958	Amber Filyah
1-3-17-122-410-950-1397-1748-1959	Corey Young
1-3-17-122-410-950-1397-1748-1960	Logan Young
1-3-17-122-410-950-1397-1748-1961	Jerrod Young
1-3-15-106-317-770-1191-1540-1807-1962	Madelyn Key
1-3-15-106-317-770-1193-1547-1816-1963	Allie Grace Gibson
1-3-16-112-363-353-836-1260-1603-1842	Russell Brent Musgrove, Jr.
1-3-16-112-363-353-836-1260-1603-1843	Jake Marshall Musgrove
1-3-16-112-363-353-836-1260-1603-1844	Emily Suzanne Musgrove
1-3-16-112-363-353-836-1260-1604-1845	Garrett Wallace
1-3-16-112-363-353-836-1260-1604-1846	Grayson Wallace
1-3-16-112-363-353-836-1260-1605-1847	Grace Gilbert
1-3-16-112-363-353-836-1260-1605-1848	Alexis Gilbert
1-3-16-112-363-353-836-1260-1605-1848A	Jay Gilbert
1-3-16-112-363-353-836-1260-1606-1848B	David Elder
1-3-16-112-363-353-836-1260-1607-1848C	Wyatt Gregory
1-3-16-112-363-353-836-1262-1608-1849	Karma Kirkpatrick
1-3-16-112-363-353-836-1262-1609-1849A	Jackson Callahan
1-3-16-113-370-879-1303-1646-1863-1964	Matthew Ramsey
1-3-16-113-370-879-1303-1646-1863-1965	Trevor Ramsey
1-3-16-113-370-879-1303-1646-1863-1966	Colton Ramsey
1-3-16-113-370-879-1303-1646-1863-1967	Olivia Anderson
1-3-16-113-370-879-1303-1646-1863-1968	Phallyn Anderson

1-3-16-113-370-879-1303-1646-1864-1969   Dakota Geren
1-3-16-113-370-879-1303-1648-1865-1970   Cole Geren
1-3-16-113-370-879-1303-1648-1865-1971   Callie Geren
1-3-16-113-370-879-1303-1648-1866-1972   Savanna Geren
1-3-16-113-370-879-1303-1648-1866-1973   Chase Geren
1-3-16-113-371-885-1320-1672-1884-1974   Neeley Benton
1-3-16-113-371-885-1320-1672-1884-1975   Luke Benton
1-3-16-113-371-885-1320-1672-1884-1976   Parker Benton
1-3-16-113-371-885-1320-1670-1885-1977   Anna Grace Owenby
1-3-16-113-371-885-1320-1670-1885-1978   Abbie Bess Owenby
1-3-16-113-371-885-1320-1670-1886-1979   Virginia Neeley
1-3-16-113-371-885-1320-1670-1886-1980   Emmett Reinier Neeley
1-3-16-113-371-885-1320-1670-1886-1981   Hayden Michael Neeley
1-3-16-113-371-885-1320-1673-1887-1982   Jacob Monroe Neeley
1-3-16-113-371-885-1320-1673-1887-1983   Amanda Neeley
1-3-16-113-371-885-1320-1673-1888-1984   Chelsie Summers
1-3-16-113-371-885-1320-1674-1889-1985   Michaela Park
1-3-16-113-371-885-1321-1675-1891-1986   Dalton Hodgson
1-3-16-113-371-885-1321-1675-1892-1987   Haley Hodgson
1-3-16-113-371-885-1321-1676-1894-1988   Olivia Hovey
1-3-16-113-371-885-1321-1676-1894-1989   Zachary Hovey
1-3-16-113-371-885-1321-1677-1895-1990   Tanner Caldwell
1-3-16-113-371-885-1321-1677-1895-1991   Haley Caldwell
1-3-16-113-371-885-1321-1677-1896-1992   Eston Caldwell
1-3-16-113-371-885-1321-1677-1896-1993   Shelby Caldwell
1-3-16-113-371-885-1321-1677-1896-1994   Keegan Caldwell
1-3-16-113-371-885-1322-1681-1902-1995   Corey Myers
1-3-16-113-371-885-1322-1681-1902-1996   A. J. Myers
1-3-16-113-371-885-1322-1681-1902-1997   Ethan Myers
1-3-16-113-371-885-1322-1681-1903-1998   Adam Murray married Julia
    2018.   Max Murray
    2019.   Stella Murray
1-3-16-113-371-885-1322-1681-1903-1999   Dusty Murray
    2020.   Trainer Murray
    2021.   Jase Murray
1-3-16-113-371-885-1322-1682-1550-1821   Ivo Aaron Miller, Jr.
1-3-16-113-371-885-1322-1682-1550-1822   Joshua Wade Miller
1-3-16-113-371-885-1322-1682-1550-1823   Jordan Miller
1-3-16-113-371-885-1325-1683-1904-2000   Taylor Bryant
1-3-16-113-371-885-1325-1683-1904-2001   Ashlynne Bryant
1-3-16-113-371-885-1325-1683-1905-2002   Dylan Grady
1-3-16-113-371-885-1325-1684-1908-2003   Caleb Lamon
1-3-16-113-371-885-1325-1684-1908-2004   Nathaniel Lamon
1-3-16-113-371-886-1326-1686-1911-2005   Gary L. Owens, Jr.
1-3-16-113-371-886-1326-1686-1911-2006   Brittany Leann Owens
1-3-16-113-371-886-1326-1686-1911-2007   Valerie Michelle Owens
1-3-16-113-371-886-1326-1686-1911-2008   Melanie Renaee Owens
1-3-16-113-371-888-1329-1240-1587-1834   Amber L. Morfield
1-3-16-113-371-888-1329-1240-1588-1835   Angel Faye Murphy
1-3-16-113-371-888-1329-1240-1588-1836   Aaron Murphy
1-3-16-113-371-888-1329-1241-1589-1837   Erick Freeman
1-3-16-113-371-888-1330-1687-1913-2009   Brayden Joe Byers
1-3-16-113-371-888-1331-1690-1914-2010   Hannah Elizabeth Murphy
1-3-16-113-371-888-1331-1690-1914-2011   Elliott Murphy
1-3-16-113-371-888-1331-1690-1914-2012   Hudson Murphy)
1-3-16-113-371-888-1331-1690-1915-2013   Jordan Dakota Murphy

1-3-16-113-371-888-1331-1691-1916-2014   Kathleen (Katie) Elizabeth Phelps
1-3-16-113-371-891-1336-1698-1926-2015   Kendall Allen
1-3-16-113-371-891-1336-1698-1926-2016   Kipton Allen
1-3-16-113-371-891-1336-1698-1927-2017   Addyson Grace Allen
1-3-16-113-371-892-845-1270-1610-1850   Destiny Pell
1-3-16-113-371-892-845-1270-1610-1851   Cameron Pell
1-3-16-113-371-892-845-1270-1610-1852   Kennedy Pell
1-3-16-113-371-892-845-1270-1611-1853   Alexis Pell
1-3-16-113-371-885-1322-1681-1903-1998-2018   Max Murray
1-3-16-113-371-885-1322-1681-1903-1998-2019   Stella Murray
1-3-16-113-371-885-1322-1681-1903-1999-2020   Trainer Murray
1-3-16-113-371-885-1322-1681-1903-1999-2021   Jase Murray

1-3-16-112-360-860   Kenzie Marr b. May 17, 1902 d. Oct. 24, 1981 (See pp. 63 and 84) married (1) Mary
Smith b. Feb. 25, 1902 d. Feb. 28, 1920 (*HAROLDDH38 at Ancestry.com*) and (2)
Beulah L. Smith b. March 30, 1908 d. Nov. 27, 1978 married Oct. 23, 1925 in
Bradley County, TN (Internet, *Ancestry.com*). (*Cleveland Daily Banner* for Sept.
26, 2017 had the following information for Ruby Marr McCusiton McCulley:
Children of Kins Marr and Beulah were (1) Frederick Marr; (2) Christine Marr
married a Lindsey; (3) Charlotte Marr married a Stafford; (4) Ruby Marr married a
McCusiton and Thomas Eugene McCulley; Children of Ruby were (1) Rosa Lee
McCusiton married Jimmy Botts and (2) Linda McCusiton Dashiell; grandchildren
were Sonya Richardson married to Frankie Richardson; Barry Botts married to
Marlene; Kevin Botts married to Lyndsay.)

1-3-16-112-361-864-1293B Gale Clebron Jones b. 1919 – d. 1993 (Internet, *Ancestry.com* by
MLEubank see p. 84 for parents and sister)
1-3-16-112-361-864-1293C Sa. C. Jones b. abt. 1919 but cannot be found in *1920 Bradley County Census*
nor in the *1930 Hamilton County Census*; he is only listed in the *1940 Hamilton
County Census.*

(Information for Jimie Eloise Swafford came from her Obituary in the *Cleveland Daily Banner*, Cleveland,
TN on March 22, 2018.)
1-3-17-122-409-946-1388   Eloise Ellis married Frank Melvin Swafford (See pp. 89 and 108)
1739A.   David Miles Swafford
1739B.   Thelma Swafford
1739C.   Frankie Swafford
1739D.   Melvin Douglas Swafford married April (stepdaughters are Mary Ellen Hyberger and
Maxine Whaley married to David Whaley and Grandchildren are Callie Grace Swafford,
Josiah Franklin Swafford and Charis Faith Swafford)

1-3-14-98-261   Landon Graham (See pp. 43 and 56) b. July 29, 1868 d. December 23, 1950 married (2)
Mattie Arrington
647A.   John Graham b. 1930
647B.   Cleve Graham b. 1933

1-3-20-140-462   Leonard Hooper b. 1921 in California m. Hazel Kinnamon (See pp. 49 and 69)
1018A.   Kinsey L. Hooper b. 1942 in Van Nuys, CA d. Cleveland, TN m. Marla D. Keithly
(*Ancestry.com* by *lunddl* and family information from Obituary found at Companion
Funeral Home, Cleveland, TN on June 7, 2018: Kurt Hooper with Nancy, Samantha &
Sydney Hooper. Kary Hooper with Michele, Amanda, Taylor & Kimber Hooper. Kyson
Hooper with Rebecca, Natalee & Teagan Hooper)
1018B.   Colleen Macuk
1018C.   Leoma Berry

Kinsey C. Hooper Civil War Diary and the Andrew Hooper Estate

Outside of the Kinsey C. Hooper Diary showing the Tongue closure open

Picture below showing the Tongue and Groove closure mechanism closed

Diary Opened

(The Civil War Diary book is the result of the work of Richard [Rick] Hooper. Rick is an active participant in the Civil War reenactment battles. He discovered this old diary in the 1970s or 1980s and researched the material to see if it was historically accurate. It was!!! The added explanations are Rick's unless otherwise noted. More information can be found in Appendix C at pp. 269 - 270.)

Historical note on the 7th & 8th Tennessee Volunteer Infantry Regiment from Company records: "On Dec. 26, 1862, at the time of Confederate General Morgan's third raid into Kentucky, Colonel William A. Hoskins, at Lebanon, Kentucky, reported the 7th Tennessee Infantry, 258 men, as part of his command, and stated he placed it in a temporary brigade along with the 12th and 16th Kentucky Regiments, to engage in an attempt to cut off Morgan." The 8th Regiment was mustered in at Camp Dick Robinson, Kentucky, May, 1863.... "Captain William C. Shelton. Co. "A". Mustered in at Camp Dick Robinson, May 16, 1863. Men from Scott and Hamilton Counties. Transferred from Colonel William Clift's 7th East Tennessee Volunteer Infantry...." (Company A included the Hoopers from the 7th Tenn.)

"The regiment (8th) was first reported December, 1862 in the Department of the Ohio, District of Central Kentucky with Colonel Reeve in command. On January 10, 1863, at Nicholasville, the regiment was reported with 21 officers, 324 men present for duty.... Since the beginning of organization the regiment had been employed on fatigue duty, building fortifications, etc. at various points in Kentucky."

The notes enclosed in [brackets] were added by Rick for clarity and background. The words per line, spelling and spacing have been copied as close as possible to the original. (Harold Reno added the Andrew Hooper Estate to the end because Andrew died about 1866. Most Civil War Pension Applications used the word Invalid, and Invalid means there was sickness or injury as a result of the war.)

(The Kinsey C. Hooper Diary was a narrow, foldable book that could be carried in a pocket. Since it was narrow, Rick tried to maintain the integrity of the writing by using a narrow column with his explanations written to the right of the diary information.)

[Rick Hooper comments: It starts on the inside cover and something has discolored it (see p. 132). Also, several pages are missing. FYI—Brothers are John, K. C., Jahew, James and William (Will) Hooper.]

December, 1862
bradley county
december 25 left home   [25th left home about 2 o'clock
a boute 2 oclo?? cra   Christmas
timas in the nit   in the night
travel on thre miles   travel on three miles]
26 laid in the snow
rained on us nite trav
Seven miles 27 mov?
in a half mile to a
rock hous Stade th??
to days and nite mov
one quarter of a mile
Staid ther one nite
one day next nite
eight miles Stad the
day tel evnin traveld
ten miles slep tog???
??si?? sno? ??????
January the first 186
travel ???????? Staid
????????????????????

February, 1863
10) got to hickman bridge on the
    Caintucky river   [Central Kentucky]
12) on fir teeg pild cresok
    [On fatigue, piled creosote]   [Fatigue was "**any unarmed labor assigned to a**
13) Detailed to hunt a beef   **soldier"** found at Internet *Civil War Talk* by *gross music*.]
14) wash day Dic Shipley got hear
15) prechin by Huse
16) on fur teeg pild cresok
17) corpral of the gard at the bridge
19) the sam   [same]
20) geog Atchley de serted com
    [George Atchley deserted company?]
22) blocked the bridg and stod
    picked corpral all nite same
23) apinted bugal man
    nite slep with close on
    F. C. Johnson apinted 2 Leut.
24) held a lection
    E. B. Fitzeared first sargent
    John Francisco sargent
    Sqire Fitzgerel 5 sargent
26) drad en field rifles
    [Drawed Enfield rifles – popular weapon]
27) prepard to burn the Hickman bridge
    on the ky river
    [This was in response to news that a
    Confederate cavalry raiding party was
    headed their way. In fact, Cluke's
    regiment, of Confederate General John
    Hunt Morgan's cavalry, was in Kentucky

from Jan. – Apr. foraging near Union
army territory.]

March, 1863
1) Sonday in spection of arms
2) finished the brest works on boons nob
    Samuel War departed this life at Nickelsville
    [Samuel H. Weir? – Nicholasville, Kentucky]
5) Speach by John B Bronlow [Probably
    Brownlow] [Harold Reno found John Bell Brownlow
            was the son of William Gannaway "Parson" Brownlow
            (Internet, *geni.com/people/Col-John-Bell-Brownlow*).]
8) preachin
12) Marion Shiflet
    John Neley
    Robert Boucher
    got to camp boon
14) i and foster started to bradfordville to see the
    boys
    [Probably D. D. Foster (Harold wonders if it was D. G. Foster?), to Bradfordsville, Ky.,
    to see?? D. G. Foster was possibly Kinsey's uncle. See pp. 15 and 20.]
15) got thar
16) foster got stalt   [?]   [Harold wonders if stalt might be salt?]
19) Started back moved to lexington
20) i got back to Camp Boon
22) i got to lexington to the ridgement [regiment]
23) moved our camp
25) detailed petroling the town
29) went to see the monuments at the grave yard

April, 1863
2) Clift tuck camand [Probably Wm Clift from
    Hamilton Co., took command of their
    company.]
3) orders to stay with reeves [Col. F. A. Reeves?]
4) vaxi nated   [vaccinated]
5) ester Sonday preaching by hues
8) left lexinton Started South past threw
    nixi ville
9) past threw Cra ville Stad at Damp dick [Camp Dick Robinson]
    roberson [Camp Dick Robinson was located
    +/- 10 miles east of Danville, Ky.]
10) James William foster got to ridgment
    past threw lancister
    camped at Stanford
    [James & Wm. Hooper and D. D. Foster?][Harold wonders if this was D. G. Foster?]
12) Saterday night & Sonday on picket
    Sonday evnen got a leter from wife [Elizabeth Geren Hooper]

    - Diary Page Missing –

May, 1863
?) went a fisin cot fore
    [Went fishing, caught 4 – a true Hooper!]
?) Sunday a tremendious rain, TJ Ross script
    got wet to cure the each

Monday I & TJ ross went and got spirets
for the sick
Murpha and Cavit went to a privet house
[Murphy & James Cavett?]
?) r d wilson departed this life horsepil
[Hospital]
5) bured r d wilson
10) Sunday Sent cavet som money
preachen in the first tennessee and our one to
12) i run for sargent and got beat
15) one of the first tennessee kild another
with a spade handle
16) musterd in the 8 rigiment
[The 7th was mustered into the 8th as
Company A]
i had to teah Cy dr Spakes   [???]
17) Sunday preachin by the chaplin of the 27
mishigan
18) monday i not able for duty
19) i not able for duty
23) Saturday all went to dicks and wash of
[Washed off in the Dix River]
i went and staid with Cavet tel Sunday
24) Monday i Sind the pay rolls   i comisary garde
J. K Geren foster & others got to camp dick rob [Camp Dick Robinson]
26) we drod our money
me and taylor went and sedd Cavet
27) Wensday w m ross taylor an others velenter
i an others starte to Somerset with horses
for the Second Tennessee
first stade at Stanford
28) this day got to the ridgment
Slept wi Sam Macinturf
29) friday starte back Staid at Stanfor pad
one dollar for mi lodgin
30) got to camp dick [Camp Dick Robinson]
31) Sunday i rote a leter home preachin by Spers

June, 1863
1) Monday we drd new guns went to see Cavit
Lenit Jack went to generl horspital
[Clint Jack, Tobitha's husband?]
?) Sunday i started a leter 2 pare shoes
1 handrchief 1 stran of beeds 3 pocket
nifes home by J K Geren
?) James Hooper give up his soerd Will [William Hooper]
others onder arest for mising roll
[Gave up his sword. Missing roll call was
obviously not a laughing matter!]
8) Monday James got his soerd back
9) Som of the boys drild with ther napsacks on
[Knapsack – back pack] an a man feched milk
n his & mixt to sel
10) Wedensday som of the boys drild with
napsacks on we moved our camp acros the pike
William Hooper & others garde eth nine

rebes prisners 17 more past by
12) friday we moved back to camp boon
13) Saterday i Jahew & Williamross wash in Ky
    river
    [Union Colonel W. P. Sanders leaves Kentucky
    and raids the Confederate scouting parties at
    Lenoir Station (City), Knoxville, Strawberry
    Plains and others from the 14th – 24th.]
15) Monday we mov our camps on sadle mules
16) the same thing James and William star to
    bradfordsville   [Bradfordsville, Ky.]
18) worked in the comisary at camp fry
19) marked in the river before diner
    [Marched in the river?]
    an after on sadedd mules   [saddled mules?]
20) garded mules
21) detald to cary muster to the gard
22) Monday i & T J Ross went to see the sick
    in the convalesons tents
[Rick Hooper: K. C. & Jahew had their picture taken at Nicholasville, Ky. too. Also on this day,
Union General Rosecrans begins to move south from Murfreesboro to harass Bragg and keep him
from sending reinforcements to Vicksburg, where General Grant has that city under siege.]
23) Tuesday I & Jahew
    went to nicholesville and
    got our likes to
    William Hooper got back
24) Wednesday nite i on spring gard
25) thirsday the 5 tennessee ridgiment of
    caverly and   [cavalry]
    first batallion got to camp fry
    John got a ax to hit Jahew and got fier
    to burn the tent
    i stop him
    [Talk about family quarrels! My favorite
    entry.]
26) friday we moved our tent acros the pike
27) i on Spring gard rained a tremendous
28) Sonday tuck John Woodaw a from our
    camps before bayomets
    [Took John Woodward from our camps
    before bayonets?]
29) William got tite i acted in his place
    [Rick discovered that "tite" was Civil War
    slang for drunk instead of constipation.]
30) i garded a hom & saw mill

**On p. 138 is a page copied from the Kinsey Hooper Diary for July 1863 at Camp Nelson, Kentucky.
See the information below the page for Rick Hooper's explanation:**

July 1863
1) James Hooper got back 2 nite and 3 day i
    garded 4 prisners
4) fired cannons befor day and at 1 oclock
    i garded 1 prisner a day and sick at nite
    got my likenes
    [July 4th celebration, complete with pictures of
    the troops. Probably too early to know about
    the dual Federal victories the previous day;
    General Robert E. Lee had been defeated at
    Gettysburg and Vicksburg fell to General
    Grant.]
6) Monday i gard a prisner
8) wednesday i garded the comisary
11) i Stod gard at the comisary
12) Sunday i not well the boyes riten leters home
    [Confederate General Bushrod Johnson arrives
    in Loudon, Tn. with 4 regiments and a battery
    of 4 Napoleon guns to protect the bridge over
    the Tennessee River.]

[Rick Hooper researched the Civil War and filled in the missing information on pp. 139 – 142: K. C. was assigned to return home and recruit in conjunction with the Federal army moving south in pursuit of Bragg; therefore, his diary skips to December 1863. A small piece of paper was found that has the date July 17, 1863 on it, and a list of miles that show him traveling 247 miles in 11 days (see below):]

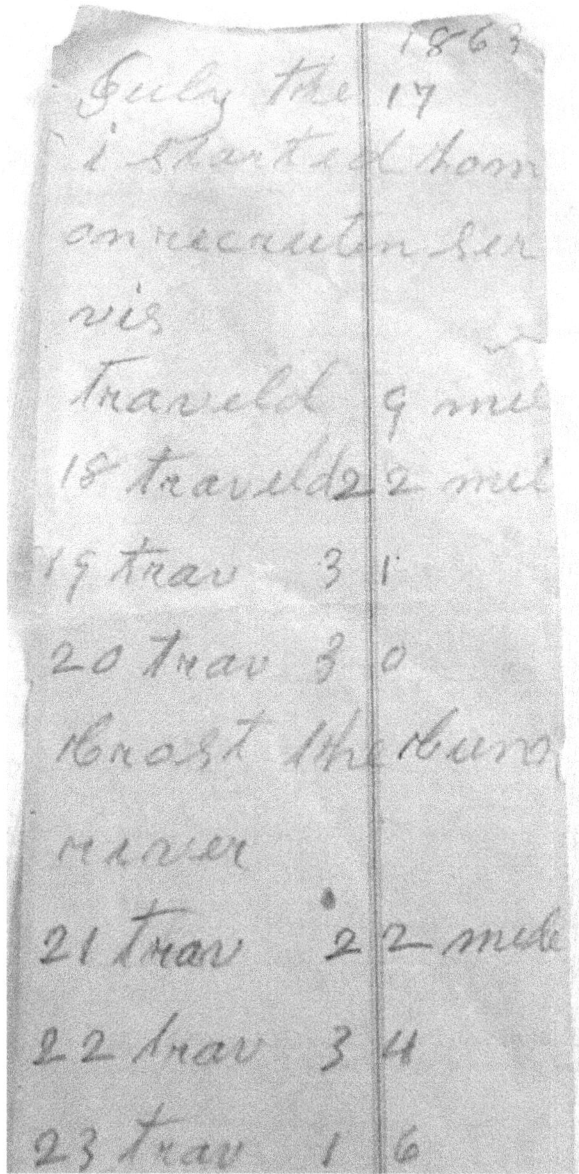

There is also a list of shoe and hat sizes – probably for brothers and friends – and a list of Corps and commanders: 20 Corps – Hooker; 4 Corps – (Sherman marked out) Howerd (Howard); 23 Corps – Scofield (Schofield); 14 – Thomas; 15 – (McPherson marked out) Logan; 17 – Blair.]
During this skip in his diary, the following events of importance occurred:

August, 1863

-(16)   Rosecrans continues his move toward Chattanooga and Union General Burnside finalizes his plan to advance out of central Kentucky into East Tennessee. (The 8th Tennessee is part of Burnside's force.)
-(20)   Orders are issued by Burnside for the 23rd Corps (which includes the Hoopers) to begin their movement from Kentucky toward Knoxville.
-(30)   Confederates withdraw from Loudon to Charleston in the face of Burnside's advance.

September, 1863

-(?) Will absent on detached service, possibly recruiting also. [William Hooper]
-(2) Burnside's Federal troops occupy Knoxville.
-(3) Confederates positioned at Candies Creek and Ross's Ford (adjoins Hooper farm).
-(4) Confederates destroy supply boats and burn the bridge at Charleston, TN., as all but one regiment on Candies Creek move to Georgetown.
-(6) Skirmish at Sweetwater
-(7) Burnside's cavalry arrives in Athens
-(8) Bragg withdraws from Chattanooga in the face of Rosecrans' advance. Union cavalry at Washington Ferry and Sale Creek.
-(9) Union cavalry scouts are sent from Sale Creek to Charleston, and also sweep through Georgetown, Brittsville and near Cleveland.
-(10) Skirmish at Athens. Rosecrans occupies Chattanooga.
-(11) President Lincoln asks Andrew Johnson (U. S. Senator from Greeneville, Tenn.) to form a Tennessee Union State Government. According to J. S. Hurlburt's book, *History of the Rebellion* (see p. 157), near this date (may have been the 9th) Union Cavalry enters Cleveland for the first time since hostilities began. They stay one night and depart through the 9th District next day, stopping long enough for a feast prepared by the loyal Union people of that area at Beech Spring. (In the No Pone Valley near the Leonard Grissom farm – Hoopers were probably there.)
-(12) Rosecrans has divided his army into 3 parts, and only due to Confederate bumbling has he avoided total destruction. He issues urgent orders to concentrate in the center near Lee and Gordon's Mill, north of Lafayette, GA.
-(15) Union reports say rebels raided Cleveland, wounding 3 men and stealing 20 horses.
-(16) Federals send 200 cavalrymen to guard Cleveland
-(18) Skirmish at Cleveland and Charleston, Union troops withdrawn to Charleston.
-(19) The Battle of Chickamauga opens with extensive casualties, but no gain on either side.
-(20) As the second day of the battle begins, it is much the same until Rosecrans issues a confusing order and leaves a gap in his line. Confederate General Longstreet, just arrived with his troops from Virginia, seizes the opportunity and pours a column of soldiers through it. The Union line is split and the right collapses. Even General Rosecrans flees for his life toward Chattanooga. However, on the left, near a small log cabin, Union General Thomas rallies his and other troops to make a stand on Snodgrass Hill. This valorous stand saved the entire Union Army from a total rout and earned him the nickname, "The Rock of Chickamauga." After dark, Thomas leads his men in an orderly retreat to Chattanooga. Total killed, wounded and missing for the Union was 16,000 and the Confederates 18,000, for a total of 34,000 casualties in two days of fighting. [**Harold Reno thinks that this was possibly the battle that James B. Allen, husband of Mary Jane Vernon Allen, was killed (see p. 249 and also the reference to *The Military Annals of Tennessee Confederate* by John Berrien Lindsley p. 255). She later married Houston Samples.**] With that ghastly numeric distinction, Chickamauga ranks as one of the bloodiest battles of the war and holds true to what some say is its ancient Cherokee Indian meaning – "River of Death."
-(21) A demoralized Federal army gathered in Chattanooga and dug in. Fortunately for them, the Confederates did not offer serious pursuit for two days, which gave the bluecoats time to fortify their position. Also on this date, a small skirmish occurred near Jonesboro, Tenn. that probably involved the 8th Tennessee. There are no details of this encounter, but the 8th was listed as being in this area.
-(23) President Lincoln orders 17,000 of General Hooker's troops to rush immediately from their base in Virginia to Bridgeport, Ala. in support of the besieged army in Chattanooga.
-(24) Union scouts from Charleston encounter Confederates on the Cleveland Road.
-(25) Advanced scouts from Charleston are attacked by greycoats on the Cleveland, Dalton and Chatata Roads.
-(26) Confederate General Nathan Bedford Forrest attacks the outnumbered Union troops at Charleston and Calhoun, forcing them to fall back to Athens, Philadelphia and then Loudon.
-(28) James Hooper submits his letter of resignation to Colonel Reeves due to "incompetency and good of the service". (Rick Hooper commented: I do wish they would have used different terminology for the reason. He resigned due to bleeding at the lungs caused by being hung by the neck! (See p. 157.)
-(30) Burnside's cavalry back to Athens and Rosecrans' cavalry to Blythe's Ferry.

October, 1863

-(9)   Another skirmish at Cleveland.
-(10) Another at Sweetwater.
-(15) Union supply wagons attacked on the Cottonport/Philadelphia Road by +/- 100 rebels.
-(16) U. S. Grant is named commander of the Western Theater.
-(17) Grant replaces Rosecrans with General Thomas, "The Rock of Chickamauga."
-(18) James' resignation is not accepted without a doctor's approval. This clearly shows it is a medical
       problem, otherwise he would have lost his rank of 2nd Lt. and there would be no need for medical
       authorization.
-(23) Grant arrives in Chattanooga to see the situation first hand.
-(25) James' resignation is accepted, effective 10 - 26. But according to his previously discussed pension
       record, he was not able to leave Knoxville until after the siege, over a month later. (He would
       receive $12/mo in 1890 for his service in the Union army. See p. 269 for more information.)
-(28) Union General Hooker's men, having reached Chattanooga and opened a "Cracker Line" from
       Bridgeport, Ala., are attacked by the Confederates in a small engagement known as the Battle of
       Wauhatchie. A marker is located on the eastbound side of I-24 at the Brown's Ferry Road/Lookout
       Mountain Exit.

November, 1863

-(4)   Bragg detaches Longstreet with 20,000 troops to attack Burnside at Knoxville. Rather than
       reinforcing Burnside, Grant decides to await the arrival of Sherman and his army from West
       Tennessee, so they can attack a weaker Bragg.
-(15) Sherman arrives in Chattanooga, and after the shocking view of Confederates on Lookout Mtn.,
       Missionary Ridge, and even Orchard Knob, exclaimed to his superior, "Why General Grant, you are
       besieged!" On this same day west of Knoxville, Longstreet makes a dash for the road junction at
       Campbell Station to gain the rear of Burnside's advanced elements – he fails by minutes.
-(19) Lincoln delivers the Gettysburg Address on the former battlefield in Pennsylvania.
-(23) In Chattanooga, Union troops participating in what appears to be a parade or drill, suddenly turn and
       charge the Confederate position on Orchard Knob, taking it easily.
-(24) Hooker's blueclad soldiers make their way up a foggy Lookout Mtn., then swinging around it, drive
       the enemy from around the Craven House in what has become known as "The Battle Above the
       Clouds."
-(25) Sherman being unable to take the left (northern) end of Missionary Ridge, Grant orders Thomas to
       attack in the middle with the objective being the Confederate rifle pits at the base. As his men
       charged across the field, shouts of, "Chickamauga!" could be heard up and down the line. The task
       was accomplished in short order, however another problem developed immediately. The soldiers
       were in the works without any cover from the fire coming down the ridge of the second line of rifle
       pits halfway up. Suddenly, the Union troops sprang from the pits and charged toward the top so
       close to the retreating rebels that the greycoats further up the hill could not fire for fear of hitting
       their own men. Confused and surprised, the Confederates did something very uncharacteristic of
       them, with the exception of Cleburn's men facing Sherman on the Union left, they broke and fled
       headlong toward Ringgold and Dalton.
-(28) Although it was a great victory in Chattanooga, life was pretty grim for the Federals and the Hoopers
       in Knoxville since Longstreet had besieged the city. Had it not been for brave Union supporters
       floating food down the Tennessee River at night to the army trapped in Knoxville, many would have
       starved to death, or had to surrender.
-(29) The morning arrived with bitter cold winds and sleet, but despite that, Longstreet's mind was made
       up; after several days of indecision, this would be the day to fight. With very little artillery support,
       the Confederates launched a "surprise attack", concentrating on a part of the line known as Fort
       Sanders (not far from present day UT campus). Burnside's men had dug a deep ditch around their
       works and strung wire from stump to stump outside that. The rebels were slipping, sliding and
       tripping all the way into the huge ditch, when to their horror, they discovered the walls were too high
       and too slick to scale – and no one thought to bring ladders! The unfortunate greybacks in the ditch
       were being shot at by Union guns simply held over the edge and pointed downward, with nothing

but their hands exposed. But worse yet, the Federals began rolling fused cannonballs over the edge; that was enough for the rebels in the ditch and they surrendered. Those that had not entered the trench retreated. Total Union losses were 700 to the Confederate losses of 1,100.

December, 1863

-(1)   Sherman is in motion to the relief of Burnside in Knoxville, and on this day writes a letter to Grant from "the near bank of the Hiwassee River", probably at the Henegar House in Charleston, Tenn. where he stopped.
-(9)   Being severely criticized for not helping Rosecrans in Chattanooga, or pursuing Longstreet toward Greeneville, Tenn. after the battle, Union General Burnside submits his resignation.
-(16) Confederate General Joseph E. Johnston is named to replace Braxton Bragg as head of the Confederate Army of Tennessee in Dalton, GA. With all the Confederate action between Chattanooga and Knoxville, the last few months were probably a little tense for K. C. since he was at home (or hiding nearby). But he survived and returned to the 8th Tennessee in December.

[Rick Hooper: We now return to his diary:]

    December, 1863
    21) i left home an started to Ridgment Staid first
        nite Scarbury in Macmin County [Scarborough]
    22) Staid at Williamsin[Williamson] same County
    23) Staid at Robert Clevelands in Swetewater valey
        [Jahew is granted a furlough for sickness.]
    24) at Knoxville
    25) at Knoxville
    26) got to Ridgment at Blains Crossroads
    27) march to the plains   [Strawberry Plains?]
[Confederate cavalry under General Joseph Wheeler – while attempting a raid on the Union line of communication between Chattanooga and Knoxville – is attacked and defeated by Colonel Long's Federal cavalry stationed at Charleston and Calhoun.]
    28) to herels ford

    January, 1864
    15) left Herels ford
    16) Staid at the plains
    17) Staid at or ner Dandradg
    18) at Dandredg
    19) Started back
    20) Staid ner the plains
    21) at the plains
    22) at Boyeds ferry
    23) at the mouth of French Brade [the French
        Broad River]
    24) at knoxville
    25) J H Mcpherson died
    26) moved on the Clinten Rode
    28) Wm Ross died   [William D. Ross]

    February, 1864
    11) left Clinten rode and am campt est of Knoxville
    20) took a scout to boyes Monton [Bays Mountain?]
        boyes 20 of them Started home

    March, 1864
    8) went to convalesson camps

[Rick Hooper: K. C. was sick at convalescent camp with rheumatism and numbing of the legs. No explanation of numbing is given. Also, on March 17th in Washington, D. C., U. S. Grant is named Lt. General in charge of all Union armies, and on the 18th W. T. Sherman is put in charge of all Union forces in the Western Theater.]

     22) left ther an went to Ridgment at Mosey Creek
        [Jefferson City]
     30) drawd money
     31) started home

     April, 1864
     1) left mosey Creek
     2) gt to bulls gap
     10) got a leter from home
     13) Capt. Shelton came to the gap
     15) zed Lansan an triel and relest
         [Somebody tried and released.]
     16) Capt. Shelton started home i started a leter
         home by hime   [Capt. – Hooper's first cousin]
         Stad in line with cotrments on from fore tel
         six oclock in morning
         [Accouterments include cartridge box, belt,
         haversack, etc.]
     17) same thing John Hooper came up from the
         peaine [?] [plains]
     18) Monday rain train did not come to take gap
     19) i and N taylor went a forgen John Hooper
         went to the plains again boyes on a Scot kild
         to rebels
         [Foraging – scouring the countryside for food –
         was common practice for both sides, and legend
         says it was the cause of naming No Pone Valley
         (no corn for a pone of cornbread). Boys on a
         scout killed two Rebels?]
     20) on picket 1 mile north of the gap
     21) boyes got from home i got a leter
         i on picket and took a scout 5 miles on the
         Rogersvill rode
         [Part of Co. A had been home on leave.]
     22) trid for a furlow sent it to General Cox
         [General Jacob D. Cox]   inspection By
         general Scofield on dres parade
[Rick Hooper: After a reorganization of the Hoopers' unit it was listed as follows: Department of the Ohio, General Schofield's 23rd Corps, Brigadier General Cox's 3rd Division, Colonel Reilly's 1st Brigade, 8th Regiment, Company A.]
     23) D G Foster come to the ridgment inspection of
         tents Started a leter home
     24) Sunday i pick salet for diner
     25) Company went on a Scout to men got Shot in
         Camp in the ankle company tore up the Rail
         Rode abuv lick Creek i eh sques [?] i wint on
         picket 1 mile on the RussellvilleRode
     26) i came to koxvill with Bagage Come to
         Knoxville with ridgment
     27) i Staid ther the ridgment went to Charleston
     28) i came down i went home

29) i staid ther
30) i went back to Charleston & was mustered for
   pay

[Rick Hooper: I think it should be noted that Cleveland was now under Union control for the rest of the war. The Hooper families finally had sympathetic soldiers in their midst!]
[Rick Hooper: As best as I can tell, this was the last time K. C., Jahew and Will would see their families for over a year (John was injured in August of this year and returned home before the others). They were now part of General Sherman's force that was preparing to advance into Georgia, with the ultimate goal of capturing Atlanta! Sherman had General Schofield (and the Hoopers) at Red Clay, General Thomas in Ringgold, and General McPherson on the south end of the Chickamauga Battlefield as they prepared to challenge the Confederates in Dalton with a force of 100,000 strong. While the series of battles and movements leading up to the fall of Atlanta received very little publicity (especially when compared to those in the Eastern Theater), the campaign itself is a fascinating study of military tactics that are still appreciated by historians and strategists today.]

   May, 1864
   3) left thar an campt at blue Springs 15 miles
   4) left blue Springs Campt at the Counsil groun
       georgia 7 miles [He is referring to the Red Clay
       Council Grounds.]
   5) Drild
   6) on pickett [Guard duty]
   7) left thar an campt at Eli Jayes Gap 7 miles
[With the rebel army in Dalton, Sherman developed a strategy of entrapment by having Schofield move south down the railroad from Red Clay to Dalton. Thomas would cut through the ridge on the west side of Dalton, and McPherson swing south and east to get behind the Confederates and cut the railroad at Resaca.]
   8) Staid all day & nite 4 miles Ringgold
   9) moved on toward dalton firen on the South &
       west at 10 oclock Six miles from dalton twelve
       in line of batel 5 miles of three Sheld us from
       the font [Front or fort?] fore miles from dalton
       at the Burger gap laid in line all nite
[The Confederate cavalry leader, General Joseph Wheeler, drew Schofield's cavalry away from the main body, and with a sudden attack, captured 150 Federals and drove the remainder back to the main line.]
   10) fell back Sheld us as we fell back back 1 ½
       miles at twelv from buzerd gap after fel back
       2 miles ferdo an Stopt then move [ferdo –
       further?] one mile north west & stopt eight
       miles from Dalton four from Ringgold Staid
       ther all nite
[McPherson encountered trouble so Sherman changed his plan and started Schofield (along with the Hoopers) from the railroad, west behind Rocky Face Ridge, south down the valley, then east to Resaca for a major attack.]
   11) after diner west on Scrumish all the company
   [Possibly their company on skirmish line since the rebels indicated an advance. The brigade was
       put in line of battle, but the enemy did not move out.]
   12) Thursday left there past tunel hill an campt
       eight miles South of tunel hill [On the road
       toward Villanow, Ga.]
   13) Friday left thar at 2 oclock in the mornin past
       threw snake gap & form line of batel at 2
       oclock an advance toward dalton lai in line all
       nite Camp in five miles of Resacher [Resaca] on
       west side

[The Confederate Army retreated from Dalton to Resaca as they discovered the Union movement to their west & south. Sherman put all three armies in motion for Resaca but arrived too late in line of battle to attack that night.]

> 14) moved on the enemy fiten from twelve til nite
> we fel back one mile an campt

[Rick Hooper: At this point, Schofield is still the left wing of Sherman's army. Confederate General Johnston assumes that if Sherman is moving his forces to the west & south of the Confederates, then in all probability he is weak to the north. Therefore, Johnston orders General Hood to attack the forces there (Schofield's) and see if he can turn Sherman's left or at least slow him down. Union forces see the Confederate positions and charge at the double quick, taking the first line of rifle pits. The 8th Tennessee is in the second line at the start, but moves to the left of the brigade to protect the exposed flank. The brigade encountered a heavy enemy resistance and used nearly all their ammunition. Unfortunately, ordinance wagons could not reach their position, so they lay in line until relieved by the 4th Corps and moved to the rear to resupply. The result of all this is the Battle of Resaca that is reenacted every year on a portion of the actual battlefield.]

> 15) Sonday moved towards the Railrode to miles
> and bilt breastworks & then moved one mile est
> and lai in line all nite the rebes attacked on the
> rite at twelve oclock in the nite & was repulst
> Rebes retret

[This attack was made to cover the sound of iron wheeled cannon and supply wagons retreating until they felt they were safe. A note should be made here that the Hoopers probably were elated that the Confederates had to retreat; remember, they were driving them farther from their homes and families.]

> 16) Monday left the batel groun crost the Railroade
> & wade Conasaga river & struck South camp on
> the Spring plase & Calhan rode
> 17) Tuesday left ther Crost Cosawatee at fields mill

travel all nite left Calhan ten miles to the rite got
    Brexfast & stat
18) Wedensday trav on south campt fiv miles est of
    Casville
19) left ther an mov on to Casville form line of batel
    & the rebes Run Campt one mile South of
    Casville

[Rick Hooper: The Confederates had designed a trap to lure Schofield's 23 Corps into an ambush by two-thirds of the rebel army. However, as was the case many times in this war on both sides, blind luck saved the day. As the Confederate army waited to the east of the road Schofield was traveling on, a Federal unit that was totally lost turned up BEHIND the rebel forces! Not knowing if Schofield's entire army was there, or still north, or even worse, farther south, the Confederates retreated in haste!]

20) friday past thru Casvill formed line of batel at
    Casvill Depot an mov towards Cartersvill firen
    in front all the way Campt at Cartersvill the
    Rebels burnt the Bridge on hito [The firing was
    from the rebel rear guard and the bridge was
    burned over the Etowah river.]
21) Saturday lai still

[The Confederates retreated to Allatoona, so Sherman takes this opportunity to rest his armies for three days and to resupply them for another flanking movement to dislodge Johnston from his strong position.]

22) Sonday left at to oclock in the nite moved up
    the river burnt one mill an one faundray fore
    miles abov Cartersvill & retur to Camps
23) Monday left Cartersville toward Rome firen
    on the left at twelv i went to the amlilan Campt
    Seven below Cartersville at the place wher the
    bridge was burnt on that day

[On this day, K. C. was assigned as a saddler in the 3rd Div., 23 A. C., which is the ambulance corps in Schofield's army. Sherman now has his armies in three columns: Schofield would swing to the west of Allatoona on the left, Thomas in the center and McPherson on the right wing. While the battle dates are correct as noted, the movements related in the diary after this are usually one day behind. This is due to the ambulance corps being behind the main army.]

24) Tuesday Crost the river on pontoons Bridges
    moved South Campt in piney wods [Crossed
    Racoon Creek.]
25) Wednesday left piney wods Crost pumkin vine
    fiten by the twentyieth Core on South of
    pumkinvine
26) thirsday our men took the front fiten all along
    the line
[Now in the area of Dallas Road and New Hope Church, west of Kennesaw Mtn. and Marietta.]
27) friday fiten in front all day
28) Saturday fiten in front all and nite
29) Sonday firen in front all day
30) Monday firen in front all day
31) Tuesday firen in front all day an nite Seventh
    day of the fite

June, 1864
1) firen in front eight day of the fite
2) thursday 8 ridgment charged the Rebes works
    lost several men
[This engagement was at Brownlow's Hill where the 8th was in the front line of attack. While it was certainly a big deal to members of the 8th, it was barely mentioned in the *Official Records*; it was just another of thousands of like skirmishes to go unnoticed in the grand scale of war.]

3) friday rain Still scrumishohin [skirmishing]
        in front tenth day of the fite
4) Saturday Rebels fell back on the left hevy
        firen in the Senter

[Rick Hooper: The Confederates start their movement to Lost, Brush and Pine Mtns. which are two miles north of Kennesaw Mtn.]

5) Sonday Rebels gone the fifteenth Corps moved
        to the left

[Being out of contact with their supply line for several days, the armies have been living on nothing but hardtack and bacon. Therefore, Sherman decides to shift them back to the east and to the railroad, so he swings Thomas and McPherson behind Schofield who is already closest to the line.]

6) Monday Sent the wonded to the railrode eight
        went to gar [guard] a train
7) Tuesday move the horspital to the Railrode an
        left [hospital] Burnt church Campt to miles est
        [east]
8) Wednesday Stade ther all day an nite
9) Thirsday Still ther rain
10) friday mov three South an campt firen in front
        rain
11) Saturday rain mov a half mile South an put up
        a horspital firen in front in site of the Rebels
        camps
12) Sonday rain rain firen in front
13) monday rain firen in front
14) tuesday firen in front 8 move to the front
        [8th Regiment]
15) Wedensday the eight made a charg an took
        the works

[The only mention of this engagement in *The Civil War Almanac*: "15 June, 1864 – Sherman's corps under Thomas, McPherson, and Schofield close in amid skirmishes on Johnston's positions near Marietta, Georgia." When the 8th Tennessee arrived at the breastworks, they found the Confederates had already evacuated them.]

16) firen in front all day an at nite the rebes
        retreated

[Confederate General Johnston abandons the smaller mountains and begins to consolidate his forces on Kennesaw Mtn. Schofield tries for the next few days to flank the Confederates.]

17) moved the horspitel to the railrode an mov up to
        miles an establish a depo hevy firen est adgident
        Reeves wonde
18) Saturday rainin hevy firen est adgident
        dide
19) Sonday Rebels fel back moved the horspitel an
        mov up three miles an establish another
        horspitel
20) monday the fiten still continues an rain to
        hevest on the left

[Sherman still testing Johnston's entire line as the Federal commanders study the awesome sight of the Confederates holding Kennesaw Mtn.]

21) tuesday Still a rainin an fiten on the left an
        senter
22) wednesday fair wether fiten on the left an
        senter
23) thursday firen on the left hevy
24) friday establish a new horspital
25) Saturday general Schofield advan his head

quarters 4 ½ miles of Merata [Marietta]
   26) advance on the right
      [Schofield is trying to flank the Confederates out
      of their strong position.]
   27) Monday hevy firen on the left
[Rick Hooper: In fact, there was firing along a ten mile front as the battle plan unfolded. Schofield was still moving farther west of the mountains, with the 8th maneuvering around a swamp. Meanwhile, rather than wait on the flanking move that was in progress, Sherman decides on a headlong attack with his middle that is meant to remind his army how to charge! And charge they did, into a withering fire of cannon and muskets from the rebels' heavily fortified breastworks. The Battle of Kennesaw Mountain cost the Union over 2,000 killed and wounded to the Confederate loss of 500. But one thing it did prove, the Federal army would charge in the face of fire as gallantly as any army ever had, or ever would.]
   28) tuesday mov the horspitel to the Achworth
   29) wedensday moved the horspitel to the next
      house
   30) Cap Shelton come to the ridgment and brot me
      a leter
[With the dead lying between the two lines on Kennesaw Mtn. for three days, Sherman asked for and received a burial armistice for his men. This was not entirely out of respect for the fallen, but was to eliminate the sickening stench that had been caused by three days of Georgia sun. A Confederate soldier later wrote, "Long and deep trenches were dug, and hooks made from bayonets crooked for the purpose, and all the dead were dragged and thrown pell mell into these trenches."]

   July, 1864
   1) Cap Started back mov on towards Atlanta
[Sherman renews his flanking tactics and starts the armies moving to the west for a run at the Chattahoochee River. The river was approximately 10 miles in the Confederates' rear and was very risky for the Federals since they would again be leaving the railroad, and even worse, with only a minimum guard left to protect their supply line.]
   2) Saturday hevy firen on the left trop pasin to the
      rite
[McPherson was moving to join Schofield.]
   3) Sonday the rebes feld back from Merata the
      pontoons pas towards Atlanta
[The Confederates, seeing the Union movement from their position on Kennesaw Mtn., started their retreat to the river in an effort to entrench before Sherman could arrive.]
   4) firen on the rite
   5) tuesday firen on the rite first brigade moved out
   6) wednesday mov to Ruff Stasion
   7) thursday mov the horspital to the an the
      Ridgment mov towards the river
   8) friday mov to the river an lae the pontoons an
      crost some troops over an put up a horspital
[This crossing was midway between Roswell and Paces Ferry at the mouth of Sope (or Soap) Creek, near present day Atlanta Country Club.]
   9) Saturday Crost river
   10) Sonday Clay Farmer got wonded i take medison
      for the diree [diarrhea?]
   11) monday i still sick an taken madison
   12) tuesday take ridgment work on the bridg
   13) wednesday finish the bridg i stillsick
   14) thirsday head quarters crost the river
   15) friday Still at the river
   16) Saturday Still at the river
   17) Sonday mov from Soap Creek Campt 5 miles
      South 15 from atlanta

[Sherman starts another flanking movement with McPherson on the left and swinging east to Stone Mountain, Schofield in the center moving on Decatur and Thomas to the right advancing toward Buckhead and Peachtree Creek.]

> 18) monday left ther an Campt at Keyes Cros rods
> on the old etocke [Echota?] rode 9 miles from
> Atlanta

[Rick Hooper: Also on this day, the Confederate soldiers in Atlanta received some bad news. While General Johnston was very popular with his own men, he was the object of scorn and ridicule by many in Richmond, including Jefferson Davis. Even though the army appreciated Johnston for bringing them this far without losing more men than their Union adversaries, the Confederate Government believed he had given up too much ground, and in order to stop it, relieved Johnston of command and replaced him with General Hood. This was very good news for General Sherman when he was told the next day, and, as was nearly always the case in this war, several Union generals knew Hood from their West Point days and had an idea of how he would proceed. In fact, Schofield had been Hood's roommate and strongly warned Sherman, "He'll hit you like hell, now, before you know it." Therefore, the probable change of strategy on the Confederates' part would be to come out and fight, not slowly and methodically retreat behind breastworks. As strange as it sounds, that was good news for the Union Army.]

> 19) tuesday left ther an took deCater an campt ner
> ther   [Decatur, Georgia]
> 20) wednesday establish a hospitel in 5 miles of
> Atlanta

[True to prediction, Hood moves out and attacks Thomas on the right flank with heavy losses and no gain. This was known as the Battle of Peachtree Creek.]

> 21) thirday i got a letter from home firen in front

[This was skirmishing associated with the Union still moving toward Atlanta. But Hood was undaunted after his first battle and was preparing a second and bolder plan.]

> 22) friday i rote a leter home the rebels drov our
> army out of De Cater we retaken deCater
> General McPherson killed

[Rick Hooper: Hood sent Hardee's corps on a south-east-north route to end up between Atlanta and Decatur and in the rear of McPherson. He also ordered Wheeler's cavalry to swing farther east and strike McPherson's supply wagons in Decatur. The attack was not a total surprise – as they had been on the alert since Hood assumed command – and met with strong and swift Union opposition. While the Civil War Confederates gained nothing in ground, they were able to deal the Union a terrible loss in the death of General McPherson. He had always been Sherman's favorite, as he believed McPherson was intelligent, bold and a hard fighter, in addition to having a flair, which he exhibited on his death. As McPherson was riding out to examine part of his battle line, he unexpectedly encountered Confederates on the road. The Confederate captain said of McPherson, "...checked his horse slightly, raised his hat as politely as if he were saluting a lady, wheeled his horse's head directly to the right, and dashed off to the rear in a full gallop." However, the good marksmanship of a nearby corporal ended McPherson's life. The Battle of Atlanta cost the Confederates 8,000 killed and wounded to the Union's 3,700.]

> 23) Saturday lucien the rebs ner Atlanta [lucien-?]
> 24) Sonday fetch in twev hundre mules that was
> capt [captured?]
> 25) firen in front ner atlanta
> 26) tuesday mov the hospital in three miles of
> Atlanta
> 27) wednesday the rebs charged the forth Core
> an was repulst

[O. O. Howard assumed command of McPherson's corps and was ordered to swing from the left flank to the right flank and move west and south around Atlanta to the railroad at Jonesboro. But on the west side he ran into opposition.]

> 28) hevey firen on the rite

[Hood attacked in force at the Battle of Ezra Church and called a temporary halt to the Union plan for Jonesboro, to which Sherman instead decided to shell the city into submission. Confederate losses were 2,500 to the Union losses of 700. However, the Confederate soldier's morale was very low indeed as is evident in a supposed exchange that night: "Say, Johnny," a Union soldier called across the breastworks into the outer darkness. "How many of you are there left?" "Oh, about enough for another killing," a Confederate replied.]

      29) friday i rote a leter with [Possibly wife or with
          something.]
      30) Saturday firen on the rite
      31) Sonday i went to the front an saw a part of
          atlanta
    August, 1864
      1) James Romines went to the horspitel move the
          horspitel an Campt at the railrode three miles
          north of atlanta
[Sherman decides to move again and starts Schofield to the west behind Howard.]
      2) tuesday left the railrode an estab a horspitel
          five miles west of atlanta
      3) wednesday firen on the left
      4) thisday firen all along the lines
      5) friday firen on the front
      6) Saturday the third division charg the reb works
          an was repulst lost 17 men out of the Company
          kil an wonde [killed & wounded]

[In a flanking move, they were attempting to cross Utoy Creek on the west side of Atlanta, the 8th Tennessee was in the middle of this charge and suffered severe casualties. Brigadier General Reilly wrote, "...I cannot, in justice, neglect to bear official testimony to the gallant and heroic conduct of the Eighth Tennessee Infantry...." Report of Capt. James W. Berry, "...the Eighth was ordered to and did charge in gallant style...being subjected to a deadly direct and cross fire, which had already decimated their ranks. Though unable to advance farther they here held their ground, bravely continuing in their exposed position the unequal fight until ordered to retire, which they skillfully did....In this serious charge the officers and men of the regiment exhibited the highest degree of bravery, discipline, and presence of mind which characterizes veteran troops."

    223 engaged, 26 killed, 5 mortally wounded, 36 wounded, 16 missing, total of 83 casualties=37%!!
        Casualties of Company A, 8th Tennessee;
    John Hooper – Cannonball wound in the stomach, abdominal peritonitis, was sick in various hospitals
        through remainder of the war (see p. 268)
    Jahew Hooper – Wounded (no details), out for one month
    Clinton Jack (Brother-in-law) – Gunshot wound to right wrist, out for remainder of the war
    Francis C. Johnston (2 Lt., replacing James Hooper) – killed in battle
    Others wounded – R. L. McPherson, Arch Fitzgerald, T. J. Taylor
    Others killed – Squire Fitzgerald, Thomas Wooden, Reese Ingle, Thomas Werick, John Skineer
    Captured – William Pierce, Samuel Massy, John Massy]

----

      7) Sonday i got a leter from home and rote one
          home the got the dead out of the rebs workes
          [Got the dead out of the Rebel works. Many
          were friends and neighbors.]
      8) monday advance
[Sherman directs his men into position as he switches to siege tactics and brings long range guns from Chattanooga. He begins firing over the heads of the Confederate soldiers into downtown Atlanta.]
      9) tuesday move the front 6 miles west of atlanta
          three from est pient [East Point]
      10) wedsday John Gufe got wonde [Guffey?]
      11) Thirsday the first Tennessee starte back
          [Their term of enlistment had expired and they were ordered home.]
      12) friday the 3 division move to the rite an come

back the rebs sheld clost to me

13) Saturday nothin past C_____ [Carnen or
Camen?]

14) Sonday nothing past C_____

15) John Hooper and D G Foster went to the
horspitel an that nite went to the railrode i
drove ambulance to the railrode

[Rick Hooper: Certainly not a pleasant task, but K. C. was taking his older brother to the railroad to be sent to another hospital. Since anything can happen in battle, and, tragically, knowing that many soldiers died of much less severe wounds than John now had, they did not know if they would ever see each other again.]

16) tuesday i got back the ridgment mov to the rite

[Back at home, Confederate General Wheeler again attacked Cleveland and Charleston from Aug. 16-19, but did not take either place.]

17) wednesday all still

18) thirsday mov to miles south

[The 8th is part of the division ordered to advance toward the rebels' left and screen the movements of the whole Union army.]

19) friday the rebs blode up one of our wagons an
busted a cannon

20) Saturday move one an a half mile south an
parke

21) Sonday Seven runaway of the eigth [Obviously,
not all members of the 8th Tenn. exhibited
extraordinary courage.]

22) Monday all stil in front

23) tuesday all stil in front

24) wednesday D G Foster went to the rere [Harold Reno thinks D. G. Foster might be an uncle.]

25) thirsday John Hooper went to the rere mov the
horspital to the railrode [John transferred to
another hospital as the entire army is now in
motion.]

26) friday the army move to the rite

[Sherman abandons his siege tactics and renews the "Grand Wheel" maneuver around the west side of Atlanta, its objective being to cut the last remaining rail line entering Atlanta from the south. Schofield's target was Rough and Ready and had the highest risk since his corps was on the left flank, and, therefore, closest to the enemy.]

27) move a lital west

28) Sonday Starte an move three miles Southwest
an park denis rin hel sent back [Dennis?? Reynolds?? sent
back?]

29) monday move one an a half miles South an
parke

30) tuesday move to miles South an struc the
mongomery rode move to miles est an parke

[Sherman described his road tactics by "...filling many deep cuts with trees, brush, and earth, and commingled with them loaded shells, so arranged that they would explode on an attempt to haul out the bushes."]

31) wednesday left thar move fore miles est an
parke in to miles of the macon rode the rode
tore up

[Schofield starts south toward Jonesboro to attack one-third of Hood's army that was isolated there. Hood had sent General Hardee to protect this area since he knew if the railroad was lost his entire force must abandon Atlanta; and true to his fear, part of Schofield's force cuts the last railroad line into Atlanta.]

September, 1864

1) thirsday left thar move fore miles South an
        struc the macon rode fiv miles north of Jones
        Boro move to miles South an parked

[Rick Hooper: Schofield moved too slowly tearing up the railroad as he went and missed the Battle of Jonesboro on the 31st, and was even late for the attack planned by Sherman for the 1st.]

2) friday left thar Stopt at to in the nite one mile
        est [east] of the macon rode fore miles South of Jones Boro

[Hardee (with part of the Conf. Army) retreated during the night to Lovejoy station, while Hood moved the remainder of the army out of Atlanta in an east-south swing to reunite the whole. Sherman pursued Hardee but found him entrenched.]

3) Saturday lai ther

[Sherman stops the pursuit and allows his men to rest while realigning and studying his next move.]

4) Sonday lai ther
5) monday left ther traveled all nite an parke at the
        railrode fore miles north of Jones Bur
6) tuesday lai ther
7) wednesday left ther an past thru ruf an redy
        parke 5 miles South atlanta distance 7 miles

[Sherman decides to occupy Atlanta and study his next move.]

8) thirsday left ther an parke at Decater dis seven
        miles i got a leter from home

[Sherman expels all citizens from Atlanta with his famous statement (though often misquoted), "You cannot qualify war in harsher terms than I will. War is cruelty, and you cannot refine it."]

9) friday i went to atlanta an back
10) Saturday Jahew Hooper came to the ridgment
        [Returning after recuperating]
11) Sonday i rote a leter home
25) i got a leter from father
26) i rote one to him an got one from home
27) i got to leters from home
29) i rote one home

October, 1864
3) left decater went to atlanta
4) left atlanta an campt at the brig on Cohee

[Hood had moved his army west and north to strike Sherman's supply line at Big Shanty and Acworth (north of Atlanta). Union troops are put in motion to counter the Confederate threat.]

5) left Chatohae an past threw Marata an lay a
        campt ner acworth
8) got to altona
10) left Altonna an campt at Cas

[Chasing Hood as he heads north along the railroad toward Dalton.]

11) left Casville an campt at Kinston [Kingston,
        Ga.]
12) left Kinston an campt at rome

[Between the 12th & 18th, several members of Company A were absent without leave, apparently going home to help with the crops. They would rejoin in mid-November. None of the Hoopers were in the group.]

14) left rome at to oclock towards Cal
15) past threw snake gap

[As more Union troops gather for battle, Hood dodges a confrontation and heads west.]

19) past threw Summervillan campt
20) got in alabama past thru Galesni an campt   [Gaylesville]

[Sherman calls a halt to the chase and awaits an answer from Grant on his proposal to march through Georgia.] **[Harold Reno found at *Ancestry.com* in the *U. S. Civil War Pension Index : General Index for to Pension Files, 1861 – 1934* a Pension Application for Caroline Vernon a widow living in TN for**

John Vernon who served in the 58th Indiana Infantry Company K. John Vernon's record listed service from Oct. 5, 1864 to July 25, 1865. Written on his Alabama tombstone was "A U. S. Soldier in Sherman's Army". See page 259 for more explanation.]

      25) left galsvillan campt at Cedar bluf

[Rick Hooper: The Confederates decide on a bold plan to invade Middle Tennessee and start through North Alabama in search of a lightly garrisoned crossing, so Sherman begins repositioning his troops.]

      28) left cedar bluf

      29) got in to georgia an campt at Cave Spring

      30) got to rome

      31) got to Calhoon

      November, 1864

      1) got to tilton

      2) left tilton

[On the home front, Jahew's daughter Josephine is born. She will marry George W. Eads. With the army, Grant accepts Sherman's proposed march.]

      4) got to Chatan [?]

      12) left Chatans ga

[Grant orders Schofield's 23rd Corps detached from Sherman's army and sent to reinforce Gen. Thomas commanding Union forces in Middle Tennessee.]

      14) go to Nashvill

[The advance of Cox's division was already in Pulaski, and on the 15th, Sherman begins his famous "March to the Sea."]

      19) left Nashvill Campt at franklin

      20) left franklin Campt at Columbia

[Hood starts his Nashville campaign by crossing the Tennessee River at Florence, Ala.]

      24) fiten ther

[Hood's cavalry reaches Columbia, and the 8th Tennessee being part of Gen. Jacob D. Cox's 3rd Division of the 23rd Corps, moves out two miles to Bigby Creek and stops the advance of Confederate Gen. Nathan Bedford Forrest.]

      25) the same

      26) the ambulances crost the river

      27) left Columbia an the   [Entry stops]

[Hood moves east and north in an attempt to gain the rear of Schofield's forces by occupying Spring Hill. Although Cox was not completely aware of Hood's plan, he knew there was a chance of being flanked and so ordered his wagons to the rear.]

      29) traveld all nite an past Spring Hill (29 marked

         out) Campt at franklin

[Due to Confederate confusion, they stopped short of the main road for the night and allowed Schofield's remaining force to slip past within sight of rebel campfires! Since the 8th Tennessee was part of Cox's force that was one of the last to leave Columbia, it is possible Jahew and William were in that night march.]

      30) the fite at franklin trav all nite an got to Nashville

[Rick Hooper: Hood was furious at the lost opportunity of defeating part of the Union army and ordered a headlong assault across a mile – long open field. The Federals were well entrenched behind their breastworks and could scarcely believe the rebel commander had ordered an attack. The 8th was in the second line near the cotton gin where some of the heaviest fighting occurred and were called upon to plug a hole in the main line during the Confederate assault. Hood's casualties totaled 6,200 to Schofield's 2,300. Hood had a larger percentage of men killed in this battle than had been lost at Shiloh, Stones River or Fredericksburg. Schofield repaired the bridge across the Harpeth River and retreated during the night for the previously planned consolidation of Federal forces at Nashville.]

      December, 1864

      15) the fite commenced

[Schofield had performed his job admirably in November by delaying Hood long enough for Gen. Thomas to put the finishing touches on his troop dispositions and supplies. When the bluecoats charged out of their works in a "Grand Wheel" movement, Hood's line began to quiver and then to slowly give ground. By the end of the day, the Confederates had given up over a mile, had Federals on three sides, and were subjected to skirmishing in the rear.]

      16) left nashvill Campt 4 miles on the Hilsbur pike

[Rick Hooper: On this day, the 8th Tennessee was part of a charge up Shy's Hill that captured several pieces of artillery and started the collapse of Hood's entire line. The Confederates broke and ran for the Franklin Pike with little regard for the emotional pleas of officers to rally and fight. Only Confederate Gen. Stephen Lee was able to collect enough men to form an effective rear guard that kept the entire rebel army from being destroyed. Also to the greybacks good fortune, was the Union armies being so mixed amongst each other that precious time was wasted just sorting out the various units so orders could be given and an organized pursuit undertaken.]

      17) Campt 8 miles on the graney white pike   [Harold thinks it might be Granny White Pike?]

      19) Campt ner Franklin

      21) Campt at franklin

      22) Campt at Spring Hill

      23) Campt at Columba

      26) crost the river

January, 1865

      2) left Columba and campt at mount plesant

      3) Campt on the mountain

      4) Campt on buffalo

      5) Campt at warns   [Waynesboro]

      6) Campt at Clifton [Clifton, TN]

[Gen. Thomas planned to winter his army where they were and await a spring campaign; however, Sherman had concluded his march to Savannah and was preparing for a run through South Carolina and into North Carolina. To execute this maneuver, Grant decided to detach Schofield's army from Thomas and transport them to North Carolina for a meeting with Sherman, and an added goal of dashing toward Virginia and the rear of Robert E. Lee's army. At the same time, the defeated rebel army was retreating to Tupelo, MS., though only at half the strength it had been just a few months before.]

      17) left Clifton

      18) at paduca [Paducah, KY]

      20) at luisville [Louisville, KY]

      22) at Cincinnata [Cincinnati, Ohio]

      23) left Cincn

      25) Crost the ohio river lebaran Com to drafton [Lebanon, OH to Grafton, WV?]

      26) ther an com to the top of Cohiate mountan

           the Cor broke damn [?]

      27) left ther past Cumberlan and harpers fery an

          [Harper's Ferry]

      28) got to washinton [Officially estimated 1,400 mile trip]

      29) mov to San Mans barek

February, 1865

      4) mov to town

[First troops of the Confederate army begin arriving in South Carolina from their Tupelo base.]

      10) left washington

      17) at alexandre [Virginia]

      18) Set sale [sail]

[Cox and much of his infantry were already on the march between Cape Fear and the Atlantic Ocean, with Wilmington, NC as their first major goal.]

      19) past Cape Hater [Cape Hatteras]

      20) got to the mouth Cap far river [Cape Fear]

      21) went roun the bar

      22) i ran a whil   [??]

      26) landed at Wilmanton North Carolina

[General Joseph Johnston was returned to command of all Confederate forces now located in North Carolina.]

March, 1865
6) left Wilmanton
9) crost new river
11) Campt in eight South of Kinston
12) moved to miles north
14) moved in ther
16) moved in Kinston
20) left Kinston
21) got to goldesber [Goldsboro, NC]
[This was the meeting place for Sherman's forces that would create an army 90,000 strong. Sherman arrives two days later and decides to rest and resupply his army.]

April, 1865
10) left golbar
[Rick Hooper: General Robert E. Lee surrendered at Appomattox on the 9th as Sherman resumes his march on the 10th.]
12) heard that lee had serenderd
[They say a messenger galloped down the road screaming the news. For those toward the back, they knew it was something good by the way the soldiers would yell and throw their hats in the air as he passed!]
14) got to Raleigh
[A flag of truce is sent from Johnston to Sherman as the surrendering process begins. That night Abraham Lincoln is assassinated. Sherman's initial terms, which were along the lines of his last conversation with Lincoln a few weeks earlier, were rejected by a Washington, DC in a state of hysteria after the President was killed. Grant was dispatched to North Carolina with orders to renegotiate on a tougher basis, and so extended the formal surrender by nearly two weeks.]
27) Johnson sorender
[The war was finally over for the Hoopers. But the task of receiving arms and paroling prisoners was assigned to Schofield, so a long delay kept the Hoopers from returning home immediately.]
May, 1865
5) left Raley [Raleigh]
6) got to Chapel Hill
8) got to graham [East of Greensboro, NC]
9) got to green bar i got a leter from home
[May have been acting as a police force for the area]

June, 1865
29) i was releved from thein [I was relieved from the thing!!]

July, 1865
3) left the Company Shops an starte for home
    change cars at Greensbro an again at danville
    an stopt at Clover Stasion [Company Shops is
    now the present day Burlington, NC.]
4) Got to lurhesvill an stai thur 24 oures
5) left thar at 2 oclock an past petersburg fore
    miles an staid all nite
6) left thar an got on the late an got to fortres
    monroe against six ninty miles an past pint
    foak out at twelve in the nite
7) got to laltime against twelve an got on the
    AMO in the evinin and started for Parkersburg
    387 miles an got to martinsville
8) got to grafton
9) got to parkerberg an laid all nite
10) got on the viola and run thirt.eight miles an then [Viola Station, KY)

got on the matisom at bufin ton i lant an run a [Madison Station, Indiana]
litel pes an stopt

11) Started agane an past galiper an got to
Cincinna left Cinc an got to lusvill

13) laid at louivilletil nite an then run to nashville
against seven on the

14)   [The date only, no entry.]

(See Appendix C on pp. 269 - 270 for a summary of 8th Infantry history on the Internet from *nps.gov/.../search-battle-units-detail.htm* 8th Union Tennessee .)

A note on K. C.'s discharge paper says, "Paid excepting transportation," dated July 28, 1865, Nashville, Tenn.   He and the other family members left Company Shops, NC and traveled to Nashville. (See the copy below of the discharge.)

Also, his discharge paper below lists the following personal information: "Said Kinsey C. Hooper was born in McMinn County in the State of Tennessee, is 34 years of age, 5 feet, 4 inches high, Fair complexion, Black eyes, Black hair, and by occupation, when enrolled, a Sadd??" [The end of the word is not legible and could be Saddler, Saddle Maker, or something similar, and is what he actually did in the Ambulance Corps, not prior to his service.]

Kinsey's pension file shows that he had trouble with rheumatism for the rest of his life, and also developed epilepsy in his later years. According to my (Rick's) preliminary research, epilepsy does not have to begin at childhood, but can develop through an injury to the head. It is possible his stay in the convalescent camp in March 1864 was due to an injury, possibly to the head. This might also explain his transfer out of the infantry. Apparently, scar tissue left from a head injury can form on the brain and cause epileptic seizures. Kinsey died June 6, 1904 and is buried in the Candies Creek Cemetery with many other family members.

Jahew Hooper's file states he contracted measles in Kentucky and because of subsequent relapses developed diarrhea, piles (hemorrhoids) and heart disease. He finished the war with the 8th Tenn. and returned to Bradley County. Jahew passed away Nov. 14, 1902 and is buried in the Candies Creek Cemetery.

(The preceding information ends the work that Rick Hooper accomplished using K. C. Hooper's Diary.) J. S. Hurlburt wrote *History of the Rebellion in Bradley County East Tennessee* which was published in Indianapolis in 1866 (Internet). On pages 220-221, Mr. Hurlburt wrote that Capt. W. McClellan and his men arrested two of the Hooper boys and took them to Charleston. The father, Mr. Hooper, followed hoping to intercede for his sons. When he was seen following Capt. McClellan, a number of the rebel soldiers caught Mr. Hooper and tied a rope around his neck, telling him he could follow his Lincolnite sons to the gallows. They pulled Mr. Hooper with the rope around his neck into the presence of his sons. On the same day William Bracket was arrested. The three men were hanged three times until they were senseless and almost dead each time. One objective was to force the men to confess to Union activities in the area. William Bracket had been reported to be aiding Union refugees. The morning of his arrest, Mr. Bracket had provided breakfast to such a person, but neither he nor the Hoopers betrayed their friends. Mr. Hooper, his three sons, and Mr. Bracket lived to see the rebellion crushed, and the rebels brought to justice. (James Hooper in his request for a pension mentioned only himself as being hanged. See his pension statement in the following paragraphs.)

The following was taken from James Hooper's application for a pension or continuation of his pension:
> State of Arkansas, County of Sebastian in the matter of Invalid (Veteran Reserve) Pension Claim of James Hooper late of Co. A of the 8th Reg't of Tennessee ON THIS 8 day of April A. D. 1889 personally appeared before me Justice of the Peace in and for the aforesaid County, duly authorized to administered oaths James Hooper whose Post Office address is Central Arkansas well known to me to be reputable and entitled to credit, and whom being duly sworn, declare in relation to aforesaid case as follows: That he is the claimant in the above entitled claim and that he enlisted in Co. B, 7 Tenn. Infty on the 11 day of Nove. 1861 at the mouth of Sale Creek on the Tennessee River under Col. Cliff. I got a commission from Col. Cliff to go back on the south side of the Tennessee River to recruit and while I was over there recruiting, I was captured by Capt. McClelland Company that was stationed at Charleston in Bradley County Tennessee and it was Capt. McClelland that hung me. This took place about 2 months after I enlisted. Capt. McClelland after the hanging said I had to join his company if I did not he would kill me. I stayed with them five or six months and when they started with us down to Atlanta I managed to get away one night and made my way back to my command the 7th and 8 Reg. were consolidated at Lebanon Ky. And I was discharged after the siege of Knoxville I believe about Jan. 1865.

James Hooper
(Signature of Claimant.)

James Hooper's pension file has sworn statements from friends and relatives in Arkansas & Missouri about how the hanging in Nov. 1861 caused him to bleed at the lungs several times a year. The witnesses said he could "do no more work than ½ a man." The file stops May 4, 1892 without any explanation. However, on May 13, 1892 a James Hooper of Central City, Ark. passed away, and that was where James lived.

John Hooper had no Civil War pension application on file. This might have indicated he was deceased prior to 1890. He had moved to Arkansas before 1870, but he continued to pay Bradley County taxes on 380 acres until 1874 (Tennessee, Bradley County, *1874 Revenue Collections Register* transcribed by Barbara Fagan, CGRS and published in Cleveland, Tennessee in 2004). A deed was registered in1894 in Bradley County, Tennessee from John Hooper (*Deed Book O* pp. 54-55). He sold 123 acres to C. F. Hooper (Charles F. Hooper) and Kinsey C. Hooper, with the… "exception of the water pond and a road on the line to dam and the dam not to be raised any higher than it is at present." This deed specifies the line crossing the K. C. Hooper mill race. This might be the hand dug mill race, and John didn't want the dam raised, perhaps, because he remembered his mother's death and the disease that the flooded creek caused. This deed could have been made while John lived but not registered until later. His son Andrew J. Hooper also served in the Civil War.

Sergeant William Hooper moved to Arkansas, Fayette County, Illinois and then to Hickory County, Missouri where he died July 14, 1918. (See pages 31 and 35 for more information.)

Clinton Jack (husband of Tabitha) enlisted August 1862 in Company A, 8th Tennessee Volunteers of the United States Army. He was in the battle and siege of Knoxville, participated in the Georgia campaign from Buzzard's Roost to Atlanta. He was skirmishing or fighting every day from April 14 to August 6. When he was at Atlanta, he was wounded in the right wrist which continued to disable him because the cut tendons caused the hand to be crooked. He was in Raleigh, North Carolina in April 1865 when the war ended. Afterward he was taken prisoner in Bradley County, Tennessee from his own home by Major Goode of Georgia, held for two days and then released. (See *Memorial and Biographical* below.)

After the war, Clinton Jack and family moved to Arkansas and then to Dallas, Texas. He died February 1902 of an apparent self – inflicted gunshot wound. Tabitha Jack, wife of Clinton Jack applied for a Pension on March 24, 1902 in Oak Cliff, Texas because her husband had served in the Civil War as a Private in Company A, 8 Regt. Tenn., and she said he died of a gunshot wound. But, in the1920 Census his name reappeared and living with his wife and their son. See the pages 32 - 33 for more information.

David Jack, father of Clinton Jack, was in the 5th Regiment, Tennessee Infantry of the Union Army and died January 21, 1863 in Nashville (Internet, *Ancestry.com, National Cemetery Administration. U. S. Veterans Gravesites, ca. 1775-2006* [database on-line]). In the *Cleveland Banner* May 5, 1866, Vol. 1 No. 34 Mary Jane Jack was listed as the Administratrix for the Estate of David Jack deceased. Mary Jane died in 1879 when she was 56 years old. The following David Jack Civil War information was found in the *Memorial and Biographical History of Dallas County, Texas* published in 1892 by The Lewis Publishing Company of Chicago on page 885 (Internet). David Jack served as a private in the 5th Army Corp of the Union Army. He was taken prisoner at Cumberland Gap and imprisoned in Richmond, Virginia at the Libby Prison from November 1, 1862 until January 1863. He died at the age of 45 from chronic diarrhea that he had contracted while in prison.

Andrew Hooper Estate:
After the Civil War, Andrew Hooper died about May 30, 1866 because his wife, Margaret, began the estate distribution, and by June 19, administrator, K. C. Hooper, reported, "The foregoing is a true account of the Inventory of sale of the property that came to my hands and sold 19th day of June 1866 of the estate of Andrew Hooper Deceased. This 3 day of September 1866 K. C. Hooper Adm. Sworn to & Subscribed before me this 3 day Sept. 1866, Joseph H. Davis Clerk." These records were found on pages 66, 67 and 68 of the *Trustees Book* of Bradley County, Tennessee for the years 1836-1876:

page 66

E. Wyles	1 Bell quilt	.75
Danis Hooper	1 oil cloth	.10
T. H. Gilbreath	1 oil cloth	1.45
Margaret Shepherd	1 oil cloth	.25
M. Graham	1 wash kettle	3.75
K. C. Hooper	1 wash tub	.80
M. Graham	1 oven	.25
K. C. Hooper	2 chairs	1.55
Tobitha Hooper	2 chairs	1.50
Tobitha Hooper	1 chair	.25
Tobitha Hooper	1 chair	.15
William Hooper	1 chair	.35
N.Elling Burg	1 lot of wool	7.87
T. H. Gilbreath	1 lot wool	2.00
T. H. Gilbreath	1 lot nails	.60

T. H. Gilbreath	1 frau (froe)	.50
E. Wyles	20 pounds soap	1.00
K. C. Hooper	1 lot soap	3.25
T. H. Gilbreath	1 barrel grass seed	2.00
Danis Hooper	1 axe	.90
Beatey Perren	1 axe	.60
Tobitha Hooper	1 wheet	.25
T. H. Gilbreath	1 saddle	3.50
Francis Hooper	1 filley	70.00
		$825.30
William Hooper	1 pr hames	1.00
William Hooper	1 fly brush	2.00
William Hooper	2 barrels	.25
William Hooper	2 lard cans	.40
William Hooper	1 fire shovel	.10
Francis J. Hooper	1 plow	.50
Danis Hooper	1 set plow gears	1.50
William Hooper	1 mattock	.50
K. C. Hooper	2 klavis	.50
K. C. Hooper	1 chisel	.25
T. H. Gilbreath	1 fly brush	2.00
Tobitha Hooper	1 fly brush	2.00
Tobitha Hooper	10 geese	2.50
Tobitha Hooper	d. chickens	1.00
Eli Fitzgerald	1 horse	100.00
		$114.50
		825.30
		$939.80

page 67

James Hooper	1 bar of iron	1.80
T. H. Gilbreath	1 bar iron	1.85
Jahue Hooper	1 cannon plow	1.50
William Hooper	1 cannon plow	3.00
Jahue Hooper	1 cannon plow	1.00
William Hooper	1 grind stone	.75
James Hooper	1 still	8.25
J. W. Beard	1 large plow	7.50
James Hooper	1 thrasher	21.25
T. H. Gilbreth	1 set black smith tools	16.50
K. C. Hooper	1 buggy	17.50
William Hooper	1 wagon	30.00
N. Elling Burg	1 wagon	8.50
E. Wyles	1 lot of dry hides	28.70
William Graham	1 yearling	4.25
Calvin Hitson	1 cow & calf	47.50
N. Elling Burg	1 cow	32.50
James Hooper	1 yoke of oxen	50.00
Thomas Hood	1 large steer	61.10
William Hooper	1 pr dog irons	.50
Tobitha Hooper	1 basket	.06
Jahue Hooper	1 table	3.00
Danis Hooper	1 table	.25
K. C. Hooper	1 lock	.25
T. H. Gilbreath	1 lot latches	.35
Tobitha Hooper	1 bed	14.00
Margaret Shepherd	1 safe	9.00

Tobitha Hooper	1 glass	.60
William Hooper	1 block	.65
S. C. Gearen	1 box glass	1.05
D. D. Taylor	putty	.15
Francis Hooper	1 bsu & c	10.00
Tobitha Hooper	1 bsu & c	12.00
Margaret Shepherd	1 bed or bell	21.00
Danis Hooper	1 bed or bell	18.00
Jahue Hooper	1 pr steelyards	.38
Wyles	1 quilt	2.00
William Hooper	1 quilt	.60
Francis Hooper	1 quilt	1.60
Danis Hooper	1 quilt	1.75
Francis Hooper	1 quilt	1.75
William Hooper	1 quilt	.75

This day came K. C. Hooper Administrator of Andrew Hooper Deceased and made settlement with the County Court Clerk of said County of Bradley which is in the following words and figures to wit. I find the Administrator chargable with the Sum of nine hundred & thirty nine & eighty cents $939.80.

page 60

I find him entitled to the following credits as for Vouchers & Receipts.

No. 1	Receipt from Thos J. Keron for notes & interest	435.25
No. 2	Note paid to Asa Fitzgerald interest included	155.42
3	Note paid to T. J. Keron including interest	17.30
4	1 Proven account by Jahue Hooper	248.18
5	1 Proven " " James Hooper	266.00
6	1 Proven " " T. E. Boucher	3.75
7	1 Proven " " Beaty Perion	3.00
		1128.90

page 61

Amount of Liabilities brot forward	939.80
Amount of credits	1128.90
No. 8 Proven account by Margaret Shepherd	7.00
9 " " William Hooper	120.00
10 " " S. H. McWhirter	115.38
11 " " Caleb Dobbs	.50
12 " " Internal Revenue Tax	20.00
13 Land to I. B. Newton for 1867	53.60
14 " " Newton for 1866	32.50
15 " " John Hooper	32.10
16 Receipt of Dr. Lewis Griffin	30.10
17 " " Dr. John C. Everett	20.00
18 Graves & Surgnine	14.50
19 Proven account of W. Ellenburg	23.75
20 1 " " Danl Hooper	50.00
21 1 " " Wm. Arnhart	10.00
22 " " " E. Wyles	14.47
23 " " " James Hooper	
Guardian for Francis Hooper	50.00
Amount paid Davis for Letters of Admr.	3.00
Paid for writing & Recording to widow part land	2.25
" " Settlement & Recording Same	1.50
	$ 1727.55
	939.80

State of Tennessee
Bradley County   Personally appeared K. C. Hooper Administrator of Andrew Hooper Dec. and made oath that the above Settlement as above made is properly and correctly made to the best of his knowledge and belief.

K. C. Hooper

Sworn to and Subscribed   Administrator
before me this 2nd day of
July 1868
Samuel Hunt Clerk

The following relate to the settlements by the Andrew Hooper heirs:

p. 65 August 5, 1865 Andrew Hooper to Thomas H. Gilbreath 240 acres for $300.00 found in *Bradley County Deed Book A*

Book A Bradley County Deeds p. 200 May 30, 1866 Margaret Hooper to John Hooper, Kinzey C. Hooper, Dialtha Gilbreath, James Hooper, William Hooper, Daniel Hooper, Francis Hooper and Tabitha Hooper, children and heirs at law of Andrew Hooper deceased for $650.00

p. 334 John Hooper to Thomas H. Gilbreath March 12, 1867 $1000.00 estate of Andrew Hooper
p. 341 $1600.00 James Hooper to Kinsey C. Hooper estate of Andrew Hooper April 3, 1867
p. 395 August 19, 1867 William Hooper to Thomas H. Gilbreath $1000.00
p. 481 K. C. Hooper sold land to R. (T.) H. McPherson January 18, 1868
pp. 624-625 Francis J. Hooper to William $800.00 from father Andrew September 10, 1868

Bradley County Deed Book C:
pp. 138-139 Dannis Hooper to K. C. Hooper on Feb. 3, 1868 the amount of $900.00
p. 246 William Hooper to Thomas H. Gilbreath January 5, 1869 the amount of $800.00

Hooper Box, Hooper Mill Owners and the Kinsey C. Hooper Estate

Some of the most important information in this book was related to a very significant discovery that Richard (Rick) Hooper made in the 1970's or 80s. Martha and Harold Reno received a phone call from Rick that he had found a box in a barn, and it had Hooper records. This chapter is mostly related to the records found in that box. Any records not found in the box are listed as exceptions.

Below are 2 pictures of the Hooper Box showing the closed box and one on the next page opened:

Hooper Box that Rick Hooper found in the old barn.

The records included Hooper Mill and other legal papers.

Hooper Box showing papers inside.

On pp. 5 – 6 is the 1837 Lewisey Melton deed which was in the Hooper Box. Another old, undated record in the Hooper box was the "A Way Bill". The paper was yellowed and the spelling was extremely hard to decipher. The title on the outside was "A Way Bill". It was a word map from Pikeville, TN to the Hickory Nut Ford on the Platte River in Missouri (Clinton County). Several families related to Andrew Hooper moved to Hickory County, Missouri about 1870. At the top of the page it said, "A Way Bill to the Missouri" (see picture below). It was not written in sentences, but rather it listed the locations you needed to know to reach Missouri.

The sheet (p. 163) was slightly browned like old, discolored paper. The only words written were "A Way bill." On the other side, the first words were "the A way bill to the missouri." Then, the directions began with the word "to" repeated before the next location. (See the picture below for the other side of the word map.)

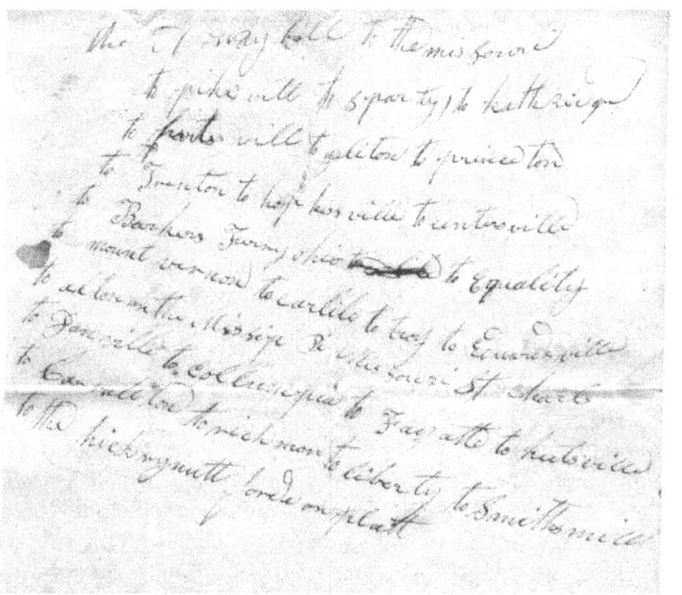

Whoever took the time to write the preceding directions must have had first-hand knowledge of the locations for shallow water (places to ford) and the ferries that could be used. See the following map that shows locations mentioned in the "A Way Bill": to Pikeville, TN; to Sparta, TN; to Carthage, TN; to Hartsville, TN; to Gallatin, TN; to Princeton, TN (Prince's Station or Port Royal); to Trenton, KY; to Hopkinsville, KY; to Centerville, KY; to Barker Ferry on the Ohio River (Internet, Pope County and Hardin County, IL); to Equality, IL; to Mount Vernon, IL; to Carlyle, IL; to Troy, IL; to Edwardsville, IL; to Alton, IL on the Mississippi; to Missouri, Saint Charles; to Danville, MO; to Columbia, MO; to Fayette, MO; to Huntsville, MO; to Carrolton, MO; to Richmond, MO; to Liberty MO; to Smithville, MO; to Hickory Nut Ford on (the) Platte (river). The word map might have been written before 1837. (Montgomery County, TN had a Prince's Station established 1782 according to Anne Goodwin of the *Hooper Compass* located between Gallatin, TN and Trenton, KY at Port Royal now [see p. 305].)

Platte River, Missouri

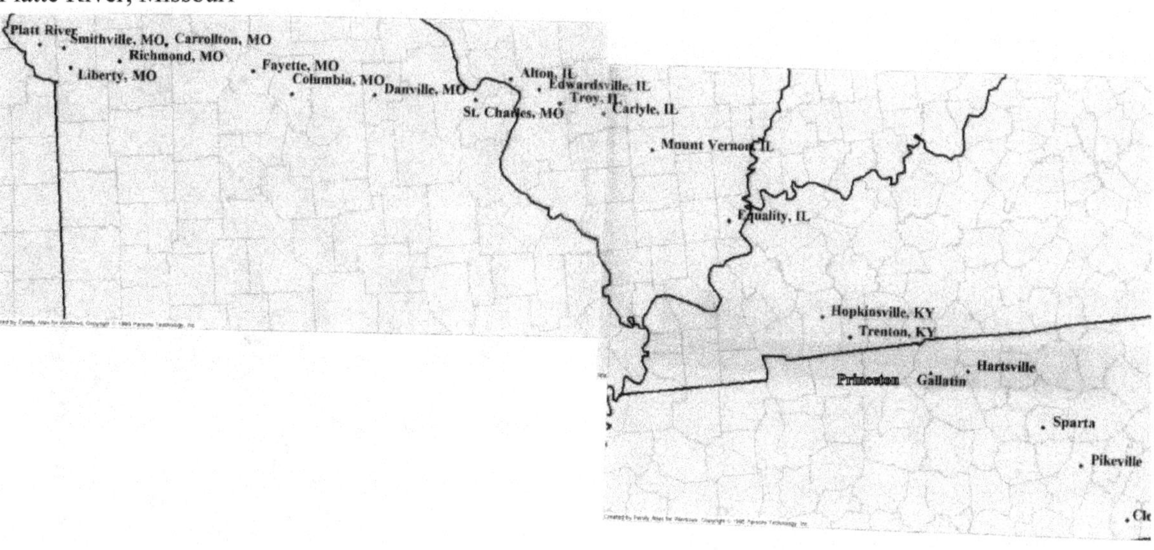

Cleveland, TN

Harold Reno created the small rough map on previous page to illustrate the locations for the different towns from Cleveland, Tennessee (lower right) to the Platte River area (on the upper left). Smithville, MO, one of the listed towns, was settled about 1828. The journey was more than a 1000 miles.

Harold Reno emailed several research facilities about the "A Way Bill" from Pikeville, TN to the Platte River. He contacted the Tennessee State Library and Archives; the Hickory County Library in Missouri; Sebastian County Library, Arkansas; Smithsonian Institution; the New York American Museum of Natural History and Anne Goodwin with the *Hooper Compass* to see if they were familiar with the word map. None were familiar with the "A Way Bill". Also, he listed the map on the Internet at *Genealogy.com*.

An Abraham Hooper family from Tennessee was a part of the early Missouri settlers before 1840 (Internet, Anne Goodwin *Hooper Compass* November 1999, Vol. 1, Issue 1, pp. 29 – 34). Perhaps this old word map was related to this family who had traveled to Missouri. Clinton County, Missouri is the actual location of the Hickory Nut Ford. Since the "A Way Bill" mentions the Hickory Nut Ford and not ferry, it must be older than 1837. In December 1837 David Hamilton was given a license to operate a ferry on the Platte River at Hickory-nut Ford according to *The History of Clinton County Missouri* by O. P. Williams & Co. and published by the National Historical Company at St. Joseph, Missouri in 1881 and found at *Google.com* and other Internet locations. (Also see Appendix G for more information.)

The records in the next two paragraphs were not found in the Hooper box, but were used for historical purposes and further explanation. The *1862 United States Direct Tax Commission* for 9th District Bradley County, TN on p. 15 found at *Ancestry.com* showed that Andrew Hooper paid taxes of $12.60 on 990 acres valued at $7200.00 and a Mill taxed at $2.10 and valued at $600.00, thus proving the existence of Hooper Mill in 1862. An 1865 reference to Hooper Mill was a Military Map (see a portion of the map on p. 270 from Internet Library of Congress *Atlas of the Battlefields of Chickamauga, Chattanooga, and Vicinity* drawn by Col. Wm. E. Merrill in 1865 and published by the U. S. Army in 1874 and 1896).

The rough drawing below was drawn by Harold Reno after visiting the Hooper Mill area on December 20, 2007 with Bill Moorhouse (see p. 189); Harold visited again March 27, 2008, March 21, 2009 and March 9, 2018 for the Culvert (below) and Sluice Gate end pictures (see p. 276). The reference numbers from 1 to 18 are the points identified on the rough drawing of the site. The references and drawings are for explanation only and not drawn to scale. The foundations can still be seen from the bridge crossing Candies Creek on County Road 308 called Eureka Road. (*Google* picture is on next page.)

1. Eureka Road to Charleston Bridge Crossing Candy's Creek
2. Candy's Creek
3. Hooper Mill Dam
4. Land separating the creek from the dug spillway
5. Dug spillway about 400 feet long
6. Open end of the spillway about 30 feet wide
7. Spillway at mill about 19 feet wide
8. Outer concrete wall about two feet wide
9. Water way between the outer wall and the middle wall six feet wide (6')
10. Middle concrete wall about two feet wide and 18 feet long with three 8" by 8" holes for supports
11. Distance between the middle wall and the inner wall eleven feet (11')
12. Inner wall about two feet wide and 35 feet four inches long with three 8" by 8" holes for supports
13. To the lower left is an old roadbed with the remains of a culvert
14. Mill foundation left eleven feet ten inches (11' 10") may have broken off
15. Mill foundation front twenty-eight feet long (28') sixteen inches to twenty-eight inches thick
16. Mill foundation right side twenty-six feet long (26') fourteen inches to twenty-five inches thick
17. Building foundation to the right fourteen feet by fifteen feet and twelve feet from mill foundation
18. There is another foundation for a house further from the mill.

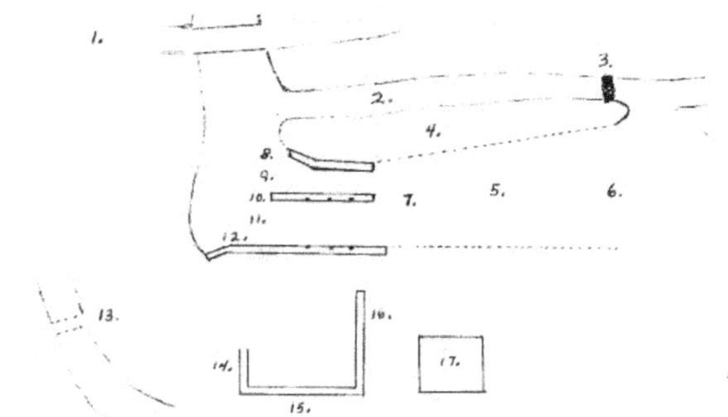

(Picture to the right shows number 13 Hand Made Culvert under old road to Hooper Mill.)

The picture below came from *Internet, Google Maps* and showed the Lower River Road (number 308) that connected Eureka and Charleston, Tennessee. Harold Reno added identifications for the dug spillway, the stone dam, and the location of Hooper Mill located at the end of the island. (See pages 183 - 184 for two pictures of the Hooper Mill.)

Also not found in the Hooper box was the *Tennessee 9th Census, 1870 Manufacturing* found at Internet *Ancestry.com* (Originals in Duke University Library). K. C. Hooper was listed as having a mill (main product "Meal"), Power (Water), Capital Investment ($750.00), One Stone (30 Bushels a Day), Custom Grinding (Corn), 9360 Bushels, Value 9360, Total Value $10,530.00. Also, a Lumber mill was listed with 1 Saw, Water powered, Sawed Logs, Quantities 50,000 (Board Feet?), Value $500.00.

(The bridge across Candies Creek close to the Hooper Mill was referred to as the Hooper Mill Bridge see p. 173 for a 1901 microfilm reference to the bridge in a court case.)

Beginning here are Hooper Mill records found in the box and arranged by dates. "October 8, 1883 I promise to pay $10.00 to the order of R. G. Cross THE HOWE MACHINE COMPANY Payable at the Bank of Hiwassee, Charleston, Tenn. P. O. Address Raht P. Office, Bradley Co., Tenn." Written on the front –Paid T. J. Knox and numbered on the back 3810. Stamped on back was "Pay (signed) H. Parsar ON ORDER FOR COLLECTION FOR ACCOUNT OF FIRST NATIONAL BANK OF CHATTANOOGA, TENN. T. G. MONTAGUE CASHIER" (the lower right corner was torn off).

"Bank of Charleston $600.00 April 1st 1886 Ninety days after we jointly promise to pay to the order of T. J. Knox cashier Six Hundred Dollars Due 7/1 No. 707" (the names were torn off).

(The following deed was not part of the collection of materials in the box, but it reflected another aspect of the K. C. Hooper family:)

Deed	This indenture made and entered into this the 4th day of August 1886 by
J. G. Stanfield and Wife	and between J. G. Standfield and Nancy Standfield of the first part and
To	and K. C. Hooper, W. P. Palmer and W. E. Lee, School Directors of the
K. C. Hooper et als	Second part witnesseth that for the love and respect we entertain for
	Educational purpose or a public School house to be used as a public

School house and none other we have this day bargained and sold unto Said Directors and their

Successors in office the following described piece or parcel of land to wit: containing about 1 acre more or less and that the School house now Stands Butted and bounded as follows to wit: on the north by Standfield and Wyrick on the East by Wyrick and Standfield and on the west by Standfield and lying in the 9th Civil District of Bradley County, Tennessee Ocoee District to have and to hold unto Said School Directors and their Successors in office for sure and we bind our Selves our heirs and assigns to forever warrant and defend free from all encumbrances whatsoever.

In witness whereof we have here unto set our hands and seals date above written.

Attest
Henry Newberry   J. G. Standfield
Margaret Newberry   Nancy A. Standfield

(At one time, Hooper Mill community had a store, houses, school and bridge see p. 173 for references.)

On a piece of paper 5 inches by 8 inches, "Recieved [sic] of Ike Hoopper in full of his acct. up till date this dec [sic] 16—1887 signed C. J. Wilson."

"$5.33 Jany [sic] 1st 1888 one day after date I promise to pay to the order of J. T. Hines Five and 33/100 Dollars E. M. Thomas. Written on the back Received on the within note four dollars this Sept. 7th 1889."

"P. O. Cleveland, Tenn., Jan. 10, 1888 bought of PALMER & GEREN DEALERS IN ALL Kinds of Undressed Lumber Mills at Eureka received of I. H. Hooper amt. in full of all notes and acts to this date that he gave to Cleveland for Geren."

"Received of I. H. Hooper $6.75 in full of Debt Due me from Henry Pew this December the 12, 1888 [signed] U. C. Melton."

"OFFICE OF B. A. EDWARDS & SON, DEALERS IN General Merchandise and Provisions, Also Wholesale dealers in Grain and Hay, Charleston, Tenn., Jy [sic] 29, 1889. 'Ike I have a note giving [sic] me by Ugene Johnson for 44.00 dollars to called against you Come to Cleveland next Saturday and we will arrange it Don't pay Johnson untill you See Me. Be Sure and Come Saturday by W. F. Barrett.'"

"$40.00 Chattanooga, Tenn. (Alabama crossed out) Feb. 2, 1889 On or before the 1st day of April 1889 for value received in one Bill of Machinery, I, the undersigned of __________ County, State of Alabama, promise to pay to the order of C. Aultman & Co. Forty Dollars payable at the office of C. Aultman, Chattanooga, Tenn. P. O. Rhatt (Raht written in) Bradley Co. State of Tenn. (Alabama crossed out) No. D10554338 (on the back) #19568 Pay Cleveland C. Aultman (lower right hand corner torn off)."

"REGULAR CHATTANOOGA AND HIWASSEE RIVER PACKET Leaves Company's Wharf Chattanooga, for Charleston, every Saturday at 7 o'clock p. m. For Kincannon's Ferry every Wednesday. The HIWASSEE SHORT LINE! SODDY COAL, IRON & RAILWAY CO., OWNERS, AND MINERS OF Steam and Domestic Coal, and manufacturers of Coke."

"Organized 1875, MINES AT SODDY, TENN. Re-organized 1887. STEAMER M. H. CLIFT OF Chattanooga, Tenn. J. C. Haley, Master and Clerk M. H. Clift Pres't. and Gen'l M'g'r. ROBT MORRISON, Vice-Pres't. J. T. Hill, Sec'y & Treas. GENERAL OFFICE: Eighth and Cherry Streets, Chattanooga, Tenn. Feb. 6, 1889 I. Hooper Trip No. 129. 4 wheels, 2 boxes, 1 pee shefte (shaft) 50 Paid H. Haly"

"OFFICE OF CIRCUIT COURT CLERK BRADLEY COUNTY A. J. FLETCHER, CLERK Cleveland, Tenn. , Feb. 8, 1889 Recd. Isaac Hooper Twenty Dollars on a note that Eugene Johnson had against him for Forty Four Dollars. W. F. Barrett, Sheriff."

"BRADLEY COUNTY, Cleveland, Tenn., Feb. 18, 1889 Received of I. H. Hooper the sum of One Dollars and 50 cents, in full, for State, County, School, Jail, Bridge and Road—(left corner torn) the year 1888, in District No. 9 of Bradley County, Tenn. M. L. Jackson Trustee"

"Recd. of Isaac Hoper [*sic*] Ten Dollars on the Dugen Johnson note this Apr. 1st, 1889 W. F. Barrett, Sheriff."

"SODDY COAL, IRON & RAILWAY CO. STEAMER M. H. CLIFT JUNE 16, 1889 I. H. Hooper Trip No. 123   2 Cog Wheals 30 Paid H. Haley"

"Recd. of I. Hooper Five dollars on a note which he owes Eugene Johnson, Cleveland, Tenn. Juy [sic] 2, 1889 W. F. Barrett, Sheriff"

"THE TENNESSEE RIVER TRANSPORTATION COMPANY, GENERAL OFFICE AND WAREHOUSE, CHATTANOOGA, TENN. Jan. the 27, 1890 Mr. I. H. Hooper To Steamer J. R. Hughes, Dr. (stamped over this is Str. M. H. Clift) TO FREIGHT ON 297 Bals (bales) Hay FREIGHT 14.85 Paid S. B. Hamsly"

"BRADLEY COUNTY CLEVELAND, TENN. Feb. 14, 1890 RECEIVED OF I. H. Hooper the sum of one dollars and 50 cents, in full, for State, County, School, Bridge and Road Tax for the year 1889, in District No. 9 of Bradley County, Tenn. $1.50 M. L. Julian, Trustee."

"Received of I. H. Hooper Thirteen & 20/100 Dollars in full of all accts. to date this the 4 day of March 1890. W. W. Beard"

"Charleston, Tenn. Spt. 23rd, 1891 Received of I. Hooper Ten Dollars Drayage and Boat freight. Kict or Keet Boat Co. by Balls"

"Warrantee Deed of W. H. Burgess to Hooper and Geren. Tax State Tax 20 County Tax 10. 30 pd. Reg. fee $1.50 STATE OF TENNESSEE Hamilton County. Personally appeared before me R. M. Chambliss, Notary Public for said County, W. H. Burgess, the within named bargainor, with whom I am personally acquainted, and who acknowledged that he executed the within named Instrument for the purposes therein contained. WITNESS my hand at office, this 12th day of Feby. 1891 R. M. Chambliss (signature) Notary Public." (See pp. 196 and 266 for a copy of this deed in Bradley County, TN related to Mount Ebal.)

"BRADLEY COUNTY CLEVELAND, TENN. May 21, 1891 RECEIVED OF I. H. Hooper the sum of one dollars and 50 cents, in full, for State, County, School, Bridge and Road Tax for the year 1890, in District No. 9, of Bradley County, Tenn. $1.50 John K. Randolph, Trustee."

Hooper Mill Store Order?
        August 17th [18]91 Bill of Goods 1 Box Soda Crackers 7, 3 doz. Box sardeens 6, 2 doz. cans Oisters 1.00, ½ box Peanuts 6, 8 boxs segars @90 for 50, candy two buckets @10, 1 box sugar cakes @10, 1 Box Lemons 4.50, 4 doz. Oranges about 30 or 40, 100 lbs. Rased Bread @3 ¾, 1 Box Raisens (marked out), 1 Bottle Pepper sauce 10, 100 lbs. Sugar Brown 5, 4 oz. Tur Taricaeid ____, 300 lbs. Ice 50, 12 Table glass large size 50, 200 Pokes one pound 10, 1 bunch Bananas !.50 (each item has X beside it) I. Hooper is written at the bottom and Chels 10 lb (the rest are written on the back), 1 Box of 11# Little Edwin Tch @28, Matches .10, Salt 90, 125# Flour #.50, 25# Lard @ 114

"E. L. & E. T. Knox General Merchandise And Grain Dealers Charleston, Tenn., ____ 189__ Received of I. H. Hooper seventeen 78/100 Owe in full of Judgem. & Cost in the case of W. S. Hunter vs Isaack Hooper obtain before W. P. Palmer on the 10 day of Sept. 1891 H. H. Brackett this Oct. 3, 1891"

"BRADLEY COUNTY, CLEVELAND, TENN., 2/25 1893 Received of K. C. Hooper the sum of Forty two DOLLARS and ____ cents, in full, for POLL (marked out), State, County, School, Bridge and Road Tax for the year 1892, in District No. 9, of Bradley County, Tenn. $42.00 John K. Randolph, Trustee"

"1894 for bank 75.00 + 500.00= 575 and on the right side 13525 + 5892= 19417"

"BRADLEY COUNTY, Cleveland, Tenn., March 26, 1894 RECEIVED OF K. C. Hooper the sum of Thirty four DOLLARS and 80 cents, in full for POLL (marked out), State, County, School, Bridge and Road Tax for the year 1894, in District No. 9 of Bradley County, Tennessee $34.50 D. H. Hambright, Trustee."

The following deed information was not found in the materials found by Richard (Rick) Hooper, but it was included because it pinpoints the location of the dam and mill race: This deed was found in *Bradley County Deed Book O* pages 54-55: John A. Hooper sold 123 acres to C. (Charles) F. and K. C. Hooper on September 4, 1894. This deed mentioned the following exceptions to the deed: the water pond, a road to the dam and the dam which was not to be raised any higher than it was at present. This land was located in the 9th Civil District of Bradley County with a corner east of Candy's creek where W. E. Lee and Raht heirs corner with Jahue Hooper. The land ran north with the Raht line one half mile and then west with the Raht line to a corner between Jahue Hooper and K. C. Hooper, Sen. one quarter of a mile. Then it ran south with said line across K. C. Hooper mill race to a corner and then west with K. C. Hooper line to a corner near his mill and then south with the Raht and K. C. Hooper line to a line to the corner and then east with the line of K. C. Hooper to a corner one half mile and then north with the line of W. E. Lee. There was also another 40 acres in the same district.

Another record that related to Hooper Mill dam was the *Chancery Court* Case in Bradley County, Tennessee found in microfilm File 991 B for the years 1900-1920 for the W. L. Ledford versus James Perry case (see p. 173 for more information from the case). John Leak in frame 1355 of microfilm was asked about Hooper Mill Dam and to describe the dam. John testified that it is a rock and log dam about three miles from the mouth of Candy's Creek and the Hiwassee River. He stated that a person could walk across the dam when the creek was low and that water spilled over it when the water was high. (Wayne Hooper told about the Hoopers digging the mill spillway, and it still can be seen when the water level is low.)

"BRADLEY COUNTY $34.80 Cleveland, Tenn., April 3, 1896 RECEIVED OF K. C. Hooper the sum of Thirty four DOLLARS and 80 cents, in full for POLL, State, County, School, Bridge and Road Tax, for the year 1895, in District No. 9 of Bradley County, Tennessee. D. H. Hambright, Trustee."

"BRADLEY COUNTY $36.24 Cleveland, Tenn., May 14, 1897 RECEIVED OF K. C. Hooper the sum of Thirty six DOLLARS and 24 cents, in full for POLL (marked out), State, County, School, Bridge and Road Tax, FOR THE YEAR 1896, in District No. 9 of Bradley County, Tennessee. I. H. Hooper son of."

> $30.00 Charleston, Tenn., Oct. 1st 1897 On or before the 1st day of Oct. 1897, for value received I [I. H. Hooper see p. 170] promise to pay to the MCCORMICK HARVESTING MACHINE COMPANY or order Thirty DOLLARS with interest at six per cent per annum from date until paid. Negotiable and payable at Cleveland National Bank. This being 1 of a series of 4 notes, executed for a McCormick Baler machine Post Office Raht 8 miles north County, Bradley, Stat, Tenn. (on the back) 40460 Sale number 706 in 1897 THIS CLAIM COMPRISES $30.00 Due Oct. 1, 1897, $30.00 Due Oct. 1, 1898, $30.00 Due Oct. 1, 1899, $35.00 Due Oct. 1, 1900

"McPherson, Tenn. May 11/97 Rec'd $30.00 in full payment for Due Bill given March 21st 1896. R. A. Palmer"

"No. 2019 Bradley County, Tenn. Feb. 14, 1898 Received of Hooper, K. C., Sr. Thirty five and 04 Dollars in full for Taxes for the year 1897, in District No. 9 bounded as follows: North Ledford, South Hooper, East Lee, West Hooper, State 8.76, County 8.76, School 8.76, C. H. 5.84, Bridge 1. 46, Road 1.46 Total 35.04 No. Acres or Town Lots 438 Value $2520, Mill $400.00= 2920 Tax Rate, $1.20 in Cleveland, $1.15 D. H. Hambright, Trustee"

"STATEMENT OF ACCOUNT Cleveland, Tenn., 12/31 1898 Ike Hooper Raht in Account With MODEL ROLLER MILLS, W. P. SYKES, Proprietor, Manufacturers of Flour, Meal, Feed, Etc. FULL ROLLER

PROCESS. January 20 50 lbs. C. L. 1.50, July 21 150 lbs. C. L. 3.60, Aug. 8 200 lbs. C. L. 4.00 for 9.10 Nov. 17 by (buy?) 705 lbs. Daeccogrd wheat 50 cts. 5.87 (under this) 3.23 Cash loaned 6.00 $9.23.”

“Bradley County Tenn., Apr. 19, 1899 No. 2526 Received of K. C. Hooper Twenty nine & 20/100 Dollars, in full for taxes for the year 1898, in District No. 9 bounded as follows: North Hooper Hooper Ledford Shelton, South Ownby Hooper Hooper Lee, East Lee Lee Hooper and Bayless, West Hooper Ledford, Ledford State 8.76, County 8.76, School 8.76, Bridge 1.46, Road 1.46 Total $29.20 No. Acres or Town Lots 448 Value $2920.00 Cash Personal 400 Total $29.20 Alex Campbell, Trustee.”

(Two pages from an old ledger were kept. The pages were 49-50.)
> **page 49.** June the 29, 1898 K. C. Hooper & I. H. Hooper to Cash $4.00, Cash 1.00, to Huse Wagame 1.55, July 22 Cash 1.00, Aug. haling mill wheat 10.00, haling logs 2 days 3.00, work on mill 7 days 2.00, Garrett Mitch .15, Lar Shafting for Mill 19.25, Aug. work on mill 4 day 2.50, I. (either I. H. or K. C. is using the pronoun I) work on mill 1 day 1.00, I work on mill 1 day 1.00, I work on mill 3 ½ day 1.75, I work on mill 1 day 1.00, I work on mill 1 day 1.00, I work on mill 1 day 1.00, I work on Mill 1 Race .40, I work on mill 1 day 1.00, I work on mill 1.00, I work on mill 1.00, I work on mill ½ day .50, I work on mill ½ day .50, going Chattanooga 5 day 7.50, I work on mill .50, I work on Mill 2 day 2.00, I work on the mill 2 day 2.00, I work on mill 1 day 1.00, Siler .25, Bill Plank work on mill 1 day .50, I work on mill 1 day 1.00, I work on mill 2 day 2.00, I work on mill 2 day 2.00, I work on mill 2 day 2.00, I work on mill 2 day 2.00, Total for Page 49 $78.35 and Written vertically on the page Setteled [*sic*] Jan. the 1, 1899,
> **page 50.** Oct. 1 K. C. Hooper I. H. Hooper to Cash by wheat $2.50, work on mill 1 day 1.00, cr. by Cash 1.00, James Grisham work on mill 11 day 5.50, George Geren work on mill 15 day 6.50, I. H. Hopper [*sic*] work on mill 1 day 1.00, Carding Loyds work on mill 6.00, arding mill work 15.00, stove pipe .25, Dr (deposit receipt) to Stove Briley 1.00, cr. by interest on bank 2.00, Dr. for the 1899 to Cash 4.00, transfer from the bank Jan. 1898 3.50, files .10, Jan. the 22, 1898 Belting 3.50, A. M. Miler on Boat lumber 3.03, Feb. the 1, 1898 work on puleys 2.00, axel grease .05, March the 1, 1898 Rope 4.95, Apr. the 16 Road lumber .48, one Block from fergson 2.00, Luther (Luther Hooper? I. H.’s son) work on mill 16 day 8.00, Total on page 50 $66.56 add to page 49 $78.35= 144.91 minus 3.50=$141.91 paid Ledford $190.86 totals $332.27, Cr. by farm rents $100.00, on the same page without comment is written 450.00 minus 332.27 equals 17.73, written vertically on this page is Settled Jan. 1, 1899

“FREIGHT BILL TO SOUTHERN RAILWAY COMPANY, DR. for charges on articles way-billed from Scottsboro Consignee Mrs. I. H. Hooper 1 carpet .52 Freight and Advances Paid Jan. 12, 1899 E. S. Petty agent, Per Robertson Cashier, (written on the back of this) 3 yds. cheese cloth, Spierces (spice) mill?, 1 ½ yds. Cashimer (cashmere) colar (collar) no. 16, one pint Whisky”

“MCCORMICK HARVESTING MACHINE CO. No. 70—(corner torn) Mr. I. H. Hoo—(torn) Raht, Nashville, Tenn. May 24, 1899 Amount $30.00 Interest from maturity Due Oct. 1/99 Dear Sir Your MCCORMICK MACHINE note falls due as above stated, and is Payable at the National Bank, Cleveland, Tenn. Yours respectfully, G. A. GARTNER, JR., GENERAL AGENT” (see p. 169)

“E. W. Borcherding The Chattanooga Saw Works MANUFACTURERS OF Circular Saws, Machine Knives, Wood Working Machinery. Chattanooga, Tenn. Jul 7, 1899 Sold to I. H. Hooper Raht, Tenn. For gurrig (gearing) thurrey 1.47 Saw 4.25 Received Payment Chatt. Saw Works”

“Regular Hiwassee and Tennessee River Packet.” (blue 1 cent documentary stamp with 7/8 (18)99 ELJ written on it) Received for Shipment by Steamer OCOEE. July 8, 189_ from I. H. Hooper MARKS OF CONSIGNEE I. H. Hooper, Ledfords Ldg. Articles 1 Wagon Weight 300 Freight 1.00, 1 Saw Weight 100 Freight .25 paid 1.00 ELJ” (See page 275 for picture of the Ocoee Steamer with the James Shelton farm in the background.)

“Sold by E. C. Atkins & Co. SHEFFIELD SAW WORKS SAWS, SAW TOOLS ATKINS ALWAYS AHEAD E. C. ATKINS & CO. INDIANAPOLIS, IND. MILL SUPPLIES INCORPORATED 1885

Chattanooga, Tenn. July 26, 1899 to I. H. Hooper Raht, Tenn. 1 (one) 16 inch Cross Cut Circ 14 Ga 2.75, 5 Lbs #4 Babbitt (price 8 cents) .40, Saw Oratr .20, total 3.35 paid JUL 26, 1899"

Office of I. Hooper No. 243, CONVERSE BRIDGE CO., CHATTANOOGA, TENN., Lumber Bill for Mouse Creek Bridge in Bradley County, Tenn. 1 span 50 feet Roadway 12 feet Approaches, 21 pieces 3 ½ inches by 12 inches 18 feet long, 2 pieces 3 inches by 6 inches 18 feet long, 4 pieces 3 inches by 6 inches 16 feet long, 6 pieces 2 inches by 10 inches 18 feet long, 1500 ft. B. M. 2 ½ inches by 6 inches to 10 inches 12 feet long, All to be good, sound, square edge White oak lumber, free from black knots and waney edges, sawed to even widths and thicknesses and to the acceptance of the Bridge Committee of Bradley Co., Tenn. and to be delivered at Bridge Site on or before Sept. 1st, 1899 CONVERSE BRIDGE CO. Chattanooga, Tenn., July 18th, 1899.

Bradley County, Tenn., Jan. 31, 1900. No. 1066 Received of Hooper K. C. Thirty six and 50/100 Dollars, in full for Taxes for the year 1899, in District No.__ bounded as follows; North Hooper Hooper Ledford & Shelton South Ownby Hooper Hooper & Lee East Lee Lee Hooper & Bayless West Hooper Hunter Ledford & Lee STATE 10.22 COUNTY 8.76 SCHOOL 8.76 BOND 5.84 BRIDGE 1.46 ROAD 1.46 TOTAL 36.50 No. Acres or Town Lots 438 Value, $2520 Tax Rate, $1.25. In Cleveland, $1.20 One mill by water $400 Total $36.50 Alex Campbell, Trustee. by D. or W. Deputy

"No. 1667 Bradley County, Tenn., Mar. 9, 1901 Received of K C. Hooper, Sr. Thirty-Seven & 50/100 Dollars, in full payment of State, County, School, Bond, Road, and Poll (marked out) Tax for the year 1900 on the following property: Dist. 9 ASSESSED TO Same ACRES 137 VALUATION DIST. 685, ACRES 180 VAL. 900, ACRES 40 VAL. 140, ACRES 61 VAL. 875, 1 Mill 400 TOTAL TAX 37.50 Alex Campbell, Trustee. By D. or W. Deputy"

(Found in the old Hooper Mill records were two, small OLIVER notebooks, one dated March 16, 1901.)
    pgs. 1 and **2** have various written numbers;
pg. 3 shoes 1 no. 6; 2 no. 5; Belting 14 ft. 10 inches 3.48 / 12=29 and 16x3=48;
pg. 4 Hogs 505; pebscet 3 yd.; sady 4 ct.; spice 5; cinnamon 5; sugar 50 ct.; candy 4 lbs.; apels ¼ B; thed 1 St. no. 6 a B; oil 1 gallon; saw; 5 log 6x6x21; 1 log 3 ¾ x3 ¾ 16; 3 log 12 ft.; 2 log 14 ft.; 1 log 11;
pg. 5 peas for Knox 4 S 515; 4 S 490; Card S 250; Amt. $15.27; 130+30=1.60; 80x4=$3.20-1.60;
pg. 6 Rilen Block 1 ½ in. 2 yd. 4 in. Amt. paid hands for Hartman 8200 ct, 2.50 ct. 50 ct. 1700-462=12.38;
pg. 7 amt paid Al Joings for H. H. Bracket for lumber $2.90 and 30;
pg. 8 Cot. Jeans 1 ½ y.; butons; coffee 2 p.; cot. checks 2 y.;
pg. 9 centrel mfg. co. Chattanooga Hugh;
pg. 10 length 25 in. wd. 15 in., neth 12 in. Eag Cores; Weling ½ yd.; Hoes 1 pair black; 1 ½ yd gamy fine; Sody 5 ct.; spice 5 ct.;
pg. 11 High of Black 6 ¾ inc.; Fran San in.; Sid Carer 7 ¼ weth of; carer 3 ft. 7 in.; md of block 2 ½ in;
pg. 12 2 cogs 2 ¼ in.; 37 1/2x3=111+ 18+2=1.31; 13 ½ x50=650+25=6.75+60+7.35+11.00+18.35-1000=8.35;
pg. 13 Bil Plank work 7 day; work 1 day; work 1 day; work 1 day; borrowed money $11.00; credit by Cash $10.00, work 1 day; work 1 day; work 1 day; work ½ day; threshing 1 day; Amt. due Aug. the 13 $18.00 ct.;
pg. 14 corn to Shelton by Milaway April 1 bus., April 1 ½ bus., May the 9 1 Bus., 20x40=8.00; 14x35=4.90; 500/35=14;
pg. 15 Honey Mar.; corn 2 B.; corn ½ B.; corn 1 B.; corn 1 B.; corn 1 B; corn 1 B.; corn 1 B.; corn ½ B.; corn 1 B.; corn 1 B.; corn 1 B.; corn ½ B.; corn ½ ; corn ½ Bushel; corn ½ ; corn ½;
pg. 16 14x20=180; 13x35=455; 5.00/35=14; 14x35=4.90; 12x20=240/160=1 80/160;
pg. 17 126x80=1.00.80; 14x40=5.60+280=840; 44x33=1452/160=9 12/160;
pg. 18 5.00/35=14 10/35; potatoes ½ Bu.,; 2 gal. Battems ani; 5 ball thread; 10 soap; 1 f. beats tuginet; 1 box starch; 1 oil gal.; nails; last two pages figures.

(the second OLIVER notebook) Mr. [March] the 16, 1901 to (two) ft. 50; cr. to ft. 70; ct. to well 50; March the 15, 1902 give note to I. H. Hooper for two hundred fifty one dollars and ninty cents; 1903 for March the 15 one hundred and sixty one dollars and twenty five cents; 11201 (money? debt? previous number written at the bottom of the page); April the 7, 1902 give note to J. Browder twenty five hundred dollars four years of date March the twelft; October the 6 give note to Gus thats for six hundred and fifty dollars" (several pages are erased or torn out).

On March 16, 1901 K. C. Hooper and Betsey J. Hooper sold Hooper Mill to Isaac H. Hooper, their son, and John L. Hooper, Isaac's son.

This agreement made this 16th day of March in the year of Our Lord One thousand nine hundred and One; between K. C. hooper Betsey J. Hooper his wife Parties of the first Part and Isaac Hooper and John L. Hooper Parties of the Second Part all of Bradley County, Tennessee, Witnesseth that the Said Parties of the first Part, hereby Covenants and agrees that is the Parties of the Second Part Shall first make the Payment and Perform the covenants hereinafter mentioned on the Part of the Parties of the Second Part to be made and Performed the Said Parties of the first Part will convey and assure the Parties of the Second Part in fee Simple clear of all Incumberances whatever by a Good and Sufficient warranty deed the following Tract or Parcel of Land and bounded as follows towith Begining On the North line of quarter Section of Section Six Township one Range, Range one west Ocoee District, and In the 9th Civil District of Bradley County, Tennessee beginning on the north line of said quarter Section at the center of said quarter and running thence south with the fence 120 rods thence west with the fence 60 rods; thence South with the fence 8 rods; thence west with the fence 20 rods; to the line of W. L. Ledford thence North 128 rods, with Ledfords line and thence East with said line to the beginning and containing Sixty One acres more or less, and Including the building known as Hoopers Mill, it is also Stipulated and agreed that Isaac H. Hooper and John L. Hooper Parties of the Said Second Part, are to have conveyed to them by these Presents the mill known as Hoopers Mill with all the fixtures and appertinances thereunto belonging also the mill race also that part of the mill race running over a Piece of land formerly owned by Jahew Hooper and to have the right of Ingress and Egress to the Same and the right to Keep the same in repair and to maintain the Present water Power and dams, both on the Portion of said real estate above described and the said Isaac H. Hooper and John L. Hooper is also entitled to a wagon road wide Enough for all Ordinary Purposes running from the South East corner of said land to the mill dam and said K. C. Hooper and Betsey J. Hooper his wife, agree and bind them selves that if the said Parties of the second Part shall first make a Payment of twenty three hundred dollars towith on the 16th Day of March one thousand, nine hundred and six with interest at the rate of six per centum per annum on the whole sum interest payable annually as follows one hundred and thirty eight dollars on the 16th day March of each and every year beginning March 16th nineteen hundred and two for a term of five years and it is further agreed that in case of failure of the said parties of the second part to make the payments or perform any of the covenants on the part of the said party of the second part hereby made and entered into this contract shall at the option of the party of the first part be forfeited and determined. It is mutually agreed that all the covenants and agreements herein contained shall extend to and be obligatory upon the heirs executers of the respective parties. In witness whereof the respective parties to these presents have hereunto set their hands and seals this 20 day March, 1901. Witnesses: K. C. Hooper, Betsey Hooper   attest: Oscar Hooper, A. J. Hooper

STATE OF TENNESSEE, County of Bradley before me, Oscar Hooper, Deputy Clerk (name and Deputy are written in and J. I. Harrison are marked out) of the County Court in and for the County and State aforesaid, personally appeared K. C. Hooper and wife Betsey Hooper the within named bargainors with whom I am personally acquainted and who acknowledged that they executed the within instrument for the purposes therein contained. And Betsey Hooper wife of the said K. C. Hooper having appeared before me, privately and apart from her husband, the said Betsey Hooper acknowledged the execution of the said Title bond (Deed marked out) to have been done by her freely, voluntarily and understandingly, without compulsion or constraint from her husband, and for the purposes therein expressed. WITNESS my hand and official seal at office, in Cleveland, this Mar. 30th, 1901, Oscar Hooper Deputy County Court Clerk. State of Tennessee Bradley County. I certify that the foregoing instrument was received this day at 3, 20, O'clock P.M. and noted in *Note Book B* page 51 and with the accompanying certificates is duly registered in my office in *Deed Book T* pages 436-437 this Oct. 8th, 1901. T. M. Caldwell, Register Reg. Fee $1.25 paid.

(In a Microfilm Record at the Cleveland Bradley County Public Library, History Branch, a Chancery Court case filed in 1901 helped to give more information about the Hooper Mill. The case was filed by W. L. Ledford against James Perry. W. A. Stephenson testified in Microfilm Frame 1333 on July 1, 1901 that there was a Hooper School House. Evidently the Hooper Mill dam was about the same distance from the Hiwassee River as the Shelton/Young dam that was mentioned by Caleb Dobbs on page 20 of this book as being about 4 miles from the river, and in Frame 1340 W. A. Stephenson testified that the Hooper dam was about 2 ½ to 3 ½ miles from the river. On July 15, 1901 Ed Ervin in Frame 1351 testified that Mr. Hooper built a boat 25 feet by 8 feet for $25.00. John Leak in Frame 1355 testified on July 16, 1901 that the Hooper Mill Dam was a rock and log dam about 3 miles from the mouth of Candy's Creek. He also said that when the water is low you could walk across the dam and when it is high, water spills over it. Ed Ervin in Frame 1364 mentioned the Hooper Bridge.)

> TENNESSEE RIVER IMPROVEMENT. ENGINEER OFFICE, U. S. ARMY, Chattanooga, Tenn., Feb. 24, 1902 I. H. Hooper & Co., Raht, Tenn. Sir: About a month ago I sent you a letter asking you to please furnish me certain information as to the kind and quantity of freight which has been transported by you, or your agents, on the Tennessee River, or any of its navigable tributaries. I make this request because I am required by law to collect and furnish this information in my annual report to Congress. I desire to ascertain not only the amount of freight transported by steamboats on the river, but also that which was moved in flatboats or rafts. It is possible that my letter, above referred to, failed to reach you or that your reply to me has in some way miscarried. If such be the case, please let me know and I will send you at once a new set of blanks to be filled out. If the matter has simple been overlooked, please give it your earliest attention. Even if you have not transported any freight on the river, this information is valuable and necessary to me, for it will enable me to take your name from the list of shippers, or carriers. Permit me to remind you that the law of Congress relating to this matter is very stringent; it compels me to collect this information, and provides a heavy penalty for those owners, agents, masters, and clerks of vessels, who refuse to give it to me. Very respectfully, John G. D. Knight Major, Corps of Engineers

"Big Spring, Tenn. April 2, 1902 Mr. I. H. Hoopper [*sic*], Raht, Tenn. Dear Sir, I want to know what you will take for four or five hundred pounds of wheat bran so please let me know by return mail and oblige. Charles Todd" [Stock trader in Meigs County, Internet, *Ancestry.com, Meigs County 1900 Census* page 5 A in District 2].

Letter from W. W. Gavitt Medical Company, to K. C. Hoapper [*sic*], dated May 27, 1903 about GAVITT'S SYSTEM REGULATOR (several brochures and letters were found related to this company).

"$35.00 on or against the 20 day of Dec. 1905, I promest [*sic*] to pay P. W. Jenkins $35.00 thirty five dollars for value received of him this Aug. the 22, 1905" [right corner torn off] [P. W. Phillip Walden]

[on a sheet of paper] "100x12 [crossed out] x6=600 ft. 2000/3=666 2/3 100x6 2/3=975 lbs. x115=11, 21, 25 [other side of paper] 85: 60:: 200x60=12000/85=141 15/5=3 85/5=17 141 3/17x85=11985+15=12000/60+$200 85x3=255/17=15"

In a small FOX CHEMICAL CO. FERTILIZERS, LOUISVILLE, KENTUCKY notebook were records from 1902-1906 involving K. C. Hooper, I. H. Hooper and John Luther Hooper. Many of the records were related to Hooper's Mill, and some of the information was repeated in the records of the Cleveland National Bank deposit book. [See pages 174 and 175 for the records.]

p. 1 J. L. Hooper last time Sept. 10   1 day, Sep. 18   ½ day, Sept 29   ½ day, Oct. 3   ½ day, Nov. the 14   1 day, Dec. last days 4, Dec. 22   1 day, Dec. 22   2 days, Jan. the 1903 last day Jan. 12   1 day, Jan. 17   1 day

p. 2 J. L. Hooper Sept. 1 R. P. .15, Sept. 1 mg. .65, Sept. 13 feed .50, Sept. 13 meal ½ bus. .38, Sept. 23 corn ½ bus. .38, Sept. 24 feed .60, Sept. 25 Corn .38, Sept. 30 mw. .65, Sept. 30 corn .21 totaling $4.00, I. H. Hooper dew (due?) J. L. Hooper $14.00-.35=$13.65-.40=$13.25

p. 3 Oct. 3, 1902 J. L. Hooper Oct. 4 feed .30, Oct. 7 cash .41, Oct. 7 corn ½ B. .25, Oct. 13 corn 1 (bu.?) .50, Oct. 14 feed .50, Oct. 21 corn ½ B. .25, Oct. 22 feed .45, Oct. 28 feed .30, Oct. 30 corn ½ B. .25, Nov. 1, 1092 [sic] feed. 50, mg. .65, corn ½ Bus. .25, corn ½ Bus. .25, corn ½ Bus. .25, corn ½ Bus. .25, corn ½ Bus. .25

p. 4 1745 written at the top of the page, feed .30, corn ½ B. .25, corn ½ B. .25, feed .35, meal 1 B. .55, corn ½ B. .25, corn ½ B. .25 ("Set" is written across the preceding entries probably meaning "settled".) Dec. 1, 1902 mq. .65, feed .30, corn ½ B. .25, corn ½ B. .25, corn ½ B. .25, feed ½ B. .30, Dec. 9 meal ½ B. .25, Dec. 11 corn ½ B. .25, Dec. 12 feed ½ B. .30, Dec. 13 corn ½ B. .25, Dec. 16 corn ½ B. .25

p. 5 Dec. 1902 written at the top of the page, Dec. 24 mq .65, totaling $3.95, I. H. H. dew J. L. Hooper on settlement Jan. the 1, 1903 Jan. the 1, 1903 $13.79, I. Hooper dew J. L. Hooper on settlement $8.00, last time Mar. 11   1 day, Mar. 12   1 day, Mar. 24   1 day

p. 6 J: L: Hooper Jan. 10, 1903 meal ½ B. .25, Jan. 14 mq .65, Jan. 26 medicine 1.00, Jan. 29 R. Phy. .45 totaling $2.35, Feb. 1903 Feb. 2 sugar .50, Feb. 12 mq .65, Feb. 14 meal .55, Feb. 23 mq 1.25 totaling $2.95, Mar. 16 meal 1 Bus. .60, Mar. 14 medicine 1.00, Mar. 20 express 3.65

p. 7 Mar. 21 mq .65 totaling $4.90, April 1903, April 8 mq .65, April 11 express $5.50, April 13 matches .05, April 15 mq 1.30, April 16 meal .30, April 28 mq .65 totaling $8.45, May 1903 May 14 mq $2.60, May 18 meal .65, May 19 mq .65 totaling $3.90

p. 8 June J. L. Hooper June 5 meal ¼ B. .17, June 6 cash 1.00, June 6 feed .12, June 11 mq .65, June 15 meal ¼ B. .14, June 19 cash .25, June 23 cash .15, June 25 flour .25, June 29 meal ¼ B. .17 totaling $3.93, July 7 J. L. Hooper, July 8 mq .60, July 9 cash .60, July 9 bran .30, July 9 meal .19, July 13 meal .37

p. 9 July 13 (cont.) flour mq $1.95, July 24 cash 1.15, July 25 cash .50, July 25 meal .75, July 29 meal .38, July 31 cash .50 totaling $7.29, Aug. J. L. Hooper Aug. 3 mq .65, Aug. 4 mq Lee 1.25, Aug. 10 mq .65, Aug. 10 meal .38, Aug. 10 mg S. 1.25, Aug. 10 meal Lee 1.50, Aug. 12 meal .38, Aug. 13 mq Lee 1.25

p. 10 Aug. 14 J. L. Hooper Aug. 14 cash 1.00, Aug. 14 meal 1 B. by Lee .75, Aug. 17 mq Lee 1.25, Aug. 21 cash 2.50, Aug. 26 mq .65, Aug. 26 meal .38, J. L. Hooper Sept. 25 mq .65, meal ½ B. .38, cash $3.75, balance 98, totaling 5.70, Oct. 31, 1903 mq .70, meal ½ B. .28

p. 11 cash $1.55+98=$2.53, flour to Lee mq 1.40 totaling $3.93

p. 12 3004-1392=16.12

p. 13 Mar. 28, 1906 Shelton corn 1460 lbs.+1662+1612=4734, 3000-1350=16.50, 3008-1350=1658

p. 14 [nothing written]

p. 15 April 14, 1906 at 53 ct, 1330+3032 (I. H. & K. C. 1702), +1324+3064 (I. H. & K. C. 1740) +3002+1310 (I. H. & K. C. 1692)=16.92

p. 16 I. H. & K. C. at 57 ½ ct, Apr. 26, 1906 Sam W. Shelton corn 200 lbs, 200, 200, 200, 200, 200, 200, 280 totaling 16.80 lbs

p. 17 April 28, 1906 at 57 ½ ct I. H. & K. C. Hooper bought corn from Shelton 274, 200, 200, 200, 200, 200, 200, 173 totaling 16.47 lbs

p. 18 I. H. & K. C. at 57 ½ April 26, 1906 corn from Shelton 200, 200, 200, 200, 200, 200, 200, 200, 85 totaling 16.85

p. 19 I. H. & K. C. May the 1, 1906 Dr (deposit receipt) 200, 200, 200, 200, 200, 200, 200, 200, 200, 200, 200, 200, 200, 200, 200, 200, 88 totaling 3.288

p. 20 I. H. & K. C. Aperi (April?) 1, 1906 200, 200, 200, 200, 200, 200, 200, 200, 200, 200, 200, 200, 200, 200, 200, 200, 96 totaling 3.496

p. 21 I. H. & K. C. May 4, 1906 Shelton corn 2962 lbs

p. 22 1908 February 19 amt. barter sold, toll Feb. 19 $7.85 c, Feb. 20 .60 ct, Feb. 25 $1.20, March 3 $3.25, March 8 $1.95, March 13 $3.75, March 27 $7.25

p. 23 845 [written at the top of the page]

p. 24 Sam Hooper 240 ft +144+69+144=597 ft +216+8.13+120=I. H. K. C. 6.93 ft

p. 25 Bates

p. 26 [nothing written]

p. 27 I. H. K. C. Bates lumber 50 ft 2x3-12, 28 ft 2x4-12

p. 28 Shaden 3 feed, 3 bran, 1 meal

p. 29 order for Thursday Allen 2 bag meal, Duff 2 bag meal, 3 bran, Rager 5 meal, Harel 3 meal, Rains 2 meal, Talar 2 meal, Rains 2 meal, Talar 2 meal, Flour 100 lbs, Kile 2 meal, Rary 3 meal, Hains 2 meal, 5 feed E. J. Slaw

p. 30 [blank]

p. 31 [blank]

p. 32 3+2+8   20, 2+1 ½ +12   18

p. 33 Darey 2 Du. 6x6, 2x9, Ser wire 19 ft

p. 34 [blank]

p. 35 [blank]

p. 36 May 23, 1906 I. H. Hooper dr. to mill for flour for Dugan 50 lbs, for Shiflett 125 lbs, meal I. H. H. 1 Bu., flour Dugan 100 lbs, flour for Bedwell 5 lbs, mal 2 bus, meal A. J. H. 1 Bu. meal, A. J. H. 1 Bu. meal, A. J. H. 1 Bu.

p. 37 Hains 5 B. meal, Rager 3 B. me, Shaden 1 B., Kile 2 bran, Shaden 5 bran, 5 feed

p. 38 I. H. Hooper pade [sic] the mill corn from Bales 2 ½ B., Newman 96 lbs

p. 39 I. H. Hooper due J. L. Hooper on Sept. work $13.80, I. H. Hooper dew the mill corn 2 B., meal 1 B., meal 1 ½ B., meal 2, corn 1 B., meal 1 B., bran 50 lbs, mq 100 lbs, meal 1 B. meal 2 B. Andy, corn 1 B. Andy, meal 1 B. I. H.

p. 40 I. H. Hooper due J. L. Hooper on work June 1 $24.55-meal 1.46=$23.09-fruit jars 16 .75=22.34-cash 9.00=$13.34, July cash 2.04=$11.30

p. 41 Dew [sic] J. L. Hooper for work in June $14.07+July 11.30=25.37, cash 15.00=10.37-Aug.15 cash 8.56=$1.81, Aug. 26, 1903 J. L. Hooper due I. H. Hooper on settlement $1.67 ct bbl .75 leaving .92 ct

p. 42 I. Hooper due J. L. Hooper on Beb work 4 April $15.80-cash 1.00=14.80-seeds .10=14.70-April 19 cash 5.05=$9.65-April 23 cash .25 leaving 9.30

p. 43 Mar. work $12.35+9.30=21.65-10.00=$11.65-1.50=10.15+Apr. 9.55=19.70-May 4 cash 2.00=17.70-May 2- cash 5.55=$12.15-May 25 cash 3.00=9.15+May 15.40=$24.55

p. 44 [blank]

p. 45 [blank]

p. 46 paid J. L. Hooper last time April 1th 1 day, April 25   2 day, May 4th 1 day, June 2   1 day, June 16   1 day, Aug. 15 ½ day, Aug. 22   1 day

p. 47 J. L. Hooper work in Jan. $19.50-taken up 2.35=$17.15, cash 4.45=12.70-cash 5.00=$7.70 Feb. $15.80- cash .85=14.95, Mar. dew J. L. Hooper $12.35

p. 48 due J. L. Hooper Nove. the 39 [sic], 1902 on settlement 10 $13.14-salt .80=12.34-oil .20=$12.14-30   .30=$11.84-500   5.40=6.24-Dec. 24 .75 =$5.69-.50=$4.19-1.70=$3.49, 224/12=19 8/12 inside the back cover is written W. F. Barrett Agt.

"Mch .[March?] 5, 1906 Received from James Hooper two&50/100 dollars in full $2.50 R. Graham, Trustee for Wd. Petty"

"Bradley County, Tennessee No. 616 Cleveland, Tenn., Mar. 23, 1907 RECEIVED OF George Geren the sum of ONE DOLLAR AND FIFTY CENTS, in full for POLL TAX for the YEAR 1906, in District No. 9 of Bradley County, Tennessee J. A. Johnston Trustee P. E. Trewhitt, Deputy"

"Charleston T. 1906 Hooper, I. H. to Cumberland Telephone & Telegraph Co., Dr. INCORPORATED Toll Messages for Apr. 1906   25 cents Date 17 TO WHAT PLACE Chatta BY WHOM Hooper .25"

"Empty envelope from THE CONTINENTAL FIRE INSURANCE CO. Contract of K. C. Hooper   Mr. I. H. Hooper Charleston, Tenn. R#2, dated Oct. 8, 1906"

The following records were found in the Cleveland National Bank book in account with I. H. and K. C. Hooper for a part of 1906-1907. On the left side deposits received were listed and on the right credits, overdrafts and vouchers:

> **Apr. 20, 1906** deposit 131.85, **Apr. 25** deposit 56.20, **Apr. 27** deposit 71.70, **Apr. 30** deposit 28.30, **May 4** deposit 34.68, **May 9** deposit 326.00, **May 11** deposit 33.50, **May 16** deposit 49.70, **May 18** deposit 49.00, **May 22** deposit 118.76, **May 28** deposit 120.15, **June 1** deposit 93.10, **June 4** deposit 30.00, **June 11** deposit 64.50, **June 16** deposit 86.55, **June 19** deposit 91.10, **June 20** overdraft 37.69, **Total Deposits** 1471.45 **June 20** by Balance 00.00, Amount to Deposit 31.85, **June 23** deposit 37.12, **June 27** deposit 35.55, **Jul. 2** deposit 65.40, **Jul. 9** deposit 135.35, **Jul. 11** deposit 30.00, **Jul. 13** deposit 60.90, **Jul. 18** deposit 44.41, **Jul. 25** deposit 40.84, **Jul. 27** deposit 97.40, **Amount Forewarded** from the first page 578.92, **Jul. 30** deposit 33.50, **Aug. 1** deposit 26.00, **Aug. 3** deposit 27.50, **Aug. 8** deposit 54.76, **Aug. 13** deposit 135.37, **Aug. 15** deposit 40.30, **Aug. 17** deposit 38.30, **Aug. 20** deposit 31.00, **Aug. 22** deposit 48.86, **Aug. 24** deposit 60.00, **Sept. 5** deposit 26.50, **Sept. 7** deposit 310.00, **Sept. 12** deposit 132.35, **Sept. 19** deposit 16.45, **Sept. 26** deposit 35.35, **Oct. 1** deposit 20.00, **Oct. 9** deposit 60.00, **Oct. 15** deposit 72.00, **Oct. 19** deposit 44.20, **Oct. 25** deposit 34.40, **Nov. 8** deposit 18.00, **Nov. 12** deposit 59.30, **Nov. 15** deposit 40.00, **Nov. 20** deposit 37.30, **Nov. 26** deposit 34.00, **Nov. 30** deposit 28.45, **Dec. 3** deposit 33.00, **Dec. 3** overdraft 140.30, **Total Deposits** 2216.01, **Amt. Forewarded** 37.69. 12/3/06 Cks listed 2178.32. **Dec. 3** deposit 29.62, **Dec. 3** deposit 25.00, **Dec. 5** deposit 91.00, **Dec. 11** deposit 44.03, **Dec. 15** deposit 20.29, **Dec. 18** deposit 30.30, **Dec. 20** deposit 20.00, **Dec. 31** deposit 34.20, **Jan. 3** deposit 25.00, **Jan. 9** deposit 40.00, **Jan 16** deposit 30.56, **Jan. 18** deposit 31.95, **Jan. 21** deposit 45.00, **Jan. 24** deposit 40.00, **Jan. 28** deposit 35.63, **Jan. 30** deposit 34.00, **Feb. 9** deposit 31.49, **Feb. 12** deposit 27.00, **Feb. 14** deposit 53.50, **Feb. 16** deposit 25.00, **Feb. 19** deposit 38.00, **Feb. 21** deposit 183.94, **Feb. 23** deposit 44.84, **Feb. 26** deposit 35.00, **Feb. 28** deposit 50.00, **Mar. 11** deposit 49.35, **Mar. 15** deposit 67.40, **Mar. 21** deposit 52.83, **Total Deposits** 1266.93, **12/03/06** by overdraft 140.30, **Mar. 22, 1907** CKs Listed 847.90, **Mar. 22** balance 278.73. **Mar. 26** deposit 42.10, **Mar. 28** deposit 25.00, **Apr. 4** deposit 53.77, **Apr. 6** deposit 70.76, **Apr. 9** deposit 35.00, **Apr. 11** deposit 45.00, **Apr. 18** deposit 50.70, **Apr. 20** deposit 32.80, **Apr. 23** deposit 44.93, **Apr. 25** deposit 43.85, **Apr. 30** deposit 34.05, **Total** 755.69. **May 17** balance 14.30, **June 6** deposit 72.20, **June 28** deposit 66.35, **May 17, 1907** Cke 741.39, **May 17** balance 14.30.

[The incorporation record was not found in the Hooper Box of materials that Richard (Rick) Hooper found, but it was included here because it pertained to the Hooper Mill information. On March 8, 1907 the Hooper Milling Company was incorporated. This record was found on pages 310-313 of the *Trust Book*:]

> State of Tennessee, Charter of Incorporation. Be it known, that J. L. Hooper, I. H. Hooper, T. L. Rogers, W. P. Sykes and Chas. S. Mayfield are hereby constituted a body politic and corporate by the name and style of the Hooper Milling Company for the purpose of manufacturing and selling flour, meal, bran, and other feed and food stuffs; and for the purpose of buying, selling and dealing in the same, and buying, selling, storing and dealing in wheat, corn and other grains. The Capital Stock of said company is to be the sum of fifteen thousand dollars, $15,000.00, consisting of one hundred and fifty (150) shares each of the par value of one hundred dollars ($100.00).

> And it shall have and may exercise all powers conferred by the laws of Tennessee upon mining and manufacturing corporations....

This corporation was also recorded in the *Bradley County Court Clerk Book B* on page 124. It was also recorded by Jno. W. Morton, Secretary of State, in *Corporation Record J8* on page 107 on April 1, 1907.

"No. 2439 BRADLEY COUNTY [torn page] PR2 1907 Received of I. H. Hooper Seventy one & 50/100 Dollars in full payment of State, County, School, Bond, Road, Bridge, Judgment and Poll Taxes for the year 1906 on the following property: DIST. 9 ASSESSED TO Hooper ACRES 61 VALUATION REAL 4000 POLL 1.50 DIST 9 Hooper ACRES 80 VALUATION REAL 100 TAX 71.20 penalty .30 total 71.50 J. A. Johnston, Trustee"

The following checks were drawn on the Cleveland National Bank unless otherwise stated: " **2/16, 1907** Pay to the order of G. W. Eads $12.55 for Wheat I. H. & K. C. Hooper (signed on the back G. W. Eads); **3/11, 1907** Pay to the order of J. E. Mayfield $39.25 I. H. & K. C. Hooper (signed on the back J. E. Mayfield and P. B. Mayfield); **Mar. 22, 1907** canceled vouchers tape corresponding to the bank book **totaling** 847.90."

Southern Railway Company Law Department, April 20, 1907. For a good and valuable consideration the contract heretofore made between me and I. H. Hooper, under which I was to be the owner of a one-half interest in the Hooper Mill (reference being here made to the deed of I. H. Hooper for a full description of the property) is hereby rescinded, and I have no right or interest in said property, after this date –This April 20, 1907-.

[The following accounts were in the back of the Cleveland National Bank records of deposits. The **May 17, 1907** deposit ended those records, so the Hooper Milling Company decided to use the empty pages at the back of the book for their records. Below are deposits, and below that are the related checks.]
May the 18, 1907, check out of bank **May 18** T. B. Powell $654.21, **May 18** J. K. Powell $364.50, **May 22** Holt Ledford $70.04, **May 22** W. L. Ledford $202.83, **May 29** S. W. Shelton $67.18, **May 31** The Wolf Co. $12.00, **Totaling** $1370.76. **June 6** W. D. Williamson $58.60, **June 6** J. L. Hooper $25.00, **June 8** A. B. Wise $3.00, **June 11** G. W. Eads $117.89, **June 11** W. Hooper $63.74, **June 20** C. L. Hooper $42.39, **June 27** J. L. Hooper $2.79, **June 27** John W. Mortan $5.00, Total $594.62. **July 5** The Wolf Co. $15.46, **July 13** Sam Graham $8.73, **July 17** Hiwassee Bank $250.00, **July 24** Sam W. Shelton $67.00, **July 25** Sam Graham $10.00, **July 31** Hiwassee Bank $6.22, **Totaling** $372.81, **Check Amt.** 2,338.19+1001.00+318.22=3667.41 Deb. $61.73. **Aug. 5** E. G. Godsey $61.73, **Aug. 5** J. D. Powell $43.80, **Aug. 6** W. P. Lang, cashier $100.00, **Aug. 8** Holt Ledford $12.30, **Aug. 9** K. C. Hooper $62.00, **Aug. 9** C. L. Hooper $57.85, **Aug. 10** Griffin Cofer $15.58, **Aug. 12** Griffin Cofer $11.39, **Aug. 13** W. D. Williamson $60.54, **Aug. 14** John T. Jewell $55.00, **Aug. 15** J. E. Carlton $25.00, **Aug. 15** J. E. Carlton $16.15, (**Aug. 16, 1907** voucher tape for 2590.55), **Aug. 17** Alley Shiflett $205.48, **Aug. 17** C. L. Hooper $7.28, **Aug. 22** E. G. Godsey $11.08, **Aug. 23** Hooper & Eads $178.68, **Aug. 31** W. P. Lang cashier $69.61, **Totaling** 1,001.00. **Sept. 2** C. L. Hooper $50.00, **Sept. 4** A. B. Wise $12.00, **Sept 4** Tom Tompson $7.61, **Sept. 4** T. L. Cartright $55.00, **Sept. 23** J. C. Williamson $35.11, **Sept. 25** The Wolf Co. $105.00, **Sept. 30** J. L. Hooper $100.00, **Sept 30** T. L. Gibson $8.50, **Totaling** 373.22. **Oct. 5** John Jewell $31.74, **Oct. the 23, 1907** Hooper Milling Co. on Dep. $44.93.

[The following were Hooper Milling Company canceled checks which related to the deposits above.]
May 18th, 1907 **No. 1.** Pay to the order of T. B. Powell $654.21 for corn Hooper Milling Co. by
    J. L. Hooper, Pres. [signed on the back T. B. Powell];
May 18, 1907 **No. 2.** Pay to the order of J. K. Powell $364.50 for corn Hooper Milling Co. by J. L.
    Hooper, Pres. [signed on the back J. K. Powell];
May 22nd, 1907 **No. 3.** Pay to the order of Holt Ledford $70.04 for corn Hooper Milling Co., by
    J. L. Hooper, Pres. [signed on the back Holt Ledford and A. J. Gass & Co.];
May 22nd, 1907 **No. 4.** Pay to the order of W. L. Ledford $202.83 for corn Hooper Milling Co., by
    J. L. Hooper, Pres. [signed on the back W. L. Ledford and Holt Ledford];
May 29th, 1907 **No. 5.** Pay to the order of S. W. Shelton $67.18 for corn Hooper Milling, Co. by
    J. L. Hooper, Pres. [signed on the back Sam W. Shelton];
May the 31, 1907 **No. 6.** Pay to the order of The Wolf Co. $12.00 for bags Hooper Milling Co.
    I. H. Hooper, Sec. [stamped on the back Walter K. Sharpe Receiver of the Wolf Company];
June the 6, 1907 **No. 7.** W. D. Williamson $58.60 for wheat Hooper Milling Co. I. H. Hooper, Sec.
    [signed on the back W. D. Williamson and W. L. Hambright];
June 6, 1907 **No. 8.** Pay to the order of J. L. Hooper $25.00 Hooper Milling Co. I. H. Hooper, Sec.
    [signed on the back J. L. Hooper and Geo. I. McCarty];
June the 8, 1907 **No. 9.** Pay to the order of A. B. Wise $3.00 Hooper Milling Co. I. H. Hooper,
    Sec. [signed on the back A. B. Wise and Maclister & Ramsy];
June the 11, 1907 **No. 10.** Pay to the order of G. W. Eads $117.89 for wheat Hooper Milling Co.
    I. H. Hooper, Sec. [signed on the back G. W. Eads and W. H. Hooper];
June the 11, 1907 **No. 11.** Pay to the order of W. H. Hooper $63.74 for wheat Hooper Milling Co.

I. H. Hooper, Sec. [signed on the back W. H. Hooper];
June the 20 **No. 12.** Pay to the order of C. L. Hooper $42.39 for wheat Hooper Milling Co. I. H.
Hooper, Sec. [signed on the back C. L. Hooper and J. W. Hooper];
June the 27, 1907 **No. 13.** Pay to the order of J. L. Hooper $279.00 Hooper Milling Co. I. H.
Hooper, Sec. [signed on the back J. L. Hooper].

In the records the following figures were found on Hooper Milling Co. letterhead which reads "J. L.
Hooper, President   J. W. Hooper, Sec. & Treas.   I. H. Hooper, Asst. Sec. & Treas. HOOPER MILLING
CO., Manufacturers of High Grade Flour, Water Ground Meal, Bran and Crushed Feed. R. F. D. No. 2
Phone 42, 1 long, 1 short Charleston, Tenn., 1907". [3 columns of figures below were on next page.]

15.16	5.00	250.00
17.25	1.65	65.00
298.08	17.63	44.45
12.27	6.50	21.71
160.00	5.00	27.50
11.43	139.00	66.66
126.40	9.92	33.00
15.00	7.54	29.50
25.21	14.53	7.67
24.50	50.00	23.00
4.00	8.80	17.61
1209.30	266.57	636.10

[Written on the same page 2,298.07 was a word like Texas
on the back of the same sheet.]

34.20		
9.60		
6.35		
8.42	471.17	
47.87	336.10	
36.85	266.57	
149.00	1209.30	
37.92	2283.14	
13.87		
8.70		2798.07
9.86		2283.14
48.67	Balance [*sic*]	$514.93
40.06		
19.80		
$471.17		

[After this, I. H. listed himself as President, and Luther was not mentioned except for his name on a few
checks. Possibly, Luther began to trade in the Futures Market after this, but he was still connected to the
mill because Albert talked about working with Luther at the Mill and driving the truck that Luther bought
and used at the Mill. Luther was a miller in the *1910 Bradley County Census for District 2* on page 3 B.]

June the 29, 1907 **No. 14.** Pay to the order of John W. Morton $5.00 for tax Hooper Milling Co.
I. H. Hooper Pres. [signed on the back Jno. W. Morton, Secty. (Secretary) State];
July the 5, 1907 **No. 15.** Pay to the order of The Wolf Co. $15.46 for clothes Hooper Milling Co.
I. H. Hooper, Pres. [stamped on the back Walter K. Sharpe Receiver of the Wolf Co.];
July the 13, 1907 **No. 16.** Pay to the order of Sam Graham $8.73 for wheat Hooper Milling Co.
I. H. Hooper, Pres. [signed on the back Sam Graham and J. M. Cofer];
July the 17, 1907 **No. 17.** Pay to the order of the Hiwassee Bank $250.00 Hooper Milling Co. I. H.
Hooper, Pres. [stamped on the back the Hiwassee Bank, Charleston, Tenn. J. E. Quisenberry,
Cashier];
July the 24, 1907 **No. 18.** Pay to the order of Sam W. Shelton $67.00 for corn Hooper Milling Co.
I. H. Hooper, Pres. [signed Sam W. Shelton];
July the 25, 1907 **No. 19.** Pay to the order of Sam Graham $12.40 for wheat Hooper Milling Co.

I. H. Hooper, Pres. [signed Sam Graham and J. M. Cofer];

July 29, 1907 **No. 20.** Pay to the order of O. B. Wise $3.00 Hooper Milling Co. I. H. Hooper, Pres. [signed O. B. Wise and MaClinty & Ramsey];

July the 31, 1907 **No. 21.** Pay to the order of E. S. Godsey $10.00 for wheat Hooper Milling Co. I. H. Hooper, Pres. [signed E. S. Godsey and Sam W. Shelton];

July 31, 1907 **No. 22.** Pay to the order of the Hiwassee Bank $6.22 for Morgan & Hamilton Hooper Milling Co. I. H. Hooper, Pres. [stamped by The Hiwassee Bank, J. E. Quisenberry, Cashier];

Aug. the 2, 1907 **No. 23.** Pay to the order of J. A. Maddux $9.53 for wheat Hooper Milling Co. I. H. Hooper, Pres. [signed J. A. Maddux and G. W. Marshall & Co.];

Aug. 5, 1907 **No. 24.** Pay to the order of E. S. Godsy [sic] $60.73 for wheat Hooper Milling Co. by J. W. Hooper, Sec. [signed E. S. Godsey];

Aug. the 5, 1907 **No. 25.** Pay to the order of J. D. Powell $43.80 for wheat Hooper Milling Co. I. H. Hooper, Pres. [signed J. D. Powell];

Aug. the 6, 1907 **No. 26.** Pay to W. P. Lang Cashier or order $100.00 for credit on note Hooper Milling Co. I. H. Hooper, Pres. ["paid" on back];

Aug. the 8, 1907 **No. 27.** Pay to the order of Holt Ledford $12.30 for corn Hooper Milling Co. I. H. Hooper, Pres. [signed Holt Ledford];

Aug. the 9, 1907 **No. 28.** Pay to the order of K. C. Hooper $62.00 for wheat Hooper Milling Co. I. H. Hooper, Pres. [signed K. C. Hooper];

Aug. 9, 1907 **No. 29.** Pay to the order of C. F. Hooper $57.85 Hooper   Milling Co. by J. W. Hooper, Sec. [signed C. F. Hooper];

Aug. the 10, 1907 **No. 30.** Pay to the order of Griffin Cofer $15.58 for wheat Hooper Milling Co. I. H. Hooper, Pres. [signed Griffin Cofer];

Aug. the 13, 1907 **No. 31.** Pay to the order of Griffin Cofer $11.39 for wheat Hooper Milling Co. I. H. Hooper, Pres. [signed Griffin Cofer and J. M. Cofer];

Aug. the 13, 1907 **No. 32.** Pay to the order of W. D. Williamson $60.54 for corn Hooper Milling Co. I. H. Hooper, Pres. [signed W. D. Williamson, C. C. Gibson, H. C. Melton and R. A. Palmer];

Aug. 14, 1907 **No.** – Pay to John T. Jewell or order $55.00 for – Hooper Milling Co. by J. W. Hooper, Sec. [signed John T. Jewell];

Aug. the 15, 1907 **No. 34.** Pay to the order of J. E. Carlton $25.00 for wheat Hooper Milling Co. I. H. Hooper, Pres. [signed J. E. Carlton and J. M. & W. L. Hambright];

Aug. the 15, 1907 **No. 35.** Pay to the order of J. E. Carlton $16.15 for wheat Hooper Milling Co. I. H. Hooper, Pres [signed J. E. Carlton, W. H. Hooper and Sam W. Shelton];

Aug. the 17, 1907 **No. 36.** Pay to the order of Alley Shiflett $205.48 for corn Hooper Milling Co. I. H. Hooper, Pres. [signed Alley Shiflett, W. H. Hooper, and K. C. Hooper];

Aug. the 17, 1907 **No. 37.** Pay to the order of C. F. Hooper $7.28 for balance on Morgan Timber Hooper Milling Co. I. H. Hooper, Pres. [signed C. F. Hooper];

Aug. the 22, 1907 **No. 38.** Pay to the order of E. S. Godsey $11.08 for corn Hooper Milling Co. I. H. Hooper, Pres. [signed E. S. Godsey and J. H. Epperson & Wm.];

Aug. the 23, 1907 **No. 39.** Pay to the order of Hooper & Eads $176.68 for corn Hooper Milling Co. I. H. Hooper, Pres. [signed Hooper & Eads];

Aug. the 31, 1907 **No. 40.** Pay to the order of W. P. Lang cashier $69.61 for Morgan & Hamilton draft Hooper Milling Co. I. H. Hooper, Pres. [signed "paid"];

Sep. the 2, 1907 **No. 41.** Pay to the order of C. F. Hooper $50.00 Hooper Milling Co. I. H. Hooper, Pres. [signed C. F. Hooper]);

Sept. the 4, 1907 **No. 42.** Pay to the order of O. B. Wise $12.00 Hooper Milling Co. I. H. Hooper, Pres. [signed O. B. Wise and Maclister & Ramsy];

Sept. the 4, 1907 **No. 43.** Pay to the order of Tom Tompson $7.61 for wheat Hooper Milling Co. I. H. Hooper, Pres. [signed Tom X (mark) Tompson   witness C. F. Hooper];

Sept. 23, 1907 **No. 45.** Pay to the order of J. C. Williamson $35.11 for corn Hooper Milling Co. I. H. Hooper, Pres. [signed Sam W. Shelton and J. C. Williamson];

Sept. 25, 1907 **No. 46.** Pay to the order of The Wolf Co. $105.00 for Seauser Hooper Milling Co. I. H. Hooper, Pres. [stamped Walter Sharpe Receiver for The Wolf Co.];

Sept. the 30, 1907 **No. 47.** Pay to the order of J. L. Hooper $100.00 for wheat Hooper Milling Co.

I. H. Hooper, Pres. [signed J. L. Hooper];
Sept. the 30, 1907 **No. 48.** Pay to the order of T. F. Gibson $8.50 for corn Hooper Milling Co.
I. H. Hooper, Pres. [signed T. F. Gibson, C. C. Gibson and J. H. Epperson & Rn.]

"No. 1913 BRADLEY COUNTY, TENN., MAR. 3, 1908 Received of I. H. Hooper Six & 76/100 Dollars in full payment of State 35c, County 30c, School 40c, Bond 40c, Road 12c, Bridge 3c, Judgment 10c, and Poll $2.00, Taxes for the year 1907, on the following property: DIST. 2 ASSESSED TO Hooper ACRES 80 VALUATION REAL 100 PERS. 180 TOTAL TAX 6.76 J. A. Johnston, Trustee"

"BUREAU OF INFORMATION 109 S. Cherry St. Galesburg, Illinois 2/8/09. I. H. Hooper, Cleveland, Tenn. [On the envelope, Cleveland was marked out and Charleston substituted.] Will you kindly give your opinion of the financial standing, character, integrity and habits of Delia Baker & father S. I. Baker of Charleston, Tenn. R#2-Box#1. We will treat this information with STRICT CONFIDENCE and trust you will treat this inquiry the same. Respectfully, FRED H. CARTAN Mgr. Bureau of Information"

At various times, land was used as collateral in order to borrow money. The following note was signed by I. H. and Ella Hooper to raise $1200.00 on March 9, 1909 (the Hooper Mill burned in May and this loan was not fully paid until 1915):

> For the purpose of securing and making certain the payment of a certain note for the sum of twelve hundred dollars executed at even date herewith by I. H. Hooper, payable to the order of the Cleveland Bank & Trust Co., due one year after date, providing for the payment by the maker of reasonable attorney fees and costs of collection in case said note is not paid at maturity, and suit for its collection is instituted and for the purpose of securing and making certain the payment of any note or notes given and accepted in renewal of the said indebtedness, we, the said I. H. Hooper and wife E. C. Hooper have this day bargained and sold and do hereby bargain and sell, transfer and convey unto J. E. Mayfield, Trustee and his successors and assigns forever the following described real estate, to wit:-

> Beginning on the north line of a quarter section of section six township one, range one, west, Ocoee District and in the 9th Civil District of Bradley County, Tennessee and beginning on the North line of said quarter section at the center of said quarter and running thence south with the fence 120 rods; thence west with the fence 60 rods thence south with the fence eight rods thence west with the fence 20 rods to the Ledford line, thence north 128 rods with the Ledford line thence east with said line to the beginning, containing sixty one acres more or less, and being the real estate conveyed to I. H. Hooper by M. L. Ross, Adm., of K. C. Hooper, decd., and later a one-half interest was conveyed by I. H. Hooper to K. C. Hooper their half interest in said real estate; but there is excepted and reserved from the above description two acres more or less which contained the mill & c. and which has been conveyed by I. H. & K. C. Hooper to the Hooper Milling Co.

The deed just mentioned was registered in the Register's Office of Bradley County, Tennessee (below).

> To have and to hold the same unto the said J. E. Mayfield, Trustee and his successors and assigns forever.

> We covenant that we are lawfully seized of the said real estate; that is free and unencumbered and that we have a good right to convey it; and we will forever warrant and defend the title to the same against the lawful claims of all persons whomsoever.

> Now if we shall pay said note for $1200 or renewal thereof at or before maturity then this conveyance is to be null void and of no effect. But in case we shall fail to do so, then said Trustee is hereby authorized and empowered after giving thirty days notice in writing on the Court House Door in Cleveland, Tenn., of the time, terms and place of sale to expose said real estate to public sale at said Court House Door and sell the same in bar of the equity of redemption homestead and

dower, each and all of which rights we expressly waive and renounce and make a deed to the purchaser.

After paying the costs, fees and expenses incurred in the execution of said trust said trustee will first apply the proceeds of sale to the payment of said note for $1200 or renewal and the balance if any pay to us. We expressly waive the oath and bond of the trustee and agree that we will keep all buildings on said premises insured against loss by fire in some reliable insurance Company in an amount not less than $500.00, and to have the loss if any made payable to the holder of said note for $1200.

In case of foreclosure it is expressly agreed that the occupant of the premises will become the tenant at will of the purchaser.

Witness our hands on this the 29th day of March, 1909. (signed) I. H. Hooper and E. C. Hooper

State of Tennessee Bradley County Before me P. B. Mayfield, a Notary Public in and for the County and State aforesaid, personally came I. H. Hooper and wife E. C. Hooper the within named bargainors, with whom I am personally acquainted, and who acknowledged that they executed the within instrument freely, voluntarily and understandingly, without compulsion or constraint from her said husband, and for the purposes therein expressed. Witness my hand and notarial seal, duly affixed at office in Cleveland, Bradley County, Tennessee, this the 29th day of March 1909. [signed] P. B. Mayfield Notary Public

Filed this day at 2:20 P.M. and noted in *Note Book B* Page 155-this March 30th 1909. E. M. Morrison Register   Reg. Fee $1.50 Paid

Cleveland Bank and Trust Co. $1200.00 March 29th 1909 One year days after date we jointly and severally promise to pay to the order of the CLEVELAND BANK AND TRUST COMPANY Twelve hundred & 00 DOLLARS at the CLEVELAND BANK AND TRUST CO., Cleveland, Tennessee, for value received. In case we fail to pay this note at maturity and suit shall be instituted for collection, we agree to pay reasonable Attorney's fee or Commission charges for collecting. Secured by deed of trust of even date. I. H. Hooper paid 1915 (handwritten date Mch. 29/1913) (on back) #659 int. paid to Mch 29th, 1911, Mch. 29, 1910, Interest paid to Mar. 29, 1912—This Apr. 17, 1911, Int. Paid to Mch. 29th, 1913—This Apr. 17, 1911, Int. paid to Mch. 29th, 1913, This April 6th, 1912, Interest paid to March 29, 1914 This 4-5-13, Int. paid to Mch. 29th, 1915 this 4-18 1914.

[The next set of checks began March 1909 with No. 1 and were not signed Hooper Milling Co.]
>Mar. the 3, 1909 **No. 1.** Pay to the order of Sam W. Shelton $616.70 I. H. Hooper [signed Sam W. Shelton]
>Mar. 3, 1909 **No. 2.** Pay to the order of Louis Geren $279.37 for corn I. H. Hooper [signed Louis Geren];
>April 23, 1909 **No. 3.** Pay to A. W. Henry $125.00 I. H. Hooper (signed A. W. Henry); [checks 4 and 5 are missing]
>May 1, 1909 **No. 6.** Pay to K. C. Hooper $75.00 I. H. Hooper [signed K. C. Hooper]

Barbara Fagan, Director of the History Branch and Archives at the Cleveland Public Library, discovered the following article published June 4, 1909 in the *Journal and Banner* on page 1 in Cleveland, Tennessee:

HOOPER'S MILL BURNED

Caught Fire at an Early Hour Mon-
day Morning and Was
Destroyed
[May 31, 1909 would be a Monday date.]

The Hooper Milling Company suffered a heavy loss by fire at an early hour Monday morning and was totally destroyed together with 3,000 bushels of wheat. The loss was at least $9,000 with $4,200 insurance on the mill and equipment. Only a few days before the fire, however, an application for $3,000 insurance on the wheat had been taken by an agent of an insurance company, but up to the time of the fire the policy had not been delivered. If this holds, the Mesrss. J. Hooper and son, James, will not loose *[sic]* more than $2,500, otherwise they will be damaged in excess of $5,000. It is not known how the fire originated, but is thought it started in the dust room.

[Checks continue from p. 181. The dates jump from May 1, 1909 to July 3, 1909 possibly due to the fire.]
July 3, 1909 **No. 7.** Pay to Minnie Cuningham $8.00 I. H. Hooper [signed Minnie Cuningham];
July the 10, 1909 **No. 8.** Pay to James Calhoun $6.00 I. H. Hooper [signed James Calhoun];
[check 9 is missing],
Sept. 9, 1909 **No. 10** Minie Cuningham $2.75 I. H. Hooper [signed Minnie Cuningham, C. L. Wrinkle and S. F. Reeder];
Nov. 9, 1909 **No. 11.** Pay to J. W. McCarty $25.00 I. H. Hooper [signed J. W. McCarty and Bulen & McCarty];
Nov. 12, 1909 **No. 12.** Pay to the order of A. U. Miller $10.00 I. H. Hooper [signed A. U. Miller and Sam W. Shelton];
Nov. 15, 1909 **No. 13.** Pay to A. U. Miller $20.00 I. H. Hooper [signed A. U. Miller and C. S. Gibson];
Nov. 16, 1909 **No. 14.** Pay to A. H. Everet $10.60 for sawing lumber in full of act I. H. Hooper [signed A. H. Everett and J. R. Everett];
Nov. 16, 1909 **No. 15.** Pay to J. W. McCarty $50.00 for corn I. H. Hooper [signed J. W. McCarty];
Nov. 17, 1909 **No. 16.** Pay to Ples Bedwell $10.00 for George Geren I. H. Hooper [signed Ples Bedwell and Homer Thomas];
Nov. 20, 1909 **No. 17.** Pay to W. P. Lang cashier $25.00 I. H. Hooper [signed "paid"];
Nov. 26, 1909 **No. 18.** Pay to Minie Cuningham $10.00 I. H. Hooper [signed Minnie Cuningham];
Nov. 27, 1909 **No. 19.** Pay to J. W. Crow $5.87 I. H. Hooper [signed J. W. Crow];
Dec. the 2, 1909 **No. 20.** Pay to A. J. Hooper $6.00 I. H. Hooper signed A. J. Hooper and W. H. Hooper];
Dec. 8, 1909 **No. 21.** Pay to J. C. Guinn $20.12 for corn I. H. Hooper [signed J. C. Guinn and B. L. Atchley and Son];
Dec. the 10, 1909 **No. 22.** Pay to Sam W. Shelton $5.00 I. H. Hooper [signed Sam W. Shelton];
Dec. the 11, 1909 **No. 23.** Pay to Chattanooga Feed Co. $34.75 I. H. Hooper [signed Pay to the Order of Any Bank, Banker or Trust Co.];
Dec. 14, 1909 **No. 24.** Pay to Minie Cuningham $11.00 I. H. Hooper [signed Minnie Cuningham and Sam W. Shelton];
Dec. the 14, 1909 **No. 25.** Pay to Louis Geren $60.94 I. H. Hooper [signed Louis Geren and N. C. Ziegler];
Dec. 15, 1909 **No. 26.** Pay to I. H. Hooper $10.00 I. H. Hooper [signed I. H. Hooper];
Dec. the 15, 1909 **No. 27.** Pay to Brint [Bryant] Hardware Co. $32.50 for wire I. H. Hooper [stamped Bryant Hdw. Co.];
Dec. the 15, 1909 **No. 28.** Pay to T. A. Barnes $20.00 for insurance note I. H. Hooper [signed Pay to the Continental Ins. Co. of New York R. W. Barnes];
Dec. 22, 1909 **No. 29.** Pay to Albert Hooper $10.00 I. H. Hooper [signed Albert Hooper];
Dec. 28, 1909 **No. 30.** Pay to J. W. Hooper $2.60 I. H. Hooper [signed J. W. Hooper];

The following post card was written by Phoebe to her father C. W. Buck from Pennsylvania. C. W. was a Millwright at the Wolf Company (suppliers of mill equipment) and possibly was working on Hooper's Mill after it burned May 31, 1909. The card was dated January 1910. [This card is also on p. 220.]
January 1910
Card: North Main St. Chambersburg, PA
Postmark: Chambersburg, PA

To: Mr. C. W. Buck
         Charleston, Tenn.
              Hooper Milling Co.
              R.F.D. #2
         Dear Papa, ma will write you today some time. Had company until so late last night. Baby & I
         wanted to leave at noon but it is pouring down rain all morning. Wish you could have been here
         too.
              Loviable [sic]
              Phoebe
[Hooper Mill checks continue.]
         Jan. 1, 1910 **No. 31.** Pay to A. H. Gilbreath $2.77 I. H. Hooper [signed A. H. Gilbreath and Sam
              W. Shelton];
         Jan. 3, 1910 **No. 32.** Pay to I. H. Hooper $5.00 I. H. Hooper [signed I. H. Hooper];
         Jan. 3, 1910 **No. 33.** Pay to A. J. Cartright $20.00 I. H. Hooper [signed A. J. Cartright, B. L.
              Worley & Son and Randolph & Parkinson];
         Feb. the 21, 1910 **No. 34.** Pay to Chattanooga Feed Co. $15.60 I. H. Hooper [signed Chattanooga
              Feed Co.];
         Feb. 26, 1910 **No. 35.** Pay to J. A. Johnson Trustee $20,00 for taxes I. H. Hooper [signed J. A.
              Johnston, Trustee].

Not found in the Hooper box was the picture of Ethel Hooper (below) which showed the layout of the home
place of Isaac Hooper, and how it related to Hooper Mill. Did the mill have two stories before the fire?
Notice the two pictures below which showed the bottom row of windows parallel with the porch on the
building with one floor above it (close-up picture is on the right). Aunt Gertrude always said that Luther
redesigned and enlarged the mill after it was rebuilt. Did the new mill building have three floors instead of
two above ground? Notice the size of the building to the right of the mill, and the direction it was turned.
The picture on p. 184 seemed to show a low, long storage building while the upper picture showed a
building turned parallel to the mill. Ethel on p. 242 in 1907 looked about the same age as the picture below
when she would have been 19. (Richard (Rick) Hooper believed that Hooper Mill was taller first and then
rebuilt as the lower mill building. Harold Reno wondered if it was 2 stories first, then 3 stories and then
finally a smaller building when TVA bought it on October 18, 1938?)

The picture of the Hooper Mill above definitely showed the three stories above ground plus a lower area where the mill wheel was located. Probably it would have been an undershot mill or a turbine because of the amount of fall in the dug spillway. Notice Candy's Creek reflection to the left of the concrete walls.

"Merchants Bank, CLEVELAND, TENN. IN ACCOUNT WITH I. H. Hooper, Sep. 18, 1909 Dep. 300.00"

"No. 2606 BRADLEY COUNTY, TENN., Apr. 19, 1910 Received of I. H. Hooper Five 10/100 Dollars in full payment of State 35c, School 40c, Bond 40c, Judgment 5c, Road 10c, Bridge 5c, and Poll $2.00, Taxes for the year 1909, on the following property: DIST. 2 ASSESSED TO Hooper ACRES 80 VALUATION REAL 75 PERS. 218 TOTAL 4.82 P.& cost .28 Total 5.10 J. A. Johnston Trustee, Alfred Beavers Deputy."

"No. 2907 BRADLEY COUNTY, TENN., Apr. 19, 1910 Received of I. H. Hooper 41/100 Dollars. In full payment of State 35c, County 30c, School 40c, Bond 40c, Judgment 5c, Road 10c, Bridge 5c and Poll $2.00, Taxes for the year 1909, on the following property: DIST. 2 Gresham ACRES 5 VALUATION PERS. 20 TAX .33, P. & cost .08 Total .41 J. A. Johnston Trustee Alfred Beavers Deputy"

"FIRST NOTE OFFICE WESTERN DEPARTMENT THE CONTINENTAL INSURANCE CO. OF NEW YORK 280 LA SALLE STREET Chicago, Ill., NOVEMBER 18, 1911. Mr. I. H. and A. K. [Albert Kinsey] Hooper. Charleston, R.#2. 14. DEAR SIR: Your note given for first payment for Insurance in this Company under Policy No. 741339 will fall due on the first day of DECEMBER. Dear Sirs: Enclosed herewith I hand you $22.80 to pay my FIRST NOTE given for insurance under Policy No. 741339. Agent Box Bros. & Co."

"Deed James Calhoun and wife to I. H. Hooper State Tax $2.00 + Probate Fee .15=$2.15 paid Filed May 7, 1912 in *Note Book B* page 213 and recorded in *Deed Book 3*1 pages 135-136, E. M. Morrison Register, Mayfield & Mayfield Attorneys-at-law, Cleveland, Tennessee, Reg. Fee $1.50 Paid"

For and in consideration of the sum of TWO THOUSAND DOLLARS ($2000.00), of which the sum of SEVEN HUNDRED DOLLARS ($700.00) is paid in cash, and for the remainder of which I. H. Hooper has at even date herewith, executed his three (3) promissory notes, as follows: One for the sum of FIVE HUNDRED DOLLARS ($500.00), due on or before December 1st, 1912, and one for the sum of FIVE HUNDRED DOLLARS ($500.00), due on or before December 1st, 1913, each of said notes bear interest from date and provide for the payment by the maker of reasonable attorney fees, or commission charges for collection, in case the said notes are not paid at maturity and suit for their collection is instituted, said notes are payable to the order of JAMES CALHOUN AND LILLY CALHOUN, and the payment of the same in full, is secured by a vendor's lien which is hereby expressly retained upon the real estate herein after conveyed, we, JAMES CALHOUN and wife, LILLY CALHOUN, have bargained and sold, and do hereby bargain, sell, transfer and convey unto I. H. HOOPER, and his heirs and assigns forever, the following described real estate, to wit:

A certain tract, or parcel of land located in the old EIGHT CIVIL DISTRICT, of Bradley County, Tennessee, beginning at the northeast corner of Section 4, Township 1, Range 1, West of the Basis Line Ocoee District, and running thence south 62 degrees east, running through the center of the barn, sixty (60) poles; thence south 61 degrees east, one hundred and thirty-one (131) poles to the center of the creek; thence down the creek with the center of the pike; thence west with the pike, to the line of Mrs. Bates's land; and thence with the township line to the beginning point (a correction was entered here) "Should read 'with Mrs. Bates' line to the beginning point.' On Feb. 5th 1913, Hooper executed a deed of trust to secure a note to J. P. Elkins and corrected the description in it."

Also another tract, or parcel of land, beginning at the southwest corner of Bayless's land, at a rock with the pine pointer and running thence north 64 degrees west, sixteen and one-half (16 ½) poles to the rock in the road with a black oak pointer; thence up the road north 12 degrees east, eighteen (18) poles, to the pike; thence with the pike westwardly to Bayless's line; thence south 23 degrees west, with Bayless's line to the beginning.

Both of the above described tracts being a portion of the real estate conveyed to the grantors by G. G. Moore and wife, by deed, which is registered in the Register's Office, of Bradley County, Tennessee, in *Deed Book No. 27*, pages 449-50, to which reference is here made.

TO HAVE AND TO HOLD the said real estate unto the said I. H. Hooper, his heirs and assigns forever.

We covenant that we are lawfully seized of the said real estate; that it is free and unincumbered [sic], and that we have a good and lawful right to sell and convey the same, and we will forever warrant and defend the title thereto against the lawful claims of all persons whomsoever.

Witness our hands, this May 7th 1912. Signed James Calhoun and Lillie Calhoun. (The debt was paid Feb. 5, 1913, according to the paid notes. Int. paid on note to Mar. 1/13.)

Some information from the King Medicine Company was kept in the box also:

KING MEDICINE COMPANY 3207 Colorado Avenue, CHICAGO, ILLINOIS This certifies, that we have this day delivered to Mrs. Ella Hooper a treatment for Neuralgia Kidney Liver Change of Life Stomach Bad Blood, and believe if said medicine is taken as directed, that it will effect a cure for the above named malady, and if said medicine fails to cure, we agree to pay the above named party the sum of $3.00 on receipt of signed statement witnessed by three responsible persons who are personally acquainted with the physical condition of above named party, and knows said party to still be suffering with above named malady. This guarantee expires Oct. 20/1912 KING MEDICINE CO. Per J. C. Parker Deliveryman

"The Hiwassee Bank. $9.75 Charleston, Tenn. 2/5, 1914 six months after date I promise to pay to the order of I. H. Hooper Nine 75/100 Dollars Wm Grecewaters"

"CLEVELAND NATIONAL BANK $200.00 Oct. 14, 1914 ninty [sic] days after date we jointly and severally promise to pay to the order of Cleveland National Bank Two Hundred Dollars at the CLEVELAND NATIONAL BANK, Cleveland, Tennessee, for value received. I. H. Hooper, Albert Hooper, J. L. Hooper, J. M. Hooper Rec. Jan. 12/1915:"

To secure and make certain the payment of a note drawn at even date, By I. H. Hooper, payable to J. P. Elkins or order, for the sum of FIFTEEN HUNDRED DOLLARS ($1500.00), due One (1) year after date, bearing interest from date and providing for the payment of attorney fees by the maker if not paid at maturity and suit is instituted, and to secure all notes given in renewal thereof, we the said I. H. HOOPER and wife, ELLA HOOPER, have sold and do hereby sell, transfer and convey unto P. B. MAYFIELD, Trustee, the following real estate to wit:
A certain parcel or tract of land, with improvements thereon, situate in the Old Ninth Civil District of Bradley County, Tennessee, and containing Fifty-nine (59) acres, more or less, and beginning on the north line of the Quarter Section, at the center of the quarter, and running thence south with the fence, sixty (60) rods; thence south with the fence, eight (8) rods; thence west with the fence, twenty (20) rods to the line of the W. L. Ledford land; thence north with the Ledford line, one hundred and twenty-eight (128) rods, and thence east with said line to the beginning.

There is excepted however, from the above tract, a tract containing Two (2) acres, more or less, heretofore conveyed by us to the Hooper Milling Company by deed registered in the Register's Office of said County and reference thereto is made for a complete description.

Said real estate is the property conveyed to us by M. L. Ross, Administrator &c., less the two acres described, by deed registered in said Register's Office in *Book X* pages 296-7.

TO HAVE AND TO HOLD the said real estate unto the said P. B. MAYFIELD, Trustee, his assigns and successors forever. (K. C. Hooper Estate is on pp. 189 – 192.)

"Trust Deed I. H. Hooper & wife to P. B. Mayfield Trustee, March 2nd, 1915, *Note Book B* page 267 and recorded in *Trust Book V* pages 61-62, B. G. Lawson Register by Chas. H. Ward Dep. Register, Mayfield & Mayfield Attorney's-at-law, Reg. Fee 150 paid [1.50]"

We covenant that we are lawfully seized of said real estate; that it is free and unencumbered; that we have a good and lawful right to sell and convey the same and will forever warrant and defend the title thereto against the lawful claims of all persons whomsoever.

Now if we shall pay said note for FIFTEEN HUNDRED DOLLARS ($1500.00), and all notes given in renewal thereof at maturity this conveyance will be null and void, but if we fail to do so, then said Trustee is hereby authorized and empowered, after giving thirty (30) days' notice in writing, of time, terms and place of sale, by poster on the Courthouse Door in Cleveland, Bradley County, Tennessee, to expose said real estate to public sale at said Courthouse Door and sell the same at public sale, to the highest bidder for cash in hand, in bar of the equities of redemption, homestead and dower, each and all of which rights we expressly waive and renounce and make a deed to the purchaser.

From the proceeds of sale, the Trustee will first pay all costs, fees and expenses incurred in the execution of this trust. He shall then pay said note, or renewal thereof, and the balance, if any, pay to us.

It is stipulated that all insurance against loss by fire covering said buildings on said lands, are to be made payable to said J. P. Elkins, as the holder of said note to the extent of his interest. We waive the oath and bond of the Trustee and agree in the event of foreclosure under the terms of this instrument, that the occupant of the premises will immediately become the tenant at will of the purchaser.

WITNESS our hands, this March 2nd, 1915. I. H. Hooper and Ella Hooper

$1500.00 March 2nd 1915, One Year after date we jointly and severaly [*sic*] Promise to pay to the order of J. P. Elkins Fifteen Hundred & No/100 Dollars at the CLEVELAND NATIONAL BANK, Cleveland, Tennessee, for value received with interest from date. Secured by deed of trust of even date herewith. Signed I. H. Hooper (on the back of this note) received interest on the within note to March 2, 1916, received interest on the within note to March 2, 1917 For value received I hereby transfer this note together with the deed of trust and lien securing the same to W. T. Beaty, without any recourse to me in law or equity. This May 3, 1917, J. P. Elkins, Interest Paid to May 3, 1917, interest Paid to May 3, 1918, interest paid to May 3, 1919, interest paid to May 3, 1920, 5/3/21 interest paid for 1921, 5/3/23 interest paid for 1922, 6/7/24 paid by Albert 55.00 + 35=90.

"Mr. I. H. Hooper Dr. to HALL BROS. CO. Farm Implements CLEVELAND, TENN. Mch. 22-17 Balance to Mch. 3.17 $29.69"

HENRY GENNETT, President. HARRY GENNETT, 1st V. Pres. T. J. CAMPBELL, 2nd V. Pres. FRED GENNETT, Sec'y. CLARENCE GENNETT, Treas. THE STARR PIANO COMPANY ATLANTA, GA., MONTGOMERY, ALA., PENSACOLA, FLA., STARR, RICHMOND, TRAYSER, REMINGTON, GRAND, UPRIGHT AND PLAYER PIANOS, THE STARR PHONOGRAPH, THE STARR LIBRARY OF PERFORATED MUSIC ROLLS, THE STARR LIBRARIES OF PHONOGRAPH RECORDS. DISTRICT HEADQUARTERS 1820 THIRD AVENUE, Birmingham, Ala., A. G. FORBES DISTRICT MANAGER, 11/9/17 Miss Ella Hooper, Charleston, Tenn. Dear Miss Hooper, We are sorry to find that you have not yet settled your August dues on piano. You sent us $50.00 in September, which was credited to your February dues, but you are yet past due $50.00. Please send us check or money order for $50.00 by early mail, and after this sum is credited your account will be in good shape until February first next. Yours truly, The Starr Piano Company H. Moore, Auditor

Found in Hooper Box on a small undated piece of paper with no date was "40 acres in Section 5 T 1 R1 on the west corner of N W V, 120 a (acres?) in Setion [sic] 32 of T 1 Range 1 South E V". (This could possibly be related to land in McMinn County.)

Issac Houston Hooper and his son John Luther Hooper bought the mill on March 16, 1901. On a few of the Hooper Milling checks after the incorporation in March 1907, J. L. was President with I. H. Secretary. Shortly after that I. H. became President. J. L. continued to be connected to the mill, but he began to trade in the futures market and became interested in politics. In a Circuit Court case dated July 9, 1915, Road Commissioner A. C. Vest was accused of illegally being on both the Pike Road Commission and also Poorhouse Commissioner. In this court case J. L. Hooper was said to be the Chairman of the Pike Road Commission. In the *Cleveland Herald* on February 22, 1917, J. L. Hooper was listed as being Chairman of the county Pike Road Commission. Evidently some road graders had been bought and the newspaper had made accusations about the legality of the purchase. In the *Cleveland Weekly Herald* on April 5, 1917, J. L. Hooper said he had sold his mill and farm property to his brother K. C. Hooper, but it probably should have said Albert Kinsey Hooper. The article stated that Mr. Hooper had been Chairman of the Pike roads Commission for the past six months (see pages 213 – 214). When John Luther Hooper sold the mill to H. H. Brackett in 1919, he was President of Hooper Milling (p. 191).

Hooper Mill Stones Found at John and Glenda Cantrell's Log Cabin. (See Appendix D 273 - 274.)

Below is a picture of the three concrete support walls of Hooper's Mill with Candy's Creek to the left. See page 165 for a site drawing. The picture also shows the dug sluice/spillway with trees across it . A picture on the next page shows a close-up of the dug sluice/spillway.

Remains of the Hooper Mill foundation on Candy's Creek in Bradley County, Tennessee. The undershot or turbine wheel might have been between the two left foundations and the building would have been built above the foundation (see notches in concrete for floor joists) and extending to the right in the picture above. Look at the picture of the building (p. 184) and you can barely see part of the foundations at the rear and the lower part of the building sitting on lower concrete foundation. The dug sluice ditch that is visible above at the upper end of the concrete directed the water from the dam to the undershot wheel or turbine that would have been to the rear of the building. Notice Candies Creek to the left of the picture.

The close-up picture below shows the dug sluice/spillway with trees that have fallen across it.

The upper foundation was more than six feet tall where side of the mill sat. (Bill Moorhouse [about six feet tall] was standing beside the upper concrete foundation in the picture.)

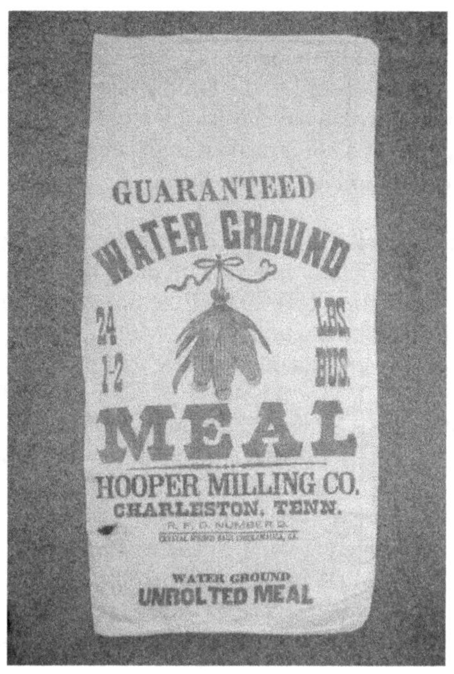

This is a picture of the Hooper Milling Co. meal sack. The mill sold water ground, unbolted meal not only locally but also to other places in the area of Chattanooga, Tennessee.

(When Harold Reno was interviewing J. L. Hooper, Jr., he mentioned that two black men who worked at the mill were Bob Gaines and Jack Mack. Jack could be John Mack? He also mentioned that John Luther Hooper owned a Saxon automobile at one time, and it caught on fire and burned. On the Internet at *Google.com* Books, K. D. Saulpaw sold Saxon cars in 1915 in Calhoun, TN according to *Automobile Topics* Vol. 34 No. 1 p. 443 published in New York Aug. 14, 1915. See p. 54 for Karl D. Saulpaw.)

John Luther Hooper in White Truck 1912-1918 (the truck company was named White – see p. 240)

Luther Hooper (p. 190) had his picture made in the Hooper Milling Company truck in Cleveland, Tennessee. This was the first truck in Bradley County. (When Martha and Harold Reno took Billie and Earl Hooper [Luther's daughter-in-law and son] to the Smithsonian in Washington, D. C., Earl looked at an old White truck on display and said, "My dad had a truck like that.") The truck picture on previous page was the same truck that Albert Hooper was talking about in the chapter related to Gertrude and Albert on page 240. These trucks were built from 1912 to 1918.

As stated earlier, the first record that listed a mill related to the Hooper family was the 1862 tax record (see p. 165). From the beginning the sons evidently helped with the mill. Did the mill exist before 1862? Possibly it did, but the Andrew Hooper court case against the Shelton/Young Mill that ran from about 1854 to 1855 did not list another mill close to the Shelton/Young Mill on Candy's Creek. The case did not end until almost 1856, and K. C. Hooper represented his father at that point.

After Andrew Hooper, the next owner was Kinsey C. Hooper who operated Hooper Mill from about 1866 to 1901(see p. 166). K. C. and Betsey J. Hooper sold the mill March 16, 1901 to Isaac H. Hooper and Luther Hooper for $2,300.00 plus interest (see pages 172 – 173 for deed). This included 61 acres of land at the mill site. On March 8, 1907, Hooper Mill was incorporated as Hooper Milling Company, and it was valued at $15,000.00 with 150 shares valued at $100.00 each. Luther Hooper became President, and I. H. Hooper became Secretary (see pages 178 and 187 for information).

Close-up of Edward Townsend Map from 1901 showing Cleveland, Candies Creek (blue), old roads and dark smudge for Hooper Mill

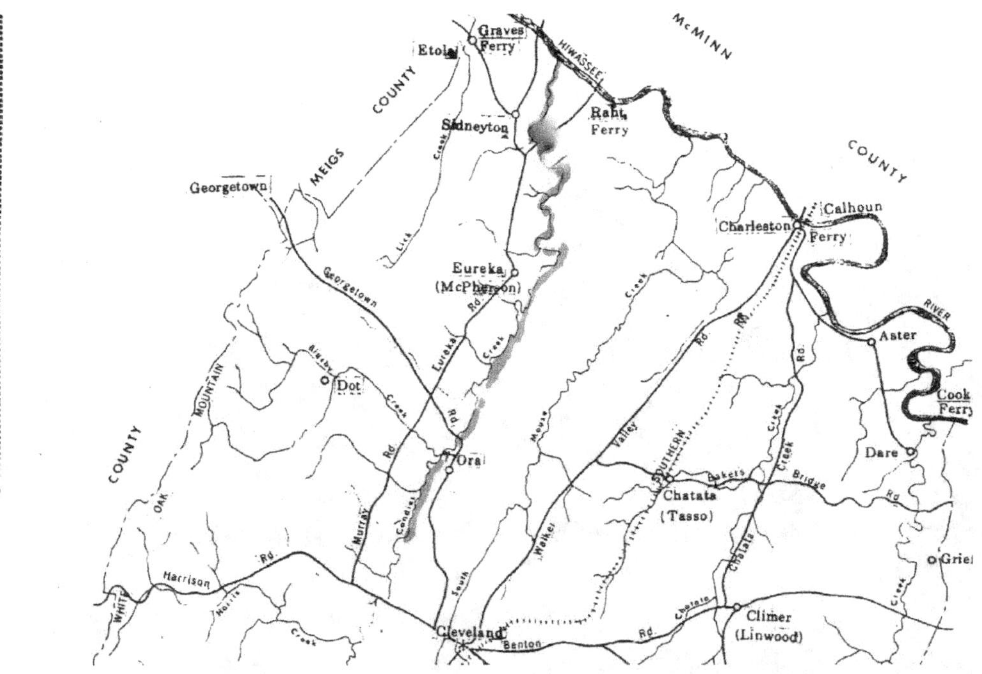

The Hooper Milling Company ended on November 28, 1919 when the Hooper Mill with 2 acres of ground were sold for $12,000.00 to H. H. Brackett who married (1) Ethalinda Hooper and (2) Jessie Pierce. This included the mill, dwelling, warehouse, barn, and all the equipment (*Deed Book 27* page 418 and *Deed Book Y* pages 626-627). The sale was handled by Luther Hooper, President of Hooper Milling Company.

In the *Note Book D* on page 248 and in *Deed Book 60* page 135, H. H. Brackett and his wife Jessie sold the Hooper Mill to Cleveland National Bank on April 7, 1926 for $3500.00. Cleveland National Bank then sold the mill to Ernest Thompson and Arthur Thompson on August 5, 1933 for $838.38 as recorded in *Note Book D* page 248 and *Bradley County Deed Book* 60 page 136. The final sale occurred October 18, 1938 when Ernest Thompson and his wife Anna along with Arthur L. Thompson and his wife Beatrice sold the mill to the Tennessee Valley Authority for $1682.21 recorded in the *Bradley County Deed Register*

Volume 60 page 136 and in *Bradley County Book of Deeds Volume 61* on page 15. Annie Hooper Thompson was the daughter of K. C. and Elizabeth Geren Hooper's youngest son Andy, so the mill was still in a family related to the Hooper family. (See pages 277 – 284 Appendix E for the final records.)

K. C. Hooper's Will was found in *Bradley County Wills Vol. 2 1883-1908* pp. 491-492. Because of the settlements of the Will of K. C. Hooper, a deed was registered in the *Bradley County Deed Register Volume 39* on pages 517, 518 and 519, and the children were listed as S. I. Baker, Jennette Baker, I. H. Hooper, Ethalinda Brackett, H. H. Brackett, A. U. Miller, Martha Miller, and A. J. Hooper. This was dated March 8, 1911. This was also recorded in Dallas County, Texas on March 20, 1911 because H. H. Brackett and Ethalinda Hooper Brackett lived there.

The Hooper Mill was not mentioned in the settlement because Isaac H. Hooper and his son, John Luther Hooper, purchased 61 acres which included the mill on March 16, 1901. Mt. Ebal was also not mentioned because I. H. Hooper and J. K. Geren, Jr. purchased the 80 acres February 16, 1891 from W. H. Burgess (p. 196). I. H. then purchased the land from J. K. on September 31, 1891. (See page 198 - 199 for the deed.)

WILL OF K. C. HOOPER.

This July the 16, 1903.
In dividing the land of K. C. Hooper between the Heirs, Etha Linda and her heirs is [sic] to have the south half of the home farm divided east and west about 68 ½ acres for the sum of seven hundred and fifty dollars to be paid March the 16 1906 with rents till then then [*sic*] and then make all the heirs equal.
K. C. Hooper.

This July the 16, 1903
In dividing the land of K. C. Hooper between his heirs Jeneta Baker and her heirs is to have the north half of the home place about 68 ½ acres for the sum of SIX hundred dollars to be paid March the 16 1906 with rents till then and then make all the heirs equal.

K. C. Hooper

This July the 16, 1903.
In dividing the land of K. C. Hooper between his heirs Martha Miller and her heirs is to have the north half of the upper farm about 80 acres the line to be run east and west and fifteen acres on the south side bounded on the west by Mrs. McPherson on the south by Ada Ownsby (Addie Hooper Ownbey) for the sum of eight hundred and seventy five dollars to be paid March the 16, 1903 with rents till then and then make all the heirs equal.

K. C. Hooper

This July the 16, 1903
In dividing the land of K. C. Hooper between his heirs A. J. Hooper is to have the south half of the upper farm running east and west and five acres on the south side bounded on the south by Martha Miller for the sum of eight hundred and twenty five dollars to be paid March the 16, 1906 and then make all the heirs equal with rents till then.

K. C. Hooper.

PROBATE, NOVEMBER TERM, 1904.

Be it remembered that on this the 12th day of November, 1904, (p. 492) before the Honorable Jacob Smith, Chairman of the County Court of Bradley County, Tennessee, the heirs-at-law of K. C. Hooper, deceased, by their attorney W. L. Humphrey produced in open Court a paper writing purporting to be the last will and testament of K. C. Hooper, Sr., lately deceased, bearing date of July 16, 1903, having the name of K. C. Hooper subscribed thereto, and there being no subscribing witnesses there the said attorney for the heirs of said K. C. Hooper allege that said will and every part thereof was in the handwriting of said K. C. Hooper and that it had been found since the recent death of K. C. Hooper along with his valuable papers, and said heirs allege it to be a holographic will (handwritten), and moved the Court that the same be admitted to probate and record as the last will of said K. C. Hooper, deceased.

And it duly appearing to the Court from the testimony of M. L. Ross, Thomas Caldwell and J. W. Hawk who are credible and reliable personages who are disinterested in the disposition of said estate; that said paper writing was found among the valuable papers of K. C. Hooper, deceased, shortly after his death, and that said K. C. Hooper's handwriting was commonly and generally known by his acquaintances, and that said paper writing and every part thereof including the signature was in the handwriting of said K. C. Hooper, deceased, and that said K. C. Hooper was of sound mind and memory; and it further appearing that said K. C. Hooper lately died in Bradley County, Tennessee, and that his usual place of residence at the time of his death was in said County, it is also adjudged. And it is adjudged and declared by the Court that said instrument is the true, whole and last will and testament of the said K. C. Hooper, deceased, and the Clerk is directed to file and record the same, together with this order of probate.

Since Kinsey C. Hooper died without a proper will, the handwritten will was accepted. M. L. Ross was concerned that there might not be enough money to satisfy the debts, so he proceeded under that assumption until the estate was settled. On page 42 of *Insolvent Estates 1889-1947* (Bradley County), the following record was found:

To the Clerk of the County Court of Bradley County, Tennessee
I, as Administrator of the Estate of K. C. Hooper, Sr. deceased, do hereby suggest the Insolvency of the Estate of K. C. Hooper, Sr deceased.
This 12 day of Jan. 1905

M. L. Ross Adm'r.

Since it appearing to the Administrator that that [*sic*] the amount against said estate will amount to more than the personal property belong to said estate.

[The following newspaper article was published in the *Cleveland Herald* on February 15, 1905.]
Insolvent Notice
To the Creditors of the estate of K. C. Hooper, Sr., deceased.

The inventory of the estate of K. C. Hooper, Sr., deceased, having been suggested to the Clerk of the County Court of Bradley County, Tennessee, notice is hereby given as required by the order of said Clerk to all persons having claims against said estate to present and file the same with the Clerk of said Court in Cleveland, Tennessee, authenticated as required by law, on or before Tuesday, June 20th , 1905 or be forevered barred.
M. L. Ross, Admr.
This Feb. 15, 1905 Pr. Fee $4.00

M. L. Ross of K. C. Hooper, Sr. deceased, having duly suggested the Insolvency of the Estate of said K. C. Hooper, Sr. deceased;

THEREFORE, I, J. I. Harrison Clerk of the County Court of Bradley County, Tennessee, do order you M. L. Ross, Administrator of K. C. Hooper, Sr. deceased, to give notice in the *Cleveland Herald* and also at the Court-house door, in the town of Cleveland, Tennessee, for all persons holding claims against the Estate of the said deceased, to come forward and file them with me, as Clerk aforesaid, for a pro rata distribution, on or before the 20th day of June 1905.

This 15 day of Feb. 1905

J. I. Harrison Clerk.
STATE OF TENNESSEE, BRADLEY COUNTY

I, J. I. Harrison Clerk of the County Court of said County, do hereby order you M. L. Ross, Admr., of K. C. Hooper, Sr. deceased, to file with me in my office as Clerk aforesaid, a true and perfect Schedule of the amount of said estate, consisting of the available funds, choses in action [personal rights not reduced to possession, but recoverable by suit at law, as money due on bond, or note or other contract] and other effects, including the Real Estate, on or before the 20th day of June 1905.

This 15th day of Feb. 1905.

J. I. Harrison Clerk.

Another record was found in the *County Court Settlements, Administrators Oct. 1895-Aug. 1908* on pages 563-564 in Bradley County, Tennessee:

Formal settlement of M. L. Ross Adm. Of the Estate of K. C. Hooper, Sr. decd.

To the County Court Clerk and the County Court of Bradley County, Tenn.

M. L. Ross Adms. Of the estate of K. C. Hooper dec'd. submit the following as his final settlement of   said Estate.

He is chargable with the following sums to amount received from sale of personal property as per acct. of sales, recorded in inventory book page 214   176.03
For sale of mare later   60.00
"   "   " corn to I. C. (I. H.?) Hooper   11.00
"   "   " 4 bu. Peas to I. C. (I. H.?) Hooper   4.00
"   "   " hay   4.25
Collected of I. C. (I. H.?) Hooper in account for land
   which the said K. C. Hooper had made him   908.00
Title bond for as follows – Cash
   and by amount allowed him for his share   696.00
   of said Estate
By Amt. allowed him for the share of Lon Hooper
   and Oscar Hooper heirs at Law of James Hooper,
   which share was deeded to him   696.00
By Amt. paid by Ethalinda Brackett as the amount
   her land was valued at above one share   54.00
By amt. paid by Martha Miller being the amt the
   land she got in the will was valued at above one
   share in said Estate   179.00
By amt. paid by A. J. Hooper as the amount the
   land he took in the will was valued at above
   one share in said Estate

                For Amt. Charges $2917.28
This Administration is entitled to the
   following credits for disbursements
Amt. pd. J. I. Harrison Clerk for letters and
   recording will   8.50
Amt. pd. J. I. Harrison for publishing notice
   of insolvency   5.00
Amt. pd. Edwards & Son for funeral expenses   9.40
Taxes   31.00
Amt. pd. K. C. Hooper, Jr. for note against Estate   <u>33.60</u>
         Amt. Frd. $2917.28   117.50

Page 564

Amt. Brot. Frwd.	$2917.28	117.50

Apr. 3, 1906   Amt. paid W. H. Hooper on note   4.90
July 1906   "   "   J. L. Hooper on note and acct.   19.93
Apr. 3 "   "   "   Sam Shlton on store acct.   12.57
July   "   "   "   I. H. Hooper on acct.   9.95
Nov. 16, 1905   "   "   W. L. Humphrey Atty. Fee   5.00
Apr. 19, 1906   "   "   W. L. Humphrey "   "   20.00
Apr. 10   "   "   "   R. W. Palmer on acct.   3.00
July   "   "   "   J. H. Gilbreath Doctor Bill   2.00
June   "   "   "   W. L. Ledford on note and
       Mortgage   428.00
   "   "   Clerks for this Settlement   2.50
   "   "   allowed Adm. For service   107.93

Amount paid heirs at law and legatees under the will
To I. H. Hooper, a son one share retained out of his
   Amt.   696.00
To I. H. Hooper one share purchased from Lon
   Hooper and Oscar Hooper the only heirs of James
   Hooper a share retained out of his acct.   696.00
Amount paid A. W. Miloway, Gdn. Of the minor
   heirs Alice Miloway, a daughter   696.00
Amt. paid Jenette Baker, Bal. on her share, she
   having received land under the will valued at   600.00   96.00
Vouchers are hereby filed $2917.18   2917.28
Martha Miller a daughter, A. J. Hooper and
   Ethalinda Bracket all received their share
   in said Estate in land by the will and paid
   an over plus to me as above shown .
Sworn to and subscribed before me this Jan. 2, 1907
       Jacob Smith,   M. L. Ross adm.

The debts were paid, so the estate was solvent. Since there could have been questions about the legitimacy of the handwritten will, the Executor probably filed for Insolvency to protect the estate assets.

The Wonder of the World. America's Mount Ebal Or the Handwriting on the Buried Wall and the Isaac Hooper Estate

The first time that Harold Reno heard of Mount Ebal which was located in Bradley County, Tennessee, he was riding with Earl Cook Hooper and his brother John Luther Hooper, Jr. As they were approaching the intersection of Lower River Road (308) and Eureka Road (306) in Bradley County, Tennessee, J. L. mentioned Mount Ebal. Harold asked where it was located, and they gestured in a general way and told him we would walk to see it one day. But, the day never came, and in the intervening years he became aware that it was an anathema to the family to discuss it. Later Richard (Rick) Hooper and Harold discussed it, and Rick discovered the location and visited the site.

The land where Mount Ebal was located was part of the Ocoee District. Because of the legal separation of Caroline Law Burgess and Doctor William Harvey Burgess in Hamilton County, TN, Caroline made a Quit Claim Deed to dower and homestead rights in the Ocoee District for land in Ranges two, three and seven. (See Appendix A for Ocoee Land Purchase information pp. 263 – 266.)

Possibly, William H. Burgess sold the land where Mount Ebal was located. On August 1, 1890, Caroline E. Burgess entered the following Quit Claim Deed in *Bradley County Deed Book L* on pages 534-535:

> **Quit Claim**   For the consideration of one dollar I, Caroline E. Burgess wife of
> **Caroline E. Burgess**   W. H. Burgess & heirs do by these presents quit claim and release
> **To**   forever unto the said William H. Burgess and unto our heirs Mary,
> **William H. Burgess**   Jessie, Annie, Joe and Libbie and to his and their assigns all of my dower
> and homestead rights in and to the lands owned or ever owned by the
> said William H. Burgess in Ranges two [2], three [3] and seven [7] of the Ocoee District, State of
> Tennessee. This conveyance is made in order that the said party of the second part may freely
> traffic in said lands….

W. H. Burgess' deed for 80 acres more or less dated February 12, 1891 was Notarized in Hamilton County, Tennessee (see p. 168). W. H. Burgess sold the land to I. H. Hooper and J. K. Geren, Jr. for $200.00. This was recorded on February 10, 1891 in *Bradley County Deed Book L* on page 536. **(The deed did not refer to the land as Mount Ebal.)** Dr. W. H. Burgess was listed as an Alloph Doctor on his death certificate June 26, 1913 (Internet, *Ancestry.com, Directory of Deceased American Physicians, 1804-1929*).

(The Quit Claim above included the land in the deed below for Range 2 in the Ocoee District.) In *Bradley County Deed Book L* on page 536 and *Bradley County Deed Book A* page 233 was the following deed:

> For the consideration of two hundred dollars, I, William H. Burgess, do by these presents sell, transfer and convey unto I. H. Hooper and J. K. Geren, Jr. and to their heirs and assigns forever the west half of the South East Quarter of Section Twelve in Township One North and Range Two West of the Basis Line in the Ocoee District and State of Tennessee, in Bradley County, Containing eighty acres of land, more or less. Retaining a lien to secure a $150.00 note of the purchasers. To have and to hold the said lands with all their appurtenances forever. And I do by these presents warrant the title to the said venders to be free from all encumbrance, and agree to defend it against the legal claims of all persons whatsoever. In witness whereof I have hereunto set my hand and seal this 10th day of February A. D. 1891 W. H. Burgess [signature] State of Tennessee Bradley County. I certify that the foregoing Deed was received this day at 11 ½ O'clock A. M. and noted in *Book A* page 233 and with the accompanying certificate is duly registered in my office in *Book L* page 536 Feb. 16, 1891 P. C. McCamy, Register
> **(See p. 266 for the Hamilton County and Bradley County Deed from Hooper Box.)**

The first reference to "the wall" was found in *The Cleveland Weekly Herald* p. 3 on April 16, 1891, titled "The Alleged Wall." It tells about Ike (Isaac H.) Hooper of the 9th District, bringing some of the stones found near Hooper's Mill which had strange markings thought to be a form of writing. Mr. Hooper said the wall was about 2 ½ feet thick, built of stones about two feet square and ten inches thick, placed on the edge and cemented together in three tiers of stones to form the wall, and the strange characters appeared only on the west face of the middle tier, protected by the stones outside. The characters were only found in one section about eight feet in length. The wall was traced for about two hundred yards with protruding stones that stood about six inches above the ground at regular intervals of about twenty feet. The writing might be some ancient language, or the alleged wall may just be a natural strata.

Engravings 1, 2 and 3 below were dated May 1891, and they were drawn by Dr. A. L. Rawson.   Albert Leighton Rawson, who was very important to the story of Mount Ebal, was a very educated man who was an artist, illustrator of the Bible, novelist, author of *The Bible Handbook,* worked with various secret religious groups, traveled to Arabia, spoke Arabic, and was a friend to mystics. He was involved in Theosophy (god wisdom) and a free thinker. He traveled with Madame Blavatsky who created the Theosophical movement which sought to join all religions into one showing the unity of man and god.

Another newspaper article was published in *The Cleveland Weekly Herald* on June 4, 1891 titled "The Buried Wall." The article surmised that a Mr. Ralston [*sic*], hired by the Smithsonian institute, was in Cleveland to sketch a section of the wall. Mr. Ralston [*sic*] felt that the characters resembled writing found in Massachusetts which had recently been deciphered. He said that the wall is genuine and had been made by man. He also said a Smithsonian expert would soon be sent to try to read the characters on the rocks.

A newspaper article dated June 7, 1891 in *The Sun* was published in New York and found on the Internet at The Library of Congress in the section *Chronicling America*. A. L. Rawson used drawings to illustrate the article. In the article on page 30 using the byline "Memphis June 3" a question was asked, "Is It Natural or Man-Made?" This is the central point for all the articles related to the archaeological find near Cleveland, Tennessee.

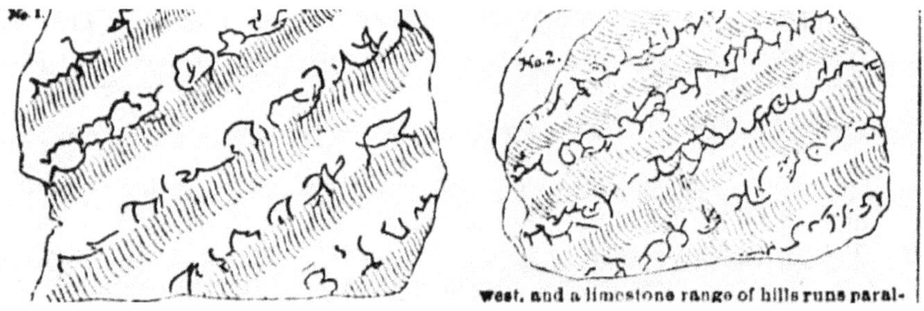

Engravings 1 and 2 above illustrate the inscriptions found on the west side of the middle tier of stones which were protected by a layer of stones on the outside (illustration below).

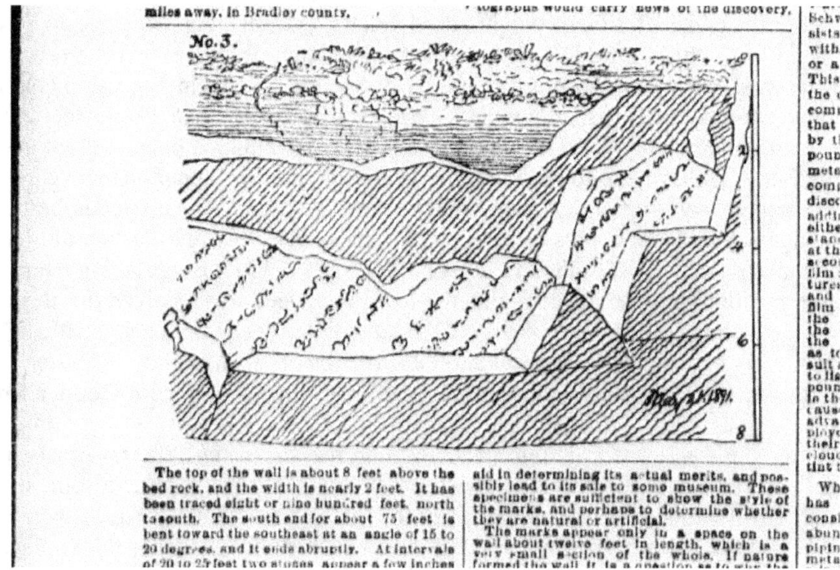

The top of the wall is about 8 feet above the bed rock, and the width is nearly 2 feet. It has been traced eight or nine hundred feet, north to south. The south end for about 75 feet is bent toward the southeast at an angle of 15 to 20 degrees, and it ends abruptly. At intervals of 20 to 25 feet two stones appear a few inches aid in determining its actual merits, and possibly lead to its sale to some museum. These specimens are sufficient to show the style of the marks, and perhaps to determine whether they are natural or artificial.

The marks appear only in a space on the wall about twelve feet in length, which is a very small section of the whole. If nature formed the wall it is a question as to whether

Engraving number 3 (previous page) showed the top of the hill with a scale on the right showing a depth of 8 feet. It also showed the three layers or tiers of stone with the writing protected by the outside layer which hid the inscriptions. Number 3's date of May 21, 1891 corroborates the previous article even though Rawson is spelled Ralston.

Engraving No. 4 shows a close up of one of the marks half normal size.

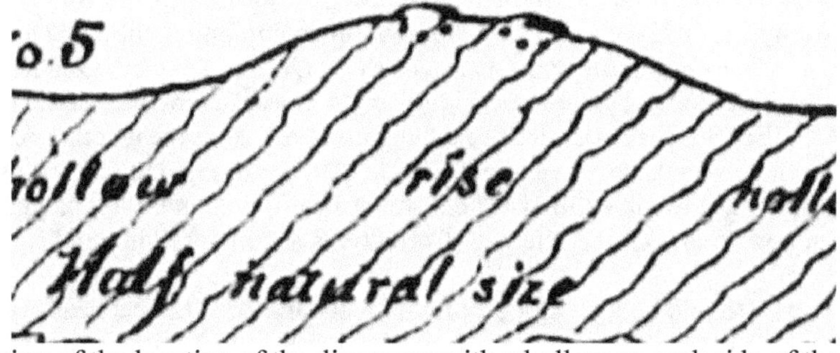

Number 5 is a drawing of the location of the discovery with a hollow on each side of the raised area.

Dr. Rawson stated that Mr. Hooper (Ike) was suspicious and would not allow pictures to be taken. He would only allow drawings even though Mr. Rawson urged him to allow photographic proof to carry news of the discovery. It also mentions a partner who was probably J. K. Geren who was half owner.

J. K. (Joel) Geren, Jr. and his wife sold their 40 acres of the W. H. Burgess purchase to I. H. Hooper on September 31, 1891. Since the original price was $200.00, J. K. increased his $100.00 investment to $1000.00 in about seven months (found in the *Bradley County Deed Book T* on pages 601-602):

        Deed   This indenture entered into this day by and between J. K. Geren, Jr.
J. K. Geren, Jr. & wife of the first part and I. H. Hooper of the second part. Witnesseth that
        To   for and in consideration of one thousand dollars to me paid in hand by
I. H. Hooper   I. H. Hooper of the second part the receipt whereof is hereby
                       acknowledged. I, J. K. Geren, Jr. of the first part have this day
bargained and sold and by these present do transfer and convey the following described land or real estate towits to I. H. Hooper with all its protuberances of whatever kind belonging to said land and bounded as follows on the North by the lands of T. H. Gilbreath, on the West by the land of W. P. Eads, on the South by the lands of W. P. Palmer, on the East by the lands of William McPherson and laying [sic] in the 9th Civil District of Bradley County, Tennessee my half of the West Half of the South East Quarter of Section twelve in Township one North and Range two West of the Basis Line in the Ocoee District containing forty acres of the above described land to

have and to hold the same forever and I, J. K. Geren, Jr. and I, J. K. Geren, Jr. [*sic*] do further
covenant with the said I. H. Hooper to warrant and defend the title to said land against the lawful
claims of all others whomever.

In witness whereof I set my hand and seal This 31ˢᵗ day of September 1891.

J. K. Geren (Seal)

Nettie Geren (Seal)

On October 22, 1891 another article appeared in *The Cleveland Weekly Herald* titled "The Buried Wall." It
stated that a Professor, a biologist, and Dr. (David Starr) Jordan (noted Smithsonian ichthyologist), a
geologist, had decided that the wall was a natural formation, but the inscriptions had been cut by some pre-
historic people. They related the writing to the mounds further south. They had not been able to interpret
the inscriptions but would make a report to the institute.

The first articles in 1891, correctly identified I. H. Hooper as the finder of the wall. For some reason, A. L.
Rawson started using wrong information such as Chatata while trying to identify the Mount Ebal location.
R. J. M. Only (the Illustrator) on page 208 of this book drew the map which showed the railroad below
Charleston where it ran through Chatata, but he also showed where the ferry crossed the Hiwassee River at
Ledford Island which was several miles from Chatata and Charleston; Dr. Rawson started using J. H.
Hooper instead of I. H. Hooper, and changed the name of the newspaper from *The Cleveland Weekly
Herald* to the *Cleveland Express* which was wrong. These three errors appear over and over in many
articles from this point forward. Changing the "I" to a "J" might be explained by how the letters look when
written. Maybe Isaac's son, John Luther, was also helping, so J. H. should be J. L?

In HARVARD UNIVERSITY LIBRARY of the MUSEUM OF COMPARATIVE ZOOLOGY number
8422 Exchange dated July 21, 1892-February 25, 1902 was the compilation entitled *TRANSACTIONS OF
THE NEW YORK ACADEMY OF SCIENCES LATE LYCEUM OF NATURAL HISTORY VOLUME XI
October, 1891, to June, 1892* Edited by the Recording Secretary, assisted by the Publication Committee
NEW YORK: PUBLISHED BY THE ACADEMY. On pages 26 – 29 at the meeting of the New York
Academy of Sciences which was dated November 9, 1891, with19 present and chaired by A. A. Julien, a
paper was presented by A. L. Rawson entitled "The Ancient Inscription on a Wall at Chatata, Tennessee":
(A copy of this meeting was found on the Internet. Corrections are enclosed in brackets.)

> Mr. J. H. Hooper [should be I. H. Hooper] found what appeared to be a headstone to a grave, on a
> wooded ridge on his farm, in Bradley County, Tennessee, about thirteen miles from the railroad at
> Cleveland. He dug around the stone, expecting to find a name, but instead found only curious
> unknown letters or marks. He dug deeper and uncovered other stones that formed a wall of three
> courses, in all about two feet thick, eight feet high, and about sixteen feet of its length, as
> measured from the north end, was covered with the letters, arranged in wavy, nearly parallel and
> diagonal lines. The wall was traced and examined in many places for a distance of nearly a
> thousand feet, its course marked on the surface by stones like No. 1, projecting a few inches
> above the surface of the ground, and twenty-five or thirty feet apart. Seventy-five feet of the south
> end of the wall ended in a hollow of a hill.

> In March, 1891, the *Cleveland Express* [*The Cleveland Weekly Herald*, another example of wrong
> information] printed a short account of the discovery, written by Mr. Carson of that place, who
> had seen the wall. In the *Sunday Sun*, New York, June 7ᵗʰ, I published a short notice of the find,
> with engravings made from my sketches made at the place, May 21ˢᵗ. The engravings in this
> article are from my sketches corrected by photographs. The stone is dark-red sandstone, and the
> wall lies along the crest of a ridge of that kind of stone which trends north and south, flanked by
> limestone east and west, and extending from the Hiawassee [*sic*] River north to Chattanooga,
> south where it dips below the bed of the Tennessee River.

> The surface of the west side of the inner course of stones is cut into rounded ridges with hollows
> between, and the characters are raised on the crest of the ridges, and are from two to three inches
> in width, with a few larger groups.

Mr. J. Hampden Porter says, in a letter from Chatata, October 21st : "It is not a wall but a red sandstone ridge, faced with red, slaty, and yellow clays to an unknown depth. No implements and no traces of previous excavations have been found." The faces of the other course of stones are level and not cut into grooves. Between the courses is found a dark-red cement, which is probably formed of red clay with salts carried down by water. Mr. Porter says: "As a rule inscriptions are intended to be read….I do not remember any instance of a designed concealment like this."

The architect of the Pharos at Alexandria, Egypt, cut his name on the stone, covered it with plaster, and moulded Pharaoh's name in the covering. Time tore off the plaster and exposed the builder's name. This concealment in Tennessee may have been effected in time of invasion or some great social calamity.

Eight hundred and seventy-two characters have been examined, many of them duplicates, and a few imitations of animal forms, the moon and other objects. Accidental imitation of oriental alphabets are numerous.

The rock was chiseled in the form of letter intended, a hard cement worked in and raised above The surface, and a cement placed, in its surface is engraved there. The bird or other animal is The largest of that kind of figures that is found on the wall. Some of these forms recall those on the Dighton Rock, and may belong to the same age. How many other hidden inscriptions there may be in this, the geologically oldest continent, it is impossible to say but delightful to conjecture. This wall would be a valuable and interesting addition to the Metropolitan Museum.

Considerable discussion followed the reading of this paper, and was participated in by Drs. Julien and Bolton, and Prof. Martin and others.

Another article found on the Internet written by A. L. Rawson was published in the *American Antiquarian and Oriental Journal* January – November 1892 in Vol. 14 pages 221-223 Edited by Stephen D. Peet, Ph. D. with basically the same ideas repeated again including the wrong identification of I. H. Hooper as J. H. Hooper which might be J. L. Hooper. Also this article and the preceding article explain why several have searched in Chatata valley for Mount Ebal. The following is quoted from the article found on page 221:

A cousin of Mr. Hooper carried me in a buggy from Cleveland, thirteen miles to Chatata, where Mr. J. H. [I. H. or J. L.] Hooper, who found the wall on his farm, resides. We arrived late at his house and were entertained all night. After supper the stones were mentioned, and one they had at the house was shown to me, and I transcribed the marks. In the morning six or eight more stones, about sixteen or eighteen inches across, and irregular in fracture and about ten inches thick, were shown, as they lay under a rude shed where the children at play could injure them.

The Internet article continued on p. 221--Mr. Rawson stated that the ridge was about a mile from the Hooper home, and that the marker stones were about twenty-five to thirty feet apart for a distance of about a thousand feet. At the north end of the ridge was the inscribed section of wall.

(Cont. p. 222) Isaac Hooper had been working on the ridge when he saw a standing stone that had a number that looked like an eight, and he thought it might mark a soldier's grave. But after digging it out, he was surprised to see the marks on the stone were not readable. As he dug, he discovered a formation of brown or red sandstone in three thicknesses of about ten inches each with the "writing" on the middle course, west side. The lines of drawings were diagonal ascending to the right, cut on the narrow ridges of the rock. The "letters" were from one and one half inches to two inches in size and not of an uniform depth varying from an eighth of an inch to an inch in depth. A few were larger and appeared to be pictures of animals.

Mr. J. Hampden Porter visited on October 21 (1891) and concluded that the characters were created by someone; therefore, they are not the result of nature. He had identified 825 symbols placed in such a fashion of forms recurring, so that he determined that the chances of accidental origins were very small. He said that some figures were of the old and new moon and even the serpent and thunder bird.

As you look at the 17 page book that Isaac Houston Hooper had copyrighted in 1893, you will see some drawings of the inscriptions found on the wall. Also on page 212, there are two postcards that Earl Hooper kept: one might be a picture of the writing and the other a picture of four men at Mount Ebal. The two men in suits might be the experts who visited and the two workmen might be John Luther and Isaac H. Hooper.

The title for this chapter was taken from the Copyright, October 13, 1893 and kept at the Library of Congress. Elsie O'Neal found a copy of the Copyright which was kept at the Cleveland Public Library in the History Branch in Cleveland, TN. This page helped translate the title page on 204:

> No. 45897 y (or v.) Library of Congress,
>   Copyright Office, Washington.
> To wit: Be it remembered,
> That on the 13" day of October anno domini 1893, Isaac Houston Hooper, of Charleston Tenn. has deposited in this Office the title of a Book the title or description of which is in the following words, to wit:
>
> The Wonder
of the
World.
America's Mount Ebal
or the
Hand Writing on the Buried
Wall.
Written by R. J. M. Only
1893
>
> the right whereof he claims as proprietor in conformity with the laws of the United States respecting Copyrights.
>
>   A. S. Spofford
>   Librarian of Congress.

Richard (Rick) Hooper mentioned that at least one of the stones was taken to the Smithsonian Institution, and we wondered if they still had the stone. Unknown to Rick and Harold Reno, Roy G. Lillard also wanted to know.

Local historian, Roy G. Lillard, became interested in the stone and wrote to the Smithsonian. He received a letter in 1976 from the Smithsonian that explained the return of one of the stones (Elsie O'Neal at the Cleveland Public Library History Branch helped locate the Mount Ebal folder.):

> National Museum of Natural History   Smithsonian Institution
> WASHINGTON D. C. 20560   TEL. 202- 381-5758
> Dec. 27, 1976
>
> Roy G. Lillard, Chairman
> Social Science and Business Division
> Cleveland State Community College
> Cleveland, Tennessee 37311
>
> Dear Mr. Lillard:
>
>   The stone item you referred to was returned to the owner, Isaac H. Hooper on April 19, 1902. It resided at the Smithsonian from 1900-1902 and measured 17"x11"x6."
>
>   There seems to have been a question as to whether the 'markings' constituted an inscription and probably, for that reason it was returned.
>
>   Sincerely,

George E. Phebus
Supervisor
Processing Laboratory
Department of Anthropology

After finding the information in the History Branch of the Cleveland Public Library related to Mount Ebal, the decision was made to find the book published in 1893. Harold Reno wrote to the Tennessee State Library and Archives to request a copy of "The Wonder of the World: America's Mount Ebal, Discovered by I. H. Hooper" and received the following letter:

January 22, 2008
Floyd H. Reno
3418 Ramblewood Circle
Cleveland, TN 37312

Dear Mr. Reno,

I am writing in regards to your request for a copy of "The Wonder of the World: America's Mount Ebal, Discovered by I. H. Hooper". This publication is listed in the Bradley County section of the Bibliography of Tennessee of Tennessee Local History Sources, found on hold copies of all the items that are listed. I regret to say we do not have a copy of this publication in our collection. For this reason, we are returning your check for $6.50.

I did a search and was only able to locate a copy of this book in one library in the United States;
The American Museum of Natural
  History
79th Street and Central Park West
New York, NY   10024
(212) 769-5100
Please let me know if I can be of further assistance.

Ronald A. Lee
Tennessee State Library and Archives

On January 25, 2008, Floyd Harold Reno emailed *speccol@amnh.org* with the following request:
I am presently writing a book about my wife's great-grandfather, Isaac Houston Hooper, and her grandfather, John Luther Hooper, and their attempt to develop Mount Ebal in Bradley County, Tennessee. In my research, I discovered that a 16 page copy of the pamphlet titled: The Wonder of the World America's Mount Ebal or the Hand Writing on the Buried Wall published in 1893 is available at The American Museum of Natural History. The reference number is RF-38-1. Is there a way that I can send a dollar a page and have you photocopy it and mail it to me?

I appreciate any help you can give.

Thanks,
Floyd Reno

Floyd received the following reply on January 30, 2008:
Ingrid Lennon-Pressey *ingrid@amnh.org*
floydr9903@bellsouth.net
Re: FW: Mount Ebal Tennessee
Wed, 30 Jan 2008

Mr. Reno-
Yes please send payment in the form of a check or money order made out to: AMNH Library/ILL and mail to:
Library/ILL

American Museum of Natural History
79th St. @ Central Park West
New York, NY 10024-5192

Thank you,
Ingrid

Then, in a follow-up, it was decided that the photocopy could not be done, so they decided to copy the booklet and mail Harold a copy.

Mary DeJong *mdejong@amnh.org*
Tue, 5 Feb 2008

Thanks for your inquiry to the American Museum of Natural History Library. We can send you a photocopy of the booklet. There is also a plate that accompanies the booklet; the plate is entitled: "The Wonder of the World : America's Mount Ebal, discovered by I. H. Hooper, 1891. The ... picture shows the inscription or tablet rock, found in Bradley County, Tennessee, U. S. A."

This plate is too large to photocopy, so we will copy the booklet.

Please provide your address.

Thanks
-Reference Desk, AMNH Library

I also received the following that explained why the photocopy was impossible, so they decided to scan the booklet and mail me a copy.

Ingrid Lennon-Pressey
Dear Mr. Reno,
Thank you for your interest in our collections. The pamphlet America's Mount Ebal or the Hand Writing on the Buried Wallis [sic] is in our Rare collections.

Unfortunately we do not photocopy our rare materials, instead we scan and send them via email.

Therefore the fee is $20 for the first 10 pages and a $1 for each additional page.

Please let me know if we should proceed.

Thank you,
Ingrid

My reply: "Yes, Thanks [*sic*] you so very much. Do I send the money first? If so give me the address or method of payment.

Floyd Reno"

Then I received the following after sending the money to pay for the scan:
Barbara Mathe' *bmathe@amnh.org*
Monday, Feb. 11, 2008

I have forwarded your request to our reference staff. Please let me know if you don't hear back from them.
Barbara Mathe'
Museum Archivist and Head of Library Special Collections
American Museum of Natural History Library

Central Park West @ 79 Street
New York, NY 10024
phone: 212 769-5419

On the following pages are copies of the 17 page document written by Isaac H. Hooper and found at the American Museum of Natural History Library in New York City. The title page was extremely dark, but the following accurately depicts a translation of the original (see p. 201 for Copyright information):

**THE
WONDER
OF THE
WORLD.
AMERICA'S MOUNT EBAL
OR THE
HAND WRITING ON THE WALL
THE OLDER SANDSTONE
TESTIFES THAT MAN IS AS OLD AS THE
OLDEST IN AGE
LETTERS OF THOUSANDS OF TIME FOUND
CARVED IN A WALL 2 X 20 FEET BEDDED
IN A RIDGE OF SHALE 100 FEET THICK
FOUND BY I. H. HOOPER NEAR CLEVELAND
BRADLEY COUNTY TENNESSEE**

R. J. M. ONLY CALHOUN TENNESSEE

Return Jonathan Meigs Only of McMinn County did the drawings in the short 17 page book and used the initials for his name and his last name, RJM Only, to sign each one.

[To make the reading of the book easier, Harold Reno has provided the page numbers as listed in the booklet and written the words in bold print that are on each page. Page 3 below is rewritten on p. 205. Page 10 was written as 01, and he noted that by using the term [*sic*] to indicate it was quoted as written.]

3

**THE WONDER OF THE
WORLD.**
42-153149 0+3

THE ROCK INSCRIPTION, shown in the central illustration, of the large engraving, is the most wonderful Archæological discovery known to the literary world; because of the Geological position which it occupies.

The searcher after the truth of history, imbeded in the geological strata of the earth; or amid the ruins of buried cities, lying deep in volcanic ashes, cinders and lava; are aware that their findings have greatly modified the unreasonable claims of some Geologists. Their extravegant claims have staggered, stunned stupeified and stung, the students of Theology, and the defenders of the Mosaic, record, of the origen of the world, of the vegetable and animal, kingdoms, including man, with his domestic

THE WONDER OF THE
WORLD.

The Rock Inscription, shown in the central illustration, of the large engraving, is the most wonderful Archaeological discovery known to the literary world; because of the Geological position which it occupies.

The searcher after the truth of history, imbedded in the geological strata of the earth; or amid the ruins of buried cities, lying deep in volcanic ashes, cinders and lava; are aware that their findings have greatly modified the unreasonable claims of some Geologists. Their extravegant claims have staggered, stunned stupeified and stung, the students of Theology, and the defenders of the Mosaic, record, of the origin of the world, of the vegetable and animal, kingdoms, including man, with his domestic [end of page 3 with the sentence continued on page 4 below]

p. 4 animls [*sic*]. Many good men have been horified [*sic*] at the blsphemy [*sic*] and boldness of the geological Evolutionist's claims, because there had never been, any fossil of man his work not of his domestic animals found below the Tertiary, the seventh geological, period of the worlds history. Some learned Christians have been driven into the fogs of speculation and doubt concrning the purpos[e] of the writings of Moses, in the book of Genesis.

Illustration: No. 7 by **RJM Only** [RJM Only drew the illustration above before he used it in the book and numbered the drawing No. 7; his drawing in the book numbered No. 1 is on p. 207.]

Era of Man	[shown by]	Fossil of Man
Mammalion Age	"	**Fossil of Beasts**
Age of Reptiles	"	**Fossil of Reptiles**
Carbonifarus Age	"	**Coal fields**
Devonian Age	"	**Rock inscriptions**
Age Mollusks	"	**Fossil of Shells**

Universum interior
Estimated period of Time
From 10,000,000 to 680,000,000 years

p. 5 The above geological map, will give an idea, of the teachings of those who criticise the statements of Moses, and will also show the geological dispositon of the wonderful discovery made by I. H. Hooper.

This writing impresses the saying of Job "O, that my words were now written! oh that they were printed in a book!

That they were graven with an iron pen and lead (laid) in the rock forever. Job 19:23,24

Likewise that of David, when he said "Truth shall spring out of the earth; and righteousness look down from heaven".
Psalm 85:11

Also: the command to Joshuah, "And thou shalt write upon the stones all the words of this law very plainly'. Deut. 27:8

These Scripture references, show the possible importance of the inscription on the Buried Rock of America's Mount Ebal, should the Philologist, ever succeed in giving to the world what is there written.

That it is the writing of some one well acquainted with letters cannot be doubted.

6

The claim set up by some Geologists, that vegetable and animal life is from 10 000 000 to 680 000 000, of years older than man, and the above diagram of the geological periods, should give place, to one like to that on page seven; showing all of the geological formations, going on at the same time, and that the age of man, is equal to that of fern, fish and fowl. The fact that this writing is in the center of the Devonian age, is of its self, evidence sufficient to sustain the record of Moses, though we never learn what has been written on these stones

Carved in the soft sand stone at the bottom of the bed of a lost ocean, in the morning of history; then again flooded by the return of the waters, and then coverd by the sedimentary deposits of more than a thousand years; then lifted high above the water by volcanic force, where for 2000 years it has lain hidden in these East Tennessee, hills until God has seen proper to bring it to light. The Scripture references on page seven, will be read here with interest.

7

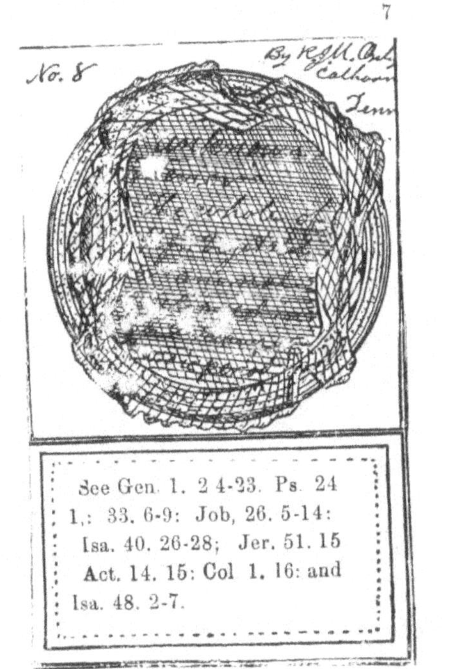

See Gen. 1. 2 4-23. Ps. 24
1,: 33. 6-9: Job, 26. 5-14:
Isa. 40. 26-28; Jer. 51. 15
Act. 14. 15: Col 1. 16: and
Isa. 48. 2-7.

The above cut is intended to show the

p. 6 The claim set up by some Geologists, that vegetable and animal life is from 10,000,000 to 680,000,000, of years older than man, and the above diagram of the geological periods, should give place, to one like to that on page seven; showing all of the geological formations, going on at the same time, and that the age of man, is equal to that of fern, fish and fowl. The fact that this writing is in the center of the Devonian age, is of its self, evidence sufficient to sustain the record of Moses, though we never learn what has been written on these stones.

Carved in the soft sand stone at the bottom of the bed of a lost ocean, in the morning of history; then again flooded by the return of the waters, and then coverd by the sedimentary deposits of more than a thousand years; then lifted high above the water by volcanic force, where for 2000 years it has lain hidden in these East Tennessee, hills until God has seen proper [sic] to bring it to light. The Scripture references on page seven, will be read here with interest.
Illustration on p. 7   No. 8   by RJM. Only   Calhoun, Tenn

Unknown
[unreadable]
The whole of
life (?) vegetable
animal
[unreadable]
[unreadable]
---aic period

See Gen. 1. 2 4-23. Ps 24. 1,: 33.6-9: Job, 26.5-14: Isa. 40.26-28; Jer.51.15 Act.14.15: Col 1.16: and Isa. 48.2-7.

The above cut is intended to show the [end of page 7 with idea continued on page 8 below]

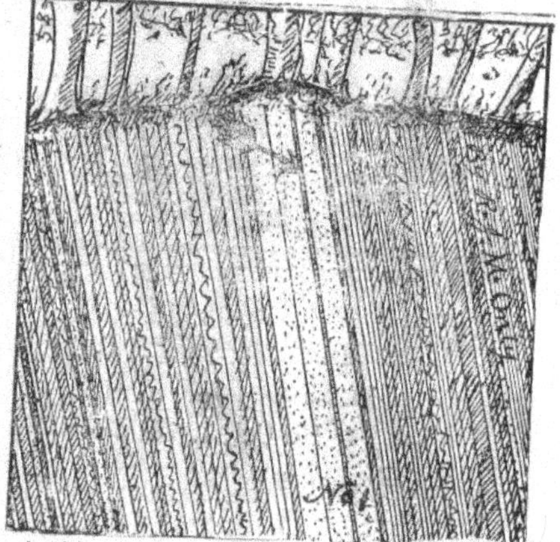

p. 8 possible manner in which portions of the earths crust are elevated or depressed.

The cut below, shows a cross section of the ridge, in which the rock is found.

The arrow, shows a ledge of Old Red sand stone: on the west, or topside of the middle strata the writing is found. [Picture above, Arrow is top center pointing toward right hand dark vertical line in white. Illustration shows trees at the top and the writing says No. 1 by R. J. M. Only.]

A thin strata, of sand stone separates the letters from the top strata; and a thin coat,

p. 9 of sut and ashes over the letters allows the thin rock, mostly to peel off, leaving some, letters filled with the ashes or pumice, stone. In the blank rows on the engraving the thin cement, has not peeled off.

While copying the letters; I knocked off portions of the cement, and with a camel's hair brush, cleaned out the dust, from the letters, to the depth of about the eighth of an inch.

Some who have heard more of this stone than they have seen; criticise by calling the letters the trails of worms. The samples, in the illustration, on page 10, are about one third the full size, and plainly show the manner in which they were cut, and the marks of the tool, with which they were carved. The large character, showing several angles at which the tool, was held is of its self sufficient, to convince any real critic.

The best of Geologists represent that the 400 miles of Tennessee, from the Alleghanies, to the alluvial drifts, of the Mississippi, show almost a complete map of the ge- [word finished on page 10]

ologial ages and they place, the valley, of East Tennessee, in the Devonian, age; and the slates, ores, marble-, lime stones, clayes shale-, old red sand stones and fossil sustain them; and these are the means by which it is proposed to distinguish one age from another. Were it not known when

these letters were invented, there would be made the wildest of claims regarding the age of man: but the facts being known, that---

many of these letters were invented less than 4500 years ago, will not only prevent extravagant claims of that character, but will also: place the men who carved these letters in an age antedating Mr. Winchell's Pre-Adamites, so called: if we follow his course of reasoning.

The range of hills at the top of the large drawing shows the general appearance of the country, and the flag, marks the place.

Below is an enlarged image of the above map found in "The Wonder of the World" book:

p. 01 [10] [*sic*] ological ages and they place, the valley, of East Tennessee, in the Devonian, age; and the slates, ores, marble, lime stone, clayes shale, old red sand stones and fossil sustain them; and these are the means by which it is proposed to distinguish one age from another. Were it not known when [Illustration No. 4 by RJM Only] these letters were invented, there would be made the wildest of claims regarding the age of man; but the fact being known, that---p. 11 many of these letters were invented less than 4500 years ago, will not only prevent extravagant claims of that character, but will also: place the men who carved these letters in an age antedating Mr.

[Alexander] **Winchell's Pre-Adamites, so called; if we follow his course of reasoning.**

The range of hills at the bottom of the large drawing shows the general appearance of the country and the flag, marks the place. [The letters and close-up map are on previous page 208. The map shows the Hiwassee River running into the Tennessee River with the boundary of James County and Bradley County being close to Mt. Ebal. Meigs and McMinn Counties are shown north of the Hiwassee. Calhoun and Charleston with the railroad at Chatata, several miles away, were also in the illustration. The map shows a hand pointing to the location of Mount Ebal. The Illustration is No. 6 by RJM Only.]

p. 12 The map above is apart of the Hiwassee valley. The dark square shows the location of Mount Ebal, and is about seven miles from Charleston, Tenn. [page 208 has map in this book]

The Island at the mouth of Hiwassee, is where the statuary or stone images, shown below were found. Seven of them were plowed up in the ruins, of an earthen templ [*sic*] in 18(92). The clay tablet shown on 14 page was also: found there. [Under the drawing is written Statuary found in 18?? (unreadable) the island at the mouth of Hiwassee Drawn by RJM Only. The Illustration of the pots below has **No. 2 by RJM Only**]

p. 13 Below are found illustrations of pottery made of clay, and pounded shells. These were found within two, or three miles, of Mount Ebal: but the same class is found in all the river valleys of East Tenn.

These are only a few of the many evidences of a habitation, and civilization, of this country ages before the wigwam of the Indian, was pitched among the silent hills, of America. What this writing will reveal, or [Sentence is finished at the top of page 14 on the next page.]

The map above is apart of the Hiwassee valley. The dark square shows the location of Mount Ebal, and is about seven miles from Charleston Tenn

The Island at the mouth of Hiwassee, is where the statuary or stone images, shown below were found. Seven of them were plowed up in the ruins, of an earthen templ in 1892. The clay tablet shown on 14 page was also: found there.

13

Below are found illustrations of pottery made of clay, and pounded shells. These, were found within two, or three miles, of Mount Ebal: but the same class is found in all the river valleys of East Tenn.

These are only a few of the many evidences of a habitation, and civilization, of this country ages before the wigwam of the Indian, was pitched among the silent hills, of America. What this writing will reveal, or

[The pictures at the top of the next page (page 210) are examples of statues that have been found which are similar to the above drawings in "The Wonder of the World". The two statues on the left were found on the Sellers Farm in Wilson County, Tennessee. Internet credit was given to Jefferson Chapman, Ph.D. Frank H. McClung Museum, University of Tennessee, Knoxville. The three statues on the right were found on the Internet at the Smithsonian, National Museum of the American Indian; Georgia Department of Natural Resources Parks and Historic Sites, Stockbridge, Georgia. The five statues are representative of the R. J. M. Only drawings in the book which are seen on this page.]

p. 14 the story it will tell; or the great earthquakes, wars, and epidemics, which wrought the ruin, of those who were here, can only be matters of speculation until further excavations and science will reveal the truth. [Illustration No. 5 by R. J. M. Only is the basket weave above.]

State of Tennessee
   Bradley county
   I Arthur Traynor, Judge of the circuit court for the 17th. Judicial District of Tennessee Hereby certify that I have carefully [p. 15] examined the pictures, and prints, made from the rocks' found by I. H. Hooper, in 1891-- and pronounce the pictures, and prints offered for sale by I. H. Hooper and W. F. Duncan, true copies as stated of the Rock inscription. I further certify, that I. H. Hooper and W. F. Duncan of Chatata Tenn. are citizens of Bradley county Tenn. who own, the curiosity, with whom, I am personally acquainted would not in my opinion, attempt to deceive any person, or the public by putting fraudulent pictures on the market. Given under my hand and seal in Cleveland Tenn. July the 1 st 1894.
                   Arthur Traynor Judge &c.
State of Tennessee,
   Bradley county,

I A. J. Fletcher, Clerk of the Circuit Court in and for Bradley county Tennessee Hereby
certify that Arthur Traynor, whose genuine signature, appears to the foregoing certificate is
the Judge of Circuit Court for the 17 th Judical District of Tennessee, and whose official acts
are entitled to full faith and credit; and I know the other facts, my self. Given under my
hand and seal of office in Cleveland Tennessee July 31 1894
A. J. Fletcher, Clerk, Seal.

16

I certify that the letters, and the large
drawing is as near correct, as I could make
in two weeks. The row of letters, on the
left a c from Webster; those on the right,
are from clay tablets. found in the West.

The cuts, on the 17 th page and inside of
cover are from drawings made by Mr Porter
of Washington; and that on the last page,
of cover is from a photograph of a part of
the Rock.   R. J. M.Only.

There are a few errors. which were overlooked in proof reading. They were noticed too late for correction

COPY RIGHTED OCTOBER 1893, AND
FOR SALE BY I. H. HOOPER
CHARLESTON TENN.
W. F. DUNCAN GENERAL AGENT.
CHATATA, TENN.
DRAWN BY R. J. M. ONLY,
CALHOUN, TENN.

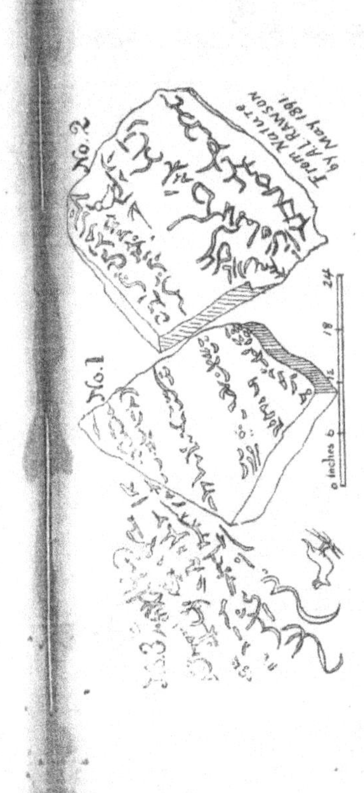

p. 16 I certify that the letters, and the large drawing is as near correct, as I could make in two
weeks. The row of letters, on the left are from Webster; those on the right, are from clay tablets.
found in the West. [Harold Reno thinks the previous reference to Webster (left page) means
dictionary, and the "tablets found in the West" refers to p. 197 where the writing was on Ebal's west side.]

The cuts, on the 17 th page and inside of the cover are from drawings made by Mr. Porter of
Washington; and that on the last page, of cover is from a photograph of a part of the Rock.   R. J.
M. Only. [The photograph on the last page of the cover was not printable, so it is missing.]

There are a few errors, which were overlooked in proof reading. They were noticed too late
for correction.   COPY RIGHTED OCTOBER 1893, AND FOR SALE BY I. H. HOOPER
CHARLESTON, TENN. W. F. DUNCAN GENERAL AGENT, CHATATA, TENN. DRAWN BY
RJM. ONLY, CALHOUN, TENN.

[p. 17 is not numbered. Picture on page 211 right side shows three examples of J. Hampden Porter's
drawings of the Mount Ebal writing from *Nature* by A. L. Rawson May 1891 on page 27.]

(The R. J. M. Only who did the drawings for the book was Return Jonathan Meigs Only who was listed as a
Painter in the *McMinn County, Tennessee 1880 Census*, House Painter in the *1900 Census* and Architect in
the *1910 Census*. Also found on the *Internet Archive* was the *Official Record of the Holston Annual
Conference, Methodist Episcopal Church, South, Eighty-Second Session, Held at Bristol, Tenn.-Va.,
October 11-17, 1905* which said that R. J. M. Only was not a member and not ordained. Zella Armstrong
said that he was part Cherokee, but Harold Reno found no proof. R. J. M. Only did submit records to try to
prove that other families were of Cherokee ancestry. One of those families was the Madison Hawk family
submitted by Ralph Jenkins on Nov. 20, 1998 and found on the Internet at *Genealogy.com*.)

Above is a scan of a post card that was possibly a picture of part of the wall at Mount Ebal which I. H. Hooper and W. F. Duncan hoped to sell (from Earl Hooper estate). The lines angle across the stone from lower left to upper right. Notice the Illustrations on pages 197 and 213 which showed the writing being angled instead of straight across. Some of the symbols found on 197 and 213 can also be recognized.

Since the date for the picture is unknown, John Luther Hooper (see his picture p. 246) may be holding the handle of a pickaxe, and I. H. Hooper (see picture p. 218 which shows I. H. with a moustache) may be holding the shovel; the two men on the left might be scientists such as J. Hampden Porter, Dr. David Starr Jordan, A. L. Rawson or two of the other scientists.

Many pictures have been drawn to illustrate the wall and the writing. One picture (see below) also
attempted to show the "flatiron" stone at the surface that was found first. This would be the first stone that
Isaac Hooper found and also would represent the other stones that marked the wall on the ridge. Some
newspaper articles based the distance between the stones at 25 to 30 feet, and other articles extended that to
50 feet between each of the surface marker stones. Notice the angle of the writing which was said to
extend from lower left to upper right: (R. J. M. Only drawing No. 1 page 207 is very similar.)

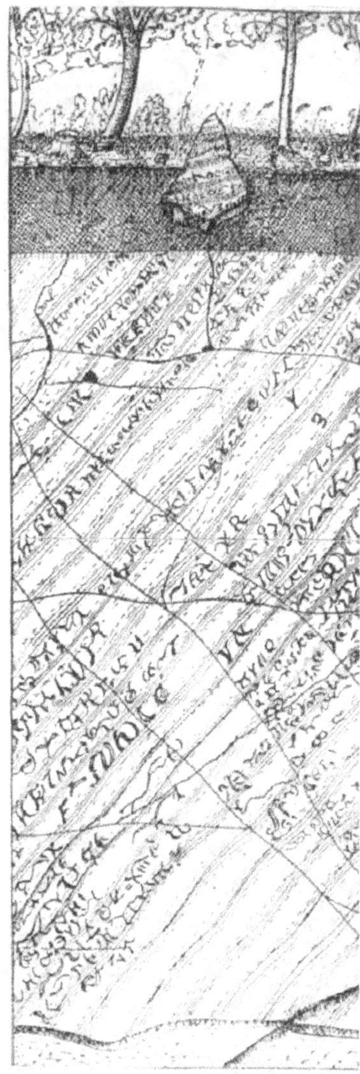

One place this illustration was seen was the October 23, 1920 article in *The Cleveland Herald* on page 2.
After the initial excitement, the wall was left alone until about 1920 when more articles appeared in the
Chattanooga Times and *The Cleveland Herald*. One of the reasons that there was no development from
1900 to 1920 could be the Smithsonian refusing to acknowledge the authenticity of the writing on the stone
sent to them (see pages 200 - 201). Other reasons the Buried Wall might have disappeared from
speculation were the deaths of A. L. Rawson in 1902 and Isaac Houston Hooper in 1915. Also the First
World War intervened and might have dimmed the exploration. Luther Hooper, the son of Isaac Hooper,
also became involved in politics for a time in addition to being a futures trader, and this might have slowed
interest. The following was an article published in *The Cleveland Herald* on February 22, 1917 on page 1:

HOOPER SPEAKS IN SELF DEFENSE
Chairman of Pike Commission Explains Presence of Road Machinery Here.

PURCHASE WAS APPROVED, BUT SHIPPING WAS DELAYED

The Herald is in receipt of the following communication from Mr. J. L. Hooper, Chairman of the county Pike Road Commission. Mr. Hooper's letter is self explanatory, but the Herald comments on it.

Editor *Cleveland Herald*,
Cleveland, Tenn.,
Kind Sir:

I notice it is charged in the *Cleveland Banner* that I, as chairman of the pike road commission, had overstepped my official authority. I want to say right here and now, I have never bought a single piece of machinery without the approval of at least one of the other members of the board. Mr. Durkee and my self bought the graders, but on condition that the county court voted another twenty-five thousand dollars, as they had told us they were going to do. But at the first regular time for county court, after we placed our first order with Mr. John Logan of Knoxville, the court was tied up or any way didn't give us any more money, so I thought the grader business was over, but the court later issued the bonds and Mr. Logan shipped the machinery; which throws the matter in rather an awkward shape, but will say we need the graders. We have a big tractor that Mr. Hardwick bought when on the commission that has sufficient power to handle both machines, and our idea was to take the tractor and two graders and widen our roads, for it is well known they are too narrow and we have proved by experience, that the graders we now have are not sufficient for the work and further we have the engine and why not use it for this purpose instead of having teams to do inferior work. We havn't got enough graders anyway, even of the smaller sizes and these two graders would make us a complete power outfit for road building with only one team to be used for the sprinkler. These graders were bought very reasonable, fifteen hundred dollars for the two machines, with a credit of two hundred dollars for some old discarded machinery, which makes the machines cost us only thirteen hundred dollars, which is a bargain.

Further, Mr. Logan says that he dosen't [*sic*] want the county to have the machinery if they don't want it. He is going to unload the machines at his own expense and show the good people of the county what they will do, and when once put in operation in Bradley County, and the people see them work, you will hear quite a different tale to what you are hearing by a certain bunch of smart Alecks and know-it-all's, and further I invite every one that reads this statement to examine yourself, and if you find that you are clean, and clear of mistakes, cast the first stone, for I will still be here for a few days anyway, and will also pass around by the Banner office, and would ask that when I do, to please tap me lightly with that clean and perfect stone.

I am yours for more and better roads.
J. L. Hooper, Com.

With the political problems taking his time, J. L. Hooper made another decision before April. In the *Cleveland Weekly Herald* on April 5, 1917 another article appeared:

HAS SOLD PROPERTY

J. L. Hooper has sold his milling and farm property to his brother, K. C. Hooper [Albert] and contemplates removing with his family to the north. Mr. Hooper was born and reared in the county and has been promment [sic] for a number of years in public affairs. For the past six months he has served as Chairman of the Pike Roads commission. The fact that he was preparing to leave the section was responsible for his name not being before the court for re-election along with other members of the court, it is said. Mr. Hooper has a number of friends in the county who will be sorry of his decision to leave this section.

(Harold Reno did not find a record of this sale of Hooper Milling Company. Luther and Maudie did move for a time to Chicago, Illinois, according to postcards and letters on pages 224 - 225 of this book.)

By November 21, 1920 J. L. (John Luther) Hooper, Sr., the son of Isaac H. Hooper, was part owner of the farm where the ridge was located (see pp. 217 - 218 for the other heirs). He exhibited one of the stones at the Glenn Hotel opposite the Terminal station according to the *Chattanooga Times* article. The article had the discovery dates wrong and seemed to say that the discovery was only about six years ago. Also the article referred to A. L. Rawson as if he were still alive, but he died in 1902. J. L. Hooper, Sr. said that historians from New Zealand, Italy, Japan, Cuba, France, Spain and other countries had visited the farm. A week later on November 28, 1920, Jane Snodgrass, a writer for the *Chattanooga Times* wrote an article on page 27 entitled "Buried Wall in Bradley County Attracting Nation-Wide Interest." The wall was reported to be 700 feet long and over twenty-two feet deep. She stated that archaeologists said the wall was over 4000 years old. She also referred to the idea of the two lost tribes of Israel that A. L. Rawson thought might have been responsible for the writing.

In another article in *The Cleveland Herald* on December 3, 1920 that copied an earlier article in the *Chattanooga Times*, a statement was made that Professor Rawson believed that the lost tribes of Israel had crossed into America by way of the Bering Strait. J. L. Hooper, Sr. further stated that Professor Rawson was confident that the translation will soon be finished (A. L. Rawson died in 1902). He further stated that when that happens, the Rockefeller Institute and the British museum would vie with other institutions for possession of the tablets (sandstone rock inscriptions?).

Another article from Washington, D. C. on December 3, 1920 was reprinted in the *Chattanooga Times* on December 4, 1920 on page 13. This article made reference to the November 28 article in *The Times* that was referenced above that stated that the wall was a puzzle to officials of the National museum (yet the letter from the Smithsonian written in 1976 and copied on page 201 - 202 of this chapter seemed to say that the Smithsonian in 1902 decided that the wall inscription was not writing). According to this *Times* article, Frederick Giddings of the James building in Chattanooga had brought the wall to the attention of the museum. The Smithsonian contacted Mr. Giddings and said that no statement could be made until someone was sent to study the wall (in 1902 J. Hampden Porter from the Smithsonian did visit and looked at the wall as referenced by A. L. Rawson on page 200 of this chapter). W. E. Myer of Carthage, Tennessee, reputed to be an archaeologist and ethnologist, was present at the Smithsonian and was asked about the wall. He said that he would not make a comment until he had studied the images. His book *The Stone Age Man of the Middle South* was to be issued by the Smithsonian Institute in the next few weeks.

On page two of *The Cleveland Herald* December 23, 1920 another article entitled "Record of Lost Race" referred to the wall as the Hooper wall and stated that further research might be hampered because Professor Rawson had died, and his research papers had burned. The article stated that this would probably be the end of the project unless some other research society became interested. Several articles made reference to A. L. Rawson being the translator of the Moabite Stone, but that also is an exaggeration. Also, hieroglyphics and the ancient language of Israel had been mentioned.

Richard (Rick) Hooper said that his Grandfather Arnold Hooper told him about taking people to the site. He lived on Eureka Road just north of Roy Caldwell's place. He said he charged visitors a small fee to take them in a buggy. He could vaguely remember hearing the archeologists/historians or whatever they were talking about the theory of the lost tribe of Israelites. There was also talk around that time that the materials (stone) to build the wall could have come from upper East Tennessee and people had associated that with the Melungeons. There was a surge of interest in the Melungeons late in the 1800's, and that probably added to the mystery. Granddad Hooper just laughed it off and said he thought the wall was something related to older Indians. (Mound Builders had been suggested.)

In an effort to develop the Mount Ebal site, John L. Hooper, Sr. decided to have an annual picnic day at the site (p. 216). Once while I was talking to Earl Hooper and J. L. Hooper, Jr., they mentioned that their father brought a flying jenny to entertain the people who came. This was a form of carrousel probably powered by a mule, but it could have used a gasoline engine for power. (The information and picture of a simple Flying Jenny with wooden benches, on the next page, were found on the Internet at Mountain Village 1890 Bull Shoals, Arkansas. A favorite place for young men to bring their young lady friends for some courting, the Flying Jenny was one of the first carousels. It was powered, not by electricity but by mule power! The mule would have been hitched to the center pole of the carousel, which she would walk round and round, causing the swings to go round and round, too. The mule usually was a female, called a jenny, hence the nickname for this type of carousel.)

Rick Hooper's grandfather, M. Z. Miller, mentioned that there was a short-cut to Mount Ebal that ran through his property and the day they had the picnic he was upset. Rick thought that maybe he was upset because he was not making any money from the people using the short-cut.

Another newspaper article was printed in the *Chattanooga Times* on August 2, 1921 and also in *The Cleveland Herald* on August 5, 1921 on page 2 written by J. D. Clemmer related to his impression of the wall after attending a picnic. He said the picnic was held on July 29 and 30 about a half mile east of the wall. He went on the describe the wall:

> The east side of the ridge is gravel or chert, the west side is, colored talc layers and shale, but the ridge top has several strata of hard sandstone in almost vertical layers, the dip being a little westward. Between two brown layers of a few feet thickness is a gray layer about a foot or two thick, which stripped off some twenty feet deep and maybe sixty feet long is the famous "wall." A cross-cut entry to the pit coming from the west slope of the hill serves to cut into and expose several small strata of colored talc, one narrow streak being very soft and red. A barb wire fence surrounds the excavation, except at the entrance. Covering the western face of this gray sandstone strata so far as exposed are practically continuous lines of "writing," or "hieroglyphics," ordinarily two or three inches in height, and spaces between about the same, except that some "lines" of the "script" run together, while further on it will branch into two rows. The script lines run diagonally up to the right or south side of the exposed face of this natural strata. The other two sandstone strata closely lie against the one called the "wall." This "wall," or stratum continues downward into the earth, and in both directions as a part of the natural stratification to indefinite but great distances.

> The only curious part about the "wall," which is nothing more nor less than a hard natural stratum of sandstone, consists in the curiously shaped "writing" or "hieroglyphics" which cover all the surface of the stratum so far exposed, and these "script lines" are curiosities indeed.

He went on to say that he thought the rocks were the work of nature and not of man. He said that at one time the rocks were horizontal and that the water that covered them had done the work. He said that vines or other vegetable lines were replaced by the remains of a sandy lake or ocean bottom or maybe a beach.

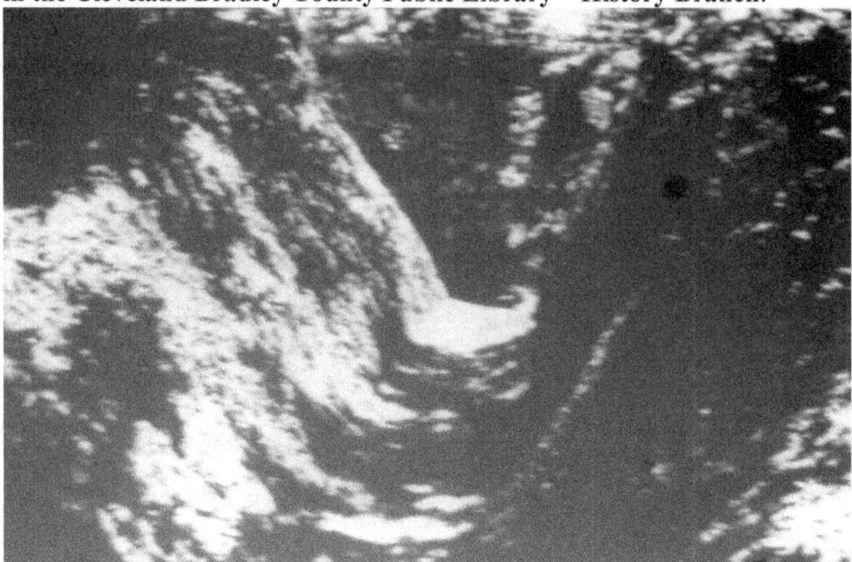

J. D. Clemmer "View of Wall" (See the reference on page 215.)

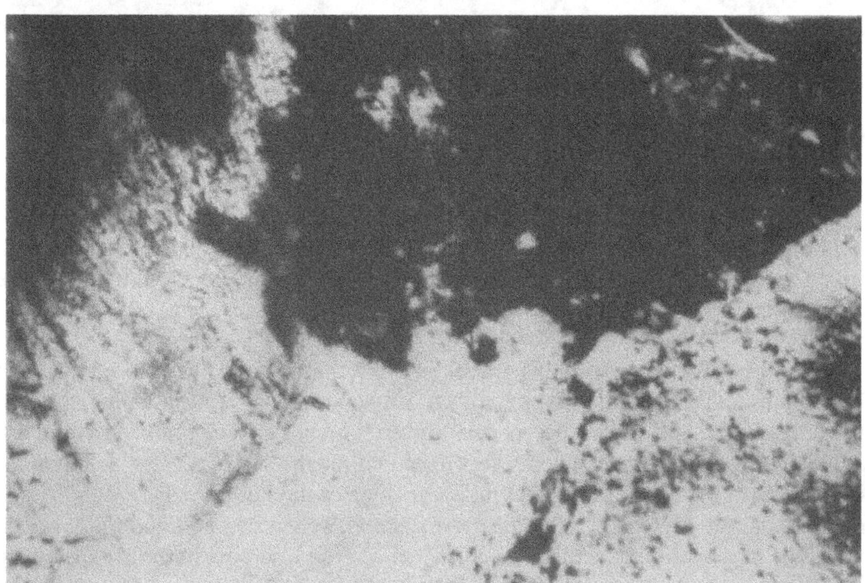

On September 25, 1921, J. L. Hooper, Sr. and his wife Maudie conveyed their interest in the lands of I. H. Hooper to James W. Hooper, a brother, for $200.00.

One strange story that has been told about Mount Ebal involved a strange noise that was heard when the men were digging at the site. William Hooper recounted that a strange ringing noise started, and the workers were so startled that they dropped their picks and shovels and fled. This same story was told by J. L. Hooper, Jr. and Earl Hooper, also.

Except for the mentioned newspaper articles and the short book, little can be found related to what happened to Mount Ebal.

A Warranty Deed was made July 9, 1927 from E. C. Hooper et als. to W. L. Humphrey which mentioned that the two tracts were I. H. Hooper's, and he died Intestate (without a will). The heirs were Lena

(Lennie) Geren (husband G. W. Geren), Lillie Calhoun (husband James Calhoun), Rosa Hooper (husband K. C. Hooper), James W. Hooper (wife Mary Taylor Hooper), Ethel Taylor (husband James B. Taylor) Albert Hooper (wife Pearl Beaty Hooper), Gertrude Brewer (husband J. L. Brewer) and J. (John) L. (Luther) Hooper (wife Maudie Shiflett Hooper). (J. L. had already sold his part to his brother J. W. for $200.00 in 1921.)

Tract 1 in District 2 contained 60 acres and Tract 2 had 85 acres more or less. The buyer agreed to pay $6000.00, to assume a $1500.00 loan owed to W. T. Beaty (see pages 186 - 187 for the 1915 loan) and to pay the remaining $4000.00 to the heirs (J. W. received double since he bought J. L.'s part.).

These two tracts were deeded back to the Hooper family by W. L. Humphrey and wife Maud E. Humphrey on June 12, 1928 for $10.00 as found in *Deed Book 49* pages 26-27. The land was then sold to Albert Hooper for $3100.00 on June 12, 1928 with the same $1500.00 still to be paid to W. T. Beaty as part of the sale. Albert made a promissory note for $1600.00 to pay the rest of the money. This was recorded in *Deed Book 55* on pages 426-428 in Bradley County, Tennessee. In the deed, the family decided not to sell the development rights to Mount Ebal: **"Our interest in Mount Ebal wall and right to and from same and to develop the same is reserved."**   (The bold print was for emphasis and not used in the document.)

On page 246 of this book, Albert Hooper made the comment that "there should never have been a rock taken out of that [place]." Mount Ebal has been an embarrassment to many in the Hooper family.

Isaac Houston Hooper Estate:
After I. H. died Intestate (no will) before October 5, 1915, an inventory of the estate was listed with the Bradley County Clerk for *Inventory of Estates* on page 360.

This picture of Ella Allen Hooper and Isaac Houston Hooper was provided by Carolyn Hooper Bryant.

Inventory of all the goods and chattels of the estate of I. H. Hooper deceased.

--Money—
None at all

--Good Debts—
Small store accounts amounting to about $100.00 or $150.00

--Live Stock—
One (1) mare, five (5) head of mules, nine (9) head of cattle including cows & calves, eight (8) head of hogs

--Tools and Farming Implements—
One (1) buggy, one (1) mower, one (1) hay-rake, cutting harrow, several plows & plow stocks, and several small tools and implements

--House Hold Goods—
One (1) lot of household goods and kitchen furniture, such as is exempt from execution.

--Store—
One (1) small stock of groceries and general merchandise worth about $300.00, one (1) pair of scales, two (2) show cases, a small lot of hay and grains probably all exempt property.

Ella Hooper by Sol. [Solicitor]

State of Tennessee   Ella Hooper as administrator makes oath that the foregoing is a just bill
Bradley County   and perfect inventory of the good and chattels of the estate of I. H. Hooper
                            that has come or ought to have come to her hands as Administratrix of the
estate of I. H. Hooper, deceased, by due Diligence.
                            Ella Hooper
Sworn to and subscribed before me, this Oct. 5th 1915
                            Jno. G. Hearing, Clk.

Another document was on page 500 of Bradley County, Cleveland, Tennessee in the *County Clerk Guardians Administrative Settlements Volume 5 for the years January 1906 to November 1920*:

Partial Settlement of Mrs. Ella Hooper Admrx of estate I. H. Hooper Decd.

Charges

1916			
Sept. 1		To Amt. from L. L. Ross in payt stock goods	$374.00
		" " realized from sale farming implements	130.00
16		" " " " " 2 young mules	225.00
		" " " " " 1 pr. " " Albert Hooper	300.00
		" " " " " 6 hogs Epperson Bros.	74.00
		" " " " " 6 head Jas. Hooper	115.00
		" " " " " hay Rymer Bros.	34.64
		" " " " " corn J. L. Hooper	105.00

Credits

1915			
Mch. 29	Hiwassee Bank Int. on note	$15.00
Apr. 24	Barnes Mfg. Co.	5.75
May	Jno. G. Hearing Clk. Cost of Apelot (Administration Cost)	3.00
June 16	J. F. Harmsh Acct.	50.00

	J. W. Shelton on Acct.	4.00
" 29	D. G. McLane Funeral Expenses	52.50
Aug. 23	J. H. Jarnagin Acct.	31.00
Nov. 29	Insurance	22.80
1916		
Jan. 4	Edwards & Son Acct.	4.60
May 2	Hiwassee Bank on note	251.40
Aug. 1	W. C. Lee on Acct.	5.65
" 29	Merchants Bank	250.00
" "	" "	50.00
	" "	30.00
	Cleveland National Bank	
	On note	109.00
Sep.	J. P. Elkins Int. on note	105.00
Oct. 7	Interest on note	6.75
	State and County Taxes	
	for 1916	24.01
	Insurance 1916	18.64
1917		12.09
	J. P. Elkins on note	105.00
May 3	J. P. Elkins on note	17.00
Nov.	Hall Brothers	46.80
1918		
Mch. 26	W. L. Humphrey on Atty. Fee	5.00
Jan. 1	Bryant Hdwe. Co. acct	13.49
	Mr. A. Ross & Clark	10.00
	Charles Hooper on acct.	14.05
	J. A. Keller on acct	4.00
Mch. 26	Balance in the hands of	
	Administratix	90.11
		1357.64

There are still outstanding debts
of about 1600.00
and no years support has been allowed

Mrs. Ella Hooper

(See page 218 for the final disposition of the area known as Mount Ebal. It is still owned by an heir of the Hooper family.)

Below is a rock found in the Mount Ebal area by Frankie and Joe Conar. Martha Reno is holding the sample which shows markings that may be similar to those found by Isaac Hooper.

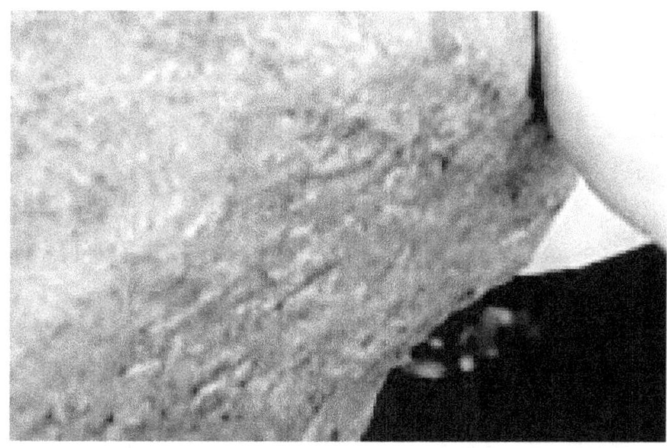

John Luther Hooper's Post Cards and Letters

After Willie (Billie) Tennessee Jenkins Hooper died, a box was found that was tied with a thick blue string. (See p. 247 for Billie's comment.) When the box was opened, post cards and letters were found that date from 1910 related to Maudie Bell Shiflett Hooper and John Luther Hooper. Luther and his father Isaac were owners of Hooper Mill, and Luther was a futures trader who traveled several months out of the year with other traders across the Midwest pooling their money and investing in grain and in other commodities.

Evidently, John L. Hooper, Sr. traveled with Earl Voorhis, Diel, and W. W. Deck while buying Future Contracts. He also knew Earl Cook and J. H. McReynolds from the Chattanooga area. Gertrude Hooper made a comment about a Board of Trade, and I thought of another comment made by Aunt Gertrude (who always bragged on her brother John Luther) that J. L. Hooper had a seat on the Board of Trade (see p. 246). (In conversations with Martha and Harold Reno, she would say a seat on the Chicago Board of Trade.) John Luther and Maudie did live for awhile in 1920 in Chicago, but there was no proof he had a seat (see pp. 224 – 225). The Uhlmann Grain Company did have a seat on the Kansas City and Chicago Boards of Trade, and Luther seemed to be associated with them for at least part of the time (pp. 230, 233, 234).

After the Stock Market Crash of October 25, 1929, someone mentioned that Luther had friends who killed themselves after losing money. On July 6, 1930, Luther told his wife Maudie that this would be the worst winter we have seen and dollars would look as big as wagon wheels to the average man (see p. 233).

The card notations will include the date, address, postmark and the message. Since most of the writing was on picture cards, a description of the card will also be given. Some of the cards said very little but indicated where Luther was traveling. The first card was written by Phoebe to her father C. W. Buck from Pennsylvania. C. W. was a Millwright at the Wolf Company (suppliers of mill equipment) and might have been working on Hooper Mill after it burned May 31, 1909. This card also appears on pp. 182 - 183.

January 1910
Card: "North Main St. Chambersburg, PA"
Postmark: Chambersburg, PA

To: Mr. C. W. Buck
         Charleston, Tenn.
         Hooper Milling Co.
         R.F.D. #2

Dear Papa, ma will write you today some time. Had company until so late last night. Baby & I wanted to leave at noon but it is pouring down rain all morning. Wish you could have been here too.

         Loviable [*sic*]
         Phoebe

December 20, 1912
Card: "Cincinnati Southern Railroad Bridge over
          Ohio River, Cincinnati, Ohio
          Christmas Greetings"
To: Charleston, Tenn.

Hello Pearl. How are you getting along these times, Pearl? Hope you will have a good time for Christmas. J. L. is walking **[John Luther Hooper, Jr. was born in 1911]** can go any where he wants to. When I go to cook for Christmas, I will remember last year. Come down and see me and we will have a good time.

         Bye, Bye
         Maudie Hooper

December 23, 1912
Card: "Merry Christmas"
Postmark: Birchwood, Tenn.

To: Mrs. Maudie Hooper
         Charleston, Tenn.
         R.F.D. #2

Excuse this delay as I have not been feeling so well for the last few weeks. Can't walk yet. You don't know how I would enjoy a visit with you during Holidays but can't come. Hope I will be able to make your next visit more pleasant.
        With best regards to all.
        Annie Watkins

January 14, 1914
Card: "Glimpse of Coney Island from the Lake, near Cincinnati, Ohio"
Postmark: Cincinnati, Ohio

To: Baby Earl Hooper
         Charleston, Ten. [sic]

Hope you are well.
        Papa   **[John Luther Hooper, Sr.]**

January 14, 1914
Postmark: Cincinnati, Ohio

Mrs. J. L. Hooper
Charleston, Tenn.

Good luck.
        J. L. H.

December 17, 1914
Card: "Signal Mountain Inn, Near Chattanooga, Tenn."
Postmark: Chattanooga, Tenn.

To: Mrs. J. L. Hooper
         Charleston, Tenn

Tell Albert [Albert Hooper] be shure [*sic*] and come to Cleveland Friday. I will meet him there.

J. L. H.

July 17, 1915
Card: "Rainbow Falls, Walden's Ridge,
         Chattanooga, Tenn."
Postmark: Chattanooga, Tenn.

To: Mrs. J. L. Hooper
         Cleveland, Tenn.
         (Charleston was written in.)

Guess who?

[Undated and not postmarked but placed here because the business was registered Aug. 9, 1916:]

"The Seasons Greetings with Best Wishes
The Brouse-Skidmore Grain Co."
Cincinnati, Ohio
Henry M. Brouse   Earl F. Skidmore

Best Wishes

     Nanlee Bunch

January 16, 1917
Card: "Hutchinson Hall and Tower, University of Chicago"
Postmarked: Charleston, Tenn.

To: Mrs. Martha Shiflett
       Georgetown, Tenn.
       R no. 1

Hello, hope all are well. Don't come after me till three weeks is out. Wright [*sic*] me a post card back. I am going to school. I never went yesterday it was so icey. Well I recond [*sic*] this is all. (unsigned)

February 7, 1917
Card: "Birthday Greetings"
Postmark: Georgetown, Tenn.

To: Mr. Jim Shiflett
       Georgetown, Tenn.

Hello, how are you? Fine I guess. I am all o.k. I am sending you a card to let you know tax paying day is Friday, so come down. [Only 5 % of the population paid taxes in 1917.]

     Dennie Shiflett

May 29, 1917
Card: "At the Animal Pens, Grant Park, Atlanta, GA"
Postmark: Atlanta, GA.
To: Miss Sarah Elen Hooper
       Georgetown, Tenn.
       R no. 1

Hello, sister. How are you? We are all o.k. Will be home tomorrow. The boys are having a good time down here. They went and saw all the animals in the park. [John L., Jr. and Earl Hooper]

     By, By
     Mama

May 29, 1917
Card: "For the Freedom of the Seas" (handwritten: Harrison Hooper his flag)
Postmark: Atlanta, GA.

To: Mr. Harrison Hooper
       Charleston, Tenn.
       R no. 2

Hello, Harrison. We are all the same. Will be home tomorrow on 42. The boys are having a good time down here. [John L., Jr. and Earl Hooper were the "boys". (Harrison Hooper was born in 1903)]
>So By, By
>Mama

December 25, 1918
Card: "Best Christmas Wishes"
Postmark: Charleston, Tenn.

Harrison Hooper
Charleston, Tenn.
R #2

Dear friend how are you? I am fine. What is old santa going to bring you? Wishing you a merry Christmas and Happy New Year's. Your friend.
>Guess who?
>By, By   ans.

December 19, 1919
Card: "Wm. Penn Home" (handwritten "Wishing you a merry xmas.)
Postmark: Charleston, Tenn.

Mr. Harrison Hooper
Charleston, Tenn.
R.R #2

Dear Friend—will ans. your card received Wednesday: there will be a Xmas tree at Center Point Xmas night. Bring everybody and come.
>A friend
>Florence

December 29, 1919
Card: "The Old Abe Lincoln Log Court House, Decatur, Ill."

Hooper Milling Co.
Charleston, Tenn.

I and Mr. Woods are here tonight on business for our company. This is Sunday night.

December 29, 1919
Card: "New Orlando Hotel and Powers Building, Decatur, Ill."
Postmark: Decatur, Ill.

Hooper Milling Co.
Charleston, Tenn.

Maudy, I wish you was with me here to night. So long old girl.

[The next 6 entries were from Maudie Hooper in Chicago to her children Harrison (b. 1903), Sarah Ellen (b. 1907), John L., Jr. (b. 1911), and Earl (b. 1913).]
1920
Card: "Polk Street Depot, Chicago"

Here is the Depot that I come in & didn't know any body. I went to the traders aid for information.

1920

Card: "Illinois Central Depot, Chicago"
This is where we aim to go to come home. It goes by Cincinnati.

____

1920
Card: "Northwestern Passenger Station, Chicago"

This is where we went Sunday morning. It sure is a fine place.

____

1920
Card: "Rothchild & Co., Chicago"

I have been through this building by my self. Believe me it [*sic*] some store. You can look all day.

____

1920
Card: "Double Deck Motor Bus, Chicago"

Here is the wagon that papa calls the cattle wagon. We ride down on the lower part going out and on the top carriage we go up at the back end.

____

Fred Van Orman, Pres.   Geo. W. Stowe, Vice Pres. & Mgr.
Hotel Victoria
Fire-Proof Construction
Everything New
Victoria Hotel Co.
Clark & Van Buren Sts.
Half Block from LaSalle
St. Station
250 Rooms $1.50 and up
European Chicago

Monday AM 8 1920 **[Pansy was a nickname for Sarah Ellen "Biddy" Hooper.]**
Hello, Pansy, how are you all getting along by this time. Alright I hope. We are well at present. Well it is raining up here this morning. Well I haven't got any letter from you all yet. Write me often and tell me how you all are getting along. Papa said we would leave the last of the week for home. Well I have seen most all of Chicago except the Armour Packing House & Sears & Robuck [sic] Store. He said he would go out there some evening when the market closed. We went out to Jackson park yesterday morning & over cross the river to the first Depot Station in Chicago. All the trains there go west. **(p. 2)** Went to the water works out at Jackson park where the water is pumped out of lake Michigan an run through the big machines and then over the city. It is some show. Sister, I have been through all the big stores. Up here all the girls your size are wearing lace slippers like mine. When it quits raining I am going down the Rothchild big store. It is almost 20 stories high & over across the street is the Speigel May store co. It is 1[one] whole block. I have been over at Bradys office. **(p. 3)** Tell grandma & granpaw we like our new home alright. Papa said he would move us to Chattanooga any time we wanted to move if that is next week or we could stay and put up our fruit that's just with us. Harrison, he wants you to come up here and stay a month with him. Tell the little boys papa said to look at the elephant on his watch chain. He would bring them one when he come. They are white pearl. We had ½ dozen pictures made will send you one will bring the others when I come. Papa said for you to go to the store and get some oats to eat. You can ride the elevated street car all over Chicago for 8 cts. Go over the park for 10 cts. We will try to go to Chattanooga on Saturday. I want grandmaw & sister to go in the stores there and up the elevators. I will bring you all something when I come. Tell J. L. to be good till I come. They have got big red banana up here big as your arm. I will bring some home. Write me often. If we are gone the letters will be returned. I will write you again tomorrow will let you know what day we will leave here.
                    With love to all
                    Mama [Maudie Bell Hooper]

____
February 17, 1923
Card: "Birthday Greetings"

____
July 30, 1923
(Envelope) Mr. J. W. Cooper
                310 Holston Nat'l Bank Bldg.
                Knoxville, Tenn.

(Back of Envelope) In case of accident notify Harrison Hooper Georgetown, Tenn.

____

December 22, 1923
Card: "Christmas Cheer
            Bringing all kind thoughts and wishes and
            the Seasons Greetings"
Postmark: Benton, Tenn.

J. L. Hooper
Charleston, Tenn.
Rt. # 3

Just a line to let you know I am thinking of you.
            Love,
            Grandmother [Ellen Allen Hooper to J. L. Hooper, Jr.?]

____
July 31, 1924
Card: "The Craven House and Point Lookout, Lookout Mountain, Tenn."

Miss Inez Murphy
Spring City, Tenn.

Not to surprise you but to remind you of a friend.

        S. E. Hooper

____
December 2_, 1924
Card: "Best Christmas Wishes"
Postmark: Charleston, Tenn.

________ Hooper
Charleston, Tenn.
RR no. 2

Wishing all good wishing for a Merry Xmas.

        Laton

____
December 23, 1924
Card: "Here's a right good wish and hearty too
            For a Merry Christmas to all of you
            Christmas Wishes"
                Clara M. Geren

Postmark: Cleveland, Tenn.

Mrs. Maude Hooper
Route 3 (Charleston marked out), Georgetown, Tennessee

Clara M. G.

____

Miss Hazel Branam
Charleston Tenn. RR 3

Best wishes for

S. E. Hooper

____

Meg Ross
Charleston Tenn. Route

Best wishes

Sarah Ellen Hooper

____

Miss Sarah E. Hooper
Georgetown Tenn.

Best wishes

____

Ollie & Bula Millaway
Georgetown Tenn. R. F. 1

Best Wishes

Sarah Ellen Hooper

____

December 22, 1925
Card: "May the Yule-tide season bring
              Happiness and Good Cheer"
Postmark: Birchwood, Tenn.

Mrs. Maudie Hooper
Georgetown, Tenn.
R. 1

Wish you all a Merry Xmas & Happy New Year.

        Mary Randolph

____

March 3, 1926
Card: "Florentine Dining Room, Hotel Gibson, Cincinnati, Ohio"
Postmark: Cincinnati, Ohio

J. L. Hooper
Georgetown, Tenn.

How is the pigs?

____

March 3, 1926
Card: "Hotel Gibson, Cincinnati, Ohio"
Postmark: Cincinnati, Ohio

Mrs. J. L. Hooper
Georgetown, Tenn

Expect to leave here tomorrow for Dixie.
       Best wishes
       Papa

———————————

1926
Graduation Invitation:
Card: Clara Mae Geren

Mr. & Mrs. J. L. Hooper and Family
Mrs. Maude Hooper
Route 3 (Charleston marked out) Georgetown, Tennessee

Class 1926
The faculty and Senior Class
of
Bradley County High School
request the pleasure of your company at the
Tenth Annual Commencement Exercises
on Tuesday, May twenty-fifth
at eight o'clock
High School Auditorium
Cleveland, Tennessee

———————————

December 24, 1926
Card: "Christmas Greeting
       Just to say, Merry Christmas
       And Happy New Year, too!
       Just to say, no day passes
       That I don't think of you!"
Postmark: Benton, Tenn.

J. L. Hooper & Family
(Charleston marked out) Georgetown, Tenn.
R. # 3

Lots of Xmas wishes.
       The Brewers   [Gertrude and John]

———————————

No date
Card: "Best Wishes"

Miss Nanlee Bunch
207 Covel St.
N. Chattanooga, Tenn.

Best wishes for a happy new year.

       Sarah Ellen Hooper

———————————

1928
Road Map: "Standard" Road Map of Tennessee, Arkansas, Louisiana, Mississippi Alabama, Georgia and

228

May 9, 1928
Graduation Invitation:
Cards: Alvin A. Taylor
             Dennis K. Taylor
Postmark: Cleveland, Tenn.

Mr. and Mrs. J. L. Hooper and Family
Georgetown, Tennessee
R.F.D. # 1.

The Faculty and Senior Class
of the
Bradley High School
request the honor of your presence
at the
Commencement Exercises
Tuesday evening, May twenty-second
at eight o'clock
nineteen hundred and twenty-eight
High School Auditorium
Cleveland, Tennessee

1928
Card: "Comanche Indians, Near Chichasha, Okla."
Postmark: Caldwell & F.T. Worth

Mrs. J. L. Hooper
Georgetown, Tennessee

Very dry here but light rain here to day, and turning cool. Good crops here.

Yours
J. L. H.

December 21, 1928
Card: "Merry Christmas and Best Wishes for the New Year"
             Elsie

Mr. J. L. Hooper
Route 1
Georgetown, Tennessee

December 22, 1928
Card: "May you abide in the glow of happiness at
             Christmastide and throughout the New Year"

Mr. & Mrs. J. G. White
Postmark: Cleveland, tenn.

Mr. & Mrs. John L. Hooper
Georgetown, Tennessee

No date
Card: With the best wishes for happiness at

Christmas time and during the coming year

granmother [*sic*]

December 23
Card: "James Point, Signal Mountain, Chattanooga, Tenn."
Postmark: Chattanooga, Tenn.

Mrs. J. L. Hooper
Georgetown, Tenn.
R. # 1

Dear mama, we are in town now. Earl is enjoying his self fine. Will be up Xmas.
    With Love

    S. E., C. M. & Earl   **[Sarah Ellen McDowell, Claude McDowell & Earl Hooper]**

December 24, 1929
Futures Letter: "Grain Letter Branch Office
            The Uhlmann Grain Co. of Chicago and Kansas City.,
            607 Tradesmens National Bank Blg. at Oklahoma City.,
            Phone 3-2841; L. D. 279; W. W. Deck, Manager, December 24, 1929"
Postmark: Oklahoma City, Okla.

J. L. Hooper
Georgetown, Tenn.

The Uhlmann Grain Company and their Oklahoma City office force wishes to each one, a Merry Christmas
and a Happy New Year.

Grain Belt Forecast: Dakotas, Nebraska and Kansas mostly fair tonight....
Argentine: Government estimate published today indicated export surplus new crop wheat 58,800,000
bu's.
Chicago Cotton Close: Wheat:...   Kansas City:....

No date:
Card: "Bull Fight Mexico City"

From Papa to Mama Hooper

February 18, 1929
Card: "Group of Military Monuments, "Iowa," "Wisconsin," "New York." on Lookout
            Mountain and Chickamauga Park, near Chattanooga, Tenn."
Postmark: Chattanooga, Tenn.

Mrs. J. L. Hooper
Georgetown, Tenn.
R. # 1

Sun. night
Dear Mama made our trip back alright. Will write again soon.

    S. E. & C. M. **[Sarah Ellen McDowell and Claude McDowell]**

May 1929
Graduation Invitation:

Card: Marvin B. Hooper
Postmark: Cleveland, Tenn.

Mr. and Mrs. J. L. Hooper and Family
Georgetown, Tennessee
Route 1

> The Faculty and Senior Class of
> Central High School
> of
> Bradley County
> request the honor of your presence
> at the Commencement Exercises
> Tuesday evening, May the twenty-first
> at eight o'clock
> High School Auditorium
> Cleveland, Tennessee

____
Graduation Invitation:
Card: Boyd M. Hooper

> The Faculty and Senior Class of
> Central High School
> of
> Bradley County
> request the honor of your presence
> at the
> Commencement Exercises
> Tuesday evening, May the twenty-first
> at eight o'clock
> High School Auditorium
> Cleveland, Tennessee

____
June 7, 1929
Card: "George Peabody College for Teachers, Nashville, Tenn."
Postmark: Nashville, Tenn.
Mrs. J. L. Hooper
Georgetown, Tenn.

I have stoped [*sic*] off in Nashville on my way back from the west. Hope to be home Sat.
    Gby
    J. L. H.

____
1929
Letter: "Skirvin Hotel
    Skirvin Operating Company
    Proprietors
    Oklahoma City"

    J. L. Hooper
    Georgetown, Tenn.

    Thurs. Eve
    Dear Mama and boys, I am well hope you are all the same. Got your letter. I went to see about your business at Sears Roebuck. They had shiped [*sic*] the stuff out yesterday so they said. They

had gotten it misplaced and had never shiped it out it out but they they [*sic*] finally traced it up. Well I may not get off on Saturday for home but will come in time for Xmas. The market is maxing very fast and I want to make all I can before I leave here. I will write you again Sat. if I don't leave for home.

J. L. Hooper

December 21
Card: "Christmas Wishes
              A Happy Christmas and New Year
              A heartfelt wish and most sincere"
Postmark: Benton, Tenn.

Mr. & Mrs. J. L. Hooper & Family
Georgetown, Tenn.

Mother [Ellen Allen Hooper]

January 26, 1930
Card: "General Bragg's Headquarters, Missionary Ridge, near Chattanooga, Tenn."
Postmark: Chattanooga, Tenn.

Mrs. J. L. Hooper
Georgetown, Tenn.
R # 1

Dear Mama & Budor (Brothers?), we are in town now have just got here. Made our trip back alright. Will write again soon.
          Love,
          S. E. & C. M. **[Sarah Ellen Hooper McDowell and Claud McDowell]**

July 6, 1930
Cards: "Souvenir of Tulsa, Okla."
Postmark: Oklahoma City, Okla.

Mrs. J. L. Hooper
Georgetown, Tenn.
Various scenes in Tulsa, Oklahoma

July 6, 1930
Letter: "The Mayo in Tulsa
              Six Hundred Rooms Each with Bath"
Postmark: Oklahoma City, Okla.

          Mrs. J. L. Hooper
          Georgetown, Tenn.

          Sun. Eve
          Dear Mama & Boys
          I am feeling fine to day. Have been feeling better since friday [*sic*] can breath good. Seems as though a great load had been taken off of me in some way. I don't feel like the same person it feels so good to breathe good and free, but am going right on with the treatment for awhile yet. I hope to get all o. k. before I stop. Well I notice you said in your letter that Harrison had come home and looked bad. I am not surprised at all. I told you when He went down there that he could not live there. I don't think He will make good with White either for people will not buy swings this time of year enough to justify him to try to sell them. **(p. 2)** Money is hard to get now

and is going to be worse later on. This in my opinion is going to be the worst winter we have seen in manyayear [*sic*]. Dollars will feel and look as big as wagon wheels to the average man. Well I and Earl Voorhis went over to Tulsa Sat. morning on business. A very good town but not up with Okla. City by a lot. Never let Mrs. Rogers know I was in the city. We came back this morning in time for church. Halcome preached a fine sermon. Am going again to night. Wish you was here to go with me. Hope you are well by this time. I look for a buisy [*sic*] week this week. We get a cotton report on Tuesday and the grain report on Thursday, and all ready had three holidays. Glad the boys are fencing off **(p. 3)** the meadow for the stock. That will be fine. **[Luther had drawn an arrow toward the sixth floor picture on the letterhead and "my room" was written.]** Sorry to hear of Calhouns sickness even though he hates me. It is all the worse to and for him self. Did his father get well? You never wrote me only you said He was verry low. Taylor is coming out of the kinks or he is getting in a worse one one [*sic*]. Lucky that George Geren had his inshurance [*sic*]. Diel and his family and his brother in law have gone to Colorado on a visit and to organize a pool up in Denver. They have sent me $600.00 so for and looks like they will do well they say up there. Earl Voorhis gave me a check to day for $2000.00 more for the pool. Hope I get a good move this week. Write me all the news.
by by to all
       Papa XXXX

July 11, 1930
Card: "Cafe Trianon, Hotel Muehlebach, Kansas City, MO."
Postmark: Kansas City, MO.

Mrs. J. L. Hooper
Georgetown, Tenn.

Arrived all o. k. this morning. Hot and dry here. Hope to see you soon.
       With Love,
       J. L. Hooper

July 12, 1930
Letter: "Uhlmann Grain Co.
          Members: Chicago Board of Trade
          Kansas City Board of Trade
          Minneapolis Chamber of Commerce
          New York Produce Exchange
          Winnipeg Grain Exchange
          Kansas City, MO."
Postmark: Oklahoma City, Okla.

Mrs. J. L. Hooper
Georgetown, Tenn.

At the office Sat. Eve
Dear Mama & Boys, I am feeling very well today hope you are all well. I and Mr. Deck went to Kansas City Thursday evening on the train, it was hot got there Friday morn 7:45 a.m. Staid [*sic*] for the market so when it closed, I caught a big trymortored [*sic*] (trimotored) plane and came back to Okla City. Left there at 3 p.m. got here at 6:15 p.m. They was 12 of us on the plane all men. I shure [*sic*] had a funny feeling when the plane started to go up. It bucked and swerved. I shure did wish that I never had started, but when we got up 9000 ft. the plane moved along perfectly smoothe [*sic*], nothing but just a roar from the engines. We went up above the clouds it shure looks scarey. When you run into the clouds, but they are pretty **(p. 2)** an automobile looks like a big speck from that height. It was cool up there, it was so hot in Kansas City I didn't want to stay ther [*sic*] over night. they say that they can't sleep only in the morning. Any way I am here and safe I thought of you and would of liked for you to of been along but guess you would not of went up with me. Mr. Deck stayed said he would come on the train. I am sending you the little pack of

cotton that they give all the passengers to put in their ears also part of my ticket you can keep them
for a souvenir   if you choose to. Well the market is working very well. Say shall I come home
or will you come out here and when can you come?
       By By to All XXXX

July 14, 1930
Letter: "Uhlmann Grain Co.
           Kansas City, MO."
Postmark: Oklahoma City, Okla.

Mrs. J. L. Hooper
Georgetown, Tenn.

Dear Mama & Boys
I am feeling verry [*sic*] well to day it is clouds here this morning and is cool here at night. Hope you are
all well. According to our weather report here, you had a rain ther Sunday hope so any way. I am sending
you my air plane credentials to keep for a souvenir. I may never ride on another one. I think it would be
best for you to come out here as I can attend to my tradeing better here. Guess you got my letter this
morning.
       By By
       Papa XXXX

July 3, [1930]
Card: "Hall of Records, Chamber St., New York"
Postmark: Cleveland, Tenn.
Mrs. J. L. Hooper
Georgetown, Tenn.
R. 2.

Dear Auntie—Uncle Jim died last night at 11 o'clock. Funeral at Charleston—1 o'clock, Friday afternoon.
Will all meet and leave Mclains funeral home at 1 o'clock Friday—be sure & be there.
       Dennis Taylor

**[James Madison Calhoun died at Speck Hospital from Paralyses on July 2, 1930. The amount of the
McLain's Funeral Home bill was $477.00 which included the coffin, Clark Vault, Burial Robe and
Opening Grave.]**

March 11, 1931
Letter
Mrs. M. B. Hooper
Georgetown, Tenn. R#1

R#3 Cleveland, Tenn.
Mar. 11 – 1931

Dear Children
Just to let you know that I am still in the land & want to see you all real bad & would have but the weather
& roads would not permit. I never knew you were sick Mauda till you were better, do hope you are still
better. Be sure & don't neglect your self. I am just so home sick to see you all. I guess when I do get to
come I just stay till you all get tired of me. Tell Earl & Jay I was so proud to see in the paper where they
had their 8th grade certificate. How are you getting along? Luther, would love to see you. Tell Harrison &
Jewel to come over to the 5th Sunday meeting Stansbery is coming up to preach that day. Wish you all
would come. Well my feet & ankles are some better. They are not swelled so bad but I can't walk good
get my Heart beats to hard **(p. 2)** makes my ears puff so hard have to be careful what I eat but am geting
[sic] some strength along so I hope to see you all soon. Am at Ethels so good by. Write soon.

Lovelingly Mother **[Ella Allen Hooper died 1935.]**

Georgetown Tenn
March 21th (19) 31

Mrs. J. L. Hooper,
Dr. Hughes had me add Pepsin enough to drops so you could take Teaspoonful at a dose. The Iron may effect [sic] your teeth. You can take it in a cane **[Cane sugar?]**.

Yours truly
J. T. Smith MD

(Maudie Bell Shiflett Hooper died April 3, 1931.)

July 15, 1937
Postmarked: Cincinnati, Ohio

Harrison Hooper
West Side Filling Station
Cleveland, Tenn.

Dear Son & Family
I aimed to of written you yesterday but was out of the city on Business and got back to late to get mail off. We are having a general meeting of all of our prospects tomorrow. Things looks good to me here at present and you know how cautious I am from now on. I will write you again tomorrow, and tell you how & what we have done. Write me Gen. Delivery.

As ever Papa

August 5, 1937
Card: "From the Government Building, Cincinnati,
        Ohio"
Postmarked: Cincinnati, Ohio

Mr. & Mrs. Earl Hooper
Georgetown Tennessee

Arrived O.K. Papa is well. Raining here today.

Love,
Harrison

December 23, 1937
Card: "New Phoenix Co. Lexington, KY."
Postmarked: Lexington, KY.

Lexington K. Y.
Dec – 23 – 1937

Earl & Billie, J. L. & Loise, Harrison & Jewell, Mc & S. Ellen, Barbara Sue & Baby June

I am well as common. Hope all are well there. I am sending you a little xmas. I aimed to send send [sic] it by Harrison but He never stoped off here last night on the bus. I met the bus as He said to do. Guess He went home on the train. The white handkerchiefs are for you boys; the colored ones for the girls, the boxes for the Grand Babies. **(p. 2)** I would of liked to come home for xmas but I am buisy as I can be at present. Hope that I can come to see you later on and spend a few days with all of you. I am going to Cincinnati to night to get some of my clothes. From there I will go to Louisville K. Y. I would like to hear from all of you while I am there. You write me the first of the week in care of the Cherokee Hotel Louisville KY **(p. 3)** and tell me all the news. I will be looking for a letter from all of you when I get there.

This letter is to all.
As ever
Papa

(Luther continued to live until October 25, 1953. As an older man he lived where ever he could including at his cousin's house [Boyd Hooper]. Finally he lived with John L. Hooper, Jr. and died at his son's home.)

____

The following are cards with no dates and no postmarks:
Card: "A Joyous Easter"
       Each year the spring returns bringing new
       life; so may new joys ever follow each other
       throughout all time for you!

____

Mr. J. L. Hooper
Charleston, Tenn. R.R. 3

I have three little baby goats. You ought to be over here and see them. Boyd H.

____

Card: "With the best of Good Wishes for Christmas Cheer,
       Health, Peace and Plenty and a Joyous New Year."

Mr. and Mrs. Buford W. Goins

____

Card: "Suppose you had a friend that loved you very dearly
       who never wrote a line; don't you think he'd be acting queerly?"

____

Hello Sam
Received your card. Was glad to hear from you. Oh! I bet you had a time in town.

____

Card: "The joys of the Yuletide season;
       Happiness cheer friendships true;
       Prosperity in all undertakings--
       Are the sincerest of wishes for you."

Mr. and Mrs. H. K. Cook

____

Card: "Christmas Greetings
       Accept my hearts best wishes.
       They are fervent, warm and true;
       May the Fairest gifts life offers
       Be the sort it offers to you!"

Mrs. Norah McDowell

____

Card: "May all the Perfect Joys combine for you
       In a Merry Christmas"
J. Howe

____

Card: "For wheresoever I looked, the while,
       Was nature's everlasting smile."
                       Bryant [Author of quote on preceding page]

Mrs. Gladys Hooper
809 W. 17th St.
Cleveland, Tennessee
C/O W. H. Hooper

Hello Gladys
Just a few lines not to surprise you but gently remind you.

"A Friend" –
19.5.8.
Guess Who

____

Card: "Senior High School, North Little Rock,
          Arkansas"

9-8501
Mrs. Hicks Arnold

____

Card: "City Park, Charleston, S. C."

Mrs. J. L. Hooper
Charleston, Tennessee

Margaret Shamblin

____

Card: "Goat Nursing a Baby, Mexico"

From Papa to Earl Hooper

____

Card: "Abraham Lincoln's Old Home, Springfield, Illinois"

The Gertrude

[The signature of "The Gertrude" was a perfect end to the chapter because the next chapter is Gertrude Hooper Brewer talking to her brother Albert Hooper.]

Conversations with Gertrude Hooper Brewer and Albert Hooper

Conversations with Gertrude Hooper Brewer, her brother, Albert Hooper, their nephew Earl Hooper and his wife Billie Jenkins Hooper took place in 1975 at the home of Martha Hooper Reno and Harold Reno in Georgetown, Tennessee. It began with a discussion of sugar cane being processed in Florida. Harold Reno recorded and transcribed the conversations, but since some talking was taking place in the background and sometimes interruptions happened, Harold tried to include only the main line of discussion while leaving out the background talking and leaving out the interruptions.

Albert: It's cut up **[sugar cane]**. I don't [know] how they get it going in that blamed truck. I reckon they have a way of getting that there seed away over at the refinery. They might have had a place in there where the top falls into itself.

Harold: Chopping it up about a foot long?

Albert: Yeah, that's what it looked like to me chopping it up about a foot long. It was between West Palm Beach and Fort Myers. We come right through the center.

Harold: Were they blowing it into trucks or something the whole time?

Albert: It's like putting up silage. In a way it's just a different way of blowing it in. They've got a blower that blows it into the trucks. Well, they take it over to refineries, just press that juice out of there, cut that up and refine it some way. I never went over to the sugar refinery. If I had time we would have gone over there. I would loved to have seen it. I would imagine it's all brown sugar when it's....

Harold: Is that a different kind of cane to what we have up here?

Albert: It looked to be like some of our old orange type cane [we] used to have. I don't know; I didn't pay too much attention. I just know it was sugar cane. It looked like our old cane.

Harold: Did you ever raise much cane up here?

Albert: We used to. They'd raise it, but we don't no more. Yeah, they used to have good cane patches. Didn't they Earl. Yeah, used to have good cane patches didn't they Earl. Yeah, they'd make sorghum, 100 gallons, the old farmers would a piece, lots of them. There's an old cane mill below Etowah, the last one I seen. They make molasses up there yet. Plumb old sorghum—I 've been by there when they make them, this side of Etowah in McMinn County.

Earl: Yeah, there was one over here on the Wilson farm. That fellow Stokes, he made some over there.

Albert: Well, they ground that old cane with a mule to it and now they pull it with a tractor or something, but they used to drive that old cane with that old lever, them old mules going round and around. Now, they've got one at up there at that cove way back there, Cades Cove. Yeah, that old mill up there, I seen that. They've got an old corn mill up there grinding this corn, old corn rock, old water mill, Cades Cove.

Harold: They bring the water down on the wooden plume.

Albert: Old water mill, Cades Cove.

Harold: Did you ever hear about the tornado—it just went above that mill. They were in there working. They said they heard it go through. Tore the trees off.

Albert: It did a lot of damage in different places.

Harold: Yeah, it has done damage in about all the states around here. That was bad last year when those hit.

Albert: Well, that was bad there in Cleveland. In South Cleveland, down through there tore up all up all them good houses just like this one. Took the roof off them.

Harold: We were there at school, and we saw that cloud go around it. Just barely missed that school **[Bradley Central High School]**. If it had hit there that would have been too bad **[April 3, 1974]**.

Albert: Well, Conasauga River School got blown away, you know. They had a good school there.

Harold: Do you have any idea why that was called a signal tree up there on that knob?

Albert: Well, it was the tallest tree on them knobs. The best I recollect, called the signal tree. They said you could see, well, the incline [at] Lookout Mountain. They said you could see it from there.

Harold: But, you don't know if they ever used it to signal anybody or anything?

Albert: No, don't know that they did. That was back yonder when I used to come over to Earl's grand daddy's, old man Shiflett.

Harold: Where did he live?

Albert: He lived—J. L.'s got the old home place, ain't he Earl.

Harold: Oh, is it the old house across from J.'s there?

Earl: No, that's where Uncle Jim (Shiflett) lived. Grandpa lived right up on top of the hill there where that old house is.

Albert: His grandfather had an old house.

Earl: You know where J's house is there?

Harold: Not where you lived—is that the same one? Yeah, I know where is....

Earl: Not the same house.

Albert: That's the grandpa Shiflett place there. I've eat good many a meal there in there. Your grandma was a good cook.

Harold: Shifletts must have had a big place here.

Albert: They had a good place in there. Uncle Jim Shiflett, old man John and all of them. Uncle Jim used to spay hogs, Earl, and come to our place and spay over there at the Hooper Mill, no telling how many.

Earl: Yeah, I have seen him spay them.

Albert: I have lived through it all **[b. May 3, 1890 d. Jan. 31, 1978]**. A lot of stuff went on in my time.

Harold: You think time changed that much?

Albert: Oh, it has changed, yeah. I can recollect there in Cleveland there on Inman Street—I have seen it two inches deep in blue mud. Blue mud—they would have gravel there, have four horses, the old mill wagon teams, that stretcher team knock that mud back teams that britching thing on the back of the horses, and it would look like mud. Old Joe Hawks transfer team—Earl, he had two or three wagons, you know, Cleveland Transfer Company. I can recollect them horses. Old Campbell Jones worked three abreast on the fire wagon.

Harold: What kind of horses were they?

Albert: Good ones—the best you could get, Old Campbell Jones....

Harold: Were they these, the kind that had big feet?

Albert: No, they didn't use them—they used a keener grade of horses than that. They couldn't run them big ones like them horses they kept. Old Fire Bell, the best horse he ever had got Campbell motion to whip at him and he fell. Hit behind his fore leg and killed him just that quick. Campbell, they said he went to bed, went home and went to bed that day like to killed him. The night the college burned, he broke a two dollar halter when the alarm went to go to that wagon. He knowed his business. Old Hawk, they called him. Yeah, they said he tore up a two dollar halter when that alarm went in. That liked to have killed Campbell when he lost that horse. The next one he got was Old Fire Bill.

Harold: Was he the only man that took care of the fire wagon or....

Albert: Yeah, livery stable there and had them harnesses hung up and they fell on the horses—just jerk a, and them horses run under them harnesses, jerk a trigger, and it fell on them. Slap them hames together and look out when they came out of there, they came out of there in a lope. Well, they done it. Yeah, yeah, I've seen them run.

Earl: Them horses knowed what to do when they heard that alarm, didn't they?

Albert: Yeah, they knowed what it was.

Harold: How many did you say, four?

Albert: Three. Three—you worked two awhile in a big wagon and then they put three in abreast—one in the middle and one on each side. Had three abreast. They would bust them streets wide open. They would run pretty good. Catch that brake on that fire wagon, and he would stop it. That's the only way they had then. They didn't have these here fire trucks—they had horses. Well, they had them in Chattanooga that way too.

Harold: Well, how much water could he carry on there?

Albert: He didn't carry it. They had this, they had this city you know where they hooked them hose up. They had about, I don't know how many hoses. Yeah, yeah, they had them big fire plugs and always have them around the city you know. They couldn't carry no water on them horses. No, he couldn't do that. They pulled a wagon and a pump on it. They would pump that water.

Harold: Was it a manned pump?

Albert: No, no, it pumped it some way. Yeah, them old hoses was big old long hoses.

Earl: What was it—gasoline operated motor, was it?

Albert: No, I don't know how that run, Earl, I forget. Had suction some way.
Harold: Well, when did they get their first fire truck out there?
Albert: Well, now, I forget. I forget what year it come in there.
Harold: Was it in the 20s or 30s? Pretty late?
Albert: No, it was in the 20s, I believe, yeah.
Harold: Did you say his [Earl's] father was the first one to have a truck? Or what did you say?
Albert: Hooper Mill Company bought first White truck that come Bradley County **[see page 190 for picture]**. His daddy—I drove for him in 1914. Luther drove it all the time, and when he wasn't on it, I drove it. I worked for him. I drove that old right hand drive, four cylinder motor. You could hear that little old motor cry, buddy. It would get it. I tell you what we done. One night he had 500 bushels of meal sold or 600 to them down in Chattanooga. The corn needed to go and he shipped that corn and he lacked 94 bushels and a half getting it. All night we ground that night until eleven o'clock. He loaded me 50 bushels of meal for Cleveland the next morning. He lit out that night to Chattanooga. All right, he got up there to Uncle Andy Hooper's, Earl, going around that and he stove the front end off that—the truck flipped over. I didn't more get straightened out in the bed until he come back and said, "Get your horses. Every time I go to pull back I'm going in the ditch with the back end. Bring old Mack and Deck. Hook them to me in the road." And they wouldn't quit either. Now in the dark I took that old wagon, hooked them old wagon handles and hooked that logging chain to back end of it. And I says now when I speak to them you let it have it. I said I want to tighten that chain. I spoke to old Mack and Deck there in that road, and all you could hear were Mack and Deck's feet. I drug him back up in the road, and he said, "You stay here until I get around that old mud hole at Frank Johnson's, and I'll be all right." I stood there and heard that old horn when he went around it. I went on back and got in bed around twelve or one o'clock. I had 50 bushels of meal to load the next morning and go to Cleveland. Well, I slept four or five hours and got up and loaded it. Went on to Cleveland and got it unloaded over there. Earl, old Cal Hardwick always made the best chili of anybody, and I decided to eat me some chili, and old Luther Pruitt—I knowed him down there—he came along said, "Albert, I seen your truck in Chattanooga while ago when I caught the train to come home." I knowed Luther had got there. I had them horses, and I came in about nine or ten o'clock that night. That's the way we had to work. Yeah, I knowed when he went around that mud hole. You could hear that little motor just stand there. Boys, it would sing—it was a good one, right hand drive now, buddy; four gears, solid tires—back tires had a groove in them about three inches apart, slick tires. They weren't like those you get now.
Martha: What were your parents' names?
Albert: I. H. Hooper—Isaac Houston—I believe was his name. My mother's name was Ellen. She was an Allen. I don't know what her father's name was. I have heard them say. I don't recollect it.
[Aunt Gertrude and Billie Hooper had brought old pictures, and they discussed who was in each picture. Billie's are included in this chapter; we did not get copies of Aunt Gertrude's.]
Gertrude: Baby, Alvin Taylor, Marvin Hooper, Jim and Mary, Marvin and Roy, Alvin and Billie—wasn't he handsome? **[Gertrude mentions several pictures that are on the following pages.]**

Alvin Taylor

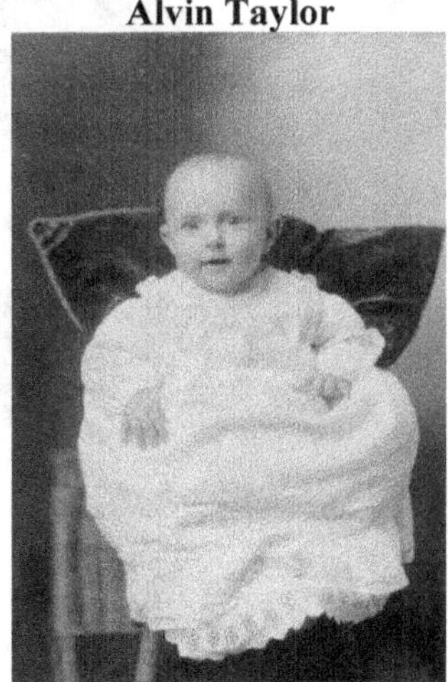

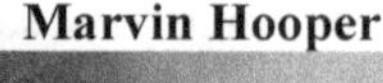

Marvin Hooper

Jim, Mary, Marvin and Roy Hooper

Albert: We know him.
Gertrude: I think Earl looks like him.
Albert: Lillie and Ethel—Lilly was the last one to leave home.

Gertrude, Lillie and Ethel Hooper about 1907 in front of their home

Gertrude: And I went to the little outside toilet and cried all day. I shut myself up in the toilet. Isn't that awful? That's Brackett. I just nearly know it is. Bruce....

Brackett Hooper

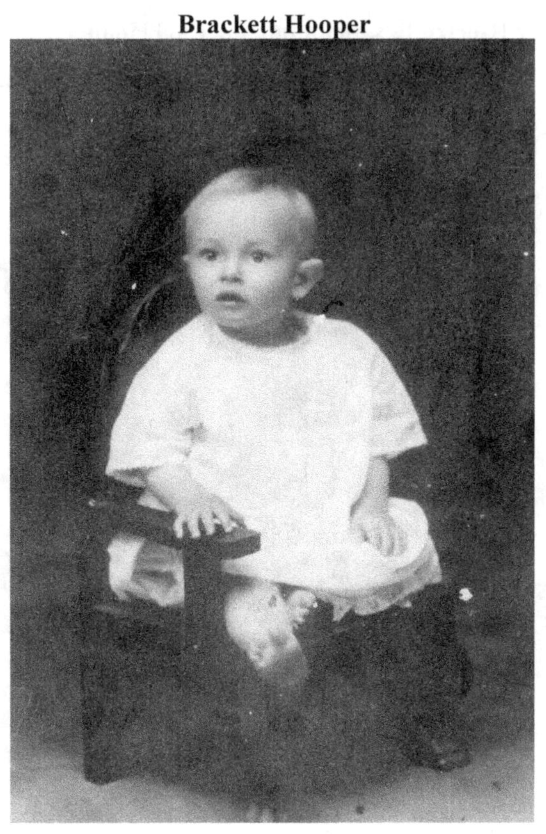

242

Bruce Hooper

Albert: Yeah, old Bruce.
Gertrude: J. L. and Early Boy **[Gertrude's nickname for Earl Hooper]**.

Earl and J. L. Hooper   **Sarah Ellen and Harrison Hooper (not discussed)**

Albert: J. and Earl. **[Sarah Ellen and Harrison Hooper were not discussed.]**
Gertrude: You know his mother always called him Early Boy, and I still do too. I don't know him unless

it is Uncle Jim Grissom.

Albert: I know who this is, but I can't think of his name. That ain't Uncle Jim Grissom.

Gertrude: That's Lilly, Aunt Lilly—that's the oldest one I've ever seen of Aunt Lilly.

Lilly/Lillie Hooper

Billie: That's grandma Shiflett—Aunt Belle Shiflett.

Martha: Isabelle Shiflett.

Albert: That there's Mr. Shiflett's mother? I just can recollect her. I tell you where I seen her at. I don't know if that was Roe Cofer or old man Sherdin who was selling goods. She was down there, and they called her Aunt Belle Shiflett.

Isabelle Hays Shiflett 1827-1901

Gertrude: You all know who that is? That's me. **[Gertrude brought pictures which are not in the book.]** Momma said, told me about this picture—said, who had a big department store on the corner there where Stampers were? Roberts, they took me in there to get me some shoes and set me upon the counter. They wanted to have my shoes on me before they made my picture, so they took me in, and Mrs. Roberts was in there—said, "Why don't you take the baby on

244

before she gets so tired and have her picture made?" So, momma said I was real tired when
they made that.

Billie: I don't know that one.

Gertrude: That's Aunt Rose—that's Rose when she is young.

Rose Hooper

Billie: There's one with a doll—who is that?

Gertrude: That's Ethel. Law, Billie, I would give the world for some of these pictures. Law, all of ours
burned when Lennie's house burned. Lennie had all the old pictures.

Ethel Hooper

Albert: She had old phone books, and they burned up. She had one of every kind from way back.

Gertrude: That is Luther. I don't know who that is. And somebody, but I don't know that man with him.

Earl:　　　Was he a big buddy with some Woods man, Uncle Albert? You remember?
Gertrude: I bet he was on that Board of Trade.
Albert:　　Earl is named after Earl Cook. Earl used to come up there a whole lot. Earl Cook and McReynolds—that's either him or old man McReynolds. I don't know which it is. **[Earl Cook and J. H. McReynolds ran a brokerage business in Chattanooga, Tennessee. They were members of the Chicago Board of Trade and were sued in 1917 for dishonest schemes to defraud investors by E. A. Colclough. The Georgia Supreme Court reversed the original guilty verdict after an appeal was made (Internet *Google.com Books* in the *Southeastern Reporter,Volume 92* by the West Publishing Company, St. Paul, MN on page 206, 1917).]**
Gertrude: That must have been Cook with Luther.
Albert:　　That's either Earl Cook or McReynolds. I forget which. I believe it's Earl Cook.
Billie:　　Then here you know when Mr. Hooper had that thing about Mount Ebal.
Gertrude: Oh, there is Mount Ebal.
Albert:　　You know there should never have been a rock taken out of that. Missed it way back yonder. Lord, you could have....
Earl:　　　That's my mother and grandpa and grandma Shiflett.

Maudie, Martha and John Shiflett

Billie: I've got post cards from all over the United States that Mr. Hooper had, you know, that he sent from Oklahoma City. **[This was the box we found after Billie's death. See pp. 220 - 236.]**

[The next group of pictures were brought by Aunt Gertrude, and no copies were available.]

Gertrude: That was Aunt Rose's 75th **[Rosa/Rose Hooper 1958]** birthday at my house. Everybody brought her a peony rose. I had a party for her. Nearly about everybody gave her a dollar, naturally. So, when she left—doesn't this sound like her—she said, "Well, I had a pretty good holiday; can you do this again next year?" Here are some pictures I brought from home. That is me and Grace Rymer. That's her table; she had a brunch last year. Carolyn sent me this last Christmas. That's me going down the receiving line. She had that made.
Billie: Earl, Uncle Jim Calhoun.
Gertrude: Aunt Lillie and Uncle Jim—that old Ford.
Albert: That old Ford, yeah, that's it. That's that old home there at Charleston. That old home there at Charleston is still holding its own.
Gertrude: Beautiful, pretty as it ever was.
Albert: That old T Model.
Gertrude: Old T Model—I've taken many a ride in it.
Albert: It was pretty good. It hauled lots of people around Charleston there. They ride that there to Hooper's Mill from Charleston.
Gertrude: And Carolyn and Steve took this over my farm. Steve's airplane and I didn't know they had it. They brought it up there before they left. And this was my door at Christmas time.
Albert: Good looking [picture of a] cow, isn't she?
Gertrude: 90 pounds a day, and that's my hall at Christmas.
Billie: There is Aunt Lillie, you said, wasn't it with that big hat?

Lillie Hooper

Gertrude: Yes, with the big hat. That was Mary Geren's hat; she borrowed it.

Albert: Old Mary Geren, she used to come to our house. She always dressed up, didn't she.

Gertrude: Oh, they borrowed clothes from her to have their pictures made in, you know.

Albert: Sula Geren was an lumber man at the Cleveland chair company. He learned me how to grade lumber.

Harold: How are you kin to the Gerens?

Albert: Well, my grandmother on the Hooper side was a Geren. I guess her name was Elizabeth. It's on the tomb rock there at Eureka. No, I don't **[know her father's name]**. I've heard she had a brother, Uncle Joe Geren; he was an old fellow. He and my grandfather was brother-in-laws. You know where Uncle Joe lived? You know that barber shop there on that steep curve going to Cleveland where there used to be a store there—Harris Brothers? He owned that farm above the road there. That's where his old home was. He owned that a good while, Uncle Joe Geren. I can recollect that Cleveland before that was built there—when there was one little log cabin right above where that motel is going toward Cleveland, about half way there. Log cabin stood there. That's all there was and on the other side there—let's see old McQueen bought it. Hamilton owned it on the right there, and now and then it's all built up where the electric is and everything else. I've seen clover there knee high.

Martha: I'm still confused about this Allen. Anything you can remember about that part of the family, I wish you could tell me.

Gertrude: That was momma's daddy. Ella Allen.

Albert: And Uncle John Allen—he left there the day you **[Gertrude]** were born, and I never did see him any, anymore. He came out on the end of the porch. Said "she has hair that long" bragging on you. I don't know where is—we don't know where he's buried at. Don't even know where he went. That was my mother's brother. Luther was named after him. Earl's daddy is named after him, J. L. Hooper.

Gertrude: Don't you think he was killed?

Albert: Never did hear from him no more.

Gertrude: That's why I know he must have been killed. When I was a kid he ran a store on East Ninth Street. I was a little fellow and my daddy taking us all down there in a surrey. We drove horses, and Aunt Laura would give me candy to get me to dance, and I could dance pretty good. I can recollect that. And Uncle John Allen—I have heard him tell it, you know, that they had two grades of coffee then, Arbuckle and Lion coffee—they had that on the post. Well, in the back warehouse they got that coffee in big 300 pound barrels or more and put it back there. Well, we had to sack that coffee; they put Lion coffee and Arbuckle coffee in different pokes, and it came out of the same barrel. Said one fellow came in and said, "I want Lion coffee." All right, we had it and said the next one came in said I want Arbuckle's, and yeah we had it and all came out of the same barrel. That shows you what people is. Now I can recollect that; Uncle John telling that. Give Jim Hooper and me—I tell you what—he bought a mare, and I swapped a watch for some way; Old Tobie we called him—well, that's been a long time ago, and he **[John]** give Luther Hooper a shot gun. Have you still got that or anybody yet? He gave Luther a good gun, and he said, "Albert, I'll give you"—going to give, but he died. I never got my present. I'll give you yours last. He always give us boys a present. That was the time I seen Uncle John was on the porch the day she was born. **[See pages 255, 256 for information on John W. Allen b. abt. 1856.]**

Gertrude: Well, how old were you then Albert?

Albert: Ten years old.

Gertrude: Yeah, because if I was just born you were ten years older than me.

Albert: I was ten years old in May, and you were born the 15th.

Harold: Could that Geren be Isaac Geren? Elizabeth's father, your grandmother's father?

Albert: I don't know. I forget. I have heard them talk about him.

Gertrude: Are you talking about the Hooper genealogy or the Geren?

Albert: She was a Geren; my grandfather's wife was a Geren.

Gertrude: Well, that's the one they're trying to get Clara Mae in on. She couldn't get in on mine. They changed the rules—Ethel went in on it, Eula **[Taylor]** went in on it, everybody, and Clara Mae sent hers in, and they wouldn't take it. This is my DAR paper. Isaac Hooper, that is our daddy, he was born in 1858 and died in 1915. His wife was Ella Allen Hooper born in 1862, died in 1935, was married in 1878. She and daddy were married—it would be a 100 years now in three years. This Ella Hooper was the child of James B. Allen, that's her daddy, born 1832—I've got it all. I'll go on down. You know I paid five dollars apiece to get this run. Here is the letter right here; it says, "We received your application, Mrs. Brewer, and the fee for searching the bonds is $2.00 a couple in one county and $5.00 for searching all Revolutionary soldiers", so I paid $5.00 a piece to get all these searched. But, I promised momma I would go in the DAR, and I worked at it until I got it. And I tell you, it took me about two years to work it all up. All right, they said James B. Allen was born in 1832, and he died in 1865 **[See pages 140 and 255 - 256 for information about James.]**.

Martha: That's the one you told me, when I talked to you, died in the Civil War ?

Gertrude: That's right.

Albert: The last time they saw him, he was sitting in Knoxville by a tree eating parched corn. I have heard Luther, my oldest brother, talking about it. Well, my mother talked about it.

Gertrude: Now this came from Washington—the pension department. That's where I got it; now, they knew him. They knew him because he sent a pension in you see. **[Since James B. Allen died during the Civil War he did not apply for a pension. His father-in-law John Vernon and brother-in-law John Callaway Vernon did apply.]** All right now, Jane Vernon Allen was his wife. She was born in 1837 and died in1905, married in 1853. Mary Jane Vernon Allen was the child of John Vernon. **[Aunt Gertrude lived with her mother Ella Allen Hooper and great-grandmother Caroline Carter Vernon, so the names are probably accurate.]**

Albert: That was grandmother.

Gertrude: That's going way back before we were born. Born 1815; they didn't live to be very old, died in 1857 **[This seemed wrong since John Vernon and Caroline were alive in 1880 in James County, TN.]**. See he died in his 30s, and his wife Caroline Carter Vernon—heard mom talk about grandma Carter.

Albert: Yeah, she was a Carter.

Gertrude: Caroline Carter Vernon, 1818—she died in 1850. **[Caroline Carter Vernon lived with Houston and Mary Jane Vernon Allen Samples in 1900, and she was 85 years old.]**

Albert: Who was that died in 1850?

Gertrude: Caroline Carter Vernon. **[As stated previously, this is confusing because John and Caroline were living in *Bradley County in 1860 in Dist. 6 p. 30, Jackson County, Alabama at Scottsboro in 1870 p. 4, James County, Tennessee 1880 in Dist. 4 p. 34*, and Caroline was still alive in 1900 in *Bradley County Dist. 9* (Sheet 3B).]**

Billie: Aunt Gertrude, are your feet warm enough?

Gertrude: Yeah, they're fine, Billie.

Billie: She's got an afghan there she could put over you.

Gertrude: No, they're fine. I have to have my toes out. Married in 1836. They were just married 24 years. Now, then, John Vernon was the child of Thomas Vernon, and that's the one Clara Mae tried to get in on after they turned her down on Richard.

Martha: Now Thomas and Richard were brothers?

Gertrude: They were brothers, and I went in on Richard.

Albert: Gertie, there is a Cal [John Callaway] Vernon in there.

Gertrude: Now I am just getting this one line.

Albert: Well, all right.

Gertrude: They sent me about six names that fought in the Revolution, and naturally, I had to take one of those to go in on, see, to go in the DAR. The reason I chose Richard, he was a big officer, and the others were just privates.

Albert: He was a Vernon?

Gertrude: Richard Vernon, I'll read you about him.

Albert: Well, that is what I know—them Vernons was in that war, and their feet all got frost bitten and that's how come them South. They came down here to get their feet cured. I've heard Luther talk about it.

Gertrude: I must have inherited my feet from them.

Albert: I've heard Luther talk about Uncle Cal Vernon. All of them said they had one—Luther knew a lot about them, you know.

Gertrude: Now where are we Martha?

Martha: Thomas Vernon.

Gertrude: John Vernon was the child of Thomas Vernon. Thomas Vernon was born in 1789—went
another $5.00; it cost me several hundred. I think I got all this information for about $120.00.
I bet now it would be $500.00. I think it was $120.00. I was teaching at the time, and I know I
would go home and work some on it, and then put it up and work another night.

[On the recording, the grandfather clock strikes 3 o'clock.]

Thomas was born in 1789 and died in 1842, and his wife was Nancy Baker Vernon—she was
born a Baker—Nancy E. Baker born in 1792 and died in 1881, and she married in 1812
[*Ancestry.com* Dec. 21, 1812 in Prince Edward County, VA]. I remember one time I sent
something in to them, and they wrote back and said, "She didn't die at the right time." Said,
"Go over your records again. She didn't die at the right time." I know I laughed about that and
momma laughed—momma was living when I did all of this, and I would read it off to
momma, you know, and she would tell me how many she remembered the names of.

[See p. 262 for explanation 3 for Lieutenant Thomas Vernon who served in War of 1812.]

Albert: Well, she did.

Gertrude: She didn't know them, but she would say, "I know about him," but she laughed when she said
didn't die at the right time.

Albert: Well, grandma Vernon—I've carried her breakfast to her many a morning and (she) had that
old rocking chair and had a board here—she was teetotally blind. That's right I can recollect
that good.

**[Harold Reno comments: There was confusion in some of Aunt Gertrude's DAR records, or at least
it seemed so. In 1975 she was 75 years old and Uncle Albert was 85 years old. In this interview, Aunt
Gertrude mentioned that Clara Mae Geren Caldwell had tried to enter the DAR using Gertrude's
information, and she had been turned down. There was a Thomas Vernon in Monroe County,
Tennessee who was in the Revolutionary War. Vernon records seemed to indicate that this Thomas
and Captain Richard Vernon of North Carolina were cousins. According to Duane Boggs on
Genforum.com, Thomas Gaines Vernon was born March 23, 1752 in Lunenburg County, Virginia
and died about 1841 in Monroe County, Tennessee. This Thomas Vernon had a brother named
Richard who married Esther Hamilton, but they remained in Charlotte County, Virginia. I can find
no proof either way, but John who was living in Bradley County, Tennessee in 1840 and in 1860
seemed to be related in some way to the Vernons from Virginia and North Carolina who moved to
Tennessee about 1815. See p. 256 for a possible connection to Richard in Charlotte County, VA.]**

**[Harold wondered at first if John might have been the son of Thomas Vernon, Jr. and Leticia Witten,
but Vernon records do not list that connection. John Vernon who was born about 1815 married
Caroline Carter before 1840 because their daughter, Mary Jane Vernon, was born April 1833
according to the *1900 Census of Bradley County*, Tennessee (Candies Creek Cemetery Apr. 1839). A
son, John C. [Callaway] Vernon, was born May 1837 according to the *1900 Census of Loudon
County, Tennessee*, but in other Censuses he said he was born 1841. This is the Cal Vernon that
Uncle Albert makes mention of several times during this conversation. He was in the 5th Infantry
Regiment, Company I of the Union Army during the Civil War. He lived at Philadelphia, Tennessee
in Loudon County and died March 28, 1904. His adopted son, John Carl Vernon, who might have
also been called Cal, was listed as a merchant on the World War I Registration Card. See pages 257,
258 and 262 for 3 possible Vernon explanations. See pp. 255 – 262 in this book for more information
on the Vernon, Carter and Samples families.]**

Gertrude: We got to watch our eyes too. She had...what is it you can go blind with now?

Albert: I don't know what it was, but grandmother Vernon was blind. She stayed at our house. That
was my mother's grandma.

Gertrude: They put her on the train to go visit somebody.

Albert: Aunt Tish in Alabama and Aunt Josie Wallingsford. **[Using Uncle Albert's information, I
was able to find the families of Latitia and Josephine in Alabama. See pages 260 – 261 .]**

Gertrude: Well, they had to—well, they had to, see she was blind. They would put her on....

Albert: I can recollect some names, Wallingsford....

Gertrude: I never had contact with that. Well, anyway, momma would tell me....

Albert: You know Clint Caroll that Berry Cartwright killed? He got into, Clint was always high strung, mean. Aunt Josie Wallingsford's son shot him, but he didn't kill him. He had been shot before Berry did. That's what they said; they got into it. He must have been kind of mean— mean to fight. Wallingsford.

Gertrude: What's your last date, Martha?

Martha: I've got the marriage date on Nancy and Thomas Vernon.

Gertrude: Married 1812 **[Dec. 21, 1812]**. Now there were two Thomas Vernons. He had a brother, Thomas, and child named for him. Said Thomas Vernon was the child of Richard Vernon.

Martha: Now wait a minute. This Thomas that was born in 1789 was the son of Richard?

Gertrude: Born in 1758 and died in 1840. Richard lived a long time. I've got "about" written over this date; they weren't sure about it, but they took it. And his wife was Betty Wooten Vernon, and that is as far as it goes. **[Harold Reno comments: Betty Wooten Vernon was not accepted by "Vernons of Rockingham and Stokes" found in *Vernon Vignettes Vol. 7 No. 3* on p. 13 Sept. 1976 on the Internet as a wife of Capt. Richard Vernon. They suggested that the Richard Vernon in the DAR record was the son of Lt. Isaac Vernon. This Richard Vernon married Betsey Wooten.]** Now that is Richard's wife, and she was born in 1760, and she died in 1830, and they married about 1778, but we could never get the real date on that, but they took it. I was afraid they were going to keep me out. Oh, they are so strict. Now, I'll read you what they said about Richard. That's the one I went in on.

Harold: What was that story you started to tell a little while ago about her getting on a train?

Gertrude: Oh, that was my great grandmother that was blind. Well, momma said she wanted to visit this daughter in some place in Alabama, and so they would have to put her on the train. She was completely blind; nobody went with her. But they would put her on and put her in the care of the conductor, and when he got her to this little town where her daughter lived, they would meet her and take her off of the train, see, and she would stay several months with them when she'd get down there, but she would go just about once a year or every two years, but she was blind—grandma Vernon that was blind.

Albert: You know it was said every conductor, they said, knew her on the road.

Gertrude: Yeah, she went everywhere under the conductor's care.

Albert: She went and got some people lived up, aunt, well, Uncle Cal Vernon lived in Philadelphia **[Tennessee]**.

Gertrude: She went there, too.

Albert: Oh, yeah, they would put her on the train, and them conductors take her and take care of her until she got there.

Gertrude: Yeah and then they would meet....

Albert: Write Uncle Cal when she would be there, and he would meet her.

Gertrude: And they would take her off, she said. Think of going that far blind. Wasn't she brave?

Albert: Then, she went to Alabama to see her other daughter.

Gertrude: Yeah, she went everywhere.

Albert: Aunt Josie Wallingsford and Aunt Tish.

Gertrude: But, she would stay a long time when she would go; she would stay several months with them.

Albert: And come back stay with grandma Samples, you know, some and stayed at our house some.

Gertrude: Law, she stayed at home a lot.

Albert: I know she did.

Gertrude: I don't remember, but I heard momma telling it.

Albert: I remember. I carried that breakfast to her many mornings.

Gertrude: I don't remember a thing about it. I remember—the only thing I remember—about grandma Samples, I must have been awful mean little young un.

Albert: Yeah, I can recollect that.

Gertrude: I was four years old. I threatened to burn her with a poker.

Albert: You know what—you know what grandmother said, "Hey, Ella, come here and get this here poker."

Gertrude: I was so mean; I know.

Albert: Well, now, she wasn't. You were just about three years old when you was doing that.

Gertrude: And Lilly would always run and grab me and pick me up and take me.

Albert: And when you was four years old in May, I took you to school in that fall over at Mount Harmony. We walked and I would take across foot logs and look after her.

Gertrude: You would have to carry me.

Albert: I looked at—she was never no trouble. She would play with the little girls out there. They all liked to play with her. So, the night Clara Mae was born, they was at our house, and my mother brought her upstairs and slipped her in the bed with me.

Gertrude: Four years old.

Albert: And the next morning when Clara was born she kind of squalled out, and that thing said, "I heard something." I said, "you lay down here." I recollect that. I'm glad you laid down. Finally, my mother come, and they got everything fixed and said let her come on down. I can recollect it.

Gertrude: I was giving him a fit. I wouldn't go back to sleep.

Albert: Why, no, you just laid there and kicked all the time in the bed—"I heard something." I've had a great life in a way.

Gertrude: You took care of me. Now, what was my first teachers' name? Miss Nannie Scoggins wasn't it, Albert?

Albert: Yeah.

Gertrude: She was my first grade teacher. I wasn't in any grade when I was four. I just went over there.

Albert: You would get up there in class. Miss Nannie was a good religious woman. She wouldn't play nothing—just let you sit there with them.

Gertrude: But, now in the first grade I learned to read and when Miss Nannie went home (she lived up at Sweetwater and I remember that yet) she came to my house to tell me goodbye, and she told momma that I was the best reader in the first grade, and she brought me a prize. And, you know what the prize was? A blue hair ribbon. Oh, I thought that was the prettiest thing I ever saw.

Albert: Well, now you know what she got me? I've got it at home. I reckon there yet, Ethel's got one.

Gertrude: Spelling—something for spelling.

Albert: Ethel taken her the advanced spelling and I got it in the other next to it.

Gertrude: Well, I got it for reading.

Albert: When Carrie Ledford...I tied. Pa kept me out to work for three weeks. I wouldn't have...I wouldn't have tied with her, but we had a big family, and they'd get in a tight...they called on me.

Gertrude: Yeah, you had to stay out. They didn't keep me out.

Albert: I had to work. Carrie came in here a year or two ago.

Billie: What did she give you, Uncle Albert?

Albert: A Testament...it's a little one.

Gertrude: Well, I was just...oh, I was just five or six...I got a blue hair ribbon for being the best reader in the first grade.

Albert: Miss Nannie Scroggins, she was a good teacher.

Gertrude: I remember she said to momma...she said, "I hope you send this child on to school."

Albert: Why, we had, Billie, we had spelling matches, Mount Harmony...Friday evening, you know and old preacher Phelps, he'd been a teacher 24 long years. You may have heard?

Billie: Was he a school teacher?

Albert: Yes sir, yes sir and he was a preacher and Jim Hooper...I remember Jim...he got them tangled up there some way. "Set them down, sister Nancy set them down." That's what he called her. Jim Hooper'd go around hollering that.

Billie: He would get up to preach, and he didn't have to use the Bible—he had it memorized.

Albert: No, he knowed it...he knowed it.

Gertrude: Are you all working on the Geren's too? Clara Mae is.

Martha: Well, see, if this Elizabeth Geren, who was your grandmother ties in, then I would be interested.

Albert: Grandmother Hooper.

Gertrude: I was going to read about the Vernon that was the highest one in the army. He became a Colonel. These others just remained privates. That is why I chose him. I would have gone in on any of them.

Albert: They were all brothers, weren't they?

Gertrude: Yeah, brothers and sons.

Albert: Now, Luther told me reason Uncle Cal [JohnCallaway] Vernon told him, of course I was smaller, but he said the reason we come south our feet got froze bit up north. Now, Luther told me this.

Gertrude: Might be true.

Albert: Yeah, Luther knowed them things...he recollect them.

Gertrude: I wonder how Richard got so far up and the others didn't.

Albert: Well, he might just have stepped on up like a lot of other people having to fall in line there.

Gertrude: You have read in history about Lighthorse Harry haven't you? All right this is what I went in on and what Martha could. Richard Vernon, Captain, he was captain of a company known as Captain Vernon's Company of Militia. Lighthorse Harry, he was captain of that. His company was ordered by Colonel James Martin to collect deserters and delinquents and on November 8, 1781, he was ordered by the governor to raise ten horsemen and cause them to rendezvous—what is rendezvous, march? And cause them to rendezvous at Salem on November 13 and to protect the General Assembly in that state. See, his company protected the whole assembly. From February 15 Richard served as a lieutenant in Captain John Peaks regiment and was out against the Cherokee Indians. He was in the battle of Moncks Corner, and from February 1, 1781 he served as Captain in Colonel Martin's regiment, and he continued to serve under Colonel Martin and Colonel Paisley until the close of the war, so you see he was still in then when it was over. That ought to get anybody in.

Martha: All right, now, Clara Mae is the daughter of one of your sisters?

Gertrude: Aunt Lennie—see she started out with her daddy, Lennie's husband, George Washington [that is old George] he was born in Bradley County. Aunt Lennie married a Geren and George was born in 1877. So, you see she started out there and then they said Mary Hooper Geren was the child of Issac Hooper, that's Lennie—Mary Lennie—her name was Mary born in 1850 died 1915 and his wife Ella Allen Hooper—see that's right along with momma.

Martha: Have you got anything that traces the Geren thing back on her's yet?

Gertrude: No, she has now because she couldn't get in on this, so she is working on the Geren line now to see if she can get in on it.

Albert: She might get through Uncle Joe Geren back there.

Gertrude: Well, that's what she's trying, but no telling when she will ever get through because it took me two years.

Albert: Well, Clara will work at it.

Gertrude: Well, she says she doesn't know what to do next. She calls me all the time—every time she gets a letter. I said Clara Mae this is going to break you up—long distance calls—it is long distance.

Albert: Well, I never understood what caused the Vernons to come South. Luther told me about that. Uncle Cal [John Callaway] Vernon—see Uncle Cal Vernon—him and Aunt Betty lived at Philadelphia [Tennessee]. That's where grandma Vernon would go to.

Gertrude: Well, Richard is the outstanding one of the Vernons. I read all about every one of them.

Albert: Well, them others, they was all alright. They was all warriors they said. That's what Luther told me, and he knowed them pretty well. He heard Uncle Cal talk about it, don't you see?

Martha: Well, who, now, would Uncle Cal have been?

Albert: Well, he was that there one's brother that I [and] Gertie is talking about.

Martha: It was Richard and Thomas' brother?

Gertrude: I don't know the one he's talking about. I never got anything on him. They just sent me the ones.... :

Albert   Luther told me about Uncle Cal telling that's the reason they come south about their feet being frost bit up there and everything. Come down to see if it would help.

Harold: Well, do you know any stories about the Hoopers?

Albert: Well, I don't know none about the Hooper only, but my grandfather was a Hooper.

Martha: I wonder if any Hoopers served in the Revolutionary War that we would be related to? That's what I want to find out.

Gertrude: No, I don't think so because I tried that, and I didn't get anywhere with it at all.

Albert: Grandfather Hooper served in the war you know.

Gertrude: I believe it was the confederate war, wasn't it—not the Revolutionary War.

Martha: Who? Kinsey?

Albert: Yeah.

Martha: I found a thing up there that said that there was a Kins Hooper from Bradley County in the Union Army.

Albert: That's right.

Harold: Kinsey C. Hooper.

Martha: In the Civil War?

Gertrude: Now that was the Civil War. This is the Revolutionary.

Albert: No, that was the Civil War wasn't it?

Harold: Well, who was Kins father, Kinsey?

Albert: Well, I don't know. Uncle Jace Hooper [Jace—nickname for Jahue b. 1830's?] and my grandfather was brothers. [Barry Hooper has a picture of the Jace Hooper reunion.]

Gertrude: Well, that is as far back as we know, isn't it Albert?

Albert: Yeah.

Harold: You know anything about an Andy Hooper? Oh, a long time ago?

Albert: Well, now there was one Andy Hooper I believe—he was a brother to them I believe. That's where Uncle Andy got his name.

Gertrude: I guess he was his daddy was a brother to Kins and....

Harold: Well, was there a John?

Albert: Yeah, Uncle John Hooper years ago killed himself a drinking, and he said he had always wanted to drink good liquor and wouldn't hurt nobody. I've heard them laugh about it. I've heard them talk about him. Grandpa and Uncle Jace were both in the Civil War.

Harold: Let me show you. This is the *1850 Census* here in Bradley County (Compiled by Ellen Ann Westerberg Campbell). I'll show you these names down through here that we are talking about. Now, is Andrew old man Andrew who was 45 in 1850? Here is John Hooper who has a son named Andrew, and John is 24, so he could be a child of this one. And then over here on this page is [Kim] Kin Hooper and Elizabeth. And this Kin is born in 1830. He is twenty years old.

Martha: That's him. That's your grandpa—that Kin Hooper right there.

Harold: I believe they put an "m" there, and it should have been an "n".

Albert: Yeah, that's it, I guess.

Harold: Cause the age here is about right.

Albert: Yeah, well now that spells Kin, ain't it.

Harold: Yeah, Kim [Kin]. How here these names—that's the reason I was wondering if John and Kim were brothers, and if they were sons of Andrew. That's what I was wondering about.

Albert: Now they could have been. Now there is another Hooper right in these. Sam Hooper's daddy and I forget his name. Sam Hooper, there's a Sam Hooper.

(This is the end of the tape made in 1975 when Martha and Harold Reno were beginning to work on the Hooper genealogy. Much of this information has been used to locate the relatives who lived in Bradley County and in other parts of the United States because of the excellent memories of Gertrude and Albert.)
A newspaper article in the *Cleveland Herald* on December 29, 1922 on page 2 reported on the marriage of Gertrude Hooper to J. L. Brewer:

The wedding of Miss Gertrude Hooper and Mr. J. L. Brewer was solemnized Thursday 2:30 o'clock in the Study of the First Baptist church Chattanooga Tenn., In the presence of only a few close friends, Rev. J. W. Inzer officiated using the ring ceremony.

The bride wore a becoming going away suit of Navy veldeen with squirrel trimmings and accessories of gray. Her flowers were Brides roses and valley lillies.

Mrs. Brewer is the attractive daughter of Mr. and Mrs. I.H. Hooper of Charleston and for the past year has been a teacher in city schools of Chattanooga. Through her charming disposition she has won many friends both in Bradley and Hamilton Counties.

Mr. Brewer is principal of Polk County High School and supervisor of Polk County School. He is a man of sterling character and through his success in Polk County has won him a host of friends.

Mr. and Mrs. Brewer left immediately after their marriage for Florida, Cuba and other Southern points.

Hooper, Vernon, Allen, Carter and Samples Families

The following information wascompiled from various sources but based on Gertrude Hooper Brewer's DAR information related to the Hooper, Vernon, Allen, Carter and Samples families of Tennessee: Isaac Houston Hooper, son of Kinsey C. Hooper and Elizabeth Geren Hooper, married Ellen Caroline Allen on June 8, 1877 in Bradley County, TN. James B. Allen, father of Ellen Caroline, was born about 1832 in Monroe County, TN to William Allen (born about 1796 in North Carolina, and he died after 1860) and Margaret Jane (born about 1800 in Tennessee and died after 1860; a Willam Allen married Margaret Ault on Feb. 16, 1815 in Knox County, TN according to *tstmarie1* at *Ancestry.com*). According to Aunt Gertrude Hooper Brewer, James died in the Civil War (p. 249). In the "Memorial Rolls" extracted from *The Military Annals of Tennessee Confederate* by John Berrien Lindsley, a James Allen was killed in action at Chickamauga, Georgia on September 10, 1863 (this date and the age of Ellen in the *Bradley County 1870 Census*, 8 years old seemed to correspond). He was in the 12th Battalion, Tennessee Cavalry, Company B. In the *1850 Census of Monroe County, Tennessee* in District 4 House 366, William Allen (53 born in North Carolina) and Margaret (50 born in Tennessee) lived with James 18 born Tennessee, Watts 16 born Tennessee, Charity 13 born Tennessee, John 11 born Tennessee and William 7 born Tennessee. In the *1860 Census for Monroe County, Tennessee* in District 4 on page 31 were James Allen 28, M. J. 21, J. W. 4 and M. E. 1. William Allen was in District 3 page 27: Wm Allen 70 worth $200.00 born NC, Jane 70 born TN, W. Allen 21 Laborer born TN and Jacob Fisher 17 Laborer TN.

James Allen's father, William Allen, was the son of John Allen who died in 1832 in Monroe County and Elizabeth Martin Allen who was born about 1762 and died in Monroe County, Tennessee July 11, 1849 according to *Southern Campaign American Revolution Pension Statements* found on the Internet. John Allen's Pension Application was numbered R 113 and was transcribed by C. Leon Harris. William filed a request for a widow's pension as the survivor of a Revolutionary War veteran. At *Google.com Books* on the Internet a book titled *Monroe County, Tennessee: History Revealed Through Biographical and Genealogical Sketches of Its Ancestors* by M. Secrist published by Lulu Press in 2013, John Allen's biography revealed that Elizabeth Martian [Martin] Allen made her will on March 23, 1834, and she left her estate to James Allen the son of William Allen. In the *Southern Campaign* information on April 29, 1848, Elizabeth Allen appeared before James Montgomery, a Justice of the Peace and made a declaration to obtain the benefit of the provision made by the Act of Congress that passed July 7, 1838. She stated that she was the widow of John Allen a private in the New Jersey line in 1776 or 1777. She said he then moved to North Carolina and participated in the battle of Cowpens under Captain Scott. She further stated that she married John Allen in 1781 or 82. John died in 1832. On March 8, 1850, William Allen of Monroe County, Tennessee appeared and declared that he was the son of Elizabeth Allen deceased. He claimed the pension for himself and his brother Andrew Allen under the act of July 7, 1838. William Allen stated that his father always signed his name "John Allen, tailor" to distinguish him from other John Allens. William also stated that his father's occupation was a tailor. On April 3, 1854, William Allen appeared before the Monroe County, Tennessee court to declare that he was the administrator of the Estate of Elizabeth Allen and that he was 62 years of age. He said his father was a Captain of a company in the North Carolina Continental Service in the war of the Revolution in 1777 from the county of Guilford. He said his mother's name was Martin before she married John Allen. He said his mother died July 11, 1849 leaving two sons, Andrew and himself, William. He said if his father was given land for his service, it was "fooled away." Another record was found on the Internet in Virgil White's *Abstracts of Pensions of Revolutionary War Files* in Appendix A page 350: John Allen, tailor, had a widow who applied for a Pension and testimony was provided by Samuel Evans. He said John was in Guilford County at enlistment and served as a captain at Monmouth, NJ, Charleston, Battle of Ramsour's Mill, Gates' defeat at Camden, Battle at Guilford Courthouse, Battle of Ninety-Six and at Hillsborough. After his mother's death, William filed papers stating that she was survived by his brother Andrew, 64 years old, and himself, 62 years old.

According to Aunt Gertrude Hooper Brewer and Uncle Albert Hooper, M. J. (who married James B. Allen) was Mary Jane Vernon, the daughter of John Vernon and Caroline Carter Vernon. (Vernon information follows on the next pages.) After James B. Allen died in the Civil War, Mary Jane married James Houston Samples on Sept. 18, 1869 in Bradley County, TN. In the *1870 Census for Bradley County*, Tennessee in District 7 page 19, James H. (Houston) Samples (37 Carpenter) and Mary J. Samples (32) lived with John

W. Allen 14, Mary E. Allen 11 and Ellen C. Allen 8. The ages would also agree with the possibility of James Allen dying in 1863 during the Civil War (see pp. 140 and 249). In the *1880 Bradley County Census* on page 47 in District 6, Houston Samples 52, Mary J. 39 and Mary E. Allen 19 (daughter) were listed. Next door to Houston was Matthew Samples who was possibly the father of James Houston **(see p. 262)**. The daughter Mary E. Allen married James Grisham in Bradley county on October 24, 1883 and in the *1900 Census* on page 3B in the 9th District, James was a widower born July 1854, Maymie, a daughter, born July 1884, Ellen, a daughter, born May 1889, John, a son, born May 1891 and James, a son, born January 1894. In the *1840 Bradley County, Tennessee Census* (compiled by Sheridan Randolph), William Samples age 60-70 on page 54 was listed along with Matthew Samples who was 30-40 on page 39. A William Samples, in *Goodspeed's History of Tennessee* published in 1887 by Goodspeed Publishing Company of Nashville, Tennessee on page 802, was listed as a carpenter and cabinet maker when Bradley became a county. William probably trained Matthew Samples who may have been his nephew.

Great-aunt Gertrude Hooper Brewer and great-uncle Albert Hooper were able to have second person information related to the Carter and Vernon families of Bradley County, Tennessee because Caroline Carter Vernon lived until 1900 with her daughter Mary Jane Vernon Allen Samples and her second husband Houston Samples. Albert would have been able to talk to grandmother Samples and his mother, Ella Allen Hooper, daughter of James B. Allen and Mary Jane Vernon. (Harold Reno has accepted that some of Gertrude's information was accurate, but because of her desire to have an officer as an ancestor in the Revolutionary War, he believed she deviated from Thomas Vernon, whom she designated as the father of John Vernon, to Captain Richard Vernon from North Carolina who settled in Williamson County, Tennessee with his family. Captain Richard Vernon did have a son Thomas Pleasant Vernon born in 1790, but he had no children listed on the *Williamson County 1830 Census*. On page 252, Gertrude said, "I was going to read about the Vernon that was the highest one in the army. He became a Colonel…. These others just remained privates. That is why I chose him.")

So, by using information on the Internet, the following is a short history of the Vernon family. Three Quaker brothers named Vernon came with William Penn to colonize the land he had received in the New World. From these three the southern branches seem to have been developed. Robert, Thomas and Randall Vernon were born in England and were the sons of James Vernon and Hestor Brown Vernon according to the *O'Guinn Family Website.*

Information at the *Lt. Andrew Crockett Chapter of the TNNSAR* and other locations on the Internet stated that Robert Vernon who settled in Chester in the Pennsylvania settlement of William Penn had a son Thomas who was expelled from the Quaker Settlement and moved to Cub Creek, Virginia with a group of Presbyterians led by the Calhoun family and Caldwell family. This Internet website also disagreed with other Vernon researchers by saying that the father of the three brothers was Hugh, and he came with his sons on the ship *Friendship* in 1682. Other websites said that James Vernon was the father of the three sons, and James's father was Hugh. Robert's son Thomas, Sr. married Mary, according to Internet, Quaker records. Thomas Vernon, Jr. married Lattice Key Chamberlain daughter of Moses and Elizabeth Key in Providence in the County of Chester, Province of Pennsylvania on August 31, 1734. (*Friends Historical Collection* [Quaker] is the official depository for the *records* of North Carolina Yearly Meetings found at Guilford College in the Hege Collection. The FHC number is 0020457 Item #8.)

Other information from the Internet *O'Guinn Family Website* about the Vernon family stated that Robert Vernon married Elinor Minshall. His son Thomas (1686 England - 1758 Charlotte County, Virginia) married Mary Brown and their children were: (1) Richard (1711 Nether Province, Chester County, Pennsylvania -1795 Madison, Virginia) who married Sarah Tinsley; (2) Jonathan (1712 Chester County, internet - June 1805 Stokes County, North Carolina) married Rebecca Worth; (3) Thomas (1713 - ?) married Sarah Gaines or Nancy Harrison; (4) Robert Vernon (1715 - ?); (5) Lt. Isaac Vernon (1721 - 1782 or 87) married Elizabeth Austin and then Jane Caldwell; (6) Rebecca (1721); (7) Hannah (1727); and (8) James (1730- 1802) married Eleanor Caldwell (according to many Vernon sites, James was the father of Captain Richard Vernon of the Revolutionary War).

Harold Reno (compiler of this book) has decided that at least three possible explanations exist for the John Vernon of Bradley County, TN ancestry: the first is related to Thomas Vernon b. 1713, and the second is related to Lt. Isaac Vernon b. 1721. The third possibility is on p. 262 and is connected to Richard Vernon b. 1746 who was the oldest brother of Thomas Gaines Vernon who died in Monroe County, TN.

(1.) The first explanation involved the third son listed on the previous page, Thomas, who married Sarah Gaines and/or Nancy Harrison and had the following children: (A) Richard (1746-1839 Charlotte County, Virginia) married Esther Hambleton; (B) Thomas Gaines Vernon (May 23, 1752 Charlotte County, Virginia and died in 1841 Monroe County, Tennessee, Revolutionary War veteran and usually listed as Thomas Gaines Vernon) married Nancy Hicks; and (C) Robert (December 25, 1768 Charlotte County, Virginia and died March 3, 1851 Bledsoe County, Tennessee) who married Elizabeth Hambleton. Thomas and Robert along with an Obadiah Vernon moved to Bledsoe County, Tennessee before 1818, and Thomas moved to Monroe County, Tennessee before 1830. (The Vernon information can be found many places on the Internet. One place was Bill Anderson at *wander.2006@gmail.com.*)

Before Bledsoe County existed, the area was part of Roane County, Tennessee. According to *Bledsoe County, Tennessee: A History* by Elizabeth Parham Robnett published by Mountain Press in Signal Mountain, Tennessee in 1993 on pages 12-13, a petition was presented to Roane County Court in 1807 for George Skillern to construct a grist mill in Sequatchie Valley. One of the signers was Thomas Vernon. One of the earliest records that mentioned several of the Vernon family in Tennessee was a Petition in Bledsoe County, Tennessee dated February 21, 1813 which related to John Miser, Tobias Long, Wm Bleavins, Robert Long, John Julian and William Hail who had provided security for Joseph Pate's appearance, and he forfeited (left?). Signers of the petition included Thomas Vernon, Jr., James Vernon, Harrison Vernon and Thomas Vernon, Sr.

On February 12, 1818 Robert Vernon and Obadiah C. Vernon purchased 98 acres in Bledsoe County, Tennessee for $350.00 from Charles J. Love of Fairfax, Virginia. On February 2, 1819 Thomas Vernon purchased 45 acres in the same county from John Tollett and paid $75.00. The land of Robert, Obadiah and Thomas bordered each other. Harrison and Miles Vernon bought 293 acres on August 1, 1823 in Bledsoe County. Harrison sold land at various times: November 13, 1826 Nathanial Painter bought 50 acres for $80.00; August 1828 Hercules Ogle bought 27 acres for $81.00. Harrison also bought 65 acres for $227.50 on both sides of Sequatchee [*sic*] Creek on March 9, 1828 from Robert Maitland of New York through Robert's attorney, John McIver. Robert Maitland was mentioned later when the estate of Harrison Vernon was settled in Meigs County, Tennessee.

The Revolutionary Soldier, Thomas Vernon, who lived in Monroe County in 1830 and 1840, had several young males and females living in his household. His oldest children have been named by the Vernon family genealogists, but in 1830 there were five included in his Census listing who were 15-20, and one of those was a male who was 10-15. Since Thomas stated that he was living with his children in the 1830s, he was probably living with his son Thomas, Jr. in Monroe County and his family. In the Monroe County, Tennessee *Deed Book K* on pages 95-96 and microfilm page 701 a Deed of Gift from Thomas Vernon, Sr. to Thomas Vernon, Jr. stated that for "natural love and affection" Thomas, Sr. gave to his son, Thomas, Jr. a negro woman Chassa and her three children: Rachel, William and Adam on March 2, 1838. Thomas must have died about December 1841 because his Revolutionary War Pension as listed in *U. S. Pensioners 1818-1872* for East Tennessee on page 128 for 1833-1849 on *Ancestry.com* seemed to end.

According to Aunt Gertrude's information, Caroline Carter married John Vernon, and in the *1840 Census of Bradley County, Tennessee* (compiled by Sheridan Randolph) a John Vernon was listed twice: the first reference was found on page 43 where John Vernon was listed between John Carter, Sr. and John Carter, Jr. (see p. 262 for Levi Carter from Wales who might be the father of John Carter, Sr.):
> John Carter one male 60-70 (1770s)   one female 15-20 and one 50-60
> John Vernon one male 20-30 (1810-1820) one female 0-5 and one 20-30 (Mary Jane Vernon
> was born in the 1830s.)

The second John Vernon entry in the *1840 Bradley County, Tennessee Census* was found on page 40 and the only difference was the additional young male who could be John C. Vernon. There is no definite proof that Caroline Carter was the daughter of John Carter listed in the 1840 Census (see next page):

p. 40 John Vernon one male 0-5, one male 20-30 and one female 0-5 and one 20-30.
As part of the first explanation of John Vernon to Thomas Vernon based on Gertrude's DAR information, Monroe County, TN records showed more about the Vernon family relationships. On April 27, 1844 in *Monroe County Book N* on page 281 and Microfilm page 264, Thomas Vernon, Jr. sold to James W. Vernon (son of Thomas, Jr.) of Rhea County, Tennessee for $1550.00 (money which Thomas owed to him) a family of slaves which Thomas, Sr. in 1838 had willed to his son, Thomas, Jr. They included a negro woman named Chassa about 29 years old and her four children (three children in 1838): Rachel 13 years old; William 11 years old; Adam 9 years old; and Sophia 2 years old. This was witnessed by William A. Witten and J. B. Peters. Possibly, Chassa and some of her children were part of the slaves listed in *1850 Laclede, MO Slave Census* owned by James W. Vernon who was living with Thomas.

In the *Meigs County Court Minutes for 1836-1841* on page 15 another son of Thomas Gaines Vernon was mentioned. He was Harrison Vernon mentioned in several records. May 10, 1836 when the Court appointed a jury to lay off a road from Rosses Ferry Road, to Samuel F. Gerreld's Mill, to Ransom P. Kerr's, to Hiram Sharp's ferry on the Hiwassee River, to John Rogers and then to Harrison Vernon's. In the records for June 9, 1836 on page 20 a second class road might be established from Roses/Rosses Ferry Road, to Hiram Sharp's ferry on the Hiwassee River to Harrison Vernon's. By March 6, 1837 Harrison had died because on page 51 the Court ordered that Miles Vernon, Sr., another son of Thomas Gaines Vernon, be appointed administrator of the estate of Harrison Vernon, deceased.

Miles Vernon finished the settlement, including the selling of personal property that Harrison owned in Bledsoe County, Tennessee on June 29, 1839. The estate was valued at $1781.84 ½. After accounting for bad debts and fees, the estate had $578.59 to divide. Vernons mentioned in the settlement who possibly were Harrison's wife and children included Mary Vernon (daughter?), Polly Vernon (wife of Harrison and daughter of Robert Vernon?), William (son?), T. and J. (sons?). The information was extremely hard to read. A John H. Vernon was listed as having two children in Meigs County, Tennessee in the School District 8 in June 1838. In District 1 for the Meigs School District 1 (below the Hiwassee River) for the school year July 1844, John Vernon had 1 school age child listed. The tax record for Meigs County for October 6, 1845 recorded that John Vernon had moved from the County and the tax was .37 ½.

It would make sense that John Vernon and his family stayed in Bradley County, Tennessee during the 1850 Census time period, but they can't be found in the Census record. Aunt Gertrude, who had the opportunity to talk to her grandmother Samples and Gertrude's mother Ella, had good information about grandparents and since Caroline Vernon lived to be 85 and lived with her daughter, Mary Jane Samples, Gertrude had the benefit of that information. Gertrude stated that John Vernon's father was Thomas Vernon (might be Thomas Vernon, Jr. who married Letitia Witten, but John was not listed as their son). Possibly, a Thomas Vernon was the father, but proof is lacking (page 262 explanation 3).

(2) There was a second also unproven Vernon family explanation for John Vernon's ancestry, and it traced back to Lieutenant Isaac Vernon of the Revolutionary War who had a brother named Thomas who was part of the same family. Thomas Vernon, Sr., father of Lieutenant Isaac and the Thomas mentioned on p. 256 in this book, left the Quaker Community and moved to Cub Creek in VA with the Caldwell settlement. Lieutenant Issac Vernon was the son of Thomas, and Isaac married possibly (1) Elizabeth Austin and (2) Jane Caldwell. The son, Lieutenant Isaac Vernon, fought in the Indian Wars and in the Revolutionary War. Possibly his sons Thomas and Joseph fought and died in the Revolutionary War. Much of the information was found in Vernon information on the Internet at *freepages.genealogy.rootsweb.ancestry.com/quaker-vernons* with Isaac's will listed on p. 54. Sons included Nehemiah 1743-1828, Joseph b. 1745 (died Rev. War?),Thomas Vernon b. 1750 (died Rev. War?), Jonathan 1760, James 1771 m. Elizabeth Davidson, Richard Vernon (1773), Isaac 1774, Frederick, and George 1785.

Lieutenant Isaac Vernon's Will was made in 1787. Before his death he provided for his grand children that were orphaned children of his deceased sons. He deeded 248 acres to John and Isaac sons of Joseph Vernon, and 136 acres on the North side of the Mayo river to Richard, Elizabeth and Nancy children of his son Thomas. So possibly his son Thomas might be the one that Aunt Gertrude should have used (Internet, *Wiki Tree* by Bob Nichol on March 8, 2013). If so then Thomas' son Richard would be the one that married Betsey Wooten and not Captain Richard Vernon that Aunt Gertrude chose. A third possibility was discovered and explained on p. 262.

On page 54 (*freepages* listed previously) was the information about Isaac's son Joseph who was born 1745 at Thornbury, Chester, PA and died about 1782 in North Carolina according to the *O'Guinn Family Website*. His two sons John 1775 or 1779 and Isaac 1777 were mentioned in family records related to Isaac's grandsons on p. 54 of *freepages.genealogy.rootsweb.ancestry.com/~quakervernons* which related to Thomas Vernon of Caldwell Settlement Cub Creek, Virginia.

John Vernon, son of Joseph Vernon, was born Jan. 31, 1779, in Orangeburg, South Carolina, and died 1850 in Amite, Louisiana. He married Sarah Sims or Sarah Lemuel and their children were Josiah 1791, Lemuel 1795, Joseph Feb. 12, 1798, Absolem 1803, Elizabeth 1810, Sally, Joanna, Ann, and Noah b. abt. 1805 according to *familytreemaker.genealogy.com/users/a/n/d* in The Vernons of Missouri, Information about John Vernon by Bill Anderson

In the same Bill Anderson article, Josiah Vernon was born on Dec. 28, 1791 in Rockingham, North Carolina and died Jan. 5, 1870 in Wayne County, Illinois. Harold Reno thinks that since there were Josiah, John, Absolem and Joseph Vernons in Bradley County Tennessee early Tax Lists, and Josiah and John Vernon were in the *1840 Bradley County, Tennessee Census* (compiled by Sheridan Randolph) that John might be the related to one of these brothers.

In the *Rockingham County, North Carolina Census of 1830* on page 51, Josiah Vernon had 2 males 5-10 and one male 30-40 with females two 0-5, one 5-10 and one 20-30. On the same page was Nehamiah Vernon with males one 0-5, one 0-10, one 40-50 and females one 5-10, one 10-15, one 30-40. On page 53 Absolem Vernon was listed with males one 0-5, two 5-10, one 20-30 and females two 0-5, one 30-40. On page 109 at *Ancestry.com* is Joseph Vernon with males one 0-5, one 5-10, one 20-30 and females one 0-5, one 5-10, one 10-15, and one 40-50.

In 1837 in District 1 of Bradley County, Tennessee Josiah Vernon and John Vernon paid taxes; in District 2 William Vernon paid. In 1838 in District 1 Namh (Nehemiah) Vernon, Absolom Vernon, Josiah Vernon and John Vernon paid; William Vernon paid in District 2. In 1839 in District 1 Joseph Vernon and John Vernon paid; in District 2 William Vernon paid. A William Vernon was mentioned in Harrison Vernon's death. All of these Vernon names seem related to the Vernons from Rockingham County, North Carolina.

On page 41in the *1840 Bradley County, Tennessee Census* (compiled by Sheridan Randolph) were Josiah Vernon with males two 15-20, one 40-50 and females two 10-15, one 20-30, and one 30-40. Josiah married Lavena Simon in Meigs County, TN on March 1841 (Bill Anderson information listed above). In *1840 Bledsoe County, Tennessee Census* (Internet, *Ancestry.com*) on page 151 is Absolem Vernon with males one 10-15, two 15-20, one 30-40 and females one 0-5, one 5-10, one 15-20, one 40-50, and one 50-60. He probably died in 1870 in Wayne County, Illinois. Josiah is probably not John's father.

After John Vernon appeared in Bradley County, TN in 1840, he might have moved to Georgia because in the *Bradley County, TN 1860 Census* (Maud C.'s birth place was GA), then to Lawrence County, Indiana (Anna Vernon's marriage in 1866 Internet *Ancestry.com, Alanna_62*), then to Jackson County, Alabama before 1870, to James County, TN before 1880 and then died Oct. 2, 1887 in Scottsboro, AL according to *FReid9169* at *Ancestry.com* who found a tombstone at Staples Frazier Cemetery with John Vernon's name. His birthday was listed as Aug. 11, 1812 and written on his tombstone was "A U. S. Soldier in Sherman's Army". *Ancestry.com* in the *U. S. Civil War Pension Index : General Index for to Pension Files, 1861 – 1934* listed a Pension Application for Caroline Vernon a widow living in TN for John Vernon who served in the 58th Indiana Infantry Company K. John Vernon's record listed service from Oct. 5, 1864 to July 25, 1865 (see pp. 152 – 153). This Application was dated July 5, 1889. His wife Caroline was living in Bradley County, TN in 1900, and according to Albert and Gertrude traveled to Alabama to see her daughters and to Philadelphia, TN to see her son. Harold believed also that Anna Vernon Chaney moved to Alabama and died there. According to *Oakcrstvet* and *WPursley at Ancestry.com* for the Bruner and Pursley families, Anna's name was Anna Emma M. Vernon.

Internet *Ancestry.com 1860 Census of Bradley County, Tennessee* District 6 page 30: **Mary Jane Vernon had already married James B. Allen and moved. See page 255 for 1860 Census information.**

John Vernon	46	Farmer	North Carolina
Caroline Vernon	44		North Carolina
John C. Vernon	19		Tennessee
Nancy R. Vernon	14		Tennessee
Anna M. A.	10		Tennessee
Margaret L.	8		Tennessee
Maud C.	8		Georgia
Josephine	6		Tennessee
Samuel	2		Tennessee

(Uncle Albert's memory of Aunts Tish and Josie living in Alabama proved to be important.)

Internet *Ancestry.com 1870 Census of Jackson County, Alabama* in Township 4 Range 5 page 4:

Vernon, John	54	Farmer	$100.00	South Carolina
Vernon, Caroline	53			Tennessee
Vernon, Margaret L.	16			Tennessee
Vernon, Josephine	15			Tennessee

Margaret L. might have been Margaret Latetia because Internet *Jackson County Marriage Records* listed Latetia Vernon marrying William Andrew on September 20, 1870 on page 905. Something must have happened because Maggie Andrews was living with John and Caroline Vernon in the *1880 James County, Tennessee*, and she was listed as Grand Daughter (see next page). Latitia would be the Tish that Albert talked about on pages 250 and 251.

Internet *Ancestry.com 1870 Census of Jackson County, Alabama* Town of Scottsboro page 31:
Andrews, William   28   Brick Mason   England

In the Internet *Jackson County, Alabama Marriage Records* Josephine Vernon married John W. Wallingsford on November 3, 1872 on page 151. W. L. Andrews was listed as Surety. Uncle Albert remembered the name Wallingsford and that Caroline would travel to Alabama to visit them. Some of the following information was difficult to find, but Harold felt it was related to the John Vernon family.

Internet *Ancestry.com 1870 Census of Jackson County, Alabama* Town of Scottsboro page 14:
Wallingsford, Jn.   22   farm laborer   Virginia

Internet, *Ancestry.com 1880 Census Jackson County*, Alabama Boyds Switch page 7:

Wallingsford, Jn.	33	Laborer	Virginia	Virginia	Virginia
Wallingsford, Hester J.	23		Tennessee	North Carolina	Tennessee
Wallingsford, William	8		Alabama		
Mary	2		Alabama		
Charles E.	baby		Alabama		

Mrs. Josie Wallingsford married William Pendergrass on March 14, 1897 in Jackson County, AL.

Internet *Ancestry.com 1900 Census Madison County, Alabama* Huntsville District page 79:

Pendergrass, William		July 1872	Farmer	Alabama	Alabama	Tennessee
Pendergrass, Josephine	wife	March 1852		Indiana	Indiana	Indiana
Wallingsford, Annie	step daughter	July 1885		Alabama	Indiana	Indiana
Wallingsford, Kate	step daughter	May 1891		Alabama		
Wallingsford, George	step son	June 1893		Alabama		
Wallingsford, Johnie	step daughter	April 1895		Alabama		

Annie Ella Wallingsford married George Washington Pendergrass, and she died Aug. 15, 1969 in Guntersville, Marshall County, Alabama. George W. died Dec. 19, 1980. Their children were Lit Pendergrass, son, b. 1910, Flossie Pendergrass b. 1913, James E. Pendergrass b. 1916, Dovie Pendergrass b. 1921, Adell Pendergrass b. 1923 and Emma Pendergrass b. 1926 (*mrundle09 Ancestry.com*). Another son George Andrew Wallingsford married Fannie Pendergrass daughter of Thomas and Martha Pendergrass. Fannie was born August 1884 and died 1964 in Jackson County, Alabama. Their children were Oscar Wallingsford b. 1918, John Wallingsford b. 1920, Ruby Wallingsford b. 1923, Edna Wallingsford b. 1927, George Wallingsford, Jr. b. 1929, Porter Wallingsford b. 1932 and Charles Wallingsford b. 1935 (*lwallingsford1 at Ancestry.com*). Johnie Wallingsford was born Feb. 14, 1894 and died May 1, 1935. She married Willie Vann Berry, and they had Waillon Berry b. 1920, Rayford Berry 1921, Inez Berry 1923, Samuel W. Berry 1924, Louise Berry 1926, Harrold Berry 1928, Kenneth Berry 1930 and Billey Wayne Berry 1935 dau. (*bstaehr at Ancestry.com*).

J. C. Vernon married Elizabeth Wyate on November 10, 1864 in Monroe County, Tennessee on page 152.
   Internet, *Ancestry.com 1870 Census of Lawrence County Indiana*, Perry Township on page 4 of Springville Post Office:

       Vernon, John C.   29   Farmer   Tennessee
       Vernon, Jane E.   28   Tennessee

John C. and Elizabeth Vernon lived in Lawrence County, Indiana until about 1890 when they moved to Loudon County, TN. J. C.'s parents, John and Caroline Vernon, must have lived in Indiana before 1864 as shown by his Civil War record (pp. 152 – 153 and 259). John and Caroline's daughter Anna Vernon b. abt. 1850 married Aaron Chaney in Lawrence County, Indiana in Perry Township on Oct. 4, 1866. Aaron and Anna M. lived in Jackson County, AL in 1880, and Anna died there on June 12, 1898 according to *Oakcrstvet* and *WPursley at Ancestry.com* related to the Bruner family and Pursley family information.

   Internet *Ancestry.com 1870 Lawrence County, Indiana* at Perry Township on p. 17 Springville Post Office:

       Aaron Chainey   23   Farmer Ohio
       Emma   21   Tennessee
       Jackson County, AL 1880 Census 1st District p. 17
       A. L. Chaney   34   Ohio   Ohio   Ohio
       Emma   wife   33   TN   NC   NC
       Malinda   dau.   8   IN   Ohio   TN
       Doella   dau.   4   AL   Ohio   TN

After Emma died, Aaron continued to live in Jackson County, Alabama. Internet *Ancestry.com 1900 Jackson County, AL* on Sheet 15B the following were listed:

       Aaron Chaney   Head   Mar. 1847   Wd.   Ohio   Ohio   Ohio   Farmer
       William H.   Son   Sept. 1880 S.   Al.   Ohio   TN   Farm Laborer
       Tommie   Dau.   July 1885 S.   Al.   Ohio   TN
       Polly   Dau.   Mar. 1890   S.   Al.   Ohio   TN

Harold Reno didn't find any more information about Latetia and William Andrews. The *1880 Census* below listed Maggie Andrews who was living with John and Caroline. She was listed as granddaughter.

   Internet *Ancestry.com 1880 Census of James County, Tennessee* Civil District 4 page 34 B:
       Vernon, John   64   Tennessee Virginia   Virginia
       Vernon, Caroline 62 Keeping House   Tennessee Tennessee Tennessee
       Andrews, Maggie   9   Grand Daughter Tennessee Tennessee Tennessee

   Internet *Ancestry.com 1880 Census Lawrence County, Indiana* Springville District 9 page 6:
       Vernon, Callaway   40 Blacksmith   Tennessee North Carolina North Carolina
       Vernon, Elizabeth J.   40   Tennessee Tennessee   Virginia
       The Census listed Elizabeth as having Spinal Disease.

John C. Vernon filed November 1890 in Tennessee for a Civil War pension. He was listed Invalid (as most Civil War Applications indicated),and Invalid means there was sickness or injury as a result of the war on his Civil War Pension Application. John Vernon was listed in 1891 as a male voter in Loudon County.

   Internet *Ancestry.com 1900 Monroe County, Tennessee* District 5 page 1:
       Vernon, John C.   May 1837   farmer Tennessee North Carolina North Carolina
       Vernon, Elizabeth   December 1839   Tennessee Tennessee   Tennessee
       Vernon, John C. Adopted son March 1895   Texas   Tennessee   Tennessee

In 1904 after John Callaway Vernon died, Elizabeth J. Vernon received a pension for her husband John C. Vernon who served in the 5th TN Infantry during the Civil War. On the Internet in Loudon County, Tennessee in the Corinth Church Cemetery, J. C. Vernon Union Veteran was buried. He died March 28, 1904. Elizabeth J. Vernon wife of J. C. was buried in the same cemetery with the following dates: October 4, 1839 and February 29, 1916.

Internet *Ancestry.com 1900 Census of Bradley County, Tennessee* District 9 and House 44:

Samples, Houston		1833	67	Tennessee	Unknown Unknown	Carpenter
Samples, Mary		April	67	Tennessee	Unknown Unknown	
Vernon, Carline	Mother	January	85	South Carolina	Unknown Unknown	

(See Houston Samples and Mary Jane Vernon Allen Samples bottom of page.)

(James Houston Samples might be the son of Matthew Samples and Nancy as stated previously. In the *1850 Bradley County Census* in House 72 were Matthew Samples 45, Nancy 52, Caroline 18, Granville 16, Leatha J. 14 and William 12. Houston was already studying wood working with his uncle William Samples and living with him. In the *1880 Bradley County Census* Houston Samples was living next to Matthew Samples age 70 and his wife Margaret on page 47. Mary Allen and Houston Samples married Sept. 19, 1869 in Bradley County, TN. See pp. 255 – 256 for more information.)

Houston Samples   **Mary Jane Samples**   **Candies Creek Cemetery**
1830 - 1902   **Apr. 22, 1839 – Dec. 30, 1905** (Internet, *Find a Grave,* Laurie Wilson
                              Feb. 3, 2014)

Internet *Ancestry.com 1910 Loudon County, Tennessee* District 4 page 11:

Vernon, Elizabeth J.		69	Tennessee	Tennessee	Tennessee
Vernon, John C.	son	15	Texas	Texas	Texas

The last census record related to Josephine Vernon Wallingsford and William Pendergrass was in *1910 Marshall County, Alabama* in Precinct 8 on page 1 A found on Internet *Ancestry.com*:

Pendergrass, Will	38		Alabama	Alabama	Tennessee
Pendergrass, Josie	57	wife	Alabama	unknown	unknown
Wallingsford, Kate	21	step daughter	Alabama	Alabama	Alabama
Wallingsford, Johnnie	16	step daughter	Alabama	Alabama	Alabama

(3.) This is the third explanation for Aunt Gertrude's DAR record. Harold Reno has looked at the Vernon family information again, and he noticed that Gertrude Hooper Brewer said that John Vernon who married Caroline Carter was the son of Thomas Vernon and Nancy Baker. One Vernon did match several of her references: Thomas Vernon who was born in 1789 and served in the War of 1812 did marry a Nancy Baker on Dec. 21, 1812 in Prince Edward County, VA (*Ancestry.com* - found little information see p. 249). **(If the tombstone in Alabama is John Vernon son of Thomas and Nancy Baker Vernon, the August 12, 1812 birth date might be questioned because of Census Records. The census records for John and Caroline Vernon indicated that John was born from 1814 to 1816 but many errors exist in Census records.)** Thomas was the son of Richard Vernon who was born about 1746 and married Esther Hambleton in VA. On the internet *russvernon47* at *Ancestry.com* wrote that Richard Vernon had a fine Rev. War record, having been in Valley Forge, Battle of Monmouth, the Seige of Yorktown, and others. The Thomas Vernon in Monroe County, TN who served in the Revolutionary War was a brother to the Richard b. 1746. There was no definite proof of any of the Vernon family information related to John Vernon in Bradley County, TN. Even with all the Vernon family information, there was very little agreement. Part of this information was found on the Internet at *wc.Rootsweb.Ancestry.com/cgi-bin/igm.cgi?op*. Great-aunt Gertrude Hooper was correct about Vernons being in the Revolutionary War; the possibility exists that 5 of the brothers were in the war. She just chose the wrong Vernon.

John Carter b. abt. 1760 may be the son of Levi Carter b. abt. 1736 in Wales and d. 1811 in Greene County, TN. On the Internet, *Family History of Levi Carter* by E. V. Carter Schnegelberger, typed and rearranged by Charles Barnum, sent to Kathy Beaudry in January of 2004 listed Levi's children as: Rachel b. 1754, Caleb b. 1756, Levi 1758, John 1768, Jesse 1774, Joseph 1776, Susannah 1780 and Elijah 1786. John Carter, Sr. and John, Jr. in the *Bradley County, TN 1840 Census* p. 41 have unproven ancestry.

Appendix A: Ocoee District or Purchase

[Internet] OCOEE LAND DISTRICT *Submitted by Phebe Morgan (phebem@comcast.net)*
The Ocoee Land District is that portion of land south of the Hiwassee and Tennessee Rivers to the State of Georgia, along the Georgia border and East to South Carolina. Before the New Echota Treaty, this land was part of the Cherokee Nation. It was ceded to the United States when the treaty was ratified on May 23,1836. The removal of the Indians began in 1837 but the "Trail of Tears" was not completed until 1838. However, many white settlers had been occupying the area for years.

The 21st Tennessee General Assembly on October 18, 1836 established the Ocoee Land District, and the following year the 22nd General Assembly set up the guidelines for the claims to the land. The first Entry Taker, Luke Lea, was elected by the General Assembly and instructed to set up his office in Cleveland, Bradley County, on the first Monday in October 1838. At that time, he was to receive any and all claims to land in the Ocoee District. P. J. R. Edwards was named the first register and he was to issue grants to the claims certified by Luke Lea.

To file a claim, anyone except a member of the Cherokee Nation could file within the first two months for a claim of 160 acres at the rate of $7.50 per acre. Those with prior claims, known as occupants, had three months in which to file their claims. After the first five months, all claims could be made for 160 acres at $5.00 per acre. At two-month intervals, the rate was reduced. At the end of nineteen months, all claims were reduced to one cent per acre or to the highest bidder. Some lands were sold for as little as one-fourth cent per acre and as high as $105.00 per acre.

John B. Tipton and his deputies started the land survey in the spring of 1837: John C. Kennedy, J.C. Tipton, Thomas H. Calloway, J. F. Cleveland, and John Hannah. The base line for the survey began at a large mass of limestone on the Hiwassee River opposite Charleston and ran 20 degrees west of south to the Georgia border, passing through Cleveland. From this line they surveyed Range Lines at six-mile intervals with Range Seven being the last Range east or west. The Ranges were then divided into Townships of six miles square. These were numbered from north to south. To further sub-divide these sections of land, each township was divided into thirty-six sections of 640 acres each, or one-mile square. The thirty-six sections were numbered from east to west. If a section did not contain the exact amount of land or number of acres, they were treated as if they did.

(The maps on pp. 264– 265 which show most of the Ocoee Purchase, helped to locate Andrew Hooper's land in TI Section which was left [west] of the Base Line, Section 6. The Base Line was in Charleston, Tennessee.)

Ocoee Purchase Land Sales—Andrew Hooper purchased land in T1 West of Basis Line on Candy's Creek. Eventually he owned more than 960 acres (see p. 20 where John Hooper said Andrew owned 920 acres and p. 165 for *1862 United States Direct Tax Commission* on 990 acres). On this land various people lived including his children and the people who rented his land. After his death about 1866, his last wife Margaret was in charge of the final disposition along with his son Kinsey C. Hooper. In order to equalize the inheritance, money was paid by heirs to other heirs, in lieu of land. By not recording the first 160 acres that Andrew purchased from Lewisey Melton in 1837 but waiting until 1839, Andrew probably saved $880.00 which was a large amount. Andrew paid $320.00 to enter the 160 acres which was $2.00 per acre instead of the $7.50 that was to be paid during the first 5 months (see pp. 6 – 7).

The map on the next page of the Ocoee District showed the 36 squares in each Township. Each square was a mile on each side and contained 640 acres. Andrew Hooper's land was in T1 (Township 1) which was west of the Basis Line. Mount Ebal was west of that in T1 North.

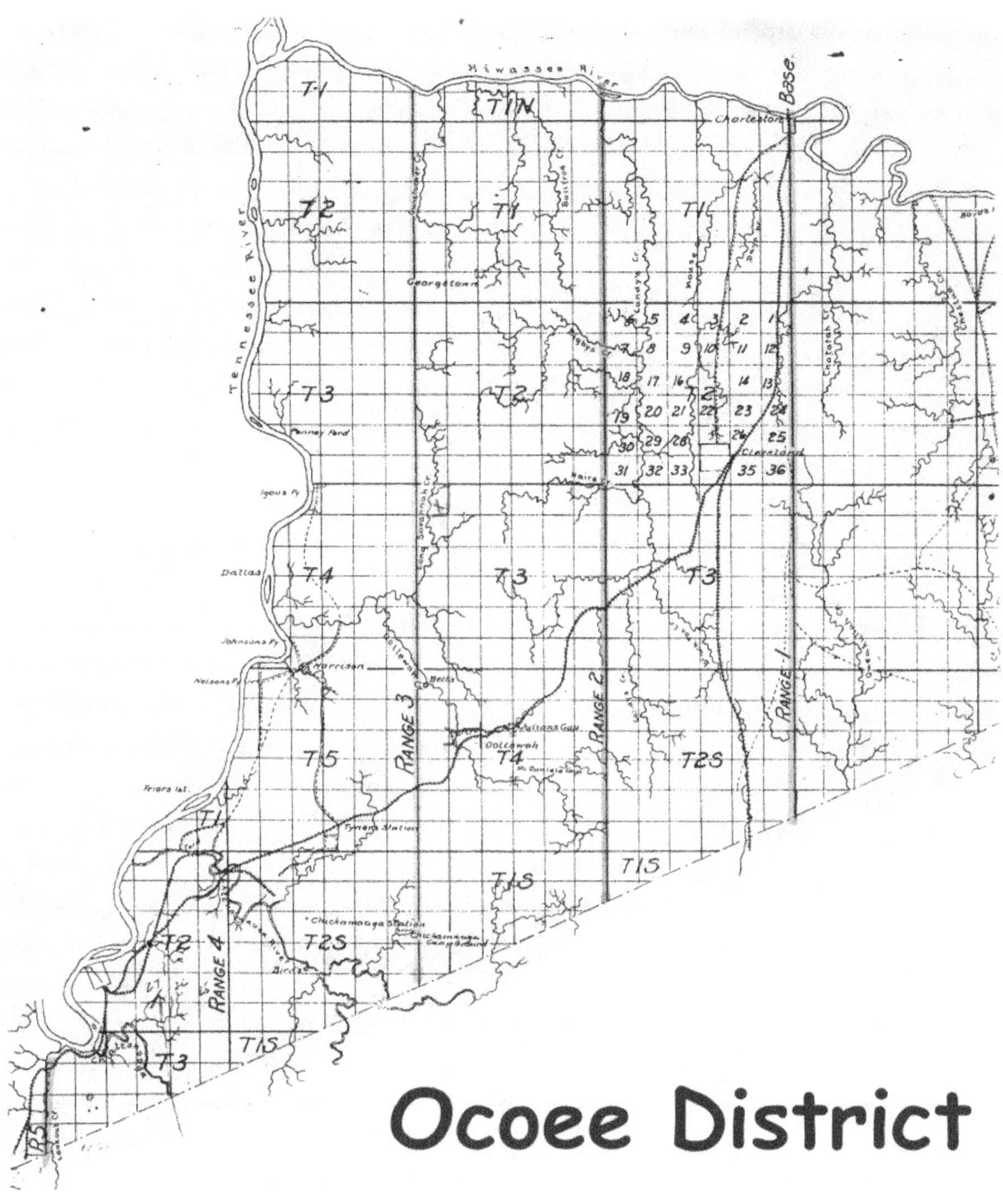

Ocoee District

Map Submitted by Phebe Morgan
phebem@comcast.net

See the next page for a close-up of the Andrew Hooper Ocoee Grants on Candies Creek. James Shelton also received Grants close to Andrew. Andrew's land was found to the left in Sections 6 and 7 where the creek curves with James Shelton to the far left edge. Shelton Mill could have been in that area. Also, James Shelton had entered more land that is below Andrew Hooper on the map.

David Johnson provided the map below on April 14, 2015 on the Internet at
tngenweb.org/marion/archive/deeds/Ocoee/Ocoee_plats.

The Ocoee Map below shows the location for Andrew Hooper land on Candy's Creek with James Shelton Grant to the left where he built the dam before 1840 which flooded Andrew's land.

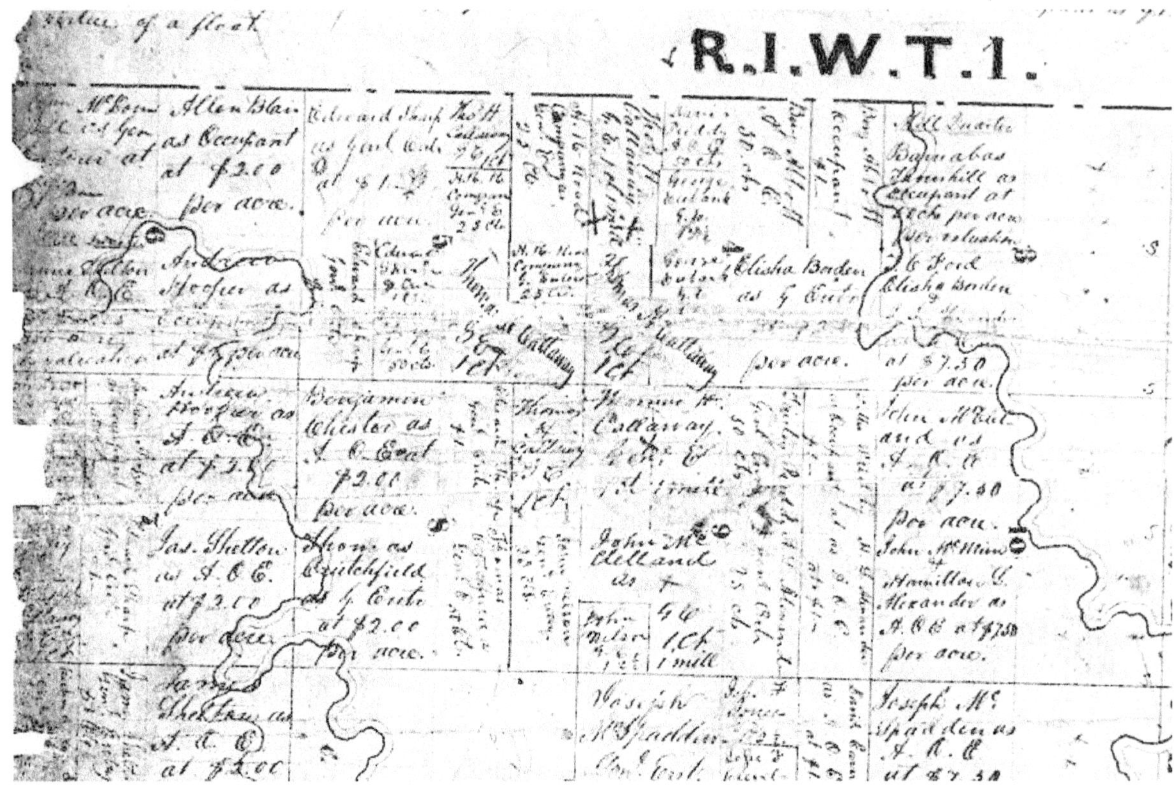

The following was taken from the Internet, *Acts of the State of Tennessee Passed by the First Session of the Twenty-Second General Assembly* page 9 published by S. Nye and Company at Nashville in 1838 and found at *Google Books*. Especially notice the highlighted part requiring 2 witnesses because Andrew Hooper on pp. 5 – 6 had to prove he owned the land he bought from Lewisey Melton in 1837.

Sec 8 That It shall be the duty of all and every person or persons whether they enter as occupants General or Enterers to produce to the entry taker at the time of making the entry a minute description in writing of the piece, parcel or tract of land…designating the range township section and quarter section and also the corner of the quarter section at which they may wish to begin. And all those who may wish to avail themselves of a preference or priority of entry under the provisions of this act shall be required first to produce to **Said entry taker the depositions of two respectable persons taken before some Justice of the Peace in the county Where the land lies setting forth That Said deponents are acquainted With the piece or parcel of land Intended to be Entered and With The person or persons wishing to make the entry and That I or They was or Were in the actual possession of and Residing upon** the same at the passage of this act and It shall be the duty of the entry taker upon any person or persons wishing to make an entry and being Entitled to the same as aforesaid and producing to the entry taker a location setting forth minutely as aforesaid to record the same in a well bound book by him to be kept for That purpose;…. at *Google Books*

In the Hooper Box that Richard Hooper found, the following Ocoee District deed was found, and it seemed to be related to the Mount Ebal story (pp. 196 – 220). The deed was recorded in Hamilton County and Bradley County, Tennessee:

Warrantee Deed
W. H. Burgess
    To
Hooper & Geren
Tax
State Tax   20
Co   "   10
       30 pd
Reg fee $1.50 paid

STATE OF TENNESSEE.
Hamilton County,   PERSONALLY APPEARED before me R. M. Chambliss
Notary Public for said County W. H. Burgess
The within named bargainors, with whom I am personally acquainted, and who acknowledged that
He executed the the within named Instrument fro the purposes therein contained.
    Witness my hand at office, this 12th day of Feby, 1891
          R. M. Chanbliss
          Notory Public

For the consideration of two hundred dollars, I, William H. Burgess, do by these presents sell,
transfer and convey unto I. H. Hooper and J. K. Geren, Jr., and to their heirs and assigns forever
the west half of the South East Quarter of Section Twelve in Township One North and Range
Two West of the Basis Line in the Ocoee District and State of Tennessee, in Bradley County,
containing eighty acres of land, more or less. Retaining a lien to secure a $150.00 note of the
purchasers. To have and to hold the said lands with all their appurtenances forever. And I do
by these presents warrant the title to the said venders to be free from all encumbrances and
agree to defend it against the legal claims of all persons whomsoever. In witness wherof I
have hereunto set my hand and seal this 10th day of February, A. D. 1891
          W. H. Burgess

State of Tennessee   I certify that the fore
Bradley County   going Deed was received
             This day at 11 ½ Oclock
A. M. and noted in Book A page 233 and with the Accompanying certificate
is duly registered in my office in Book L page 536
        Feb. 16" 1891   P. C. McCamy

Appendix B: Wilhite/Wilhoit Family, Hooper DNA and Sarah Hooper Shelton

The following was taken from Terry Hatfield's work on the Jerg Wilhite family which was found on the Internet at *homepages.rootsweb.com.ancestry.com/~george/jergwillheitnotes*. Adam Wilhoit's father was Conrad Reuban Wilhoit who was born about 1737 in Orange County, Virginia and died in 1806 in Campbell County, Tennessee. Conrad was listed as a Patriot in the Revolutionary War with the DAR number of 489209. Conrad married Elizabeth Broyles on December 3, 1758 in Culpepper County, Virginia. Children of this marriage were Adam, Solomon, Julius (who was in Bradley County, Tennessee before 1840), Matthias, Samuel, Reuban, Elizabeth, Frances, Rosina, Elijah and Simeon. Conrad Wilhoit's father was Tobias who was born July 15, 1708 in Schwaigern, Wurttemberg, Germany and died about 1762 in Orange County, Virginia. Tobias and Catharine Walkye also had Michael, Jessee, William and Mary. The father and mother of Tobias were Johann Willheit (christened January 25, 1671) and Anna Hengsteller. Johann lived at Schwaigern, Germany but moved to St. Mark's, Orange County, Virginia where he died November 26, 1738. (Jerg Wilhite was an earlier ancestor, but he was not included in this book.)

According to *Wilson-Moore.com/getperson.php?personID=15254* Research on the Internet, on 16 November 1778 Adam Wilhite and his wife, Missy, sold their 50 acres of land (Culpepper County, VA) to Bryant McGrath. Before 1782 Adam's family moved with his father, Conrad Reuban Wilhoit, to Washington County, North Carolina (now TN). On 29 September 1783 "Adam Willhight" received a land grant for 200 acres in Washington County. In 1785 Adam was taxed for the 200 acres in Greene County (Greene County created from Washington County in 1783). The land was surveyed on 7 January 1787. On 18 March 1789 Adam received Land Grant #863 for 200 acres of land on Nolichucky River on Camp Creek described as being in Washington County, but recorded in Greene County. (Camp Creek lies wholly in Greene County). On 8 March 1793 he received Land Grant #350 on Beaver Dam Creek in Hawkins County (recorded 11 April 1808 in Knox County). On 19 August 1793 Adam sold 12.5 acres on Camp Creek to John McDonald. On 30 January 1796 Adam bought land on Dumplin Creek in Jefferson County from Alexander Swagerty. The deed witnessed by Matthias Wilhite and Ezekiel Wilhite (*Deed Book Q*, page 100). At *Ancestry.com* Larry Wilhoite (*LarryWilhoite46*) listed Adam's last land grant dated 5 March 1798 in Jefferson County. On 15 December 1815 the Sheriff of Jefferson County sold at public auction 156 acres of land belonging to "Adam Wilhite" to satisfy writs of execution (one for $75 and one for $78.50 in favor of William Eaton against Adam Wilhite and John Wilhite) to Edward Ruth/Routh (p. 25 showed that the Seabourns sold land also to a William Eaton). This wording would probably indicate that John Wilhite was either a son or brother (*Deed Records M-N, 1814-1816*, pages 261-264). On 17 September 1816 Edward Ruth (Routh) of Knox County sold to "James Wilhite" of Jefferson County 156 acres of land for $300 (same land referred to above and recorded on 7 June 1818). The inference was that James Wilhite was the son of Adam Wilhite and that he repurchased the land for his own use (*Deed Book O*, page 304). (Most Adam Wilhite researchers believe Adam died in 1815, so James was probably buying it for himself. See p. 25 for James and John Wilhite who witnessed the marriage of Joseph Seaborn to Mary Wilhight.)

The Germanna Record No. #13 found at Internet *Rootswebs WorldConnect Project: Selvage and Peterson Families* indicated that the probable children of Adam and Missy were Ezekiel, John, Nancy, and James who married Comfort Stansbury. Research by *lawrpaul@erols.com* has questioned whether James, who married Comfort Stansbury, was the son of Adam. It was believed that James (Adam's son) married Peggy Baker and that he later married Susan Cate. Additional daughters have been identified by Terri Jean Adams GEDCOM File (Internet from *Lawrence Genealogy* by Paul E. Lawrence): one daughter married William Hickman; Avy Anne married Thomas Cate; Barbara married Samuel Cate; and Elizabeth married Joshua Cate. (See pp. 25 – 26 for another list of children which included Mary who married Joseph Seabourne. The *Wilson-Moore.com* research also listed Joseph Seabourne.) It was believed that Adam died before December 1815 in Jefferson County, TN. Family tradition provided by Terri Jean Adams of Florida said there was a grandparent that drowned while crossing a river and the body was never recovered. According to Marge Wilhite, publisher of *The Wilhoit-Wilhite Connections*, family records of descendants of Madison Willhite (projected grandson of Adam) state that Madison Willhite drowned while crossing the river. Since nothing was mentioned about the incident in the his obituary, it may be that the family tradition was referring to Adam Wilhite. Since no corpse was found, Adam was presumed dead by the state in Jefferson

County in December 1815.

Wade Glascock, Hooper DNA Projects Manager, reported on the results December 28, 2002 at *hooperconnections.com/wademessage.* He wrote, "so far the Hooper DNA project has shown that James Hooper (born 1745 from Union County, KY), Jesse Hooper (born 1758 from Davidson (Cheatham) County, TN), Absalom Hooper (born 1764 from Haywood County, NC), Dr. Enos C. Hooper (born 1796 from Graham Co., NC and Monroe Co. TN), Andrew Hooper (born 1805 from Bradley Co. TN) and Absalom Hooper (born 1807 from Polk Co. TN) were all relatives."

Below is Sarah Hooper Shelton death information and a story about her from a relative.

Birth: 1795
        Ducktown
        Polk County
        Tennessee, USA
Death: 1851
        Riceville
        McMinn County
        Tennessee, USA

I do want to tell you a little story my grandmother Perrin told me of our Grandmother Sallie. When Uncle Bill was about three months old, she had a violent attack of homesickness, I suspect was no different from we other women (me at least). So perhaps worried Grandfather into consenting for her to take her baby and go see her folks. So her horse was saddled; her carpet bag, herself, baby and rifle were mounted, and with her faithful dog she ventured forth to see her mama and to show her baby. Really she must have been a brave woman, for there were bears, panthers, wolves, and Indians lurking along the path. But Grandmother was a mountain woman, nothing frail about that ancestor of ours. Well she stayed three months with homefolks and was ready to come home. She thought of all the reasons she did not want to brave all those terrors, even though she had her trusty rifle and faithful dog. So she wrote Grandfather to come and fetch her home. Manlike he obeyed her request as a command...
-From a letter at hand from Catherine Shelton (Henninger) about Sarah Hooper.
(Found at *millerfam7* at *Ancestry.com*)

Appendix C: 8th Tennessee and Hooper Family Civil War Service

(The following information was found on the Internet at *nps.gov/.../search-battle-units-detail.htm* 8th Union Tennessee where the National Park Service listed Battle Unit Details. This again showed the accuracy of the Kinsey Hooper Diary and the information that Rick Hooper added on pages 132 – 161.)

OVERVIEW. Organized at Camp Dick Robinson and Camp Nelson, Ky., November 11, 1862, to August 11, 1863. Attached to District of Central Kentucky, Dept. of the Ohio, to June, 1863, 2nd Brigade, 4th Division, 23rd Army Corps, Army of the Ohio, to July, 1863. 2nd Brigade, 1st Division, 23rd Army Corps, to August, 1863. 2nd Brigade, 3rd Division, 23rd Army Corps, to September, 1863, 2nd Brigade, Left Wing Forces, 23rd Army Corps, to January, 1864. 1st Brigade, 3rd Division, 23rd Army Corps, to February, 1865. 1st Brigade, 3rd Division, 23rd Army Corps, Dept. of North Carolina, to June, 1865.

SERVICE.--Duty at Nicholasville, Ky., Camp Dick Robinson, Camp Nelson and Lexington, Ky., until August, 1863. Burnside's Campaign in East Tennessee August 16-October 17. At Greenville until September 19. Carter's Depot September 20-21. Jonesborough September 21. Watauga River September 25. At Bull's Gap and Jonesborough until December. About Dandridge January 16-17, 1864. Strawberry Plains January 22. Duty in East Tennessee until April. Atlanta (Ga.) Campaign May to September, 1864. Demonstrations on Dalton May 5-13. Rocky Faced Ridge May 8-11. Battle of Resaca May 14-15. Cartersville May 20. Operations on line of Pumpkin Vine Creek and battles about Dallas, New Hope Church and Allatoona Hills May 25-June 5. Operations about Marietta and against Kenesaw Mountain June 10-July 2. Lost Mountain June 15-17. Muddy Creek June 17. Allatoona June 18. Noyes Creek June 19. Cheyney's Farm June 22. Olley's Farm June 26-27. Assault in Kenesaw June 27. Nickajack Creek July 2-5. Chattahoochie River July 6-17. Buckhead, Nancy's Creek, July 18. Peach Tree Creek July 19-30. Siege of Atlanta July 22-August 25. Utoy Creek August 5-7. Flank movement on Jonesboro August 25-30. Battle of Jonesboro August 31-September 1. Lovejoy Station September 2-6. Pursuit of Hood into Alabama October 3-26. Nashville Campaign November and December. Columbia, Duck River, November 24-27. Columbia Ford November 28-29. Battle of Franklin November 30. Battle of Nashville December 15-16. Pursuit of Hood to the Tennessee River December 17-28. At Clifton, Tenn., until January 15, 1865. Movement to Washington, D.C., thence to North Carolina January 15-February 9. Operations against Hoke February 11-14. Fort Anderson February 18. Town Creek February 20. Capture of Wilmington February 22. Campaign of the Carolinas March 1-April 26. Advance on Goldsboro March 6-21. Occupation of Goldsboro March 21. Advance on Raleigh April 10-14. Occupation of Raleigh April 14. Bennett's House April 26. Surrender of Johnston and his army. Duty at Raleigh and in the Dept. of North Carolina until June. Mustered out June 30, 1865.

Regiment lost during service 2 Officers and 48 Enlisted men killed and mortally wounded and 1 Officer and 226 Enlisted men by disease. Total 277.

Below is additional information related to the service of John Hooper, Kinsey C. Hooper, Jahue Hooper, James Hooper,William Hooper, and Andrew J. Hooper (son of John and Sallie Farmer Hooper).

John Hooper Civil War Service information found at *Ancestry.com* by *dhooper1*.

Joined 8th Regiment on Dec. 25, 1862 at Nicholasville, KY and enlisted for 3 years. He was present in Company A from Oct. 31, 1862 – April 30, 1863. On August 6, 1864 he suffered an abdominal wound (cannonball wound p. 150) and was in the hospital at Marietta, GA. On Nov. 16, 1864 he was admitted to Jefferson General Hospital in Jeffersonville, Indiana for chronic bronchitis and phthisis (pulmonary tuberculosis). On March 1, 1865 he was assigned to Armory General Hospital in Washington, D. C. and furloughed for 30 days on March 10, 1865 because of surgery. Dr. A. Linis Griffin found him to be suffering from chronic rheumatism and was not ready to return to duty. He was discharged July 25, 1865. John's rank was Private throughout the war.

Kinsey C. Hooper Civil War Service information found at *Fold3*.

Kinsey was 34 years old when he was mustered in on Dec. 25, 1862 at Camp Dick Robinson, KY. He joined the 8th Regiment Company A for 3 years. In May and June 1863 he was present; in July and August he was absent while recruiting in TN. In Sept. and Oct. 1863 he was absent recruiting by order of Col. Young. From Nov. 1863 until April 1864, he was present. In May and June 1864 he was absent and detached as a saddler with 3rd Division 23 AC. From July 1864 until he was mustered out on June 30, 1865 at Company Shops, NC, Kinsey was present. He drew $36.45 with a Bounty due of $100.00. Kinsey's rank was Private throughout the war.

Jahew Hooper Civil War Service information found at *Fold3*.

Jahew was 28 years old when he traveled to Camp Dick Robinson at Nicholasville, KY to be mustered in on Dec. 25, 1862 for 3years. He was in the 8th Regiment Company A. He was present from May to Oct. of 1863. He was absent Nov. and Dec. 1863 due to sickness. Jahew was present from Jan. 1864 to Aug. 1864. Then he was absent due to sickness at Marietta, GA. He was present from Sept. 1864 until he was mustered out on June 30, 1865 at Company Shops, NC. He drew $104.16 and had a Bounty due of $100.00. Jahew's rank was Private throughout the war.

James Hooper Civil War Service information found at *Fold3*.

James was 23 years old when he was mustered in at Huntsville, TN on July 6, 1862 for 3 years. He was in the 8th Regiment Company A. (According to his Pension Application made in Sebastian County, Arkansas on April 8, 1889, James was commissioned by Col. Clift in Nov. 1861 to go back across the Tennessee River and recruit. While he was recruiting, he was captured by Capt. McClelland and hanged until he agreed to join the Confederate army. After five or 6 months he escaped and returned to the Union Army. See page 157 for the application.) James was appointed Second Lieutenant on Oct. 20, 1862. From May 1863 until June 1863 he was present. For July and August there is no record. During Sept. and Oct. 1863 he was absent with leave. Second Lieutenant James Hooper's resignation was accepted by order of Major General Burnside to take effect Oct. 26, 1863. He was mustered out at Company Shops, NC on Oct. 25, 1865.

William Hooper Civil War Service information found at *Fold3*.

William was 21 years old when he was mustered in at Camp Dick Robinson at Nicholsville, KY on May 13, 1863. He joined for duty and enrolled at Huntsville, TN on Oct. 31, 1862 for 3 years. He was in the 8th Regiment Company A. From Oct. 31, 1862 until April 30, 1863 he was present. He became Second Sergeant on Aug. 8, 1862 and was present from May 1863 to Sept. 1863. In Sept. and Oct. 1863 he was absent doing detached service. From Nov. 1863 until Feb. 1865 William was present, and on Jan. 1, 1864 he was promoted to First Sergeant by order of Capt. James W. Berry. He was present from March 1865 until he was mustered out on June 30, 1865 at Company Shops, NC. He drew $149.61 and had a Bounty due of $100.00.

Andrew J. Hooper Civil War Service information found at *Fold3*.

John Hooper's son joined the Union Army on Oct. 11, 1864. He was in Company A 5th Regiment. On Dec. 1, 1864 he was transferred from Company A by order of Col. S. B. Boyd. In March and April 1865 he was present. He was mustered out at Nashville, TN on July 14, 1865. He was paid for his enlistment $77.96, and he was due $66.66. *Flowermom121* posted on *Ancestry.com* Andrew J. Hooper's tombstone information in Hopewell Cemetery at Tunas in Dallas County, MO: he was born March 22, 1846 and died September 5, 1923. His tombstone also listed his Civil War Record as Private, Company A 5th Regiment Mounted.

Map below was drawn by Col. Wm. E. Merrill in 1865 and found at Library of Congress (see p. 165).
It showed Hooper's Mill on Candy's Creek with Charleston and Calhoun to the right.

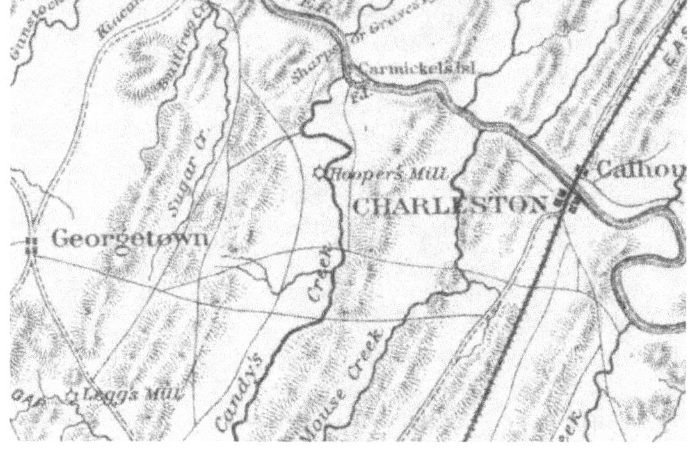

Appendix D: Wolf Company Catalog circa 1910, Hooper Mill Stones, OCOEE Steamer Picture and Hooper Mill Sluice End Channel

On September 11, 2009, Harold Reno submitted an Internet order for the Wolf Company Catalog that was printed circa 1910; this order was placed with The Henry Ford Museum and the Benson Ford Research Center in Dearborn, Michigan. Since C. W. Buck from the Wolf Company at Chambersburg, PA was working at the Hooper Mill in January 1910 (see pp. 182 - 183 and 221), it seemed likely that he was working on the rebuilt Hooper Mill (fire was May 31, 1909).

The Postcard from Phoebe to her father C. W. Buck placed him at the Hooper Milling Company, Rural Route 2, Charleston, Tenn. in January 1910. In the *Franklin County, Pennsylvania 1910 Census* at Chambersburg Ward 5 on sheet 7, Charles W. Buck was listed as a Millwright at The Wolf Company. Checks to pay for items bought from the Wolf Company can be found for 1907 on pp. 177 – 179. The checks were for sacks and for clothes. One check for $105 did not specify for what the payment was.

The pages in this Appendix are for illustration purposes. On pp. 187 – 188 and pp. 273 – 274 are pictures of two millstones that Glenda and John Cantrell have from the Hooper Mill. It seems that one of the stones is the bottom, Stationary Stone or Bedstone and the other is the top Running Stone which grinds the grain.

Cover of circa 1910 Catalog

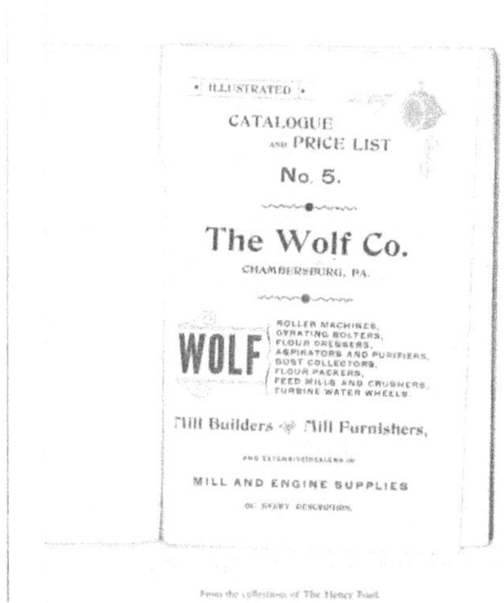

Information after Cover Page

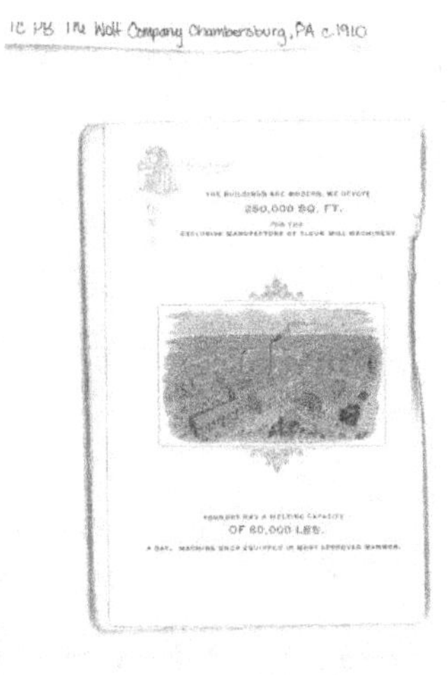

Wolf Company Factory Picture

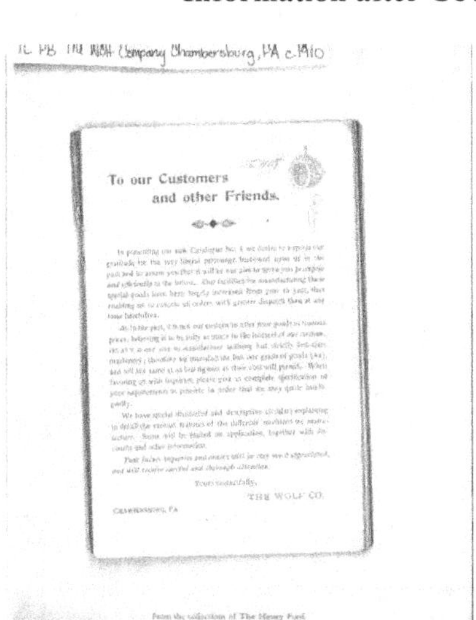

Letter thanking all the patrons

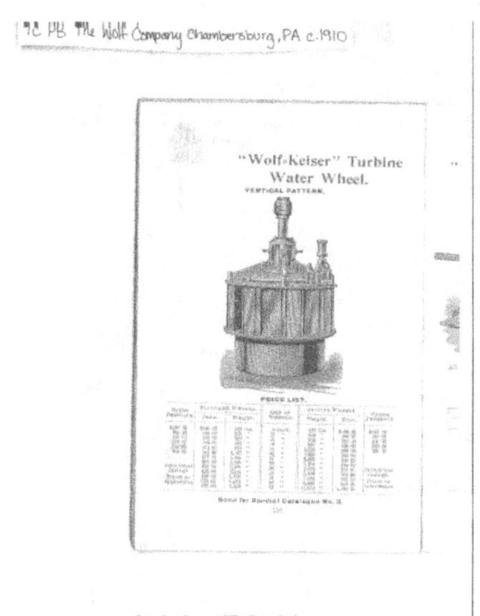

Wolf Company Water Wheel Turbine   **Kenan Mill in Alabama with its turbine**

The Wolf Keiser turbine which was made in 2 styles, a standard and a special, was built in 13 different diameters. The standard wheel was built for high and scant water supply and the special wheel for head with plentiful water supply where a wheel running at a high rate of speed is desired. Both standard and special wheels were built in both horizontal and vertical types. The Imperial friction clutch that was stated to be positive and powerful in action and to combine all the best features that experience suggest was made in 10 sizes capable transmitting from 7 to 350 hp at 100 revolutions per minute. Both the Volf Keiser turbine and Imperial clutch wee made by the Wolf Company of Chambersburg, Pa. (*The Engineering and Mining Journal* Vol. 74 published Oct. 4, 1902 p. 456 *Google.com Books*,).

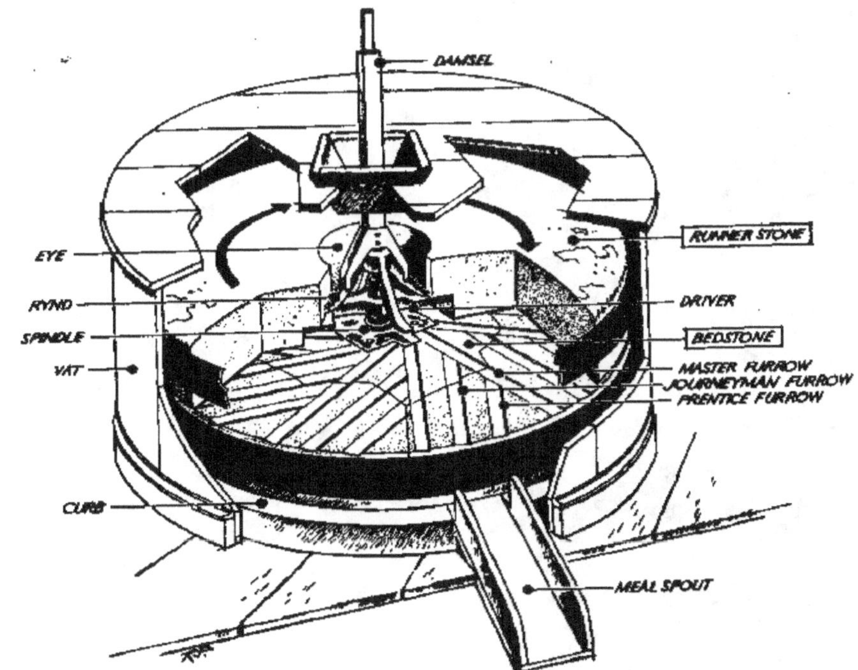

Cutaway Drawing of Millstones in Use.

This cutaway shows the grinding action of two millstones with a right hand dress. The mill information is from the Internet *The Art of the Millstones, How They Work* by Theodore R. Hazen copyright 2001.

The pictures on pp. 273 and 274 are Hooper Mill stones owned by Glenda and John Cantrell.

This is the Hooper 40 inch Stationary Millstone or bottom Bedstone with a Spindle. The thickness of this stone is 6 inches. The close-up of the Spindle is below.

Close-up of the 3 inch Spindle in the Stationary stone or Bedstone.

This is the top Hooper Mill 40 ½ inch stone with the Bale in the center of the Runner Stone which turns and can be raised or lowered to adjust the distance between the stones in order to grind the grain. The thickness of this stone is 10 ½ inches. See the close-up below.

This shows the Bale in the center which extends 3 inches on each side into the millstone. The Spindle of the bottom Stationary stone would extend through the Bale. Paul B. Flory explained the steel banding of the stones: First, the true circumference of the stone was taken, and a steel band was riveted and welded to that size in the shop. This "hoop" was then taken to the stone, where a large fire was made, and the "hoop" was placed until the "hoop" was a "cherry red"; then, it was applied or "shrunk" on the stone, similar to an iron tire applied to a wooden felloe of a wagon wheel. This iron band served a dual purpose: it protected the stone from breakage in transporting, and also it was a safety measure to prevent it from flying apart while in operation in a mill (Internet, "Old Millstones" by Paul B. Flory).

Picture showing the Hooper Millstones and the Spring House at Glenda and John Cantrell's.

The picture of the OCOEE Steamer was found at the Internet address *Ancestry.com Millerfam7*: one person in the picture was identified as "the person 4th from the right is Henry D. Saulpaw - married to Sarah Elizabeth (Dolly) Shelton daughter of John Ellsworth Shelton son of James Shelton."

Prater's Mill at Varnell, GA showing the sluice gate with mill dam to right. Part of the building sits over the Turbine location (Pictures taken Oct. 9, 2016).

Hooper Mill foundation from Sluice Channel end March 9, 2018 where the sluice gate would be located in the indentions on this end. The center and left foundations probably held building.

Appendix E: Final TVA Disposition of Hooper Mill Owned by Earnest Thompson and Arthur Thompson

On the internet at *Ancestry.com* the records for final disposition of the Hooper Grist Mill/Brackett Grist Mill/Thompson Grist Mill purchase were found. The Tennessee Valley Authority started the purchase in 1936, and it was completed in 1939. The title of the record was *U. S., Tennessee Valley, Family Removal and Population Readjustment Case Files, 1934 – 1953* . See pages 191 - 192 for the sale of Hooper/Brackett mill to Ernest Thompson and his brother Arthur Thompson. After 78 years, the Hooper/Brackett/Thompson Mill ceased operation.

TVA 978 – Revised 2/17/36

		FAMILY CASE RECORD	Tract No.	CR 870
Date 11-30-38		FACE SHEET	Map 75	
Worker			County Bradley	
			Contour above	
Name	Thompson		Code OWN-1	

Address	Rooms	Tenure	Name and Address of Landlord
Charleston, Route 2	2	Owner	

Years at Present Address 7   In County   Land Acquisition Status:
No. in Family 5   Adults 2   Children 3   Contracted September 1938
Marital Status: M x S   D   Sep   W   Closed October 18, 1938
School   Church   Referred Condemnation
Military Service   Union   Order of Possession

Information concerning Family: Relief Status   Race White

First Name Father & Mother	Rela- tion- ship	Date of Birth	Place of Birth	Highest School Grade	Condition of Health or Physical Defects
Earnest		34			Mill Operator
Anna					
Children:					
Lottie Lee		10		4	Mt. Harmon, 38-39
Marie		6		1	" " "
Edwyna		4			

Others in Household	Occupation	Dependency

Relatives--Including Children away from Home:					
Name	Address	Relation- ship to	No. of Dependents	Employment	On TVA Land

Bradley County Register's Receipt for the Deed for Thompson Grist Mill made October 18, 1938 to TVA.

TVA 630

$ 1,682.21

Tract No. CR-870

75

TENNESSEE VALLEY AUTHORITY

REGISTER'S RECEIPT FOR DEED

This is to certify that on this, the __18__ day of __October__, 193_8_, at __1:30 P.__ M, a general warranty deed, bearing date of __18__ day of __October__, 193_8_, executed by

EARNEST THOMPSON and wife, ANNA THOMPSON
ARTHUR THOMPSON and wife, BEATRICE THOMPSON

and conveying to the United State of America a certain tract of land in the ___Second___ Civil District of ___Bradley___ County, Tennessee, containing __3.3__ acres, was duly filed and noted for record in my office at ___Bradley___ County, Tennessee.

J. W. MURPHY
COUNTY REGISTER

October 19, 1938 TVA notice for no wood to be cut on the 3.3 acres that Earnest Thompson sold. Letter from L. N. Allen, TVA Assistant Coordinator specifying cut-off date of December 31, 1939.

TENNESSEE VALLEY AUTHORITY

CHATTANOOGA, TENN.

October 19, 1938

Mr. Earnest Thompson
Bradley County
Tennessee

Dear Sir:

The Tennessee Valley Authority has purchased the premises now
occupied by you, known as Tract CR-860, under a contract by
the terms of which you are privileged, if you wish, to remain
in possession of these premises until December 31, 1939.
We feel sure that you understand such privilege carries with
it certain obligations on your part, including the duty to
protect the property of the Authority as though it still belonged
to you.

As you know, after the date on which you signed the Purchase and
Sale Contract, there is to be no timber cut on the land except
firewood for your own domestic use. In order to assist in pro-
tecting this property, we hope you will immediately notify Mr.
John W. Peters, Chief, TVA Public Safety Service, Chickamauga Dam,
Tennessee, or Mr. W. J. Arrants, Reservoir Family Removal Section,
705 James Building, Chattanooga, Tennessee, if it comes to your
attention that anyone is cutting timber, trespassing, or damaging
or destroying this property in any way. We solicit your cooperation
in this matter.

Yours very truly,

TENNESSEE VALLEY AUTHORITY

L. N. Allen
Assistant Coordinator

Summary revised February 17, 1936 for Thompson's Grist Mill contract and sale.

TVA 978 - Revised 2/17/36

FAMILY CASE RECORD
FACE SHEET

Date 11-30-38
Worker Arrants

Name Mill, Thompson's Grist

Tract No. CR-870
Map 74
County Bradley
Contour
Code

Address	Rooms	Tenure	Name and Address of Landlord

Years at Present Address In County
No. in Family Adults Children
Marital Status: M S D Sep W
School Church
Military Service Union

Land Acquisition Status:
Contracted Sept 38
Closed Oct 18, 38
Referred Condemnation
Order of Possession

Information concerning Family: Relief Status Race

First Name Father & Mother	Relation-ship	Date of Birth	Place of Birth	Highest School Grade	Condition of Health or Physical Defects
Children:					

Others in Household			Occupation	Dependency

Relatives--Including Children away from Home:

Name	Address	Relation-ship to	No. of Dependents	Employment	On TVA Land

December 6, 1938, January 18, 1939, June 7, 1939 (Recheck), October 24, 1939, November 7, 1939, and December 12, 1939 TVA summarized the plan for Earnest Thompson to relocate. The location was listed as the Charleston-Blythe Ferry Road at Candies Creek Bridge.

THOMPSON, EARNEST   CR-870

12-6-38
West.

LOCATION. On Charleston-Blythe Ferry Road at Candies Creek Bridge.

TENURE. Mr. Thompson lived on this tract for the past seven years, during which time he has operated a water power grist mill and cultivated some land on this tract and other tracts in the immediate community.

PLAN. Mr. Thompson has no plan for relocation but expects to purchase a small farm and move his buildings prior to the date for surrender of possession. He has not yet decided whether or not to continue operating the grist mill.

1-18-39
Hunt.

RECHECK. Mr. Thompson thinks he will farm on this tract until July or August, at which time he will probably remove the building from the tract.

10-24-39
Barnett

RECHECK. The worker visited this place prior to this time. Mr. Thompson has been looking for a place to locate his mill but has been unable to do so. Most of the mill building has been wrecked. Mr. Thompson stated that he planned to sell the mill. He has no definite plans for relocation. However, he thought he would find a place soon.

11-7-39
Barnett

RECHECK. Mr. Thompson has purchased a place on the Charleston-Blythes Ferry Road where he is having a house built. The family expects to move to this location about November 20.

12-18-39
Barnett.

CLOSING ENTRY. Mr. Thompson has moved to his place which he has recently purchased. Mr. Thompson does not think that he will be able to operate his mill during the coming year, and he has no regular employment at present. Record closed.

*6-7-39
Hunt

RECHECK. The worker has contacted this family twice since the last entry. So far no definite removal plans have been made, and at the time of the last visit the worker suggested to Mr. Thompson that it was time he should begin to think of a suitable place for relocation.

Typed Summary of the last two pages (pp. 283 – 284) of Barnett's Final Report to TVA for December 6, 1938 and November 20, 1939 including the Closing Entry about the mill equipment being moved and may be sold if possible. **Record closed**.

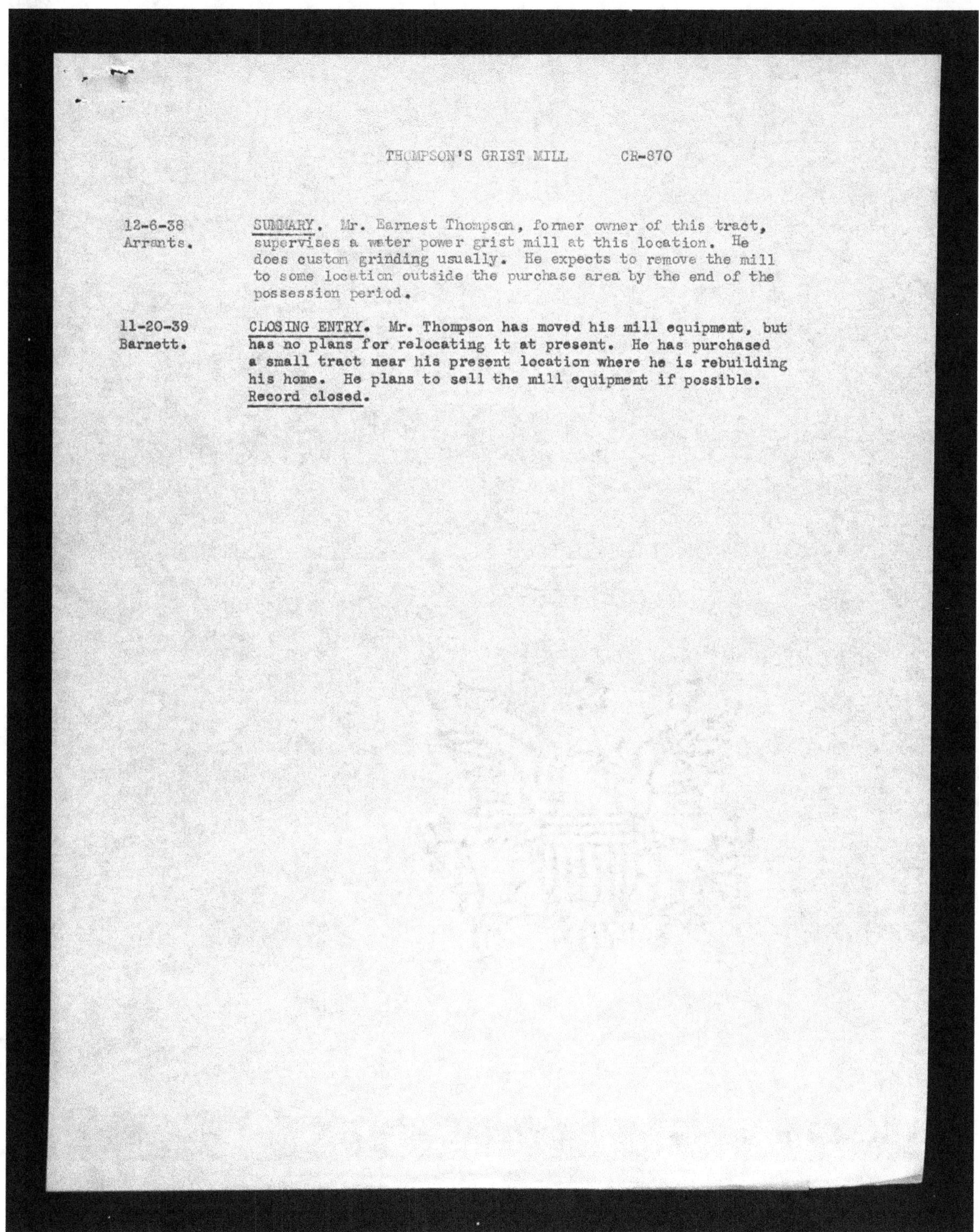

THOMPSON'S GRIST MILL   CR-870

12-6-38
Arrants.

SUMMARY. Mr. Earnest Thompson, former owner of this tract, supervises a water power grist mill at this location. He does custom grinding usually. He expects to remove the mill to some location outside the purchase area by the end of the possession period.

11-20-39
Barnett.

CLOSING ENTRY. Mr. Thompson has moved his mill equipment, but has no plans for relocating it at present. He has purchased a small tract near his present location where he is rebuilding his home. He plans to sell the mill equipment if possible. Record closed.

Barnett's written notes which were typed on p. 282.

TVA 982 (RFM)
Tennessee Valley Authority

OWNER
~~RENTER~~

NAME *Thompson's Grist Mill* TVA CODE

ADDRESS

HAS REMOVED FROM TRACT NO. *CR-870* COUNTY *Bradley*

MOVED TO PROPERTY OF *Mill not Repeated*

COUNTY   DATE MOVED *11-1-39*

COMMUNITY

POST OFFICE ADDRESS

AGENCIES AIDING IN REMOVAL

REMOVAL WORKER *Barnett* DATE REPORTED *11-20-39*

IN WORKER'S OPINION IS RELOCATION SATISFACTORY?

DO YOU RECOMMEND A FOLLOW-UP BY SOME SERVICE AGENCY?

REMARKS

Barnett's written notes which were typed on p. 282.

TVA 952 (RPM)
Tennessee Valley Authority

OWNER
~~RENTER~~

owne

NAME *Ernest Thompson*   TVA CODE *Own+1*

ADDRESS *Charleston R2*

HAS REMOVED FROM TRACT NO. *CR-870* COUNTY *Bradley*

MOVED TO PROPERTY OF *own*

COUNTY *Bradley*   DATE MOVED *12-14-39*

COMMUNITY *Centerpoint*

POST OFFICE ADDRESS *Charleston R2*

AGENCIES AIDING IN REMOVAL —

REMOVAL WORKER *Barnett* DATE REPORTED *12-18-39*

IN WORKER'S OPINION IS RELOCATION SATISFACTORY? *yes*

DO YOU RECOMMEND A FOLLOW-UP BY SOME SERVICE AGENCY? *no*

REMARKS *Purchased small tract near Centerpoint*

Appendix F: Additional Boggs Family Information

Found at Internet, *Ancestry.com, Find A Grave* related to Susan Hooper.
A. C. Boggs
Birth: Apr. 16, 1842
Death: Dec. 25, 1911
                Hartshorne
                Pittsburg County
                Oklahoma, USA

Civil War Veteran
Co. A, 19th Louisiana Infantry

A. C. Boggs, one of the oldest citizens of Hartshorne, died at his home in the south part of the city on Christmas Day, after an illness of almost two years. Mr. Boggs was seventy years of age, and had lived here for the past twenty years. In the early days he ws a pumper for the old Choctaw Coal Co., and for the past twelve years, he had been in the employ of James Brazell. He was a man who make and kept friends, and always had a good word for everybody. He was one of the oldest subscribers of *The Sun*, having taken the paper continuously since its first issue seventeen years ago. On July 4, 1909, while harnessing his team at his home, he was stricken with paralysis, and since that time, he was bedfast, and gradually grew worse until the end. The funeral services were conducted by Rev. E. P. Eubanks pastor of the M. E. church, and interment was made in the city cemetery. Two daughters and one son, survive him. They are Mrs. Jim Lloyd, Mrs. Tom Woods and Henry Boggs, all of this city.
The Hartshorne Sun, (Hartshorne, Okla.), Vol. 18, No. 1, Ed. 1 Thursday, January 4, 1912

Susan Hooper Boggs   (See pages 38 and 48 for family information.)
Birth: May 9, 1861
            Arkansas, USA
Death: Dec. 20, 1930
            Hartshorne
            Pittsburg County
            Oklahoma, USA

Susan Lincoln Hooper Boggs and husband
Alexander Cavett Boggs!
My great grandparents (MilleBelle added this to *Find A Grave, Ancestry.com* on Oct. 3, 2006).

Appendix G: Emails Exchanged Between Anne Goodwin of the *Hooper Compass* and Harold Reno

This last Appendix was based on Emails exchanged between Anne Goodwin of *Hooper Compass* and Floyd Harold Reno working on the Andrew Hooper family.   Anne's comments are printed with *italicized* type.

(I contacted Anne Goodwin about Andrew Hooper's September birthdate. She directed me to contact C. J. Giarratano, so I did on Feb. 8, 2014, and she did not know. Factually, an A. Hooper was in McMinn County, TN Dec. 14, 1826 when he bought 40 acres square of land [most likely means 40 acres and not 40 acres square which would be a large amount of land]. In 1827 and 1832 Andrew sold land to his brothers-in-law James and John Seabourn. Later, Andrew sold land to Thomas Smart as acknowledged in Thomas' will. In McMinn Andrew paid taxes on 120 acres. Anne Goodwin said the 1996 *Journeys through Jackson* used the date; this was in the Martha E. Hooper Pedigree Chart, daughter of Jahew Hooper and Mary McPherson prepared by Carol Kern Giarratano. Then I discovered that Mary Hooper Crocker in her book *A Glimpse into the Past* published in 1993 about Absolom Hooper also used the September 23, 1805 date.)

> Posted By: Harold Reno
> Email: floydr9903@att.net
> Subject: Andrew Hooper born about 1805
> Post Date: May 19, 2014 at 08:03:13
> Message URL: http://genforum.genealogy.com/hooper/messages/4275.html
> Forum: Hooper Family Genealogy Forum
> Forum URL: http://genforum.genealogy.com/hooper/

I am still interested in where the definite birth date of Andrew Hooper was found. See next page.
*****

> *Posted By: Anne Goodwin*
> *Email:*
> *Subject: Re: Andrew Hooper born about 1805*
> *Post Date: September 11, 2014 at 08:40:26*
> *Message URL: http://genforum.genealogy.com/hooper/messages/4283.html*
> *Forum: Hooper Family Genealogy Forum*
> *Forum URL: http://genforum.genealogy.com/hooper/*

For future readers, who will see the above posting after the opportunity to respond ceases [September 30, 2014], I would like to clarify some of the issues about the birth date in question.

As early as 1996, a birth date of "23 September 1805" was circulating and being published for Andrew Hooper of east Tennessee. [The 1996 version in "Journeys through Jackson," which is a publication of the Jackson County, NC Genealogical Society.] For some time, I used that birth date for my own records, but Mr. Reno helped me realize that even others who have used that birth date were uncertain of the original source.

The approximate year of birth is not much in question-Andrew Hooper appears on the 1850 Bradley County, Tennessee census as aged 45, born in TN.
Earlier, in 1840 Bradley County, he was aged 30-40.
In 1830, he lived in McMinn County and was aged 20-30.
All these records are consistent with his birth year having been about 1805.

The exact date of 23 September 1805 suggests that somewhere, at some time, someone had access to an obituary, probate document, family record, or an inscribed tombstone for this Andrew Hooper. Any of those data sources might reveal more clues about the parentage of this Andrew Hooper, born 1805. Another possibility is that another man named Andrew Hooper really did

have that birth date, but was a different person living in another place, and some early researcher in the 20th century just assumed the day and month were for this east TN Andrew.
In the last decade and a half, much more has been learned about the ancestry of the Monroe, Polk, and Bradley County Hoopers. In fact, yDNA testing has been done for descendants of this man, with exact matches to at least older Hooper men who also resided in east Tennessee and western North Carolina.
[see http://www.hooperconnections.com/dnatable.html and compare entries at lines 1-08 through 1-32]

Thus, candidates exist for the paternal lineage of Andrew Hooper, b. about 1805.
Learning the original source of the birth date for Andrew Hooper just might allow a re-examination of that source in light of the newer understanding of his origins.
****

(Floyd Harold Reno continued to search for the origin of the date of Andrew Hooper's birth; Anne sent me a book, *A Glimpse into the Past* by Mary Hooper Crocker published in 1993 which also used the date. Barry Hooper on p. III in *Acknowledgments* solved the problem: Kenneth Cress' mother, Thelma Eloise Tillery Cress [a great grandchild of Jahew Hooper], told Kenneth that September 23, 1805 was the date.)

On 3/4/2016 10:34 AM, Harold Reno wrote:
Thanks for your work!!!! I just read your reasoning about Thomas Hooper not being Absolom's father. Very clearly written and very reasonable. I am still working to finish Andrew Hooper of Bradley County, TN. No proof of parentage just know that Andrew's mother died at his new home in Bradley County, TN about 1840; Andrew's first wife, Martha Seabourn Hooper, died about the same time along with 2 sons . Testimony (see below from book) stated that Andrew married Martha Seabourn, Mary Foster, and Margaret ? ? The testimony was about Andrew's flooded land and people dying.

Thanks again for all your work!!!!
Harold Reno

John Hooper (son of Andrew Hooper) testimony below.

Under examination by the Respondent's Solicitor, he stated that his grandmother (Hooper) was in her sixty's when she died. He said that his mother died over fifteen years ago (1839), grandmother died about fourteen years ago (1840), his first brother died twelve years ago (1843), another brother died ten years ago (1845) and the other brother died twelve months ago (1854). When he was asked about his first step-mother's death, he said she died August a year ago (August 1854). (That means that Andrew Hooper was married to Martha Seaborn about 1825 in McMinn County, Tennessee; married Mary Foster about 1840 in Tennessee and Margaret (last name unknown but a Seabourn cousin) about 1854. (If Margaret was a cousin, could she be a Beaty and related to Polly Wilhite Seaborn whose mother might be Missy Beaty?)

To
Harold Reno
03/04/16 at 4:02 PM

Harold, I owe you several responses. Will try to work on this weekend. Also, have I mentioned or have you seen the Absolam Hooper [my ancestor, the RW soldier] pass to work as a blacksmith among the Cherokee? It adds some new light to the interactions between the earlier NC Hoopers and Cherokees. Also gives me hope there are more details hidden in Bureau of Indian Affairs and its predecesor agency files Why couldn't "respondent" have given a name to his grandmother?????Grrrrr. A Mrs. Hooper in her 60s who died 1840 could be wife of either old Andrew or Clemmons. Though Clemmons in 1840 may have lived further from the younger Andrew, since Clemmons moved back to NC then. The 1830 and 1840 census for Clemmons suggest his wife b. in 1780, she's not with him in 1850 nor is she buried in any known family plot in NC. The combined census records for the spouse of Andrew Hooper of Cocke Co., suggest his wife was born 1774, so she would have been in her middle 60s if she died in 1840. Sigh. If only John Hooper had been more specific....
Anne

To editor@hoopercompass.com
03/11/16 at 8:04 PM
from Harold Reno <floydr9903@att.net> On 3/11/2016 8:04 PM, Harold Reno wrote:
I read this Goodspeed biography several years ago while researching the Andrew Hooper family. Dialtha
Hooper (born 1830s) to Andrew Hooper and Martha Seabourn married Thomas Houston Gilbreath whose
father was probably Mahon Gilbreath/Galbreath from Jefferson County, TN. If so maybe Thomas
Galbreath was Mahon's father. Since Cocke County in 1797 came from Jefferson County, maybe John
Gilbreath's information was related to his father and not his mother. But Thomas Hopper and Charles
Hopper were in Jefferson County, TN in the late 1700s and early 1800s.

To
Harold Reno
03/15/16 at 8:12 AM
from Editor <Editor@HooperCompass.com> I've interspersed several comments below in green lettering
[Changed to Italicized.] *I'm not sure of the parentage. Do not have the opportunity just now, but am
interested in the TN Gilbreath family because I am related to a family out of North and South Carolina in
the 1700s, the Gilreaths/Gilbreaths [proven family members adapted either/both spellings after 1800].*

Anyway, John was Andrew Hooper's grandson and maybe Dialtha's family came from Jefferson/Cocke
County area? Here is the short entry from *rootsweb.ancestry.com*. (The entry is **Bold** and indented.)

> **JOHN H. GILBREATH, M. D. , is one of Marion county's popular and efficient physicians
> who has gained an enviable reputation and placed himself in the front rank among the
> medical practitioners of southeastern Tennessee by years of faithful and persistent effort. he
> has striven to improve upon his early methods, as every physician must do to keep pace with
> the new discoveries in medical science, and profit by his own experience and observations.
> His studies did not cease with the beginning of his practice, but have continued year by year,
> and this is no doubt one of the reasons why he occupies the prominent place he does in the
> minds of the people.**

> **Dr. Gilbreath was born in Bradley county, Tenn., March 15, 1860, a son of Thomas H. and
> Dialtha (Hooper) Gilbreath. Thomas H. Gilbreath moved with his parents, when a boy of ten
> years, from Cocke county, Tenn., to Bradley county, Tenn. He taught school during the early
> part of his life and was also a farmer.**

> **He served for a time as a member of the county court, and was conservative in his political
> views. Dialtha Hooper was born in Bradley county, Tenn, and they were both members of
> the Cumberland Presbyterian church. They both died in February, 1894, the father on the
> eleventh and the mother on the thirteenth, and the former at the age of sixty-two years and
> the latter at the age of fifty-six years.**

*There could easily be some obituary information in Cumberland Presbyterian records, such as church
newspapers. During the WPA era, I think Tennessee made some major efforts to preserve and transcribe
church records. Unfortunately, those several transcripts were carbon copies, so very limited in number and
dispersion-mostly a copy went somewhere near the record location and another copy to TN archives. LDS
did acquire microfilm copies of many of the transcriptions; a few are online. I have not checked this
possibility, however.*

> **The family is of Irish descent but several generations have been born in America.
> Dr. Gilbreath, the subject of this sketch, is the fifth in order of birth of a large family of
> children, five of whom are now living. He spent his school days in Bradley county, Tenn.,
> and at Charleston and Calhoun, in McMinn county, Tenn.**

*I had the above part of the bio in my notes already, but stopped after the reference to teaching. Will have to
add back the stuff below, which actually gives some possibility for added non-county records.*

> **He then taught one term of school and then began the study of medicine under Dr. Lee at
> Birchwood, and then under Dr. Dunham, of Bradley county. He began his practice in**

Bradley county, but in 1883 he moved to the Sequatchie Valley and located just above Whitwell. On the opening of the coal mines he moved to the city of Whitwell, and during the years a887 [*sic*] and '88, he was engaged in selling goods in that city in partnership with W. C. Shirley. In 1894 he returned to Bradley county, his old home, but stayed only a few months, and since that time has made Whitwell his home and base of operations.

Socially he affiliates with the Masonic fraternity in the capacity of Master Mason, and in politics he is a conservative Republican. As a man and citizen he is held in the highest respect and esteem by all who have the pleasure of his acquaintance, and as a physician and surgeon he is recognized as one of the leaders of his profession.

The Masons kept detailed records; most, however, were secret records. In those limited cases where the records have become available to the public, they are invaluable because the Masons were extremely interested in family history and ancestors. It would be worthwhile to try to locate the lodge in which he was a Master Mason and to then determine whether that lodge has such records, or whether they may have given their earliest records to the state lodge or to TN archives. I doubt that he would have known much about his Hooper great-grandfather, but probably had heard about his grandfather Andrew Hooper from Dialtha. Lodges in Bradley County and in Marion County, TN might have held his papers.

March 18,1888, Dr. Gilbreath was united in marriage to Miss Darthula Jane Andes, daughter of W. L. Andes and their home has been blessed by the advent of a family of three children, upon whom they have bestowed the following names: William Walter, Elbert Hughston and Bula.

Will send thoughts on Andrew Hooper's widow Margaret in a later email today.
AnneG

To
Harold Reno
03/15/16 at 4:13 PM
from Editor <Editor@ HooperCompass.com>

I have wondered for some time, and previously have written about this, but I think Andrew Hooper's final wife Margaret might have been a woman listed on the 1850 census in Bradley County.

Based on her 1860 and 1870 census listings, the woman who became Andrew's widow never seemed to be listed with a child "born of her body." Thus, I have assumed that in 1850 she was either a spinster, or a widow whose husband died early in their marriage, before Margaret married Andrew. She seemed to be available for marriage in the mid-1850s to become step-mother to younger Hooper children, so I've thought it likely she was living somewhere in Bradley County for the 1850 census.

That is why I looked for a woman named Margaret, aged about 35, born in TN, living in a situation without obvious offspring of her own, in Bradley, Polk, McMinn, Monroe counties. This is the most interesting person I found under those assumptions:

1850 Bradley County, TN p. 271B, 26th Subdivision, 9 Dec,
1899/1899
Brimer, William 55 TN farmer $650
 Lavinia 25 TN
 James 18 TN farmer
Carson, Margaret 35 TN

[House Number] 1902/1902
 Elizabeth Hooper 35 TN
  William 18 Farmer TN

Lavinia 16 TN

John 11 TN

This Margaret Carson is not apparent on the 1860 TN census, at least not as Margaret Carson. But note that the 1850 Margaret Carson in the Brimer/Brymmer household is quite near to Elizabeth Hooper. That Elizabeth Hooper - with child Lavinia in home - was a daughter of William Brimer/Brymmer, Sr. Elizabeth's son William R Hooper married in Monroe Co., TN in 1858 and eventually lived in MO. Elizabeth, Lavinia, and John Hooper all disappear from TN after the census.

See http://chroniclingamerica.loc.gov/lccn/sn84024443/1850-10-04/ed-1/seq-4/#date1=1836&index=9&rows=20&words=Hooper&searchType=basic&sequence=0&state=Tennessee&date2=1853&proxtext=%22hooper%22&y=16&x=5&dateFilterType=yearRange&pag e=1 accessed June 16, 2013

Athens Post, *Sept 20 1850, page 3, column 2,*

Notice

William Tucker, Administrator of William Brymer, decd, vs.

John Brymer, Amos Brymer, Elizabeth Hooper and husband Thomas Hooper, Nancy Thornton and husband Wiley Thornton, William Brymer, Jr, Vina Brymer, Telitha Brymer, Joseph Brymer, Polly Ann Brymer, and James Brymer an infant, and his regular guardian James Hankins,

Proceedings to sell lands to pay debts

In this cause, it appearing from the allegations in the petition filed in the County Court, September session, 1850 of Bradley County, that the defendant Amos Brymer is a non-resident and citizen of Texas, and Nancy Thornton and husband Wiley Thornton, and William Brymer, Jr., are non-residents and citizens of Arkansas, it is ordered that publication be made in some public newspaper requiring the non-residents Amos Brymer, Nancy Thornton and husband Wiley Thornton, and William Brymer, Jr. to appear at the next term (October term, 1850) of the County Court of Bradley county, Tennessee and make defence of said petition, if any they have, or the same will be taken for confessed as to them, and set for hearing accordingly. John H. Robertson, Clerk County Court, Pradley [sic] County, Ten. Sept 13, 1850--4t Pr's fee $5   103

(After Anne Goodwin sent the email above, I found the following newspaper article that she referenced at *Chronicling America* which is an excellent website that was referenced on pp. III. and 198.)

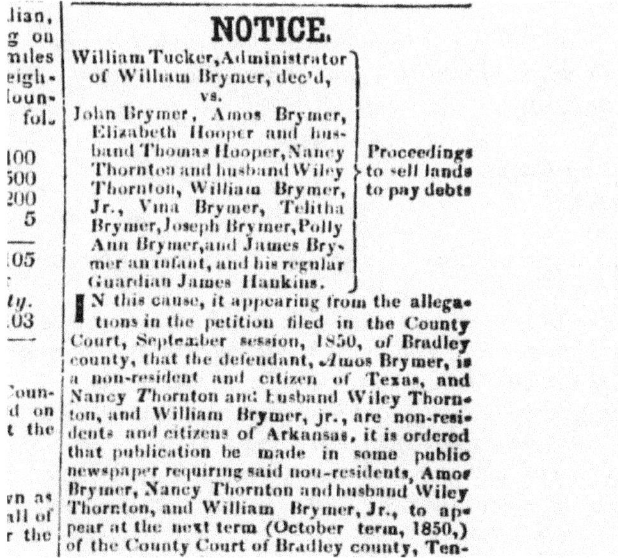

NOTICE.

William Tucker, Administrator of William Brymer, dec'd,
vs.

John Brymer, Amos Brymer, Elizabeth Hooper and husband Thomas Hooper, Nancy Thornton and husband Wiley Thornton, William Brymer, Jr., Vina Brymer, Telitha Brymer, Joseph Brymer, Polly Ann Brymer, and James Brymer an infant, and his regular Guardian James Hankins.

Proceedings to sell lands to pay debts

IN this cause, it appearing from the allegations in the petition filed in the County Court, September session, 1850, of Bradley county, that the defendant, Amos Brymer, is a non-resident and citizen of Texas, and Nancy Thornton and husband Wiley Thornton, and William Brymer, jr., are non-residents and citizens of Arkansas, it is ordered that publication be made in some public newspaper requiring said non-residents, Amos Brymer, Nancy Thornton and husband Wiley Thornton, and William Brymer, Jr., to appear at the next term (October term, 1850,) of the County Court of Bradley county, Ten-

(Continued on the next page.)

Court, September session, 1850, of Bradley
county, that the defendant, *Amos Brymer*, is
a non-resident and citizen of Texas, and
Nancy Thornton and husband *Wiley Thornton*, and William Brymer, jr., are non-residents and citizens of Arkansas, it is ordered
that publication be made in some public
newspaper requiring said non-residents, *Amos
Brymer*, *Nancy Thornton* and husband Wiley
Thornton, and William Brymer, Jr., to appear at the next term (October term, 1850,)
of the County Court of Bradley county, Tennessee, and make defence to said petition,
if any they have, or the same will be taken
for confessed as to them, and set for hearing
accordingly.   JOHN H. ROBERTSON.
     Clerk County Court, Bradley co., Ten.
Sept. 13, 1850—4t   Pr's fee $5   103

Salt ! Salt !! Salt !!
JUST received, a good lot of King's and
Sack Salt, which we propose selling cheap
for cash.   BRADFORD & DODSON.
Athens, September 6, 1850—tf   102

32 Boxes Virginia Tobacco !
PUT up in boxes about 100 pounds each,
6 lumps to the pound. just received and
for sale low.
     McEWEN & GILLESPIE.

Notice that the 1850 census entries at #1899 include William Brimmer/Brymer, Jr, and his younger sister Lavinia "Vina" Brymer, and brother James Brimer [who by the newspaper was still under age 21 "an infant" in September 1850]. The close neighbor 3 doors later is Elizabeth (Brymer) Hooper, widow of THOMAS HOOPER. These Brymers are offspring of William Brymer, Sr. who was born around 1775-80.

The Thomas Hooper who was married to Elizabeth Brymer had been born about 1810 in TN or GA, married before 1835, and died between 1840 and 21 Nov 1845. Notice his 1830 and 1840 neighbors:
1830 Monroe Co., TN page 145
line 8 William Brimer 2000101-1110001
*   line 12 John Brimer 0001-1001*
*   line 13 Thomas Hooper 0001-0001*
1840 Bradley County, TN p 49,
* line 21 Thomas Hooper 020001-10001*
* line 22 Edward Hooper 1120001-011101*

The 1830 Wm Brimer is the senior William above, whose land was to be sold 1850; John Brimer was an older son of that William and is mentioned in the legal notice of Sept 1850, and Thomas Hooper and Elizabeth (Brymer) had obviously married recently in 1830.

There is a legal record associating Brimers and another Hooper:
http://www.tngennet.org/monroe/chancery/changeya.htm

No.86)   Filed 27 Dec. 1837 Amos Brimer and Vesta Brimer vs Jesse Leming, E.C. Hooper and Executors of Jos. Callaway
[E C Hooper is Dr. Enos C. Hooper][a biography of one of Amos Brimer's sons in TX identified the wife as maiden name Vashti Hopkins; Amos and Vashti are buried in Burleson Co., TX with dates for A.R. Brymer May 1, 1813-Jan. 31, 1891 and "Vashti, Wife of Amos Brymer" Jan 22, 1815-May 24, 1884]
The Amos Brymer in the newspaper post and Monroe County lawsuit notice had left for Texas in 1847; he and wife Vashti took with them his sister Elizabeth's son named Enos M Hooper.
Ennis M Hooper married in Burleson Co, TN in 1852 for his first marriage, later divorced in 1860s and remarried, was still in Burleson County in 1880, eventually moved to Lee Co., TX. On the 1900 census in Lee County, Enos M Hooper indicated he had been born in July 1830 in Tennessee. He died in 1906 in Lee County, TX.

There are also two Hooper women who married in Burleson County in the same timeframe:
1) Elizabeth Hooper 1854 to David Roark [I've never been able to locate either party a census record, but a David Roark was on an 1855-1860 Burleson Co tax lists-he owed only poll tax, no land.] The bride Elizabeth Hooper possibly could be the widow of Thomas Hooper.

2) A. Tyler to Melvina Hooper 1853 [possibly is the Lavinia "Vina" Hooper aged 16 in 1850 Bradley County][no appropriate couple in 1860 Burleson Co., TX].

So, a long explanation to show that there IS a Hooper and Brimmer connection in east Tennessee.

There is ALSO a connection between Thomas Hooper and Andrew Hooper:
Deed, Bradley Co., TN 21 Nov 1845, attachment to the suit of William Brimmer against the estate of Thomas Hooper. Mentions that there is no personal property to be found in the county, but there is a tract of land:
NE 1/4 section 12, Twp (unreadable), range two west... 160 acres
Case concerns debt to A. P. Brimmer of $8.19 1/4 cents interest, and also $1.35 judgement. Jan term 1846 land order sold to satisfy debt and sale held 10 March 1846 by order of circuit court of Bradley, and also to pay sum of $4.45... land "struck off to William Brimmer" for $25.63. Afterwards, to wit on this 18 day of February 1848, Andrew Hooper (apparently also creditor of Thomas Hooper) land from the said William Brimmer at the price of $27.09 and raised the bid to $10.55, the whole sum $37.53 ... thus sheriff sells lands of Thomas Hooper to Andrew Hooper 3 May 1848.
Thus, the deed suggest a strong chance that Thomas Hooper and Andrew Hooper of Bradley County were either brothers or else first cousins, with brother being the more likely relationship to explain the debt actions.
That means Elizabeth (Brimmer) Hooper may have been the widowed sister-in-law of Andrew Hooper. So, in 1850, she may have been living on the land, formerly that of her husband, which Andrew Hooper had bought in 1848.

Which makes it all the more important that there was the woman MARGARET Carson, b. ca 1815 in TN, living in the William Brimmer, Jr. 1850 home without any apparent offspring with her. The woman is NOT an heir of old William Brimmer, Sr., as shown by the lawsuit notice of 1850. Which makes it look as if she may have been a teacher or nurse or weaver or cook for that family. And which makes it look as if she'd have been available to marry in the 1850s. And she'd have been closely acquainted with the Hooper family by 1850.

All the information fits to match what would be expected for Andrew Hooper's final wife Margaret _____, b. ca 1815 in TN.

And IF the widowed Mrs. Andrew Hooper is this former Margaret Carson, it could even be that she later on sought out the Brimmer/Hoopers in Texas. We do know that Margaret, Andrew Hooper's widow, was in Bradley County in 1870 with her married stepdaughter:

1870 Bradley Co., TN Eighth Civil District, page 350b, 6 Aug 1870, Cleveland PO, #136/136
Jack, Clinton 25 TN farmer $1000/550
  Tabitha 19 TN keeping house
  Charles H. 1 TN
Hooper, Margaret 55 TN
and not with that same Jack family when they were enumerated in Arkansas in 1880. A Jack child born 1874 was born in TN while an infant born 1880 was born in Arkansas. The Jacks moved on to Texas where a child was born in 1891 and were in Dallas in 1900. Clinton and Tabitha are both buried at Oak Cliff Cemetery there.

Did Mrs. Margaret Hooper die soon after 1870, or did she move elsewhere before the 1880 census? I don't know. What is sure is that she got as far as Arkansas with the Jacks. Did she possibly go on to Texas?

What if she had gone to visit Brimmer friends and Hooper relatives who were still living in Burleson County in the 1870s? Because it is possible that she could be this bride recorded in later Burleson County marriages:

3) **Margaret Hooper to James Benedict** 1875 [cannot locate either party on 1870 or 1880 Texas census, and it is certain this Margaret could not be a child of Ennis M Hooper, the only other Hooper then in

Burleson].

All this long-winded explanation just something full of possibilities for you to consider.
AnneG

(While looking at Anne's Monroe Chancery Court information, Harold found this entry which is possibly related to other people in this book: James Shelton, Singleton McKeel, Absalom Hooper and Garrett Foster from 1837. **No.77   Inj. Bill   Filed 3 May 1837 Singleton McKeel and James Shelton vs Absalom Hooper and Gharrett Foster   Bradley** [My interpretation is an injunction was filed in Monroe County, Tennessee involving Singleton McKeel who lived next to James Shelton in McMinn County, Tennessee. Also, Absalom Hooper, brother to Andrew Hooper and Sarah Shelton, was included in the injunction along with Garrett Foster (Jarrett Foster) from the newly established county of Bradley in Tennessee.] Internet definition for Injunction is from Cornell Legal Information Institute: "An injunction is a court order requiring an individual to do or omit doing a specific action. It is an extraordinary remedy that courts utilize in special cases to alter or maintain the status quo, depending on the circumstances, particularly where the defendant-party must stop its course of action to prevent possible injustice and irreparable harm to the plaintiff.")

On 6/27/2016 9:17 PM, Harold Reno wrote:
I am perplexed about Andrew Hooper's land grants in the Hiwassee District in McMinn County, TN. He started with a 40 acre grant that was misstated as 40 acres square. (I know the area was divided into 40 acre sections.) Anyway after the received the 40 acre square grant, he sold land to two brother-in-laws: James Seabourn and John Seabourn. He also assigned in 1839 more land to Thomas Smart that Andrew had received in 1828.

Andrew Hooper this day enters as general enterer [not living on the land] 40 acres square in the Southwest corner of the Northwest quarter of Sec. 34 of Tract Township 4 Range 3 West of the Meridian in the county of McMinn, Tennessee Dist. beginning on the Southwest corner of said quarter Dec. 14, 1826 40 acres A. Hooper. I do certify the above to be a true copy of the records of my office Dec. 14, 1826 Nat SmithNat Smith Ent. Taker. [If this were 40 acres square as stated it would be 1600 acres, so it is most likely just 40 acres.]

To
Harold Reno
06/29/16 at 8:09 AM
from Editor <Editor@HooperCompass.com> I cannot really answer your questions. I just have not studied the extant land records for McMinn/Bradley sufficiently to tell whether there is a mysterious land gain. Perhaps, however, I can offer so some discussion which will make the question even more confusing.I do not have reference to this tract in my notes for Andrew, so this is new to me.

It is possible that entry really was a total 1600 acres. If so, that probably accounts for the later acreages he sold. More likely, he had other land acquisitions from entries and deeds.

Without further research, I am not sure exactly where Andrew Hooper's 1826 land lay, or whether a part of it spread over to what became Bradley County once Bradley was created. I realize that Hiwassee District surveys were not supposed to run across the Hiwassee River into what then still belonged to the Cherokee, but then again, the tracts were supposed to be drawn up as square tracts, regardless of the lay of the land.

Also confounding things, historically, not all the acreage in a warrant for survey or in an entry developed into a single grant to the enterer- there is an example of Andrew Hooper [the older one] getting his 50 acres entered in Cocke County in 1811 based on part of an original certificate for 100 acres held in July 1810 by James Patton and Andrew Irwin. [That is, it appears Patton and Irwin paid for a warrant for survey in 1810, then Hooper bought part of that right granted by the warrant, and then Hooper had the surveyor mark the land sufficiently that Hooper then could take the paperwork to the Register office in Knoxville and enter the land that eventually matured into the grant to Hooper. Several similar examples come from Natchez/Nashville Absalom Hooper's land records in the NC military survey area over in now Middle Tennessee.]

(Internet, This Frederick Smoot paper first appeared in the *Middle Tennessee Journal of Genealogy and History* Volume X, Number 3, Winter 1996~97)

Frederick Smoot wrote in 1996: In 1825, "another register...to be denominated the 'Register of the Hiwassee District,' who shall keep his office at Athens, in the county of M'Minn ..." Also in that year, the register of the Hiwassee District was to copy any Hiwassee District record that was in the land office at Knoxville. There is no extant original extant map of the Hiwassee District, however there is a TVA redrawing of an 1851 map. (TSLA map #408)

So one explanation would be that Andrew Hooper the 1826 enterer was your "Johnny-on-the-spot" guy who was available outside the door of the register's office in Athens as soon as it opened. Thus, he'd have been ready to make his entry on the best land for a mill site or for a forge or for a ford, so he secured the land with seed money from family members, with the understanding that they would later pay for the actual costs to get final title to the land.

For Ocoee District (created 1836), I have the following references to someone named Andrew Hooper. I am uncertain that all are the same man, but certainly it seems that there were a lot of acreage.

Andrew Hooper, of Bradley Co., land granted 1839, 160 acres, Ocoee District. Recorded in Book B, page 176, Grant #657, Entry #679, entered 5 August 1839.

Andrew Hooper, of Bradley Co., land granted 1839, 160 acres, Ocoee District. Recorded in Book B, page 272, Grant #753, Entry #790, entered 7 August 1839.

Andrew Hooper, of Bradley Co., land granted 1841, 40 acres, Ocoee District. Recorded in Book F, page 48, Grant #2966, Entry #3093, entered 3 June 1841.

Andrew Hooper, of Bradley Co., land granted 1842, 40 acres, Ocoee District. Recorded in Book H, page 387, Grant #4377, Entry #4324, entered 6 Dec 1841.

Andrew Hooper, of Polk Co., land granted 1842, 80 acres, Ocoee District. Recorded in Book H, page 765, Grant #4755, Entry #4798, entered 29 Jan 1842.

It could be that some of these lands had been part of earlier entries or were adjacent to earlier holdings of McMinn.

Frederick Smoot wrote in 1996 that:

"There were survey conflicts between the Ocoee and the Hiwassee Districts, involving the exact placement of the dividing line between the two Districts. This involved islands in the Hiwassee River and similar claims among other things."

Much later, on his 1862 tax assessment, Andrew's federal tax assessment was high compared to most owners. US Internal Revenue Assessment Lists 1862-1874, TN (T227) Bradley, at Familysearch.com as accessed Apr 2016: (Internet, Family Search, Tennessee, Bradley County, 1862 United States Direct Tax Commission)

1862 act, 9th District Bradley, image 16 of 74
Andrew Hooper 990 acres, Value 7200, mill, value 600
K C Hooper 90 a, value 600

John Hooper 80 a, value 360

I am not sure when Andrew obtained all that land of 1862 [because I have not looked at extant deed records]. Certainly, he did hold a lot of land, compared to the common farmer, in the ante-bellum period. One suspects he was locally prominent and could have been mentioned in many places [letters, journals, store accounts] which might have survived in private hands.

Andrew also paid taxes on another 120 acres while he lived in McMinn County, TN.
Yes, I have him reporting 120 acres for his 1836 taxes. But....I am not 100% certain this was the same Andrew. I have [from http://www.rootsweb.com/~tnmcmin2/TaxList18362.htm]

*Andrew Hooper, 120 acres, value $200, **no poll tax**, tax 0.30.0, district 9*

The lack of poll tax is why I worry about identifying this Andrew Hooper.
Generally, in most early states, to avoid being subject to the poll tax, a white male of legal age had to be something like [in some jurisdictions] 1) a minister [religious exemption], 2) sometimes a miller [occupation vital to a community], 3) not living in an area subject to the county jurisdiction [i.e., holding land in the area but living in another county; living in an area still under Indian control; living on federal land such as a U.S. military fort], 4) too handicapped to earn a living [blind, completely lame], or 5) overage [usually involving a local jury declaring the individual too old, rarely being an automatic exemption, and usually someone at least 60 or more]. Of these, 3-5 were the more common exemptions, with 1 and 2 being much less common. I don't really think anywhere in TN had the occupational exemptions, but am uncertain there. [Old Microfilm showed Andrew Hooper paid Poll in 1829 and 1831.]

So, it is possible this 120 acres of Andrew Hooper was for the Andy Hooper, b. 1760-70, who was on the 1830 Cocke Co., TN census. The poll exemption then could be from his non-residence and being overage.

The non-poll Andrew Hooper might otherwise be the Andrew J. Hooper who was son of Margaret (Hooper) Hooper and her first husband John Hooper, though I think Andrew J. Hooper was too young to own land in 1836 [his birth year as given by him varies between 1818 and 1823]. In the later 1830s, Andrew J. Hooper seems to have lived on Ball Play Creek in Monroe County per his own testimony made in 1879. If he had been the McMinn owner, then he could have been underage for poll taxes and non-resident as well. The question here would be how he could be liable for land taxes [without involvement of a guardian] while too young for the poll tax. [E. G. Fisher Library in Athens, TN has old microfilm: Andrew paid 1829 & 1831.]

Or, even less likely, this non-poll-paying guy could be Andrew Hooper, born 1792 and son of my ancestor Absalom. That Andrew was in Haywood Co., NC 1810, in Hall County, GA 1820, back in Haywood in 1830, then in Union Co, GA in 1840. He died in Union in 1849. He had considerable interactions with the Cherokee, moved around a lot, got patents in GA in 1820, might have been interested in TN too since he had a sister [Margaret (Hooper) Hooper] there. So he too might have been an absentee landowner for McMinn and thus not subject to a poll tax.

These several possibilities lead to the question - if Andrew b. ca 1805 wasn't the district 9 McMinn landowner of 1836, what happened to that 120 acres and where was Andrew b. 1805?

Sorry, I know this hasn't helped at all.
Anne

Editor <Editor@HooperCompass.com>
To
Harold Reno
08/05/16 at 2:56 PM
I am so sorry to have taken so long to respond. I'll add some comments interspersed with your message:

On 8/1/2016 10:50 AM, Harold Reno wrote:
I have already thanked you for all the work related to the Hooper family. Below is information related to the publication I told you I was working on.

Will I be able to purchase a copy of your book? I am not sure whether you intend to just put it in libraries or if you also intend to offer it to interested kin.

This book relates to my wife's family and Andrew Hooper born about 1805.

Has your wife had a autosomal DNA test done yet? If not, at least for today, FamilyTreeDNA.com is offering reduced pricing for their FF test, I think under $70. It would be interesting to see whether she and my family might have any shared pieces of DNA.

We all descend from NC Absalom Hooper, who likely was uncle to Andrew Hooper b. 1805.

We have lots of matches at the 3-5th cousin level who descend from NC Absalom Hooper or from NC descendants of Clemmons Hooper, but there are almost always other intermarriages with other NC families where we can't be sure whether the segment is from a Hooper or from another one of our in-common ancestry.

We have small pieces of DNA which match to two people who descend from the Nashville Hoopers. Those people do not seem to have any intermarriages in their ancestry in common with my ancestry, other than via the Pistol Creek Hoopers. I am amazed that even a small matching segment of DNA could be in common - because the common Hooper ancestor would be someone born 1740 or earlier! But it does further prove the kinship between the Hoopers of Nashville and the Hoopers connected to Absalom and Clemmons and their brothers.

The book includes old records discovered by Rick Hooper and the Pedigree Chart created by Barry Hooper. The chapters are:

Early Hooper History and Andrew Hooper Land Grants
Andrew Hooper Court Cases
Seaborn/Seabourn and Wilhite/Wilhoit Families
Andrew Hooper's Children
Hooper Family Outline of Descendants (Pedigree)
Kinsey C. Hooper Civil War Diary and the Andrew Hooper Estate
Hooper Mill Owners and the Kinsey C. Hooper Estate
The Wonder of the World. America's Mount Ebal or the Handwriting on the Buried Wall and the Isaac
      Hooper Estate
John Luther Hooper's Post Cards and Letters
Conversations with Gertrude Hooper Brewer and Albert Hooper (transcript)
Hooper, Vernon, Carter and Samples Families
Appendix A Ocoee Purchase
Appendix B Wilhite/Wilhoit, Hooper DNA, and Sarah Hooper Shelton
Appendix C 8th Tennessee and Hooper Family Civil War Service
Appendix D Wolf Company Catalog circa 1910 and Hooper Mill Stones
Appendix E Final Disposition by TVA of Hooper Mill Owned by Earnest Thompson and Arthur Thompson
Appendix F Additional Boggs Family Information
Appendix G Emails Exchanged between Anne Goodwin of *HooperCompass* and Floyd Reno
Index

I'm pretty interested in the Wilhite/Wilhoits. I have family out of Virginia's Germanna Colony who intermarried wth Wilhoits in Culpeper and Madison Counties, VA before 1800 [but no Wilhoits that I know of in my direct ancestry]. A branch of the Wilhoits also was in northwestern NC and northeastern GA interacting with other families I research.

As you see, it is related to Andrew Hooper of Bradley County and his descendants. I acknowledge that little is known about the early Hoopers who are related to him. Several chapters relate to records discovered within the family. Several maps and pictures and maps are included.

It is especially the records discovered within the family that are important to publish and disperse among interested family members. I really, really want to see your book!

Many years ago, Martha and I visited Sherman Reno in Denver, Colorado who had spent years working on my Reno family. I asked why he had never published and he said there was enough wrong information already out there so he was not going to add to it. This book will be as accurate as I can make it after researching from the 1970's until now. But there will probably be errors in it. I am looking at possible publishers and trying to decide who will do the best job.

Martha and I published the *History of the Thomas N. Turner Farm in Meigs County, Tennessee* in 2007 which included farm journals from 1885 to 1925 and local genealogy. At that time I did not understand that we were compilers but now I recognize that I am a compiler of information and will acknowledge it as such. A lady who worked with Gateway Press in Baltimore helped us with the process but that part of Genealogical.com was closed and she left for another company. So this is the second book I have worked on. I sent copies of the first book to various libraries and will do the same with this one.

Anyway, Anne, I wanted you to know what the book entails. Again I appreciate all the work you do.

Harold Reno

On 5/6/2017 11:41 AM, Harold Reno wrote:
Ann, I know you are busy, but I was just rereading the Hiram Hooper material.

May 12 at 10:11 AM
Always busy.

In the many years since I wrote about Hiram, lots more records have become available to me, so I can confirm most of what you wrote below.

I believe that the son of Dorcas and Hiram Hooper whose name was James lived beside James Shelton in McMinn County, TN in 1870.

Reba Bayless Boyer, 1970, Monroe County, Tennessee Records, 1820-1870, vol. 1, p. 44, "Marriage Records,"
1858, Nov 7, James Hooper to Nancy J. Reed, by William Wadkins, J.P.

The couple appear on the 1860 census in Blount Co., TN [location may have significance for my message I'll send later].

1860 3rd District, Blount, TN:
James Hooper age 20, b. Tenn
  Nancy J., age 18,b.Tenn
  *Rebecca Lain, age 19, b. Tenn**
This appears to be a double listing for James, since he appears in his mother's Monroe Co., TN home too. However, his married sister Pernecia likewise appears in their mother's home in 1860, despite the fact she was married by 1850 and mother to several children by 1860. This fact suggests to me that the enumerator merely asked Dorcas for the names and ages of all her children, rather than making clear that he meant the children who lived with her for the census year.

**Some researchers think this would be Nancy's sister, meaning that Nancy's maiden name was Lain/Lane. I suspect that instead, Rebecca was staying with the family prior to the birth of their son Jeff, and was merely helping Rebecca during her confinement.*

I also think that his sister, Lorina, whose name in the Census was spelled something like Lorinia was living with him.

1870 McMinnCounty, Tenn. :
James Hooper, age 29, b. Tenn.
  Nancy J. wife, age 26, b. Tenn.
  Jeff age 10, b. Tenn
  James age 7, b. Tenn.
  Robert, age 2
  Laura, 4 months
Hooper, Lorina, age 24 house keeping
Here, I would think that James called in his spinster sister to be the helper during and after his wife's

confinement.

I do not know where Dorcas lived in 1870.

Neither do I, likely she was working as a domestic in several households and managed to be missing from all of them when the enumerator came. On her location, we do have this info:
[per pension testimony] in 1868, she swore her residence was "on Tennessee River about 15 miles from Madisonville the county seat of Monroe County, Tennessee," and she lived there since 1 Jan 1861. (Pensioners on the Roll 1 Jan 1883 [per Senate Resolution of 8 December 1882], page 319: Dorcas Hooper #962, Charleston, Bradley Co., TN widow, $8, Oct 1868). (Hiram Hooper died of fever 13 Aug 1847 at Perote, Mexico while serving in the Mexican war; this was found at *Genealogy.com* by Anne Goodwin.)

I believe in 1880, Dorcas aged 71 and Lorina (spelling looked like Luiza) were living in Marion County, TN. James, the son, and his wife, Nancy Jane Reed Hooper, were also in Marion County but not living with Lorina and Dorcas. There is a cemetery named Sardis close to Whitwell, TN where a broken tombstone for Dorcas Hooper is listed.
Several grandchildren of Dorcas, offspring of Hannah, are also buried at Sardis. See end of this message. I believe the photo of the tombstone for Dorcas, as posted at findagrave.com, indicates "wife of Hiram"

It is possible that Lorina moved to White County, TN with a Nephew, William J. Morrow, and his wife Laura in 1900. The death record for McMinnville, TN says that Laura Hooper Morrow was born in 1871 and died in 1951 and her father was James Hooper and her mother Nancy Jane Reed. I have no proof but names and ages seem to indicate a westward movement across TN.
1900 White Co., TN 14th District, Bon Air Town, page 269b, #46/47
Morow, William J 34 TN TN TN Sept 1865 miner-coal md. 7
Laura, wife, 29 TN TN TN Nov 1870 md 7, mother 2/0
Hooper, Lorina, aunt, 54 March 1846, single
By now, Lorina would have a lot of experience as a nurse. Notice that Laura is mother of 2, but none living. Same story in 1910 - Aunt Lorina would be a big helper for the couple.

1910 White Co., TN 14th Civil District, Bon Air, page 166b, 16 April, #30/30
Marrow, William 39, md 1, 17, TN TN TN miner, coal mine
Laura, wife, 36, md 1, 17, mother 3/0 TN TN TN
Hooper, Lorina, aunt, 62, single TN TN TN
The above entries seem pretty specific that Lorina Hooper was an aunt.
The two women are buried in same cemetery:
n.b.: notice in 1900 and 1910 how Laura fibbed about her age, despite her appearance as born Dec 1869 on her 1870 listing above. Her tombstone [and death certificate] shows the questionable year of birth, just like her spinster aunt.

Laura Morrow
Birth: Nov. 27, 1871
Death: Mar. 10, 1951
Wife of Will Morrow
Burial:
Wesley Chapel Cemetery
Viola
Coffee County
Tennessee, USA
Created by: Judyanne Waters
Record added: Aug 14, 2009
Find A Grave Memorial# 40669237

Lorina Hooper
Birth: Mar. 28, 1844

Death: May 23, 1919
Burial: Wesley Chapel Cemetery
*   Viola*
*   Coffee County*
*   Tennessee, USA*
* Created by: Judyanne Waters*
Record added: Aug 14, 2009
Find A Grave Memorial# 40669869
Show original message

The Andrew Hooper book is in the final stages. Again there is no solution to the ancestry except DNA evidence and common names being used. Perhaps the compilation of information will help someone.

Thanks for all your work.

Harold Reno

By the way, Dorcas's daughter Hannah had a late marriage as a third and final wife:
Hannah Hooper to A. J. Moser 14 Feb 1874 Louden Co., TN
http://www.tngennet.org/monroe/pmoser.htm [accessed 25 April 2009] "Peter Moser, Son of Francis Moser and Elizabeth Miller"
Andrew Jackson "Jack", "Blind Jack" Moser b. ca 1832 d. ca 1900
married
1. Ruth C. Swanson Mar 15, 1851
2. Mary Cannon July 28, 1870
3. Hannah Hooper Feb 14, 1874
[I haven't found the marriage record, but about the same time, Polly Ann Hooper married West Mosier, per their info from the 1910 Marion Co., TN census.]

1880 District 11, Monroe, Tennessee   Source: FHL Film 1255272   Page 79D
Jackson MOSER   Self   M   M   W   48   TN   Fa: TN   Mo: TN blind and has to be led
Hannah MOSER   Wife   F   M   W   41   TN   Fa: TN   Mo: TN
John W. MOSER   Son   M   S   W   7   TN   Fa: ---   Mo: ---
William MOSER   Son   M   S   W   5   TN   Fa: ---   Mo: ---
Hugh MOSER   Son   M   S   W   2   TN   Fa: ---   Mo: ---
**Washington HOOPER   SSon   M   S   W   17   TN   Fa: ---   Mo: ---*
**Robert HOOPER   SSon   M   S   W   13   TN   Fa: ---   Mo: ---*
**Nathaniel HOOPER   SSon   M   S   W   11   TN   Fa: ---   Mo: - blind in left eye*

**I have no idea whether these three boys were illegitimate offspring of Hannah or whether Hannah had married a Hooper cousin who died by 1874.*

Andrew Jackson Mosier is listed on the 1890 veterans census for Monroe County and was shown as blind. I would suspect that there was some kind of pension for him eventually, but have not tried to followup on that idea.
However, at least two of the Hooper boys ALSO made the migration to Marion County, TN by 1900:

Washington Hooper to Katie Ramsey 2 Jun 1883, Marion Co., TN
1900 Marion Co., TN
Hooper, Washington 1864 TN
* Willie, wife Nov 1872, md. 10, 4/4*
* Nellie E, dau July 1891*
* Ida L, dau May 1893*
* Oscar J, son Aug 1895*
* William P, son April 1898*

Several death certificates make it clear Hannah's Moser/Mosier/Mozier offspring made the Marion Co., TN migration:

name: Wess Mosier
event: Death
event date: 02 Nov 1920
event place: Whitull, Marion, Tennessee
gender: Male
marital status: Married
race or color: White
age: 52 Kate 1871 TN
Abb 1885 TN
May 1886 TN
Robert 1890 TN

1900 Marion Co., TN, 15th Civil District, page 138b
Hooper, Robt Nov 1868 md. 10

birth date: 12 Feb 1868
birthplace: Tn.
father: Jack Mosier
father's birthplace: Tn.
mother: Hanes Hooper
mother's birthplace: Tn.
occupation:
burial date: 04 Nov 1920
informant:
additional relatives:
digital folder number: 4184006
image number: 523
film number: 1299720
volume/page/certificate number: v 36 cn 509
"Tennessee, Death Records, 1914-1955," index and images, FamilySearch
(https://familysearch.org/pal:/MM9.1.1/NS5S-C4L : accessed 16 Dec 2012), Wess Mosier, 1920.

name: J. W. Mosier
event: Death
event date: 23 Jan 1933
event place: Victoria, Marion, Tennessee
gender: Male
marital status: Married
race or color: White
age: 66
estimated birth year: 1867
birthplace: Lowdon Co., Tenn.
father: J. W. Mosier
father's birthplace: Lowdon Co., Tenn.
mother: Polly An Hooper
mother's birthplace: Lowdon
occupation: Miner/Coal
cemetery: Sadis Hill Cem. [sic, really is Sardis Cemetery at Whitwell, Marion Co., TN]
burial date: 24 Jan 1933
digital folder number: 4184143
image number: 676
film number: 1876800
volume/page/certificate number: cn 8166
"Tennessee, Death Records, 1914-1955," index and images, FamilySearch

(https://familysearch.org/pal:/MM9.1.1/NSJZ-858 : accessed 16 Dec 2012), J. W. Mosier, 1933.
name: William Mosier
event: Death
event date: 28 Sep 1934
event place: Whitwell, Marian, Tennessee
gender: Male
marital status: Married
race or color: White
age: 52
estimated birth year:
birth date: 10 Feb 1882
birthplace: Monroe County
spouse: Mary Mcgowan Mosier
father: Jack Mosier
father's birthplace: Monroe County
mother: Hannah Hooper
mother's birthplace: Marion County
occupation: Coal Miner
cemetery: Walker Cem
burial place: Whitwell, Tenn
burial date: 30 Sep 1934
digital folder number: 4184426
image number: 827
film number: 1876818
volume/page/certificate number: cn 23316
 "Tennessee, Death Records, 1914-1955," index and images, FamilySearch
(https://familysearch.org/pal:/MM9.1.1/NS4J-BV4 : accessed 16 Dec 2012), William Mosier, 1934.

*I have something more to write about Hiram and Dorcas and their associates, another thing linking them
to the Missouri Abraham/Isaac/Jacob/Letitia Hooper siblings who migrated from Sevier Co [where Hiram
was enumerated 1830] to Platte County, MO. That has to wait until a later message.*

Will try to get that second message out this weekend. Sorry for the delay in responding.

Harold Reno <floydr9903@att.net>
To
Anne Goodwin_
Nov 3 at 10:35 AM
Anne, sorry to bother you, but I mentioned an old piece of yellowed paper found in the Hooper Box many
years ago. I am still working on the Andrew Hooper family of Bradley County, TN. Today while working
on the name Hardin, I discovered that Hardin County, IL was the location of Barker's Ferry which was
mentioned in the old word map document. I have written to several libraries and asked if they ever heard of
a Word Map from Tennessee to Hickory Nut Gorge and no library was familiar with the map.

This morning I discovered that in the Hardin County, IL history, Barker Ferry was listed in 1813 and 1814,
1817 and 1819. James Ford a local criminal evidently who was killed in 1833 also had a ferry in similar
location later. The old map mentions Hickory Nut Ford in Missouri and not Ferry. The ferry was created
about 1837.

I am about to decide that the old Word Map is older than I first thought. I also noticed that the History of
Hardin County, IL written in 1939 for their Centennial included a road from Barker's Ferry to the
Salines where there was a salt deposit close to Equality, IL which was also a part of an old
Indian trail. Equality is also included in the word map.

If you have any thoughts about this 1819 to 1837 time period and the map, let me know. I know Abraham
Hooper was an early settler close to the Missouri area. I am including the page (see below) that I have

written and the crude map I drew illustrating the area.
Harold Reno

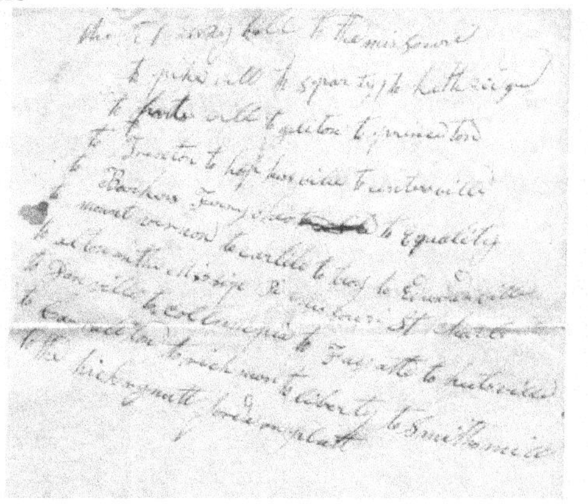

This sheet was slightly browned like old, discolored paper. The only words written were "A Way bill." On the other side, the first words were "the A Way bill to the missouri." Then, the directions began with the word "to" repeated before the next location. (See the picture below for the other side of the word map.) (See pages 163 – 165 for more information.)

Whoever took the time to write the preceding directions must have had first-hand knowledge of the locations for shallow water (places to ford) and the ferries that could be used. See the following map that shows locations mentioned in the "A Way Bill": to Pikeville, TN to Sparta, TN, to Carthage, TN, to Hartsville, TN, to Gallatin, TN, to Princeton, TN (Prince's Station close to Port Royal), to Trenton, KY, to Hopkinsville, KY, to Centerville, KY, to Barker Ferry on the Ohio River (Hardin County, IL), to Equality, IL, to Mount Vernon, IL, to Carlyle, IL, to Troy, IL to Edwardsville, IL to Alton, IL on the Mississippi, to Missouri, to Saint Charles, MO, to Danville, MO to Columbia, MO to Fayette, MO to Huntsville, MO to Carrolton, MO to Richmond, MO to Liberty, MO, to Smithville, MO, to Hickory Nut Ford on the Platte. (Anne Goodwin of the *Hooper Compass* wrote that Prince's Station may be Princeton, TN.)

Platte River, Missouri

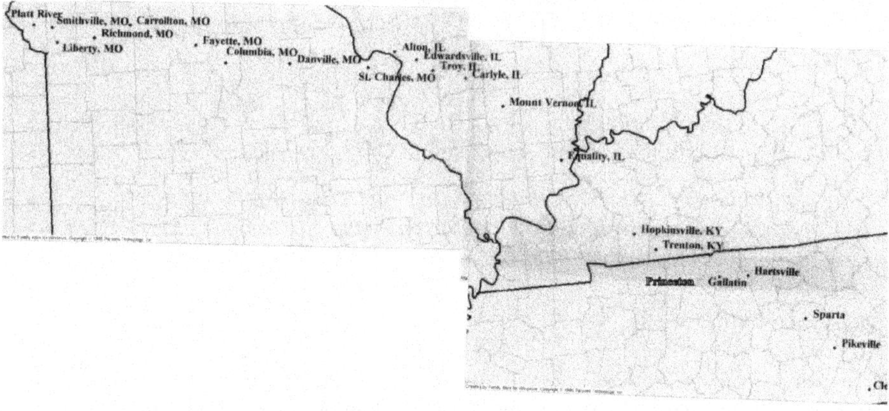

Cleveland, TN

See pp. 164 – 165. Harold Reno created the small rough map above to illustrate the locations for the different towns from Cleveland, Tennessee (lower right) to the Platte River area (on the left). Smithville, MO was settled in 1822. [Barker's Ferry existed until 1819 and Hickory Nut Ford ended in 1837.]

Answer from Anne Goodwin November 3, 2017
Editor <Editor@HooperCompass.com>
To
Harold Reno
Today at 10:59 AM

Oh Harold, I wish I could take the time for a complete answer and documentation. Just can't now.

*You talk about someone with whom I am familiar. The **James Ford (b. ca 1770, d. 1833)** you mention has some connection to the earliest Hoopers of the James (Indian fighter) line and both the early Absaloms (Nashville one and NC one) line. The connection is via the Pennington family and the Prince family, in-laws of Hoopers in VA/SC circa 1770s-1810. Some of the Penningtons/Princes seem to have been fellow migrants to KY around the area of Princeton (named for the Princes) along with the Enoch Hooper family and/or with John Lewis (who brought with him from NC a boy named Enos Hooper, who was nephew of Enoch). John Lewis later married widow Mrs. Ann _____ (Hooper) Kinging, the mother of Enos, in KY. Significance of Ann and Enos is that they had lived in early Tryon/Rutherford Co., NC in exactly the area where NC Absalom (my ancestor) was born and within 5 -10 miles of where James (Indian fighter) Hooper lived.*

But it is a long, long story to explain the kinships and connections, which go back to early northern VA, to the sons of Virginia surveyor Thomas Hooper (d. 1724).
I have so much to accomplish right now that I can't take more time for genealogy.
Anne

To
Harold Reno
Nov 8 at 2:57 PM (2017)

I am still swamped with details to attend to. Been that way for ages.
However, I found something I wrote in 2015 and cannot find evidence I ever sent it to you. It shows that the map details a number of spots known to the lineage of Hoopers who flourished near the North Pacolet River in NC/SC around 1765-1800. One branch of that group - likely offspring of Andrew Hooper of Cocke Co., TN 1830 - ended up at a spot on the end of your word map, and were there beginning in the 1830s. So, to be sure you do see it, here is the yet unfinished answer I started over 2 years ago:

On 3/10/2015 12:41 PM, Harold Reno wrote:
<snipped>   (Anne used "Snipped" to indicate she is making references to specific parts of my email.)
...a copy of the Word Map to the Platte River. Andrew Hooper of Bradley County, Tennessee had five sons who moved to Sebastian County, Arkansas and to Missouri about 1870. In Hooper family records this word map on yellowed paper was found.

I am attaching a copy of the Word Map and a rough map I put together which show the locations listed on the word map. My locations may not be in the correct counties, but should be close.

You've sent me the map before and I don't remember thinking I saw much that was notable.
HOWEVER, this time it strikes me differently. Also have some questions where I cannot read the writing or you don't have it on your map. And maybe I have some identifications.

1) second line of bill "to sparty, to kathridge"?
could that second place be Carthage, TN? Sparta is county seat of White County, Hartsville is county seat of Trousdale County, and Carthage is seat of Smith County lying between the other two places. Carthage was a river port at the confluence of the Cumberland and Caney Fork [Sparta lying on the Caney Fork] and something of a transportation hub in the mid-1800s. Gallatin, TN also lies along the Cumberland.
2) third and fourth lines "to Princeton to Trenton to Hopkinsville" *Trenton is a small town in Todd County, KY, and Todd County is next door east of Christian County, KY. Hopkinsville is seat of Christian County, KY. There is a Princeton that is seat of Caldwell Co., KY. That Princeton seems out of order for this map. Still, note that Christian county formed around 1797, Livingston from Christian about 1799, Caldwell from part of Livingston around 1809 or so.*
Caldwell/Livingston/Christian Counties KY are a SIGNIFICANT HOOPER AREA in our lineage.
Let me go off in a discussion of who these people were and why they were significant.
Enoch Hooper, the one who married Letitia Bearding in SC, served as Indian spy in Revolution, lived in upper NinetySix/Pendleton District to about 1797 -- he moved to the area near Princeton about 1797-8,

lived there and was Justice of the Peace, also owned a tavern, settled in a part that became Caldwell Co. Enoch Hooper had a nephew named Enos Hooper b. 1788 SC for whom Enoch became guardian in about 1802, taking him from the custody of one John Lewis, who had moved to KY from Spartanburg District, SC.

Enos Hooper's custodian John Lewis is the same John Lewis who married Anna _____ (Hooper)(Kinging) in Caldwell Co., KY in 1806. Anna is the woman for whom Anny Hooper's creek [now Hooper's creek], a tributary of the North Pacolet River, was named. That river runs from now Polk [then Rutherford] County, NC into Spartanburgh County, SC. This was within walking distance of the area where RW soldier Absalom Hooper, my ancestor, said he was born.
Most of Mrs. Anny _____ (Hooper) (Kinging) Lewis's records were in NC where she owned a mill that was the last residence before the road south entered into South Carolina. Hooper's creek joins the North Pacolet River in South Carolina within 10 miles of where James Hooper [born 1740s VA, he also served as Indian spy/fighter in Revolution] lived until he moved about 1802-3 to Henderson, now Union Co., KY. Anna _____(Hooper)(Kinging) had been widowed 1788 or 1789, and remarried John Kinging who died ca 1797 Rutherford Co., NC. She had a son John King Kinging born 1790-94 NC who later moved to Stewart Co., TN by 1813 [on the KY/TN line, below Caldwell County, KY and above Humphreys County where sons of James Hooper Indian fighter had settled circa 1818. Early in 1806, before her final remarriage in KY, Anna leased her NC mill for 10 years. She died between 1810 and 1816 and her last son John Kinging, then of Stewart Co., TN, came back to NC in 1816 to deal with the end of the lease and the sale of the mill.

The woman Anna was born between 1740 and 1755 and is listed on the Caldwell Co., KY 1810 census. In NC, she also had known sons William Hooper [born sometime between 1755 and 1774 (probably closer to 1774), and a son James Hooper, born 1774/1777. Both these men appear on the 1800 Rutherford Co. NC census. The last time I can identify her son William Hooper in NC is in deeds in Rutherford Co., NC dated February 1806 and then in a court case apparently brought in April 1808. Anna's son James Hooper remained in Rutherford County in 1810, with no sons and 2 daughters and then disappears from that area.

It isn't 100% proved that Anna was the mother of the Enos Hooper who was involved in the custody issue in KY, but...it's pretty much a given that her Hooper husband, who was dead before 1790, had been a very close relative to Enoch Hooper. The most likely scenario is that her Hooper husband was Enoch Hooper's brother.
Enoch Hooper left KY after April 1810 and migrated up the Ohio and then down the Mississippi River to Mississippi and died circa 1813. His widow Letticia (Bearden) Hooper was in MS to about 1818-9; then she moved back eastward to Marengo Co., AL where she died in the 1820s or so near her daughter.

Enoch Hooper's nephew Enos Hooper remained in Caldwell Co., KY until his death in 1860; Enos had 5 children and 4 of them were still in that general area in the 1860s; the survivors of the Civil War still there in the 1870s and later. It is entirely possible that Enos Hooper's offspring still had contact with Hooper relatives in TN.
Also, other Hoopers made land claims in same area in Livingston Co., KY, but the land claims are about all we know about them: In 1806, sequential land claims were made by Mary Hooper 400 acres; Rhoda Hooper 400 acres; James Hooper 400 acres, and Anny Hooper 400 acres. The 400 acres to James Hooper was sold to a Bearden relative of Enoch Hooper's wife, making a suggestion that these land-claiming Hoopers really were Enoch's kinsmen of some degree. The 1806 date may be an indication that these Hoopers were relatives, perhaps children, of Mrs. Anna _____ (Hooper)(Kinging) Lewis.

A William Hooper owed taxes on 183 acres in Caldwell Co., KY 1811. Could be the son of Anna. Back in NC, there were several land deals where her son William Hooper sold his land in Rutherford County in February 1806, and then he disappears. James Hooper, the son of Anna, was still in Rutherford County in 1810, but note that the land claim for James Hooper 400 acres in KY was sold to the Bearden relative. James Hooper had married Mary Matthews in 1798, and perhaps she was the Mary Hooper listed first in the KY 1806 land claims. William Hooper in 1800 Rutherford County, NC had a wife aged 26-45 and an eldest daughter aged 10-16 - these two women might account for the land claims in KY in 1806 in behalf of Rhoda and Anna Hooper.
And there was Elcey Hooper [female] who married 1807 Livingston Co., KY to a William McClanahan [a William McClanahan had bought land in Greenville Co., SC from the father of Leticia (Bearden) Hooper

in 1793; the Beardens had moved to KY about 1798].

There was also a William Hooper who married 1824 Caldwell Co. to a Mary Campbell, with no later record.

Back to Princeton. [Please remember, this email relates to the pp. 300 – 301 *A Way Bill to the Missouri*.]

Princeton, KY is named for William Prince, a Revolutionary war officer in SC, born 1752 in VA. He was a son of John Prince, Esq., and named a son, perhaps significantly, Enoch Prince.
William Prince's brother Francis Prince had married Sarah Bounds, who was a sister of the Sinah Bounds who had married [probably second wife] and was widow of James Hooper, who had died in Frederick Co., VA between 1756 and 1760. The Bounds and Prince families can be shown in northern VA in the 1750s. Sinah (Bounds) Hooper remarried William Wadlington and moved to TRYON County, NC between 1762 and 1770. Her sister Sarah's husband Francis Prince appears in Tryon County court records in January 1771 and was made executor of his father-in-law George Bounds's will in April 1772. It is not clear whether Sinah (Bounds) (Hooper) Wadlington had Hooper children. If so, they would have been born in northern Virginia between about 1745 and 1760 and would likely have moved to the NC/SC area around 1762 or so. Those potential Hooper children would have had first cousins in the Prince family and would have been shirt-tail relatives of the William Prince for whom Princeton, KY was named.
But there may have been another Princeton in TN, no longer known by that name today.

Before he went to KY, William Prince moved from Spartanburg, SC to Montgomery Co., TN, which IS on the way between Gallatin, TN and Trenton, KY. His brother Francis Prince had become the county registrar there and was still such in 1805. Francis and William built a blockhouse there near present Port Royal, TN, located on the Sulphur Fork of Red River about 1782. The Red River eventually flows into the Cumberland River, which flows into Kentucky until near Paducah, where it enters the Ohio River.

In Montgomery Co, TN, William Prince's wife died and he went back to SC and brought back with him other early settlers of Montgomery County. Some of those settlers later moved on to Caldwell Co., KY, evidence that the riverway was a thoroughfare leading from TN to KY. In the early years, the Prince blockhouse in Montgomery County was called Prince's Station, but may also have been called Princeton. Francis Prince, the brother-in-law of Sinah (Bounds) (Hooper) Wadlington, was on an 1800 tax list in the same small tax district with William Hooper (this one was the one closely associated with Natchez/Nashville Absolam Hooper, and probably the son or less likely the nephew of that Absolam). So there is lots and lots of association with a spot named Princeton and Hoopers who belong to our family line.
3) Line five, Barker's Ferry Ohio to Equality
Barkers Ferry on the Ohio River was at the west end of the Cave-in-Rock bluff on the Ohio River. The ferry crosses the Ohio river into present Hardin County, IL.
4) last two lines, "to Liberty to Smithville to the hickory nut ford on the Platte."
THIS is the pay dirt.
Liberty is in Clay County; Smithville in Clay and Platte Counties.
The Hoopers in Clay and Platte County began settling there in the later 1830s. They were
a) Abraham Hooper, Sr. [b. 1790/1900, d. 10 Feb 1847, married 20 an 1824 in Cocke Co., TN, had eldest son named "Clement" Hooper. Several times in early Cocke County, Abraham Hooper was chain carrier for land surveys. In March 1831, he was one for a grant there to Andrew Hooper.
He had a daughter born in TN in November 1833; the next child was born Sep 1836 in MO. He is listed in Platte County, MO on the 1840 census. Also on the 1840 Platte Co., MO census was William St. John [husband of Letitia Hooper, she born 1812/13 in TN] and Jacob Hooper.
Abraham died during the Mexican war in New Mexico; his estate back in Missouri was administered by Jacob Hooper with Isaac Hooper as his security.
b) Jacob Hooper
c) Isaac Hooper
d) Letitia Hooper

Appendix H: Additional Descendants Names:

Barry Hooper contributed these corrections:

1-3-15-109-341   Henry Miller b. Nov. 1892 married Sept. 14, 1913 in Bradley County, TN to Mae Messer b. abt. 1898
- 808.   Thelma Miller b. 1914
- 809.   Lillard Miller (dau.) b. abt. 1920
- 810.   Luetta Miller b. abt. 1922
- 811.   Cecil M. Miller (dau.) b. abt. 1924
- 812.   Opal P. Miller b. abt. 1926
- 813.   Essadine D. Miller b. abt. 1928
- 813A.   Alvada b. 1930
- 813C.   Joyce Miller b. 1935
- 813D.   Loyce Miller b. 1935

1-3-15-109-344   Lawrence Miller b. July 13,1898 married Cecil Varnell b. abt. 1898
- 814.   Rathburn Miller b. March 27, 1920-d. Sept. 1, 1989
- 814A.   Opal Miller b. 1921
- 815.   Herman H. Miller b. August 19, 1924-d. July 24, 2006
- 816.   Cash Edward (Chub) Miller b. Nov. 26, 1926-d. May 3, 2003
- 816A.   Ailene Miller b. 1937

1-3-15-109-344-814A   Opal Miller married Kenny Hixson (WW II Veteran)
- 816B.   Jane Hixson married Al Slater
- 816C.   Barbara Hixson married a   Wilson
- 816D.   Randall Hixson (Died in Vietnam.)
- 816E.   Nancy Hixson married a   Bowman
- 816F.   Gary Hixson married Brenda

1-3-15-109-341-808-1222   Jay H. Hooper married Doris Lankford
- 1568.   Debra L. Hooper
- 1568A.   Hugh Hooper married Eileen Roark
- 1568B.   Ronnie Hooper
- 1568C.   Phillip Hooper
- 1568D.   Doris Ann Hooper married James Franklin Liner

1-3-17-122-410-949-1223   William Hooper married Jean
- 1568E.   Scott Hooper
- 1568F.   Angela Hooper

INDEX: